KT-561-038

HAROLD MACMILLAN

Charles Williams

Weidenfeld & Nicolson

LONDON

First published in Great Britain in 2009
by Weidenfeld & Nicolson

1 3 5 7 9 10 8 6 4 2

© Charles Williams 2009

All rights reserved. No part of this publication may be
reproduced, stored in a retrieval system, or transmitted, in
any form or by any means, electronic, mechanical,
photocopying, recording or otherwise, without the prior
permission of both the copyright owner and the above publisher.

The right of Charles Williams to be identified as the author of
this work has been asserted in accordance with the
Copyright, Designs and Patents Act 1988.

A CIP catalogue record for this book
is available from the British Library.

ISBN-13 978 0 297 8 5194 3

Typeset by Input Data Services Ltd,
Bridgwater, Somerset

Printed in Great Britain by
CPI Mackays, Chatham ME5 8TD

The Orion publishing group's policy is to use papers that
are natural, renewable and recyclable products and made
from wood grown in sustainable forests. The logging and
manufacturing processes are expected to conform to the
environmental regulations of the country of origin.

Weidenfeld & Nicolson

The Orion Publishing Group Ltd
Orion House
5 Upper Saint Martin's Lane
London, WC2H 9EA

An Hachette UK Company

www.orionbooks.co.uk

HAROLD MACMILLAN

Also by Charles Williams

The Last Great Frenchman – A Life of General de Gaulle
Bradman
Adenauer
Pétain

For Jane

DUDLEY PUBLIC LIBRARIES	
000000323569	
Bertrams	12/08/2009
AN	£25.00
DU	

Contents

List of Illustrations

'All the world's a stage,
And all the men and women merely players;
They have their exits and their entrances;
And one man in his time plays many parts ...'

Shakespeare: *As You Like It*
Act 2, Scene vii

Preface

'It is not given to human beings, happily for them, for otherwise life would be intolerable, to foresee or to predict to any large extent the unfolding course of events. In one phase men seem to have been right, in another they seem to have been wrong. Then again, a few years later, when the perspective of time has lengthened, all stands in a different setting. There is a new proportion. There is another scale of values. History with its flickering lamp stumbles along the trail of the past, trying to reconstruct its scenes, to revive its echoes, and kindle with pale gleams the passion of former days.' Thus Winston Churchill in a generous and moving Parliamentary tribute following the death of Neville Chamberlain in November 1940.

What was true then is true now. Harold Macmillan was revered at his death as a great political figure. Yet, as the years passed and the star of Margaret Thatcher rose, he was derided by her acolytes. Now, at the beginning of the twenty-first century, 'Thatcherism' itself is on the wane. The Conservative Party seems to be turning its back on the fierce ideology which dominated its domestic agenda in the final two decades of the last century and to be embracing much of what Macmillan stood for. The 'perspective of time' has certainly lengthened. Equally certainly, it will lengthen again. There may thus never be a wholly right moment for a reassessment of Macmillan's life and his place in the historical pantheon – as a British and, indeed, European leader – but this would seem to be as good a moment as any to make the attempt.

Much, of course, has been written about Macmillan (a great deal of it, in fact, by Macmillan himself). Biographers have thus had a wealth of material to digest. It is always profitable, however, to go back to official, primary documents. This is particularly true in the case of Macmillan, given his tendency, in Rab Butler's rather mischievous expression, to 'irregularity over the facts'. In doing so, I have tried to present as fair a picture as possible. Others will no doubt judge whether I have succeeded.

Pant-y-Rhiw   April 2009

Part One

PROLOGUE

1

'The Old Rogue'

It was the kind of ceremony that the English feel they do particularly well. On 10 February 1987 the full panoply of political Britain was on display in Westminster Abbey in dignified remembrance of the recently deceased Prime Minister, Maurice Harold Macmillan, the first Earl of Stockton. The morning, unusually for a London February, was bright and crisp. The colour in the Abbey – a multitude of flowers, careful illumination of the high altar and sanctuary, the red coats of the band of the Grenadier Guards perched in the organ loft, the flamboyant purple of the Archbishop of Canterbury's cassock and mitre as well as the gold of the minor clergy's vestments – all contrasted well with the black dresses and suits worn by the distinguished mourners. Without a doubt, it was a splendid scene, and one of which, as was generally agreed, Macmillan himself would have approved without demur.

Nor would Macmillan have been disappointed by the quantity and quality of the attendance. Three former Prime Ministers, seventeen Cabinet Ministers, 234 Members of Parliament and 141 Peers, including three Dukes, graced the occasion. The Diplomatic Corps was there in force, as were representatives of all the many organisations, not least Oxford University, to which he had been, in one way or another, deeply attached. Above all, the Queen was represented by the young looking Prince of Wales, escorted from the Great West Door of the Abbey by the Dean of Westminster, first to meet the clergy of the Chapter and then to make his way past the assembled crowd – the seating in the Nave divided into two opposite sides for the occasion – to his place in Quire. Other distinguished mourners had preceded him on his voyage – not least the Prime Minister of the day, Mrs Margaret Thatcher, in a black dress and a resplendent wide-rimmed black hat. For the outside public their entrance, and indeed their every movement, was recorded by television cameras to the accompaniment of a solemn commentary from Mr David Dimbleby.

As might be expected, the service itself followed a predictable pattern. It was not a time to take any risks. After the band of the Grenadiers had played familiar pieces by J. S. Bach ('Sheep may safely graze', 'Air on a

G String', 'Jesu, joy of man's desiring') and the 'Nimrod' from Elgar's *Enigma Variations*, and after the Choir had sung their Sentences, Macmillan's Order of Merit was carried – albeit somewhat nervously – through the Nave and up to the Sanctuary by three of his great-grandsons. There followed the Bidding, a fanfare and then the National Anthem. The hymns, starting with 'I vow to thee my country' (written, as Mr Dimbleby helpfully informed the viewing public, by a former High Commissioner in Ottawa), continuing with 'He who would valiant be' and ending with the 'Battle Hymn of the Republic' (in honour, it was explained in case there was any doubt, of Macmillan's American mother), were beyond any reproach.

The lessons and prayers, too, followed a conventional pattern. The address by Lord Home of the Hirsel recited the facts of the Macmillan life, reporting that he was 'always, in whatever role he was cast, a man of style'.[1] After prayers, a Blessing pronounced by the Archbishop of Canterbury, the Last Post, and the 'Grenadiers' Return' from the flute and drum section of the band, the company made their way out into the bright sunlight to the accompaniment of more *Enigma Variations* (oddly, as it happened, ascribed in the Order of Service to Handel).

All in all, political Britain left the Abbey on that day with satisfaction that honour had been done to one of their own. Nevertheless, there were some discordant voices. It was noted that since Macmillan had died during the Parliamentary Christmas Recess the tributes in both Houses of Parliament were delayed until the New Year, leading one journalist to point out that the gap between his death and Parliamentary tributes allowed the press to start printing 'debunking material'. But, he went on, 'the old rogue had seemingly taken account of that. [The memorial services (one in Oxford and one in London)] ... will provide an opportunity for rebunking.'[2] Others pointed out that Lord Home's address, delivered in his dry voice and read with the aid of his half-moon spectacles sitting uncomfortably on his nose, was uninspiring to the point of boredom and that even Mrs Thatcher was caught on camera apparently on the verge of sleep, although her head was obscured, as was fitting, by her extensive hat. More to the point, however, was the stark criticism levelled at the whole event by left-wing tabloids. It represented, as one unkindly pointed out, 'the last gasp of Tory England'.[3]

In fact, there was some truth in the jibe. By 1987 the 'Tory England' which Macmillan had cherished had been for some time under severe bombardment from the Thatcherite political artillery – as he himself had pointed out in a speech made not long before his death. But whatever the complaint from the proponents of what passed for 'Tory England', it was hardly noticed that their archetypal Englishman, in spite of the bright colours of St George in which in his latter years he had wrapped himself, was not more than one-quarter English. He was, in fact, give or take the odd accident of blood, a quarter Scottish, a quarter English, and fully half American.

In both his family and his political life Macmillan made great play of his Scottish ancestry. Sons, daughters, grandsons and granddaughters were dragged up to the Cock of Arran (Macmillan himself was taken there at the age of eight) to view the ruins where his Scottish ancestors had apparently led their altogether humble but dignified life as crofters. They were held to be a paradigm of how the sons of modest parentage could succeed in the wide world by nothing more than their own efforts. Nevertheless, romantic as these notions were – and Macmillan played on the theme with the greatest skill – they turn out to have had little to do with the facts. By way of a small instance, such was Macmillan's idealised view of his Scottish family history that he kept in his office a photograph of the ruin on the Cock of Arran where he claimed his ancestors lived. On more exact research, however, it turns out that the ruin in question was, of the two on the site, the wrong one.

Furthermore, the Cock of Arran itself is by no means the most important site in his family history. The McMillans (such was the spelling of the name at the time) came from the peninsula of Kintyre in Argyle, crossing the narrow channel to the Isle of Arran in the early seventeenth century. The island on which they settled and spread – the name seems to be derived from the Gaelic 'island of the mountains' – was fertile grassland on the coasts and in the glens leading to the steep and barren hills. Farming was almost entirely of livestock – 'not a gay life to the superficial eye of a stranger'[4] – cows, sheep and goats. In winter, when the sun rarely shone, there were indoor jobs to be done – nets to be made for the herring catch and yarn to be spun. In spring, the soil had to be tilled and the animals turned out. Summer was the time for collecting peat, fishing, collecting kelp and, above all, for building and restoring the dry-stone houses with their heather thatch.

Life was certainly hard, but it was far from unbearable. In many respects it was preferable to life in the industrial towns and cities of mainland Scotland. Nor were those living on the island – some five thousand by the end of the eighteenth century – simply ignorant peasants. As was written at the time, 'the whole inhabitants belong to the Established Church and are sober and well disposed people.'[5] In fact, Arran, lying as it does between the Kintyre peninsula and the Ayrshire mainland, was in the middle of the shipping lanes running in the Firth of Clyde. Many young men went to sea and, when they returned, the sailors brought news of the outside world – and of territories on the other side of the Atlantic which promised a better life. Some even took up the challenge. In 1829, for instance, a group of islanders (including a group of McMillans) left to settle in Quebec.

The first of Macmillan's ancestors to be traced in Arran is Daniel, who died in 1751 and is buried in the churchyard of Sannox, on the eastern shore of the island. Daniel's son, Malcolm, was born in North Sannox in 1734, a settlement in the hills above Sannox itself, and lived the first forty-two years of his life there as a tenant of the Duke of Hamilton before, in 1776, being granted the lease of the Cock (west division) – a similar settlement owned by the Duke, although of even greater natural beauty, in the north of the island overlooking the Firth of Clyde. Malcolm developed into a much respected figure, not only becoming one of the principal lessees (the 'tacksman') of the settlement but also an Elder of the Church of Scotland in the nearby (in other words, within two hours walking distance) fishing port of Lochranza. He also fathered ten children, the sixth of whom, Duncan, also born in North Sannox, spent no more than his childhood and early adulthood at the Cock before marrying and settling down on the eastern coast of the island at Achag in 1793.

In 1816 Duncan and his wife Catherine Crawford left Achag and moved to Irvine on the Ayrshire mainland, together with four of his six children – two daughters having died in infancy or early childhood in 1813. The leases at Achag had expired and, on the advice of his former surveyor John Burrel, the Duke had decided to alter the size and shape of the holdings available for let. Moreover, Irvine was, after all, both safer for the children's health and offered much more for their education. It was in those days exceptionally prosperous, a Royal Burgh, with a population of over three thousand, enjoying its position as the largest seaport in Ayrshire and the main port for Glasgow and the coal mines of the Scottish Lowlands. Besides, two of Duncan's other surviving children, the elder sons Malcolm and William, were already working there as carpenters. It was no great matter to arrange for Duncan a job as a carter, transporting coal to Irvine harbour for shipment to Ireland.

Daniel, the three-year-old who had come with his father from Achag, and Alexander, a new son born in Irvine in 1818, were thus brought up in circumstances far removed from the isolation of the island life of Arran. Irvine was prosperous and sophisticated, the height of Ayrshire society of the day. The Church of Scotland was substantially in evidence, not only providing spiritual comfort and corrective instruction for the undoubtedly lamentable sins committed by its flock but also the highest standards of education for its younger lambs. Both Daniel and Alexander benefited. Not only was the education in the Church of Scotland school of the highest quality but the lessons were in English rather than Gaelic. (Alexander claimed that he could not understand the Gaelic Bible his father read to him out loud.) Finally, and conclusively, their surname had been anglicised to 'Macmillan'.

At the age of ten, in the year after his father Duncan died, Daniel was apprenticed to a bookseller in Irvine High Street by the name of Maxwell Dick – also, as it happened, member of the Burgh Council, treasurer and later Grand Master of the Irvine Freemasons Lodge, the proprietor of the *Ayr and Wigtownshire Courier* and a founding member of the local Burns club. Daniel completed his apprenticeship in 1831 and left Irvine to stay with his brother Malcolm, by then minister of a Baptist congregation in Stirling. But he soon left after showing all the symptoms of tuberculosis – necessitating a period of convalescence in Irvine with his mother and even in Arran with his aunt and uncle.

Undeterred, in September 1833 Daniel crossed Scotland and took ship from Leith to London. After wandering about looking for a job he concluded that his search was hopeless and set off for Cambridge, where he found a post with a bookseller. For the next four years he read everything that came to hand – Milton, Voltaire, Gibbon, Virgil, Carlyle, Landor, Hume, Fielding, Swift, Shelley – as well as joining a Baptist congregation in the hopes that the consequent self-improvement would help with his illness. But London was soon back on his agenda, to join up with his brother Alexander – who had lived an equally peripatetic life, not least in sailing to America and back before the mast. Their early efforts were unpromising. It was only after seven miserable years that Daniel met Augustus and Julius Hare, both Sussex clergymen, the latter at the time Archdeacon of Lewes. The two reverends were so taken with him that they lent him money to set up shop in London with Alexander as manager. Soon thereafter, the Archdeacon advised him to return to Cambridge and open a bookshop there. This turned out to be spectacularly successful, so much so that the brothers were able to buy one of the established bookshops in Cambridge. The Archdeacon's money, it was by then clear, had been well invested.

One thing, of course, led to another. Daniel, in spite of continual bouts of ill health, in 1850 married Frances Orridge, the daughter of a Cambridge chemist. (In 1851 Alexander took the same step, marrying Caroline Brimley, the sister of the librarian of Trinity College.) The brothers then set about publishing in earnest. The works they accepted were generally moralistic – but they sold well. Daniel was guided in his choices by Archdeacon Hare's brother-in-law, the Reverend Frederick Denison Maurice, the founder of the movement known as Christian Socialism. *Tom Brown's Schooldays*, Charles Kingsley's *Westward Ho!* and Maurice's own *Theological Essays* were all uplifting – as well as commercial successes. By the end of the 1850s the reputation of the publishing house was established. By 1857, moreover, Daniel had fathered four children: Frederick was born 1851, Maurice in 1853, Katherine in 1857 and Arthur in 1857. In fact, Daniel only just lived to see Arthur's birth. Attacked by pleurisy in May of that year, he lasted only a few weeks before he died on 27 June, at the age of forty-three. Maurice, his middle son and Harold Macmillan's father to be, was himself left fatherless, to be brought up by his uncle Alexander and sent, as was customary, away to school and then to Cambridge. Maurice did well there, achieving a first in Classics. He first thought of going into the Church (his father Daniel had converted late in life from the Baptist Church to the Church of England), thought better of it, and taught Classics for six years at St Paul's School in London before finally accepting the familial duty and joining the Macmillan publishing house. It was early in his career there that he went on a visit to Paris – where he met his future wife.

Helen Artemesia Tarlton Belles, to give her full name (although the spelling of 'Tarlton' and 'Belles' has varied over the years), was born in the state of Indiana – more precisely in Indianapolis – some time in the first half of 1856 (the exact date is not known, since the state of Indiana did not record births until the early 1880s). Generally known by her nickname 'Nellie' (she was named after her grandmother but the second name, Artemesia, proved too difficult to handle and quickly became 'Artie'), she spent her early childhood in Indianapolis – but in the shadow of her mother's death and of the early deaths of her siblings. Nellie was, in fact, the only surviving child of her father's first marriage.

Dr Joshua Belles, her father, had followed the example of many of the time in moving from here to there as opportunity beckoned. He was born on New Year's Day 1826 in Kentucky, but his own father – his mother died soon after his birth – crossed what was then an uncertain boundary between the states to settle in the relatively fertile plains of the sister state of Indiana, where he died in 1839. Joshua, then aged thirteen and an orphan, was taken in charge by his aunt and moved back to Kentucky. Undeterred, at the age of twenty-three he returned to Indianapolis. There he studied medicine at the Indiana Medical College, the medical department of Asbury University (a Methodist foundation later named DePauw University in honour of a particularly generous benefactor) and settled in Indianapolis as a newly qualified doctor.

But even before he had graduated, Joshua had, on 22 February 1850, married Julia Reed – for him, although perhaps not for her, a socially advantageous union, given that her family had been one of the earliest settlers in Indianapolis. As it turned out, the marital home in Indianapolis was suitably blessed, if that is the right word, with five children. None of them, apart from Nellie, survived to adulthood. In fact, the death in 1854 of a daughter, Emma, was sad enough to provoke yet another move. The Belles family uprooted themselves again and took the long trail to California, where the weather was more clement and there were good possibilities for a doctor, in the settlements after the manic pursuit for Californian gold, to make a good living. Disappointed, yet again, in this, the Belles family headed back to Indianapolis a year later. By way, as it were, of compensation for the Californian failure, Julia again became pregnant and Nellie, her last child, was born.

On 11 December 1862, when Nellie was six years old, Julia herself died. The cause was, and is, unknown, but it takes little imagination to believe that Joshua Belles must have thought that he had been cursed with some sort of plague. Be that as it may, in 1864 he decided to move again. This time it was to be to the small settlement to the south of Indianapolis by the name of Spencer. Perhaps coincidentally, his decision to move came at the time of the outbreak of the Civil War. If it was not coincidence, it was a sensible decision. Joshua Belles was a known supporter of the Union against the Confederacy, and such was the division of opinion in Indianapolis over which side to support, his move out of town made good sense. More happily, it also coincided with his second marriage (although the plague was to continue – of his four children by his second wife only two reached maturity). Nellie, at the age of six, thus acquired a new home and a new stepmother.

The town of Spencer, such as it was, had been laid out in 1820. Like Owen County, of which it is the main town, it had been named after yet another fallen hero of the 1811 Battle of Tippecanoe, which had secured Indiana from the threat of the Indian chieftain Tecumseh – Captain Spier Spencer. Since then, however, there had been little development. When the Belles family arrived there in 1864 the town had not yet been incorporated by the Indiana State authorities. That was to come in 1866. The population of the place was no more than could be expected in an equivalent English village – some six hundred. There was no railway, no street lighting and no buildings of consequence other than the brick-built courthouse, a log-built (Methodist) church and a log-built tavern with the widely displayed title of 'The Old Indian'. The residents of the town made do with 'dilapidated frame based buildings'.[6] True, it was an attractive enough place, on the banks of the White River as it slowly made its way towards the Ohio and thence to the Mississippi, but the amenities for living were not, to say the least, of great comfort.

As it turned out, Dr Belles had chosen wisely. In 1868 the Indianapolis and Vincennes Railroad was connected to Spencer. The coming of the railroad gave Spencer, as in so many other places in the United States, the lift which was needed. Not only had the property which Dr Belles had acquired – substantial, as it happened – suddenly become very much more valuable with the arrival of new and hitherto unimaginable industrial projects – but it also allowed those who benefited from the upsurge in the local economy to become great figures in the land. Dr Belles became a Freemason, an enthusiastic temperance worker, a Government Examining Surgeon, a leading member of the Methodist congregation and generally a dignitary of some considerable standing. Known for his 'above medium height ... a beard, not a heavy beard ... a very pleasant voice with a ringing tone ... [and] a rather ruddy complexion',[7] he was by all accounts a popular doctor in the town.

Nellie, too, obviously took to life in Spencer. She ran around the streets with her little dog and joined in whatever fun was going. As she grew into adolescence, she went out with the local 'beaus',[8] such as they were, borrowing a garnet ring and brooch for the purpose from her friend Emily Drescher. But she had to grow up, and, such was her father's wealth and standing that it allowed him to send her to a much grander school in Indianapolis – Miss Henrietta Colgan's School for Girls.

The question then was where Nellie would stay in Indianapolis, since it was unthinkable that she should be left on her own. As it happened, this was easily resolved. The Belles had by then become part of an extensive network of Indiana interrelated families owning property in Indianapolis and the subsidiary townships – Sanders, Wallace, Bayless, Fletcher – who formed a solid source of candidates both for Indiana State positions (including State Governors) but also for social preferment. It was therefore a simple matter for Dr Belles to request a berth for his daughter. Quite where she lodged is not known, but it would certainly have been in a house of one of Dr Belles's acquaintance.

Nellie studied singing – she had a gift for music as well as a fine contralto voice – and painting. She sang in the choir of the Methodist church and went out sketching in the streets of Indianapolis. So far, as it were, so good. But Nellie by that time was near to being a mature woman – 'tall, dark'[9] and no doubt with the flashing eyes of a somewhat rebellious temperament. In short, what Dr Belles had not expected was that Nellie, once there, might spread her romantic wings. While still at her school she met a young portrait painter (with several – although to the modern eye indifferent – portraits of Governors of Indiana to his credit) by the name of John Bayless Hill and, perhaps rather suddenly, agreed to marry him.

Her decision once accepted by her father – whether reluctantly or not is not known – she then proceeded in June 1874, at the age of nineteen, to marry 'Jackie' Hill, as he was known, in the Methodist church of Spencer. After their honeymoon the couple settled down in Indianapolis. But the marriage was not to last long. After only five months Hill unexpectedly fell ill and died in November at his father's house in Indianapolis (quite what he died of and why he died in his father's house are still unsolved mysteries). Undeterred, after her brief – and childless – marriage Nellie stayed on in Indianapolis for a year or so with the widow of a former Indiana Governor, singing, as usual, in the choir of the Methodist church. Life seemed to go on as normal. Nellie, after all, was used to bereavements. But it was far from satisfactory, and in 1876 Nellie took another decision. She wished to go to Europe. Her ambition was to study music, to improve her voice and, last but by no means least, to learn about the world beyond Spencer, Indiana. Dr Belles was persuaded, and Nellie took off on her own on a paddle steamer from New York. Her final destination was to be Paris.

Little is known about how Nellie spent her years in Paris, apart from the fact that she became fluent in French and went with friends for summer visits to the Normandy coast. Macmillan himself reported that she exhibited at the Salon and that 'she sang in concerts and at the Madeleine'.[10] He was almost certainly echoing his mother's (inaccurate) reminiscences since, while she may have sung in private houses (she was, in fact, still studying painting and music), there is no record of her in the programmes of public concerts during the years she was in Paris and she certainly could not have performed at the Church of the Madeleine (which did not allow women to sing 'even in the choir').[11] Nevertheless, she fitted well into the Paris of the *belle époque*, with its salons, its glamour and its eccentricities. Eight years in the Paris of those days turned an unsophisticated widow from Spencer, Indiana, into a worldly wise – and by then beautiful – young woman. There were many friends and, no doubt, many suitors. But the one she met at a party, and to whom she found herself attracted, was the diffident publisher from England, Maurice Macmillan.

Maurice Crawford Macmillan and Helen Artie Hill were married on 22 November 1884 in the parish church of St Mary's, Shortlands, in the presence, among others, of Alexander Macmillan. Nellie had been staying in Shortlands, now part of the London suburb of Bromley but then a village in its own right, for the purpose, while Maurice gave his address as Upper Tooting, his uncle Alexander's house. In spite of her Methodist convictions Nellie was required to accept marriage 'according to the Rites and Ceremonies of the Established Church [of England]'[12] – a special licence having been arranged to allow this to happen.

Their – extended – honeymoon took them all round the world. They called in at Spencer and continued westwards. By September 1885 Nellie was writing to her father from Australia. Finally, the long honeymoon over, the couple settled in No. 52 Cadogan Place in London. The house, along with others in Cadogan Place, had been built in the late eighteenth century as part of a development of a hitherto rural area owned by the heirs of Sir Hans Sloane and had been built on upwards in the early nineteenth century. The result was a row of tall and narrow houses on the eastern side of Sloane Street, from which they were separated by an extensive and attractive garden. The somewhat forbidding shape was accentuated by there being no bow windows – unusually for the date – and a pair of large columns supporting a balcony and a balustrade to form a handsome porch. Unlike the larger, more aristocratic residences of Mayfair and Belgravia, the houses in Cadogan Place were for the upper middle class, in other words bankers, stockbrokers – and publishers. No. 52 was thus admirably suited to the social status of the newly married couple.

Nellie threw herself into London social life with transatlantic determination. She quickly lost her American accent, gave up singing other than on very special occasions and devoted herself to amassing a substantial acquaintance. There were large dinner parties, soirées and teas. Whether she truly made friends is open to question. The parties seem designed more in pursuit of a well-defined social ambition, partly, of course, for her husband and his career but perhaps more indirectly for herself. Those invited therefore were either rich or titled – or could in the future be of use. That being so, the social occasions in Cadogan Place were not widely known to be the stuff of relaxed gaiety.

If there was little gaiety in social life there was hardly any at all in family life. In 1886 Nellie gave birth to her first son, Daniel. He was followed in 1889 by a second son, Arthur. Finally, on 10 February 1894, a third son was born, christened Maurice Harold in the church of Holy Trinity, Sloane Street. All three boys were brought up in conditions of strict discipline, as was the custom of the time. They saw more of their nanny and the cook than they did of their father or mother. Nellie herself was a demanding mother, particularly towards Harold, giving the impression that, having borne him at the advanced age of thirty-seven, she had done all that she could reasonably be expected to do other than push him relentlessly towards a suitably starry career. Certainly, affection for her sons was not Nellie's strong suit. Throughout his childhood, Macmillan later wrote, 'there was always a feeling of unease'.[13]

Nevertheless, whatever Nellie's failures in affection, the education of her sons was high on her agenda. Apart from the occasional treats – visits to the Zoo, watching the Changing of the Guard at Buckingham Palace, the Drury Lane Pantomime, summer holidays by the sea in north Norfolk and so on – the day for her youngest son was carefully regimented. There was the 'ordeal'[14] of lessons with his mother after breakfast. There was then a session at Mr Macpherson's Gymnasium and Dancing Academy, which the young boy dreaded since he was useless at all the required exercises, and an almost endless succession of French nursery maids teaching him to speak French – the mandatory language of the Macmillan household as dictated by Nellie. Finally, there was Mr Gladstone's day school, near Sloane Square, where, at the age of six or seven, he spent two years learning Latin and ancient Greek.

At the age of nine, Harold Macmillan, as was the custom of the day, was packed off to preparatory school. The chosen school was Summer Fields, then, as now, situated in attractive meadows on the northern fringes of the university city of Oxford. His father and older brothers had been there before him and it was an obvious choice. But for those who have been subjected to the experience of a boarding school at an early age, it is not difficult to understand his dismay at being dumped with his trunk at the gates of a strange and fearsome establishment. But it was worse than that. One of his father's clerks had been told to take him with his trunk to Paddington station and consign him to the care of a junior master deputed to shepherd a group of pupils on their way to their new home. It is little wonder that after his initial tea of bread and milk he broke down in tears. Even after that, he kept himself to himself – a clever, shy and at times sickly boy.

Summer Fields had been founded in 1864 unashamedly as a preparatory school for the social and intellectual élite. Its motto, taken from the Latin poet Juvenal, more or less sums up the school's vocation: *mens sana in corpore sano*. 'We believe in the Three Cs: Chapel, Classics and Cricket ... [and] a fourth C: Cold Baths.'[15] Its founder had been an enthusiastic gymnast. Fortunately, however, he had married a classical scholar. The combination of the two set the stage for one of the most successful preparatory schools of the Edwardian era – and, indeed, thereafter.

By the time Macmillan arrived, there was slightly less emphasis on gymnastics and cold baths – both of which he loathed – and more on academic achievement. Sitting behind large six-seater desks in the cavernous New Room, the boys – some one hundred and twenty of them in all – would be instructed, under penalty of the cane, in Latin and Greek. Since they were all boarders, there was nowhere for them to escape. The resulting claustrophobia led, as might be expected, to all sorts of pranks, many of them very much less than delicate. Since the boys were allowed to go swimming – naked, of course – in the River Cherwell which ran along the edge of the school's grounds, the opportunities were more or less endless. In spite of all that, however, there is no doubt that the main purpose of the school, defined by the redoubtable Dr Cyril Williams ('[I am] against all change, even change for the better'[16]), was to ensure that the pupils won scholarships to the major public schools of the day – and, in particular, to Eton. This the young Macmillan proceeded to do.

It was not quite as good as he had hoped. His elder brother Daniel had won the top scholarship and Harold could only manage third. Nevertheless, it was something to be proud of and, after the formal process of Election in July, he was deposited with his trunk – and a new uniform – at the gates of Eton College on 18 September 1906. Henceforward he was to be known simply as M. H. Macmillan KS.

Supporters of Eton College, and some critics, have maintained that the school in the period leading up to the First World War was in something of a golden age. Of course, it is a judgement which is easily made in retrospect. Nevertheless, the school was certainly blessed with some truly outstanding teachers – not least the Head Master who had replaced the terrifying Dr Edmond Warre in 1905, the more accommodating Honourable and Reverend Edward Lyttlelton, and the young Master in College, Cyril Alington. The standard of scholarship was high and in general the school 'gives to each as little and as much as his abilities and tastes demand'.[17]

That said, the entry of a new King's Scholar was, to him, full of perils. For a start, only his gown was provided by College. The rest of his uniform, tailcoat, starched collar and all – let alone a black top hat – was to be provided by his parents. On his arrival M. H. Macmillan KS was taken in charge by his seniors and subjected to a world quite different from the one he had known in the relatively benign world of Summer Fields. Newcomers in College, for instance, were regularly beaten by their seniors, the College Sixth Form, who met regularly after night prayers to summon any boy who had offended any of them for suitable chastisement. There was bullying, too, and juniors were required to serve their seniors as what were known as 'fags'. Behaviour was strictly supervised – Matron in College was in charge of washing and cleaning teeth. The dormitory in College was dark and full of possible threats. Lessons, for juniors, were not even meant to be any sort of fun. Early School, at a quarter past seven in the morning, was a matter of course. Almost worse for scholars was the ribaldry those boys who were not scholars directed at what they regarded as their social inferiors. Furthermore, nobody who was uninterested in sport was of consequence in the wider School.

None of this was, to put it mildly, to the taste of M. H. Macmillan KS. He was not interested in sport. Nor had he ever been – or ever would be. He made an effort at the bizarre and brutal encounter known as the Eton Wall Game but was clearly far from happy about it. Nor is there any record of any musical achievement of any description – nor would there ever be. In short, he was not one of the general crowd. He obviously found it difficult to fit in, other than with his immediate friends in College.

In his first – Michaelmas – school-time (as the 'half' was known in those days) he apparently fell ill. Later, Macmillan asserted that he was a victim of a 'serious attack of pneumonia'.[18] That may or may have not been so, although there are, reasonably enough, no surviving medical records of the event. Yet Macmillan's version in his memoirs has to be treated with caution. In the days before the arrival of modern drugs the only treatment available for the sufferer was a long, perhaps up to three months, period of isolation since at the time it was believed that pneumonia was infectious. In spite of this, however, M. H. Macmillan KS appears in the D1 Division lists (the first port of call for new King's Scholars) throughout the three school-times in the year 1906–7, studying Classics, English Grammar, Mathematics, Elementary French and, on Monday mornings, Divinity.

Macmillan's school career continued in a predictable – and predicted – pattern. From the lower Divisions of D1, always in the top class, he moved in Michaelmas school-time 1907 to C1, thence to B1 in 1908 and on to A1 in 1909, achieving membership of the First Hundred – achieved by academic rather than sporting merit – by the beginning of the Michaelmas school-time of that year. But at this point, there is a mystery. M. H. Macmillan KS suddenly disappeared from the A1 Division lists before Christmas 1909.

It was certainly not unusual in those days for boys to leave Eton early. But in most cases some explanation was offered to the school authorities. In this case, none is recorded. Macmillan himself claimed, 'I suffered from growing too fast, and a bad state of the heart was diagnosed. This led to my leaving Eton prematurely and spending many months in bed or as an invalid.'[19] His explanation has at least one detectable element of truth. He had grown physically, and his eyes were giving him trouble. On the other hand, whatever the 'heart trouble' may or may not have been, there is little record of this in his later life.

There is an alternative explanation for Macmillan's early departure from Eton. In his diaries, Woodrow Wyatt – later Lord Wyatt of Weeford – recounted how on 4 June 1986 he was telephoned by a friend who said '... you told her a very good story about Harold Macmillan being expelled for buggery from Eton'. Wyatt replied, 'it is quite true. J. B. S. Haldane wrote it to me. He was in the same house at Eton. Harold Macmillan has never been back as a former Old Boy who had become Prime Minister would have been.'[20]

It is certainly true that John Haldane was an exact contemporary of Macmillan in College at Eton. In fact, he arrived before Macmillan in 1905 with the First Scholarship and stayed the full course to 1911. As such, he would without a doubt have been aware of what was happening in the cubicles of the College dormitory. Furthermore, homosexuality was commonplace – John Maynard Keynes had, after all, been in love with Macmillan's elder brother Daniel. Moreover, Macmillan, judging from the photographs of the time, was a singularly attractive boy, and in those days both the granter and the recipient of such favours were regarded as equally culpable. On the other hand, Haldane had his own streak of particular malice, and by the time he was writing to Wyatt had been somewhat brutally rebuffed by Macmillan on two occasions. To add to the confusion, Haldane was plainly wrong on one count: Macmillan did go back to Eton on many occasions.

M. H. Macmillan KS finally ended his career at Eton in April 1910. The date is recorded in the College Book (an annual account of College events kept by Captains of the King's Scholars) of the summer of 1910. The book also records that 'throughout [the year] College has lived at peace with itself and with the authorities'.[21] It therefore seems unlikely that Macmillan was expelled. Nevertheless, there is no 'obituary' of him in the book, as was customary for leavers. The most likely explanation is that his mother decided to withdraw him, whether for illness or to avoid trouble is impossible to tell. Nellie certainly thought not that he had done anything wrong but that it was Eton which had let her son down. Whatever the truth of the matter, Nellie was determined that her son should go to Oxford University.

She therefore canvassed for tutors who would instruct him in the necessary skills. Many names came up in the search, and a number were tried. In the end, Nellie fixed on a young man, Ronald Knox, who had been First Scholar at Eton – leaving in 1906, the year Harold arrived. As it turned out, it was not an altogether happy choice. The young Harold was about to fall under the spell, not just of the continued possibility of homosexual relationships, but of the highest of all the high varieties of Anglican Christianity.

2

'Balliol Made Me, Balliol Fed Me'[1]

'He ... missed that last year which is so often the best for an Etonian and so perhaps did not greatly enjoy his time at Eton, but what is quite certain is that he greatly enjoyed being an Old Etonian.' Thus Lord Charteris of Amisfield, a later Provost of Eton, writing after Macmillan's death.[2] Certainly, Charteris cannot be accused of overstatement. The truth is that Macmillan was deeply unhappy almost throughout his time at Eton – even leaving aside the circumstances of his early departure. He did not like sports of any variety; he did not like music of any kind; with few exceptions, he did not particularly like his fellow Collegers; and there was constant harassment from his mother about his progress. But, equally, he did not just 'greatly enjoy' being an Old Etonian. He revelled in it. In his later years he wore to shreds the tie of which Old Etonians are so particularly proud. Moreover, and above all, he had absorbed at school, and practised thereafter, that special brand of social arrogance which was characteristic of the most dedicated Etonians of the time.

With three of his fellow Collegers, however, Macmillan did make firm friends. The first of the trio was the closest. Harry Crookshank had in fact known Macmillan before Eton, both in London, where Crookshank had his home in Pont Street, within easy walking distance from Cadogan Place, and at Summer Fields. The friendship was cemented with their arrival in College in the same year, and was to continue after Eton, the war and into Conservative politics. But it was not altogether easy. Crookshank was a much more confident boy than Macmillan, and certainly less preoccupied with his own health. He was thus a suitable antidote to Macmillan's occasionally severe bouts of depression, but, because of that, he could be something of a bore. The second of the trio, Henry Willink, on the other hand, was more introspective, at different times gregarious and withdrawn, while the third member, Julian Lambart, was even then given to the pomposity which he carried through to his career as an Eton master and subsequently Vice Provost and, according to one of his colleagues, 'all that there is of the most worthy but ... lacking in red corpuscles'.[3] What brought them together, of course, was that all of them were exceptionally clever.

Naturally enough, these friendships lapsed, at least temporarily, after Macmillan's premature departure in the late autumn of 1909 (Lambart declared himself 'shattered').[4] Macmillan had been drawn back in to his mother's embrace – and to what turned out to be a series of tutors employed to coach him in the subjects required to win a scholarship to what his mother believed to be the summit of worldly ambition, Balliol College, Oxford. In pursuit of this, Nellie had decided not just that a full-time tutor was required but that Harold should be removed to exile in their recently acquired country home at Birch Grove.

Birch Grove House, near East Grinstead in Sussex, had been bought by Maurice Macmillan in May 1906. Although Macmillan later described it as a 'small property',[5] it was in fact a very substantial estate. The cost, £13,000, was in itself large for the time. The house itself consisted, on the ground floor, of '3 Reception Rooms. Billiard Room, Lounge, Conservatory, Hall, Gun Room, Lobby, Kitchen, Scullery, Pantry etc.' and on the first and second floors, '17 Bed and Dressing Rooms, 1 Bath Room + 1 Water Closet'. It was situated in 'about 108 acres of land' of which some '16 acres' were woodland.[6] The rest of the land was cultivated by two sizeable tenant farms and there were in all nine cottages – those living in them, of course, tied to the Macmillans as owner, since their rents were subject to the services rendered to the land or to the owner's house. Given the high price, it was not certain that Maurice had bought wisely. The house had a leaky roof, the stables were in disrepair, and the Racquet court and Billiard Room needed attention. A very great deal of work had to be done to make the place even reasonably habitable.

It was in this – at the time remote and only recently finished – house that tutors were invited to live and to look after their young charge – and to cope with his mother. It was not an easy task, even if those selected had been suited to it. Nellie, for no identifiable reason, considered that former Eton colleagues of Macmillan's elder brother Daniel were preferable to all others. But, for one reason or another they did not last long, and throughout 1910 and 1911 tutors came and went. Bernard Swithinbank, for instance, was one – and seemed eminently qualified until it turned out that at Eton he had been in love with Daniel (competing, as it happened, for Daniel's affections with John Maynard Keynes). Dilwyn Knox, another of Daniel's close friends at Eton, was next in line, but he was judged 'austere and uncongenial'[7] and was quickly dismissed. The third Etonian young scholar to be tried was Ronald, Dilwyn Knox's younger brother. It was his turn to take on the sixteen-year-old boy and equip him to win the scholarship to Balliol his mother was determined he should have. The deal, as it were, was done.

Ronald Knox (or 'Ronnie', as he was always called) was, without a doubt, one of the intellectual stars of his generation. He had followed the well-trodden path of Summer Fields to Eton, where he headed the scholarship roll. His career there was a continuing and spectacular success. He won almost all the available prizes – the Harvey Verse Prize, the Latin Essay and the Davies Scholarship, only missing out on the Newcastle Scholarship, for which he came second in one year to Daniel Macmillan. The following year he was ill (the winner in that year, his friend Patrick Shaw-Stewart, was so upset that he went privately to the Provost to request that he resign the Newcastle in Knox's favour). He was also editor of the *Eton College Chronicle*, President of the Essay Society and of the Shakespeare Society, Secretary of College Debating Society and, in his last two school-times at Eton, Captain of the School.

But Knox's career at Eton had a darker side. Two junior Collegers, arriving in 1904, were of particular interest to their seniors. Both were beautiful, but the younger of the two was the more so. Around the two there developed a 'heterogeneous and infatuated group',[8] which went beyond College to the rest of the school. Within this group there was fierce competition to secure the affections of the two boys, but the competition was fiercest over the younger of the two. Ronnie was one of the infatuated group, and duly set out with determination to secure the prize of the younger boy's affections. He proceeded to exercise all his charm – to the boy – and all his authority – to his competitors. In the face of this double offensive, the competitors duly acknowledged defeat and the prize was successfully won.

Such as it was, it was a romantic tale – and, for that matter, not uncommon in the Eton of the day. But there was an unusual slant to this particular story. Ronnie, as the son of the then Bishop of Manchester, had, as might be supposed, been brought up in the traditional ambiguities of the established Church of England. But by 1904 he had already started on the path which ultimately led him to Roman Catholicism. In the summer he started to seek out those Etonians who came from 'High Church' homes – his friend Julian Grenfell, for instance, who had regularly read Thomas à Kempis's *Imitation of Christ* from the age of thirteen. He started to read the *Church Times*, the main publication of the Anglo-Catholic movement of the day. He went to Mass every other Sunday (alternating with the school service in Eton College chapel). Above all, he started to study the theology and ecclesiology of Roman Catholicism.

All that sat uneasily with his new conquest at Eton. As a result, there was much wringing of spiritual hands and agonised examinations of conscience. But, for all the inner argument, other than surrendering to the temptation of the flesh there was only one possible outcome – renunciation of worldly pleasures in order to 'have power to attend upon the Lord without impediment'. Knox therefore 'knelt down at the age of seventeen and bound myself to a vow of celibacy … I was just beginning to form close and intimate friendships … [which] … were likely to be dissolved through circumstances of separation after leaving school.'[9] Intimate friendships, such as they were, could only interfere with his spiritual life.

All in all, Knox had loved Eton as much as Macmillan had loathed it. Of course, as far as Nellie was concerned that was neither here nor there. What to her was of overriding importance was that Knox had won the top scholarship to Balliol in 1906 and had taken his place there in that autumn. His Oxford career then had matched his career at Eton. He had been, it was said, one of the most promising scholars in the memory of the College. Furthermore, the Balliol of his day was still only just past the intellectual flood tide which had placed it at the forefront of higher education for those who, whatever their origin, were without any doubt destined to run, as a matter of course, the affairs of the United Kingdom and the British Empire. Indeed, it was said at the time that there were three institutions for higher education in England: Oxford, Cambridge and Balliol. But the accolades, as Nellie was quick to realise, were not won easily.

For Ronnie Knox, the world after Balliol had any number of signposts along the road to power and glory. But, brilliant and charming though he was, he had already decided that it was not a road he wished to take. It was not as though he was not capable or, at times, willing. He had known power in the Presidency of the Oxford Union. He had nibbled at the bait of politics at the Canning Club. He could be as arrogant and as stupidly boisterous as anyone. He had joined with other Old Etonians in taking possession of the Annandale Society, a drunken dining club. It was commonplace to refer to the rest of Balliol as 'the plebs', to throw crockery about after dinners and to chase 'nonentities' off the premises of the college. He had his own 'Pleasant Sunday Afternoon Club' to which all were invited to play parlour games – charades were a great favourite – and went punting on the river with Shaw-Stewart and his friends. In short, on the surface he seemed quite prepared to join in all the fun, and even to accept the destiny of the end product of the Balliol of the first decade of the twentieth century.

But for Knox there was another side – and a greater imperative. It was almost another existence for him, far away from the frivolities of undergraduate life, and, early on in his Balliol career, he set out to explore it. For those who wished, of course, Oxford, in addition to the more worldly pleasures, then as now offered many opportunities for their other existence – the spiritual life. That was the road Knox had decided to follow. He pursued further his study of Anglo-Catholicism. In fact, the attraction for him, and for others of his generation, was simple. Without conceding the general authority of the Pope, Anglo-Catholics wished to restore the Roman liturgy in the Church of England to the point where the union of Roman Catholics and Anglicans, broken at the Reformation, could finally be achieved. In practice, of course, it meant that its adherents could indulge in the sumptuous (and hugely enjoyable) rituals which were considered appropriate to the cause. Not only that, but enthusiasm for the cause prompted Knox, not content with his own observances, to go out of his way to organise a tea party every Friday to which acolytes were invited for an exposition of the Anglo-Catholic position (they were known, in the Oxford tradition of gentle mockery of the High Church, as 'Spikes').[10]

In all this there was a particular and important relationship. Francis Fortescue Urquhart (his unfortunate nickname, for no known reason, was 'Sligger') was Junior Dean of Balliol when Ronnie Knox first arrived. As such, he was responsible for undergraduate discipline. It was a task he clearly disliked, since he more inclined to friendship with undergraduates than to imposing penalties for what he regarded as their regrettable but understandable lapses in discipline. Urquhart, as it happened, was a devout Roman Catholic – in fact, the first Roman Catholic to be elected as a Fellow of an Oxford College since the Reformation. Of all the Fellows of Balliol to whom Knox took a liking – and there were many – Urquhart was the first and, indeed, the foremost. He was not a great scholar, lived largely on his own private means, and had neither great wit nor stature, but he was affectionate, generous and charming. Needless to say, he was unmarried.

Urquhart owned a chalet in the Chamonix valley to which he invited undergraduates for reading and study during University vacations. Although he was careful not to push too hard, Urquhart used these occasions gently to promote Roman Catholicism. In 1908 Knox was one of the party. Although he was attracted – both to Urquhart himself and Roman Catholicism – Knox did not at that stage feel the attraction strongly enough to desert Anglicanism. By way of counterweight to Urquhart, in the following year, during the Long Vacation, he stayed with the community of Anglican Benedictine monks at Caldey Island. He was deeply impressed by the tranquil spirituality of the monks. In fact, he was sufficiently impressed to consider joining the community after he left Oxford. It was only on his return to Oxford and the secular atmosphere of Balliol that he came to the conclusion that his flirtation with monasticism did not constitute a true vocation. He therefore decided to seek the more conventional form of ecclesiastical career. When he left Balliol in June 1910 – with the inevitable First in Greats – he set about preparing himself for ordination as deacon in the Church of England. In the meantime, he had been offered – and accepted – a post as tutor in Classics at Trinity College, Oxford. This, it was agreed, would not be taken up before the spring of 1911.

It was this wholly unusual character that Nellie Macmillan chose as the next tutor for her youngest son. In late September 1910 Ronnie Knox duly appeared at Birch Grove, ready and apparently willing to take his pupil in charge and coach him in Latin and Greek literature, translation, verse and prose composition in both languages and the details of grammar and syntax, in order to prepare him for the ultimate destination – a Balliol scholarship. This, Knox was, without a doubt, properly equipped to do both by his academic record and from his own experience of the reality of Oxford life.

At first, all went well. The two young men found themselves to be something approaching kindred souls. The lessons at Birch Grove – under Nellie's severe eye – were completed according to schedule. But, as it turned out, there was a problem. Ronnie could not resist introducing his young charge to the delights of High Church Anglicanism. They went together to services in the one church in the neighbourhood whose liturgy met Ronnie's approval. Macmillan duly responded, not just to the liturgy but to his tutor's character. 'He was the only man I have ever known who really was a saint ...,' Macmillan later said, 'and if you live with a saint, especially a humorous saint, it's quite an experience.'[11]

This was not at all to Nellie's taste. It was all very well for Knox to be employed to teach her son how to win a scholarship to Balliol. What was not at all well was for him to subvert her son into the ways of Christianity which were offensive to the Methodists of Spencer, Indiana, to whose general beliefs she was unremittingly attached. That simply would not do. She therefore sent for Ronnie and told him that in future he must refrain from religious instruction and concentrate his mind solely on the task in hand. What had happened could perhaps be overlooked – provided that in future there was no mention at all of the disgraceful stuff which the tutor had been trying to force down her son's throat.

Towards the middle of October Ronnie wrote to his sister about this 'nerve-racking dispute'.[12] At the same time he wrote a long and plaintive letter to Nellie explaining – in which he said that 'when I first came here I thought that (for obvious reasons) it would be better if I didn't – whether in public or tête-à-tête – mention anything connected with Eton in Harold's presence' (a reference, almost certainly, to Macmillan's premature departure). Moreover, he claimed that 'it didn't matter' and, moving on from that, 'I feel that I couldn't keep up a reticence about my view of the Church'. Nevertheless, he accepted that to live in the same house would not 'be quite tolerable' and therefore suggested that he should live in London and commute to Birch Grove.[13] But Nellie would have none of it. Matters came to a head in what was obviously a series of stormy interviews. Ronnie was finally told simply to pack his bags and leave by the next train. All he could do, once he got back to London, was to write to request that his bicycle be sent to him at Oxford.

On 4 November, noted carefully as the feast of San Carlo Borromeo, Ronnie wrote a mournful letter to his sister. '. . . it's Mrs [Macmillan]. She (having made certain discoveries) wanted me to promise not to mention anything connected with religion to her son. Of course I refused; from Thursday 27th [October] to Tuesday 1st [November] we were arguing almost continually . . . So I left yesterday: they may want me to come back, but I can't do it under any promises whatsoever. The only thing which complicates the situation is that I'm by now extremely (and not quite unreturnedly) fond of the boy, and it's been a horrid wrench to go without saying a word to him of what I wanted to say.'[14] Nellie was obviously not taking any risks – in any direction.

There it was. But the enforced separation was deeply felt by both men. The truth is that Knox had been perilously close to falling in love with Macmillan (many years later he painfully set the episode down as 'one of his formative experiences'[15]) and Macmillan had in turn fallen under Knox's spell. But love, such as it was, formed only part of it. What fascinated the young man was the sudden opening of the vista of spiritual life such as he had never experienced at Summer Fields or Eton, let alone at home. It was a fascination he was never to lose.

In the autumn of 1911, having survived further tutors whose number and whose names have not been recorded, Macmillan sat the Balliol Scholarship examination. He found the whole process daunting. The papers seemed to mean nothing to him. Looking around, he noticed the other candidates scribbling away frenetically while he sat mesmerised. Quite clearly, he had missed the practice in taking competitive exam-inations which he would have had at Eton. As it turned out, his near panic was justified, since he failed to win the coveted scholarship. By way of consolation, however, he was awarded the Williams Classical Exhibition. It was a disappointment (his elder brother Daniel had won the Senior Classical Scholarship) but he could reassure his ambitious mother that he had at least placed a first step on the ladder to great things.

In September 1912 Macmillan arrived at the gates of Balliol. If he had

been expecting something resembling the entrance to Weston's Yard at Eton, he was to be disappointed. In fact, the whole college had been the subject of a large, joyless and clumsy reconstruction under the Mastership of Dr Benjamin Jowett in the last quarter of the nineteenth century. The only building which remained in its pre-Victorian splendour was the Library – and even that was partly obscured by the ugly rebuilding. On the other hand, although architecturally inept, Jowett had presided over a period of academic brilliance.

By the time Macmillan took his place among all this brilliance it had to some degree faded. Jowett's successor as Master, Edward Caird, had deliberately reduced the proportion of undergraduates from the great English public schools. The result was not a great success. Instead of getting the 'best men (in several ways) from the Public Schools and let[ting] them mix with intelligent men from Birmingham etc',[16] the result was not at all what was intended. Undergraduates split up into exclusive and mutually suspicious groups. The Balliol Etonians were, it need hardly be said, the most exclusive. They were certainly not going to mix with 'intelligent men from Birmingham' nor were they prepared to mix with men from other public schools. To be sure, a stronger Master might have taken them in hand, but Caird's successor, J. L. Strachan-Davidson, was weak and ineffectual (and anyway rather enjoyed the excesses of the young tearaways). Annoyingly, too, the young Etonian tearaways always seemed to come at the top of the scale of academic honours.

As was inevitable, it took some time for Macmillan to settle down at Balliol. For a start, the rooms he had been allocated were not to his liking. Perhaps they were better than Birch Grove House – at least alcohol was not forbidden – but he had to walk across Front Quad to get to the nearest bathroom. There was then the matter of finding his feet in the curriculum of Honour Moderations, the study of the ancient languages of Latin and Greek, to which he was committed by the terms of the Exhibition which he had won.

But after the initial hesitation, Macmillan fitted in well. To be sure, he was never a tearaway – nor would he ever be. In fact, he was rather like the friends that he made – quiet, studious and somewhat aloof. Of course, he learnt how to drink, how to joke and how to gossip, but he never, as far as is known, imitated other undergraduates in getting uproariously drunk and trying to dismantle various parts of the college or hanging up a freshman's trousers outside his window. He joined political clubs, the Canning (Conservative), the Russell (Liberal) and became a member of the Fabian Society (Labour). Since his (new) friend Walter Monckton was President of the Oxford Union for the year

1912–13 he was encouraged to join the Union. He spoke generally in support of the Liberal government of the day – in his maiden speech in February 1913 he was particularly severe on the public school system (reflecting, perhaps, his unhappy memories of Eton) – and spoke well, although at times his delivery was criticised for being mannered and his texts for being overprepared.

There is no doubt at all that Macmillan, once he had settled down, thoroughly enjoyed his time at Balliol. He made many lasting friends: Monckton, A. P. Herbert, Humphrey Sumner, Robert Cranborne from Christ Church and Guy Lawrence from Trinity. But his friendship with Lawrence was altogether different from the others. It was with Lawrence that he shared his deepest thoughts about Christianity. The reason for this was simple. Both were under the spell of Ronnie Knox, by then an ordained deacon and recently installed as Chaplain of the next door Trinity College. Knox, of course, had noticed the arrival at Balliol of his former pupil and great friend – and had quickly made contact.

Lawrence was in some ways an unlikely friend for Macmillan. To be sure, he had won all the available prizes at Winchester and had come to Trinity as senior classical scholar. As such, he was Macmillan's intellectual equal. But he was also, quite unlike Macmillan, a sportsman. He was 'tall, fair, affectionate and highly strung',[17] he played football for Oxford and he became President of the Oxford University Dramatic Society. All in all, he was an example of all that a good Wykehamist should be. And yet, like Macmillan, he was plagued with doubts about his Christianity. The question which exercised him was simple: would it not be better, instead of imitating Rome in Anglo-Catholicism, to go the whole hog and convert? This was indeed the question which had been exercising Knox for a long time. In fact, in his dispute with Nellie in 1910, she had more or less told him that he should stop pussy-footing around and go over to Rome.

Knox was accustomed to entertaining the undergraduates of Trinity – or at least those he found amusing – on Wednesdays after dinner in Hall, offering the odd mixture of port and bananas in what became known as 'Ronnie's Bar'. That was purely a secular occasion dedicated almost entirely to listening to Ronnie making his guests laugh. It was entertaining and without any pretence to spread a religious message. That came in a more serious event. 'Spike Teas', as they were called, were open to sympathetically High Church theology students, visiting clergymen and tutors from other colleges. But by the time of the arrival of Macmillan at Balliol and Lawrence at Trinity in the autumn of 1912, a 'third circle ... was beginning to form ... cleverer than the "banana eaters" and grander and gayer than the Friday afternoon "spikes"'.[18] 'It is hard to give a definition or even a description of them,' Knox wrote, 'except perhaps to say that in a rather varied experience I have never met conversation so brilliant – with the brilliance of humour, not of wit. It was of those that I first began to make proselytes.'[19] Lawrence and Macmillan were immediately recruited – and willingly so – to the third circle. It seemed altogether natural and worthy. But such was the moral climate of the times, the illegality of homosexual relations and the avoidance of the merest sniff of suspicion, that in Knox's writings, and even in his letters, they were known as 'B' (Lawrence) and 'C' (Macmillan) respectively.

Whatever the attractions of almost endless discussion of Anglo-Catholicism and its relations with Rome, work had to take precedence. Macmillan, as might be expected, studied the syllabus of Classical Honour Moderations with the greatest diligence. It was not a time for taking risks. Homer, Virgil, Aeschylus, Sophocles, Cicero, Horace, Euripides, the Greek Lyric poets, Hesiod, were all read and reread to the point – as was required – where he was able to spot a particular line or sentence from any of them, state where it came from (chapter and verse) and what its context was.

All this he did, but there is no doubt that outside his work his main preoccupation was the now tripartite relationship of Knox, 'B' and 'C' and the conundrum of whether 'the Anglican situation had become impossible'.[20] In other words, should he, or should he not, follow Knox's obvious intention to convert to Rome. Throughout 1913 and into 1914 the three of them conversed and corresponded in the most intimate terms. 'Harold dearest', started one letter, which ended 'your always loving Ronnie Knox'.[21] The letters went to and fro as did the debate about the validity of Anglican orders against the objections of Rome. True, there were some welcome breaks. In July 1913 Macmillan was invited by Urquhart to a reading party in his chalet – train to Paris, where there were two days of sightseeing, and the magic of the overnight express south, waking up to a first sight of the Alpine scenery. Yet Urquhart was himself something of a proselytiser, and Roman Catholicism even in the French Alps was not far away.

In March 1914 Macmillan sat the examination for Honour Moderations. The result was to everybody's satisfaction – a first. Yet that was not enough. He became again depressed and anxious about his future. He even talked of opting out of the summer term. Knox wrote to him to persuade him not to give up what he had achieved – and was successful. In the event, Macmillan was wise to return to Oxford. It was, after all, the best of moments in the four-year 'Greats' course, the summer term after 'Mods' when the final Greats examination is more than two years away. Needless to say, Macmillan and his friends took full advantage of what turned out to be an exceptionally fine summer. The term was thus 'devoted almost wholly to enjoyment. All that summer we punted on the river, bathed, sat in the quad, dined and argued with our friends, debated in the Union, danced at Commemoration balls.'[22]

For the Long Vacation of summer 1914 Ronnie Knox was lent the fine old house of More Hall near Stroud in Gloucestershire. It was owned by an Anglican clergyman, Charles Sharpe, who had declared his intention of founding there an Anglican Benedictine community to replace the community at Caldey which had voted unanimously to desert their – admittedly uncomfortable – Anglicanism and to swear allegiance to Rome. Knox thought the project quite splendid, and invited his 'circle' – Lawrence being the prime mover at the time – for a 'reading party' to take place in August. Knox chose the wine and Lawrence chose the chef. 'I think we shall all have a priceless time,' Lawrence wrote.[23] The one man in the 'circle' who was shy about going to the Knox reading party was Macmillan. He was worried about his mother's reaction ('his mother's apron strings', Lawrence wrote[24]). But in the event the reading party never took place, since the Oxford Long Vacation was interrupted, against all the expectations of the brilliant young men and amid the sybaritic entertainments of that summer, by the onset of the First World War.

Without them being at all aware, while the punting and bathing and dancing were all that concerned Macmillan and his friends, the shadows were steadily lengthening in central Europe. But the shadows were soon to fall on the revellers of that summer. In his memoirs, Macmillan recorded the day, or rather the night, on which he heard about the assassination of Archduke Franz Ferdinand at Sarejevo. 'It was a grand ball', he wrote, 'in the old style – carnations and smilax up the stairs, and Mr Cassani's string band, with one waltz succeeding another ... I remember coming out into the street in the early hours of the morning ... and hearing a paper-boy calling out the news ... "Murder of Arch-duke".'[25] (The story is, of course, striking – but, as it happens, suspect. The Archduke was assassinated on 28 June 1914 – a Saturday in Serbia in the Greek calendar but a Sunday in Western Europe. The news certainly arrived in London the same evening, but there was no ball on that Sunday evening in London. As such, the story either belongs to a different date – or is no more than Macmillan's ability to spin a good tale.)

In the month between the assassination and the outbreak of war, the political temperature continued to climb. For the Balliol scholars of the day there was only one feeling: when war came, they must do their duty to King and country and go to fight. This they did, but the result was truly dreadful. Out of all the Scholars and Exhibitioners of his year only Sumner and Macmillan himself were to survive the ensuing carnage. One by one, they all went. One of the last to go was Guy Lawrence – at the end of August 1918. 'When I heard about Guy Lawrence,' Knox wrote five months later, 'I was completely numbed to all feeling for three or four days, but expecting all the time that when I became unnumbed I should simply break down.'[26] In truth, it was Lawrence, the 'B' of Knox's *Spiritual Aeneid*, who was the favourite son. 'C', Macmillan, only came, yet again, second.

In spite of all the talk of love, of the letters beginning 'dearest' and ending 'your always loving' and the reading parties, there was always a certain innocence in Knox's love for 'B' and 'C', and their response. Of course, it was homosexual, but it was not homoerotic. There were perhaps the odd cuddle, the arm round the shoulder and the affectionate touch on the hand, but that was about as far as it went – in physical terms. On the other hand, there is no doubt that Ronnie Knox, whatever the nature of the attachment, was the greatest male figure of influence in Macmillan's early life – certainly very much greater than his father. Through him, Macmillan learnt the Christianity which was to stay with him for the rest of his life, not just passively but in genuine and constant devotion. If Balliol made him and Balliol fed him, in the sense that it was at Oxford that his intellectual gifts were honed and polished, it was Ronnie Knox who had shown him the rewards of a truly spiritual life. Besides, and apart from all else, Balliol and Knox together had given him enough character at least to make the attempt to stand up to his mother.

3

'I Was Very Frightened'

Macmillan's war got off to a slow start. In fact, it nearly did not start at all. In the run-up to the outbreak of war in August 1914 he was fully ready and altogether willing, echoing the almost manic enthusiasm of the day. But his health, yet again, let him down. Towards the end of July he was diagnosed with an inflamed appendix. The subsequent operation – difficult and life-threatening as it was in those days – kept him first in hospital and subsequently convalescing in Cadogan Place. Nothing could have been more frustrating. He was, of course, more than eager to follow in detail the progress of the war, but even that was denied. News of the great events of the early months of the war only reached him by sporadic bulletins, and often ill-informed reports, in the press. As Christmas 1914 loomed, with the certainty that almost all his friends from Eton and Balliol were already in France joining in what was supposed to be the fun, Macmillan's greatest concern was that he would miss the show on which, as had been confidently predicted, the curtain would be rung down at the turn of the year.

The one exception to the rush from Eton and Oxford to war was Ronnie Knox. As a clerk in Holy Orders, as he quite rightly pointed out, was disbarred from military service (apart from a chaplaincy) even if he had felt so inclined. But there was still one piece of unfinished business between him and Macmillan. All the discussion of Roman Catholicism at Oxford had been leading Knox himself, but also 'B' and 'C', to reflect on whether or not they should finally burn their theological bridges and convert to Rome. In the event, 'B', Lawrence, took the step early on in the war, Knox himself followed later on, but 'C', Macmillan, drew back, at least for the duration of the war. 'Dearest Ron,' he finally wrote on 23 July 1915, 'I am not going to "Pope" until after the war (if I'm alive).'[1] He was, after all that had happened, fully aware that to convert to Roman Catholicism would mean a major rupture with his mother. As such, his decision made good sense. He was still hoping to go to France to fight, and the one person he would write letters to – as it happened, on an almost daily basis – was his mother.

In mid-October 1914 Macmillan was just about well enough to be allowed to join up in one of the Territorial regiments of the King's Royal Rifle Corps (60th Rifles), the Artists' Rifles (formed as part of Lord Kitchener's 'New Army' volunteers mainly to accommodate out-of-work actors – and lawyers). Parades were held in the Inns of Court, though without equipment, uniforms or rifles since none were available. In this ragbag outfit Macmillan was immediately commissioned as an officer, and it was as a 2nd Lieutenant that in late November he was posted to a newly formed battalion of the 60th stationed at Southend-on-Sea. He managed to pass his medical examination on arrival – although he was worried about his eyesight (he was by then wearing spectacles almost permanently). Yet again, although it was a Rifle battalion, there were no rifles. It drilled – at the uncomfortably fast Rifle pace – on an open field even in the pouring rain, and learnt the principle of rifle fire – without rifles – in a small hall in the town itself.

As Christmas passed and his twenty-first birthday approached, Macmillan started to fret. His enthusiasm for war was beginning to wane, and there seemed to be no immediate prospect of getting into the war other than drilling at Rifle pace in a muddy field and practising rifle drill with sticks. He therefore took the matter into his own hands, approached his Commanding Officer, Sir Thomas Pilkington, to see whether he could transfer to another regiment where the chances of getting quickly to France and into action were rather better. Underlying his request, of course, it is not difficult to detect a wish to move from a battalion of inexperienced volunteers to a regiment of regulars – and a regiment of undoubted social prestige at that.

The procedure for officer transfer was set out in the King's Regulations of 1912. 'An application from an officer for exchange or transfer will be forwarded to the War Office,' it read,[2] along with detailed reasons for the request. In the light of all this, Macmillan's reaction was simple. 'Naturally I turned to my mother,' he later wrote.[3] Whatever the nature of Nellie's intervention, he was sent for and interviewed by Sir Henry Streatfeild, a semi-retired officer (and equerry to Queen Alexandra) who had been recalled as Commander of the Regimental District of the Grenadier Guards. The interview went without a hitch and the transfer was approved. In March 1915 2nd Lieutenant M. H. Macmillan was gazetted to the Special Reserve of the Grenadiers.

Life in London turned out to be much more comfortable than life at Southend. True, there were parades on the square at Chelsea Barracks – there being no uniforms, the dress was bowler hat, blue suit and umbrella or stick – but Macmillan was able to live at home in Cadogan Place and see friends from Eton and Oxford who happened to be passing through London on leave or on their way to France. Of course, it could not last, and in early July the announcement came that a fourth Grenadier battalion was to be formed, to be part of a newly constituted Guards Division. The gossip reported that Macmillan was to be part of it. And so it proved.

By mid-July the 4th Battalion Grenadier Guards, as part of the 3rd Guards Brigade, was up to strength and quartered at Bovington Camp, close to Marlow in the Thames Valley. That done, it turned out that there was little in the way of military activity for at least a month. The month, as Macmillan recorded, was 'like a perpetual garden party: glorious weather; lots of friends from London; plenty of visits to London: and, in both places, agreeable female society'.[4] But again, it was obvious that the good times could not last. On the morning of 15 August the battalion received its orders. The move was to be immediate. Late in the afternoon of the same day, the 4th Grenadiers were transported to Southampton to embark on an overnight sailing to Le Havre. Macmillan's war, up to now so long delayed, was about to begin in earnest.

It is difficult, after the long lapse of time and with the knowledge of the catastrophe to come, to recapture the sense of boisterous good humour – verging on jollity – in which the officers of the battalion embarked on their journey. After the 'other ranks' had been suitably settled, the officers were led to a 'full luncheon ... in the style of a peace-time party', presided over by 'Charles, the presiding genius of the Ritz'.[5] That done – the food all eaten and the wine all drunk – the officers retired to their quarters for a good night's sleep, which was just as well, since although their ship arrived at Le Havre at 11 p.m. the same evening the battalion was not scheduled to disembark before seven the following morning. The jollity, this time of officers and 'other ranks', was unconfined when the battalion was greeted by a rapturous crowd on the quayside.

But, as was frequently the case with new arrivals from England, the jollity soon gave way to worry and then apprehension. After a long overnight train journey from Le Havre to St Omer and a further march to the village of Blendecques, they were billeted with strangers – French, at that, many of whom did not speak English and needed Macmillan as an interpreter. There they heard the stories of the battles of the previous winter, of the German atrocities in Belgium, of the retreat from Mons and of the dreadful casualties of modern war.

The 4th Grenadiers spent the next month in training at Blendecques. Most of the training, in fact, seemed to consist of parades. For instance, the Earl of Cavan – who had resisted the formation of a 'Guards Division' on the grounds that he might lose all Guards officers in one throw but who had subsequently accepted appointment as Commander of the Division – reviewed the 3rd Guards Brigade on 17 September, in the no doubt august presence of the Prince of Wales and was greatly impressed by the 'appearance and smartness of the [4th] battalion ... [and] that the men's packs were the best he had ever seen'.[6] Furthermore, not content with his mere presence at a review, the Prince of Wales, on 21 September, 'came to see us in the afternoon having ridden over from Lumbres on a bicycle'.[7] All that must have been most encouraging, but on the day following the bicycle visit of His Royal Highness the battalion received new orders – for a more serious event. They were to form up to march towards the front, for an offensive which subsequently became known as the Battle of Loos.

Macmillan had been rather enjoying the September at Blendecques. He had been billeted at a small château owned by a wine merchant. The wine was plentiful, as was the food. He described to his mother a dinner there of no fewer than eight courses, derived 'partly from the country, and partly from Fortnum and Mason' and concluding with cigars. 'Such are', he explained, 'at present – the hardships of active service.'[8] Furthermore, towards the end of August, the other Grenadier battalions arrived, including Macmillan's Eton friend Harry Crookshank, an event which was the occasion for another dinner. ('There were 96 of us in all,' he wrote to Nellie.[9]) True, there were some less than pleasant moments. He was obliged, in his capacity as 'bombing officer', to train a group of Guardsmen in how to throw a grenade – although there were no grenades to throw and Macmillan himself had difficulty in throwing at all. There was also the unpleasant chore of censoring Guardsmen's letters home, which he found most distasteful of all.

On the evening of 23 September, the 4th Grenadiers marched in driving rain eight and a half miles east from Blendecques to the village of Lambres, arriving at nine o'clock and going straight into billets. The following day senior officers were summoned for a briefing on the general plan of battle. The village of Loos, they were told, was – or, rather, had been before it had been largely destroyed in the fighting of the previous May – a mining village at the western end of the Lille coal basin. It was towards the southern end of what was to be the line of attack. The northern point would be the equally devastated mining village of La Bassée, some six miles to the north. In between the two villages there was a stretch of uninhabited – and, thanks to the ravages of war, desolate – flat land.

All six divisions of I and IV Corps, the officers were told, would attack on a frontage of four miles between Loos village to the south and the German fortified position known as the 'Hohenzollern Redoubt' to the

north. The immediate intention was to break through the German first
and second defence systems so that a cavalry charge would reach open
country beyond. A second wave of attack by XI Corps, which included
the Guards Division, would consolidate the gains made and move on in
support of the cavalry – and encircle the important town of Lens from
the north.

Apart from the customary artillery barrage leading to the infantry
assault, however, there was to be an innovation. Artillery shells were in
short supply, so, to make up for the lack of fire power, the Commander
of the 1st Army, General Sir Douglas Haig, had authorised the extensive
use of poison gas. Chlorine gas cylinders, each weighing some 150 pounds,
had been carried in slings between poles by teams of three men from the
transporting lorries to the trenches (an average distance of one and a half
miles), where they were to sit until the arrival of a wind favourable
enough to carry the gas across to the enemy lines – and create the
necessary panic. The cylinders worked on the 'principle of a soda-water
syphon, and on opening the cock the gas rushed out in the form of a
yellowish white vapour, which developed into a greenish yellow cloud a
few feet from the pipe'.[10] The direction of the wind was therefore vital
to the efficacy of the gas attack – and thus determined even the timing
of the whole enterprise.

At 5.50 on the morning of 25 September the gas cylinders were
turned on. The gas release was duly accompanied by an intense
artillery bombardment. 'Battle commences', it was noted at Lambres,
'. . . heard very heavy cannonade at 6.30 a.m. and got news about 9.30
a.m. that the assault had been successful.'[11] It was true. The gas had
done its work, sowing panic. Unfortunately, it had not only sown
panic in the German lines but also among the advancing British
infantry. The panic was compounded by the inexperience of the 'New
Army' battalions, which had been thrown with only rudimentary
training in to the front line. Thus, although the initial assault had
been successful, those who had achieved the success were themselves
already starting to waver.

At 1.20 in the afternoon of 25 September the 4th Grenadiers paraded
and set off on their march east to the front to take part in the 'second
wave'. After a march of some ten miles they arrived at the hamlet of
Marles les Mines at about 6 p.m. They were then told to wait – as it
turned out, for six hours, sitting down in a muddy road and only getting
a mug of tea at about midnight – to allow a cavalry corps to pass through
on their way to exploit the success of the first day's assault. They finally
arrived at their destination, another hamlet by the name of Haillicourt,
at 1.30 in the morning. They were billeted in 'very dirty and crowded

billets'.[12] But there was little time to rest since, after the usual parades and cleaning of firearms, they were due to move again at 3 p.m. By the time they arrived at their destination, one of the British trench lines which had formed the platform for the initial assault, they were well and truly exhausted. There they bedded down again as best they could for the night.

On the morning of 27 September, the Grenadiers finally girded themselves for action. Their allotted task, along with other units of the 3rd Guards Brigade, was to capture and hold a small knoll directly to the east of Loos village known as Hill 70, an important landmark overlooking Loos and the plain to the north. Hill 70 had been captured in the initial assault but had then been lost in a German counter-attack. Their task was to lead the recapture and make it secure from counter-attack. To do this they had, as they quickly realised, to make their way through Loos village. The Commanding Officer, Colonel Claude Hamilton, on hearing his orders, instructed Captain Aubrey Fletcher, Macmillan's company commander, to reconnoitre the best route into and through Loos. That done, at 2.30 p.m. the battalion formed up and headed off along the road which Fletcher recommended towards the north-west corner of the village.

This was fraught with danger. Before they could get to Loos itself they were told by an artillery officer to get off the road and take cover, since they were at risk from the German artillery. This they did, but soon, during a lull in the German barrage, decided to press on. The bombardment gradually became heavier and more accurate, not least because the battalion was by then taking shelter in old German trenches – and the German artillery, of course, knew exactly where those were. What was worse, however, was that the German shells were not just high explosive or shrapnel but – most frightening of all – gas.

Further orders then came from 3rd Guards Brigade headquarters. The battalion was to advance through Loos at once. This they did – 'under heavy shell fire and through a considerable amount of gas'.[13] In the course of the advance Hamilton collapsed from gas poisoning. The second in command, Major Myles Ponsonby, quickly took over while the whole battalion stopped to put on their 'smoke helmets' (the primitive gas masks of the day).[14] The advance continued, but in the confusion of gas, smoke and high explosive a third of the battalion, including Macmillan's platoon, lost their way and, instead of going through the middle of Loos with the others, found themselves, led by Captain Morrison (known as 'Jummie'), working under fire round the northern side of Loos. The battalion was split, about evenly, in half.

Morrison's half, once there, almost fortuitously made contact with the

1st Battalion the Scots Guards, part of the 2nd Guards Brigade, whose orders had been to attack and secure the fortified point at a pithead known as Puits 14 bis, some three-quarters of a mile to the north of Hill 70. Morrison sensibly put his troops under the command of the Scots Guards. The attack was successful. Puits 14 bis was duly secured. In the meantime, however, Ponsonby had sent Captain Ridley to find the missing half of his battalion. When Ridley did finally find them he ordered them – again, perfectly sensibly – to continue to support the Scots Guards southern flank in their occupation of Puits 14 bis while being prepared, if and when they ever managed to make contact with the other half of the battalion, to move to support its northern flank in the attack on Hill 70.

It was then about five o'clock in the afternoon. But there was a further disaster. Without telling the Grenadiers what they were doing or why they were doing it, the Scots Guards had, under heavy machine-gun fire, retreated from Puits 14 bis almost immediately after occupying it. That left Ridley, Morrison, Macmillan and some 180 Grenadiers 'completely isolated'.[15] 'We lay down under heavy machine gun fire,' Ridley reported, 'and when I realised that no further advance was possible I ordered the men to crawl back and dig themselves in on the Hulloch road, which they did.'[16]

That in itself was far from easy. Apart from all else, Morrison was much too fat to crawl fast and Macmillan was suffering from a superficial but painful head wound he had received earlier in the day. Progress was slow and erratic. But worse was to come. Almost as darkness fell, Macmillan was shot in the right hand at the base of the third finger. It was agonisingly painful. Now concussed, bleeding and in great pain, he was told by Morrison to get back to a casualty clearing station. Once there, he was sent back to hospital and thence immediately to a hospital on the Channel coast and back to England.

Macmillan's war was thus interrupted – albeit temporarily, as it turned out. Needless to say, on his arrival in England Nellie took charge again. She badgered Streatfeild to get him placed in the house of a friend of hers which had been converted into a hospital. Needless to say, too, the house was in Lennox Gardens, no more than a stone's throw from Cadogan Place. Streatfeild even took the trouble to visit him in the hospital and was full of praise for the 4th Grenadiers in capturing Hill 70 at Loos, which Macmillan, of course, knew nothing about. He only later found out that the 4th Grenadiers had in fact captured the hill itself but they had advanced too far over the crest. The German machine guns had simply picked them off. None of the attackers returned.

In the Army List of October 1915 Macmillan is recorded as being, like other wounded officers, on Grenadier Special Reserve. But shortly before Christmas 1915 he was discharged from hospital and assigned to the Reserve Battalion at Chelsea Barracks. His wound had healed well (but, as it turned out, the effect stayed with him for the rest of his life, since he never fully regained the hand's former strength). He was certainly well enough to mount guard at the royal palaces, which he did. But other than that he seemed to do little more than see his friends, read his books and enjoy the excellent food and wine both at the barracks and in the nearby Guards Club. In short, 'there was nothing to do but read and lounge',[17] reflect gloomily on the growing list of his fellow officers who had lost their lives – and to see his mother.

Yet again, it could not possibly last. In April 1916 it was back to active service, with reluctance and fear, as he told his mother. He was posted this time to the 2nd Battalion the Grenadier Guards, commanded by Lieutenant Colonel C. R. C. de Crespigny (almost inevitably known as 'Crawley', such was the passion for nicknames at the time). In one sense, it was not an easy posting. De Crespigny was about as different from Macmillan as could be imagined. Bluff, full of rough humour, he was never seen reading a book, and his passions were those sports which Macmillan particularly disliked, hunting and steeplechasing – and gambling large sums of money on them and almost everything else. 'To all intents and purposes', Macmillan was to write, 'he was illiterate.'[18] Nevertheless, in another sense and whatever the intellectual differences, Macmillan knew de Crespigny to be a fine warrior and devoted to his regiment and his junior officers. He even managed to be tolerant of the bookish lieutenant who was apt to engage his fellow officers in discussions about philosophy when in the front line. In fact, Macmillan only redeemed himself with de Crespigny by engaging – reluctantly perhaps – in some appropriately boisterous behaviour in the officers' mess.

The 2nd Grenadiers were at the time doing duty as part of the Guards 1st Brigade in the Ypres salient. After the fighting in the spring of 1915 and before the dreadful battle of June 1917, the front at Ypres in 1916 was what was known as a 'quiet zone'. The duties of the battalion were simple – and, for the most part, boring: the front line, support, reserve, a short rest and then the front line again. True, minor hostilities continued more or less as a matter of course, but by the time Macmillan joined the battalion (now as a full 'Lieutenant'[19]) these were little more than sporadic exchanges of artillery fire and sniping at anyone unwise enough to put his head up above the top of the trench wall. But living conditions were as unpleasant as those at Chelsea Barracks had been pleasant. The trenches at the front were full of mud, dark and ever dangerous, and in the reserve quarters in the cellars of Ypres there were only the rats for company. Moreover, there was the 'desolation and emptiness of it all ... One can look for miles and see no human being ... But in those miles of country lurk ... thousands, even hundreds of thousands, of men planning against each other perpetually some new device of death.'[20]

But if that was merely distasteful, there was also occasional danger. For instance, on 21 April, only four days after his arrival – Good Friday as it happened – Macmillan's platoon found themselves isolated in a forward trench in broad daylight. The communications trench leading backwards was too shallow for daylight use and they had no idea as to the whereabouts of – or how to reach – units to the right and to the left. They simply had to sit where they were, in the hope that their presence would not be discovered by the German artillery. They were in luck. But, as Macmillan reported to his mother in a letter the same day, the only comfort in his loneliness and fear was in reading St Luke's account of the Passion – and that he was 'already calculating the days till my first leave'.[21] In response, Nellie tried to persuade him to ask for a staff job – which he resolutely refused to do. In spite of that, he did admit that, all in all, life was uncomfortable, intermittently dangerous and without the satisfaction of providing the prospect of a serious contribution to winning the war.

De Crespigny, too, was dissatisfied. He wanted action. Since there was none to be had on a wider scale, it was, in his and others' view, imperative to keep up the spirit of the troops (and to relieve the boredom) by sending them during the night on patrols into no-man's-land, usually in order to seize a German from his trench and bring him back for interrogation about enemy emplacements, regiments involved and their deployment. As far as encouraging morale went, the policy was, to say the least, not wholly successful. In fact, to be nominated for a patrol was to be invited to participate in the most dangerous exercise possible. Apart from the difficulty of getting through their own wire, the patrol had continually to dodge around in the light of flares – to avoid becoming an easy target for snipers or machine guns – and then cross the German wire, avoid sentries and snatch a protesting German soldier. Needless to say, the casualty rate was exceptionally high.

On 19 July, Macmillan was nominated for one such patrol. It was not designed to snatch a victim from his trench but was simply 'a reconnoitring patrol', in other words to scout around no-man's-land to see what, if anything, was going on and, of course, if they found a stray

German, to bring him in. Together with two men, Macmillan set off. In the dark, they stumbled across a group of German soldiers at work on a tunnel for a mine. 'A German sentry threw a bomb, wounding one man and slightly wounding Lieut. Macmillan in the head and back. This officer remained at Duty.'[22]

By the standards of the First World War the incident was no more than trivial. But Macmillan was obviously rather pleased with himself. He had only mild concussion, but he recorded carefully that although the battalion medical officer had offered to send him to a hospital he had declined. Furthermore, he recorded a complimentary message sent to him by the Brigadier commanding 1st Brigade, Brigadier General Cecil ('Pinto') Pereira. Yet Macmillan's wounds are not on the list for officers of the 2nd Grenadiers in July compiled by the brigade headquarters – one killed, three wounded. Nor did Pereira note the incident in his diary (in fact, he was much more interested in a visit to his headquarters by the King – and the King's indiscretion that 'Lord French and Winston Churchill were intriguing against Douglas Haig and [William] Robertson').[23]

At the end of July the whole Guards Division left Ypres and marched south – towards the Somme. On 26 July, Macmillan was sent with a Drill Sergeant as advanced party to the village of Heerzeele to look for billets for the battalion when it arrived there. The rest of the battalion waited for two hours on a siding at Ypres before a train arrived to take them part of the way to a transit camp (the rest of the way was on foot), arriving at nearly three o'clock in the morning, then setting off again the following afternoon, again on foot, to arrive late on the 27th. There they had baths (it was a 'very hot day') received 'new underclothing' and the attentions of the 'Divisional Disinfector' – and set off again on the 30th.[24]

That day set the general pattern for the march to the south in late July and the first half of August – hot days of marching followed by days of rest in billets and light training – and periodic visits from the 'Divisional Disinfector'. Apart from noticing on 10 August that 'His Majesty the King and His Royal Highness the Prince of Wales passed us in a motor car',[25] there was little excitement. Macmillan, however, had one stroke of fortune. His friend from Eton, Harry Crookshank, had turned up again to join the battalion in mid-June. They immediately agreed to share a tent. Not only that, but on the march they soon fell into the easy kind of conversation – amused and detached – of Eton and Oxford. They spent hours looking at and commenting on the scenery – the Thiepval plateau was a particular attraction – which made 'quite a nice change after Ypres'.[26]

Appreciation of the scenery and easy conversation were soon interrupted by a return to serious matters. The 2nd Grenadiers had reached
the end of their long march. On 25 August they arrived at the village of
Meaulte where they were to be billeted. Again, the conversation turned
to gloom. It was by then clear to all of them that the assault along the line
of the Somme had not gone at all well. Casualties had been horrendous; in
spite of that, the expected breakthrough had not been achieved. Another,
and even greater effort, was needed.

The future shape of the battle was by then becoming clear. The second
great push by the British Fourth Army, so senior officers were told at a
meeting on the 27th, would come in September at the southern end of
the Somme front, and the Guards Division would be part of it. The 2nd
Grenadiers immediately stepped up their training programme. 'Training
was carried on almost continually ... in spite of moderate weather
conditions.'[27] On 31 August the battalion was sent forward for three days
to dig trenches at Carnoy. As soon as they returned, they were ordered
to prepare to move at short notice. The order was almost immediately
cancelled. Over the next few days several similar orders to move were
issued and equally suddenly cancelled. It was all very frustrating. Finally,
on 10 September, an order came without cancellation, and the battalion
moved forwards, first to camp at Carnoy and then, on the 12th, to
positions on the northern and eastern side of the village of Ginchy. The
'September push' was about to begin.

The plan of battle for the 1st Guards Brigade was, on paper, com-
mendably simple. It was to attack at 6.20 a.m. on 15 September along a
front of just over half a mile, move through Ginchy to capture Objective
1 – the Green Line (a line of German trenches) – in the early phase at
6.30 a.m., capture Objective 2 – the Brown Line (another line of
trenches) – soon thereafter at 7.30 a.m., capture Objective 3 – the Blue
Line (yet another line of trenches) – at 8.20 a.m., occupy the village of
Les Boeufs and move on beyond to the Red Line (a road), which would
be taken at 10.50 a.m. The first day's attack would thus carry the British
front line forward some 3500 yards and, in doing so, strike a decisive
blow at the enemy's defensive network.

That was all very well. But before any of that could happen,
patrols discovered several previously undetected German machine-gun
positions, manned in strength in an orchard just to the north of
Ginchy and along the road leading northward to the village of Flers –
in other words, aiming at the left flank of the Brigade's eastward
attack. Obviously they had to be taken out. On the night of 13
September, therefore, the 2nd Grenadiers, holding the northern sector
of the Brigade line, were ordered to do so. No. 4 Company, under

2nd Lieutenant Tim Minchin, was detailed for the main task and two platoons of No. 2 Company, under Lieutenant Macmillan, were ordered to protect their flank and join up with them. In the event, the operation was only partially successful. A bright moon illuminated the whole affair, and Minchin and Macmillan were forced to dig in on the far side of the orchard, which they had managed to clear, leaving the machine-gun nests on the road beyond to be cleared by one of the new machines of war which were to be deployed for the first time in a major attack – a tank.

By that time, of course, the German command was fully aware that an attack was imminent. Accordingly, the 2nd Grenadiers were bombarded all day on the 14th with heavy shells. 'The line was much knocked about and the Companies all rather shaken.'[28] That account is certainly a heroic understatement. In fact, one Company's trenches were hit by a 28-inch bomb which buried half its occupants, and the casualties to other Companies were almost as bad. The whole battalion was more than happy to be relieved by two battalions of the Coldstream Guards and to retire to 'bivouac in shell holes a few hundred yards behind Ginchy where rations were given out and rum issued. Bitterly cold night and no great coats.'[29]

But there was still the main business to be done. In fact, the plan for the 2nd Grenadiers for the main attack was as simple as the plan for the Brigade. They had already been three days in the line, had been heavily shelled and had carried out the attack on the night of the 13th. They were therefore given 'what was thought to be the easiest task'.[30] They were to follow up the initial assault made by the 2nd and 3rd Coldstream Guards battalions (with a third Coldstream battalion in support) and be prepared to form a defensive left flank in case the tank had not succeeded in knocking out the machine-gun posts along the Ginchy–Flers road. When the Coldstream were clear of the first objective they were to occupy it and allow the 1st Irish Guards to pass through them. They were then to support the Irish Guards in their attack on the fourth objective. Nothing, indeed, could have been simpler.

Early in the evening of 14 September the news came through: the infantry attack was to start, after a twenty-minute artillery barrage, at 6.20 the following morning. Before dawn, the whole battalion, indeed the whole Brigade, prepared themselves in the by then familiar mixture of intense excitement and intense fear. At 5.30 a.m. they were ready. They paraded in their heavy uniforms, their webbing properly cleaned and their firearms and ammunition carefully checked.

True to the timetable, the British artillery barrage started at 6 a.m. – with an immediate response from the German artillery. At 6.20 a.m.

precisely the 2nd Grenadiers duly moved in two lines through the
German barrage and into Ginchy, where they halted – under a heavy
artillery fire, mostly directed to the south of the village but 'we were
almost blinded by the noise and the confusion'.[31] About twenty minutes
later they decided to push on out of Ginchy, took cover in shell holes
and searched for the Coldstream battalions whom they were meant to
support. Around 7.20 a.m. they moved forward again, but there was still
no sign of the Coldstream. In fact, the initial Coldstream attack had
come under machine-gun fire from the same position on the Ginchy–
Flers road that Minchin and Macmillan had tried to knock out. The
tank had obviously failed as well. 'The first waves of the assault were
literally mown down.'[32] The two Coldstream battalions, or what was left
of them (one company had only its commander and four men surviving),
and the third Coldstream battalion in support, were forced to swing left
to face the challenge.

The 2nd Grenadiers thus found themselves advancing into territory
which had not been secured. Worse still, they found a previously
undetected German trench and were badly held up and subjected to a
'German barrage of huge shells bursting at the appalling rate of one a
second ... shooting up showers of mud in every direction ... the noise
was deafening ... in addition ... fierce rifle fire'.[33] One shell fell close to
Macmillan, a piece of shrapnel wounding him in the right knee. But,
such was his adrenalin rush, 'I felt no inconvenience until later,'[34] and,
once the trench was secure, he kept going.

The battalion then moved forward again – still expecting to find the
Coldstream Guards in front of them on the first objective, the Green
Line, where the plan said they were to wait to allow the Irish Guards to
pass through. Much to their surprise they found the Green Line still
occupied by the Germans. All they could do was to deploy (with heavy
casualties in the process) and attack. There was fierce hand-to-hand
fighting. 'The centre of the Battalion ... rushed a part of the Green Line
and bayoneted all Germans they found ... almost as soon as the centre
got in the Germans began bombing down the trench ...'[35] De Crespigny
'led his battalion like a real fighter ... took one trench at the point of
the bayonet and bombed the Boche out of other trenches'.[36] In the end,
the Line was taken, and de Crespigny gave the order to clean up the
positions which had been captured and wait for further orders. There
was still, however, an annoying machine-gun nest on the battalion's left
flank. De Crespigny ordered Macmillan to take a few men from his No.
3 Company and take it out.

Half crawling, half crouching, Macmillan was on his way towards
the machine gun when he was shot. The machine-gun bullets entered

his left buttock, fragmented and lodged in his pelvis. He knew immediately that the wound was serious. There was no question of just carrying on, but the question was what he should do next. He was in no-man's-land, as far as he could tell, between the Green and Brown Lines. All he could do was to roll into a shell hole, dose himself with morphine, and wait. For a period he slept. But shells were falling all about his shell hole; twice he was covered with mud. Germans, too, were launching counter-attacks – grey uniforms running along the lip of the shell hole. Feigning death, Macmillan lay there all day, drifting in and out of consciousness. It was not until dark that a search party came for him and took him back. There was no doubt about what should happen next. As de Crespigny said: 'Well, I think you'd better be off.'[37]

It was not to be as easy as that. Stretcher-bearers were organised – one for Macmillan, another for a fellow officer, Captain Ritchie – to take them back to a dressing station in Ginchy. When they arrived there, they found that the dressing station had been abandoned. The two officers conferred, saw no reason why able-bodied Guardsmen should risk their lives for them when they should be back in the fighting, and decided to release them. The two officers then separated. At that point, Macmillan recalled, 'I was very frightened.'[38] He knew he had to get out of Ginchy or be killed in the rain of shells which were falling there. Somehow – he hardly remembered how – he managed to stumble out of Ginchy and roll into a ditch.

Macmillan was finally picked up by the transport section of a battalion of the Sherwood Foresters. In the greatest pain, and only semi-conscious, he was taken to a dressing station. The next thing he remembered with any clarity was waking up in the French military hospital at Abbeville. The hospital was overrun with casualties from the Somme, and, since he was not on the critical list, his wound was allowed to heal as it was without being drained. Unsurprisingly, it became septic. He was then examined, and deemed no longer fit for battle. He was consequently ordered to be shipped back to England.

The hospital ship landed him at Dover. A train then took him on to Victoria. There he was put into an ambulance which had instructions to take him on to a hospital in Essex. Still in pain, running a high temperature and exhausted, Macmillan refused to do as instructed and persuaded the driver to disobey his orders and take him round immediately to Cadogan Place. When he got there, by luck, Nellie was in and answered the door. She took the matter in hand immediately, summoned a surgeon of her acquaintance and had him placed in a hospital in Belgrave Square (owned and run by two American ladies,

Lady Ward and Lady Granard). As he wrote later, 'no one who has not experienced it can realise the determination of an American mother defending one of her children.'[39] There it was. Macmillan's war had ended – in the arms of his 'mother dearest'.

4

'I Do Hope It Is Alright'[1]

It is no more than commonplace to say that the Great War, as it came to be known, changed the world; and yet it is none the less true. The history, after all, speaks for itself. The United States, which had entered the war as the largest debtor nation, emerged as the largest creditor – and the greatest of the Great Powers. The British Empire, as would become clear in the course of the next three decades, was mortally wounded. The Ottoman Empire was no more. Russia had embarked on a political experiment whose outcome was unpredictable. France and Germany, and indeed all the belligerents of Europe, were exhausted. Popular opinion, too, was confused. Nobody seemed to have confidence that the war had achieved anything other than massive bloodletting or that the future held any obvious promise of better things to come. Reflecting the general mood, painting, music, literature and even politics became suddenly more fractured and uncertain.

The war left its mark, in different ways, on each individual. Those who had fought and survived had to try to awake from their nightmare. Those who had stayed behind had to try to understand what it had all been like and why so many of those who returned took refuge from their memories in brooding silence. On the other hand, for the lucky few – the very lucky few – the war had brought a surprising but precious gift. In the furnace they had experienced the intensity of comradeship in battle. They felt that they had truly been to hell together and, together, they had somehow come back. Indeed, for those who had fought and survived, and had felt the emotion, the bond thus created was to last throughout their lives.

Macmillan was one of those lucky few. He had survived – unlike so many of his contemporaries from Eton and Oxford. But he was, in fact, luckier even than most of the survivors. His two episodes of fierce battle had been short. He had twice received what many longed for – wounds which had him sent back to 'Blighty'. His nightmare had been brief, although brave and bloody. Nevertheless, he like the others had known the comradeship and, as with the others, the bond was there for life – and was unforgettable.

But all that for the moment was thankfully past, and, as he later wrote, his mind at the end of 1918 was 'concentrated on the sole question "What do I do next?".'² There was no easy answer. Hospital after the Somme had been long, painful and, above all, tedious. Admitted at the end of September 1916, he was there without a break until June 1917. An operation to remove fragments of a bullet from his back was successful but attempts to take out other bits were judged to be too dangerous. In June his surgeon told him that he would have to go back to hospital from time to time to have his wound drained but that it was most likely that he would still, for the rest of his life, have bits of metal in and around his pelvis. In the meantime, he would be free for the lightest of light duties – at least those which would not disrupt the operation of the draining tube in his upper left thigh. During this time, and for the rest of 1917 and all 1918 (he was only free from periodic visits to hospital in December 1918), Macmillan had plenty of time to reflect on what he knew was the 'sole question': what he was going to do.

The verdict, such as it was, was far from clear. Physically, he still stood tall – at just under six feet – with the bearing of a Guardsman. True, he had lost weight and his walk was still something of a shuffle. The wound in his thigh was far from healed (and, in fact, would not properly close until the early months of 1920). But, all in all, in spite of the recurring pain and the damage to his right hand from the wound at Loos, he could be reasonably pleased that he had come out of the war with no more serious or permanent injury to his body.

Apart from that, however, he had less reason to be pleased. He had at least settled within himself the problem of his religious belief. From then on he would remain a devoted servant of High Church Anglicanism without further temptation to cross over to Rome. So far, as it were, so good. But he still did not know what he was going to do. It was no good going back to Oxford – there were too many ghosts. Besides, he had left behind the boisterous side of Balliol life. The Grenadiers too, to put it perhaps a little crudely, had given him the kind of social lift that Nellie had always wished for her favourite son.

There lay Macmillan's dilemma. His birth, upbringing and background had been in the intellectual upper reaches of the middle class – very respectable, of course, but, in the brutal language of social class at the time, in 'trade'. Nellie had somehow managed, by sending him to Eton and then helping him to enter the Grenadiers, to project him into a social class a notch higher. Eton and the Grenadiers had left their mark. In fact, along with his admiration for his fellow officers, he had absorbed some of the most objectionable characteristics of the Grenadiers. 'I suppose', he wrote to his Oxford friend Robert Cranborne, 'our nasty little

Prime Minister [Lloyd George] is not really popular any more, except with the International Jew.'³ But if the social arrogance of the Grenadiers was quite manageable, and even desirable for regimental discipline in time of war, it was very much more difficult to justify in peace.

It was a dilemma which had no easy solution. There were times, during the long months in hospital, when Macmillan thought fancifully of opting out altogether and going to live in Italy 'in a villa in Fiesole, with Cypresses ... and dear Italian wines with their ravishing names. How wonderful it would be!'⁴ That phase seemed to pass, and by the time of the Armistice of November 1918, when he was able to walk with the aid of sticks, he took a less jaundiced view of the future. 'To a young man of twenty-four,' he later wrote, 'scarred but not disfigured, and with all the quick mental and moral recovery of which youth is capable, life at the end of 1918 seemed to offer an attractive, not to say exciting, prospect.'⁵ But the question remained unanswered. He still could not work out what he was going to do.

There was no question of prolonging his commission as a Regular officer even if he had been fit enough to do so. The Grenadier Regular officers wanted to take back their regiment from wartime incomers. His father invited him to join the family publishing firm, but that was too constricting. Politics was of interest, but he had no identifiable platform. Moreover, he had been disillusioned by the conduct of the war and was contemptuous of '[Lloyd] George and Beaverbrook ... Let [them and] the rest of them reconstruct to their hearts' content.'⁶ The City of London was an unknown world to which only his more aristocratic Grenadier colleagues had access. Writing for a living was, of course, out of the question.

It was in the winter of 1918 that Macmillan, encouraged no doubt by Nellie, had an idea. He was, after all, still an officer in the Grenadiers. Until he was demobilised he could still claim all the privileges – and accept the responsibilities (such as suppressing the mutinies in February 1919 of soldiers who objected to being sent back to France). Early in 1919 the solution to the main question dawned on him. Why should he not take advantage of 'a year or two of an easy agreeable existence, seeing a country where I had never been and learning something of a world about which I knew nothing'?⁷

It so happened that during the winter of 1918 Macmillan had renewed an acquaintance he had made at the Oxford Union with the Conservative Member of Parliament for West Staffordshire, George Lloyd. Although a serving Member of Parliament, Lloyd, like others, had joined up in 1914 and had served at Gallipoli and in the Middle East. In January 1918 he had returned to the Western Front to become Secretary to the newly formed Inter-Allied Council, the body set up as the main coordinating body for the prosecution of the war. From there, in August 1918 he had been appointed – surprisingly perhaps – as Governor of Bombay. As such, he was entitled to a serving officer as an aide-de-camp, and it was this post that he offered to Macmillan. It was, of course, too good a chance to miss.

But there was a problem. Macmillan had to have a medical certificate before the appointment was ratified. This was refused by his doctors, who pointed out, reasonably enough, that his wound was not entirely healed, that he still had a tube in his thigh and that to go out to Bombay in such a condition would be little short of madness. A second medical opinion gave the same result. Much to his disappointment, India was ruled out.

An alternative soon appeared. Victor Cavendish, the ninth Duke of Devonshire, godson of Queen Victoria, was one of the more cerebral – and conjugally faithful – scions of the Cavendish family. After leaving Cambridge with a modest degree he had studied accountancy and law for a brief period before moving seamlessly into the House of Commons in 1901 at the age of twenty-three (unopposed, of course) for the trad-itional Devonshire constituency of West Derbyshire. There he flourished, first as Conservative Whip and then, from 1903 to 1906, as Financial Secretary to the Treasury. He had by then married Evie Fitzmaurice, the daughter of the Marquess of Lansdowne, at the time Viceroy of India. It had all been very suitable. Even Queen Victoria was moved to write, 'the Queen hopes that they will be as happy as is possible in this uncertain world' while adding, somewhat mournfully, 'Evie will be a terrible loss to her mother.'[8] In fact, loss to her mother or not, Evie turned out to be irredeemably snobbish and a bully to all around her. The Prince of Wales thought her 'hopelessly pompous' and her brother-in-law, the Duke of St Albans, 'considered her disagreeable and authoritarian'.[9]

The story goes on from there. Victor's uncle, the eighth Duke (known for his weakness for gambling and sexual peccadilloes as 'Harty-Tarty') died in 1908. Victor thus inherited the title – and the large estates – but was immediately obliged to leave the House of Commons for the House of Lords. It was not at all to his taste. He thought that his promising political career had been unfairly cut off in its prime. When war came in 1914, he was too old to volunteer, and became no more than an infrequent attender in the House of Lords, spending most of his time looking after his estates. In 1916 the arrival of a coalition government brought him out of what by then was semi-retirement to be Governor-General of Canada. As it happened, it turned out to be an excellent appointment. As one of his contemporaries remarked, he was 'uncouth in gesture, ponderous in appearance, slow in style ... [but] ... there is a massive imperturbability about him which gives confidence. He will never let one down, never play for his own advantage, never do anything brilliant ... let us hope [he] will never do anything wrong.'[10]

In fact, the ninth Duke of Devonshire was almost the perfect Governor-General for the time. The job was no sinecure, nor did he want one. 'The Executive Government [of Canada] is vested in the [British] Crown, and is exercised by a Governor-General, appointed by the King, assisted by a Privy Council chosen and summoned by himself. The Cabinet, as in England, is a Committee of the Privy Council.'[11] Thus ran the official account of the Canadian Constitution as it was during Devonshire's term of office. In other words, the Governor-General was far from being a mere figurehead. He, aided by a full staff of officials from the Colonial Office in London, was responsible to the British Government for the wellbeing of the Dominion. In short, it was far from an easy job. Canada was, after all, an active belligerent in the war, and by the end of it was flexing the muscles of independence from the British Crown. Canadian politicians demanded separate representation at the Paris Peace Conference. Furthermore, the waves of industrial unrest which marked demobilisation in the United States were breaking over its neighbour to the north – together with some radical notions of workers' rights and political power.

But there was also the much more agreeable social role as the King's representative. For this, as a matter of course, the Governor-General needed aides-de-camp – and more than just one. During the war it had been difficult to fill the posts and Devonshire had to put up with some unsatisfactory appointments – of officers who had been severely wounded in the war and were unable to return to military service. As it happened, in all cases but one they were Grenadiers. After the Armistice the Duke was much concerned to upgrade the quality of his ADCs. Three wounded Grenadiers and a wounded officer from the Rifle Brigade were swiftly retired from post; and the Duchess was instructed, on one of her frequent visits to London, to cast the net wide for young men of properly distinguished ancestry who would wish to serve.

It so happened that Nellie had been, and still was, much taken with charity work in London. It was, after all, a convenient way of climbing up the social ladder. The particular object of her charitable intentions was the Victoria League, 'founded immediately after the death of the great Queen with the special object of drawing closer the links of personal sympathy between different parts of the Empire'.[12] Nellie had joined in 1906 and had soon become honorary treasurer – on the grounds that she was very good with money. Devonshire's mother, Lady Edward

Cavendish, was equally enthusiastic for the cause. It thus needed little effort for Nellie to mention the matter of her son's future. Almost before he knew what his job was to be, in March 1919 Macmillan found himself on the boat to Canada.

His ten months in Ottawa turned out to be 'in many ways the happiest of my life'.[13] The new ADCs, as they arrived, were adopted by the Duke's two eligible daughters, Rachel and Dorothy – until then starved of acceptable bachelor company – and led immediately into the fascinations, such as they were, of Government House social life. The atmosphere there was 'that of a large and cheerful house party, with the family, a continual flow of guests, young and old, and our own very congenial staff'.[14] Travel was available, across Canada and to New York, on duty of course, and 'there was fishing; there was boating; there was swimming; there was flirting'.[15] Flirting there was indeed in good measure. One of the ADCs, Henry Cator, who had won the Military Cross at Gillemont Farm in June 1917, found himself romantically entangled to an unsuitable lady, and the Duke had to be mobilised to disentangle him. '. . . Telegram from Jack Cator asking me to prevent Harry doing anything foolish,' the Duke noted in his diary. 'Very Awkward . . . Went for a walk with Harry. He is absolutely right & though he was once attracted to the girl it is all over & and there is nothing in it. He certainly is a most attractive boy.'[16]

It need hardly be said that Macmillan was not a good flirt. First of all, it was only early in 1919 that he had the tube removed from his thigh, and although he was firm enough on his feet to take up again the golf he had started in the first months at Chelsea Barracks before his two wounds had put an end to it he was far from physically confident. Not only that, but he had not been able to slough off the bookishness – and pomposity – which had irritated some of his fellow officers in the war. More important, however, was his almost total inexperience in dealing with women – let alone trying to attract their romantic attention. In fact, although he was happy enough in the early days to engage in Government House social life, and to enjoy it, his main interest was in Canadian politics.

By the end of 1918 these were, at the emergence from war, becoming interesting – and starting to alarm Government House. In January 1919 a rash of strikes had broken out in Ontario and Quebec. With the spring they spread across the country. For the moment, at least, the strikes were not overtly political. The grievances of the workers were understandable and, at least in part, understood: the rate of unemployment and the high cost of living. But the situation became so tense, and ensuing violence so widespread, that the government on 4 April appointed a Royal

Commission on Industrial Relations 'to consider and make suggestions for securing a permanent improvement in the relations between employers and employees in Canada'.[17] This move, however, failed to satisfy the strikers in Winnipeg (now including the police and the fire fighters) who declared the strike to be general and set up their own Strike Committee to run the city.

The alarm bells in Government House started to shrill. Winnipeg was, after all, the capital city of the Province of Manitoba. Furthermore, there were sympathy strikes throughout the country, notably in Calgary and Toronto. Devonshire, in something of a panic, reported to Lord Milner on 2 June: 'The motive underlying this movement would seem to be ... the formation of the organised workers of the Dominion into one big Union ... undoubtedly the overthrow of constitutional Government ... it was only the very firm stand taken by the Citizens' Committee, consisting of resolute citizens of standing and influence, that prevented the establishment for the time being at any rate of what would have practically amounted to a Soviet Government.'[18] That was bad enough, but the Conservative Prime Minister of the day, Sir Robert Borden, was at the Paris Peace Conference pleading Canada's case. It was only the astute manoeuvring of the Minister of Justice, Arthur Meighen, that allowed the Winnipeg strike to run its course and fizzle out.

In all these events, Macmillan played only the part of an interested bystander. As an ADC, he could have no formal role in the political responsibilities of the Governor-General. Officials from the Colonial Office made sure of that. True, Devonshire, a kindly soul, kept him informed about events. From time to time, Macmillan went to Devonshire's office in the Parliament Building and sat in the gallery to hear debates, and there were meetings to be arranged in the Governor-General's yacht. But none of that was of great consequence. In fact, however interesting the Canadian political situation, by the spring of 1919 the attention of this particular ADC was elsewhere. Flirting, such as it was, had taken pride of place.

Dorothy Cavendish, the object of his attentions, was the Duke of Devonshire's third daughter. Born on 28 July 1900, she had been brought up in the traditional manner of the English aristocracy of the time – by nannies and governesses. Her first eight years had been spent at (by Devonshire standards relatively modest) Holker Hall in Lancashire and Lismore in southern Ireland, but when the Duke inherited the great Devonshire estates in 1908 there was a different pattern of life. Once electricity (but no heating) had been installed at Chatsworth the whole family moved around, mostly in private trains and with a considerable retinue, between the great family estates of Chatsworth and Hardwick

Hall in Derbyshire, Compton Place at Eastbourne, Lismore, Bolton Hall in Yorkshire and Devonshire House in London. There were French and German lessons and ponies and golf – but little appetite for reading books. In short, Dorothy's was a life led outdoors. But it was not just a question of horses and golf. She was warm-hearted, gregarious, friendly to everybody (except when she flew into spectacular rages) and wholly without snobbery (unlike her mother). Of course, she was no beauty – tall and rather thin, with arms that seemed always too long – and her clothes sense was no better than erratic, but she was, in the jargon of the day, a 'good egg'.

As such, she was popular with the staff at Government House in Ottawa, where she had arrived, at the age of sixteen, with her father on his appointment. Wartime Ottawa, however, was hardly a joyous place for a young girl. In fact, there was not very much to do. Her brother had made a suitably dynastic marriage to a daughter of the Marquess of Salisbury in April 1917 and lived in London; her eldest sister, Maud, had married one of her father's ADCs in November 1917 but he had died of pneumonia in October 1918 leaving her a mourning widow with a three-week-old daughter: and Blanche, the next sister, was firmly attached to Captain Ivan Cobbold (whom she would marry in April 1919) and spent most of her time in England. The fourth daughter, Rachel, was the only possible participant in what might be called adolescent jollity. Anne, the fifth daughter, and the younger son, Charles, were considered a bit too young – and perhaps a bit too dull.

By March 1919 Macmillan had started to write to Dorothy when on his travels. On 20 April, Easter Day, she was 'Dear Lady Dorothy . . .' By June she had become 'Dear Dorothy'.[19] By December she was 'My darling Dorothy'. By then, Macmillan had clearly become infatuated with this rumbustious nineteen-year-old tomboy, and in early December he was so struck that he was proposing marriage. Dorothy, on the other hand, was more cautious. 'After tea,' the Duke noted in his diary, 'Harold proposed in a sort of way to Dorothy but although she did not refuse him definitely nothing was settled. She seemed to like him but not enough to accept & says she does not want to marry just yet. She seemed in excellent spirits. After dinner they went skating . . .'[20] Three weeks later, however, the deal was done. On Boxing Day 1919 'Dorothy and Harold settled to call themselves engaged', wrote the Duke[21] – and Macmillan was writing triumphantly to Nellie.

The following day '. . . Dorothy and Macmillan spent the whole day together & it is really rather difficult to have to maintain that they are not engaged . . .'[22] Nothing could be announced as yet. The truth was, of course, that Dorothy's mother Evie disapproved of the whole idea and had to be won over. She had not – but not for lack of trying – managed to attract interest in Dorothy from the Prince of Wales, who had visited Canada earlier in the year, but she still had a second string to her bow in the Duke of Buccleuch. Marriage to one of her husband's ADCs – and a commoner at that – was quite impossible. The Duke, on the other hand, thought Macmillan a perfectly acceptable suitor. During the first week of the New Year there was much negotiation, but in the end the father's view carried the day. Money, certainly, was not going to be a problem. 'As far as I can make out,' noted the Duke carefully, 'he will get £3000 a year from own sources but will be able to get more . . .'[23]

There was, however, still a question mark. Macmillan's infatuation was clear enough, but nobody could quite see why Dorothy had accepted him. Macmillan was, after all, not an outdoor person. He was intellectual, stilted and awkward in company. True, he was as upright as a Guardsman should be, but he wore spectacles (even, from time to time, a monocle), sported a slightly comical small moustache (quite unlike the Duke's flamboyant walrus shape), was hampered in his walking by his still obvious shuffle and – most noticeably – his upper lip turned upwards when he smiled, turning the smile into what looked like a snarl, revealing an uneven set of teeth. In short, he certainly was not one to turn many feminine heads. Perhaps so, but 'she was probably very flattered', as her niece Anne said later. 'He was very good company and very courtly, and Uncle Harold, quoting Plato and so on, must have been frightfully impressive. Probably Aunt Dorothy was very impressed by him being so educated, as uneducated people are always very impressed by the educated.'[24]

On 7 January 1920 the engagement between Captain Harold Macmillan (he had been promoted with a view to prospective demobilisation) and Lady Dorothy Cavendish was revealed to the world. The announcement was celebrated at a great ball in Ottawa on the 9th for three hundred guests at the Château Laurier given by the Cliffside Ski Club, of which the Duke was honorary president. The Duchess, it was recorded, wore a 'handsome black jet embroidered gown'[25] which was noted by the curious to be of the kind normally worn when in mourning. The bride to be, on the other hand, wore a cheerful dress of blue chiffon.

That done, preparations were made for the various parties and their respective retinues to leave Canada for England. Macmillan and Dorothy were the first to go, carefully chaperoned by a Miss Egerton, leaving Ottawa on 20 January to embark on the Canadian Pacific liner *Empress of France* at St John, New Brunswick. Next were the Duke and Duchess. They were due to leave on 13 February – but there was a slight hitch. The Duke was detained on business, and the Duchess had to go by herself – with the dutiful Harry Cator (now also a Captain) as escort. It was not until 12 March that the Duke felt able to sail, and this he did, again on the *Empress of France* – with his daughters Rachel and Anne and, of course, the remaining ADCs. They were, in fact, cutting it a bit fine, since the date of the wedding was announced only days after their departure from Canada. It was to be, as the press loudly announced, 'Wednesday, April 21 . . . at St Margaret's, Westminster'.[26] Moreover, the public were duly informed that it was undoubtedly to be the great social event of the London season of 1920.

On 6 April the Duke and Duchess, with all their children – and Captain Macmillan – arrived at Chatsworth to 'a real Derbyshire welcome'. All the house servants and the staff of the estate were lined up to greet them. The Duke made a brief speech of thanks for the welcome, remarking that 'after all, there was no place like home . . . Furthermore, he himself was optimistic enough to feel that, with the same sterling qualities which won for us the war, this country would be equally successful in solving all its difficulties, big and little, in the course of time.'[27] The speech was duly applauded, and members of the household and estate staffs of Chatsworth – and of the staffs of all the other Devonshire estates – presented the engaged couple with a silver tea kettle. The feudal ceremony was thus accomplished in the best of good cheer.

The silver tea kettle was not alone. It figured on the list of presents which, as was then the custom, was published in full on the morning of the wedding. But it was, it need hardly be said, among the most modest. Queen Alexandra gave a diamond brooch, Princess Mary a Sheraton table, the Duke and Duchess of Devonshire a diamond necklace, Mr and Mrs Maurice Macmillan a diamond cross and the Marquess and Marchioness of Lansdowne a Meissen dinner service. In all, there were some two hundred presents recorded and displayed at Lansdowne House in Berkeley Square where the reception was to take place – almost all of them of very substantial value. In monetary terms at least, the happy couple got off to a splendid start.

Long before the event started crowds gathered around the entrances to St Margaret's to gawp at the guests as they arrived. They applauded the carriages of the Duke of Connaught, Prince Albert (the future King George VI), Princess Victoria and Queen Alexandra – just catching a glimpse of the royals as they emerged. Inside the church no expense had been spared on the decorations. There were flowers all over the place, orange trees in the chancel (unfortunately rather obscuring the choir) and huge bunches of lilies on the altar. The congregation, of course, was seated well before the royal arrivals. Those who did not have reserved seats had to stand, since the church was packed to bursting. 'It is a long time', noted the *Bystander*, 'since I saw so many Duchesses at a wedding. In addition to the bride's mother there were their Graces of Wellington, St Albans, Buccleuch, and Buckingham and Chandos, and what is called "the general company" included everybody of note . . .'[28]

Against this onslaught of aristocracy, Nellie, in her invitations for the bridegroom's side of the church, had difficulty in competing. Her only resource was to summon authors from the Macmillan publishing house. Thomas Hardy, for instance, was dragged out to become a signatory to the wedding document. But, try as they might, the assembled authors never attracted the attention of the newspapers and their participation passed unnoticed in the following day's press.

At 2.15 p.m. precisely the bride arrived on the arm of her father accompanied by bridesmaids and pages from the family. Unlike her normal casual day-to-day dress sense, Dorothy Cavendish had taken a great deal of trouble – or at least her mother had made sure that she did. 'The bride looked particularly charming', enthused 'Mrs Gossip' of the *Daily Sketch*, 'in a cream velvet dress, draped over a petticoat of priceless old Brussels lace, and a Botticelli-shaped bodice caught at the waist with a chaplet of orange-blossoms. Her full Court train of velvet was lined with cloth of silver, and she wore a wreath of orange-blossoms over a veil of Alençon lace.'[29]

All this was very splendid, but it was noted, with some questioning, that Dorothy carried in her hand not the traditional wedding bouquet but – as though making a special petition to the Almighty – a white vellum prayer book. Waiting for her on the steps of the chancel, of course, was her chosen bridegroom Harold Macmillan, dressed suitably in morning coat and striped trousers (and a black rather than grey waistcoat), wing collar and tie – and a lily in his buttonhole. Standing with him was his best man Arthur Penn, who had been Adjutant of the 2nd Grenadiers on the Somme (where he had won the Military Cross – he was, needless to say, also an Old Etonian. Another Grenadier, the old friend Harry Crookshank, appeared as an usher). Nothing could have been more suitable. Even the Duchess of Devonshire could not have faulted it.

The service followed the traditional pattern of the Church of England. It was conducted by the Bishop of Derby (formerly Vicar of Bakewell in Derbyshire), assisted by Canon William Temple (one of Dorothy's cousins and, as it happened, a future Archbishop of Canterbury) with the Reverend John Macmillan, Macmillan's cousin, who was at the time Vicar of Kew. All went according to plan, and the vows were taken as prescribed – without any apparent hesitation. After waiting, as appropriate, for the departure of the royals, the company then made its way to the reception at Lansdowne House. That done, the married couple went off, in the usual shower of confetti, to a honeymoon in one of the Devonshire houses, Compton Place, in the agreeable seaside resort of Eastbourne.

The wedding had proved to be as advertised – the social occasion of the London season of 1920. Yet for Macmillan it was something much more important. Of course, Nellie had been delighted that her favourite son had married into the cream of British aristocracy and that she, in consequence, could hold her head high in the best of London society. For him, however, the marriage opened a new perspective on the 'sole question' of what he should do now. To be sure, there is no doubt that he was infatuated with his new wife. There is no doubt, also, that she was prepared to settle for the life of a publisher, to settle down in some country house or other with children, horses and dogs. Yet, for him, marriage into the great Tory families of Cavendish, Cecil and Lansdowne – let alone all the other duchesses at his wedding – made for a perfect platform from which to jump from publishing, which was clearly going to be his next step, into the greater arena of national politics. The question of what he should do next had resolved itself: entry into politics was no longer 'whether?' it would be so; it was much more 'how?' and 'when?'.

5

'I Had Never Been To Tees-side'

There is a photograph, taken in late April 1920, of what on the face of it seems to be a rather eccentric looking young couple. The scene is a garden. The figures are stilted and formal – he wearing a dark three-piece suit, stiff collar and dark tie, black shoes, coloured handkerchief in the breast pocket and a flat cap the shape of a pudding on his head, she in a formless jersey suit, flat lace-up black shoes and a sad looking straw hat. Both of them wear the fixed smiles of acute embarrassment. It was, of course, as *The Tatler* proudly announced, 'an exclusive picture of Captain Harold and Lady Dorothy Macmillan' on their honeymoon.[1] The garden was at Compton Place in Eastbourne. After that, under-standably enough, no more press photographs were allowed. In fact, no other photographic record has survived at all of their peripatetic honeymoon journey, which took them first to Eastbourne, then to the comparative hardships of Bolton Hall in Yorkshire and finally on to the burgeoning spring of Italy.

Although taken in the early days of their honeymoon, the Eastbourne photograph already tells a story. It is obviously posed – but posed awkwardly. The couple do not look at one another. They do not even hold hands. Dorothy's long arms hang loose to her thighs. Macmillan's are clasped together behind his back. Macmillan's embarrassed smile seems strangely defensive, as though protecting himself from some unexpected attack. Dorothy's, on the other hand, is just a fraction more relaxed. To judge from it, whatever the problems – no doubt painful – of the bullets in Macmillan's pelvis and of Dorothy's virginity, the particular requirement of a honeymoon had, it seems, been satisfactorily met. Beyond that, the photograph suggests something of a distance between the two figures. In sum, the onlooker is left with the rather melancholy impression that it is not altogether a picture of love's young dream.

Honeymoons, of course, almost always present problems. After the excitement of the wedding there is the matter of settling down to get to know one another as husband and wife. In the Macmillan case, lectures on Plato might have been fascinating to the prospective bride but less so to the new wife. If the conversation turned to horses, the new husband could have been excused interest. Yet, whatever the intellectual space between them, there is no reason to suspect that anything was going badly wrong. Macmillan was certainly enthralled with his new wife – almost embarrassingly so, judging from the ecstatic way he wrote to her in words which read like the sighings of the Latin romantic poets. On her side, Dorothy was much less given to romantic outpourings – besides, she had never studied Latin. Furthermore, she very rarely wrote letters at all. It was not something the Cavendishes did. But, for all that, there is no reason to doubt her affection at the time.

Macmillan was to be less enthralled, on their return to London, by the welcome, on one side, from his mother and, on the other, from the Cavendishes. His father, as family duty required, suitably welcomed him back as a new junior partner along with his brother Daniel and his cousin Will into the House of Macmillan in St Martin's Street. In fact, it was only the members of the family who were brought into the partnership (others who worked there were either 'servants' or, at best, 'helpers'). It was, of course, still very much a family firm and had the customary eccentricities. The senior partner was Sir Frederick Macmillan, the eldest son of the original Daniel who, along with his brother Alexander, had founded the firm. Apart from publishing, his major interests were in his chairmanship of the Beefsteak Club and in hunting foxes resolutely wherever and whenever they could be found. He also kept a splendidly large Rolls-Royce in which he arrived at the office each morning in time to read out the correspondence to the other two partners (Maurice, Macmillan's father, and George, with particular responsibility – for some reason – for theology) and decide what the firm's response should be. Luncheon was also a daily ritual. The senior partners discussed their business while the juniors sat and listened, after which they were allowed 'a glass of madeira and were fed on cake' before being dismissed.[2] As though to stress the Victorian formality of the firm, the offices were furnished in dark and gloomy mahogany.

The business itself was doing well, thanks to a large and productive list of authors and Maurice's prudent financial management. Although Macmillan started by learning how books were printed, bound and delivered to the booksellers he gradually was allowed to look after some of the firm's major authors – Thomas Hardy, Rudyard Kipling, W. B. Yeats, Hugh Walpole and, above all, Sean O'Casey and a new historian, John Wheeler-Bennett. But, however successful he was in looking after them, they were all distant figures. More and more, Macmillan became a servant to the 'daily grind'[3] of publishing – reading manuscripts of dubious value, editing proofs and supervising presentation and printing. If the truth be told, he did not find it much fun. Nor, for that matter, did his father, who used to retire to his club in the evening, to read the newspapers which Nellie was too miserly to buy for the home but also – and not least – to escape Nellie's complaints.

The complaints were not about her youngest son but about her other two sons – and their father. Maurice, her husband, would not enter into the brilliant social life which she planned; Daniel was morose; and Arthur was far too heavily Anglo-Catholic. Besides, both had married girls whom Nellie disliked. By contrast, Macmillan's marriage was just what Nellie had wanted for her favourite son. Nothing was to be too good for him. To support his publishing career, her literary afternoons – such as they were – were converted into sales conferences to find authors for her son. Lady Elizabeth Cavendish was dragooned into sheltering the couple on their return from their honeymoon while their new home – No. 14 Chester Square (needless to say, within walking distance of Cadogan Place) – was being done up. Finally, in August 1920, Nellie arranged for a series of rooms at Birch Grove to be made available to Dorothy – on the understanding that she spent a good deal of her time there.

The Cavendishes were not much better, although in a different way. Nellie was all-embracing; the Cavendishes were all-rejecting. The consensus in the family was that Dorothy had married beneath her – in particular into 'trade'. Moreover, Macmillan himself was considered hopelessly boring, always buttonholing people to lecture them on some subject that they were not in the least interested in. Her sisters – and their husbands – simply could not understand why Dorothy had married him rather than a Duke of Buccleuch. Macmillan, in turn, was too eager to ingratiate himself with them, but he could not stop lecturing and – a fatal fault – could not summon any interest in horses, the Cavendish abiding passion. He was therefore left out, and, needless to say, the more he felt left out the more he tried.

Christmases at Chatsworth, as might be imagined, were particularly difficult. Apart from the menacing presence of Evie, there were seven Devonshire sons and daughters, all of whom brought their wives and husbands, their children and attendant nannies, nursery maids, lady's maids and valets – and some their own butlers and cooks. Dorothy, of course, thought it all quite delightful. Dorothy's sisters, on the other hand, competed among themselves to avoid sitting next to Macmillan at luncheon or dinner – for fear of yet another lecture on a matter they could not understand and certainly did not want to hear about. As for Macmillan himself, although in later years he claimed to have been perfectly happy, the days must have been, according to his son Maurice, 'absolute hell'.[4]

The one Cavendish who enjoyed Macmillan's company was the Duke of Devonshire himself. Their shared interest was, as it had been in Canada, the politics of the day. In October 1922 Devonshire was appointed Colonial Secretary in the Conservative government formed by Andrew Bonar Law after the wartime Coalition had broken up over the threat of renewed war with Turkey and the subsequent General Election had been won. In November the Duke was writing that he had an 'interesting talk with Harold',[5] and it seems that this talk was one of many. In fact, there is little doubt that the conversations with the Duke, and the access at the highest level to the problems of the colonies – and Africa in particular – stimulated Macmillan to take the decision to move, if possible, into a political career. Besides, if other motivation was needed, the other Cavendishes might belittle him at the moment because he was 'trade'; but there was no gainsaying the position of an elected member of the House of Commons.

There were, nevertheless, three hurdles in his way. The first was in his domestic life. In 1921 his son Maurice was born. Dorothy was enchanted – and spent much more time with the baby than was usual – or approved of – for mothers in her social class at the time. As a matter of course, a nanny was imported. Macmillan was thus kept at arm's length from his new son. For him, as for many fathers in those days, this was welcome, difficult as he found it, as did others, openly to express paternal emotions. But then, towards the end of 1922, Dorothy announced that she was pregnant again. The problem was compounded. Family life was perhaps becoming altogether too complicated for a sudden and speculative leap by the head of the household into an uncertain career in politics.

The second hurdle was his job. He had, after all, only relatively recently joined his father, his uncle and his cousins in the family firm. He was still learning the trade, and could hardly expect them to endorse, let alone pay for, what would inevitably be an absentee partner. After some thought, the solution which Macmillan arrived at was clever – so clever, in fact, that it met the requirements of his employment and his domestic life: he would have a shot at a constituency, but only one which it was impossible to win.

But that in turn led to a third hurdle – opportunity. Although he was encouraged by the Duke of Devonshire (and pushed by his ever ambitious mother) there was no question of the Duke delivering anything more than encouragement. All his influence was to be directed to ensuring that his elder son and Macmillan's brother-in-law, Edward Hartington, was placed in a suitable constituency – specifically the Duke's old constituency of West Derbyshire – so that he could glide without difficulty into the House of Commons. Macmillan would have to find his own way.

Nevertheless, circumstances were in his favour. Bonar Law and the Conservatives had won the General Election of November 1922 which followed the collapse of the Lloyd George Coalition, but Bonar Law himself lasted no more than five months. In late May 1923 he was forced to resign owing to incurable throat cancer. But those five months had certainly been full of incident – none of it, as it happened, favourable to the government of the day. The row over German reparations had boiled over with the occupation in January 1923 of the Ruhr by French and Belgian troops. The British economy, after a post-war boom, was sliding downhill. Stanley Baldwin, the Chancellor of the Exchequer under Bonar Law and his successor as Prime Minister, was in favour of imposing tariffs on foreign imports – in other words protectionism – to solve the country's financial and economic problems. Yet he and others had campaigned in November 1922 on a platform of free trade. Baldwin felt that he was obliged to keep the promise that Bonar Law had made to seek a new mandate before any such change was made. On 15 November 1923 Baldwin duly called a General Election. Macmillan had his chance.

By that time, he had taken two vital decisions. He had decided which party he would support and he had accepted the candidature for a constituency. The first, perhaps surprisingly, was not entirely easy. Lloyd George, in spite of Macmillan's hostility over the Paris Peace Conference, had by 1922 become somebody to be admired rather than criticised. The ease of the language, the power of the rhetoric, the histrionics, all had captured Macmillan's developing political imagination. This was, he was starting to learn, the way that politicians should present their case. In fact, if Lloyd George had been a believable political presence after the 1922 General Election, Macmillan might have been tempted – whatever the damage to his Cavendish relationships – to support his cause. But there was clearly no future in it, and Macmillan, now (and as always) the realist, opted for the Conservatives. Apart from all else, that would make his life easier with the Duke – and with his mother.

That decision made, the next thing was to find, and accept, a candidature in the forthcoming General Election for a constituency which was beyond any doubt unwinnable. With some diffidence, he went along one morning to Conservative Central Office to be 'introduced to a gentleman who dealt with these matters'. He explained his intentions. The 'gentleman' replied that he had just the vacancy which Macmillan was after – Stockton-on-Tees. 'You can't possibly win it,' he said.[6] It so happened that the Chairman of the Stockton Conservatives was in London at the time, looking for a candidate. The same afternoon, the deal was done, on the grounds, as the Chairman – no doubt kindly – said, that 'no one [else] had felt inclined to waste his time or his money'. Since Macmillan had both time and money he was accepted. 'It will be a fine thing for you, my boy,' the Chairman went on, 'and you will thoroughly enjoy it.'[7]

The following day Macmillan set off for Stockton. 'I had never been to Tees-side or even Tyneside,' he later wrote.[8] There he found a world different from anything he had ever previously known. It was one of heavy industry, of poverty, of tough northern businessmen and sharp working-class humour. Baffled, Macmillan wrote out his speeches as though he was speaking to the Oxford Union – and was surprised to be heckled continuously in a language he barely understood. The whole business of canvassing was distasteful, and the campaign management of the constituency party, the quaintly named Stockton and Thornaby Constitutional Organisation, was both moribund and, where it existed, hopelessly confused. Nobody seemed to know the basic mechanics of political campaigning on the ground – least of all Macmillan. The situation was saved, after the first few days of the campaign, by the arrival of Dorothy – still nursing Carol, her first daughter and second child. She treated everybody, particularly the women, as though they were tenants or servants at Chatsworth. 'Women's gatherings, inspired by Lady Dorothy Macmillan, wife of the candidate,' trilled the local newspaper, 'are a feature of the Conservative campaign.'[9]

But the tide was against them. The traditional Tory working-class vote was starting to turn to Labour. To them the message of protectionism, which Macmillan gave out with enthusiasm, promised more in the way of higher food prices than more jobs. Nevertheless, when the votes were counted, Macmillan had done much better than expected. He lost to the Liberal by only seventy-three votes. 'We returned to London,' he wrote, 'excited, exhilarated, not disappointed, and looking forward to another fight. Of course, with such a tiny margin, we must come back to Stockton.'[10]

The electorate had, in fact, spoken with an uncertain voice. The Conservatives won the largest number of seats, with Labour second and the Liberals third. Since neither of the minority parties was prepared to support Baldwin, the choice fell on the Leader of the Labour Party, Ramsay MacDonald. On 22 January 1924, MacDonald became Prime Minister of a Labour minority government dependent on Liberal support. But such a government could not possibly last. After a few hectic political months, the Liberals withdrew their support and on 8 October the government was defeated in the House of Commons. The country was then called upon to vote for the third time in two years.

Macmillan's return to publishing had been brief, uneventful and certainly something of a let-down after the excitement of the 1923 Election. But Stockton had not been ignored. During 1924 he and Dorothy paid visits – he to go round the working men's clubs and she to go to women's tea parties. Both noted that things were gradually getting worse. Unemployment was over 20 per cent and rising. Families were only surviving by what amounted to beggary. Stockton in the late autumn General Election of 1924 was thus all the more welcoming – and by then, to Macmillan, more comprehensible. Baldwin had dropped protectionism (which in Stockton had meant 'dear food') and, late on in the campaign, had been helped by a forged letter from the president of the Communist International, Grigori Zinoviev, to British communists explaining how to go about acts of disruption and sedition. The fake letter, a godsend to Conservative propaganda, was duly obtained by the *Daily Mail*, and used to illustrate the underlying treachery of the Labour movement.

The 1924 campaign in Stockton thus 'proved lively'.[11] Meetings were rowdy – much of the heckling was simply abusive. Dorothy and the two children helped with the canvassing, which Macmillan still found distasteful. As the campaign went on it became clear that the Liberal vote was slipping and that the Labour candidate was Macmillan's most dangerous opponent. Fortunately for him, however, the Liberal held on to enough votes and the poll in the end split three ways to give Macmillan the victory by 3218. Duly elated, he and Dorothy went out on to a platform put up outside the Borough Hall and 'for the first time in my life I heard the roar from thousands of throats, acclaiming victory'.[12] Finally, the police made a gangway for them through the applauding crowd and escorted them to a tram which had been stopped nearby. They climbed to the top deck and rode triumphantly away. It was, in truth, as anybody who has experienced it knows, a moment of heady rapture.

The Duke was particularly pleased. 'Harold won by 3000,' he wrote in his diary, 'a very fine performance ...'[13] The Stockton result mirrored the trend in the rest of the country. It was a Conservative landslide. Two of Macmillan's brothers-in-law had been safely returned – Hartington (needless to say, for West Derbyshire) and the absurdly aristocratic James Stuart, who had married Dorothy's sister Rachel a year earlier – together with a few old friends such as Crookshank. In short, it was a House of

Commons in which Macmillan could reasonably expect to feel at home.

Baldwin's new government contained one very big surprise. Winston Churchill, who had fought the 1923 General Election as a Liberal (on a Free Trade platform) and a subsequent by-election as an independent, had returned to the Conservative fold to fight – and win – Epping. He was immediately projected by Baldwin into the post of Chancellor of the Exchequer. For many Conservatives, who had been loyal in Opposition, the appointment came as an unhappy blow. For Macmillan, however, it was welcome. One of his intentions as a new boy in the Commons was to hitch on to a star – and Churchill was as good a star as any.

There was, nevertheless, another star whom Macmillan still could not help admiring. Although he had no longer any substantial party base, David Lloyd George was a performer who could entrance the House. Macmillan realised – so many people at Stockton had told him – that he himself was a poor speaker: academic, portentous, lecturing, stiff and unemotional. It was not long before he was asking Lloyd George for tips. Ever willing to help a new member of the House, and seeing in Macmillan something of the future, he was happy to oblige. He showed Macmillan how to use his upper body, and particularly the full length of his arms, when making a point, and not just to flap about or stand rigidly to attention. He taught him that it was much better to make one point six times in a speech rather than six points once. Above all, Lloyd George told him not to worry if the speech went badly. 'The clock', he said, 'does not strike twelve every hour.'[14]

Macmillan had not yet learnt these lessons when he made his maiden speech in the Commons on 30 April 1925. Called at just after half past six in the evening to a full House on the debate on Churchill's first Budget Statement he was predictably nervous, and his speech reads as though it had been overprepared. Its content, however, was not quite what was expected from an uncontroversial maiden speech, and it came as something of surprise to the House when he launched into attacks, first of all on the former Chancellor, Philip Snowden, and then on Ramsay MacDonald himself. He accused Snowden of using the 'full amount of acerbity with which he is wont to speak' and of using 'the very ancient method of making up for a certain weakness in argument by a certain vigour in statement'. MacDonald fared no better. He had apparently tried to lure some of the younger Conservatives 'to range themselves under his flag'. Macmillan's response illustrates his speaking style at the time. 'If he thinks', he said in what came out as a high-pitched drone, 'that he and his party have only to offer us as the true socialism a kind of mixture, a sort of horrible political cocktail, consisting partly of the dregs of exploded economic views of Karl Marx, mixed up with a little flavour of Cobdenism, well iced by the late Chancellor of the Exchequer, and with a little ginger from the member for Gorbals (Mr Buchanan) – if he thinks that this is to be the draft given to our parched throats and that we are ready to accept it, he is very much mistaken.'[15]

The ageing Sir John Marriot, who had been deputed to make the customary complimentary remarks about a maiden speech, thought it 'very brilliant'.[16] Others thought it at the same time convoluted in its style and offensive in its content. Nevertheless, Macmillan had at least – the normal task of a maiden speech – made the House aware of his political position. He had placed himself fairly and squarely on the left wing of the Conservative Party. More precisely, in attacking MacDonald's version of 'socialism' as 'true' he left open the idea that there might be other forms of 'socialism' which he might support.

This turned out to be not far from the truth. Like others, Macmillan had decided early on to associate himself with a group of like-minded Members. It was no good grouping himself with Hartington or Stuart. Apart from the personal differences – Hartington drank too much and Stuart was forever teasing Macmillan about his pomposity (and social class) – they sat for rural constituencies which were out of sympathy with the demands of the industrial working class whose votes were crucial for success in constituencies such as Stockton. He therefore teamed up both with the loosely organised Northern Group of Conservative MPs but also, more important, with those from any part of the country whose views where similar to his. There was Oliver Stanley (son of the Earl of Derby, Etonian, married to the daughter of the Marquess of Londonderry, sitting for Westmoreland), John Loder (Etonian, son of Lord Wakehurst, sitting for East Leicester) and two Scottish MPs – Noel Skelton (Trinity College, Glenalmond, and Christ Church, Oxford, sitting for Perth) and, finally, Robert Boothby (Etonian, sitting for East Aberdeenshire).

Together they formed what used to be called a 'ginger group'. The object was to prod their government from time to time and to advance their own interests in doing so. Indeed, when one of their number was promoted (Stanley became Parliamentary Private Secretary to Lord Eustace Percy, President of the Board of Education in November 1924) they were alternately pleased for a colleague and disappointed for themselves. In the course of time, this particular ginger group attracted the soubriquet of 'Eager Young Men' (EYM),[17] which soon became the 'YMCA' (the acronym of the Young Men's Christian Association – in other words, insufferably priggish). But it was fun and, as it happened, Macmillan had something of a privileged position in the group. The reason was simple. He was a publisher and would be able to agree – or not agree, as the case might be – to publish tracts, or even books, written by his friends.

Macmillan in fact managed to combine successfully his Parliamentary duties with his job in publishing. The mornings were reserved for publishing and the afternoons and evenings for the House of Commons. But that in itself put strains on family life. He spent his weeks in London, usually dining either in the Commons or at one of his clubs, while Dorothy spent hers at Birch Grove. They only came together at weekends – even then Macmillan was often late on Friday nights – and at holidays at Chatsworth. But in 1925 even Chatsworth lost its remaining attraction. Dorothy's father, the Duke of Devonshire, suffered a serious stroke and even though he partially recovered he never regained the general bonhomie – and interest in Macmillan – which he had previously shown. As if that was not enough, Nellie at Birch Grove was at the same time starting to become almost impossible.

In 1926, just at the point at which Dorothy was having her third baby, Catherine, Nellie demanded that Birch Grove House be reconstructed. Maurice, her husband, meekly agreed. The result was a large neo-Georgian pile with a huge hall, a drawing room some twenty metres long and a series of gloomy rooms to match. Not only that, but there was no privacy for Dorothy, her husband and children, and the garden was always a subject of endless wrangling. Dorothy, according to her daughter Carol, kept 'an effigy of her mother-in-law ... in her dressing room drawer' in which she used to stick pins.[18] Finally, and most perniciously of all, Nellie persuaded her husband not only to cut the elder sons Daniel and Arthur out of the Birch Grove inheritance so that Harold would have it for his own but also to ensure that she would live there – on top of them – for the rest of her life. In sum, and even taking into consideration all her declared love for her youngest son, it is very hard, in all truth, to imagine a series of actions more destructive to his marriage.

Politically, 1926 was a bad year for the Conservatives. The miners' strike of March was followed by the General Strike in May. Fortunately, Stockton, and the North East in general, was affected by violence much less than the South of England and Wales. Macmillan was thus able to stand aside from the reaction of the Conservative hard line. But he did not fail to irritate his colleagues by his support of the conclusions of the Royal Commission, under the chairmanship of Sir Herbert Samuel, that the mine owners should come to their senses and cancel the wage cuts they were trying to impose and that the trade unions should calm down. Neither side in the dispute agreed. Baldwin then suggested that Macmillan (among others) should go to their constituencies and test the temperature. This Macmillan did and noted that, apart from the occasional incident in the mining villages, 'things seemed reasonably calm throughout the North-east area'.[19] All that was left to be done, after his return to London and before the General Strike was called off on 12 May, was to volunteer to help despatch *The Times* newspaper in the watches of the night. (He deliberately avoided the offices of the *Morning Post*, which Churchill had commandeered for the production of the inflammatory *British Gazette*.)

The miners' strike dragged on until December 1926. But the matter did not end there. The Baldwin government wanted to reinforce the judgement that the General Strike had been illegal. Macmillan, and others, agreed in principle but also wanted to ensure that the conditions for a general strike should not reoccur. During the winter they started to devise a system which was to lie in between 'unadulterated private enterprise and collectivism'.[20] The result was a short (and, as it happens, almost unreadable) book entitled *Industry and the State*. The nominal authors, although the net had been cast wide for contributions, were Macmillan, Boothby, Stanley and Loder. Among other proposals, the pamphlet argued for collective bargaining between union and employer to be given statutory authority.

The publication of *Industry and the State* in April 1927 almost coincided with the publication of the government's Trade Disputes Bill in May. The object of the Bill was, in essence, to confirm the view that a general strike was illegal. Strikes, of course, could be tolerated – provided that there was no secondary action by unions which were not party to the original dispute. All this left Macmillan in difficulty. He could not possibly argue, as he and his allies had argued in *Industry and the State*, that collective bargaining should have statutory backing while supporting a Bill which took the directly opposite view. At the Second Reading debate of the Bill in the House of Commons Macmillan, perhaps for the first time but certainly not for the last, managed successfully to face both ways. He was able to claim that the Bill should be supported but that on the other (more convincing) hand 'the inevitable psychological effect upon the delicate situation of our industrial fabric in the particular circumstances of the moment is likely to be bad . . .'.[21]

Macmillan's efforts had attracted political attention. Neville Chamberlain, not a natural ally, had written an appreciative letter about *Industry and the State*. But there was more to come. Churchill, or at least Treasury officials, had picked up a suggestion of Macmillan's in an article in *The*

Banker that in order to avoid both industrial and agricultural decline – and to counter demands for protectionist measures – agriculture and industry should be relieved of local taxation, the deficit to local authorities being met by the Exchequer.

At this point, Macmillan had a stroke of luck. His friend, colleague and (nominally) co-author of *Industry and the State*, Boothby, had been in 1926 invited by Churchill to be his Parliamentary Private Secretary. One thing then led to another. Macmillan was invited by Churchill to read the official papers which the Treasury were preparing on the reform of local authority finance. Macmillan was quick to accept the invitation. There followed an intricate exchange between Churchill and Macmillan – starting with a draft, dated 12 December 1927, of a memorandum which Churchill was proposing to submit to the Cabinet early in January 1928. On 21 December Churchill told his Private Secretary that 'Mr Boothby should arrange with Mr Harold Macmillan to read this file through in my office – if possible before Parliament rises'.[22]

Macmillan's response was composed during Christmas at Chatsworth. 'Christmas, with its accompaniment of large numbers of children to be amused and large numbers of pheasant to be shot,' he wrote ponderously, 'is not conducive to serious thought.'[23] Although the opening was, to say the least, rather silly, the content of Macmillan's letter was an impressive analysis of Churchill's proposals. In fact, Churchill was so impressed that he forwarded it to Baldwin. Moreover, he wrote back to Macmillan that 'it is always pleasant to find someone whose mind grasps the essentials and proportions of a large plan ... though you may have forgotten it – a chance remark of yours about the rating system, made more than two years ago, first implanted in my mind the seed of what may become a considerable event'.[24]

Throughout the winter Macmillan worked with Treasury officials on the proposals for derating and the taxes to be put in place of rates. The most vociferous opponent of the scheme, Chamberlain, had to be argued round (Macmillan noted the contrast between Chamberlain and Churchill – 'the cold formality of one Minister and the warm geniality of another').[25] The Cabinet had to approve and Churchill's Budget speech had to be drafted. It was not until the end of April that Churchill was able to announce the scheme to the House of Commons in his Budget Statement, in a speech 'packed with detail, yet so simple and clear that there could be no possible misunderstanding'.[26] For the young man who had been let into the secret it certainly was a great occasion.

The Derating Bill was subsequently introduced into the Commons in November 1928 and passed to the House of Lords in February 1929. Macmillan not only spoke in the Commons debates on the Budget and the Bill but also visited a number of Conservative Associations to urge them to support Churchill's reforms, since he believed that they were essential for the future of the Party. But although, thanks to Lloyd George's tuition, he was improving as a speaker in the House, he still could not avoid boring a public meeting. He addressed a meeting in Plymouth, for instance, for no less than one and a quarter hours (Lady Astor, who was present, was surprised that she had not heard 'the slightest snore').[27]

The 1924 Parliament was by then dragging to its preordained close. The government was drifting. The Conservative Party had no apparent policies to present to the electorate. Churchill wanted an attack on Labour's supposed 'Bolshevism'. Chamberlain wanted a return to protectionism. The Conservative Central Office suggested the slogan 'Safety First'. In the end, that was the theme which Baldwin, smoking his pipe and admiring his pigs, adopted. It turned out to be an electoral disaster. The government's opponents had little difficulty in resurrecting the epitaph delivered by Colonel Moore-Brabazon on his resignation in 1927: 'The snores of the Treasury Front Bench resound throughout the country.'[28]

On 10 May 1929 Parliament was dissolved. The General Election was fixed for 30 May. Macmillan realised that the tide in Stockton, as elsewhere, was against the Conservatives. In particular, the ratepayers, who had seen no benefit from the derating of farmers and businesses, received their rate demands, increased as it happened, only a few days before the poll. In an effort to stem the tide, Evie, the always formidable Duchess of Devonshire, was wheeled in to open the Empire Bazaar at the Borough Hall. True to form, she said that she was 'struck by the zeal and energy of the workers for the Conservative cause, and she congratulated them on the big efforts they were making'.[29] Nevertheless, in spite of the Duchess's intervention – and the zeal and energy she had no doubt detected – the result was very much what had been expected: Macmillan lost to the Labour candidate by 2389 votes. He felt the blow dreadfully. As he and Dorothy on the following day left Stockton railway station bound for London his face was seen at the window of the carriage – drenched in tears. The personal elation of 1924 had been turned to show the opposite side of the electoral coin – personal tragedy in defeat.

As though that were not enough, there was worse news for him in the autumn. One of the Conservative survivors of 1929 had been Boothby. To cheer Macmillan up, Boothby thought to invite him and Dorothy to his father's annual shooting party in Scotland in August. 'It was on the second day on the moors, when Boothby was waiting his turn to shoot, that he was startled to find his hand being squeezed affectionately, and turned to see a beaming Dorothy beside him.'[30] The meaning of the gesture and the smile was clear. She was out to seduce him. And, in the end, she succeeded.

6

'Why Did You Ever Wake Me?'

The Kuranstalt Neuwittelsbach in Munich is nowadays acknowledged to be one of Europe's most expert centres for the treatment of severe nervous disorders. In fact, although its circumstances have changed over time, it has a long-established reputation in the field. Founded in 1885 by Dr Rudolf von Hösslin, its speciality was unique for those days, so much so that Dr Hösslin even invented a vocabulary – the '*Hösslinsches Zeichen*' – which became the medical name for physical symptoms arising from disorders known in the early days, incorrectly of course, as 'hysteria'.[1] His treatments were naturally much in demand during and immediately after the First World War, and as a result of his successes all those who knew about such things agreed that this was the place where sufferers from those symptoms – from all over Europe – could be sure of receiving the most careful and expert attention.

The old building housing Hösslin's sanatorium was destroyed in 1945 along with all the records, but a number of photographs have been preserved by the Sisters of St Vincent de Paul, who own and run the modern hospital, enough to give an impression of the old building as it was in 1931. Originally a private house outside Munich, in a solid Bavarian country style, it was converted by Hösslin into a makeshift hospital for neurasthenic patients. Five years later, in 1890, the whole district, including the nearby Nymphenburg palace and park, was incorporated into the expanding suburbs and gradually absorbed into the great city that Munich has become. Yet even now some of the characteristics of Hösslin's original sanatorium survive. Now, as it was then, it is a haven of quiet and peaceful recovery from the wilderness of psychological nightmares.

It was to this gentle and rather solemn establishment that Macmillan was admitted on 16 September 1931 with what was clearly a serious breakdown. He was, of course, made welcome. But his first few days, under the supervision of the resident physician, Dr A. E. Lampé, were spent in bed, 'either sleeping and dozing or eating'. Various tests were carried out on blood, urine, saliva and faeces, as a result of which Dr Lampé decreed that his patient's 'organs – heart, digestive, bladder etc – are free from disease but that all are "tired". According to him I have narrowly escaped a complete nervous breakdown and I see myself at Chiswick (is it still an asylum?) or some similar place quite soon ... I lie in bed all day (most of the time in a semi-darkened room) & eat the strangest meals, of which cream forms always the main item.'[2]

The eighteen months which ended in Macmillan's breakdown had been miserable for him. He was out of Parliament, his wife was having a torrid affair with his political ally, his friends, such as they were, mostly thought him pompous and didactic – and the Cavendishes wrote him off as a failure (apart from his mother-in-law, Evie, who at first had disapproved of his marriage to Dorothy but, when her daughter strayed from what she regarded as the proper path, became an unexpected ally). Moreover, the Macmillan publishing house was still run by the senior members of the family, allowing little initiative to the junior partners who had to be satisfied with a salary of £6000 per annum. It is little wonder that during 1930 and the early months of 1931 Macmillan himself became badly depressed. Indeed, in the late spring of 1931 he was openly saying that he simply could not go on. He was even seen banging his head against a window of a railway compartment in obvious despair and, even more sinister, there were dark hints of suicide.

The proximate cause of all this was the sexual obsession of Dorothy with Bob Boothby. Macmillan was warned of this at the end of July 1929. 'I fell in with Dorothy in Belgravia this afternoon,' a friend (known only by his initials) wrote to him, 'and she confessed to me, without apparent shame, that she contemplates deserting you before long – a modern plan with which I have little sympathy', then adding, by way of some sort of jolly consolation, '... Can't we persuade you to dine [with us] whilst the inevitable legal proceedings are put in motion?'[3] Apparently, this was not to be simply a convenient arrangement such as was frequent – and accepted – at the time. '[Illicit affairs were] quite common then ...,' said Dorothy's niece. 'It was a left over from the Edwardian period, so many people had *ménages à trois* of the most discreet kind.'[4] That was not at all in Dorothy's mind. She wanted a divorce.

Moreover, she was not in the least discreet. Indeed, she was the very opposite. There were constant telephone calls to Boothby which could be overheard by anybody in the vicinity. Passionate letters were left lying about for anybody to read. They saw each other every day, frequently meeting in the open. They went away together. Needless to say, it was not long before the whole thing was widely known. But in those days the press did not hunt as ruthlessly as they do today. No less a figure than Lord Rothermere, a close friend of Boothby, took the lead in telling his editors and other proprietors of newspapers to suppress all press comment. King George V, when he heard of it, is said to have snapped 'Keep it quiet'.

There is no doubt that Boothby was an attractive and skilled lover. He had a raffish air about him which Macmillan, for one, could not match. He drove a six and a half litre, open-top, two-seater Bentley, liked jazz, was witty and full of laughter, spent summer holidays with Oswald ('Tom') and Cynthia ('Cimmie') Mosley at their palazzo in Venice and their villa at Antibes, and played golf with the Duke of York, the future King George VI. To all that was added good looks and an animal sexuality, which he was enthusiastic to flaunt – with both sexes. It is little wonder that Dorothy completely lost her head. 'Why did you ever wake me?' she asked him once.[5]

It was far from a one-way street. Boothby, too, was infatuated with Dorothy (although this did not stop him pursuing other women – and even attempting to marry one until Dorothy chased him around Europe to stop him). Nor did he show any sympathy for Macmillan, his ally and proclaimed friend. The entanglement became much more complicated when, on 26 August 1930, Dorothy gave birth to another daughter (mysteriously – and so far inexplicably – not registered until 7 October and left without a name on her birth certificate). She promptly told Macmillan that the father was Boothby.

The paternity of Sarah, as she came to be called, has never been settled. Boothby himself certainly had his doubts (for obvious reasons – not to be encumbered with an illegitimate child), and Macmillan himself (again for obvious reasons – not to admit to the humiliation of his wife's infidelity) wrote to his old mentor Urquhart ('Dearest Slig') that 'my family has just been increased by another daughter'.[6] What does seem clear, however, was that Dorothy was determined on a divorce and would use her version of the baby's paternity, whatever the truth of it, as a lever to get one.

In this humiliating mess, there was nothing Macmillan could do – just try to bury misery in work, search for a more promising constituency, take refuge in the practice of his religion and hope that Dorothy would come out of her obsession. But there was not much more he could do in his publishing job – it went on as it went on. The effort, such as it was, had to go into his political career. Yet it was difficult to know how to go about it. After his loss of Stockton in the General Election of 1929 there was clearly much ground to be made up, but it was not easy to see how that could be done. It comes as no surprise to find that his friend Cuthbert Headlam, who had lost the neighbouring constituency of Barnard Castle at the same time, had found him 'dejected'.[7] But it was no good just feeling dejected, and the two of them joined others who had lost seats in a group which became quickly known as the 'Defeated Candidates Association'. Some of them claimed that the object of the exercise was to 'ginger up' the Tory leaders.[8] The truth was that they were all, in one way or another, in search of a winnable constituency.

Almost immediately Macmillan struck what was tantamount to political gold. The sitting member for the Hitchin division of Hertfordshire, Guy Kindersley, wished to retire. Strangely enough, it was the Liberal Chief Whip, Robert Hutchison, who suggested to his friend, the Chairman of the Hitchin Conservative Association, that Macmillan would be their ideal candidate. The constituency was safely Conservative, not far from London and under the general protection of the Cecils at nearby Hatfield. There followed a protracted negotiation, Macmillan refusing the request to live in the constituency on the grounds that 'it would be a great blow to my parents since it would probably reduce the amount of time our children could hope to be with them'.[9] In spite of this rather strange objection, and under some pressure from Lady Salisbury, the Hitchin Conservatives duly nominated him, and he was able to report to Headlam on 5 December 1929 that he was 'pleased with himself having secured the Hitchin division ... He has got the seat on his own terms and Guy Kindersley is to resign in 6 months' time to give him a by-election.'[10]

In the end Hitchin, and the prospect of a safe seat for life, slipped from Macmillan's hands. The reason it all went badly wrong was Macmillan's sudden attachment to the current meteorite in the political firmament, Tom Mosley. Admittedly, there was at the time much to be said for Mosley. He was one of the most fascinating figures of the day. He appeared to have all the social and political talents. Moreover, he played to his strengths. He made a great deal – in fact, rather too much of a deal – of his wartime record in the Royal Flying Corps, claiming repeatedly that those who had fought in the war had achieved some sort of superiority over those who had not. This certainly helped him to win the nomination as Coalition-Unionist candidate for Harrow in the 1918 General Election (although his money was used generously to help as well).

Victory there in turn helped him to win Lord Curzon's second daughter in marriage. He had, in fact, been laying siege to her for more than a year. In the end, she agreed, subject, of course, to her father's approval. Curzon gave this only grudgingly (noting to his wife – ironically in the light of subsequent history – that Mosley had 'rather a big nose' and was Jewish in appearance[11]). The wedding duly took place on 11 May 1920 in the Chapel Royal, St James's Palace, in the presence of King George V and Queen Mary and other guests of the highest social distinction, including, as minor actors in the play, Mosley's friends Bob

Boothby and Harold Nicolson. The King and Queen of Belgium were so determined to be there that they astonished the social world by flying across the Channel for the event in a two-seater aeroplane.

Tom and Cimmie seemed immediately to be thrown into a life of constant pleasure among the social élite of Europe. They were to be seen at all desirable occasions, whether in Venice or Antibes, Paris or London. Money was not a problem – Tom had an income in his own right of something approaching £1 million in today's values and Cimmie brought with her the same. But quite apart from their social success Tom had come to be accepted as a serious politician. He was big enough, in fact, to be able without damage to his standing to cross the floor of the House of Commons after a series of rows over his support for Irish Home Rule, sit as an Independent and, as an Independent, win Harrow again comfortably in December 1923. Almost immediately, however, in March 1924 he changed again. Finding no satisfaction outside a political party, he joined the Independent Labour Party. Since Harrow obviously could not be held for Labour he looked elsewhere, finally winning the Smethwick division of Birmingham in a by-election in 1927.

Judging from his Election addresses, Mosley had by the late 1920s become a determined Socialist red, more or less, in tooth and claw. Even though he had inherited the baronetcy on his father's death, arousing some hostility in his Party, he fully expected to be made Foreign Secretary in the MacDonald administration of 1929. Much to his irritation he had to be content with the Chancellorship of the Duchy of Lancaster – with particular responsibility, however, for unemployment. During the next few months he managed to quarrel with most of his colleagues – and the Chancellor of the Exchequer, Philip Snowden, in particular – over his proposals, influenced not least by Maynard Keynes and supported by a fervent disciple in the Labour Party, John Strachey, to use government money to stimulate economic growth with slum clearance and to secure price stabilisation by bulk central purchase as well as the public control of banking. But even the stock market collapse of October 1929 and the subsequent economic crisis had done nothing to bend Snowden and the Labour leadership. It was then only a matter of time before Mosley resigned from the government. On 20 May 1930 he handed his resignation letter to Ramsay MacDonald – who noted that it was written in a tone of 'graceless pompousness'.[12]

Mosley then embarked on a campaign to woo Labour friends and, above all, Conservative sympathisers. The Labour friends were easy targets – Cimmie, of course (who had won Stoke-on-Trent for Labour in the General Election), Strachey and the young Welsh MP Aneurin Bevan. The Conservatives were at the outset rather less trusting, but

Oliver Stanley mobilised a group of disgruntled MPs – Boothby, William Ormsby Gore, Walter Elliott, Brendan Bracken and Terence O'Connor – and added to the list his friend and aspiring candidate Harold Macmillan. On 26 October they all met at the Astors' grand house at Cliveden to pledge their support for the Mosley agenda. On 29 October Mosley spoke in the House of Commons to urge the formation of a cross-party coalition 'to lift this great economic problem and national emergency far above the turmoil of party clamour'.[13]

Macmillan took up the cause with enthusiasm. By the beginning of December he was spotted by senior Conservatives as 'most likely to join [Mosley] ere long'.[14] At the end of the month he went again with Dorothy, Mosley – and some thirty of his supporters – to stay at Cliveden (Boothby again in attendance). 'Planning' was discussed at length, but during the course of the weekend the discussion went beyond economics to the question of whether democracy could survive. 'The main conclusion', Nicolson recorded, 'is that Parliament, though susceptible to dealing with politics, is hopeless at finance and economics ... And that unless the economic situation can be dealt with on undemocratic lines, i.e. independent of votes, we shall go smash.'[15] There is no record of disagreement by Macmillan. In fact, some of his ideas on 'industrial self government' mirror Mosley's views on Parliamentary failure.

By that time, Mosley had issued the 'Mosley Manifesto', calling for a 'national plan' and the creation of an 'Emergency Cabinet' which could override Parliament to 'carry through the emergency policy'. Macmillan approved of it – but with a note of caution: 'Whatever criticisms as to detail or as to omissions I should wish to put forward at a later stage, I welcome ... a manifesto of this kind, which at least faces facts ... I do not understand the point of view of any Conservative who does not welcome such doctrine ...'[16]

Macmillan's caution in welcoming the Mosley Manifesto in fact marked the start of a division between Mosley and his young Conservative supporters. As Boothby later pointed out, 'the young Tories never reached any kind of agreement with Mosley over his "National Plan".'[17] By the time Mosley announced the formation of his 'New Party', on 1 March 1931, all but one of the young Conservatives had come to the conclusion both that his planning proposals were too authoritarian but also, very much more to the point, that a new party had almost no realistic electoral future. Macmillan made it clear to Nicolson: '... his heart is entirely with the New Party but ... he feels that he can help us better by remaining in the Conservative ranks.'[18]

By that time it had all become too much for the Hitchin Conservatives. They consulted their sitting Member. The response was decisive. Instead of resigning, Kindersley changed his mind and said he would stay on until the next General Election. There was, as a result, to be no by-election, and no early return for Macmillan to the House of Commons. He therefore resigned his candidature in a suitably pompous letter to the Chairman, claiming that 'while everyone in the North appreciated my desire to return as soon as possible to the House of Commons, I am afraid they will judge differently of my action, if, in fact, I wait for the General Election'.[19]

It was a dreadful mistake. Macmillan had assumed that the Labour Government would last 'for another two years'.[20] He was quite wrong. Throughout the summer of 1931 the MacDonald Government teetered on the verge of collapse. By August there were discussions about a 'National Government'. On 24 August King George V held a conference in Buckingham Palace, announcing that 'the leaders of the three Parties must get together and come to some arrangement'.[21] The deal was duly done – but nobody thought it would last for more than a few months. Another General Election before the end of 1931 was pencilled into the political diary.

Macmillan had then to make it up with Stockton. As it happened, the Stockton Conservatives were surprisingly tolerant of their errant candidate. But he was only just in time. While he was still resting quietly in Munich he received a telegram from Dorothy telling him that MacDonald had requested a Dissolution and that a General Election was to be held on 27 October. Dr Lampé advised that he was not yet well enough to travel, let alone fight a General Election. Macmillan, on the other hand, felt much better. He had put on weight, and felt 'calmer and quieter. I read a little – but only old favourites. I have just finished the first 12 books of Homer's Iliad, and am glad to find that I still remember my Greek!'[22] Undeterred by Dr Lampé's advice, and, although he could only walk with the aid of sticks, in mid-October he set off for Stockton, just in time to be formally adopted – as a 'National Con-servative'. Dorothy then left Boothby to fight his own campaign in Aberdeenshire and joined Macmillan in Stockton. It was just as well, since he was having even greater difficulty than usual in making speeches. In the event, of course, it hardly mattered. Carried on the tide of what was one of the great electoral landslides in Parliamentary history, he won easily by a majority of over 11,000.

Macmillan was back in the House of Commons – and Dorothy was back with Boothby. There was certainly not much joy in that, but there was not much joy either in the House of Commons. He was still not well and, although he expected ministerial office, had to watch while his colleagues Anthony Eden, Alfred Duff Cooper and Rab Butler were rewarded with jobs. It was disappointing but perhaps salutary. In January 1932 Headlam found him 'immensely improved ... he is not nearly so superior as he used to be and does occasionally listen to what one says ... He is very clever and takes infinite pains to make himself well informed, but ... he bores people too quickly and has little or no sense of humour.'[23] That may be so, but he certainly was not idle. Another pamphlet, *State and Industry*, was circulated privately in March 1932. 'The proper substitute for the individual', it proclaimed, 'is not the State but the functioning group, substituting the initiative of the whole industry for that of the individual.'[24] So it went on – with, as was Macmillan's style at the time, a good deal of repetitive prose.

Still full of enthusiasm for his ideas for 'planning', Macmillan went to see how it was done in another country. In September 1932, he made a trip to Russia with his new private secretary and former Mosley supporter, Allan Young. When he told Dorothy of his plans she and Boothby immediately grasped the opportunity. While he was away, they took advantage of his absence to spend a fortnight together in Portugal – '... one lovely deserted beach after another to bathe from ... she brushed her hair back behind her ears & actually put lipstick on & got more radiant by the day ...'[25] The political tourists, on the other hand, went on with their dreary business. They visited Leningrad, Moscow, Nizhni-Novgorod, Stalingrad and Kharkov. But the visit was not a success. None of the great Stalinist showpieces much impressed them, and they came away even more than ever convinced that Soviet-style state planning was inefficient and had no future in Britain. Together they then sat down to compose yet another pamphlet – to be called *Reconstruction: A Plea for a National Policy* and published in late 1933 – advocating, yet again, a planning system based on industrial self-government as an alternative to what they perceived to be inefficient state bureaucracy and the inadequacy of Parliamentary institutions. In fact, it was hardly original. Many of the ideas in the pamphlet – and some of the language – were borrowed from another economist working in the same field, Arthur Salter.

By then it was winter – the bitterly cold winter of 1932–3. Stockton suffered badly – male unemployment rose to nearly a third of the workforce and four out of five children were officially declared to be undernourished. Macmillan did what he could – generous donations to charities and even personal help for those who appealed to him. In a different way, however, Macmillan was also suffering, through personal humiliation rather than personal poverty. Dorothy was still pressing for a divorce. 'I have not entirely given up hope', she wrote to Cimmie in September 1932, 'of getting Harold into a more reasonable frame of mind about divorce, but at present he is hopeless.'[26]

It was not just the humiliation of domestic life. His political career looked to be badly stalled. All his pamphlets, articles and letters to newspapers had no effect. Something else was obviously needed. Early in 1933 Macmillan decided that direct action was required. If the Government would not move of their own accord, the House of Commons must make them move. Together with Lord Melchett, the son of the founder of Imperial Chemical Industries (whose main plant was on Tees-side), Macmillan formed the Industrial Reorganisation League to promote a Bill to enable the establishment of 'industrial self-government'. Melchett managed to recruit the support of many of the most successful British businessmen and bankers. At the same time, however, another group, Political and Economic Planning, was thinking along similar lines. At a dinner at the Savoy in March 1933, at which Macmillan and Melchett were both present, the outline of a Bill was discussed. It made obvious sense, as all there agreed, for the two groups to cooperate.

When Parliament rose for the summer Recess, Macmillan had time to take a break from politics. Dorothy was not in any mood to join him on a holiday, so in September he decided to take his twelve-year-old son Maurice for two weeks, at Evie's invitation, to stay at Bolton Abbey. For the first time, father and son seemed to be able at least to communicate. Dorothy's open affair with Boothby seemed to have brought them together. Macmillan, in one of his most affecting letters of the time, wrote to Evie that he 'felt able to make a companion of him ... he means such a lot to me'. So much so, in fact, that he took Maurice soon after on a cruise around the Adriatic – again with the feeling, put in letters to his mother, that Maurice was showing himself to be a good companion and even interested in all the Greek sites which his father lectured him about.

Equally affecting, however, are his thoughts about Dorothy, poured out in the same letter to Evie. 'Dorothy certainly seems much happier & better,' he wrote in an obvious mixture of hope and despair. 'It is very hard to know what to do best for her but I suspect its best to leave her to recover from her wounds. I still (for some reason or other) love her so ridiculously, that I don't dare see too much of her. I feel its best for her to try to forget altogether – for the present – the emotional side of life and concentrate on children, gardens, politics etc. But it needs a lot of self-control as I can't stand too much of her at a time – not because I don't want to be with her but because I love her too much, and have to hold it all in ... But I do believe she is better ... The hard rebellious look seems much rarer now, and a softer quality to be returning.'[27]

If 1933 was bad, 1934 was not to be much better. In April Macmillan put on another brave face to Evie. 'Dorothy', he wrote, 'seems very well & much more serene in every way ... I think the best great thing for her is to be allowed to get through in her own way. How this will come about I can't yet tell. But I do really think that it *will* come about, in good time & given peace and calm ... She must make her own way through ... She came with me to early service – an unusual act, going beyond mere conformity ...'[28] It was a brave try, but Headlam recorded a dinner in 14 Chester Square in mid-July: 'He is such an odd unforthcoming type of man – so tremendously absorbed in himself and his own affairs ... and yet he is about the only man in the House who in other respects appears a suitable person to work with. Tonight he was far less self-centred than usual and full of ideas both political and personal ... until about 10pm when Dorothy suddenly appeared – then he shut up like a trap and became morose and silent ...'[29]

There was not even much consolation in publishing. The firm was still under the control of the senior partners and there was, naturally enough, great resistance to any form of change. Yet there was some light for the juniors. Macmillan had been allowed by his seniors to build a relationship with one of the firm's most valued authors, John Maynard Keynes. Keynes, indeed, in return made approving noises about Macmillan's plans for 'industrial self-government'. Moreover, Keynes was working on a major book designed to build a theoretical underpinning for his polemics against the economic orthodoxy of the day – and Macmillan was certainly most interested, both as a publisher and as a politician, in what his author was writing. During 1934, too, Macmillan had found a new ally. Clifford Allen, a left-wing firebrand before the war but by 1931 a National Labour supporter of Ramsay MacDonald and editor of the National Labour magazine *News-Letter* (and duly rewarded with a peerage in 1932), had formed yet another group, rather portentously baptised as the Next Five Years Group. In February 1934 the group published a document, *Liberty and Democratic Leadership*, drafted by, among others, Allen and Macmillan, intended as a response to Mosley's by then open fascism. The two worked together again on a second document setting out more specific ideas for economic reconstruction and appealing for support from all political parties for their proposals.

Yet although Macmillan was an important part of Allen's drafting team – although they were to fall out later – he still had his other enthusiasms. In fact, during 1934 and the first few months of 1935 he was burrowing away – to the point of irritating his Parliamentary colleagues – to promote the Bill for 'industrial self-government'. But the burrowing was not easy and ended – again – in failure. The idea of the Bill had already been rubbished by ministers in the National Government. There was, perhaps, still some hope since it seemed to be taken seriously by the

Conservative Party and was, in fact, studied at length by the Conservative Research Department. Finally though, in April 1935, the Bill died. A Research Department report was produced which pronounced the Bill to be too radical. Oliver Stanley, for one, said that the Bill 'would cut across Conservative principles',[30] although nobody seemed to be entirely clear what those principles were. The Bill was, after minimal debate, thus buried.

By then, however, politics had taken another turn. On 7 July 1935 the seventy-nine-year-old Ramsay MacDonald resigned, to make way for Stanley Baldwin – and another government reshuffle. Yet again, there was to be no government job for Macmillan, but there was new hope. Baldwin called an autumn General Election. After that, Macmillan thought that he would at last be rewarded with ministerial office. Much as he wanted it, however, he threw away even the possibility by writing an election manifesto for the voters of Stockton which the leaders of his Party found both objectionable and disloyal. While promising support for a Conservative Government he declared that he would continue to press for the proposals of the Next Five Years Group – which ran directly counter to the message which Baldwin was putting out. Nevertheless, Stockton returned him with a comfortable majority of just over 4000 – Dorothy playing the dutiful wife again, now that Boothby earlier in the year, in what looked like a fit of absent-mindedness, had married her Cavendish cousin. The electoral result was, of course, wholly satisfactory but it comes as no surprise to find that Macmillan's election manifesto had so irritated Baldwin that he was not even considered for a government job.

There was by then another cause for him to take on – resistance to the growing fascist movement, both in Britain in the form of Mosley and his 'Blackshirts' and in continental Europe in the form of Benito Mussolini in Italy and Adolf Hitler in Germany. Within weeks of the Election of the new Government, the Foreign Secretary, Sir Samuel Hoare, signed a pact with Pierre Laval, the French Foreign Minister, to cede large parts of Abyssinia to Italy in the wake of Mussolini's invasion. In March 1936, Hitler moved troops into the demilitarised Rhineland. It was time to put foreign affairs high up on his political agenda.

There was clearly much to do, but the question for Macmillan was how to do it. Eden, at the age of thirty-nine, had become Foreign Secretary on Hoare's resignation after the row over the Hoare–Laval pact, but he had little time for Macmillan and was overcautious about challenging Hitler over the Rhineland. Churchill was continuing his volcanic rumbling, but he was unpopular in the Party and much mistrusted, not least because of his determined defence of the British Empire at the mere suggestion of Indian independence. It was therefore time to look elsewhere for allies. In May 1936, as it happened, there was such an opportunity. G. D. H. Cole, a lecturer at Oxford of consistently and aggressively advertised socialist views, wrote an article in the magazine *New Statesman* advocating a 'British People's Front'. He took as examples the experiments in Belgium and France. But he added a new dimension. It was, he argued, the only way to stand up effectively to the fascists. To this was added the idea of working towards a suitably planned economy in order to make sure that fascism could never take hold in Britain.

Macmillan was duly persuaded by both ideas and – in an unlikely alliance – joined Cole in drafting a programme for a People's Front Propaganda Committee. A conference in Oxford was organised in July by the Next Five Years Group, under the banner of their new magazine *New Outlook*. It attracted most of the 'progressives' of the day – among them Lloyd George (who had been pursuing his own, parallel, course inspired by experience of Franklin Roosevelt's New Deal in the United States). A Committee was duly set up (including, incidentally, Boothby, Bevan and Strachey). Its central theme was to be the creation of an inter-party alliance – ranging from the Conservative left to the Labour right on a platform of resistance to fascism in all its manifestations, the protection of democracy and an economic policy (including planning) to conquer the misery of unemployment.

This was all very well. Yet much had happened in the early months of 1936 to take Macmillan's attention away from the campaign for a 'People's Front'. In February Macmillan had published, with the greatest enthu-siasm, Keynes's long-awaited great work, *The General Theory of Employ-ment, Interest and Money*. No sooner was that done, however, than the firm lost all three of its senior partners. On 3 March George Macmillan died. Four weeks later, on 30 March, Macmillan's eighty-two-year-old father Maurice, who had been almost totally blind for the previous two years and had suffered from a series of debilitating illnesses, died peace-fully at home. Then, on 1 June Frederick, the most senior of the three, died. Thus, within a period of no more than four months, the firm had lost the three who had guided it for as long as anybody could remember. Apart from the necessary business of funerals – and looking after Nellie, who took her husband's death badly (and was already showing signs of dementia) – there was the future of the firm itself to settle. Death duties complicated the succession and Macmillan and his elder brother Daniel were forced into deciding, after a long review of the family finances, whether or not the firm could be maintained as a private business. They finally did so decide, and – a relief for Macmillan – agreed between them that Daniel would take on the burden of day-to-day management, with his brother helping out when time and politics permitted.

In spite of all his problems at home, Abyssinia and the Rhineland were still uppermost in Macmillan's political mind. In May 1936 he joined the December Club, a group under the chairmanship of Churchill's friend Louis Spears, which had been formed to press for rearmament. He also took control from Allen of *New Outlook* – in a dispute which turned surprisingly bitter – to turn it into a campaigning magazine rather than an educational tract. Then, while his father was dying, he made another bruising attack on the Government – and the rhetoric was becoming ever fiercer. In a newspaper article towards the end of March he blamed Baldwin for the whole sorry episode of the Rhineland remilitarisation (not mentioning that the French were in the middle of a General Election campaign and thus unable – as well as unwilling – to react with force). Baldwin and MacDonald before him had 'elevated inactivity into a principle and feebleness into a virtue'.[31] At the end of the debate of 23 June on the matter Macmillan voted against the Government. A week later he resigned the National Government Whip. As it happened, his resignation passed without anybody noticing – or caring very much. (Baldwin took ten days to reply to his letter of resignation.) Rather to his surprise, however, and certainly to his gratification, the long-suffering Stockton Conservatives enthusiastically supported his decision.

Nevertheless, it was not a wise move. Voluntarily to resign a Party Whip, particularly a Government Whip in the House of Commons, may seem an attractive gesture at the moment but it brings with it unavoidable disadvantages. The channels of communication are severed. Information about forthcoming business is no longer available. It is more difficult to catch the Speaker's eye to be called in a debate. Finally, the erstwhile colleagues are reluctant to share the gossip which is an integral part of Commons life. All this happened to Macmillan throughout the last half of 1936 and into 1937. In short, he became, in the splendidly mixed metaphor of one of his former colleagues, 'a lone independent gun barking on the left of the Conservative Party'.[32] The whole controversy over the abdication of King Edward VIII in the last months of 1936 – and Churchill's defence of the King – in Parliamentary terms passed him by. As a further irritation, if one was necessary, Boothby's marriage had collapsed and he had turned back to Dorothy – a willing Dorothy – by way of consolation.

Macmillan's exile from his Party did not last long. He soon realised that gestures in politics, however satisfying at the time, do not come without a price. By the beginning of 1937 he was starting to count the price. It was soon time to find a way back into the Conservative fold.

The opportunity occurred when Baldwin, after successfully managing the Abdication and the subsequent coronation of King George VI, decided to retire on 28 May 1937. It took little time for Neville Chamberlain to be chosen by the Conservative Party elders as Baldwin's successor as Prime Minister. Macmillan saw his chance, and, not to put too fine a point on it, crept back on Chamberlain's coat-tails.

This put him in a very difficult position. Creeping back was not easy – it never has been – but it is all the more difficult when the leader you promise to support is notably uncongenial, systematically unfriendly and, in policies, unlikely to adopt anything that is remotely satisfactory. Macmillan was thus left in a political no-man's-land. The price to be paid to the Conservative Whips was that he would simply shut up and support the Government. In his new realism, Macmillan was learning about the nature of modern Party politics. Throughout 1937 and into 1938, therefore, his voice in the House of Commons was muted. It was time to keep quiet and to work on his own affairs.

His affairs, of course, did not preclude writing – even political writing. He therefore set about writing a political book. After much thought, he decided that the book would carry the (very substantial) title of *The Middle Way: A Study of the Problem of Economic and Social Progress in a Free and Democratic Society* (by Harold Macmillan, MP). But before *The Middle Way* could be published in June 1938 two events occurred, one marking the end of a personal voyage, the other pointing the way to a political voyage in the future.

The first event was the death, on 26 October 1937, of his mother, Nellie. Eighty-one years old, she had been wandering in her mind for some little time and finally took to her bed at Birch Grove House in the late summer. In the end, she suffered 'acute cardiac failure'[33] and died peacefully in the presence of her son Arthur. Macmillan wrote later that she had been 'a rock-like, unshakeable support'.[34] That was certainly true. But she was also domineering, protective of her favourite son and overambitious for him. Furthermore, she had never been able to get on with Dorothy ('Mrs Mac is really worse than ever,' she had written to her mother, 'and I've had nothing but a series of rows since I've been here'[35]) and had, perhaps inadvertently, contributed in no small way to his marital problems. Indeed, in her later years, as Macmillan himself acknowledged, she was not an easy person to love. Be that as it may, Nellie's favouritism to her youngest son meant, on a practical level, that his whole establishment could be moved from Chester Square to the caverns of Birch Grove House.

The second event was Eden's resignation on 20 February 1938. Eden found Chamberlain impossible to deal with – like many Prime Ministers before and since, Chamberlain wanted to be his own Foreign Secretary. The final break came over Chamberlain's overtures, behind Eden's back, to Mussolini (on the grounds, thought by Eden to be not only ridiculous but immoral, that he expected to be able to detach Mussolini from Hitler). Resignation from government meant that Eden, too, had to look for friends. Until then he had hardly noticed Macmillan. Now he was only too happy to listen to any like-minded colleague. In fact, for Macmillan Eden was at the time a more congenial ally than Churchill, who was apt to sit up late into the night with his friends and who found Macmillan unwilling to drink brandy and smoke cigars – and altogether rather boring. Macmillan thus joined the group of Conservative dissidents around Eden – known as 'Edenites' but more irreverently as 'The Glamour Boys' (Churchill's acolytes being known as 'The Old Guard').

As the full title suggests *The Middle Way* was, and is, a formidable work, in the original edition of no fewer than 376 pages of text, an Appendix giving the quantities and prices of the minimum dietary needs (totalling '20s[hillings]. 6 p[ence] for a family of man, wife, and three children' on the assumption that 'bread is baked at home')[36] and a long list of reports and books referred to. It is little wonder that Macmillan's contemporaries found it hard going. 'Harold's book is so terribly dull', was one verdict, 'that I find it almost impossible to read – let alone digest.'[37]

In fact, in some respects the book is easy enough to digest. The themes which it presents were for the most part familiar stuff – the threat from dictatorship at home and abroad, the inability of Parliamentary democracy, with its emphasis on ideological disputes, to counter it, the need to mobilise support for the middle ground where democrats of suitable moderation could unite. Added to that was a dash of Keynesian economics to spice it all up. So far, as it were, so good. Yet Macmillan had still some reservations. Government management of total demand in the economy, the Keynesian view, was necessary to secure and maintain full employment but it was not enough. 'Capitalist Planning', in other words 'industrial self-government', was still essential.

All this was little more than a general statement of Macmillan's position after he had absorbed the arguments in Keynes's *General Theory*. Where he moves on to new territory is in setting out a blueprint for what in future years came to be known as the welfare state. Every citizen, he argued, should be guaranteed an irreducible minimum standard of life. There should be a minimum wage, child allowances, the production and distribution of essential foodstuffs by public boards, housing provision and electricity (and coal) for the those in need. Yet this was not in any sense a march towards Socialism. He insisted on 'the deliberate preservation of private enterprise in a field lying outside the range of minimum human needs'.[38] In other words, Macmillan was arguing not for equality or even equality of opportunity but for what was in the future to become the firm Conservative doctrine of the 'safety net'.

The Middle Way has come to assume the cloak of legend – as a manifesto that was to be adopted by the Conservatives after the Second World War. But this was never the intention. Macmillan set out to show how democracy had to learn to deal with the threat of fascism – not by sterile party political disputes but by a determined assault on the causes of right-wing revolution. In short, its inspiration was not ideological. It was a response to the dangers Macmillan saw in his own constituency of Stockton-on-Tees. The dangers were, to him, obvious. Unless more were done to alleviate poverty there would, sooner or later, be an explosion which, on any reasonable expectation, would result in dictatorship – either fascist or communist.

Macmillan was certainly right in pointing to the danger to democracy. But he missed the point which Churchill was making – that the threat came above all from dictators outside rather than potential dictators inside. After Germany had annexed (a willing) Austria on 13 March 1938, Macmillan did little more than make speeches in Stockton about the need for a national government, or the revival of the moribund League of Nations or, preferably, both. When Chamberlain announced on 28 September that he was making a visit to Hitler the following day to negotiate a deal Macmillan stood up with others in the House of Commons to join in the general approbation. Even when Chamberlain came back from Munich with the terms of the Munich Agreement, Macmillan, later in life, remembered thinking, in relief, that 'my son would stay at school and go to Oxford in the autumn ...'.[39]

Macmillan abstained in the post-Munich debate in the House of Commons. But it took the resignation of Duff Cooper from the Cabinet at the same time to galvanise him to action. There were, of course, pamphlets – *The Price of Peace* and, in February 1939, *Economic Aspects of Defence*. At risk of offending his Party, he supported the Independent candidate in a by-election for Oxford City, Dr A. D. Lindsay, the Master of Balliol, against the official Conservative candidate, Quintin Hogg (later Lord Hailsham). He tried to get Hugh Dalton, an Old Etonian Labour MP, to mediate in a complicated scheme involving the Labour leader, Clement Attlee, and Churchill to join together to form a national government to replace Chamberlain.

But all this was to little effect. At the end of March 1939, the British Government issued their guarantee to Poland. If Poland were attacked, Britain (and France) would come to its aid. Macmillan immediately joined with Churchill, Eden and Duff Cooper in a motion demanding a national government. Seven days later, however, Macmillan was lunching at Churchill's home, Chartwell, when the news came through – it was Good Friday – that Italian forces had invaded Albania. From then on, Macmillan, with both Churchill and Eden, knew that war with Germany was inevitable. On 1 September 1939, German tanks crossed the Polish frontier. On 3 September, Chamberlain announced, in a gloomy radio broadcast, that Germany had failed to meet the terms of an ultimatum demanding its withdrawal and that 'Britain is therefore at war with Germany'.[40]

The outbreak of the Second World War was, of course, a momentous event. Yet, apart from a good deal of running to and fro – instructions for 'blackouts' and shelters for protection against the expected German air raids and so on – not very much happened. Birch Grove House, where Macmillan and Dorothy had been living more or less at opposite ends of the building, was to receive forty 'evacuees' from south London. Dorothy moved into Pooks Cottage, a small house on the estate, and Macmillan gave up Chester Square to spend his – still lonely – week in a small flat at 90 Piccadilly with dinners at the Beefsteak.

Given the lull in wartime action, there was a moment – in fact, rather more than a moment – for reflection. By the autumn of 1939 Macmillan was well into his forty-fourth year, at a time when, for most ambitious men, reflections on past events in life and future prospects are particularly appropriate. Macmillan's personal balance sheet did not make easy reading. To be sure, he could reasonably claim some successes: he had become a Member of Parliament for a difficult constituency outside the normal range for aspiring Conservatives; he had developed a genuine sympathy for the misery of the life lived by the majority of his constituents, reflected in his pamphlets and books – which, if not bestsellers, had at least attracted the attention of the political public; he had constantly maintained his belief in – and devotion to – the Anglo-Catholic version of the Church of England; and he was, together with his brother, managing a successful London publishing house.

On the other hand, he had been in the House of Commons, apart from a short interlude, for fifteen years without having been offered even the meanest political job. He bored his colleagues by constant lecturing and by an obvious absence of a sense of humour. He still had not achieved the confidence that would allow him to relax. His political views, sincerely held, were neither flesh (laissez-faire Conservatism) nor fowl (Socialism), and failed to attract more than an ephemeral following. Finally, and above all, he had for ten years lived with the humiliation of his wife's open infidelity.

It was this last, miserable, experience which without a doubt changed him over those years. He learnt to become adamant (with the support of his mother and mother-in-law) in his refusal to give Dorothy the divorce she wanted, and how to be patient in allowing her just enough rope to prevent her suddenly rupturing his marriage. The adamantine firmness he showed there was gradually translated into firmness – verging on brutality – elsewhere. For instance, the way in which he wrested control of the magazine *New Outlook* from Clifford Allen in June 1936 can only be described as brutal. He also realised that politics is not just a difficult trade but above all not for the faint-hearted. In fact, it is only for those who have the will and who at the same time are able – by being, in truth, self-centred – to surf the waves of hostility which they will encounter. The patience he had also learnt taught him that friendships come and go – and can easily break on the anvil of ambition – and that persevering conviction in political views commands respect and, with any luck, success. Paradoxically, Dorothy's dreadful behaviour had taught him the two most valuable lessons which would stay with him for the rest of his life – reliance on self and patience. She might have asked Boothby – as she did – why he had ever woken her. Macmillan might also have asked her – but understandably never did so – how it was that she, quite inadvertently, had in her turn woken him as well.

Part Two
THE FIRST ACT

7

'Very Much the Minister Nowadays'

At the outset of war in September 1939 Macmillan had little reason to be pleased with himself. True, there had been one success, if it can be called that. He had won – or at least not lost – the battle with Dorothy, in the sense that their marriage had survived her obsession with Boothby. By then, her affair had become less sexually passionate and was slowly moving towards what might be described as a gentle middle-aged liaison. Encouragingly, even the Cavendishes had in the end all come round to his side. Dismayed by Boothby's marriage to Dorothy's own cousin, they hoped, in the words of one, that '[Dorothy] will now settle down & grow fond of poor Harold again'.[1] But the battle was no more than drawn. There was still distance between them – in every sense.

There were, to be sure, some other pluses. His health had fully recovered from his 1931 breakdown, his eyesight had not deteriorated further, and the shuffle in his walk which was the result of his war wounds had, at least to some extent, become less pronounced. The Macmillan publishing business was doing well – providing him with a substantial income and, as a by-product, continued access to the rich bourgeoisie of the day (he had heard Chamberlain announce the declaration of war while cruising on a yacht belonging to Wyndham Portal, whose company produced banknotes for most of the British Empire). Moreover, thanks to the Cavendish connection, there was a suitable flow of invitations to the aristocratic shooting weekends of a fine autumn.

On the other hand, Macmillan's sudden affection in the early 1930s for his son had faded and his relations with his daughters – including the Sarah of doubtful parentage – were courteous, as always, but no more than conventional in form. In short, his life in London was one of a bachelor, at his publishing job in the mornings, at the House of Commons in the afternoons and, for dinners, various clubs – Pratt's, Carlton, Turf and, his preferred, the Beefsteak. 90 Piccadilly, such as it was, was his home and Pooks Cottage, from time to time, his weekend retreat.

That was all very well. But in his main interest, the world of politics, he was still something of a lost soul. He was not popular with his colleagues in the House of Commons – '. . . for all his intelligence . . . lacking in judgement . . . and a too facile critic of the Government and the PM' was one verdict.[2] There were, of course, speeches to be made in the Commons on the familiar themes – a planned economy and so on – but these made little impression (and, as always, caused him nervous moments, even sickness, before he rose to speak). In fact, so bleak were his prospects that at the beginning of the war he even thought of signing up again with the Grenadier Guards, only to be told, on enquiry, that he was far too old.

As usual, he was much happier in a group of like-minded colleagues, and it was the Glamour Boys which occupied much of his political attention in the autumn of 1939 and into the early months of 1940. Their purpose, not to put too fine a point on it, was not just to support Eden but to harry Chamberlain in what they regarded as his weakness in the face of an obviously implacable enemy. Although Eden himself kept a suitable distance – he had accepted a humiliatingly junior position at the Dominions Office in Chamberlain's Government – the Glamour Boys knew perfectly well that he 'still loathes the Prime Minister, whom he regards as obstinate, opinionated, rather mean and completely ignorant of the main issues involved'.[3]

The Glamour Boys lived up to their name. Not for them meetings in dusty committee rooms in the Palace of Westminster. The main figures – Leo Amery, Cranborne, Harold Nicolson, Spears, Boothby and Macmillan himself – were not to be denied the proper measures of food, wine and cigars to encourage them in their debates. Dinners were held either in the Arlington Street house of Cranborne's father, the fifth Marquess of Salisbury, or in the Carlton Club or, for that matter, in any other suitable establishment which could meet their requirements. At one such – clearly refreshing – dinner, on 17 January 1940, the group agreed that they should act against 'a group in the War Cabinet working for appeasement and at present in negotiation with Brüning [a former German Chancellor living in the United States] to make peace with the German General Staff on condition they eliminate Hitler'.[4] There was even talk of siding with the Labour leaders, mounting a challenge in the Commons and voting against Chamberlain.

Leo Amery was a leading figure in what was then beginning to look like a serious plot. Apart from all else, he had the advantage of having been Churchill's contemporary at Harrow (a dubious advantage, certainly, since 'rumour was unsure whether Amery had thrashed Churchill or vice versa'[5]) and, when he was First Lord of the Admiralty in 1923, of having defended Churchill's decision in 1915 to attack the Dardanelles. That was not the sort of thing Churchill ever forgot. Amery thus was

not only an 'Edenite' but he also commanded immediate access to
Churchill whenever he wanted it. It comes as little surprise that Macmillan hitched himself firmly to the Amery wagon. He, along with the
other Glamour Boys, had come to the conclusion that Churchill, by
then returned to government in his old post of First Lord of the Admiralty, should replace Chamberlain as Prime Minister as soon as possible –
and that Eden should be his Foreign Secretary.

As it turned out, Amery was at the time as good a patron as any. He
was always very willing to do his close colleagues a good turn. In fact,
one good turn for Macmillan came up in the late autumn of 1939. It so
happened that after a short spasm of – deliberately – unsatisfactory
negotiation between the two Governments, Soviet troops crossed the
border into Finland on 30 November. The world, of course, was suitably
outraged. But, on reflection, it was difficult to know what to do about
it. There was talk of sending supplies, food, even troops to the gallant
Finns who, failing any other news of consequence, had been adopted by
the British and French press. As a result, there was a good deal of clamour
in London and Paris for action. Wiser heads, of course, realised that the
worst outcome would be for Britain and France to join in a war against
the Soviet Union.

Chamberlain, quite rightly, was cautious. He decided to temporise –
to set up in January 1940 a Committee, to be chaired by the Finnish
Minister in London but with members of both Houses (Amery was one),
separate from government but supported by it. Rather to Macmillan's
surprise the Conservative Chief Whip of the day, David Margesson,
asked whether he would be willing to serve on the Committee (Margesson
told him that the recommendation had come from Amery). Macmillan
could hardly wait to accept – although he was sensible enough to
consult Churchill before doing so. It was, after all, the first governmental
appointment he had ever been offered.

It was not long before the Committee decided to send a delegation of
two of its members to assess the situation on the ground in Finland. To
his 'delight'[6] Macmillan was chosen as one of them. The other was the
Liberal peer Lord Davies of Llandinam. Lord Davies was, in truth,
something of an odd fish. He had sat in the Commons as Member
for Montgomeryshire, had been Lloyd George's Parliamentary Private
Secretary before being awarded a peerage in 1932, and he described
himself, among other things, as a 'landed proprietor' and as a keeper, as
Macmillan was quick to note, of two packs of foxhounds. His voice was
loud and his opinions strident. But, as it happened, he was hampered in
both by his false teeth.

On 10 February 1940 the unlikely duo, accompanied by a colonel

from the Finnish Legation in London, set off for Finland. Almost immediately, the matter of Lord Davies's teeth took pride of place. In fact,
Macmillan had not only noted the matter but had taken on a new
characteristic – an amused observer and one, moreover, who was starting
to come out of a previously impenetrable donnish (and very boring)
shell. He wrote a diary of the delegation's progress. 'Lord Davies', he
recorded on 12 February, 'has left his teeth in the train. Great confusion,
followed by much diplomatic activity . . . Lord Davies has lost his passport
. . . Lord Davies's passport has turned up but not his teeth . . . as the
Malmö train connects with the Berlin train it is thought that the teeth
have been stolen by a Gestapo agent.'[7]

Such was his new personal confidence – well understood by those
who, like him, have toiled for many years in the political vineyard and
have suddenly been blessed with recognition, even if only in a minor
way – that he felt able, while passing through Stockholm, to buy for
the purpose, and subsequently wear, a tall white fur hat for what was
announced to be the coldest winter for a hundred years. Admittedly, it
looked even then rather ridiculous, perched as it was grandly but top
heavily on his head, the rim almost covering his spectacles and the whole
thing contrasting uncomfortably with his dark moustache, sombre dark
suit and a funereal black tie. But it certainly marked another hitherto
unnoticed streak in Macmillan's character. In short, he had started to
learn to act. In this, perhaps, as in other matters, Boothby – another
actor – had again left his mark.

The Finland expedition made its way, as such expeditions tend to do,
from one ministerial meeting to another, interspersed with visits to the
front line – or as near to the front line as was expedient. Appeals for help
to the Finns were sent by Macmillan to Chamberlain and his Foreign
Secretary Lord Halifax and by Lord Davies to Lloyd George and to
the Liberal leader Archibald Sinclair. Although there were preparations
somewhere in Scotland for a Franco-British force to be shipped to
Finland, nothing much resulted from their appeals (fortunately, as it
turned out, since any Franco-British intervention could easily have led
to war with the Soviets), and their visit ended disconsolately on 22
February. After a short stay in Stockholm, Macmillan returned to London
on 3 March.

It had always been clear that the Finns, however brave they had been,
had in the end no option but to capitulate – which they duly did on 12
March. There was, of course, much lamentation (and the fall of the
French Government). When the House of Commons debated the matter
on 19 March, Macmillan joined in the lamentation, assaulting the Government for their neglect of the Finns in what his friends called 'a fine

attacking speech'[8] and Chamberlain's supporters derided as 'irritable and irritating'.[9] But he went further than that. In a carefully prepared peroration he took aim at the whole war conduct of the Government. 'It does, I think, throw a piercing light on the present machinery and the method of government. The delay, the vacillation, changes of front, standing on one foot one day and on the other the next before a decision is given – these are patently clear to anyone.'[10] The Glamour Boys, of course, were unanimous in praise.

But by that time the Glamour Boys themselves were going out of business. Now that Eden was a minister it seemed fruitless to rely on him to harry Chamberlain. Cranborne, suffering as he was from ill health, on a rare visit to London suggested a way forward – a group of 'respectable' Conservatives[11] who would bring pressure on the Cabinet – with Amery as the representative of the Glamour Boys. The whole thing – to be called 'the Watching Committee' – was to be run out of Arlington Street, and membership would be by personal invitation, in Cranborne's absence, from Lord Salisbury himself. Macmillan was naturally one of the lucky ones and was therefore present at the first meeting of the Watching Committee on 4 April. When they were all present, they unanimously declared themselves clear in their objective – to dislodge Chamberlain. They were, however, less clear on how this could be achieved. Some argued for a long haul, others for a quick strike. These were, of course, brave words, but as it turned out none of that mattered, since no sooner was the Watching Committee formed than it was overtaken by events. Only a few days after its first meeting the Germans launched their attack on Norway.

The German campaign in Norway and the British attempt to counter it were soon over. A Franco-British Expeditionary force arrived too late. It only just managed to get ashore and occupy the port of Narvik on the Norwegian west coast. That done, and with British troops still marooned there, the House of Commons on 7 May started a two-day debate on the fiasco. The debate has, rightly, gone down as one of the decisive moments in modern British history. In his opening speech Chamberlain was substantially roughed up. The afternoon went badly for the Government, but there was uproar when Amery, in the late evening, at the end of a long speech, turned directly to Chamberlain and thundered, 'This is what Cromwell said to the Long Parliament when he thought it was no longer fit to conduct the affairs of the nation: "You have sat too long here for any good you have been doing. Depart, I say, and let us have done with you. In the name of God, go!"'[12]

The second day of the debate was as rowdy as the first. At the end the vote on a Labour Opposition censure motion was the greatest shock of

all. Instead of a majority for the National Government of over two
hundred it was down to eighty-one. As the tellers' announced the result,
'there were shouts of "Resign ... Resign" ... and that old ape Josh
Wedgwood [Colonel, later Sir Josiah, Wedgwood, Labour Member for
Newcastle under Lyme] began to wave his arms about and sing "Rule
Britannia". Harold Macmillan, next to him, joined in but they were
howled down.'[13] In his enthusiasm, Macmillan rushed around buttonholing anybody who would listen and demanding support for Chamberlain's resignation. Many – understandably – found his behaviour offensive
(one Member managed to avoid him, feeling certain that 'I should have
struck [him]'[14]).

It was, of course, all very exciting. So excited were they that at 9.30
the following morning, chattering among themselves, the Watching
Committee reconvened in Arlington Street. They all agreed that
Chamberlain – who was still trying to hang on – should go, but they
could not agree, even after a good deal of animated argument, on who,
Halifax or Churchill, should take over. As it happened, what they thought
hardly mattered, since by the afternoon Chamberlain had accepted the
need for a coalition with Labour, had realised that Labour would not
serve under him and, finally, Halifax had said that he did not think he
could lead the country in wartime from the House of Lords. By the early
evening of the next day – during which the Germans had forced their
way into Belgium and France – the Labour leadership had told Chamberlain, who was still wavering, that they would serve in a coalition but
not under him. The result was inevitable. That same evening Churchill
was asked by the King to form a Government.

While Churchill was forming his Cabinet Macmillan was very much
on the sidelines. He was also very nervous. He was on the telephone
constantly, both to find out what was going on and pressing his own
claims. He learnt from Brendan Bracken, Churchill's Parliamentary
Private Secretary, that '[Bracken] sat up till three in the morning with
David Margesson going through lists. Winston was not in the least
interested once the major posts had been filled, and kept on trying to
interrupt them by discussing the nature of war ...' Macmillan had asked
Bracken what was Churchill's mood. 'Profound anxiety,' he replied.[15]

In the end, Macmillan was one of the last to be offered a government
job. Thanks, finally, to Amery's intervention, he was to be Parliamentary
Secretary at the Ministry of Supply, as junior Minister to Herbert Morrison, one of the Labour leaders brought into the Cabinet. Margesson
thought that since Macmillan had written and spoken so much about
planning production he had better have the chance to see whether his
ideas worked in practice. It was his first ministerial job, and, with the

mixture of nervousness and curiosity that accompanies such events, he duly presented himself at the offices of the Ministry of Supply on the morning of 18 May at Shell-Mex House in the Strand. There he met his new Private Secretary, introduced to him when he arrived by the Permanent Secretary, the bluff Sir Harold Brown – a nineteen-year-old civil servant by the name of John Wyndham.

It was to be the beginning of a long and, over the years, complex relationship. Wyndham matched all Macmillan's criteria for a loyal servant – among other things, he habitually referred to Macmillan as his 'master'. His pedigree was of the finest: grandson of Lord Leconfield, educated at Eton and Trinity College, Cambridge; rejected for military service because of poor eyesight but recruited to the civil service in lieu; connected, in truth, to most of the great families of England. He was, of course, a snob – but so was Macmillan. He was very short-sighted – but so was Macmillan. In all, he was 'tall, stooping, and peering through spectacles with exceptionally thick lenses . . . observer and commentator, contact man, cheerful but determined "fixer", good companion and court jester'.[16] Not the least of Wyndham's attributes, as it turned out, was his ability to cope with Macmillan's occasional fits of depression.

Macmillan was certainly pleased with his new Private Secretary. But he was much less pleased with his Minister. In fact, Morrison and Macmillan were far from a happy team. Macmillan did not take to Morrison – he regarded him as a vulgar south London barrow boy – and Morrison did not take to Macmillan – he thought him an irredeemable snob. Furthermore, much to Macmillan's irritation, Morrison was stubbornly pursuing his vendetta with Ernest Bevin.

Bevin had been appointed by Churchill to be Minister of Labour in May 1940 at the same time as Morrison was appointed Minister of Supply. But the two were hardly on speaking terms. They had started the rows over transport policy in the Labour Governments of the 1920s when Bevin was General Secretary of the Transport and General Workers Union. They had flared up over Morrison's initial flirtation with Ramsay MacDonald's National Government and it was to continue throughout their political careers. (When somebody told Bevin that Morrison was his own worst enemy, Bevin is said to have replied 'not while I'm alive he ain't'.) Yet it was a major part of the Ministry of Supply's brief to organise the supply of raw materials and labour to where they were most needed for the war effort. With Morrison and Bevin barely speaking to one another it was hardly a formula for harmonious government success. Macmillan, too, was more than open in his dislike of Morrison. Dining at the Beefsteak on 24 June – 'very much the Minister nowadays, but he says that he has arrived too late to rise very high' – while protesting loyalty to his Minister he made at least one colleague 'realise that he agrees with what I have already heard – *viz* – that H.M. is not as much a success as Minister of Supply – and cuts very little ice ...'.[17]

In the midst of these departmental rows and inter-ministerial sniping, London was hit in early September by the first wave of German bombing raids – which in all were to last throughout the winter and into the spring of 1941. For more than six weeks in September and October the raids were nightly. Macmillan recalled having to walk from his office in Shell-Mex House 'to a club in Pall Mall or St James's Street and then to my own flat in Piccadilly ... the need to grope along in the murky darkness, only occasionally illuminated by the flash of guns'.[18] In October he was lucky to escape unhurt when the Carlton Club was bombed – he and his brother-in-law James Stuart 'both admitted that they found the air raids very nerve-shaking and infinitely preferred the shelling in the trenches of the last war'.[19] In November he was hit by a taxi in the dark and knocked out. He was again lucky not to have been killed.

It is hardly surprising that Morrison was worried about the safety of his junior Minister. He wanted him to sleep along with the others in an underground shelter under the Ministry building. (After the war Macmillan, unforgivably, said that Morrison's perfectly sensible arrangements were due to his cowardice.) But Macmillan – fastidious as he was – did not take to it at all and preferred – equally unforgivably – to risk the danger in going back to 90 Piccadilly. Even that did not survive. Arriving late one night after dinner at Pratt's, he found a note from his servant (even in the Blitz servants were apparently indispensable): 'Your rooms have been blown in. I have put some things in Mr—'s room. This was a flat on the ground floor. Here I found pyjamas, dressing gown, slippers, the property of the owner of the flat, neatly arranged, with toothbrush and glass set out and towel folded in the traditional way on the washstand.'[20] The following day Macmillan moved into a flat next door. Such as it was, this was Macmillan's London life in the ordeal of the Blitz, unnecessarily risking danger for domestic comfort – with only occasional weekend visits to the difficult *ménage* at Pooks Cottage.

None of this, however, had prevented him from engaging in what seemed another clever plot. On 17 June 1940 Amery and Macmillan met to devise a plan for a reconstruction of the War Cabinet which Churchill had in large measure inherited from Chamberlain. The new junior Ministers, they agreed, should act together to impress their views on Churchill. There was a need for strong men as ministers who could command, who could sack civil servants as they wished as well as junior ministers. Boothby was in on the plot as well as a clutch of Liberals. They met at White's, in Amery's house and finally in Lloyd George's office. Duff Cooper was invited to join the plotters but wisely declined.

As might be expected, it all went badly wrong. Churchill soon got wind of the plot and sent for Amery. His message could hardly have been clearer. 'Their [junior Ministers'] business', he told Amery, 'was to stick to the job that he had given them. If anyone in the Government wished to criticise its working or its composition they should resign and criticise from the outside.'[21] The plot thereupon collapsed. Macmillan, for his part, learnt the lesson. It was about the reality of political power. It was a lesson which, in all his long life, he would never forget.

On 3 October 1940, the lesson learnt, Macmillan heard that he was to have a change of Minister. Chamberlain had resigned from the Cabinet owing to the onset of the cancer which was shortly to kill him. In the resulting Cabinet reshuffle Oliver Lyttelton, a contemporary of Macmillan in the Grenadier Guards, was parachuted in as President of the Board of Trade (and to a safe Conservative seat in the House of Commons at Aldershot), Cranborne became Dominions Secretary and, of greater interest to Macmillan, Morrison was moved to the Home Office and replaced by Sir Andrew Duncan.

As an individual, Duncan was pleasant enough. A Lowland Scot, he had been successful in the shipbuilding industry and had then migrated south. He was a kind and gentle man, with few enemies, and he moved almost seamlessly on to the Court of the Bank of England and then into the House of Commons as Member for the City of London. He then served as President of the Board of Trade before being dislodged by Lyttelton and shifted to the Ministry of Supply. As a political master, however, Macmillan did not think much of him. Although in later life he wrote kind words about Duncan, at the time he was scathing: 'smoking too many cigars', he told his friend Crookshank, 'and pale from too many *crêpes suzette*.'[22] Worse still, mischief makers spread the view that Duncan 'hates the HofC and is nervous when speaking there'.[23]

Duncan, in fact, turned out to be a perfectly competent minister. He had a good grasp of detail and a sympathetic ear for all complaints. On the other hand, competence in those days was not enough – Churchill demanded urgency. But at least Duncan started to make some sense of the Ministry of Supply – a ramshackle body which had only been formed in 1939 to coordinate provision of armaments to all three Services but in practice, because of inter-Service disputes, had the Army as its sole customer. But he was unable to resolve the disputes with Bevin over the deployment of labour or with Lord Beaverbrook at the Ministry for Aircraft Production. Macmillan, of course, wisely kept out of the disputes and busied himself with answering questions in the House of Commons, going on his travels to the Regional and Area Boards for which he was responsible and, it need hardly be said, collecting gossip when in London at his dinners at the Beefsteak.

In the early months of 1941 Macmillan noted that the production of tanks was well below the Army's requirements. Others had noted it too. In fact, it was precisely those months which were some of the gloomiest of the war. The Lend-Lease arrangement with the United States, manna from heaven to the Ministry of Supply, was not signed until March, the Soviet Union was still in alliance with Germany and Britain was on its own – and British cities were nightly being pounded by German aircraft. Even in the Ministry of Supply there were gloomy thoughts that Britain might, after all, lose the war.

The gloomy thoughts were dispersed by the arrival, on 29 July 1941, of a new Minister, none other than Lord Beaverbrook. Macmillan had come across the 'Beaver', as he was known, in the 1920s but they had never been at all close. Beaverbrook's history, of course, was well known – indeed, he had made sure it was. Born as William Maxwell Aitken in Canada in 1879, he had made his money in stockbroking before moving to Britain in 1910, where he became Unionist Member of Parliament for Ashton-under-Lyne and, at the same time starting to build a London newspaper empire. There followed a career of startling success – knighted in 1911, elevated to the House of Lords in 1917 (his coat of arms was designed by Rudyard Kipling), hectoring the staff of the *Daily Express* to make it the most feared of the national newspapers, almost succeeding single-handedly in overthrowing Baldwin's Premiership and, above all, remaining one of the few who supported Churchill when he was in the political wilderness and, consequently, as one of Churchill's lifelong friends. His energy was prodigious, his health uncertain – he was badly asthmatic and had great difficulty sleeping – physically small and ugly – 'this strange attractive gnome with an odour of genius about him'[24] – but a notoriously successful seducer. In short, like him or loathe him (both camps were fully populated) he was never one to be ignored.

This was the Beaverbrook who arrived in his Rolls-Royce at Shell-Mex House on the morning of 29 July. Only a week earlier, however, the whole landscape of the war had changed. On 22 June German armies had invaded the Soviet Union. Beaverbrook was insistent that Britain give as much military aid as possible to the Soviets. At the same time, as a member of the War Cabinet, he was advocating an invasion of France – or at least a raid in strength on the French coast – in order to detach German forces from the eastern front. Churchill was content with the aid proposal but thought, reasonably enough, that the proposal for an attack on the French coast was unrealistically premature. Nevertheless, now that Britain had a powerful ally in the Soviet Union it was all the more important to recruit another powerful ally – the United States. The Lend-Lease agreement, signed in March, had also to be made to work. The result was that Beaverbrook was as much employed by Churchill as a trusted go-between with the Soviets and the Americans as he was as a departmental minister. Macmillan, as the junior Minister, was largely left to run the place by himself.

Fortunately, the Ministry was well managed by its officials – Duncan had seen to that. All it needed were periodic fireworks from the Minister, which Beaverbrook was able to provide, and a steady hand from the junior Minister – particularly in answering questions and putting the department's case in the House of Commons – which Macmillan was equally able to provide. In fact, Macmillan was even able to keep up with the some of the other Glamour Boys who, at Crookshank's instigation, had formed a group of eight junior ministers to meet regularly – and dine lavishly – at the Café Royal. In so far as they had any specific programme it was to encourage Eden to be more assertive and, strangely, to try to establish a right to question Churchill on a regular basis about his conduct of the war. (It need hardly be said that neither of these two aspirations found favour with Churchill. In fact, after his experience in 1940, Macmillan, although enjoying the company and the dining, wisely kept his distance from their attempted machinations. He had, after all, been bitten once already.)

While officials in the Ministry of Supply were busying themselves with the details – and delivery – of the agreement signed by Beaverbrook and the Soviet Foreign Minister Molotov in early October, Macmillan, apart from his job as the Minister in charge of the programme, was working on a proposal to reorganise all the ministries of war production. Beaverbrook, like Morrison before him, was unable to get on with Bevin – Bevin used to shout at him in meetings of the interdepartmental committees set up to manage war production and Beaverbrook, the asthmatic, was no good at shouting back. All that was damaging not only to the war effort but to morale in the Ministry of Supply. 'In October', Macmillan recorded, 'the Government was under heavy fire.'[25] The solution, advocated by many in the debates in Parliament and carried forward by Macmillan, was to create a super-ministry, one which would embrace the Ministries of Supply, Aircraft Production, Ship-building, Works and Buildings and, arguably, the Ministry of Labour.

As might be expected, it took many weeks before the idea worked its way up to the top of the War Cabinet agenda. In fact, it took the Japanese assault on Pearl Harbor in December, and the subsequent German declaration of war with the United States, for it to emerge as a priority. As 1941 drifted into 1942, the matter became not just a priority but a

matter of urgency. In the end, on 2 February 1942, Beaverbrook told
Macmillan that the new Ministry would be created and that he, Beaverbrook, had accepted Churchill's invitation to be the new Minister. The
Ministry of Labour, he went on to say, would not be included. That was
a battle which Bevin had won. Furthermore – and here was the sting in
the tail – Beaverbrook confided in Macmillan that the new Ministry
would be a coordinating department only, with a small staff and no room
for a junior minister.

In the ensuing reshuffle Macmillan was given a job at the Colonial
Office to serve under Lord Moyne – formerly Walter Guinness – and
made a Privy Councillor (serious recognition at last). Fortunately, he was
also able to take Wyndham with him. The move, however, was not easy.
He knew almost nothing about the British colonies and, moreover, found
the Office itself one of 'vast caverns ... where light seldom penetrated
and ghostly steps echoed down the lofty corridors as in the aisles of some
great cathedral'.[26] Furthermore, only ten days after he had begun work
there Singapore, along with 85,000 British and Imperial troops, surrendered to the Japanese. Hong Kong had already gone as well as the
Malay States, North Borneo and Sarawak. Burma was threatened and
India and Ceylon were the obvious next targets. Sixty per cent of the
world's tin production and ninety per cent of its rubber production had
been lost.

But no sooner had Macmillan settled down with Moyne than he was
in the middle of another reshuffle. Moyne was unceremoniously bundled
out. Cranborne, too, was bundled out of the Dominions Office to make
way for Sir Stafford Cripps on his return from the Moscow Embassy. He
went to the House of Lords, taking one of the Salisbury titles, Essendon,
'by advancement' as the procedure was known, and took Moyne's place
at Colonies – to find his brother-in-law already settled in there as junior
Minister. It was another turn in the political merry-go-round. Macmillan
treated it as such and, perhaps surprisingly, was not put out by Cranborne's arrival as his superior. In fact, he rather welcomed it, since
he would keep his role of spokesman for the Office in the House of
Commons.

There was no doubt in either of their minds about the role of the
Office in time of war. It was, in Macmillan's words, 'the mobilisation of
all potential resources of the Colonial Empire, both of men and materials,
for the purposes of war'.[27] Together they decided that Macmillan would
take charge of economic and trade questions, since he had the contacts
in the Ministries of Production and Supply, and a small group was
formed to support him, housed away from the main Office in the
building which had more than one hundred years before belonged to

Lord Melbourne (Macmillan was delighted with Wyndham's agility in securing 'this beautiful house'[28]). Their job was to ensure the maximum supply of raw materials (and soldiers) from the colonies to Britain's engine of wartime.

As it happened, there were diversions from the central purpose. The first followed a report which had been compiled in the early months of the war by an old India hand – he had been Governor of the Punjab and of the United Provinces until his retirement in 1934 – Lord Hailey of Shahpur. In 1936 Hailey had toured Africa – east, west and south – and, as a result, had sat down to write what was grandly known in those days as the African Survey. The effort nearly killed him, but the work was saved by an official from the Colonial Office, Frederick Pedler, who managed to produce a (just) readable document. Early in 1940 Hailey, with Pedler in tow as his secretary, toured Africa again to report further. In June 1940 Hailey and Pedler went again to Africa to follow up their initial research. The result was a report, largely written by Pedler, entitled 'Native Administration and Political Development in British Tropical Africa'. In it, Hailey stated roundly that 'the dependencies shall be given a full opportunity to achieve self-government'.[29]

This was not at all what anybody in 1942 wanted to hear. But it was widely known that Pedler was at least a major influence in Hailey's ideas – if not the author – and the Colonial Office could not simply ignore them. The African waters had been muddied further still by Churchill, who had declared that British policies towards the colonies was covered by 'declarations' in harmony with the Atlantic Charter he had agreed with (the arch anti-imperialist) President Franklin Roosevelt. An official statement on the matter was demanded by an Opposition Member in the House of Commons in the form of a Government White Paper. To add to the inconvenience, Hailey himself proclaimed his doctrine – as one of 'Partnership' in a speech to the House of Lords towards the end of May 1942.

But when Macmillan asked his officials to prepare the White Paper it became apparent that the 'declarations' were not only in many cases unrecorded but, when they had been, were at variance one with another. 'I do not think', he minuted Cranborne, 'the P.M. can have realised the true nakedness of the land when he made the statement of September 9th, 1941 ... The declarations are not complete in themselves, nor are they free from ambiguity. They are scrappy, obscure and jejune ... The P.M. must have written the declaration on his own.'[30] The question then was how he and Cranborne could dig themselves out of a rather unpleasant hole.

Macmillan was at least partially successful in this. In a speech to the

House of Commons on 24 June he presented Hailey's ideas of partnership in the most Delphic manner – to the point where nobody was quite sure what he meant in practice. But still the matter would not go away. The dilemma, of course, was evident. There had to be some sort of political movement, if only to satisfy Roosevelt that the post-war British Empire would be quite different from the pre-war formula to which the Americans took so much exception. On the other hand, Churchill and the other Conservatives in his Cabinet were certainly not going to agree to anything which even remotely looked like the dissolution of the Empire – either in the short or the long term.

Macmillan's solution to the dilemma was nothing if not ingenious. Together with his officials he devised a plan which, in the immediate, would apply to Kenya only but which, over a longer horizon, might apply to other parts of the Empire. It was to allow local government to buy the freehold of the white-owned farms, keeping the present owners as managers of the large ones and selling to Africans the smaller ones as and when they became able to afford them. Needless to say, the authors of the plan knew perfectly well that nothing could possibly come of it in wartime. But it had the merit of solving the dilemma. It served to show, not least to the Americans, that the British Government was doing something about the Hailey doctrine of 'partnership', while making sure that nothing in practice would happen.

An easier problem for Macmillan was the matter of labour legislation. In the spring of 1942, even in the middle of the war, an international convention on the matter had been agreed. It provided for protection of conscripted labour to the Armed Forces, forced employment of labour into factories, introduction of minimum wages and safety provisions for factory workers. There were mutterings from Bevin that implementation of its provisions were essential. Macmillan and Cranborne, however, took the view that these were matters to be dealt with after the war. Any attempt to impose new labour laws in the colonies would without any question damage the war effort. That was a battle which Bevin had to lose – and he did.

In the autumn of 1942, when the tide of the war was turning at El Alamein and Stalingrad, and when the Americans were preparing to land in North Africa, the tide was also turning again in Whitehall. There was yet another reshuffle. Cranborne was asked, and agreed – partly owing to his continued ill health – to leave the Colonial Office to concentrate such energies as he had on the leadership of the House of Lords. The vacancy at the Colonial Office was to be filled by Macmillan's old colleague Oliver Stanley.

This was very bad news for Macmillan. While Cranborne had been in charge Macmillan had sole responsibility for the Office in the House of Commons. Stanley was, of course, himself in the House of Commons and would consequently take the lead role. Macmillan, in a fit of injured pride, accordingly drafted a letter of resignation. But before submitting it he was sensible enough to show it to Churchill's confidant Brendan Bracken, who advised him to stay his hand. Macmillan thought of going to see Churchill 'to talk over the question of my future frankly'.[31] Bracken told him not to be so silly. The North African landings had just taken place. There were a thousand problems for Churchill to deal with. The political future of a junior minister was certainly not one of them. Macmillan, Bracken advised, should 'swallow [his] pride and be patient'.[32] That, after some searching of conscience, Macmillan did. Oliver Stanley was duly appointed on 22 November and for a month Macmillan continued in the Office as his junior Minister.

Bracken's advice turned out to be eminently sensible. Churchill's attention was indeed focused on North Africa. The military operation was not going well and the Americans had done a deal with the fiercely Anglophobe French Admiral François Darlan in an attempt to secure a French ceasefire and, with any luck, bring the French Army over to the Allied side. Churchill and Eden agreed that the political section of the Allied Forces Headquarters in Algiers badly needed reinforcement. Their first proposal was to send Sir Alexander Cadogan, the Permanent Under-Secretary at the Foreign Office, but this found no favour in Washington. On 17 November they sent a second proposal: to send a minister comparable in status to the British Minister in Cairo. Roosevelt replied that the United States and Britain should only send political representatives with a limited remit to oversee French civil administration.

Roosevelt went further. As the American representative he nominated Robert Murphy, a State Department official who had spent ten years in Paris before the war and had accompanied the Pétain Government to Vichy. In late 1941 Murphy had been transferred to North Africa – where he had set up an apparently harmless consular network (most of his 'consuls' were in fact spies). But Murphy was not popular in London. Apart from his Vichy connections, he was known to be a Catholic of Irish origin and therefore believed to dislike Britain. It was all the more important for the British to find a politician of skill and presence who could act as a counterweight. After much deliberation, Churchill and Eden settled on the erstwhile Glamour Boy, leader of the Café Royal group and now the disgruntled junior Minister at the Treasury, Harry Crookshank.

The problem was that Crookshank did not want to go. In fact, he did not want to go anywhere. As far back as May 1942, at a dinner in the

Carlton Club, Churchill had tried to persuade him to go as Minister Resident in West Africa. Despite Churchill's persuasiveness 'and two bottles of champagne the prime minister poured down his throat',[33] Crookshank was unmovable. Similarly, when he was offered the Algiers job, which came with Cabinet rank, he turned that down too. Churchill had then to find a third choice. In the end, that turned out, rather to the surprise of his colleagues in the House of Commons, to be none other than the junior Minister at the Colonial Office, Harold Macmillan. Macmillan, when offered the job, accepted without a second thought. Indeed, at long last, he felt able at least to be moderately pleased with himself.

8

Greeks, Romans and Frenchmen

For northern Europeans the Mediterranean has always had its own magic. The bright sunlight, the tideless sea, the rays of an evening sun dancing on almost unnoticeable waves, the romance of ancient ruins, the food and wine, the sense that time is no more important than the blink of a sleepy eye – all this has over the centuries changed, for better or for worse, the lives of those from the gloomier north who have been lucky enough to experience it. Sometimes it takes time, even years, to work, but the magic was to work without much delay and with particular effect on the pasty-faced Englishman, in rimless spectacles and baggy trousers, who arrived, along with an equally pasty-faced and bespectacled Private Secretary, two secretaries, two typewriters purloined from the Colonial Office and trunks full of Gibbon, Trollope, Jane Austen and Homer, at the airport of Maison Blanche just outside Algiers on the morning of 2 January 1943.

There was, to be sure, very little magic to greet them on their arrival. The weather at the time was dreadful. There was no suggestion of 'Alger la Blanche', however beautiful the city, and particularly the crescent-shaped bay, might be in sunshine. After a bumpy journey in an antique Lockheed Hudson and an overnight stay in Gibraltar, the first hours and days were miserable. Macmillan and his party were put up in a hotel where there was hot water only for one hour a day, no heating and only one sheet for each unpleasantly hard bed. Their office was apparently to consist of two rooms in another unheated hotel. It is no surprise that Wyndham, who had been persuaded to accompany Macmillan to North Africa (the Foreign Office official assigned to him as chief assistant, Roger Makins, was to follow later), was given as his first job the task of finding somewhere better to live and work.

Nor was Algiers itself settled in any sense – either militarily or politically. On the way in from the airport Henry Mack, the British diplomat who had been seconded to the staff of Allied Forces Headquarters (AFHQ), had been gloomy in his briefing on the current state of affairs. The city administration was still in the hands of Vichy officials owing their loyalty to Marshal Philippe Pétain. Indeed, posters of Pétain were to be seen everywhere. In spite of the ceasefire negotiated by the Americans and Admiral François Darlan there were still wayward gangs of Vichyite paramilitaries – not least the official Légion des Anciens Combattants – threatening armed riot. Darlan himself had been assassinated only the previous week in murky circumstances. In short, the new Resident Minister, Mack pointed out, had to be prepared for the worst.

There was to be no pause to allow Macmillan to catch his breath and digest all that Mack had said. At 4 p.m. on the same day Macmillan was summoned to meet the Allied Commander-in-Chief for North Africa, General Dwight D. Eisenhower, in his office in the Hôtel St Georges – splendidly perched on the hills overlooking Algiers bay. As might be imagined, it was not an easy encounter. First, Eisenhower was not in a good mood. Second, Macmillan knew very little about Eisenhower's background or character, and thus had no idea how to approach him. He had been told, of course, that Eisenhower's appointment to command the 'Torch' armada was said to be due – some said entirely due – to his previous position as assistant to the US Chief of Staff General George C. Marshall. What Macmillan did not know was that Eisenhower had never commanded troops in battle, that his parents in Kansas had been Jehovah's Witnesses and pacifists – and had done their best to pass on their beliefs in biblical fundamentalism to their son – and that, most important of all, he suffered from Crohn's disease (a chronic inflammatory condition of the gastrointestinal tract which, among other things, makes for painful toiletry and consequent sudden eruptions of bad temper – and, in Eisenhower's case, when the smiling and wholly engaging mask of the Kansas boy slipped, of coarse and sometimes blasphemous language).

When Macmillan arrived, Eisenhower's mood was all too clear. He was upset. He had not been pleased by Macmillan's appointment. He thought that Mack, as civil liaison officer on his staff, was doing a perfectly good job. In fact, on 31 December he had cabled Washington and the US Embassy in London that he had been shown a telegram sent by the Foreign Office to Mack about Macmillan's appointment and he demanded to know why it had been made in the first place and what it was all about. The response came quickly – from Churchill, no less, via the US Embassy. 'Your 3670. We meant Macmillan to be in the same relation to you as Murphy, who I presume reports on political matters direct to the President as Macmillan will to me. Although *not* formally a member of your staff he fully accepts your supreme authority throughout the theater and has *no* thought but to be of service to you. I hope he and Murphy will work together so that you can relieve yourself of the burden of local politics.'¹ Moreover, Churchill had previously pressed Macmillan's other advantages: that Macmillan had had an American mother and spoke passable French (unlike Eisenhower, who spoke none at all).

Macmillan's account of their first meeting is very different. 'Considering that neither Washington nor London had informed him of my appointment (which one of his staff had heard on the radio),' he wrote to Dorothy on 7 January, 'the interview was quite a success.'[2] As is so often the case with Macmillan, the account is theatrical but substantially untrue. What was true, however, was Eisenhower's undoubted irritation at being excluded from the negotiations between Roosevelt and Churchill leading to Macmillan's appointment. He had also, as it happened, been irritated by British criticisms of his handling of the 'Torch' landings and their military aftermath (the British Chief of the Imperial General Staff, Sir Alan Brooke, wrote in his diary, 'I am afraid that Eisenhower as a general is hopeless!'[3]).

After their preliminary skirmish, the two men finally settled down to an hour's discussion about how Macmillan might help and, more particularly, about those whom he would have to deal with. Eisenhower, by then in a better temper, explained that his deputy, General Mark Clark, would be for the most part in the field, together with the senior British general who had commanded the British task force at 'Torch', Lieutenant General Kenneth Anderson. Admiral Sir Andrew Cunningham, in command of naval forces in North Africa, on the other hand, would mostly be in Algiers. More important for Macmillan, however, was Eisenhower's Chief of Staff, Major General Walter Bedell Smith (known as 'Beetle'), Captain Harry Butcher, Eisenhower's naval aide, and, of course, Murphy. As for the lesser players, Eisenhower imagined that Macmillan would get to know them well enough in due course. There was, however, one important figure that Macmillan needed to know about. After Darlan's assassination, General Henri-Honoré Giraud had been the Americans' favoured replacement and had duly been appointed High Commissioner for French North Africa and Commander-in-Chief of French forces.

On the face of it, Giraud had been an obvious choice. He had been a hero in both wars. In the first war he had fought courageously, had been left for dead on the battlefield, had been captured, had escaped and had then operated clandestinely behind enemy lines (his description of his exploits had mightily impressed Churchill when he visited Giraud's positions on the Maginot Line in 1937). In the second war, he had been taken prisoner of war again but had again escaped, sliding down a 150-foot rope from a window in the fortress of Königstein on the River Elbe in spite of lameness from an earlier wound which had healed badly. From there he had made his way through Switzerland into Unoccupied France, where he had arrived on 25 April 1942. Finally, he had been smuggled out of France on a British submarine and, after a stay in Gibraltar (arguing with the Allies about his future role in the war), he had arrived in Algiers in mid-November.

Wherever he went, Giraud commanded attention. He was tall – some six feet five inches – and walked impressively with large strides of his elegantly long legs, sporting a truly magnificent moustache curled in the form of a sabre and looking to the watching world like a proper model of a French five-star general (a rank he was happy to emphasise on every possible occasion). There were those, of course, who whispered that his brain had not grown in proportion to his body, but there was no doubt that he was a grand figure, in every sense, and one who commanded respect. As such, he was admirably suited to serve the American purpose – to find a successor to Darlan who would bring the 120,000 French troops in North Africa over to the Allied side without too much argument.

Lurking in the London background, nevertheless, was the almost equally tall figure of General Charles de Gaulle. In fact, Macmillan had met de Gaulle twice – and, perhaps surprisingly, had been impressed by his courtesy. That, of course, was in the days when de Gaulle had been welcomed by Churchill and Eden as the only Frenchman of any rank who had protested against the 1940 Armistice and who had fled to London to raise the banner – uncertain at the time – of Free France. Once the tide of the war had changed and the battalions of Free French troops had shown that they too could fight, the name had been changed to Fighting France – and de Gaulle himself had changed with it. He was no longer dependent on British charity. The days of mere survival were over. The future of post-war France was now firmly on his agenda.

On being told of 'Torch', of which he had been kept in ignorance, and of its unsatisfactory aftermath, de Gaulle had set out his stall. On 31 December 1942, after Darlan's assassination and Giraud's appointment, Fighting France issued a statement to Reuters news agency setting out their position. There could be no military cooperation, it said, without political unity. Anything else would lead to 'a large number of Frenchmen [fighting] side by side with the Allies without any French interest [being] represented during the war or at the moment when the war would come to its end'.[4]

De Gaulle, not for the first time and certainly not for the last, had seen what others had failed to see. Roosevelt's strategy was to ensure that US forces, on their first engagement in the European war, met with success. Any political manoeuvre – whether with Darlan or Giraud or anybody else – was subordinate to that end. Furthermore, Roosevelt's old friend William Leahy, who had been US Ambassador in Vichy, was insistent in his view that Pétain was the best bet for bringing the French people to side with the United States. De Gaulle, in this context, was just an unpleasant nuisance. Yet de Gaulle had realised that time and circumstance were on his side – the more so since his emissary, Jean Moulin, was on the point of bringing the Resistance in France under the Gaullist banner.

By mid-January, Wyndham had succeeded in finding 'a rich and sumptuous villa' as living quarters for Macmillan and his party. True, nine members of the refugee Jewish family who were living there had to be evicted but the lady of the house saw no difficulty in that. Moreover, she volunteered to leave them her housemaid and – 'unspeakable glory' – her cook. 'The females', in other words the long-suffering secretaries Miss Campbell and Miss Williams, 'will live (it is hoped) in oriental seclusion, as in a harem.'[5] Yet no sooner had they all settled down there and Macmillan had started to take the political temperature of his American and French allies than he was summoned to a great event which was to take place at the Moroccan coastal city of Casablanca.

On Friday 13 January Macmillan set off in Eisenhower's aeroplane. The journey was certainly eventful – three of the four engines failed from time to time during the flight – and it was with relief that they all landed safely. When they arrived, knowing by then that it was to be a conference at the highest level between Churchill, with his posse of generals, and Roosevelt, with his larger posse of generals, to determine the future conduct of the war, they were escorted to 'a curious kind of settlement [Anfa]', about two to three miles outside Casablanca itself, 'consisting of rich villas belonging to Moroccan millionaires, centring around a three-storey hotel'.[6] Roosevelt and Churchill (with Macmillan in attendance) were to stay in villas while the staffs were put up in the hotel. The whole place was surrounded by an impenetrable fence.

The question at issue between Roosevelt and Churchill was simple: whether to use success in North Africa as a springboard for an invasion of Italy (as Churchill and his generals wanted) or whether to conserve forces for a 'second front' in northern France (as Roosevelt – and, for that matter, Stalin – wanted). There was, of course, a minor matter: what to do about French North Africa. On the great issues, Macmillan was not consulted. This was not because he was ignored. It was simply that the whole thing seemed to turn into 'a mixture between a cruise, a summer school and a conference'.[7] Churchill spent most of the day in bed playing 'bagatelle and bézique by the hour' – Macmillan dubbed him 'The Emperor of the East' – while Roosevelt, 'The Emperor of the West', also spent most of the day lying 'in a great bed on the ground floor' of his villa.[8] Both seemed obviously to be enjoying themselves. Meetings between the two, once the staffs had 'come out of school at five o'clock or so'[9] in the evening, went on late into the night.

On the evening of his arrival Macmillan was summoned to meet Roosevelt. After making his way past the searchlights and the 'horde of what I believe are called G-men' he was ushered into the presence. 'The President was particularly charming to me,' his letter to Dorothy continued. 'There was a great deal of joking about me being the publisher both for him and for the Prime Minister. There was a lot of bézique, an enormous quantity of highballs, talk by the hour, and a general atmosphere of extraordinary goodwill.'[10] Macmillan was quite clearly drenched in Roosevelt's famous charm. It was only much later in his life that he reflected on the meeting, claiming that Roosevelt was 'absolutely insincere'.[11] Of course he was. That was part of Roosevelt's technique – and Macmillan, like many others, fell for it.

By 16 January the two leaders had agreed that Italy would indeed be the next target and that there would be no second front in 1943. They were then ready to turn their attention to North African politics. Giraud and de Gaulle were both summoned. Roosevelt, who was not in the least interested in the French politics of North Africa, turned the whole thing into a schoolboy joke. 'We'll call Giraud the bridegroom,' he told Churchill, 'and I'll produce him from Algiers; and you get the bride, de Gaulle, from London, and we'll have a shotgun wedding.'[12]

Giraud, of course, responded immediately, arriving in Casablanca the following day. De Gaulle, even after Eden and Cadogan had done their best, refused to leave London. He replied that 'the atmosphere of an exalted Allied forum . . . [was not] . . . the best for an effective agreement'.[13]

In fact, de Gaulle's true position was even tougher. Two weeks before, he had sent a long telegram to Félix Éboué, the Governor-General of the Congo, one of the French colonies which had rallied to the Free French. 'Roosevelt', he wrote, '. . . hopes that Giraud will make himself sole master of the situation and that thereafter it would be possible simply to place us under his orders, but various things occurred to block the plan. First of all, Giraud has displayed an extremely [one word, perhaps, fortunately, illegible] political stance, falsely placing himself between Vichyites and Gaullists . . . He has not been able to establish a real authority [and] his decisions and declarations have appeared incoherent . . . [Furthermore] the people of Vichy in North Africa . . . have made Giraud prisoner . . . they keep their psychology and above all their posts.'[14] In other words, not only would de Gaulle refuse to meet Giraud at the behest of the Allies (he had offered four times to meet him face to face on French territory) but there could be no possible union of French forces while Vichyites remained in any position of authority.

Churchill, needless to say, was furious at de Gaulle's refusal – the more so since Roosevelt was quick to mock. He cabled Eden that he should tell de Gaulle that if he failed to turn up at Casablanca the consequences would be dire: North Africa would be settled without him and he would be removed from the leadership of Fighting France. Eden, on the advice of the War Cabinet, toned the message down. It was then considered by the French National Committee who, in turn, advised de Gaulle not to upset Roosevelt. Finally, de Gaulle went to see Eden to say that he would go, although he was being invited, without warning, to discussions of which he knew neither the programme nor the conditions. He was only going because he could not decently refuse an invitation from the President and Prime Minister. The warning, however, was ominous – as it was meant to be.

De Gaulle arrived at Fedala military airport, just outside Casablanca, on the morning of 22 January. He was met by an American general and driven in an American car with the windows smeared in mud to prevent him being seen to the enclave at Anfa and to a villa which had been specially requisitioned for the purpose. It was heavily guarded by American sentries. He was then taken to lunch with Giraud (who greeted him brusquely – '*Bonjour, Gaullè*) where he refused to sit down until American sentries were replaced by French, kept up a barrage of barbed comments and then stalked back to his villa.

His first visitor there was Macmillan. He had come to invite de Gaulle to a meeting with Churchill in the Prime Minister's villa. De Gaulle was courtesy itself. Either he thought that it was not worth having a row with Macmillan or he felt that the invitation was what he had come for and should therefore be graciously accepted. With Churchill, however, it was different. It was, as Churchill later wrote, 'a very stony interview'.[15] De Gaulle complained about the American bayonets surrounding him on French soil. If he had known that would happen, he certainly would not have come. Churchill started shouting 'this is an occupied country' and, in his own brand of French, '*Si vous m'obstaclerez, je vous liquiderai.*'[16] De Gaulle started shouting back. It was only when they had both calmed down that Churchill told de Gaulle of the scheme for the future government of North Africa which he and Roosevelt had agreed. Giraud would be supreme military commander, and he and de Gaulle would be joint chairmen of a governing committee. Other members would be General Alphonse Georges, General Charles Noguès, General Pierre Boisson and General Marcel Peyrouton.

It could hardly have been worse. Georges had been a general in the defeated French Army of 1940, Noguès was a sly and unreconstructed

Vichyite at present Resident General in Morocco, Boisson had defended Dakar against the Free French in September 1940, ordering his troops to fire on fellow Frenchmen, and Peyrouton had been a member of Pétain's Cabinet, then Vichy Ambassador in Buenos Aires before being brought back to be Governor-General of Algeria. Furthermore, he was one of those who had signed de Gaulle's death warrant in 1940. In fact, the plan was little short of ridiculous. De Gaulle replied that it must have been drawn up at the intelligence level – quite respectable for what it was, he admitted – of American sergeant majors but that it had nothing to do with reality. Fighting France was certainly not going to let itself be submerged in a Vichy-dominated Committee. With that, de Gaulle simply got up, politely asked if he could now take his leave – and left.

Macmillan thus had his first experience of de Gaulle's confrontational method of negotiation. It was certainly not something he had come across before, and for an urbane British politician and diplomat, with a fondness for Jane Austen and Trollope, it was rather shocking. Moreover, he had never before seen Churchill in a temper – which was equally shocking. Yet, much as he admired Churchill, he was in turn starting to admire the stubborn General. Where before he had been patronising to the French, treating them as many Englishmen of his day and class used to treat foreigners – as beings of a strange and slightly unruly disposition – he was now prepared to see de Gaulle (but certainly not Giraud) as a serious leader who was just, perhaps, what France needed.

De Gaulle's subsequent meeting with Roosevelt changed nothing. Roosevelt's message was the same as Churchill's. De Gaulle went back to his villa – and wrote in his own hand a letter to Commandant Loys Tochon, a Fighting France sympathiser (and former pupil of de Gaulle at St Cyr) in the garrison of Casablanca. 'I am here,' he wrote,

> brought by the Anglo-American areopagus shut in within these boundaries. As far as we are concerned, the object is to oblige Fighting France to subordinate itself to General Giraud and accept the system and the people in place [here] ... The real reasons are as follows: in the first place, the American desire to ensure at whatever cost the triumph of the American team which you know and whose objective since the Armistice is to maintain Vichy in the victory; in the second place, the desire of the Americans to establish in North Africa, and if possible throughout the Empire, while waiting to establish it in France, a French authority which can only exist thanks to them and which consequently can refuse them nothing ... England, and above all its Prime Minister, support this policy, not very willingly but by force, since the pressure in all areas exerted by Washington on London

reaches an intensity and character [which are] literally unbelievable
... the atmosphere they have created here ... recalls that of Berch-
tesgaden ... I will certainly not accept the American scheme ... I do
not know how things will turn out ... it is perfectly possible that the
blindness and anger of the Americans and the English will put me in
such a situation that our action becomes impossible ... In the extreme
hypothesis of a rupture, there is no doubt that Washington and
London will present the matter in their own way, in other words
heaping insults on me ... I will then have little scope for informing
France and the Empire. This is why I am sending you this letter ...
make it public ... [17]

Although Macmillan had come to believe in de Gaulle as a possible
future leader, he had not yet grasped the essence of de Gaulle's message.
In the same letter to Tochon, de Gaulle (not that Macmillan ever saw
the letter) was quite specific in his reference to Giraud. 'I find in Giraud
a man whose stature and tone can be impressive but has on me, militarily
and politically speaking, the effect of a ghost from 1939. He does not understand either the fact that France is in full revolution precisely against the
system and the men of Vichy or the danger that he himself presents to
the sovereignty of France in the Empire, and tomorrow to national
independence, in putting himself in the hands of the Americans.'[18]

Soon after writing that letter, de Gaulle was summoned to another
meeting with Macmillan and Murphy. They had been charged with
producing, and getting agreement to, a communiqué along the lines of
the Roosevelt–Churchill plan. All evening and well into the night they
went through draft after draft, all of which Giraud accepted and all of
which de Gaulle rejected. As night drew on, word came that Roosevelt
had been dining with the Sultan of Morocco and General Noguès the
previous evening and had discussed with them the post-war future of a
Morocco free of French influence. That was enough for de Gaulle. The
night meeting was quickly abandoned. The next morning de Gaulle told
Macmillan and Murphy that the French Empire was not, and never
would be, up for disposal by Anglo-Saxons.

There then was another de Gaulle–Churchill meeting. 'Owing to Mr
Churchill's dispositions, we had an extremely bitter interview. It was to
be the roughest of our encounters in the whole war.'[19] Macmillan listened
while Churchill told de Gaulle that he was finished, that he would be
denounced in the House of Commons and discredited. De Gaulle listened politely – with the odd sally of his own. There followed the absurd
scene of Giraud and de Gaulle shaking hands – in a picture which was
immediately flashed around the world – with Roosevelt shouting *'encore'*.

Finally, a communiqué, almost entirely drafted by de Gaulle but approved by Giraud, was issued. It 'stated the obvious: that Frenchmen should unite to fight beside the Allies against the Axis'.[20] On that note, the Casablanca conference came to its sudden and sullen end.

All in all, Macmillan had had a good conference. He had pleased Churchill. He had made progress with de Gaulle (the evening after everybody else had left the two had a cordial dinner together). Even Eden was complimentary, and he had, moreover, made friends with one of Roosevelt's most influential advisers, his envoy-extraordinary, Harry Hopkins (Murphy was still another matter). In fact, there was a strange postscript to Casablanca. Macmillan had picked up from Hopkins that Roosevelt had signed documents – based apparently on drafts by one of Giraud's most sinister allies, the vegetable oil producer Jacques Lemaigre-Dubreuil – committing the United States and Great Britain to recognising that the French Commander-in-Chief in Algiers would have the 'right and duty to preserve all French interests in the military, economic financial and moral plane'. Furthermore, Giraud was to be given the job. Shocked at Roosevelt's duplicity, Macmillan managed to get copies of the documents out of Murphy – who had not read them before they were signed – and insisted on sending them to London, where they were immediately and angrily disavowed. Four months later they reappeared with de Gaulle given equal status to Giraud. Macmillan's view of Roosevelt after that was never quite the same.

Macmillan described the atmosphere at Casablanca in the second of his long letters to Dorothy, a series which was kept up for the rest of the war (and which were published as his *War Diaries*). Their style, unlike that of his pre-war writings, follows that of the Finland diary – perceptive, amused and detached – which makes for easy and enjoyable reading, like letters from a brother to a favoured sister. Dorothy's letters back are sisterly as well, but less informative (always starting 'My dear Harold' and ending, simply, 'Love, Dorothy'[21]) and for the most part talking about the flowers at Pooks Cottage. She did, however, note that she had picked up, no doubt from one of her brothers-in-law, that at Casablanca '[Churchill] was delighted with you and thinks you are doing amazingly well ...'.[22] After that, she went on to discuss the problems of the partridges. Macmillan in turn reported to her that he was settling in to his villa, which 'is almost out of the town, and you hardly see the town from it ... you look out upon the blue waters of the Bay on the one side, and backwards to the hills and mountains on the other'.[23] Moreover, Makins had arrived and the 'very nice man' from the Foreign Office, Pierson Dixon, who had been standing in, would be bringing his letter back to London.

The serious business, of course, continued. In mid-February Macmillan sent a long despatch to London. In it, he argued more emphatically than before that some form of unity of all the French who were fighting the Axis was essential. In the short term it would make the use of North Africa as a military springboard for an attack on continental Europe much easier, and in the long term it was in Britain's interest for there to be a stable France. That would depend on there being no civil war, and that, in turn, depended on the unity of the army of liberation. But he worried about Giraud, 'the timidity, the wobbling, the whoring after Vichy, the right-wing political flavour of the administration ... and the hesitating, vacillating, double-faced policy which lasted now since Darlan's elevation and assassination ...'[24] In truth, although he meant it as a criticism of Giraud, it was as much as anything a scathing critique of the Americans.

Macmillan's despatch was well received in official London, although, given its length, it was submitted to Churchill by Eden with some diffidence. Senior Foreign Office officials were particularly pleased, both with the quips in Latin (recognised, of course, with knowing smiles) and with Macmillan's critique of the Americans (it was just after the moment when Roosevelt's signature to the Giraud documents had arrived in London). Churchill, however, was not altogether pleased. He was still furious with de Gaulle and threatening – yet again – to get rid of him (without ever quite managing to do so). In fact, the domestic London difficulties rather suited Macmillan, since he had come to believe that after the fireworks at Casablanca everybody should have time to calm down.

It was then time for another delicate task. Churchill instructed Macmillan to go to Alexandria in order to bring over the French naval squadron which, under its commander, Admiral Godfroy, had been holed up there in neutrality since the defeat of France in 1940. Together with Wyndham, the French Admiral Jacques Missoffe and his flag lieutenant, Macmillan boarded an old Lockheed Hudson at 1.15 on the morning of 22 February. To get the plane off the ground, Macmillan, the heaviest of the party, was asked to sit up front with the pilot – a louche-looking, gum-chewing Australian. Halfway down the runway the plane had just left the ground when, to Macmillan's consternation, the pilot shut down the throttle, landed heavily and braked. But it was all too late. The plane skidded off the end of the runway, lurched sideways and ended up in a ditch.

At that point nobody was hurt. The pilot and navigator escaped immediately through an emergency exit. Wyndham and the two French officers opened the door at the rear and walked out. It was then that the plane caught fire – with Macmillan still in it. He managed to scramble over the various control levers separating him from the pilot's seat and get to the emergency exit. Impeded by his heavy Ulster overcoat he was slow in getting through what was little more than an escape hatch until, with one last heave, he was out, rolling on to the wing and then to the ground.

By that time his face was badly burned. Fortunately, his spectacles had protected his eyes and his coat had protected his body – though not his legs. Equally fortunately, Makins, who had stayed behind to see Macmillan off, was still there to organise the rescue party. Macmillan was taken to the first-aid station at the airport and thence on to Maison-Carrée Hospital, where at about half past ten in the morning he was taken to the operating theatre. There, while he was under general anaesthetic, a surgeon opened the blisters on his face, removed the burnt hair of his moustache and from his head, and made 'a sort of mask ... of bandages and plaster' which the nurses put over his head.[25] That done, he was, of course, obliged to stay in hospital – where he wrote an account of the whole episode to Dorothy. In truth, although he only admitted to great pain where the nerves in his cheeks had been exposed, he was lucky to escape with his life. It came as no consolation to learn while he was in hospital that the cause of the pilot's panic was the failure by a mechanic to remove a cover to the air passage leading to the speedometer – a minor affair which could have been rectified by the navigator when the plane was in the air.

Undeterred, and still wearing his mask, Macmillan took off again – only six days later – for Cairo on 28 February. His mask was finally removed there on 3 March – after ten days – leaving his hair 'a curious kind of porridge colour' and his forehead with 'lovely new [pink] skin like a baby'.[26] His lips, however, were badly swollen and very far from healed. He also had to spend a day in bed to recover from delayed shock. But he was just well enough to take the train to Alexandria to spend a few hours with Godfroy – over dinner discussing partridge shooting and the First World War. That done, it was time for a short break. On 8 March he and Wyndham left to spend three days in Malta – to be royally entertained in beautiful weather by the Deputy Governor, Admiral Sir Ralph Leatham. Macmillan was able to rest, do some sightseeing and, above all, according to his letters to Dorothy, admire the flowers and the shrubs.

When the two arrived back in Algiers, they found that much had happened. On 23 February, Fighting France had issued another declaration restating their position of December. Even more important, a new character had come on stage – Jean Monnet. At Anfa, Roosevelt had promised Giraud that the United States would provide arms to re-

equip the forces under his command. Monnet was the perfect person for
the job. His career had begun as a salesman for his family's brandy
company in the Charente. As a young man he had moved to London
during the First World War to help in the procurement of American
arms for France and Britain, had then shifted to the League of Nations
as Deputy Secretary-General, then to investment banking, then back to
Washington as vice-chairman of the British Supply Council. There he
had built up an extensive network of contacts in the Roosevelt administration (including a close relationship with Hopkins). Among his many
virtues in Roosevelt's eyes was that he disliked de Gaulle. But above all
he worked behind the scenes, avoiding public rows (he never stood for
elective office) and cajoling rather than shouting. Small in stature – and
somewhat fastidious (he reminded at least one British observer of Agatha
Christie's Hercule Poirot) – in Algiers, of course, as Macmillan was quick
to note, he had the advantage of being French.

Monnet had soon realised that there was no conceivable possibility of
uniting the different French factions while the measures imposed by
Vichy were still in place. He had been sent by Roosevelt to help Giraud,
but he knew that Roosevelt had at Casablanca pronounced Giraud to be
a 'dud'.[27] Moreover, he was aware that Murphy and his superiors in
Washington, thanks largely to British efforts, had only reluctantly come
round to the view that the previous policy of propping up Giraud by
himself was no longer viable. Monnet therefore started to use his very
considerable powers of persuasion on Giraud to get him to repeal the anti-
Semitic legislation, to release all political prisoners, to abolish political
censorship of the press and to re-establish the laws of the Fifth Republic.
If Monnet's silver tongue was not enough there was always the stick: no
liberalisation, no guns. In fact, Macmillan had spent 'two and a half
months of work'[28] preparing precisely the project which Monnet was
about to bring to final fruition. In Macmillan's official report, '[Monnet]
arrived, a deus ex machina (in this case a Liberator) at the psychological
moment; or (to change the metaphor) he was the small and efficient
catalyst which precipitated the solution.'[29]

At five o'clock in the afternoon on 13 March, Makins and Sam Reber
(Murphy's deputy) were called round to Monnet's flat. 'When Sam and
I appeared,' Makins later said, '[Monnet] said "we must turn General
Giraud into a liberal . . ." we then went all over [the speech] . . . we kept
it up until 1 a.m. . . .'[30] Giraud objected to much of it, brought in one of
his aides, André Labarthe, to rewrite part of it – and in the end agreed.
The speech was delivered in the evening of 14 March at a meeting in
Algiers of Lorrainers and Alsatians – some five to six hundred of them.
It was delivered in 'a simple and soldierly style, with no attempt at

oratorical effect'.[31] Although there was no oratorical effect there was no doubt about the political effect. The 'New Deal', as Macmillan baptised it, was born, and the way was now open for substantive discussions between the Gaullists and the Giraudists.

An invitation was accordingly sent to de Gaulle. Quite properly, it was sent through General Georges Catroux, the five-star general who had arrived in Algiers to lead the Gaullist side in preparatory talks. Macmillan liked Catroux. He thought him '*très fin, très souple*, and all that. A good diplomatist, a man of the world, with a very high standard of personal comfort, a French snob (princesses and all that) and yet a broad, tolerant liberal view of life.'[32] (With a suitable change of nationality, of course, Macmillan could easily have imagined that the description might apply to himself.) Yet just at that moment, when he was most needed in Algiers, Catroux took off to Syria and was not to return until the end of March.

It was all very frustrating. Although he and Murphy had agreed to keep out of the negotiations as much as possible Macmillan at least was anxious that the favourable tide should not be missed. In fact, as he wrote later, he was in too much of a hurry, still believing that it was a matter, now that the issues dividing the two sides had been largely resolved by the New Deal, of the two generals sitting down and putting together the mechanics of union. He still had not understood the true nature of the dispute between the two protagonists – Giraud's conviction that a military defeat of Germany was all that mattered, de Gaulle's equally strong dedication to the 'revolution' in France after victory. Fighting France in London had noted this. 'Macmillan', ran a note based on information from a sympathetic British official in Algiers, 'has the best of intentions; but he has absolutely no understanding of the complexities of French internal politics.'[33]

Nor was it at all clear what game Murphy was playing. At times he seemed to be working along the line agreed at Casablanca – the union of the two French factions. At other times he seemed to encourage Giraud to believe that he had complete backing from the United States and could ignore de Gaulle. What had obviously filtered down to him from Washington was Roosevelt's dislike of de Gaulle, shared by his Secretary of State, Cordell Hull, and his deputy, Sumner Welles. Roosevelt also showed openly his contempt for the French collapse in 1940. He demonstrated this at a dinner with Eden in Washington on 22 March. '[After the war] armaments should be concentrated in the hands of Britain, the United States and Russia ...,' he pronounced. 'The smaller powers should have nothing more dangerous than rifles ... the three powers should police Europe in general ... a new state called "Wallonia" would include the Walloon parts of Belgium with Luxembourg, Alsace-Lorraine and part of Northern France . . .'[34] Eden was deeply shocked. He knew perfectly well that Churchill would never accept any of that. For Britain, a strong post-war France was essential as a buffer against a possibly resurgent Germany and a victorious Russia.

At the same time, Eisenhower was doing his best to keep the focus on the conditions for successful military operations. In his view, there had to be at least a degree of harmony among the French. Confusion in Algiers would lead to military weakness in the next operation – clearing the enemy out of Tunisia. At the weekly meetings of his Political and Economic Council – Macmillan and Murphy were both members – he was at pains to emphasise the point. In fact, Giraud and his allies had not gone very far in implementing the programme of the New Deal. True, some prisoners had been released, the major obstacles (including the vegetable-oil magnate, Jacques Lemaigre-Dubreuil) removed and political censorship and anti-Semitic laws softened. Since implementation of the New Deal was a pre-condition for French unity, Eisenhower wanted more vigorous action. There was, after all, still a long way to go, and what had been done was only a small and uncertain start.

The remainder of the month was spent waiting for Catroux to return from Syria and take charge of events. From time to time there were rumours that de Gaulle himself was expected but they all turned out to be without foundation. Macmillan noted 'the continual atmosphere of strife, incompetence and intrigue which surrounds us in Algiers',[35] and it was with obvious relief that he escaped from Algiers to visit the headquarters of General Sir Harold Alexander, Eisenhower's Deputy Commander-in-Chief. 'He has quite extraordinary charm,' Macmillan noted. Then there was another expedition. On Saturday 27 March the weather was perfect, and he and Wyndham set off on the two hundred-mile journey by car into the mountains to see the town of Sétif and, more particularly, the ruins of two Roman imperial settlements – one dating from the time of Trajan and the other from Septimius Severus – and of a fifth-century Christian town. 'A long but very enjoyable day,' he told Dorothy. 'We slept in Sétif having brought our bedding rolls and blankets with us.'[36] They were, in truth, behaving just like a couple of schoolboys.

While Macmillan and Wyndham had been away at Sétif, Catroux had reappeared in Algiers. When he saw Macmillan, he told him that de Gaulle wanted to come to Algiers to take charge personally of the negotiation with Giraud but that he was determined to prevent such a potentially disastrous move. Macmillan agreed but thought that Eisenhower should be persuaded to write, as one soldier to another, asking de

Gaulle to postpone his departure to allow preparations for the Tunisian campaign to proceed smoothly. Macmillan drafted the telegram, Eisenhower agreed – and off it went. It went down badly. De Gaulle was furious, recalled Catroux and issued a statement claiming that he had been prevented from going to Algiers by the American Commander-in-Chief. (As Butcher put it, 'the louse ruthlessly rushed into print.'[37]) In the eye of the storm, Macmillan sat in his office receiving a 'continual stream of French callers: (a) Giraudists; (b) Gaullists; (c) Neutrals; (d) Giraudists, with sympathy for de Gaulle; (e) Giraudists, without sympathy for de Gaulle; (f) Gaullists, with sympathy for Giraud; (g) Gaullists, without sympathy for Giraud. I just sit and murmur from time to time – "*Oui, monsieur – comme vous dîtes, l'union française est indispensable*".'[38]

After a period of studied calm, Catroux finally went to London on 8 April to deliver Giraud's offer to sit down with de Gaulle and discuss the mechanics of setting up a joint administration. On 15 April Fighting France replied. A central provisional authority for France and the French Empire must be set up at once – and no leading Vichyite should be part of it. On 27 April Giraud replied. A council of seven members, chosen by him and de Gaulle, was acceptable provided that it made decisions by majority vote, that Vichyites were not excluded and that Giraud himself retained the two posts of co-President and Commander-in-Chief. On that basis, de Gaulle was invited to meet Giraud – not in Algiers (the stated reason was not to disrupt military operations in Tunisia but the underlying fear was a Gaullist *coup d'état*) but at one of the two large American airbases, Biskra or Marrakesh.

Up till then, Monnet had been careful to guide Giraud's footsteps. He had been particularly assiduous in drafting Giraud's messages to de Gaulle. Most of his work, however, was done at Tipasa, another bay about fifty miles to the west of Algiers 'beside the soft and shining sea, in a beautiful setting of Roman ruins, scented by wild thyme, under a clear Mediterranean light, with a profusion of flowers and birds. You will find Monnet there ... he lives in a little hotel of a kind one might find anywhere in Provence. There is an abundance of melons, aubergines and mullets to eat, washed down by a fresh local rosé wine ...'[39] That, of course, was all very well. But it did mean that from time to time, due to distance and poor communication, there were slips. Giraud's invitation to de Gaulle was one of them. Macmillan, too, failed to spot it. In fact, he was busy urging Churchill and Eden 'to use all your influence to persuade de Gaulle to accept this invitation without demur ... Things have not been easy here in the last few days ... My friend Murphy has I suspect been acting with something less than candour ... [but] has now fully accepted the position ... If [de Gaulle] hesitates I think he is lost.'[40]

De Gaulle, of course, exploded. The invitation to meet another French general – and to decide the future of France – on an American airbase was altogether too much. On 4 May, on Fighting France radio he made a violent personal attack on Giraud and condemned his administration root and branch. The language he used and his methods, as Monnet wrote to Hopkins, were worthy of Hitler. Catroux threatened – again – to resign. Giraud said he would retract the invitation and never again negotiate with de Gaulle. Macmillan was called in again. At a meeting in the evening of the 5th Macmillan, with Murphy present, told Giraud, Monnet and Catroux that 'they could not really break off a negotiation simply on the ground that one politician made an offensive remark about another ...' The joke fell flat. Macmillan tried another one. 'For a great country to remain divided,' he told them, 'because no one could decide whether the negotiation should take place in London or Brighton seem[s] to me absurd.' In the end, they calmed down, except for Murphy who had been shocked by Macmillan's flippancy (and 'who, of course, didn't particularly want the union to come off anyway').[41]

During the following two weeks, both while waiting for a further message from de Gaulle – who had realised his mistake and was trying to make amends – and composing Giraud's reply, Macmillan was a constant visitor to Tipasa and Monnet's hotel: with Wyndham on 9 May ('the sea was quite clear and not too cold ... we bathed naked ... and ... sunbathed afterwards ...'[42]); again on the 12th to talk it all over quietly; by the 18th it has become (possessively) 'our little quiet hotel, our beautiful secluded bay, and our Roman city'.[43]

The Mediterranean was clearly having its effect. Macmillan even wrote to Dorothy that he would be glad to finish with the French and get on with something else. But his task was far from finished. Giraud's reply was at least conciliatory: collective responsibility of the Executive Committee with joint presidency; a limited life for the Committee which, as soon as France was liberated, would hand over to a provisional government constituted under the provisions of the law of 1872 (which provided for representatives of elected Councils in areas still unoccupied by the enemy to choose a government); initially, six members, two chosen by each co-president, leaving three places to be filled by the six already on the Committee. The position of the Vichyites was not mentioned.

Although the Monnet/Macmillan draft (reluctantly accepted by Giraud) was conciliatory, events were again drawing the two sides apart. De Gaulle had been heartened by the news on 15 May that Moulin had succeeded in forming a National Council of the Resistance and that in its first declaration it had affirmed that de Gaulle should become President of a Provisional Government with Giraud as Commander-in-Chief. Giraud, for his part, had been encouraged by the military successes in Tunisia (the Germans surrendered on 12 May) in which his French troops had played a – admittedly minor – part. Furthermore, Murphy was urging Roosevelt to bring de Gaulle to heel. Roosevelt accordingly bombarded Churchill, on his arrival in Washington, with requests that de Gaulle be sacked. On 21 May Churchill transmitted the request, for urgent consideration, to the War Cabinet. Eden and Attlee – they had by then heard of de Gaulle's success with the French Resistance – replied that a breach at this stage would turn de Gaulle into a martyr and that the War Cabinet was, again, refusing to ditch de Gaulle.

On the previous day a great victory parade had been held in Tunis to mark the success of the Tunisian campaign. Macmillan thoroughly enjoyed it. Some 30,000 troops took part in the parade, which was led by the 'great naval and military and Air Force swells ... but in closed cars'. Macmillan and Murphy followed perched on an open 'sort of superior jeep ... as in a Roman chariot ... Immediately in front of us were the flags of our respective countries – the Stars and Stripes and the Union Jack – and (since we had the flags and were the only people who could actually be seen) I can tell you that our procession through the streets of Tunis was like driving through Stockton on polling day ... When the people saw our flags, they cheered and waved and threw flowers. We cheered and waved and kissed our hands to the ladies on the roofs and in the windows and on the street. It was a magnificent progress ... If ever I am forced out of English public life, I shall certainly put up for Mayor of Tunis.'[44]

But there was to be no let-up. On 21 May Macmillan flew to London with Wyndham and Catroux in Eisenhower's aeroplane, lent to him for the purpose. After a stop for the night in Gibraltar and an awkward train journey from Portreath in Cornwall where the plane had landed, he arrived in London on the morning of Sunday the 23rd and went straight to Pooks Cottage to see Dorothy and his children.

Monday saw a round of visits to report to Eden and Foreign Office officials – and a meeting with de Gaulle. Since he had won almost every argument, de Gaulle could afford to be at his most benevolent. He sent a friendly message to Giraud accepting his programme. Macmillan paid another visit to Pooks Cottage before leaving again with Wyndham for Algiers on the afternoon of the 27th. De Gaulle followed two days later. The bride, as Roosevelt kept on calling him, was finally to arrive at the door of the church. The ceremony at the altar, of course, had still to be accomplished – which, indeed, was not to be easily done.

Macmillan had achieved his first objective, and in doing so had shown considerable skill in diplomacy – hitherto not by any means his strong suit. True, he had made some mistakes. He had failed to object to Peyrouton as Governor of Algeria – in fact, he seems rather to have liked him. He had not understood de Gaulle at all, either in person or in his agenda. In fact, his early dealings with the French, even Monnet, were often confused by his lack of experience, and hence his lack of finesse, in French internal politics. Conscious of this – a rare admission – he had tried to keep out of the maze and leave its exploration to Catroux and Monnet, but that had proved impossible. Once engaged, however, he had learnt quickly and, above all, was starting to show that most precious of a politician's gifts – the art of timing.

Physically, too, Macmillan had found some of the Mediterranean magic. The pink skin had developed a healthy tan. Swimming, along with the food and the wine, had broadened his body. That, in turn, had led to a certain relaxation of the spirit. He had become more confident, less uptight. Moreover, his expeditions with Wyndham had brought a companionship which until then had been strange to him. If romantic adventures had no place in his life – there were many elegant ladies in Algiers at the time but they were unable to elicit a spark of interest – at least Wyndham was, perhaps, the next best thing.

There were flaws, of course. He still seemed unable to think and write crisply – his despatches, unlike his diaries, were notoriously prolix and full of rather mannered classical references. That, however, was no more than a venial sin. Rather more serious was his attitude towards others, in particular the French. Deep down, it was unpleasantly patronising. He was far too well mannered to betray this openly – it was only to those whom he instinctively trusted that he would come out into the open. Eton, Balliol and the Grenadier Guards had seen to that. But they, too, had worked both ways – the good manners they had inculcated were joined umbilically to an equally inculcated, and unjustified, sense of superiority. It showed in his letters, in his conversation with his British colleagues and in some of his judgements. De Gaulle, for instance, knew perfectly well that Macmillan referred to him in private as the 'bride' and that he liberally used his code name 'Ramrod' – and it was not the sort of thing de Gaulle ever forgot.

This attitude was not confined to the French. He was also patronising to the Americans. For instance, he showed his colours most clearly to Richard Crossman, during Crossman's secondment to the Ministry for Psychological Warfare, when he arrived in Algiers during May to set up an office there. 'We, my dear Crossman,' he said at their first meeting, 'are Greeks in this American empire. You will find the Americans much as the Greeks found the Romans – great big, vulgar, bustling people, more vigorous than we are and also more idle, with more unspoiled virtues but also more corrupt. We must run AFHQ as the Greek slaves ran the operations of the Emperor Claudius.'[45]

Yet all in all Macmillan could be pleased with the job he was doing. He was certainly enjoying it. Furthermore, he was receiving plaudits from Churchill and Eden and, not least, from Eisenhower (whom he was too sensible to patronise). Indeed, when he left for London on 21 May Eisenhower had said to him: 'Come back as soon as you can. I don't want to be without you.'[46] But whatever the satisfactions of the last five months he was aware that the major task was to come. Although he was perhaps not fully aware of it, he was about to become the midwife to the birth of post-war France.

9

'A Marriage Has Been Arranged'[1]

Just before midday on Sunday 30 May 1943, in a blaze of Mediterranean sunshine, General de Gaulle arrived at the dingy French military airport of Algiers-Boufarik. To be sure, it was not a particularly triumphant return to French territory; nor was the General's mood particularly sunny. He was obviously nervous, and was still resenting the clear implication that he was only allowed on to what he regarded as his home turf by leave of the British and American occupiers. Had he known it at the time, he certainly would have been even more irritated by Churchill's arrival at the official airport of Maison Blanche on the previous Friday. In fact, Churchill's purpose was to review arrangements for the invasion of Sicily – baptised Operation 'Husky'. Nevertheless, he was tempted, as a sideline, to play best man at the de Gaulle–Giraud wedding, which was by then a virtual certainty although, as he himself put it, 'we [can] count on de Gaulle to play the fool.'[2] Perhaps wisely, however, at the last moment he had asked Eden to join him in Algiers. Eden, he felt (rightly), would be more suited to the part.

Although Churchill was dog-tired after the flight from Washington, he set about trying to resolve with Eisenhower and Marshall, who had been his companion on the long journey, some of the problems that planning for 'Husky' had thrown up. Not the least of the problems, as it turned out, was Macmillan's future position. Once Sicily had been taken, the plan went, there was to be an Allied Military Government of Occupied Territory (AMGOT) under the leadership of General Alexander – the general in charge of 'Husky' operations. As it happened, AMGOT had already been formally set up in Algiers, and Alexander, nominated as its head, had been entitled, as a matter of course, to nominate Francis Rodd, a Balliol contemporary of Macmillan and now Lord Rennell, as British Chief Civil Affairs Officer. This in turn had led to the complaint in Washington that 'Husky' was already becoming far too British-led. To have a British Cabinet Minister there as well, treading on some very sensitive American toes, was, in the Washington view, quite out of the question.

But Eisenhower and Bedell Smith were firm. Macmillan must, they asserted, stay in his job, whether that meant continuing for the present as Resident Minister at AFHQ, Resident Minister for the new French authority or, in the future, as Resident Minister to a Sicilian or Italian AMGOT or whatever it might turn out to be. Moreover, the whole matter of the French union was still to be resolved – while military planning for 'Husky' was in its most intense phase. In short, Macmillan was simply too valuable to Eisenhower who, after all, was only trying to do his job – to get on with the war – and could not afford to be diverted into political quagmires. After pleas from both Eisenhower and Bedell Smith, Marshall was persuaded. Macmillan would stay in post, he confirmed – and he undertook to bring Roosevelt round.

Eisenhower, of course, knew perfectly well that de Gaulle's arrival in Algiers would lead to any number of Mediterranean squalls which Macmillan would have to ride. It was no good relying on Murphy. He was caught in the middle of what Macmillan called the 'fatal dualism'[3] of American attitudes towards the French in North Africa. After Casablanca, official United States policy was to encourage the union between the de Gaulle and Giraud factions. Roosevelt, on the other hand, quite apart from his almost paranoid dislike of de Gaulle (shared by his Secretary of State, Cordell Hull), could not be moved from his belief that American lives would best be saved by regarding French North Africa as an occupied territory – to be no more than a quick platform for an assault on the continent of Europe. For this purpose, Giraud was more than adequate and French union was unnecessary and possibly destructive. In fact, not only was Murphy caught in the middle of the argument but Churchill – always anxious not to upset Roosevelt – was as well. As before, it was only the resolute defence mounted by Eden, Attlee and the War Cabinet that stopped him from supporting Roosevelt and breaking with de Gaulle even as late as May 1943.

The first squall blew in almost immediately. On the evening of 31 May, the day after de Gaulle's arrival, Macmillan went to see Monnet to catch up with what had happened so far. Monnet reported that he had had a long talk with de Gaulle the previous night – not ending until two o'clock in the morning – that de Gaulle's mood 'seemed to vary from comparative calm to extreme excitability ... clearly very hostile to the Americans and, to a somewhat less extent, to the British ... Monnet still finds it difficult to make up his mind whether the General is a dangerous demagogue or mad or both.'[4] Later in the morning, Monnet reported, an embryo French Committee had met, but there had been no agenda, which had allowed a rambling discussion – and had given an opportunity to de Gaulle to demand the resignation of Peyrouton, Noguès and Boisson before substantive negotiations could begin.

After berating Monnet about the incompetent conduct of the meeting, Macmillan sat down to think about de Gaulle's true agenda, which he was by now starting to understand. In fact, it became very much more specific when he and Murphy went on the following day to see de Gaulle at his villa, the Villa des Glycines (whose relative modesty in their eyes contrasted favourably with Giraud's sumptuous Summer Palace). De Gaulle, in a perfectly quiet and pleasant manner, not only set out his views on the constitution of the proposed Committee but determinedly explained his real purpose. At the time of the Revolution, he said, the Royalist Army was torn in conflict with divided loyalties. Similarly, the French Army of today was, after 1940, divided in the same way. Subsequently, after the Revolution and the Napoleonic era, the Army had stood, throughout the long years of the Third Republic, as the ultimate guarantor of the Constitution. That should, and would, still be its role in the future, but for it to do this successfully all the old generals had to be got rid of and the Army reconstituted – so as to provide the base for a resurgent post-war France run by 'young and untried men ... if the soul of France were to be saved'.[5]

This lesson in French history undoubtedly much impressed Macmillan. 'He is a more powerful character', Macmillan concluded, 'than any other Frenchman with whom one has yet been in contact.'[6] But, just as calm seemed to have settled, there was another surprise. That same evening Peyrouton resigned as Governor-General of Algeria. There was, to be sure, a good deal of confusion about how it all had happened and what it all meant, but what became certain was that de Gaulle, without any obvious justification, had made great political capital out of the event by leaking it immediately to the press – without telling Giraud. From being a quiet and pleasant lecturer de Gaulle now appeared as a political villain. At that point, Macmillan decided that something more than just friendly and interesting conversation was required. Somehow or other, de Gaulle had to be brought back into what the Allies – or, to be more accurate, Macmillan's view of the Allies – considered to be the proper line. In short, he decided that it was time for him to put on a performance.

It was to be the first of many in his life, and it was certainly a bravura show. When de Gaulle came to see him at four o'clock in the afternoon of 2 June he first reproved the General over his handling of the Peyrouton resignation – and then launched into his act. He first asked whether de Gaulle would mind if he spoke in English. He then went straight to his own history in the First World War. Like many other Englishmen (conveniently, he omitted to mention his Scottish and American parentage – these, of course, were useful but only on other more suitable occasions), he had fought and been wounded three times on French soil. He had lost many of his best and dearest friends in that struggle and, in doing so, had formed a friendship with France which could never be broken. He had broken with Baldwin and Chamberlain and joined Churchill in the move to rearm and to reject Munich.

Furthermore, he went on, he thought his views on social matters were very like de Gaulle's own, and in England as in France there were old men who looked backwards rather than forwards to the future. We needed young men with young minds. The future, he asserted in an outpouring of what at least passed for emotion, would be wholly different. Great wealth would pass away. Property would be held in trust for the benefit of the people, but we hoped to see the transformation from one society to another without revolution or disturbance. Men of progressive opinions, in both England and France, should work together and inspire the necessary changes. He had followed all that de Gaulle had done with the greatest sympathy and admiration. Of course, there were differences between their two countries. England had not suffered a great defeat and the ignominy that followed that defeat. Nevertheless, he implored de Gaulle to take courage and 'not to miss so great a moment in his own private history and the life of France'.[7]

Macmillan, of course, was hardly – if at all – sincere in what he himself described as a harangue. (Churchill, for one, would certainly have been astonished to hear Macmillan's view of the future ownership of property.) But that is not the point. It was a performance, and de Gaulle, as always, much admired performances. The General replied solemnly – in French – that he would pay much attention to what Macmillan had said ('whether he meant it or not,' Macmillan was quick to note[8]). In fact, the two protagonists had quite obviously enjoyed themselves. Nevertheless, in spite of that (or perhaps because of it), the 'harangue', in terms of real politics, turned out to have served its purpose.

'The events of 1 June to 2 June', Macmillan reported later, 'had been so fantastic that all those who had participated in them were either ashamed or exhausted.'[9] There were rumours of armed conflict between the two factions. Catroux had resigned and had then withdrawn his resignation. Giraud had threatened to call off the whole thing. The press magnified every rumour, however absurd, into a certainty. Finally, Macmillan and Murphy felt it necessary to give a press conference, after the 'harangue', to emphasise 'the part which we both, on instructions, were playing, namely to facilitate the conditions under which French union could be achieved. We also said that we intended to continue working for this object even it the present attempt failed.'[10] The press conference, together with the 'harangue', did the trick. On the morning of 3 June Macmillan took Eden for a bathe and lunch at Tipasa. After lying naked in the sun for a while they got dressed, looked round the Roman town and ate at Macmillan's 'little hotel'. Just as they were looking forward to a long afternoon sitting over their wine and coffee, Macmillan received a telephone call. 'The French Committee for National Liberation (FCNL) had been painlessly constituted and French union achieved.'[11] Their leisure thus rudely interrupted, they drove back at pace to Algiers to find out what had gone on.

Later in the afternoon, René Massigli, de Gaulle's foreign affairs adviser, called on Macmillan to tell him the day's news. The Committee had been duly formed, he reported, with de Gaulle and Giraud as co-Presidents, Generals Catroux and Georges, Monnet, André Philip and Massigli himself as members. The Committee announced itself as the sovereign French authority, replacing the old Imperial Council which had elected Darlan (and, for that matter, Giraud), until metropolitan France had been liberated, when it would give way to a Provisional Government. There was no place for the Vichyites. 'In parting,' Macmillan later wrote laconically, 'M. Massigli confided to me that at the conclusion of the Committee meeting of the morning General de Gaulle had embraced General Giraud. Thus ended a French political crisis on a classic model. It augured ill for the future work of the Committee.'[12] But what Massigli did not report, and Macmillan did not at the time notice, was a provision slipped in that the Committee would be 'completed by the co-option of other members'.[13]

So far – at least for the moment – so good. In honour of the event, on the following day Admiral Cunningham hosted a large lunch. Strangely, no Americans were invited (as Butcher sourly noted). Churchill, Eden and Sir Alan Brooke were there for the British, and all the members of the Committee were there for the French. Churchill, who had been swimming in the morning and seemed much rested, made an affecting speech about 'Victorious France' in his unique mixture of English and French vocabularies. Giraud replied, followed by de Gaulle (a 'really moving little speech, chiefly about the Prime Minister's personal attributes'[14]). Eden followed on in perfect French (very much better than Macmillan's) and Georges wound up with a reference to Joan of Arc which caused much merriment – Churchill shouting that it was the Burgundians and not the English who had done the dreadful deed.

After all the excitement, and a farewell to Churchill, it was time for a break. On the Saturday afternoon Macmillan and Wyndham went off on another of their weekend trips. Leaving the heat of Algiers

they were driven up into the mountains to the winter ski resort of
Chréa – some 2000 metres above sea level. The views were spectacular,
and Macmillan noted that, apart from the late flowering jacaranda
trees, the lowland was barren and colourless but at Chréa the alpine
flowers, as well as pansies and violas, were full of the mountain
springtime. They were lent a chalet, ate their meals in the military
mess there but otherwise were looked after by their driver and batman,
spent Sunday resting and walking in the cool of the day – and talking
of anything but the events in Algiers. 'It really was an indescribably
lovely spot.'[15]

It was a short but certainly a very welcome break. But no sooner had
they arrived back in Algiers on the Monday morning than they learnt
that the FCNL had met in secret on the Sunday and doubled itself in
size. Macmillan and Murphy were caught wholly unawares. On further
investigation it turned out that three more Gaullists and three more
Giraudists had been appointed. Nevertheless, although that seemed on
paper to preserve the balance between the two factions, Monnet was
more and more drawn to de Gaulle, and a newcomer, a young civil
servant who had escaped from Vichy, Maurice Couve de Murville,
seemed astute enough to sniff the way the wind was blowing – and would
be careful to trim to it.

On Thursday 10 June there was yet another squall. At half past nine
in the morning Macmillan called on Giraud to be shown a letter from
de Gaulle tendering his resignation as President and member of the
Committee. Later in the morning Catroux told Murphy and Macmillan
that de Gaulle had resigned because he found too much opposition to
his views, because the Allies were 'out of sympathy with him' since his
associates appointed to the Committee the previous Sunday had not been
allowed to leave England, and, lastly, because of his 'violent dissatisfaction
with the recent declaration in the House of Commons the official text
of which he has not even seen'.[16]

Macmillan, Murphy, Catroux and Monnet, by then veterans of these
Mediterranean squalls, girded themselves for action. In the afternoon
Macmillan went to see de Gaulle suspecting, along with Murphy, that
de Gaulle was putting on a performance (subsequently admitted by de
Gaulle in his memoirs). He explained that Churchill's speech was no
more than the normal account a Prime Minister is expected to give to
the House of Commons. (This was not true. Churchill had also
announced that in future the British Government would switch its
funding from Fighting France to the FCNL – in fact a clever way of
ensuring that if de Gaulle walked out he would walk out into private life
without any financial support.) Monnet put in his word with Massigli

and Murphy was doing his best with Giraud. In the course of his talk with de Gaulle, Macmillan told him of a new development. On the Saturday King George VI, under the code name 'General Lyon', was due to arrive in Algiers for a round of troop inspections. De Gaulle would, of course, be invited to meet the King but he had to understand that the visit, and its security implications, would take up much of the time of British officials, including himself. Although this was undoubtedly calculated to imply to de Gaulle that he, Macmillan, as Resident Minister, had more important things to think about than French tiffs, it had a certain amount of truth. As Butcher wrote in his diary, 'for the past several days there has been a considerable "flap" amongst the British. Although normally quiet, matter-of-fact and staid, they have planned for the arrival and tour of the King as if it were the second coming of Christ to Jerusalem.'[17]

The 'flap' continued right up to the King's arrival on 12 June at Maison Blanche. But it did not end there. The King was tired and feverish, and, moreover, was surrounded by courtiers who Macmillan thought were both incompetent and ridiculous. It took a good deal of persuasion by the Resident Minister to get agreement on the King's programme. Nevertheless, by the evening the King had sufficiently recovered to be able to dine with Eisenhower, Cunningham, the Secretary of State for War, Sir James Grigg, and the attendant courtiers. The dinner, by good fortune, was a great success, not least because after dinner the King took Eisenhower aside and presented him with the Grand Cross of the Order of the Bath. 'General Eisenhower was very delighted, and we all shook hands with him and renewed our congratulations.'[18]

On the King's programme for the next day, apart from two or three hours' rest, was a lunch with Giraud, de Gaulle and Catroux, with Macmillan and Murphy (and the courtiers) in attendance. After the lunch de Gaulle asked Macmillan what he was going to do with his afternoon. Macmillan replied that he would probably drive out to Tipasa for a swim. De Gaulle asked if he could come too. 'So I had three and a half hours', Macmillan reported to Dorothy, 'of driving, walking in the ruins, and continuous talk with this strange – attractive yet impossible – character. We talked on every conceivable subject – politics, religion, philosophy, the classics, history (ancient and modern) and so on.'[19] (Later, in his memoirs, Macmillan wrote of de Gaulle, in full uniform and perched on a rock, watching while he swam naked in the sea. This account, of course, differs from his contemporary – and full – letter to Dorothy and may well be one of Macmillan's historical embellishments.) But at the end of the long conversation Macmillan thought that de Gaulle was ready to give the Committee another try. De Gaulle for his part thought that he had made his point clearly enough and that he was now ready for further battles in the Committee to get what he wanted. In short, his resignation from the Committee, if suitable arrangements were negotiated, might be withdrawn.

For the next week or so, Macmillan was kept busy with his court functions as the resident Cabinet Minister. His duty was to accompany the King and to give him guidance and advice whenever he was asked or whenever he felt it necessary. There was, however, one break in his task when the King went off to review the troops of the British Eighth Army. While the King was away, and Macmillan stayed in Algiers, Eisenhower set out to do his best to broker a settlement between de Gaulle and Giraud. The issue, of course, like many others of the Algiers day, was both militarily simple and politically complex. But, in essence, it was about which of the two generals should run the French Armed Forces.

Eisenhower's task was made more difficult by continued assaults from Roosevelt about de Gaulle. In fact, he was so irritated that on 18 June he complained to Roosevelt, 'it is my earnest belief that the local French difficulties in reaching workable agreements have been magnified in certain reports to you . . .'[20] In other words, Murphy, yet again, had been sending the wrong signals. In the face of this riposte, Roosevelt in the end relented on de Gaulle – but not before he had sent a few more violent telegrams. Roosevelt had also, as it happened, relented on his opposition to Macmillan continuing in his job. To confirm this, Bedell Smith went so far as to show Macmillan a telegram from the President acceding to Churchill's request that Macmillan stay with Eisenhower in Sicily and on into Italy. Much cheered by this, Macmillan had time to berate the correspondent of the *Daily Herald*, Victor Schiff ('a horrid little French Jew'[21]), for misreporting events, before leaving Algiers to join the King on the cruiser HMS *Aurora* for the review of the British Mediterranean fleet. It was only on 21 June, after an enjoyable and – be it said – to him eminently satisfying, cruise in the company of the King that Macmillan returned to Algiers. He was just in time to learn of the decision of the FCNL on the matter of French military command. Giraud, it turned out, was to be Commander-in-Chief of all French forces in North and West Africa and de Gaulle was to be Commander-in-Chief of French forces in the territories formerly under the control of Fighting France. Eisenhower promptly signalled Marshall that he was pleased with the arrangement. At least it allowed him to reassure the President that his requirements had been met – that de Gaulle should have no control over French forces in North Africa. Yet what he failed to realise was that Giraud's strategic decisions would always be subject to review by the FCNL, which was becoming more Gaullist by the day. Macmillan, for his part, realised that only too well and, rightly, concluded that the arrangement might just serve for the time being but could not possibly last for long.

On 24 June the King left Algiers. Quite apart from the relief that the visit had gone well and that there had been no untoward accidents, Macmillan had an unexpected bonus. During the King's stay he and Wyndham had moved into a new villa, much more luxurious than the old. 'We are really spoilt here,' Macmillan wrote to Dorothy. 'We have *far* too much food and drink, and John seems to collect servants, like some people collect postage stamps.'[22] But no sooner had the King left than political Algiers was in new confusion. Boisson, it appeared, had unexpectedly resigned as Governor of Dakar and Giraud had first accepted and then refused the resignation. Yet another squall was blowing in.

The Boisson affair sparked Roosevelt to action yet again. He was determined to keep Boisson in Dakar. Churchill, yet again, supported him. 'It is rather shaming to see the P.M. taking this line,' wrote Eden's Private Secretary, Oliver Harvey. 'He would do anything now to blacken de Gaulle. He will not face the fact that Giraud, Georges and Boisson mean nothing to the French. Giraud and Boisson are marked off as American puppets. Giraud and Georges are silly old fools and Boisson is a Vichyite who employs a private Gestapo, but the Americans find him easy and wish in any case to make a post-war base of Dakar ... They want a "comfortable" pre-war Europe of Pétains ...'[23]

Not content with his attempts to keep Boisson in post, Roosevelt stepped up his support for Giraud. On 2 July, in response to a personal invitation from Roosevelt, Giraud left Algiers, to be fêted in Washington as though he were a favoured prince – tea with the Roosevelt family in the White House garden, an official dinner the next day, talks with senior State Department and Department of Defense officials, visits to munitions factories, press conferences and so on. Giraud, of course, could not help but be impressed. Nevertheless, he had left de Gaulle in sole charge in Algiers, and de Gaulle was quick to take advantage. There was a purge of Vichyites in the administration, and those in charge of Camp Hadjerat in the Sahara, where Gaullist supporters had been kept in the most dreadful conditions, were arrested. But also, and much more important, de Gaulle went on a tour of North Africa to show himself to what he considered to be his people. Some in the FCNL thought this to be unwise, but his tour, as it happened, was, in every sense of the phrase, a spectacular success. If there had been any doubt, either in his mind or in the minds of his supporters (such as Macmillan), about his popularity they were firmly laid to rest. Wherever he went he attracted large and enthusiastic crowds. At the end, the highlight of his tour was without a doubt his speech in the Place du Forum in Algiers on Bastille Day, when his call for national renewal and unity of a people at war was cheered to a truly thunderous echo.

By the time Giraud arrived back from America on 25 July, fresh from the delights of America, his position in Algiers had been fatally undermined. In fact, de Gaulle's sharks were even then starting to circle. At the meeting of the FCNL on 31 July Giraud was informed that he had been guilty of representing himself in Washington as the sole authority in the French Armed Forces – omitting to say, as he was bound, that ultimately he was responsible to the Committee. In the light of this clear offence, the Committee decided that Giraud would remain a co-President but he would only preside over meetings of the Committee when it was discussing national defence. All other meetings would be chaired by de Gaulle. Furthermore, as Commander-in-Chief he would be formally and legally bound to respond to the newly named Committee for National Defence – of which de Gaulle, of course, was chairman and which contained a clear majority of Gaullists.

That done, or more or less done, Macmillan's attention shifted north-wards to Sicily and on to Italy. 'Husky' had been launched on 10 July (Macmillan had secretly told de Gaulle about it the previous evening and noted that 'he certainly wanted to impress me with the quiet role that he was now playing and the almost saintly character of his patience'[24]) and, after some initial difficulties in landing, was proving successful. It was time for Macmillan's staff to be enlarged – Harold Caccia, another young high-flyer in the Foreign Office, was sent out to look after the Italian side while Makins remained Head of Mission in Algiers. It was also time to set up a residence and office for the purpose in Tunis. Wyndham was despatched as advance party, and on the day 'Husky' was launched Macmillan and Caccia joined him. Macmillan was quite pleased to be moving. 'It is rather fun,' he wrote to Dorothy, 'for I am beginning to get very bored with the French and their affairs and very disgusted at the stupidities of London and Washington regarding them.'[25] Tunis, too, proved altogether more pleasant than Algiers. He and his party were allocated one wing of the Consular Residence – a large hall with a fine marble floor and a painted ceiling, a dining room, four bedrooms (and, as he carefully noted, some servants' rooms) and a large covered terrace – the other wing providing another room for Alexander's headquarters as well as an officers' mess. Wyndham had already managed to find some furniture and two nice rugs 'sent by two leading Jews ... in recognition for what I am supposed to have done for the Jews in North Africa!'[26]

But, however pleasant the living arrangements, there was serious work to be done. Mussolini resigned on 26 July just as Eisenhower was preparing the assault on the Italian mainland. As part of the preparations Macmillan and Bedell Smith were required to compose a speech which Eisenhower could broadcast to tell the Italians what the invaders proposed to do. Since the Allies could not agree among themselves – the Americans wanted another AMGOT and the British wanted a new Italian Government – this was far from easy. Macmillan, reflecting Churchill's view, thought that King Vittorio Emmanuele of Italy (or possibly his son, Crown Prince Umberto) and Marshal Pietro Badoglio should be allowed to get on with the job. Smith, under pressure from Eisenhower, was inclined to agree – but was worried about the response from Washington.

All this coincided with a hectic telegraphic debate about the terms to be proposed for an Italian armistice. The Foreign Office in London was conducting a dialogue with Washington on a comprehensive document which would settle military and political matters once for all. The negotiation, as might be imagined, was slow and from time to time rather ill tempered. In Algiers, Macmillan could do nothing but wait. But on 31 July, when Macmillan, Makins, Wyndham and Crossman were still sitting around in the heat of the Algiers summer waiting for an agreed directive from London which had been due five days earlier, Macmillan took a decision. 'At our meeting in his villa', Crossman recalled, 'everyone was cursing London and Washington until Macmillan quietly proposed that since neither the British nor the Americans could get any policy directive from home we should draft our own Anglo-American Directive to ourselves and send it via the Combined Chiefs of Staff to the White House and No. 10.'[27] Thus were born what came to be known as the 'short terms'. (The 'long terms', it need hardly be said, were those in negotiation between the Foreign Office and the State Department.)

As if all this was not enough, there was another simmering dispute between London and Washington over whether, and to what degree, the two Allies would officially recognise the FCNL. Churchill was pressing for this, and had suggested a formula to Roosevelt. This turned out to be much too enthusiastic for Roosevelt, who was hardly prepared to allow any form of recognition while there was a chance that de Gaulle might blow up and leave the field to Giraud. Eisenhower was so worried that these two arguments would hold up – and, if there were another French explosion, possibly wreck – his plans for the assault on Italy that he asked Macmillan to go to London to try to sort things out. Macmillan was glad to go, partly to escape the oppressive heat but not least to establish his own future position. He had cabled Eden on 3 August on the matter. 'In the event of formal recognition of the French Committee,' he wrote, 'you will have to consider whom you wish to appoint as the British accredited representative.' He himself did not want the job since he wanted to remain a Minister. His suggestion was that he should be the first accredited representative but he would hand over to a 'professional diplomat' when AFHQ moved from Algiers to the mainland of Europe. At that point he would remain 'as a camp follower with them' (Macmillan's rather arch way of saying that he wanted to continue as Resident Minister with Cabinet rank at AFHQ[28]).

By the time Macmillan arrived in London Churchill had already left for the conference with Roosevelt at Quebec, where the question of recognition was due finally to be resolved. On arrival, much to his pleasure, Macmillan received a note from Eden agreeing to his suggestion for his continuing for the foreseeable future as Resident Minister with AFHQ. Furthermore, in discussions with Eden, he managed to get agreement from him, somewhat reluctantly in view of Macmillan's rather high-handed approach, to proceed with the 'short terms' and wait until those had been agreed before presenting the Italians with a further dose of the 'long terms' (which still had to be settled).

On his return to Algiers on 15 August Macmillan found that the Italian negotiations were continuing, although in a somewhat roundabout way, in Lisbon. There was nothing much he could do to help things along, and, since all French affairs were in suspense awaiting a decision from the Quebec conference on recognition, he decided that it was time for him and Caccia to pay a visit to Alexander's headquarters in Sicily. In spite of the intense heat (drier but hotter than Africa – Macmillan found himself some short-sleeved naval shirts and khaki shorts), there was a good deal of classical sightseeing to be done in neighbouring Syracuse and evening bathing with Alexander (naked, of course). As always, Macmillan much enjoyed his visits to Alexander (now known, in letters to Dorothy, as 'Alex' and 'charming, gracious, interesting and helpful as ever'[29]). Back again in Algiers on 25 August, Macmillan learnt that the Quebec conference had decided that the Allies would recognise the FCNL but in two different forms. The texts were sent to Algiers the following day. Both the British and the Americans recognised the Committee as 'administering those French overseas territories which acknowledge its authority', and '[took] note, with sympathy, of the desire of the Committee to be regarded as the body qualified to ensure the administration and defence of all French interests'. The United States, however, qualified that by adding that 'the extent to which it may be possible to give effect to this desire must however be reserved for consideration in each case as it arises', and went no further than admitting 'recognition of the FCNL as functioning within specific limitations during the war'.[30] As it turned out, that seemed good enough for the French and the French press. De Gaulle, for instance, 'seemed genuinely delighted and was really most friendly'.[31] That was also enough for Macmillan, who now felt able to turn his full attention to the Italian negotiations.

'I have sent some pretty good telegrams home,' he wrote to Dorothy on 26 August, 'and expect instant dismissal.'[32] In fact, although it had not got as far as dismissal, there is no doubt that he was starting seriously to irritate Eden. 'Macmillan and Eisenhower are being incredibly wooden and obstructive over the armistice arrangements,' Harvey wrote in his diary on 1 September. 'Eisenhower is in a fright over his operations and seems now to think the Italians must be won over to us. We are heading for a new Darlanism and what a row it will cause. We blame Macmillan for being stupid over this. He at least should have more sense. The only way to get anything out of the Italians is to go on hammering them.'[33]

Macmillan, of course, claimed that the situation on the ground was not understood in London. But he was walking along a difficult road. Badoglio was proving to be at best a bent if not a wholly broken reed. Even after the armistice had been signed by Badoglio's emissary, General Castellano, on 3 September at Alexander's headquarters, and even after the first assault on the mainland, on the same day, proved successful – a bridgehead on the toe of Italy opposite Messina – he was not able to promise more than token support. Furthermore, the more substantive invasion, on 9 September at Salerno, just south of Naples, provoked from Badoglio no more than silence. It was not until Eisenhower sent a brusque message that he was going anyway to announce the armistice and its terms that Badoglio made the required announcement on Rome radio. But that was far from the end of the matter. The Italian armistice led to several aftershocks.

The first was an uprising in Corsica by some 15,000 Corsicans (who had, in fact, been secretly armed by the Allies). On hearing the news, Giraud ordered two French destroyers with commandos on board to help the uprising. Although he had sought the permission of AFHQ, he had failed to inform de Gaulle or the FCNL. The second was a move by the British Middle East Command in Cairo to take over the Italian-occupied islands in the Aegean on the grounds that they would serve as a useful base for a further assault on Greece itself. The third was the continued insistence by both London and Washington that the 'long terms' of the armistice should now, and at last, be presented to the Italians. The fourth, the most important from Macmillan's point of view, was a move in the Foreign Office in London to start to cut him down to what they thought to be reasonable size. This, apparently, was to be achieved by appointing two diplomats to senior posts with ambassadorial rank to the Mediterranean – Duff Cooper to FCNL in Algiers and Noel Charles to an 'Allied Advisory Council' which was on the agenda to oversee the running of Italy. Furthermore, they were planning to send General Sir Frank Mason-Macfarlane, the Governor of Gibraltar, as head of the British Military Mission to Italy. There were, in fact, to be three conduits through which London could make its views known – two of them by-passing Macmillan.

All this was happening while Macmillan and Murphy, together with a motley crew of British and American officers, were trying – in some desperation – to find the Italian Government of Marshal Badoglio. At first they thought it would be at Taranto, which had been cleared of German troops by an American commando brigade. It was then rumoured to be at Brindisi, also cleared of Germans, where King Vittorio Emmanuele, Badoglio and his ministers had apparently fled after the announcement of the armistice. That turned out to be the case, and Macmillan and Murphy drove to Brindisi on 15 September. There they met with Badoglio and other Italian ministers and, as a result of their discussions, they decided that it would be sensible to send Lord Rennell and the American General Julius Holmes, head of the Military Government Section of AFHQ 'to work out a *modus vivendi* for the area in which the Italian Government found itself, something between the full AMGOT system and Italian self-government'.[34] Needless to say, the Foreign Office was not told about this. Macmillan was treating the matter as within his remit as Resident Minister responsible to Churchill – and had deliberately left Caccia behind in Tunis. He returned to Algiers late on 25 September to be faced with yet another squall – this time the fallout from Giraud's Corsica venture. There was to be a row in the Committee, on the grounds that Giraud had behaved irresponsibly, if perhaps not illegally. As a veteran of such squalls, Macmillan knew that it was no good him or Murphy intervening in the French row. Any intervention would have immediately allowed de Gaulle to play the card of 'Allied interference in French affairs'. On the other hand, if Giraud resigned altogether there would be a major crisis. For the moment, as it happened, all was on hold. There was to be a pause while the Consultative Assembly which the FCNL had summoned could meet and give its opinion on the future construction of the Committee itself. (The fact that there was a large representation from the Resistance told heavily, of course, in de Gaulle's favour.)

Macmillan and Murphy spent the next few days in Brindisi preparing a meeting between Badoglio and Eisenhower due to take place in Malta to sign the final version of the armistice – the 'long terms' – and settle Italian military contribution to the campaign in Italy. Macmillan and Murphy presented the 'long terms' to Badoglio and his ministers in Brindisi, with the explanation that they were under strict instructions to get the document signed when they all arrived in Malta. There were, of course, as they admitted, bound to be Italian objections – not least about Italy's ability at present to live up to its commitments set out in the document. Nevertheless, as Macmillan carefully pointed out, Eisenhower had the power to modify the application of its provisions. This was enough to satisfy Badoglio and the King. When the whole party moved to Malta to meet Eisenhower and Alexander on board the British warship HMS *Nelson*, there remained little to negotiate and, amid general expressions of goodwill on all sides, on 29 September the 'long terms' were duly signed.

Macmillan then decided to go to London. Apart from a morning at Birch Grove – not least to see how Maurice's wife Kate was doing in the late stages of her pregnancy – he thought that there were some loose ends which needed tying up. But Eden himself was preparing for a stop in Algiers on his way to a conference of Foreign Ministers in Moscow. 'Macmillan has suddenly turned up to A. E.'s fury!' wrote Harvey. 'We wanted him at the other end to prepare for us in Algiers. He is being packed off again. Macmillan is anxious to maintain a sort of *droit de regard* over all our French and Italian relations from his post at Eisenhower HQ. A. E. does not wish to encourage this ... I can't think why he dislikes Macmillan (though he is certainly a bore) and is even jealous of him.'[35] Macmillan was indeed duly 'packed off'. But, as it happened, he was by then quite seriously ill, with diarrhoea and headaches, in what turned out to be a severe form of gastroenteritis. By the time Eden and his party arrived in Algiers Macmillan was spending most of his time in bed. Fortunately, Eden was preoccupied, not with the French affairs which he had come to review but with the sudden failure of the British attempt to take and hold the Aegean islands. Cos, Leros and Samos had been taken but Cos had just been retaken by German troops and it was only a matter of time before Leros and Samos fell too. Furthermore, in spite of Churchill's hectoring, on 9 October Eisenhower turned down a request for further resources to be allocated so that Rhodes could be taken. His reason was simple.

The news had just come through that the German armies in Italy were going to defend a line south of Rome. For Eisenhower and his fellow commanders-in-chief it was a question of choosing 'between Rhodes and Rome'.[36]

Macmillan's illness lasted the best part of two weeks. Once he stopped working, moreover, he admitted to feeling homesick and depressed. But he was cheered by Dorothy's telegram announcing the birth of a grandson. 'Are they really going to call it Alexander?' he asked Dorothy.[37] (The baby, apparently, was to him still an 'it'.) He was also just well enough to see Cordell Hull who was passing through and to say goodbye to Admiral Cunningham, who was leaving for London to take over as First Sea Lord. Even then, however, his doctor told him not to eat solids and, when he went with Makins to Tipasa, not to swim.

The illness finally relented and, although he was still feeling rather weak, Macmillan set off for Italy again on 25 October for a four-day tour. After seeing Alexander in his headquarters near Bari, he and Murphy were driven across Italy to the headquarters of General Mark Clark just south of Naples ('far the most intelligent American soldier I know').[38] From there they went into Naples to see the operations of AMGOT HQ. Macmillan officially reported to London that AMGOT was doing an excellent job. Privately, however, in a memorandum to Eden, he was scathing.

His private view was certainly shared in London. In fact, the performance of AMGOT was something of an embarrassment. Many local fascist officials had been retained in post and there was little sign overall of orderly government in the areas which had been liberated. Rennell, too, seemed not up to the job. 'Rennell had better abandon military government and devote himself to grouse shooting,' wrote one aggrieved American officer. 'He doesn't know what really hard work at a desk means ...'[39] Even Churchill was getting restless. 'Could you find out for me', he minuted Cadogan, 'whether the word Amgot in Turkish means camel's dung or something equally unpleasant?'[40]

Enough was enough for the Foreign Ministers' meeting in Moscow. The plans for governing Italy were changed. AMGOT, under Alexander as Military Governor, would continue but only in the territory immediately behind the armies. The rest of liberated Italy would be governed nominally by the King and his Government but in practice by an Allied Control Commission. This Commission would continue to act until such time as the Supreme Allied Commander felt ready to relinquish a part or, in the end, all of its territory. An Allied Advisory Council for Italy was to be formed as an overall supervisory body, to include 'High Commissioners' from France, Greece and Italy as well as from the three major belligerents, the United States, Britain and the Soviet Union. That done, there was, of course, much jockeying for position by those who were already in place. On 5 November, for instance, Francis Rennell, 'a great prima and a prime intriguer',[41] came to see Macmillan to secure support for his promotion to become president of the Control Commission. Macmillan listened carefully – without committing himself – not least because his own position was still in doubt. (In the end, Rennell failed to get the job, resigned from AMGOT in a sulk and went back to England.)

Eden called in at Algiers on his way back from Moscow. The atmosphere, as he told Massigli in a meeting with Macmillan on 10 November, had been good – much better than before. The Soviets had recognised that they would need a great deal of help in reconstructing their battered country after the war ('In Ukraine all the towns had been completely destroyed and nothing remained of Stalingrad – which [Eden] had overflown'[42]) and that help would have to come from the industries of the West. On specific matters, apart from Italy, he said they had agreed that the existing three-power Mediterranean Commission would be transferred from Algiers to London, would change its name to the European Advisory Commission and would deal with the administration of liberated Europe and post-war Germany. France, it appeared (much to Massigli's and, later, de Gaulle's disgust) was to be excluded from the Commission.

During his stay in Algiers Eden was briefed by Macmillan on the first meeting of the French Consultative Assembly on 3 November. Macmillan and Murphy, along with the new Soviet Ambassador, Alexandr Bogomolov, had sat in the gallery. There had been a long debate about the membership of the FCNL. The upshot was that a small committee, headed by de Gaulle, was given the task of reconstructing it. All existing members of the FCNL were required to place their resignations in the hands of the new committee. Furthermore, the committee's remit was to ensure that the 'civil power' and the 'military power' were definitely and finally separated. In other words, the Commander-in-Chief was to be subordinate to the civil government. When the committee reported, Giraud accepted its proposals, even if he had not read them, that he himself, while remaining Commander-in-Chief, not only had to resign as co-President but his membership of FCNL as well. When he heard all this, Eden told Massigli that 'personally he was not at all disturbed; but it was not certain that some "eliminations" would not arouse from M. Winston Churchill or Washington, some unpleasant reactions'.[43] So, indeed it turned out. In fact, it subsequently took all of Eden's diplomatic finesse to persuade Churchill not to make the demotion of Giraud yet another pretext for breaking with de Gaulle. On 15 November Macmillan was summoned to Gibraltar to meet Churchill on board the battle cruiser HMS *Renown*. Churchill was on his way to Cairo for a meeting with Roosevelt, to prepare for their subsequent joint meeting with Stalin in Teheran. But, even then, there was a more immediate Mediterranean squall – this time not in North Africa but in Lebanon. It so happened that in July 1943 Catroux, wearing his hat as commissioner there for Fighting France, had agreed, as a result of strong British pressure, to hold elections in Syria and Lebanon. In spite of subsequent French claims that the British had rigged the elections, the results were decisive – and not to the French liking. In short, in both Syria and Lebanon Nationalist parties were elected with very large majorities.

The upshot in Lebanon was that the new government in October announced their intention to change the constitution in a way which would effectively end the French mandate which been in position since 1920. The French Ambassador to Lebanon, Jean Helleu, immediately flew from Beirut to Algiers to seek instructions, but while he was away the Lebanese Chamber on 8 November passed the Government's proposals by 48 votes to 0. On his return, Helleu immediately, and on his own initiative (he was known to drink heavily and, indeed, 'cease to be lucid at certain hours of the day'[44]) mobilised the Army, moved in and threw the Lebanese President and his ministers in jail. In the ensuing uproar, riots in Beirut were put down with ferocity by Senegalese troops.

There were, of course, protests from the United States, the Soviet Union and neighbouring Arab countries, but the whole matter might have been quite easily settled had it not been for the presence in Lebanon, on a roving commission there with ministerial rank, of Louis Spears. The problem was not only was Spears Churchill's friend – and used his position without shame – but that he had taken a violent dislike to de Gaulle (whom he had shepherded to London in June 1940). Spears denounced Helleu's actions as 'inadmissibly dictatorial measures, taken against a small and defenceless people' and sent a barrage of messages to the Foreign Office, copied to Macmillan, calling for British intervention.[45] This was enough in turn to prompt de Gaulle to send a message to Helleu in support. (His message was, in fact, not entirely supportive. Indeed, it was – perhaps intentionally – Delphic.) 'The forceful measures you have seen fit to take' – it went, 'were no doubt necessary. At any rate, I consider that they were necessary, since you have taken them.'[46] Macmillan had discussed the matter with Catroux, who, as it happened, was on the point of leaving for Beirut to calm everything down. Catroux told him that Helleu had made a complete fool of himself – he had not even asked Algiers for authorisation. But on the other hand it was important to stop Spears making trouble, not least because he was trying to bully his fellow minister Casey in Cairo to take unilateral action. During his overnight stay on the *Renown*, therefore, Macmillan used much of his time with Churchill trying to persuade him that Spears was up to no good. 'The PM did not much like this,' Macmillan wrote later.[47] But that was not surprising. Churchill never liked disparaging comments about his friends and Spears was certainly an old friend. It was only when Macmillan said that, if handled carefully, de Gaulle would be outvoted in the FCNL that Churchill visibly cheered up and agreed to let the matter pass.

Macmillan had been right. On his return to Algiers he found among the telegrams waiting for him a proposal from London to deliver an ultimatum to the French which demanded the immediate recall of Helleu and the immediate release of the President and his ministers. By the afternoon of 20 November Casey had formally presented it to Catroux. Macmillan was about to give a copy of it to Massigli but was advised to hold on to it for the moment. It would be easier to bring the Committee round, Massigli told him, without a British ultimatum. The ruse worked. As it turned out, all went according to plan and the FCNL – with only a telegram from Catroux, and no British ultimatum, in front of them – voted the way both Macmillan and Massigli had wanted. Only de Gaulle and two of his supporters voted against Massigli's motion.

Macmillan reported all this to Churchill when he met him on 24 November in Cairo on the eve of the conference. Churchill, it need hardly to be said, was particularly pleased that de Gaulle had been defeated by his own colleagues. On the margins of the conference, moreover, Macmillan had persuaded Eden that French interests in Lebanon and Syria should not be threatened, that Britain should only be represented at ambassadorial level – and that Spears should be told to calm the Lebanese down (although Macmillan was doubtful whether he would be much good at it – 'being a popular hero in the Levant has rather gone to his head').[48] There was one matter in Cairo, however, on which Macmillan did not get his way. After the fiasco of the British attempt to take the Aegean islands it had become clear that two separate commands in the Mediterranean – one, Allied, in Algiers and another, British, in Cairo – made little sense. To resolve the problem, William D. Leahy, Roosevelt's Chief of Staff after his return from ambassadorial duties in Vichy, put forward a plan for an overall supreme command for the whole of the European theatre. Leahy's suggestion was considered 'ridiculous' by the British, and Churchill 'sent back [a] strong telegram

... with his views as to the absurdity of the proposal'.[49] That debate over, it was finally decided that there would be a unified Mediterranean command and a separate command for the cross-Channel invasion of France (to be named 'Overlord') planned for 1944.

On their way back from the Tehran conference the Allied caravans stopped again in Cairo, where Macmillan, after an interval in Algiers (and a bibulous dinner there with the Soviet Deputy Commissar for Foreign Affairs, Andrei Vyshinsky) went to meet them. It had been agreed at Teheran that 'Overlord' should have priority over the Mediterranean campaign. The question to be resolved in Cairo was who was to command it. After much debate about the relative merits of Marshall and Eisenhower, on 4 December Roosevelt decided that Marshall was too valuable to him in Washington and plumped for Eisenhower. That in turn raised the question of who would replace him as commander in the Mediterranean. To preserve a balance, he had to be British. As it turned out, it was to be a contest between only two candidates: Alexander and the current Commander-in-Chief Middle East, General Sir Henry ('Jumbo') Maitland Wilson.

The military view was that Wilson was the man for the job. Brooke, the Chief of the Imperial General Staff, was loud in his support. It turned out that he had a particularly low opinion of Alexander. 'Charming as he is [he] fills me with gloom,' he wrote in his diary. 'He is a very, very small man and cannot see big ...'[50] Macmillan, on the other hand, when consulted by Churchill (much to Brooke's displeasure), thought differently. 'I do not of course know whether General Alexander has the military qualities most suited to the duties of a C-in-C in such an organisation,' his minute to Churchill ran, 'but I feel strongly that these points should be weighed ... has learnt the quite difficult art of managing Americans ... has ... the art of simplifying problems ... has the simplicity of character and the concentration on the sole purpose of war ...'[51] Churchill told him to go round and see Brooke to state his case. This he did. But Brooke was dismissive. 'He [Macmillan] came round to see me for an hour this evening and evidently does not even begin to understand what the functions of a Supreme Commander should be. Why must the PM consult everybody except those who can give him real advice!'[52] So that, as it were, was that. On that matter, Macmillan went back to Algiers empty-handed. Wilson was duly appointed, first to be head of AFHQ and subsequently as Supreme Allied Commander Mediterranean (SACMED). He was to take up his appointment on 8 January 1944, just after Duff Cooper's arrival as British Ambassador to the FCNL. In other words, there was to be, at the beginning of 1944, a wholesale changing of the Algiers guard. The Allied Advisory Council for Italy,

The boy at home in Cadogan Place, carefully posed.

At Eton: the 4th of June 1907

An undergraduate reading party in Austria in 1913, Macmillan relaxing in the centre

The reading party in the mountains, Macmillan in a Mexican hat

Ronnie Knox

The 4th Battalion, Grenadier Guards, at Marlow, August 1915, Macmillan standing second from right

The battle of Ginchy on the Somme, September 1916

Nellie Macmillan

An advanced dressing station
on the Western Front in 1916

Dorothy, in foreground, on a
yacht with her family in 1916

The honeymooners

The Cavendish Christmas of 1930, Macmillan standing on the far right

In 1934, the middle of
the Boothby crisis

Bob Boothby's wedding to
Dorothy's cousin, Diana
Cavendish, in 1935

The Kuranstalt Wittelsbach in Munich, 1931

Mosley and the Blackshirts in East London, October 1936

Macmillan and Beaverbrook returning from Moscow, October 1941

Macmillan and 'Alex' waiting for Churchill at Casablanca, January 1943

Eden, Churchill and Macmillan, Algiers, May 1943

Churchill, Archbishop Damaskinos, Macmillan and Alexander under siege
in Athens, Christmas 1944

Macmillan as Minister in Churchill's caretaker government of May 1945

too, was eventually set up, with Macmillan duly nominated as its UK High Commissioner (his third title – in addition to 'Resident Minister' and Political Adviser to SACMED). The move from Algiers to Italy was now clearly imminent.

There were, however, matters to be dealt with before that could happen. In fact, the run-up to Christmas and the New Year proved particularly difficult. First, on his way back from Cairo on 13 December Churchill fell ill with pneumonia, suspected pleurisy and an irregular heart rhythm. He was so ill that his doctor, Lord Moran, 'thought the PM was going to die ...'[53] But no sooner had Churchill – holed up in Tunis – begun, almost miraculously, to recover and to start sending telegrams round the world than, on 21 December, the FCNL decided to arrest Peyrouton, Boisson and the former Vichyite Pierre Flandin and put them on trial for treason.

Roosevelt's reaction to the news was both unexpected and violent. He cabled Eisenhower to direct the FCNL to take no action against the three men. Churchill, in support, called Bedell Smith from Tunis and bellowed loudly (in Macmillan's hearing), 'Keep Harold up to the mark. He is much too pro-French. He will not carry out my policy or my wishes. I rely on *you*!' For the first time, Macmillan was deeply offended. As he wrote, 'This makes life interesting but exhausting. It is really getting beyond a joke, and much as I love Winston, I cannot stand much more.'[54] In the end, calm, as usual, was restored. De Gaulle agreed that there would be no trial of the three Vichyites before the liberation of France and a legal and constitutional government had taken the place of the FCNL. Moreover, the FCNL accepted in addition the Allied request that all French forces should come under the overall command of the Allied Commander-in-Chief.

On Christmas Day 1943, after attending church, crowded with troops, Macmillan flew to Tunis and was driven straight to the villa where Churchill was staying. There he found the Prime Minister presiding over a 'magnificent Christmas dinner ... clothed in a padded silk Chinese dressing-gown decorated with blue and red dragons – a most extra-ordinary sight'.[55] After the long feast, Churchill retired, but in the evening, at around eleven o'clock, he sent for Macmillan. He listened patiently to an explanation of what was happening in Algiers. Then it was time to make everything up. 'Then he took my hand in his in a most fatherly way and said "Come and see me again before I leave Africa, and we'll talk it over".'[56] It never happened, but Macmillan at that point knew that he still, whatever the Mediterranean squalls, had Churchill's confidence. By the time Duff Cooper arrived on 3 January to take up his post Macmillan was ready to leave Algiers. He had never much liked the climate – he much preferred the milder weather of Tunis – and was always more than willing to escape to Tipasa for a bathe and an afternoon in the Mediterranean sun or to drive with Wyndham up into the hills to look at the scenery, the flowers or, preferably, a Greek or Roman ruin. Moreover, during the last months of 1943 his health had not been good (he had latterly developed an unpleasant eczema) and he was starting to miss England.

Nevertheless, there is no doubt that 1943 had been very much his most successful political year to date. He had shown deftness in handling his American colleagues and skill – albeit sporadic – in his dealings with the French and his British superiors. He seemed, too, to have become likeable – even, on occasions, charming. Some of it, of course, was acting – even to the point of dissembling – but much of it was genuine, particularly with Eisenhower. Moreover, he had commanded both loyalty and affection from his staff, particularly from Wyndham, of course, but also from Makins and Caccia. Makins, for instance, was quickly won over. Soon after his arrival he wrote to his wife 'this is the toughest job I have ever had ... Fortunately Harold Macmillan is really excellent, he has all the right ideas, good judgement, and a keen sense of humour, and he never gives me a moment's anxiety.'[57]

Macmillan had also acquired the habit of writing friendly, and sometimes congratulatory, notes to the French and to the Americans, and many have survived. They were mostly well meant, but from time to time they sound mannered and even, on occasions, oleaginous if not positively feline. They are, of course, quite different from his letters to Dorothy, which were discursive as well as witty (in what might be described as a Balliol way). Even those letters, however, were not as discursive as his despatches. In fact, by the end of the year these were starting to bore their Foreign Office readers – and Churchill was asking for them to be reduced to one page for his attention. Quite unlike his letters to Dorothy and his diaries, not only were they discursive but they were ponderous – and at times pompous. In writing his last despatch from Algiers, for instance, he commented, in relation to the political crisis in Lebanon, that 'It is the unhappy fate of the English people to be misunderstood. But we must also recognise that these misunderstandings are based on the curious way in which history seems to work itself out.'[58] This was by way of introducing a passage about Gladstone's views on South Africa. At the heart of this, of course, was a rather lonely life. In spite of an early invitation, Dorothy refused during 1943 to join him in Algiers. She preferred to stay at Pooks Cottage – and, apparently, to continue to see Bob Boothby. In fact, the one morose note in Macmillan's letters to her refers to Duff Cooper bringing his wife, Lady Diana Cooper, with him to enliven the social scene. Loneliness, too, contributed to moments of depression which Wyndham had to cope with. Most important of all and whatever the reason – loneliness and the lack of a companion who might advise him as an equal – he also started to show, from the middle of the year onward, a certain high-handedness.

Indeed, two events illustrate the point. Just before Operation 'Husky', Macmillan received a telegram from Churchill ordering the immediate arrest of Peyrouton. '"You all know", he told his morning staff meeting, "that this might produce something like civil war and could well stop the invasion of Sicily … so there is really only one thing to do with this telegram and that is to consign it to the flames." And with these words he dropped the telegram into the fire behind him.'[59] So runs Crossman's report of the incident. There is no reason to doubt it. On the other hand, it says much for the loyalty of his staff that no word of the burning of the Prime Minister's document filtered back to London. If it had, Churchill's reaction would certainly have been fearsome.

The second event had much more serious implications, as it affected the whole conduct of the war. In October there was a report from Giraud's office that an emissary had arrived from Vichy with the message that old Marshal Pétain was prepared to leave France (and go anywhere other than North Africa where his life would obviously be in as much danger as Darlan's) and, moreover, would release the French Armed Forces from their oath of loyalty to him. When this message finally arrived on Macmillan's desk he was dismissive. 'There are no advantages', he noted in his own hand to Makins, 'in Pétain's escape. The only reason for taking him out of France wd be to execute him as an arch traitor. This is very dangerous stuff indeed. We must act with great circumspection.'[60] Indeed it was dangerous stuff – and Macmillan decided to suppress it. Murphy was not told, let alone Eden or Churchill. It takes little imagination to predict the reaction of Roosevelt and Leahy, or, indeed, Churchill, if the message had been passed on to them. If genuine (which is by no means certain but Macmillan obviously suspected it might be – he called it 'dangerous stuff' indeed), it would have provided a perfect weapon to use against de Gaulle and to dislodge him.

Macmillan's critics at the time – for instance, Eden's acolytes (not yet Eden himself, who wrote a generous message to Macmillan on his leaving office in Algiers) – thought him pedantic and a bore. That was no more than a reflection of the pre-Mediterranean Macmillan. A much more serious criticism, from Eden himself and with accusations not just of high-handedness but of personal disloyalty, would come in 1944. But as one of his earlier critics had predicted in 1940, by the end of 1943 he might have become just a little bit 'bigger than ever for his boots!'[61]

10

'People Get Very Peculiar After a Time'

On 1 May 1944 Dorothy Macmillan arrived in Algiers. She had agreed, after sidestepping invitations which had been extended ever since January 1942, to join her husband – for a limited stay of perhaps no more than two months. Until then, of course, she had expressed her clear preference to remain in England, mostly at Pooks Cottage but with excursions to London as occasion required. As might be imagined, her journey to wartime Algiers, as the wife of a Cabinet Minister, took much detailed organisation and was subject to the customary delays of military flight schedules and security procedures. In the event, the delay in her arrival, about four hours or so, was such that Macmillan himself was too busy to meet her at Maison Blanche – and sent John Wyndham in his stead. It was not a good start. But there was not much better to come. Although she was tired after her flight, she was greeted with the news that there was a dinner party that evening for Sir Keith Murdoch, an Australian newspaper owner, and about ten others.

Dorothy thus discovered early the kind of life she was expected to lead in North Africa. As she wrote rather plaintively to her mother on 17 May, 'one never knows how long these social meals will take, and I don't particularly want to attach myself to any one organisation because ... there is a good deal of squabbling.' The only pleasant note in her letter was that 'we have been out for two nights to an Inn in a delicious place, where there are some rather good Roman remains'. It was, indeed, Tipasa. For Macmillan, of course, the place had a special magic. He had bathed there naked with Wyndham, Monnet and Eden, had walked for hours with de Gaulle in the ruins of the Roman town in almost endless talk, had eaten the olives and drunk the wine of the 'little hotel' in the Mediterranean sunshine. Dorothy, on her first encounter, was much more prosaic. She had noted that the 'W.C.s dont [sic] pull, which is much worse than having none'.[1] The romance of the place was not for her. Moreover, not only was she impervious to the magic of Tipasa but, unlike Duff Cooper's wife, Diana (also the daughter of a Duke), Dorothy took almost no interest in the politics of the North African day. If before the war she had disliked her husband's membership of the House of

Commons, the dislike was very clearly transferred to the even less interesting AFHQ.

Had she taken more of an interest she would quickly have realised that by the time of her arrival her husband had succeeded in projecting himself into becoming one of the chief actors in the drama of the Mediterranean war. In fact, even at the time of her arrival his plate of problems seemed to be full to overflowing. First, and certainly foremost, was the steady deterioration in relations between the two Allies. This had not been General Wilson's fault, although he was clumsy in his political touch. But while Eisenhower was in post in Algiers, the Joint Chiefs of Staff in Washington had been broadly prepared to accept his authority and support his decisions. On their side, those in London had known that Macmillan, as Eisenhower's adviser, would ensure that Eisenhower's authority would be exercised (more or less) in line with British policies. With a British General – a British Cabinet Minister as Political Adviser – running AFHQ, there were many in Washington who began to think that there was too much Britishness about the whole thing. Ever suspicious of British imperialism, they believed that Britain's underlying purpose was to establish a position in the Mediterranean which would carry over into the post-war period. That, in the American view, should not be allowed to happen. Anxious to preserve Anglo-American harmony, Macmillan thus found himself riding a particularly difficult (and occasionally pantomime) horse.

The second problem had arisen from the failure of the Allies to manufacture a unified political authority to support the unified military command decided at Cairo in December 1943. In truth, Churchill himself had muddied the water by appointing Lord Moyne as Resident Minister in Cairo answerable, like Macmillan, directly to himself. There was thus a separate, and wholly British, political power centre within the military territory under the command of the Anglo-American AFHQ. Needless to say, Moyne and his skeletal military staff were more than enthusiastic in pursuing adventures in the eastern Mediterranean which they considered to be their province. General Wilson, having learnt his lesson in the Dodecanese fiasco of the autumn of 1943, was firmly opposed to any such adventures – and Macmillan duly supported him. The dispute was at times fierce, and by March 1944 Moyne's staff were reporting to London that relations between Cairo and Algiers were 'extremely acrimonious'.[2]

The third problem, for Macmillan personally, had been, and still was, Eden himself. The Foreign Secretary was becoming tetchy. He found himself dealing with conflicting ministerial views from Macmillan and Moyne, on to which, of course, Churchill's own opinions were imposed more or less at random. Pierson Dixon, who had become Eden's Principal Private Secretary in place of Oliver Harvey, recorded in his diary that there was a 'latent crisis' in the Foreign Office over the whole Mediterranean arrangement. This in turn aggravated Eden's distrust of Macmillan's increasing assertiveness. 'AE's [Eden] feelings about HM [Macmillan] are really the difficulty.'[3] Macmillan himself seemed quite prepared to rub salt on the wound. He continued to play his Churchill card – that as a Cabinet Minister he was accountable only to the Prime Minister (a point which Churchill was happy to confirm). Moreover, when Sir Noel Charles was plucked from the British Embassy in Brazil in March 1944 to become High Commissioner in Italy, he commented airily 'the more ambassadors I have to manage the merrier',[4] a long distance from the Foreign Office view of a direct line to their own Ambassador without interference from the Resident Minister.

The fourth problem, not that Dorothy apparently noticed it, was Macmillan's own health. While the military (and political) action had been in North Africa his job, although frequently stressful, had not involved much travelling. With the war's centre of gravity moving north Macmillan found himself with an enlarged geographical remit. Not only was he obliged to travel much more – in uncomfortable and often dangerous aircraft – but there were many more telegrams to read, answers to compose and despatches to write, meetings to chair and, as Dorothy had found out, official and unofficial dinners to entertain passing generals, politicians and foreign dignitaries. It is little wonder that during the early months of 1944 Macmillan's health had turned quite sharply for the worse. The eczema which had been a worry in late 1943 became a serious problem in January 1944. His hands were very painful and there were eczema spots on other parts of his body. His back was suffering from the discomfort of flying and, as he put it himself, 'I [feel] very tired. I really need a rest.'[5] Indeed, it was just before his fiftieth birthday on 10 February and a subsequent flare-up of his eczema that his doctor had told him that he must take a break of at least a month.

Churchill, when asked for his permission, had agreed, and Macmillan had left Algiers for London on 12 February for leave of a month. But it had not been a restful holiday. There had been much to do in London and little opportunity to spend time at Birch Grove. Even when there, the atmosphere had been uneasy. Carol was proving something of a concern to Dorothy – she was to be married in April – and Dorothy herself was not at her most cheerful. In fact, Macmillan was worried enough to write, on his return to Algiers, to her sister-in-law, that he wanted 'to take this opportunity of thanking you for your immense kindness to Dorothy during all her troubles. She tells me that she could never have managed at all without you. You know how much I care about Carol and how anxious I have been about her ... I hope all will work out for the best.'[6] There was, too, time to be spent at Chequers for a convivial weekend with Churchill, when, among other jollities, Churchill began to smoke Turkish cigarettes, 'saying that they were the only thing he got out of the Turks ... then we had to listen to most of Gilbert and Sullivan on the gramophone, before retiring at 3 a.m.'.[7]

Almost immediately after his return to Algiers on 9 March Macmillan set off on his travels again. (Fortunately, Wyndham had by then found a solution to the discomfort of flying – an inflatable mattress, known as a 'Li-lo', on which Macmillan could lie on the floor of the aircraft.) It was yet another trip to Naples – and a spectacular view from the air of the eruption of Mount Vesuvius – to tell Badoglio that there could be no change in the status of his Government, whatever the Soviets might say (without consulting their Allies they had suggested bilateral Soviet– Italian diplomatic relations), until Rome was liberated. From there it was on to Cairo for meetings to discuss with Moyne and his staff the delivery of relief to the Balkan countries as and when the Germans were driven out and to try – unsuccessfully – to clarify the responsibilities in the matter of AFHQ in Algiers and the Balkan Affairs Committee which Moyne was proposing to set up in Cairo.

April had, in its turn, brought another set of French problems. The FCNL on 4 April passed a decree establishing its President (de Gaulle) as the final authority in matters relating to organisation and employment of French Armed Forces. Giraud promptly declared his intention of resigning. Macmillan received the news during yet another trip to Naples, decided that there was nothing he could do about it all and that anyway it was Duff Cooper's problem. After an exchange of telegrams with Makins – 'Giraud has been an unconscionable time dying. Let him die' – to which Makins replied, 'Ambassador Cooper is taking the affair so calmly that he has gone to the desert whence his staff are feverishly trying to extricate him'[8] – the matter was left there. (As it happened, much to Macmillan's annoyance, Giraud asked whether he could retire and live in England.)

By mid-April Macmillan was again feeling tired. As Makins had pointed out in a letter as early as March, 'our political operations in Italy have far out-stripped our military achievements, and this has made more difficult the application of co-belligerency ... both the Minister and I are much exhausted by our wild rush around the Mediterranean.'[9] Furthermore, Macmillan was not only feeling tired – more and more, his diaries record that he 'stayed in bed all morning'[10] – but on occasions depressed and even maudlin. For instance, in a rare outburst of emotion – and self-flagellation – he wrote to Dorothy on 16 April: 'I cannot write now what I would like to – but I read and re-read your letter and could see Dorothy Cavendish – first a little girl I never knew with pigtails – then Canada – and then the young woman and always that love of trees and woods and streams which I (poor fool) dared to imprison in the stucco and railings of Chester Square. Dear, dear Dorothy – please forgive me.'[11]

All this had been, and was, the background to Dorothy's arrival in Algiers on 1 May. The country was strange, her husband was tired, in poor health and stressed. Sudden social events were sprung on her. If that was not enough, she was also, as it happened, greeted by a plague of locusts. 'They have done a great deal of damage,' she wrote to her mother, '... [they] have eaten miles of vegetables. ... It is an extraordinary sight when they come in clouds.' More cheerful was the visit from her elder sister Maud, who had been roaming around North Africa and Italy in a tartan skirt, staying with any general she could find ('[she] is in very good form ... All the old Generals love her'). But she went on to write, 'Harold has got very busy again, which he seems to enjoy. We had hoped to be able to get a tiny cottage by the sea that we could go to in the evening, as it is a much better rest.'[12] That, in the end, proved impossible, and Dorothy had to make do with the villa – and the locusts.

Thus was Dorothy's initial view of Algiers life. And indeed Macmillan, it is true, was busy – but perhaps not enjoying it as much as she supposed. Moyne had gone ahead with setting up the Balkan Affairs Committee in Cairo. In turn, this had spawned a number of sub-committees. On 22 May Lincoln MacVeagh, the US Ambassador to the Yugoslav and Greek governments-in-exile in Cairo, lodged an official complaint with Moyne, on the grounds that the US had not been consulted (and thought, anyway, that this was another example of British imperialism). When this was reported to London, Churchill decided that the American complaint should be ignored. This in turn provoked a more energetic complaint from the State Department, delivered by Murphy to Macmillan on 6 June. There was then quiet discussion between them and General Wilson – and the 'Balkan Committees' were, on Wilson's orders, quickly disbanded.

The whole affair provoked a fierce letter from Makins to Sir Orme Sargent, the Deputy Head of the Foreign Office in London. 'My dear Moley,' he wrote (Sargent was often, in the gentlemanly conviviality of the Foreign Office, known as 'Moley'). 'This Balkan Committee affair would never have happened if the directive to Macmillan had been drafted to take proper account ... of the necessity of making the political authority of the Resident Minister coterminous with the military authority of the Supreme Allied Commander ... Next, Italy. The appointment of [Noel] Charles was rushed through without really giving Macmillan time either to comment or advise ... Then Yugoslavia ...' Working himself up to a lather of elegantly phrased indignation, Makins went on, 'Harold Macmillan is far too generous and public spirited a man to comment on this sequence of events, but its cumulative effect is overwhelming and he cannot fail to have been struck by the apparent distrust on the part of the Office of him and his staff ... no one has done or could have done more in the last eighteen months to carry out the policy of H.M.G., and in particular that of the Foreign Secretary ...'[13] Sargent dutifully passed Makins's letter on to Eden, who found it 'revealing and disgraceful'.[14]

There was to be yet another spark to the dispute. In AFHQ there was by then a Political Warfare Bureau, responsible – such had been the expansion of the organisation – to the Information and Censorship Section. True to the division of jobs between the two Allies, the latter was headed by an American appointee and the former by a British appointee. Under those arrangements, the Political Warfare Executive in London, with Sir Robert Bruce Lockhart as its head, had appointed Lieutenant Colonel Paul Vellacott, a former Headmaster of Harrow School and Master of Peterhouse, Cambridge, and head of political warfare in Cairo, to the post in Algiers. Soon after he arrived, Vellacott started to demand that his Bureau be taken out of the hierarchy to be free-standing – accountable directly to General Wilson. Macmillan, reasonably enough, considered that the Americans would be needlessly offended over what was, after all, a minor issue. He told Vellacott so – in fact, rather brutally. Vellacott understood the message – and promptly resigned.

This provoked a furious signal from Eden and Brendan Bracken, the Minister of Information, insisting that Vellacott be reinstated. 'We find it hard to understand', went their signal, 'why the necessities of Anglo-American cooperation should require the surrender of the control of political warfare to the Americans in an area which is now a British command and in which British interests are paramount ...'[15] The row, of course, was absurd, but Macmillan only managed to avoid Vellacott's reinstatement by suggesting – in a suitably devious way – a reorganisation of political warfare responsibilities between Algiers and Cairo so ingenious as to require much complicated staff work. That done, the whole matter disappeared off Eden's agenda.

At the same time there had also been an upset in Rome. The city had fallen on 4 June (Macmillan, the Old Etonian, sent a congratulatory telegram to General Alexander, the Old Harrovian, 'It was ... thoughtful of you, as an Old Harrovian to capture Rome on the Fourth of June', to which Alexander replied 'Thank you. What is the Fourth of June?'[16]). Against Macmillan's advice, General Mason-Macfarlane had invited the King of Italy and Marshal Badoglio to go to Rome immediately to proclaim the new Government. As Macmillan had expected, the reaction of Roman politicians to the old Marshal – and to the King for that matter – was very hostile, to the point where Badoglio was forced to admit that, with his record of complicity with Mussolini, he should give way to an admittedly weak, but untainted, liberal, Ivanoe Bonomi. Churchill, who had supported the King and Badoglio and had only read about the fiasco in the morning newspapers, was understandably furious. '[The] P.M. said "If Macmillan had been there this would not have happened".'[17]

As if all the Mediterranean problems were not enough, a parochial British drama was being played out against the backdrop of the even greater one of the long-awaited invasion of northern France, Operation 'Overlord'. Everybody was more than usually tired and, consequently, more than usually bad-tempered. Macmillan, however, was not only tired but worried. He badly needed to resolve the simmering disputes with Eden and the Foreign Office and to read Churchill's mind on the future of the Mediterranean war now that the whole focus was on the liberation of France. With all this in mind, without asking permission and after sending Dorothy off on a week's trip by car to Tunis, on 20 June he left Algiers for London.

By the time he arrived in London another inter-Allied dispute had risen up the agenda. It had been agreed in December 1943 at Teheran that 'Overlord' would be followed by an invasion of southern France (under the code name 'Anvil'). Nevertheless, on 7 June 1944 Alexander had sent a telegram to Churchill – copied to Wilson at AFHQ – advocating an offensive (under the code name 'Armpit') to strike north-eastwards from Italy towards Vienna through the so-called Ljubljana Gap in the Alpine range. It was possible, Alexander argued, for the British to get to Vienna before the Russians, thus forestalling a communist takeover of Austria and probably, for good measure, Hungary, Italy and Yugoslavia as well. Churchill was much taken with the idea, not least because he, and the British Chiefs of Staff, thought that 'Anvil' was a waste of both time and resources. When Macmillan arrived in London on 22 June the argument was in high temper. American officials in AFHQ and, once they heard about it, the whole of the US administration from the President downwards, were suspicious of British motives – a return, they thought, to the old imperialism. Macmillan found himself in difficulties. He was in favour of 'Armpit', and he had been asked by Alexander to promote the scheme in London. But in the light of American displeasure it was not a task which he at all enjoyed.

Apart from the inter-Allied dispute over 'Armpit', there were the difficult fences to be mended, or at least jumped over, with Eden. Macmillan had not told Eden about his proposed visit to London – and Eden was, reasonably enough, badly put out. By then he was becoming not just tetchy but irritated, and on occasions rather more than irritated, by what he considered to be Macmillan's abuse of his position. '[He] is ... interfering with Italian and Balkan affairs,' Bruce Lockhart wrote, 'and is upsetting our representatives, Noel Charles and Lord Moyne ... Anthony said: "We already have two Foreign Secretaries [i.e. himself and Churchill]; I am not going to have a third!"'[18] Complaints on the matter to Churchill, however, got short shrift. In fact, Churchill took some obvious pleasure in reaffirming – against Eden's plaintive criticisms – that Macmillan was accountable only to him and not to the Foreign Office.

In the event, Macmillan's June visit to London turned out to be wholly unproductive. Not only did Roosevelt brush aside Churchill's advocacy of 'Armpit' and insist on 'Anvil' but Macmillan's attempts to allay Eden's suspicions failed miserably. 'He is still quite adamant,' Macmillan wrote of their meeting on 27 June. '[He] seems to think that I want to be Foreign Secretary everywhere. I quite see his point of view; I told him, frankly, that if I were Foreign Secretary I would secure the liquidation of all Ministers Resident wherever and whoever they might be.'[19] It was hardly, to say the least, the most tactful remark to make to the sensitive Eden. It merely strengthened the belief among Eden's supporters that Macmillan was playing above himself – and that in truth he had got his eye on the Foreign Secretaryship. Nor, judging from Macmillan's self-confident mood of the time, were they wholly wrong.

By 29 June Macmillan was back in Algiers. He had just had time to collect news about his family. Dorothy had been very worried, so she said, about 'the children and these new bombs' and was 'so glad that Harold had been home and seen exactly what it is really like'. (Macmillan in fact professed himself unmoved by the V1 'flying bombs'.) But on his return, Macmillan found a rather disgruntled wife. She had, to be sure, enjoyed her trip to Tunis, but although 'I have not had time to discuss my plans with Harold yet ... I expect that I shall be home fairly soon.'[20] In other words, she was getting tired of Algiers – and bored with having little to do.

There was, however, more to do in July. On 21 July AFHQ moved from North Africa to Italy. Macmillan moved out of his villa in Algiers and settled into the – even grander – Villa Carradori at Posillipo on the outskirts of Naples, 'a delicious place above the bay', Dorothy reported. Her return home, in fact, had been postponed for her to help with the move. Since the house in Algiers had to be kept going 'in full swing until we left half of our stuff got delayed on the way . . . and we had to get two houses this [Italian] side running the day we arrived . . . Luckily we were lent an aeroplane [by General Wilson] and the last load consisted of 14 people, including an Ammamite [sic] and a Sudanese (these did not belong to us) one dog, three kittens and four hens, who laid two eggs on the way.'[21] (Macmillan, as he did frequently, used author's licence in his memoirs, in this case to turn the four hens into one egg-laying parrot.)

The second house was a small cottage in the little village near the great palace of Caserta, where AFHQ was to be housed, as it turned out, for the rest of the war. The palace itself was a vast, and somewhat absurd, triumph of Italian rococo – more than three thousand rooms, four great courts, with a mass of fountains, statues, follies, fish ponds, lakes and temples in the enormous garden. Nevertheless, whatever its extravagance, it was certainly a suitable place to receive King George VI, who arrived on 23 July at the start of a tour of the Italian front. There was a great reception in the banqueting hall in the centre of the palace for Allied officers and Italian dignitaries. Macmillan claimed, rather obsequiously, to have been particularly impressed by the way the King shook hands with each guest but even more, on the King's return to Naples, by 'his retentive memory and detailed knowledge of all that was going on'.[22]

King George VI was quickly followed by Churchill, who was on yet another Mediterranean trip – not least to witness at first hand the 'Anvil' landings in the south of France. He arrived at Naples on 11 August accompanied by Pierson Dixon. But Dixon had come on a separate mission from Eden (about which Churchill knew nothing). Macmillan was quick to sense that something was wrong and soon discovered that 'Dixon's real job in coming out here is to wind up the post of Resident Minister, Mediterranean . . . If only Anthony [Eden] had told me straight out that he wanted to get rid of me I would willingly have resigned . . . but I do resent being got out by the back door . . . I shall now fight to the bitter end.'[23] His method of fighting, he decided, would be to compose for Churchill a long memorandum on the whole future of the Mediterranean command.

On the face of it, his memorandum addressed the problem of a possible breakdown of German resistance in the Mediterranean theatre. But the message it contained was more immediate. The War Cabinet had on 8 August approved a plan to despatch a British force to Greece. The question then at issue was whether the British force would come under General Wilson at (Anglo-American) AFHQ in Italy or General Sir Bernard Paget at the (wholly British) Middle East office in Cairo. As Macmillan pointed out in his memorandum, the answer to that question would have implications for the command structure in the Mediterranean (and even beyond) right up to the end of the war.

Moyne, backed by Eden, argued for the wholly British answer. Macmillan, unsurprisingly, argued for the joint Anglo-American answer. But by then he knew that the British Chiefs of Staff had, even before Churchill left London, supported his case. In those circumstances his memorandum was supremely – and, be it said, elegantly – devious. First of all, it put the question in unambiguous terms. 'Is it the desire of His Majesty's Government to treat the Mediterranean Command as a whole for policy questions; that is to say, do we wish an Anglo-American integrated Command to operate ... for all countries [at present under AFHQ]? Or is it our policy to keep it in respect of some parts and not in respect of other parts? ... If we wish to exclude the Americans from certain parts of it, the Command should be divided' and 'the political and economic control should be coterminous with the military control'. In other words, Moyne should run the eastern Mediterranean (as Eden wanted). On the other hand, 'If, however, it is suggested to keep the Mediterranean as a single integrated Anglo-American Command ... a Foreign Office official representative can be appointed Political Adviser to General Wilson ...' At that point, Macmillan seemed to be offering his head on the block. But, he went on, 'Alternatively we could continue to have a British Resident Minister at Allied Force Headquarters who would have a general responsibility to the Prime Minister and the Foreign Secretary for carrying out the main objectives of His Majesty's Government.'[24]

It was no contest. Churchill was certainly not going to override his Chiefs of Staff, lose Macmillan as his Mediterranean eyes and ears and damage further his difficult relations with Roosevelt. Macmillan was to stay; the idea of splitting the Mediterranean Command was rejected and, at a meeting in Caserta on 20 August, Brooke agreed that he and his colleagues '[saw] the necessity of dealing with the Balkans as a whole and support the idea of transferring Greek questions and the Greek command *directly* [Macmillan's emphasis] to AFHQ from Cairo'.[25] It was left to Churchill to announce the decision at a press conference at the British Embassy in Naples on the following day.

'I fear Anthony may not like the decision,' Macmillan smugly wrote in his diary. 'Poor Bob [Pierson] Dixon seems rather alarmed ... He came out with orders to abolish me. In the first day's work he has given me Greece. Tomorrow he has got at least to get me out of Italy! Roger [Makins] is triumphant.'[26]

By then, it was time for Dorothy to go home. She was worried about her family, particularly Carol, and felt 'very guilty about having left her to do so much ... Harold thinks I had really better go home now ... I have certainly had a wonderful rest, and had a most thrilling and interesting time,' but 'it is a tiring life here ... also it is really hot here now ... also I find that they have not put anyone else in to do my work and I really cant [sic] leave that any longer.'[27] Macmillan, in his turn, summed up her visit. 'Her time with me has done her a lot of good and I think she thoroughly enjoyed it. It was certainly very nice for me to have her.'[28] It was not, to be sure, the most enthusiastic endorsement, but it was the best he could do. His diary for 24 August, the day of her departure, was rather more forthcoming: 'It is very sad to lose her.'[29] But he failed nevertheless to write – even to himself – that he would miss her.

Soon afterwards, at the end of August, Bob Murphy left AFHQ. He was to become American Adviser to the German Control Commission, a post which he saw as a promotion. Macmillan was sorry to see him go, although he recognised that Murphy was right to accept the offer. After an initial period of mutual suspicion – caused, as much as anything, by the differing views of their political masters – they had arrived at a good working relationship. Macmillan was much more doubtful about Murphy's replacement, Alexander Kirk. Worse, however, was the scheduled departure in September of Roger Makins. This was 'a great loss – even a great grief ... He has been a most loyal supporter in all my difficulties and a most agreeable companion and friend ...' Makins's replacement, Christopher ('Kit') Steel, 'will, I think, be agreeable and efficient. But he has not got that rapier-like brain combined with that almost monastic devotion to duty which makes Roger such a unique figure in the public service.'[30] To add to Macmillan's gloom at the time, he learnt on 24 September that his brother-in-law, Bill Hartington, had been killed in action.

But there was little time for moping. The British force was on its way to Greece under the command of Lieutenant General Sir Ronald Scobie. On 4 October, after some alarums, they landed on the Peloponnese coast and started to pursue the retreating Germans northwards. Macmillan, in a state of great excitement, decided that it was time for him to follow them to Greece and, on 13 October, he embarked on the cruiser *Orion* (superstitiously, however, the ship did not sail until one minute after midnight – 13 October was a Friday). A substantial flotilla of some forty ships was assembled – a further seventy were coming from Alexandria – and, slowly so as to allow the minesweepers to clear their passage, it made its way around the southern coast of the Peloponnese and headed for Athens. By nightfall of 16 October the *Orion* and half the flotilla were anchored in Phaleron Bay and looking across at Athens. Indeed, the following morning Macmillan was up early and spent some happy hours looking through field glasses at the Acropolis and the Attic hills behind. A quiet day on board ship had cheered him up. 'A lovely evening – after a nice bright sunny day. The setting sun on the Acropolis is a wonderful and thrilling sight.'[31]

It was not until 18 October that Macmillan was able to get in to Athens itself. Early in the morning he picked up Reginald ('Rex') Leeper, the British Ambassador to the Greek government-in-waiting – Leeper had in fact been waiting around himself for some time, first in Cairo and then in Naples – and together they were driven to the Grand Hotel in Constitution Square to witness from one of its balconies the formal appearance of the (provisional) Greek Prime Minister, George Papandreou. The scenes of enthusiasm bordered on the hysterical, but Macmillan was quick to note that the Greek resistance fighters – the communist dominated Greek People's Liberation Army (ELAS) – were still armed to their discoloured teeth and chanting anti-monarchist slogans. Since Churchill had, against the advice of Eden, General Wilson, Leeper and Macmillan himself, determined that the King of Greece, then in London, should return in triumph to his kingdom, Macmillan saw nothing but trouble ahead.

So it turned out. Churchill in mid-October had been in Moscow haggling with Stalin about the degree to which each belligerent could exercise predominant influence over the liberated countries of Eastern Europe. After much wrangling, both about the practicality of dividing Eastern Europe on what was little more than the back of an envelope (it became known as the 'percentage agreement') and about the percentages themselves, the Soviets conceded that in the case of Greece the 'percentage' should be 90 per cent Britain and the US to 10 per cent the Soviet Union. Armed with this agreement Churchill on his return from Moscow stopped overnight in Naples on 21 October and told Macmillan, by then back from Greece, that it was more important than ever to press on with the Greek operation – including humanitarian relief (baptised, of course, 'Operation Manna') – and, as he went on to minute Eden when back in London, 'not hesitate to use force in support of the Royal Hellenic Government under M. Papandreou'.[32]

This was not at all what Macmillan wanted to hear. But his difficulties were compounded by the news that Wilson was no longer able to give him support. Early in November General Wilson had been posted to Washington in place of the recently deceased Field Marshal Sir John Dill. To be sure, Macmillan was pleased to hear that Alexander was to replace him (and, in the process, to be promoted to the rank of Field Marshal) but knew well that it would take some time for Alexander to be fully briefed about the situation in Greece. There was still, after all, a campaign to be fought in Italy. A further visit to Athens – this time for the stabilisation of the Greek currency and a picnic with Wyndham on the plain of Marathon, where we 'mused ... upon the mutability of human affairs'[33] – confirmed Macmillan in his fears that Greece was on the brink of civil war. From there it was back again to Italy, but it was not until 18 November (after a morning audience in Rome with Pope Pius XII) that he finally caught up with Field Marshal Alexander at his headquarters in Ancona to brief him on the whole complex of problems that he would now have to face in Greece.

That done, it was time for another visit to London, this time with a stop in Paris, arriving at Northolt airport on Friday 24 November. After lunch, he was driven down to Birch Grove – the main house by then not yet fully habitable – for a late dinner, went shooting the following day ('We did Wheeler's, Brigham's and Hopgarden Shaw before lunch. After lunch, Stripes, Round Wood, and then Buttocks Bank up into Smalls and Smalls Wood back ... We got sixty-five pheasants and a woodcock or two ...'[34]). Church at Horsted Keynes on the Sunday was followed by a family lunch at Pooks. Yet the war had to go on, and after the weekend he was back in London and on business. There were the usual meetings, lunches and dinners – one, for instance, in 10 Downing Street to hear Churchill read to his Ministers the King's Speech which was to be delivered at the State Opening of Parliament the next day.

That was all very well. But by 5 December it had become clear to Macmillan in London, as he noted in his diary, that 'the Greek news is really bad. It looks now like civil war.'[35] It was true. On 1 December General Scobie had ordered ELAS to hand in their arms. They had refused. The ministers of EAM, their political wing, resigned from the Papandreou Government. There were calls for strikes and armed insurrection against the Government. By 5 December, in fact, an outright left-right bitter and unforgiving civil war had erupted between ELAS and Papandreou supporters.

On 10 December Macmillan and Alexander, who was also visiting London at the time, flew out of the Air Force base at Lyneham, Wiltshire, first to Italy and then, the next day, to the smaller Athens airport of

Kalamaki, the larger airport at Tatoi being in insurgent hands. Much to their surprise they were met by two tanks – one for Alexander and one for Macmillan – and driven through sporadic sniper fire to Scobie's headquarters where Alexander was to be briefed. Macmillan went on to the British Embassy. There he was told that insurgents held about four-fifths of Athens and its port of Piraeus. The Embassy itself was besieged, with an anxious Leeper and some fifty staff inside it. There was no heat, no water apart from the baths, which had been sensibly filled before the insurgents drained the reservoir on which the Embassy depended, and no light. Sporadic negotiations with the ELAS insurgents for a truce had come to nothing.

For Macmillan and Leeper (and, indeed, Mrs Leeper and the staff) this was to be their home until military reinforcements could arrive. Telegrams from London told them that the War Cabinet had met three times and on Eden's recommendation had decided that there should be a regency, with the Metropolitan of Athens, Archbishop Damaskinos, at its head, but that Churchill was still supporting the claims of the King of Greece – accusing Damaskinos himself, quite unfairly, of being a Quisling. Moreover, Churchill was constantly firing off telegrams to Scobie urging him to use maximum force if necessary (without appreciating that Scobie had little force to use – but he had managed to secure Kalamaki airport and most of the port at Piraeus). Macmillan and Leeper, Churchill shouted, were two 'fussy-wuzzies'.[36]

In the middle of all this Macmillan was able to make a trip back to Naples on 20 December – driven again to the airport in a tank – before returning to Athens the following day. On Friday 22 December, however, there was another twist in the story. Churchill suddenly decided that he would go to Greece himself to take charge. The next day he went down to Chequers and told his Private Secretary, John ('Jock') Colville, to make the necessary arrangements. He also told his wife, Clementine, that he might not be staying for what, after all, would be the last family Christmas of the war. Mrs Churchill went up to her bedroom, where she was found by her sister 'in floods of tears'.[37] Throughout the next day there was therefore much family argument, and it was not until after lunch on the 24th that Churchill finally made up his mind.

At one o'clock in the morning of Christmas Day 1944, Churchill and Eden, with the customary supporting staff, took off from Northolt for Athens. Alexander had been summoned from Italy and arrived by sea – the weather had been too bad to fly – in time to go out to Kalamaki airport with Macmillan and Leeper to meet Churchill's aircraft. It was bitterly cold – a biting wind from the Attic hills – and they had to stand around for about half an hour, stamping their feet to keep warm. When

Churchill's party finally arrived Alexander persuaded them to stay on board the aircraft and hold their meeting in comfort and warmth. During some two hours of discussion Macmillan and Leeper explained the plan they had concocted – to summon a conference 'generally representative of Greek political opinion', including 'ELAS delegates'.[38] Damaskinos would preside but Churchill would be the convener of the conference and would see fair play. Churchill, after some hesitation and much questioning, finally agreed to the plan.

Churchill's party then left for Piraeus in armoured cars (Colville's driver began the conversation with him by remarking, 'the last man who sat where you are sitting died yesterday morning'[39]) and were transferred by boat to the cruiser *Ajax*. Damaskinos and Giorgios Papandreou, the politician most trusted by the Allies, were both summoned and were ferried across to the ship with Macmillan and Leeper to be greeted by the ship's carol party lustily singing 'The First Noel'. Papandreou went in to see Churchill straight away, while Damaskinos 'who is a magnificent figure,' reported Colville, 'and obviously has a great sense of humour' swapped stories with the staff. The *Ajax* officers produced a bottle of ouzo, 'a nauseating Greek liqueur tasting like a cheap cough mixture', and offered drinks all round.[40] The result was that by the time Damaskinos got in to see Churchill everybody seemed to be in a particularly good mood. Churchill immediately took to Damaskinos and even thought that he would make a good regent – much to Macmillan's relief. Eden, on the other hand, became more cautious. It took until 2 a.m. for him to be persuaded – but by that time everybody (except Churchill, of course) was exhausted. But at least it had been agreed to hold the conference.

It finally began just before five o'clock in the afternoon at the Greek Ministry of Foreign Affairs. But it did not go smoothly. No ELAS delegates had turned up. Damaskinos had finished an elegant opening address, and Churchill had spoken for about five minutes, 'when there were noises off and three shabby desperadoes ... came into the dimly lit conference room'. These turned out to be the ELAS delegates. They were welcomed, in silence by the Greek Government delegates but effusively by Churchill. 'The P.M. was only prevented from rushing to shake the ELAS people by the hand by Field Marshal Alexander's bodily intervention.'[41] The conference then began all over again. Churchill, when it came again to his turn, said that the objective was peace, an amnesty and economic rehabilitation. One of the ELAS delegates replied that he hoped for peace between Greece and Britain. There was then a succession of mutually congratulatory speeches from the Greek delegates – and the British left the meeting for the Greeks to discuss among themselves. This was done – with a good deal of noise – until the meeting broke up in time for dinner at half past ten in the evening.

The conference reconvened the next morning with an enlarged cast. More delegates had been invited. The Archbishop reported to them all that at the meeting on the previous day an agreement had emerged in favour of a regency. This agreement was immediately endorsed by all delegates, although there were some who wished to wait until ELAS had agreed the terms of Scobie's offer of truce. The Archbishop then read out the demands that ELAS had put to him – which everybody apart from the ELAS delegates thought wholly unacceptable. With that, the conference was adjourned. It seemed, mysteriously, that a deal had indeed been done. The Archbishop then reported to Churchill that Papandreou had resigned, that he was prepared to become regent and that a new government would be formed as soon as the regency was in place. Churchill was still fussing about the attitude of ELAS and thought of staying on in Athens for another day, but Eden and Macmillan succeeded in persuading him that it was much more important for him to see the King and secure his agreement to the regency. Finally, having issued the necessary press releases, the whole party, Macmillan included, then left for Naples.

1944 thus ended – at least for Macmillan – on a high note. There was, of course, a government to be formed in Greece and Italian problems were piling up – the food ration, the housing situation, local elections, transport difficulties and the links with partisans in the north of the country. But these were all manageable. On the plus side, Macmillan had also acquired a new title (not that he wanted it) – President of the Allied Control Commission in Italy. Above all, however, the negotiations in Athens had brought with them a reconciliation with Eden. The Foreign Secretary had recognised the skill with which Macmillan had organised matters and, above all, his ability to use his influence with Churchill and to use it for their joint purpose.

On the other hand, Macmillan was very tired and not very well. He was often sleeping late in the mornings and his eczema had not gone away. But almost more important than anything was the thought, and the worry, that the war was coming to an end – and that it was time to give serious consideration to his future.

On 5 October, Duff Cooper had written to Macmillan that since he had given up a political career and returned to the Foreign Office (to become British Ambassador in Paris) his constituency of St George's Westminster would become available at the General Election which would take place once the war had ended. If Macmillan were interested,

Cooper would gladly put his name forward. Macmillan replied that he was indeed interested. Stockton was, after all, a long way away and, at the age of fifty-one, he was too old to risk not being a member of the new House. By December, matters had got to the point where Macmillan, on his visit to London, had seen the St George's Westminster Conservative Committee. 'I gave them my position quite frankly,' he noted in his diary, 'I sought nothing but would accept if asked.'[42] In other words, he was now too grand to be a supplicant.

It was, on the face of it, a piece of supreme arrogance. But it is also revealing. By then, Macmillan thought himself a fine catch for any Conservative constituency. Not only that, but by March 1945 he was noting that '[Stockton] is a really dreadful prospect. I have scarcely been near Stockton for five years. I have no agent, no association and no funds! ... It seems my fate to try to get away from Stockton, but never to achieve it.'[43] In fact, by then he was committed to Stockton. He had received a letter from Beaverbrook (prompted, there is no doubt, by Churchill) telling him on no account to give up Stockton for St George's and assuring him that if he lost Stockton whoever won St George's would be immediately sent to the House of Lords to make way for him. 'Poor Dorothy!' he noted after making up his mind to accept Stockton. 'Those weary journeys to the North are still worse under the conditions of railway travel in England today.' Stockton, in other words, was bound to be a perennial nuisance until he could safely lose it.

The early months of 1945 rolled forward. The February summit conference at Yalta and President Roosevelt's death in April came and went. Events of the Mediterranean were gradually becoming less pressing and urgent as peace approached. Both Greece and Italy were settling down. There was more time for sleeping in the mornings and for leisurely visits to the great Greek and Roman archaeological sites. March the fourteenth, for instance, was (it was a Wednesday) a 'red-letter day ... an absolutely halcyon day – blue sky, no wind, no clouds ... The pale light blues of the sea as we passed Eleusis and the Bay of Salamis were marvellous.' Macmillan and Wyndham were on another expedition – through the northern Peloponnese and down to Tiryns and Mycenae. 'I will not try to describe', he wrote to Dorothy, 'these wonderful remains of a magnificent civilisation ... The drive back to Athens was as beautiful, in the evening light, as can be imagined.'[44] As April glided into May and the news of Hitler's death and the German surrender came through it was also a time for rejoicing – and for farewells.

Before Macmillan could leave the Mediterranean, however, there was an episode which would come back to plague him in later life. After the German surrender on 7 and 8 May 1945 there were many unpleasant messes to clear up. But the horrors of Belsen and Auschwitz drew public attention away from other minor – and almost peripheral – catastrophes in other parts of Europe. One of these occurred in the south Austrian province of Carinthia during the second half of May. Carinthia was the last major stretch of land to be occupied. The Soviets, under Marshal Fyodor Tolbukhin, had stopped (somewhat over their agreed line) in their assault from Vienna in the northeast; the British Eighth Army, under General Sir Richard McCreery, had not yet completed its advance through the north of Italy; and the Yugoslavs, by then well organised under the communist Marshal Josef Broz Tito, had not yet got to where Tito wished them to be. Carinthia thus lay open.

Tito, of course, had been supported by the Allies. Macmillan himself had met Tito at lunch in Caserta in August 1944 – without much enthusiasm. In September Soviet forces had linked up with Tito's partisans, after which Tito became more assertive in his territorial ambitions. By the end of February 1945 he was becoming more strident. He was claiming the port of Trieste and a large slice of Carinthia (and its neighbour Istria on the Adriatic) as properly belonging to Yugoslavia after the war. To reinforce his claim, by early May Yugoslav troops had made their way north to the outskirts of the Carinthian capital, Klagenfurt.

But there was a further complication. The Yugoslav advance had pushed before it a motley group of anti-communists who had been resisting, under German leadership, Tito's advance and who were (rightly) terrified that Tito and his troops would be merciless if they were caught. At the same time the Soviet advance had led to another motley group, in this case various units of Cossacks and 'White' Russians who had been fighting against the Soviets, also to seek refuge in Carinthia. Finally, there were droves of German soldiers determined to seek their own refuge with the Western Allies rather than fall into the hands of the Soviets. By mid-May they too were heading for Carinthia.

Even on the day of the German surrender, Churchill fired off a telegram to Alexander about Tito's territorial claims. A 'steady gathering of British or British-controlled forces on the front', he telegraphed Alexander, '... is most likely to maintain peace and most convenient if unpleasantness arises'. His telegram went on to take a swipe at the Soviets. 'Let me know what you are doing in massing forces against this Muscovite tentacle, of which Tito is the crook.'[45] It was, and is, clear that what was exercising Churchill and the Chiefs of Staff (and Alexander and Macmillan) about Carinthia had nothing to do with the fleeing Yugoslavs or Cossacks or lost German soldiers. The whole question was how to stop Tito occupying and holding on to territory in the expectation that the Soviets would support him in any future peace settlement. If they could not stop him it was difficult to see how, without the use of force, he could be dislodged.

This was the problem which Alexander addressed at his meeting with Macmillan, Kirk and others in Caserta on the morning of 10 May. Tito had made a counter-proposal, offering free user rights of Trieste and a kind of military condominium provided Yugoslavia was acknowledged as sovereign over the part of the Italian province of Venezia Giulia which they had occupied. That was obviously unacceptable. A reply was sent to that effect. At the same time military planners were starting to work out the forces necessary to eject the Yugoslavs should that prove necessary. The next day Macmillan sent a telegram to Churchill summing up the options – try to contain Tito by diplomacy or be prepared for military action against Tito (and possibly his Soviet patrons) – and Alexander sent another to the Combined Chiefs of Staff: 'In the event of hostilities against Yugoslavia, I must know on what divisions I can rely. I would be glad if you would consult the US, UK, New Zealand, South African, Indian, Brazilian, Polish and Italian Governments.'[46] Alexander also asked Macmillan to go to the headquarters of the Eighth Army at Treviso, near Venice, find out at first hand from General Richard Loudon McCreery what was happening and, if necessary, go on to see his subordinate generals, General Charles Keightley, commanding 5 Corps, and General John Harding, commanding 13 Corps.

On the morning of Saturday 12 May Macmillan and Philip Broad, a Foreign Office official who had been with the Greek government-in-exile when it had been in Cairo and was now on Macmillan's staff at AFHQ, flew from Naples across the Apennines to Treviso. There they found McCreery worried at being unable to use force against the infiltrating Yugoslavs and having to stand by while they set up local governments of their own and occupied all the public buildings. Although a New Zealand unit had managed to get to the port area of Trieste in front of the Yugoslavs, the rest of the town was in Yugoslav hands. Rather deflated by McCreery's gloom, Macmillan and Broad went on to see General Harding at his headquarters near Monfalcone ('a splendid castle,' Macmillan noted, '. . . on the sea with a delightful garden and beautiful view . . . a wonderful display of blue irises'[47]). Harding was more cheerful. He claimed that he would be able to hold on for a few weeks to allow diplomacy to resolve the problem. With that news, they went back to Treviso, drove into Venice and dined there at the Grand Hotel. Not a word had been said about Cossacks or Yugoslav refugees.

The next morning Macmillan and Broad continued their journey, this time over the Alps to Klagenfurt and Carinthia. There they found a similar situation, except that units of 5 Corps had succeeded in reaching Klagenfurt a few hours before the Yugoslavs and had been able to secure the main buildings. Nevertheless, when British troops put up posters announcing their military government the Yugoslavs simply tore them down and put up their own. Macmillan also noted the problem of the influx of surrendered Germans into Carinthia – 'nearly 400,000 ... not yet disarmed ... Moreover, among the surrendered Germans are about 40,000 Cossacks and "White" Russians with their wives and children. To hand them over to the Russians is condemning them to slavery, torture and probably death. To refuse, is deeply to offend the Russians, and incidentally break the Yalta agreement. We have decided to hand them over (General Keightley is in touch and on good terms with the Russian general [Tolbukhin] on his right ...' Macmillan also noted that 'To add to the confusion thousands of so-called Ustashi or Chetniks, mostly with wives and children, are fleeing in panic in front of the advancing Yugoslavs ...' But there was no equivalent decision about what to do with them. In fact, the substantive business of the visit was 'a conference with the general and his officers covering much of the same ground as those with Generals McCreery and Harding yesterday. He gave us his story and we gave him ours.'[48] In other words, the main business of the day, which had taken no more than two hours, had been what should be done to counter the Yugoslav infiltration. That concluded, Macmillan and Broad flew back to Treviso and from there on to Caserta.

On the following day General Sir Brian Robertson, Alexander's Chief Administrative Officer at AFHQ, held a meeting to decide how to follow up the decision taken by Macmillan and Keightley in Klagenfurt the previous day. McCreery had asked that morning for clear instructions. During the day Robertson discussed the matter with Alexander Kirk, Macmillan's American political number. Kirk was unhappy about handing over the Cossacks without his Government's approval – and sent a telegram to the State Department in Washington asking for instructions. Robertson told Kirk that the matter was too urgent to wait for the State Department to respond and, on that very evening, sent an order out that 'All Russians should be handed over to Soviet Forces at agreed point of contact established by you under local arrangement with Marshal Tolbukhin's HQ ...'[49] Robertson's order was, in fact, ambiguous. Not all the 'Cossacks' were Soviet nationals (to be repatriated under the agreement at Yalta) although all of them, one way or another, could be classed as Russian. Like Macmillan in Klagenfurt, Robertson assumed that all of them should go back – although a determined sifting process would have discovered that some 10,000 out of the 40,000 were not Soviet nationals at all. Robertson's order went on to say that Yugoslav nationals who had served in German forces should be handed over to Tito's partisans. In the last provision, of course, Robertson made no attempt to rely on any Macmillan recommendation (or decision) since there had been none.

On 14 May Macmillan 'stayed in bed or lounged in the garden all the day'.[50] Robertson's order was sent just after 6.30 in the evening. It was marked as approved by the British Resident Minister. Macmillan himself could not possibly have seen it while he was lounging in his garden. The only conclusion must be that Broad had signed it off for him in his absence. Broad knew that it was consistent with what Macmillan and Keightley had decided in Klagenfurt and that, on any interpretation, Yugoslavs who had fought for Germany probably, in view of the known German atrocities in Yugoslavia, deserved what they got.

In the end, the repatriation of both the Cossacks and the Yugoslav refugees was dreadful – and shameful. In spite of orders demanding no use of force, in spite of orders countermanding the Robertson order, and in spite of American proposals to take charge of many of them, the Cossacks were handed over to the Soviets and the Yugoslav refugees were handed over to Tito's forces. The circumstances of both 'repatriations' by 5 Corps have been recounted in graphic and horrifying detail. There is no doubt that they were a truly dreadful blemish on the record of British forces in the Second World War.

Much ink has flowed, and many legal fees incurred, in trying to pin responsibility for the outcome on the various players – not least on Macmillan himself. None of these has been entirely successful. As for the Yugoslav refugees, Macmillan wrote to Sir Percy Grigg, the Secretary of State for War, on 18 May, referring to the problems faced by 5 Corps, that one of them was 'dealing with . . . Yugoslav refugees, deciding which, if any, are to be handed back to the Tito troops'.[51] Nothing that happened thereafter has supported any conclusion that Macmillan was in any way implicated in the repatriation or in the deception it ultimately involved. As for the Cossacks, however, there is ample evidence – his own diary – to show that Macmillan was indeed party to the decision taken at Klagenfurt to send them back and that the decision was taken in the full knowledge of what almost certainly awaited them. Beyond that, nevertheless, he was not party to the final acts of the drama and was unaware of the horrors of the final event – which took place after he had left Italy for good on 24 May.

In spite of this, there is no doubt that Macmillan's attitude towards the Cossacks was callous – bordering on the contemptuous – of those who were, after all, fellow human beings. In fact, if that is the real charge, he never admitted it. In later life he was unrepentant. When questioned in 1982 on British television, he simply stated that the Cossacks were 'rebels against Russia' and, even more tellingly, '[they] were practically savages'.[52]

This was to be the last chapter in Macmillan's war. It leaves an unpleasant taste. Yet it is only a part, albeit an important one, of how the political Macmillan had developed in the nearly two and a half years he had been in the Mediterranean. The boring pedant political London knew in the 1930s had turned into the accomplished politician of the mid-1940s. By the time he returned to London to take up the unlikely post of Minister for Air in the interim administration pending the forthcoming General Election, he was a senior figure in the Conservative Party with a record of wartime success.

None of this had come without some personal cost. Apart from Dorothy's four-month visit and Wyndham's companionship, his life had been one of domestic loneliness. Relaxations had been few. He read voraciously – but always the familiar English favourites. There was no Goethe, Proust, Dostoyevsky, Cervantes or Dante. There was no music, no sport, no chess or even crosswords, no sex (as far as is known) and few cigars (he took up smoking cigarettes). Visits to archaeological sites and gardens, of course, were joys to be recorded in detail – in long letters to the absent Dorothy and equally long entries in his diary. It was all there was to combat the bouts of depression which assailed him from time to time.

Beyond all that, he had certainly toughened up. His treatment of Vellacott and his callousness towards the Cossacks had revealed, at the age of fifty, a character trait which had hitherto been hidden – the ability to ignore, often brutally, those who stood in his way. He had also smartened up. The baggy trousers had given way to well-tailored suits. Even the spectacles were, on occasions – for instance, press conferences with Churchill – discarded. His moustache and hair were kept carefully trimmed. True, he could do nothing about his teeth and the snarl when he smiled (Colville noted, 'I don't like the would-be ingratiating way in which Macmillan bares his teeth'[53]) and the shuffle was still there. But the Mediterranean – the sun, the food and the wine – had not only bronzed his skin (and, in the end, taken care of his eczema) but filled him out physically. This was no longer the Balliol-educated don. This was somebody who gave the appearance of a serious political figure.

The problem, of course, was managing a return to post-war England. As Dorothy wrote to her mother in June 1944, 'He will find England very small when he has to settle there again!' Even more trenchantly, in the same letter she went on, 'I think there is no doubt that this is a funny place and people get very peculiar after a time.'[54] That may well be so. The Mediterranean has strange effects. But Dorothy had a point. It certainly was a different Macmillan who arrived back in England at the end of May 1945 – to fight for his place in the unwanted constituency of Stockton-on-Tees.

Part Three
WAITING IN THE WINGS

11

A Stranger at Home

'Harold may yet succeed Winston. He has grown more in stature during the war than anyone. I have known him now, off and on, for sixteen years. He was always clever, but was shy and diffident, had a clumsy handshake and was more like a wet fish than a man. Now he is full of confidence and is not only not afraid to speak but jumps in and speaks brilliantly.'[1] Thus Robert Bruce Lockhart, an old acquaintance, early in 1946. Yet the second half of 1945 had not been easy. As Dorothy had predicted, Macmillan had difficulty in settling back to the dreary life of post-war England. As he himself later wrote, 'I felt myself almost a stranger at home.'[2] The house at Birch Grove was still a mess and would take time to restore to anything resembling comfort. Dorothy was still emotionally distant (and still uncomfortably attached to Boothby) and the birth of successive grandchildren made little impression. Besides, his son Maurice had started to drink too much.

Moreover, Macmillan felt out of touch with the political times. Britain, whatever the enthusiasm that greeted peace, was exhausted. Almost everything was rationed, cities still bore the scars of the intensive air raids, and people, after the first welcome for a Labour Government, were becoming progressively more gloomy about the future. Furthermore, Macmillan saw for himself, on a visit to Germany as Secretary of State for Air, the almost total destruction which was the war's legacy there. On top of all that he had to fight an election in which he was, even at the outset, doubtful of success. All in all, the Mediterranean, and the excited optimism of the final moments of the European war, seemed a very long way away.

The campaign of June 1945 turned out for him to be as dull as the weather. Conservative meetings were, of course, reasonably well attended, and Dorothy dutifully did her support work, but there was no spark – there was no rowdy heckling, no demonstrations and, most noticeable of all, the women on the doorstep were either angry or moodily silent. Churchill had hoped that the Election could be won on the back of gratitude for wartime success – but he made a dreadful mistake in a radio broadcast appearing to compare Labour with the Gestapo. Finally, the whole momentum of the campaign was lost by the knowledge that the overseas Service vote would take three weeks to collect and bring back to Britain. The result was that a desultory campaign led to a cloudy polling day on 5 July – and then to an unhappy wait until 26 July before the result could be known.

In the event, on the day Stockton declared early. In spite of a turnout of four out of five electors on the register it took less than an hour to count the ballot papers. Macmillan and Dorothy, having taken the afternoon train from London, arrived only minutes before the result was announced by the Mayor of Stockton from the balcony of the Town Hall. An unexpectedly small crowd there heard that George Chetwynd, the Labour candidate, had polled 27,128, Harold Macmillan, the Conservative candidate, had polled 18,464 and Gordon Evans, the Liberal candidate, had polled 3718. After a perfunctory vote of thanks to the Mayor as returning officer (Macmillan, seconding the proposal as the losing candidate, said dryly that it was 'his sixth contest of Stockton and he had won three and lost three'³) he and Dorothy immediately took the night train back to London. It had been a most depressing evening, and on the way back Macmillan could only reflect that his Parliamentary career was, at least for the time being and possibly permanently, at a rather inglorious end.

The outlook was indeed dismal. Losing a seat in the House of Commons, as Macmillan had found before, is an event which carries its own kind of trauma. Yet previous experience did not make it easier. Furthermore, he was now not just out of Parliament but out of office. Moreover, the Macmillan publishing house, his point of refuge during previous gaps in his Commons membership, had suffered like everybody else during the war and needed rebuilding, but Macmillan himself had little enthusiasm for the task. His brother Daniel would have to bear the burden. He had lost touch with his family during his two and a half years in the Mediterranean and could find no comfort there (even if he was so inclined). In short, he had little idea where he should turn and what he was now going to do.

In fact, he had an immediate stroke of luck. Sir Edward Campbell, who had represented the constituency of Bromley, Beckenham and Penge for many undistinguished years and who had been almost ceremonially re-elected, had quite unexpectedly died before his victory could be announced. Leaving aside the undoubted sorrow of his erstwhile colleagues and his constituents, there was, as a result, a plum Conservative vacancy. Of course, many put their names forward, but the front-runner, as it happened, was not a rejected former Member of Parliament but Churchill's own son, Randolph. The Bromley Conservatives assumed that he came with the full support and endorsement of his father. In fact, it is certainly true that only a word from Churchill himself would have secured him the nomination. But no word came.

On 17 August Randolph wrote to Macmillan. 'The day after the poll was declared,' his letter went, 'I asked the Chairman of the Bromley Conservative Association to place my name before his Selection Committee. I have only just heard that your name is also before them. Not only am I sure that your name would be preferred to mine, but also I would wish it to be, in view of your very great claims to be in this Parliament. I have accordingly written to the Chairman asking him to withdraw my name.'⁴ There was, of course, more to it than Randolph simply withdrawing his name. The Bromley Conservatives could recognise a nod and a wink when they saw one. Macmillan was obviously Churchill's favoured candidate – and was duly nominated. Once that was done, Churchill himself sent a fulsome letter of support, saying that 'the electors of Bromley, Beckenham and Penge will render good service to the Nation at this juncture by returning you with a large majority'.⁵

Bromley was not only a safe seat but it was much more to the post-war Macmillan taste than the dreariness of Stockton-upon-Tees. On the south-east of London but only twelve miles or so from its centre, with carefully cultivated gardens and parks, it had been a haven for the middle classes of the 1930s. The rows of identical houses were much prized homes for those who commuted into London for work but wished the quiet or at least the resemblance of countryside in the evenings. For the curious visitor – if there were any – Charles Darwin's house was a feature, as was the park where the Crystal Palace had finished its uncomfortable – and finally fatal – journey after the Great Exhibition of 1851. For the devotees of Free France (not that Macmillan ever noticed it) there was the modest house in Petts Wood where de Gaulle had taken refuge in the autumn of 1940. All in all, it was a constituency where, it need hardly be said, it was much more profitable to be a relation of the Cavendishes than the descendant of a Scottish crofter.

Macmillan slipped into the part of patrician candidate easily enough and Dorothy, of course, was an even greater electoral asset than she had been in Stockton. After his nomination as prospective candidate at the end of August, he set about rebuilding the moribund Conservative organisation and patrolling the suburban streets to meet his future electors. He did, however, face a difficulty. Outright opposition to the Labour Government was what his Conservative supporters expected, but in his own pamphlets and speeches before the war he had, after all, preached much of what they were doing. He could hardly go back on all that now. The result of his dilemma, as it turned out, was an election address which reads as a strange amalgam of *The Middle Way* and his other pre-war writings with some political pepper thrown in as spice for the immediate purpose. As he later put it himself, it 'no doubt puzzled the electors'.[6]

Nevertheless, puzzled or not, the electors of Bromley, Beckenham and Penge did their duty, and on 20 November 1945 Harold Macmillan took his seat in the House of Commons, introduced – as though to cock a snook at the Labour ranks opposite him – by two Eton College contemporaries, Harry Crookshank and Harry Willink. As a Privy Councillor, too, he duly sat in his place on the Opposition Front Bench. But his return to Parliamentary life was again not to be easy. He found Commons procedures, after all the years of absence, unfamiliar. Moreover, Churchill's method of conducting Parliamentary opposition was, to say the least, bizarre. Every other Wednesday he entertained some fourteen of his closest colleagues to a large and bibulous lunch at the Savoy Hotel, apparently to discuss forthcoming business. No portfolios, as such, were allocated. It was generally assumed that Eden would lead on foreign affairs and that Stanley and Lyttelton would lead on economics and finance, with support from Butler and Macmillan himself as occasion required. None of that, however, prevented any of them from speaking on other matters as they felt so moved.

Inevitably, there were grumbles. Many felt that Churchill had lost touch with the House of Commons, that his attendance was infrequent – or that he was too fond of provoking Parliamentary rows instead of making speeches about future policy. 'He is not in fact leading the Party,' Cranborne complained to his father. 'He just comes down to the House to make a big speech or have a row, and then returns again to the country.' There was also, above all else, the matter of Churchill's own future. He had, after all, turned seventy and had fought an exhausting war. When Lord Woolton (a surprisingly successful Minister of Food during the war) was invited to become Chairman of the Conservative Party in the spring of 1946, he 'sent out his spies all over the country, & they have all come back with the same report. Everywhere, people are asking: "when is Winston going to retire?" It isn't that they don't love him and revere him for what he did in the war. But they regard him as a reactionary in home politics, & that is the one thing they won't stand.'[7]

Churchill, of course, had no intention of retiring. Nor did Macmillan want him to. He had put in much effort during the war in cultivating their relationship and, give or take the odd explosion, had largely succeeded. In fact, Churchill himself had taken the trouble not just to write to Macmillan in his support at Bromley but to speak for him during the by-election campaign. Moreover, although others – even Beaverbrook –

found Churchill 'very difficult to deal with', Macmillan thought that Churchill had 'mellowed'. '"One always had to be patient with Winston",' Bruce Lockhart reported him saying, '"and wait for one's chance to speak. It rarely produced an immediate effect, but eventually he would come back to one's point and show that he had appreciated it" ... He implied rather smugly that he knew how to manage Winston.'[8]

Others, as it happened, had difficulty in managing Macmillan. Although he spoke well in the Commons he had taken on some irritating mannerisms. Dressed in the Parliamentary (at least for Conservatives) uniform of the day – short black coat, black waistcoat with a watch chain carefully threaded through the appropriate buttonhole, white shirt with stiff collar, black tie and striped trousers – he put his hands to the lapels of his jacket and spoke as though he were addressing a theatre audience. His voice had become lower in tone and he had assumed, consciously or not, a pronounced drawl. His face had taken on the features of aristocratic and world-weary contempt – hooded eyes, a mouth slightly turned down under a carefully clipped moustache and, of course, the snarl which passed for a smile when he was making a joke. All this had the effect not only of annoying his Labour opponents (which was half the point) but from time to time of annoying his own supporters. 'One of his clever, well prepared speeches which are always worth listening to, even though his manner of delivering them always irritates me,' was one comment. 'He is so profoundly certain that he is doing the job so well and that H[arold] M[acmillan] is the man to back.'[9] Furthermore, he had fallen into his old habit of lecturing his colleagues in the House of Commons Smoking Room. 'Harold Macmillan,' wrote one, 'with whom I had a talk in the Smoking Room (or rather whom I heard talking, for, as usual, one has little chance of saying anything oneself) ...'[10] The lectures, it need hardly be said, were not always welcomed by those who spent their time listening to them.

All in all, Churchill's Front Bench in the early years of opposition could not easily be described as a happy ship. Eden was as ever frustrated – and in the spring of 1946 openly asked Churchill to retire in his favour. Lyttelton and Stanley were old friends but found it difficult to share the finance portfolio without stumbling over one another. Crookshank performed well in the House of Commons but was suspected of plotting Churchill's removal. Cranborne was in the House of Lords, where he would stay for ever – not least because he inherited the title of Marquess of Salisbury on his father's death in the summer of 1947. Moreover, none of them, apart from Churchill himself, particularly liked Macmillan. Eden, especially, was both suspicious and jealous. 'When I mentioned Harold Macmillan,' Bruce Lockhart reported, 'he drew in his horns at once. Said he was a flabby creature. I think that he is a little jealous of Harold. In this respect he is like a woman; he fears a potential rival.'[11]

But at least they were, for the most part, from Eton (and Oxford) and were former Grenadier, Coldstream or Scots Guardsmen or, in Eden's case, a Rifleman from a most socially acceptable Green Jacket regiment. All had fought in the First World War, and there is no doubt that at least some of the old tribal loyalty still held good. The odd man out from the tribe, of course, was Richard Austen ('Rab') Butler. He was neither an Old Etonian nor a former Guardsman or Rifleman. He had been only twelve at the outbreak of the First World War and, anyway, at the age of seven in his childhood in India he had been thrown from a pony in an accident which left his arm so damaged that it disbarred him permanently from military service. He had also been educated not at Eton and Oxford but at Marlborough and Cambridge – and had been an open and avowed supporter of the Munich Agreement of 1938. Nor did he like the Beafsteak, Pratt's or the other clubs where Macmillan and others used to exchange gossip. Finally, he spoke – in a voice that was a little too high in pitch – in ways which could best be described as Delphic, and was, on private occasions, often gloriously indiscreet. The Etonians, with their customary snobbery, referred to him as the 'Rabbit'.

Yet Butler had certainly made his political name during the war. He had showed himself to be the equal of anybody – Macmillan included – in intellect and, above all, he had laboured away in the Board of Education from the summer of 1941 onwards and had produced, negotiated and put through Parliament – almost without the rest of the Government taking much notice – what became the 1944 Education Act. There was no denying Butler's achievement. He had, almost single-handedly, overseen a thoroughgoing reform of the English educational system. In fact, apart from the report of Sir William Beveridge, published in December 1942, on Social Insurance, it was the one measure which the Government could point to in 1945 as setting the stage for post-war reconstruction. In opposition after 1945, it was Butler rather than Macmillan – for all Macmillan's insistence on *The Middle Way* – who emerged as the leader of the Conservative left wing. In fact, in the jockeying for position if and when Churchill finally decided to call it a day, Butler was seen as a credible successor. It comes as no surprise to find some who were determined to ensure that the following day would never come – when 'the Rabbit will come into his predestined kingdom'.[12]

Towards the end of 1946 Macmillan decided to escape the dreadfully cold English winter weather of the time and to visit India. The Macmillan publishing house had spawned branches in Calcutta, Bombay and Madras, and it had been many years since any member of the family had visited them. But there was now a particular, and political, reason. The Prime Minister, Clement Attlee, had announced that the question of India's future was one which fell to be decided by the Indians themselves. It was therefore of commercial importance, as well as political interest, for Macmillan to see at first hand which way the Indians might be preparing to jump. Besides, if only as a matter of curiosity, he had never been to India before.

Since Dorothy had no intention or wish to go with him, Macmillan sought out his old Mediterranean travelling partner, John Wyndham, and invited him along. As it turned out, at the time Wyndham was free. He had been posted to Washington after the General Election of 1945 to take a minor role in negotiations for a United States loan to Britain and, those completed, had returned to London – to be offered a further posting to Cairo. Rather than go to Cairo he decided, at the age of twenty-five to retire altogether from the civil service. Since there was no shortage of family money, he was well able to live without a job. Still devoted to 'Master' or, as he had now become, 'Uncle Harold', Wyndham accepted Macmillan's invitation with alacrity. The pair then duly set off, Macmillan armed with, among other books, his copy of the *Confessions* of St Augustine. They first flew to the oil port of Abadan in Iran ('one horrid desert knoll after another[13]), went up to Teheran for a depressing meeting with the Iranian Minister of Labour, returned to Abadan and hitched a ride on an oil tanker bound for Bombay, arriving there on 24 January 1947.

Their week in Bombay was filled mostly with Macmillan's business affairs. The firm's managers there, rather against his expectations, were optimistic about the future for educational publishing after independence and felt that English, rather than Hindi, would remain the first language in schools for some time to come. Furthermore, although the Bombay press had worked itself into a frenzy of anti-British bitterness, this was not reflected in discussions with the Bombay politicians.

The same was true in Delhi. Yet Macmillan had a sense of unease. Staying in the huge and opulent viceregal palace with the Viceroy, Field Marshal Lord Wavell, he noted that 'all power is oozing away and only the shell is left ... the outward symbols of imperial power remain ... at home there are too few servants; here there are really too many'.[14]

In fact, he did not think much of Wavell. Charming and cultivated, to be sure, Wavell was no politician and the leaders of the then dominant Congress Party could twist him around with their sophistries. On the other hand, Macmillan was certainly impressed with Pandit Nehru and with Mohammed Ali Jinnah (the first 'exquisite and even flowery in taste', the second 'thin, almost emaciated, with long bony fingers and a strangely shrunken, skull-like head"[15]). Jinnah sombrely warned him that a united India was no longer a possibility and that civil war was unavoidable. Jinnah's warning was then suddenly and brutally illustrated when Macmillan and Wyndham moved on to Calcutta, where 'the killings were on a scale quite beyond what we were led to believe at home'.[16]

In sum, Macmillan did not like India. He found Indians for the most part snobbish and unsympathetic (and, of course, un-Christian), and he thought the remnants of the British Raj faintly ridiculous. But on their way back through Cairo, he heard the news that Wavell had been removed as Viceroy and replaced by Lord Mountbatten. Moreover, the British Government had expressed its clear intention to hand over India to independence no later than June 1948. For him, this was tantamount to retreat. On his return to London he told a colleague that he regarded 'the Indian situation as the most alarming matter of the moment. He has been in India recently and the conditions were pretty bad – now they are infinitely worse – absolute chaos will result if we go – and what is to become of our own people and their business interests under Indian rule?'[17] In truth there was not much more to say.

Macmillan had escaped a good part of the hard winter but he had missed some important weeks in internal Party politics. The conference of October 1946, gloomy as it still was after the defeat of 1945, had made it clear that some sort of new direction was needed for the Party ever to return to what they regarded as its rightful role – governing the country. The lesson of 1945 was taken to be that the electorate would go to almost any lengths to avoid a return to the economic conditions of the early and mid-1930s – for which it held the Conservatives largely responsible. The strength of feeling at the conference was such that Churchill felt impelled – reluctantly, since his inclination was always to avoid policy commitments in opposition – to appoint a committee to study the whole matter. In order to keep the thing in reasonable order, he also made sure that its membership was politically heavyweight. The Chairman of the committee – to be known as the 'Industrial Policy Committee' – was Rab Butler, in his capacity as head of the Conservative Research Department, and there were to be four other members from the Parliamentary Front Bench – David Maxwell Fyfe, Stanley, Lyttelton and Macmillan himself. Four backbenchers were appointed to complete the membership.

Butler was quite happy to take on the task, but it did not prove easy. Lyttelton, for instance, grumbled that he did not think there needed to be much change at all, while Macmillan, on the other hand, 'insisted on reading out chunks of his book' (*The Middle Way*).[18] Butler's solution to his difficulties was, as was his style, ingenious. He asked each member of the committee to visit and report on the views of Conservative industrialists in a particular area of the country (thus keeping them away from full meetings). Macmillan, naturally, was invited to survey the northeast of England.

That task, and his visit to India, kept Macmillan at a suitable distance from the contentious moments of committee debate. But there is no doubt that his views, even sometimes from a distance, were a major influence on the committee's findings. The document, called – perhaps, in today's language, somewhat portentously – an *Industrial Charter*, was completed and sent in page proof to Churchill in late April 1947. It followed much of the essence of *The Middle Way* – central planning, governmental oversight of the wage-price mechanisms, workers' rights, acceptance of the nationalisation of coal, the railways and the Bank of England and, in Macmillan's words, 'the maintenance of full employment, to sustain and improve the social services, and to continue the strategic control of the economy in the hands of the Government, while preserving wherever possible the tactical function of private enterprise'.[19] But it was not, as some had hoped, a detailed statement of policy.

This in turn led to a problem. Macmillan wrote later that Churchill gave the document his earnest attention. Butler wrote rather differently: 'his ultimate imprimatur was not so much obtained as divined.'[20] Eden launched the document at a rally in Cardiff in mid-May, but the press were in no doubt that the main authors were Butler himself and Macmillan. The problem was that any attempt to push the *Industrial Charter* through the Party Conference the following October as a firm Party commitment rather than as a mere intellectual construct would be extremely difficult without Churchill's wholehearted – and vocal – support. And that was by no means guaranteed.

In the event, Macmillan showed at the conference in Brighton another hitherto unsuspected quality: deft, and democratically ruthless, Party management. He had become president for that year of the National Union of Conservative and Unionist Associations and, in that capacity, he took the chair at the conference – and hence called amendments and speakers. The National Union had put forward for debate, apparently out of caution, a motion from a young Member of Parliament, Peter Thorneycroft, welcoming the document but referring to it as no more than a basis for discussion. Macmillan then chose an amendment tabled by Reginald Maudling, an aspiring Parliamentary candidate and, more important in the circumstances, one of the secretaries to the committee, an amendment which called on the conference to accept the *Industrial Charter* as 'a clear statement of the general principles of Conservative

economic policy'.[21] Maudling presented his amendment as no more than
a matter of drafting. Thorneycroft, in the meantime, had been fixed – and
promptly announced that he would accept the Maudling amendment. As
a result, the substantive motion before the conference incorporated the
Maudling amendment. By the time Butler came to wind up the debate
the conclusion was already determined – the *Industrial Charter* was to
become the firm guide to future Conservative economic policy. In the
vote, there were only three dissenting voices.

When Churchill came to draft his speech for the last day of the
conference he asked his speech writer to put into his speech five lines or
so about the *Industrial Charter.* His speech writer, as it happened, turned
out to be Maudling. The lines were duly drafted but Churchill, when he
read them, slowly and with by then the greatest attention, turned to
Maudling and said, 'But I don't believe a word of this.' Maudling,
however, was up to the occasion. 'But, sir,' he replied, 'this is what the
conference adopted.' Churchill 'took refuge in a discontented grunt.
"Oh well," he said, "leave it in."'[22] That done, on the same evening, after
the conference had approved the motion, Churchill summoned Butler
and his wife to his suite in the Grand Hotel. '"Well, old cock, you have
definitely won through," he said; "I wish now to toast your victory."'
Butler's account goes on: 'Pol Roger was produced and I realised then
what the psalmist meant when he sang "My cup runneth over".'[23] Thus
did the *Industrial Charter,* in bubbles of champagne, become the central
stone of the Conservative acceptance of the Labour agenda. The post-
war consensus, as it came to be known, was born.

The birth, however, was hesitant and, to some extent, difficult.
Although the conference had voted in the way Butler and Macmillan
wanted, the Party activists were far from convinced – and some were
upset at what was perceived, rightly, as a clever piece of political leger-
demain. 'I find', wrote a Parliamentary colleague shortly afterwards, 'that
this pinkish portion of our Party are more prominent but less popular
than they used to be.' But the political realities were recognised – with,
it is true, a note of political cynicism. 'If and when we come back to
power,' he went on, 'it will be time enough to decide how much Govt.
intervention in the conduct of industry is required . . .'[24]

The press response was divided. By far the most hostile gunfire came
from Beaverbrook. In his view the whole thing was 'Socialism'. At first,
his editors were slow to grasp his message – in fact, their broadsides took
some time to develop the firepower which Beaverbrook demanded. All
this, of course, was most welcome to Butler and Macmillan. But Macmillan was certainly not going to let Butler take all the credit. He
managed to make it clear to journalists that he was at least the joint

author of the document and, in his writings, had been the guiding spirit. 'Crossbencher', in one of the Beaverbrook newspapers, wrote as much in what was meant to be a hostile and sarcastic piece. 'This report', his piece ran, 'is a triumph for Mr Harold Macmillan. [He] once wrote a political treatise called *The Middle Way*. This is the second edition.'[25]

Even before the October conference, in fact almost immediately after the publication of the *Industrial Charter* in May, Macmillan had started along another path. In September 1946 Churchill had made a speech at the University of Zurich in which he had appealed for 'a kind of United States of Europe' and, specifically, for Franco-German reconciliation. He was, however, careful to allocate to Britain, along with America and possibly the Soviet Union, the role of 'sponsor' to the enterprise – whatever it might turn out in the end to be.[26] In other words, Britain should encourage but not participate. Following Churchill's speech, on 14 May at the Albert Hall in London, the United Europe Movement was launched to a packed audience and a platform presided over by the Archbishop of Canterbury. Churchill, in full flow, announced that Europe was 'the fairest, most temperate and most fertile area of the globe' but now 'it is a rubble-heap, a charnel-house, a breeding ground of pestilence and hate'. The task, he declared, was one 'of reviving the glories and happiness of Europe and her prosperity'.[27] Churchill, nevertheless, rather to Macmillan's disappointment, was careful to avoid anything which could remotely be called a specific programme.

A committee was then duly formed, to be named the 'United Europe Committee'. Churchill invited Macmillan to serve – and the invitation was immediately accepted. The prime mover, however, was Churchill's son-in-law, Duncan Sandys, but apart from Macmillan the committee also included David Maxwell Fyfe, Lady Violet Bonham Carter from the Liberal Party – and Bob Boothby. Eden, on the other hand, wanted none of it; nor did the Labour Foreign Secretary, Ernest Bevin. Cranborne (now Lord Salisbury) was also sceptical, later calling the thing a 'pantomime' and a 'talking shop for cranks'.[28] Macmillan, for his part, engaged with enthusiasm, partly to please Churchill but partly, too, because he was convinced by the objective. In fact, there was reason for his enthusiasm. The European Recovery Programme – known as Marshall Aid – was announced in June 1947. At the end of October Belgium, the Netherlands and Luxembourg formed a customs union (Benelux), and at the turn of the year negotiations started for a treaty binding Britain, France and the Benelux countries to mutual defence. The move towards European integration seemed to be gathering pace.

The pace quickened. By December 1947 similar committees had been set up in other European countries. After some tortuous negotiation an international committee was established and the whole renamed as the 'European Movement'. It was only a matter of time, and further negotiation, before all the countries involved agreed to send delegations to move towards a closer form of cooperation. The stage was set for a European Congress – to meet in The Hague in May 1948.

There is no doubt that Macmillan had by then come to feel that he had a particular flair for foreign affairs. He had, after all, been almost his own Foreign Secretary when he was in the Mediterranean, and had thoroughly enjoyed it. He had spoken as equals to kings and presidents – let alone the British Prime Minister – and he knew he had done well. But there was another bonus. His domestic life was little short of dismal. He lived during the weeks when the House of Commons was sitting by himself in a bachelor London flat. His meals were in the House of Commons or at the Beafsteak or Pratt's. Weekends were mostly spent at the house at Birch Grove but he and Dorothy lived at opposite ends of the house. Church, of course, was, as always, a consolation, but it takes little imagination to see that journeys away from London, particularly to the Europe he knew and whose history he revered, had special attractions. It was to these attractions that he was to be drawn when The Hague Congress finally assembled. Besides, if he was to be a stranger at home, engagement in Europe only served to thicken further what had already become a redoubtable political – and personal – skin.

12

'This New Opportunity'

'Opposition is hell.'¹ Thus a former Labour Minister in the late 1980s at one of the high points of the Thatcherite tide. Although it seems extreme, the reason for his outburst is easy to explain. In the British political system it is the convention that ministers who are to form the executive arm of government are selected from among members of the legislature, in other words either from the House of Commons or the House of Lords. The result of this convention is that those who make politics their main career almost always look to government office as its fulfilment. The most ambitious, of course, look to the higher reaches of Cabinet and even of No. 10 Downing Street. Consequently, deprivation from governmental power, for those who have known it or aspire to it, causes corresponding, but sometimes surprisingly intense, personal anguish.

To be sure, there are some who are content to be modest backbench members of one or other of the Houses of Parliament, but since the Second World War, certainly in the House of Commons, these seem to have become a rare breed. Macmillan was emphatically not one of them. For him, a political career had become, in the years after the end of the Second World War, almost all-consuming. Publishing took no more than a lowly second place. But in the years of the Labour Government there was for him none of the raw pleasure of power which he had become used to during the war. In the House of Commons there was little opportunity to do other than to debate, and, although he had learnt to do so with confidence and skill, as those years rolled by he quite clearly became progressively more frustrated.

Frustration soon turned into irritation. For example, his attacks on his opponents – and sometimes on his colleagues – became more impatient as well as more personal and waspish. In turn, as often happens, his verbal assaults provoked hostility from his targets. True, the House of Commons has never been shy of personal attacks (Churchill himself was a master of the art), but those who engage in them to excess always risk Parliamentary unpopularity. This turned out to be true for Macmillan. Many Labour members, victims of his taunts, started seriously to dislike him. Some even took to playing some unpleasant (and schoolboy) pranks. When, on one occasion for instance, he went to the Smoking Room he was met by a group chanting 'Good Night, Tories!'[2] He braved it out, found himself a chair and sat down. Almost immediately he got up to get himself a drink only to find when he returned that a Labour member had occupied his chair. Oddly enough, what made the prank more telling was that the group was led by a Labour Old Etonian whom Macmillan thought to be something of a fellow spirit, Hugh Dalton.

Frustration – and, equally, irritation – also transferred itself to his family. Things were not going well. The big house at Birch Grove had been let in 1945 to a boys' preparatory school, and the family had transferred from Pooks Cottage to Gosses, another house on the estate. Dorothy was by then in rumbustious command. 'Lady Dorothy's furies were dramatic,' it was said, 'though seldom directed at Harold himself. In her determination to do what pleased her and do little that displeased her, she allowed her liking and disliking of people too free a rein, especially within her own family.'[3] Boothby was writing to her almost every day, and when Macmillan was in residence she 'was always the first down to breakfast to snatch up the letter, lest Harold should see it'. When Macmillan was away, she went from time to time to London to stay in Boothby's flat and when he was away for more than a few days there were malicious spirits who said that the pair – unlikely as it seems given the circumstances of the day – had taken off together to Italy.

Moreover, his children were neither happy nor settled. By the end of the 1940s Maurice was showing all the signs of serious alcoholism. His wife, Katharine – or 'Katie', as Macmillan affectionately called her – had fallen out with Dorothy and, since she was living in a cottage on the Birch Grove estate, was subjected by her mother-in-law to frequent harassment and family rows. Carol, who had been such a problem during the years of war (Macmillan had even suggested that she should go to Algiers in the hope that 'she could marry John [Wyndham] – which would be very agreeable, for he already treats me like a father'[4]), although married to a successful insurance broker, Julian Faber, was still reported as having her mother's 'capacity for irritable boredom'.[5] Catherine showed all the signs of Macmillan's depressions until she married Leo Amery's son Julian in 1950. Almost worst of all, Sarah, although Macmillan had been particularly affectionate towards her, was living on the edge of breakdown. She was convinced – not least because she was constantly told so – that she was Boothby's daughter. On one occasion, for instance, when she was dancing with a clumsy young man who apologised for treading on her toes and, in his blushes, apologising the more earnestly given her father's political status, 'she exclaimed with furious misery:

"You're dancing with the most famous bastard in England. Everyone knows I'm Bob Boothby's daughter."[6]

Under all those circumstances, it is hardly surprising that Macmillan looked for something which would bring a measure of cheer to what was in danger of becoming a badly depressing life. The House of Commons, after all, had not much to offer, Gosses not altogether welcoming, his wife unfaithful, his family irritating, the seemingly endless dinner circuit of the Beefsteak, Pratt's, Turf and Carlton boring and his flat lonely and dismal. (In fact, one day Katharine found, when paying him a visit, that the lampshades had obviously not been dusted. She wrote 'dust me' on one with her finger – only to find, two weeks later, the words still there and the lampshades undusted.) It was only the weekends shooting which, during the season, were undiluted pleasure.

As it happened, at that point he had another piece of good fortune. The United Europe Committee and its continental sisters, together known as the European Movement, decided to hold a grand congress of their supporters in order to move their project forward. It was to be held, it was announced, in The Hague at the beginning of May 1948. Churchill was to be the congress's president and the great and (more or less) good from throughout Western Europe who supported the idea of a United Europe were to be invited. Several former Prime Ministers, more than twenty-five former Foreign Ministers, bishops, industrialists, trade unionists, scientists, poets, economists were to be there, together with representatives of all political parties except, it was carefully pointed out, communists. Macmillan was duly invited by Churchill to be a member of the Conservative delegation – and immediately accepted.

Along with more than seven hundred delegates from all non-communist Europe, Macmillan arrived in The Hague on 7 May 1948. In among the apparently prosperous delegates (almost all male, of course, in suitably dark suit and tie) the British immediately found themselves at a severe disadvantage. They had only been allowed the twenty-five pounds permitted to those taking holidays abroad, and were forced to take most of their meals on food tickets provided by their European friends. In addition, they noted that the shops, unlike those in Britain at the time, were well stocked and well frequented. 'Such', Macmillan commented sourly, 'are the fruits of victory.'[7]

The first plenary session of 'The Congress of Europe', as it wished to be known, was opened with much self-congratulation in the medieval (but suitably restored) Knights' Hall of the Netherlands Parliament Buildings. Churchill made the first major speech (after first gallantly kissing the hand of Princess Juliana of the Netherlands), outlining what he saw as the purpose of the gathering. In fact, he went very much further than he had in Zurich eighteen months earlier. 'Mutual aid in the economic field and joint military defence', he proclaimed, 'must inevitably be accompanied step by step with a parallel policy of closer political unity.' 'It is said with truth', he went on, 'that this involves some sacrifice or merger of national sovereignty. But it is also possible and not less agreeable to regard it as the gradual assumption by all the nations concerned of that larger sovereignty which can alone protect their diverse and distinct customs and characteristics ...'[8] In other words, he was coming down on the side of 'federalism' rather than 'confederalism' in the argument which raged during the week (and which, of course, has been raging ever since). Churchill's view was then reflected in the text of the Political Resolution, passed unanimously on the final day: 'The Congress recognises that it is the urgent duty of the nations of Europe to create an economic and political union in order to assure security and social progress.'[9] Although he did not himself speak, there can be no doubt that Macmillan, whatever he may have later said, was at that moment without a doubt a fervent supporter of its federalist tone.

After that, it was time for him to go home – perhaps reluctantly, since he had enjoyed himself in The Hague. On the way home, however, there was a nearly fatal accident. He, along with five other delegates (including Peter Thorneycroft and two Liberals, one of whom was Lady Violet Bonham Carter), was given a lift in a small aircraft hired for the purpose. They took off in a storm, but they emerged safely from that and all was well until they were starting the landing run into Croydon airport. The pilot then told his passengers that he was unable to lower the undercarriage. However unpleasant their surprise at the news, they remained comfortingly calm while the aircraft circled around to use up fuel. Macmillan, looking out of a window, nervously saw the fire engines and ambulances parading on the airfield ('all this nostalgically recalled to me my Mediterranean days') and prepared for the worst. Fortunately, the pilot managed to land without disaster and they all jumped out safely – Thorneycroft and Macmillan crying out 'Women and Liberals first!' 'If the worst came to the worst,' Macmillan noted, 'they would provide a convenient cushion.'[10] (In this near catastrophe, it is worth noting that neither his wartime courage nor his post-war wit had deserted him.)

The Hague Congress had produced two important results: a general agreement for a European Assembly and a programme for what eventually became the European Convention of Human Rights. For the second, the European Movement set up an International Judicial Section, under the chairmanship of the French jurist Pierre-Henri Teitgen – with Maxwell Fyfe as the British member. For the first, it was left to the governments of Britain, France and the Benelux countries to work out some sort of arrangement for an Assembly. Inevitably, there were delays (and much reluctance from the British Foreign Secretary, Ernest Bevin), and it was not until January 1949 that the five governments reached agreement – and not until May that a constituent conference could be called in London to agree the final text of a Statute.

Macmillan, in the meantime, had, in the autumn of 1948, been invited to lecture both in Germany and in Italy where, according to his memoirs, he found 'growing enthusiasm for the European idea'.[11] Where he went – and the scope of his lectures – is left mysteriously unclear, but it is certainly true that the Congress of Europe had caught the imagination of young people in continental Europe. In fact, many hundreds had voluntarily turned up in The Hague – and some at least were vociferously disappointed that the results had been in their view so meagre. Their enthusiasm, of course, was directed at a new, federal European construct. At the time, Macmillan, full of encouragement as he was for their ideas (whatever his later doubts), was certainly regarded by them as something of a hero.

When back in London, however, he quickly realised that a large majority of the Conservative Party, let alone the Labour Government, was in no mood for federalism. The Government's view, of course, might be what it might be, but it was the view of his own Party which made him pause. If he was to pursue his ambitions within the Conservative Party, there had – to put it as gently as possible – to be from time to time some convenient adjustment to his opinions depending on his audience. His view on federalism was consequently delicately modified, so much so, in fact, that he was unblushing in supporting the Statute that finally emerged. In fact, it was wholly inter-governmental in nature. There was no trace of federalism. The 'Council of Europe', as it was to be named, was to be made up of a decision-making body, a Committee of Foreign Ministers (on which the British insisted on a veto of any measure which they found not to their taste), and a consultative body, an Assembly of Parliamentarians from the constituent countries (the original five plus Italy, Ireland, Norway, Denmark and Sweden – Greece and Turkey were to come in later).

There was then the question of who should be appointed to the Assembly. On the formula as agreed, the United Kingdom was allotted eighteen members. As might be imagined, there was a good deal of agitation about who would be appointed by the United Kingdom to serve in the Assembly. These were, after all, plum political jobs – with the added enticement of unlimited foreign travel. In the end, it was duly agreed that eleven of those would be Labour, six Conservative and one Liberal. As a matter of course, the Conservative group was led by Churchill, with Macmillan as his unofficial deputy. Along with them were Maxwell Fyfe, Ronald Ross (representing Northern Ireland), David Eccles and, as seemed almost inevitable in Macmillan's life, Bob Boothby.

Macmillan always much enjoyed the meetings of the Council of Europe Assembly. Even before the first meeting in August 1949 he had praised the Congress of Europe – perhaps too extravagantly – as 'a landmark to future historians'. 'It is more important, perhaps,' he had gone on to say, 'than any other event in the second half of this century',[12] and he later described the first Council meeting as 'a thrilling moment'.[13] More prosaically, it allowed him show off the acquaintance he had made during the war of a number of European politicians. On top of that, for a few weeks of the year he could escape the austerity of post-war Britain for the relative luxury of Strasbourg.

At the time he was not at all clear why Strasbourg had been chosen as the seat of the Council. It had only a small airfield and was at least six hours' train journey from Paris. On the other hand he grew to see its advantages. Since there was not much to do apart from the work of the Council, members of the Assembly came to know each other very much better than they would have if the Council seat had been in a capital city such as Paris or London. There were two good hotels where most of the British members would stay (Churchill, of course, had his own villa) and the food, as always in Alsace, was both abundant and excellent. So abundant was it, in fact, that British stomachs, used to the exiguous rations of home, were at first unable to cope. 'Until we began to get into practice,' Macmillan wrote to Dorothy, 'one portion of meat was enough for three of us.'[14] It was more than enough, indeed, for his daughter Catherine, who had been persuaded to accompany him to the first meeting (in the absence, of course, of Dorothy). In fact, she made something of a stir. 'One of my Italian friends', Macmillan later wrote to Dorothy, 'congratulated me on my speech, saying "you are a fortunate man. You have made the best speech of the debate, and you have the prettiest daughter – like an angel."'[15]

The first meeting on 10 August 1949 was certainly exciting. Herbert Morrison, then Leader of the House of Commons (and leader of the Labour delegation to the Assembly), made an attempt to dragoon all British members into a disciplined group, an attempt which first Macmillan and then Churchill bluntly rejected. Then, after the former Belgian Foreign Minister, Paul-Henri Spaak, had been unanimously elected President, Morrison did his best to get the genial Government Chief Whip, William Whitely, elected as one of the four Vice-Presidents ('as Caligula made his horse Consul,' Macmillan wrote to Dorothy[16]).

That manoeuvre failed as well, thanks to Churchill's furious intervention in favour of Whitely's opponent and the rumour, assiduously spread by Macmillan, that Whitely had never before crossed the Channel.

Leaving aside the electoral shenanigans, the main subject for debate in the Assembly was the fiercely aggressive nature of the Soviet Union, which had been trying during the previous months to strangle Berlin by blockade. There were even proposals for a political treaty to work along-side the defence treaty which had formed the Western European Union. Yet Churchill produced something of a sensation when, in the debate on the political future of Europe he ignored everything else and made the main theme of his speech the necessity of bringing the then fledgling Federal Republic of West Germany into the Council of Europe. 'In a dramatic outburst,' Macmillan later recorded, 'looking around the hall, he demanded almost fiercely "Where are the Germans?" He pressed for an immediate invitation to the West German Government to join our ranks.'[17] For many of his listeners, of course, whose countries had been brutally occupied by the Germans only a few years before, the idea was shocking. In fact, if anybody other than Churchill had suggested such a thing he would have been shouted down. As it was, having launched his diplomatic grenade, Churchill left Strasbourg the next day. It was only on leaving that he put Macmillan in charge of the Conservative group – with the strict instruction to work for an invitation to West Germany to join the Council as soon as possible. It was not a task which, initially, Macmillan much enjoyed.

But it was not just a matter of the past, gruesome though that had been. Many were worried about the possible resurgence of a revanchist Germany. They had, after all, seen it all before. The new West German Chancellor, Konrad Adenauer, had committed his country to work with the United States and their Western European allies but he was known to be determined to restore the Federal Republic to what he regarded as its proper place in the international community. That in itself was enough to make some of his neighbours nervous.

As it happened, there were other plans in the diplomatic air. Jean Monnet, Macmillan's old acquaintance from Tipasa, had become, at de Gaulle's invitation, head of the Commissariat au Plan, the French plan-ning organisation. As such, he seemed to be able to roam far and wide outside the particular brief for which he was responsible. Ever interested in international affairs, he had noted the debate in December 1949 in the economic committee of the Assembly of the Council of Europe – at the request of the French Foreign Minister, Robert Schuman – which resulted in a proposal for intra-European organisations for coal, iron and steel, and in due course for electricity and transport. Since the Assembly was no more than consultative, nothing much came of the proposal. But it did sit comfortably with the ideas which had been in Monnet's head for some time. In fact, when he had met Macmillan even as early as July 1944 he had stated firmly that 'the whole future of Europe depends upon the solution of the German problem and the effective reduction, not merely for the first few years when peace is assured but over a long period, of the German war potential'.[18] He therefore set about persuading Schuman of the merits of a plan to do just that.

In the meantime, Macmillan's campaign to secure for West Germany membership of the Council of Europe was coming to fruition. The matter had been debated in the Assembly on 5 September 1949. In preparation for the debate, Macmillan had decided that it was time for another of his (by then carefully crafted) stage performances. 'I had changed from my old flannel suit into a black suit and stiff white collar,' he later wrote, '(I have a feeling that when one is to speak one should be properly dressed – especially if one is to make a speech of dramatic importance). The perspiration was dripping from me at every pore – but fortunately my speech was short.'[19] It may have been short but it was certainly dramatic. In the middle of it he produced a Minute which Churchill had sent to Eden in October 1942. 'Hard as it is to say now,' Macmillan's voice sank to a tone of reverence as he read it, 'I trust that the European family may act unitedly as one under a Council of Europe. I look forward to a United States of Europe in which the barriers between the nations will be greatly minimised and unrestricted travel will be possible. I hope to see a Council consisting of perhaps ten units, including the former Great Powers . . .' At that point Macmillan paused for effect. In fact, he was about to leave out the next passage, which reads in the original '. . . with several confederations – Scandinavian, Danubian, Balkan, etc – which would possess an international police and be charged with keeping Prussia disarmed'.[20]

It was a supremely clever trick. Churchill, of course, had only suggested that the 'United States of Europe' should be a series of 'confederations' and that 'Prussia' (i.e. Germany) should be kept permanently disarmed. The bit that Macmillan read out seemed clearly to imply that Churchill had suggested something approaching a federal Europe and that 'Europe' should include 'the former Great Powers' – of which Germany, of course, had been one. In fact, the trick was so clever (some would say it verged on the dishonest) that his listeners believed that they were indeed hearing Churchill's inspiring wartime voice – not realising that the voice had been edited, very carefully, by Macmillan. All in all, the Assembly was so impressed that it passed without demur resolutions allowing the creation of a standing committee of the Assembly to deal on its behalf with the Committee of Ministers to invite West Germany to membership. This was done, although it was not until the following spring that a formal invitation was issued to the Federal Republic.

By late 1949, Macmillan's attention, like that of all British politicians, was turning to the prospect of a General Election due in the next few months. Nothing excites British politicians more than the prospect of a General Election. Attlee announced that there would be no Election before Christmas – which, of course, led to a general belief that it would come soon after that. So it turned out, and Parliament was dissolved on 3 February 1950. The race began.

Macmillan was bullish about the result of the race. His own constituency had been reduced in size on the agreed formula (it was now to be known only as Bromley) but his majority was secure. This left him free, since Dorothy was, as always, doing her dutiful work on his behalf, to join the national Conservative campaign. Speaking to a meeting of candidates, agents and Party officers at Newcastle on 28 January, just before the dissolution but in the general knowledge that the Election was imminent, he was reported by one of his colleagues as being 'somewhat cocksure, I thought ... the idea being that our manifesto is a winner'. There was then some doubt. 'I wonder,' the colleague went on. 'My fear is that the working man won't change his attitude until he is in want – and that is not yet.'[21]

In the event, the campaign turned out to be almost wholly devoid of interest. The electorate was clearly polarised – Labour voters fearing a return to what they perceived as the dreaded 1930s, Conservative voters eager to throw out the 'Socialists' who they believed were diabolically responsible for the continuing austerity (the pound sterling had only recently been devalued). Neither group was listening to the other's arguments. But as the campaign wore on, it became clear, not least from the Gallup poll, that the result would be too close to call. In the end, excitement took hold on the night of polling day, 23 February, and lasted through the following day as the results came in. Finally, it emerged that in the new House of Commons Labour would have 315 seats, the Conservatives 298, the Liberals 9 and the Irish Nationalists 2. In the evening of 24 February Churchill finally conceded defeat. 'I listened to Mr Churchill's brave but broken voice with a pity so deep I began to cry bitterly,' mourned one unsuccessful Conservative.[22] Yet it immediately became clear that with an overall majority of only six the Labour Government could not last for a full term and that another General Election could not be long delayed. Macmillan himself, as he had expected, won Bromley easily with a majority of 10,688.

But he was still out of office. Deflated by the outcome, he turned yet again to the Council of Europe. As it turned out, there was much to do. Monnet's plans were moving ahead at speed. On 11 May there was a meeting in London between Bevin, Schuman and Dean Acheson, the United States Secretary of State, called to discuss a joint response to continued Soviet hostility and to reinforce their determination over Berlin. The meeting, however, was dominated by Monnet's plans for pooling the coal and steel industries of France and Germany under a supranational high authority. Schuman had announced these as French Government proposals only two days earlier. Bevin was furious, accusing Schuman and Acheson of plotting together behind Britain's back in Germany's favour. Attlee, however, was more cautious and gave Schuman's initiative at least a guarded welcome. On 15 May Monnet and his close colleague Étienne Hirsch arrived in London to explain the plan in greater detail to Sir Stafford Cripps, the British Chancellor of the Exchequer, and Treasury officials. But four days of explanation failed to convince the sceptics. Macmillan, in his turn, found the Cripps response shocking. In a speech in Bromley on 17 May, he said that he found the Schuman proposals 'an act of high courage and of imaginative statesmanship ... I hope that British statesmanship will at least be equal to this new responsibility and this new opportunity.'[23] This was followed up by letters to the press (attracting, of course, an attack from Beaverbrook in response).

On 23 May, however, the negotiating climate changed again. In what was only their first meeting, Monnet and Adenauer agreed in one swoop all the main points of the Schuman Plan. At first, Adenauer was 'not self-assured ... Clearly he could not believe that we were really proposing full equality; and his attitude was still marked by long years of hard negotiation and wounded pride.' But when they finished, Adenauer 'rose to his feet. "Monsieur Monnet," he said, "I regard the implementation of the French proposals as my most important task. If I succeed, I believe my life will not have been wasted."'[24]

The German enthusiasm was certainly not replicated in London. On 25 May the British Government responded to the French that they would be prepared to enter into negotiations but, as a later message made clear, without any commitment. In other words, it was refusal. This was confirmed by Attlee in a statement to the House of Commons on 13 June. Macmillan, speaking again in Bromley, said that 'this has been a black week for Britain ... the political importance of the Schuman Plan far outweighs its economic or industrial aspects. Its purpose is the unity of France and Germany. With British participation, this will secure peace ... without British participation Franco-German unity may be a source not of security but of danger.'[25]

Macmillan then wrote to Churchill, pleading with him to raise the matter in the House of Commons. His argument was that the Labour Government's dilatoriness offered the Conservatives an opportunity which could not be missed. 'Without you', he wrote, 'there would be no Council of Europe, no Committee of Ministers, no Consultative Assembly, no Strasbourg. This is the first and supreme test. You cannot let down all Europe … We must support the principles of the Schuman Plan … to secure the peace of Europe … This is a crisis for Europe. It is also a crisis for you and the Party …'[26] Churchill responded to Macmillan's (perhaps rather overblown) rhetoric – and was rhetorical in his turn in the debate which took place on 26 and 27 June. 'On the question of sovereignty', Macmillan recorded, 'he repeated Eden's [earlier] words. He was prepared without any hesitation to consider, and if convinced to accept, the abrogation of national sovereignty involved, provided the conditions and the safeguards were satisfactory.'[27] In a final flourish he proclaimed that 'the Conservative and Liberal Parties declare that national sovereignty is not inviolable and that it may be resolutely diminished for the sake of all the men in all the lands finding their way home together'.[28]

Churchill's speech, for all its final flourish, was overshadowed by a statement by Attlee, taken immediately afterwards, announcing, in the soberest of moods, that the armies of North Korea had invaded the Republic of South Korea and that the Security Council of the United Nations had recommended all UN member states to give whatever assistance was necessary to resist the attack. It was against this background that Attlee's reply to Churchill on the Schuman Plan was brief and that the Government won the subsequent Division by a comfortable majority.

Macmillan nevertheless persisted. But, in truth, he was now starting to hedge his bets. For all his encouragement to Churchill to 'support the principles of the Schuman Plan' it had become plain to him that although the bulk of the Conservative Party would follow Churchill in whatever he said or did, the same would not be true of him. Together with Eccles, therefore, he started work on a plan which would find favour with the Party and which he could in due course present to the Council of Europe.

The starting point was the rejection of the supranational element in the Schuman Plan. The Macmillan–Eccles plan, as it came to be known, made the pooling of the coal and steel industries subordinate to decisions by the Committee of Ministers in the Council of Europe – thus preserving the national veto – and allowed any country involved to withdraw at twelve months' notice – or be expelled. In explaining this new approach to a journalist, Macmillan was loftily critical of Monnet himself. He was, of course, an old acquaintance and 'was a delightful person but with a foible for constructing enormous constitutional blueprints that had hardly any practical application'.[29] It was Macmillan at his worst: patronising, as he had been in North Africa, and, as it happened, mistaken (Monnet's 'constitutional blueprint' is still going strong after over half a century). But he was almost even more patronising when he spoke in August 1950 to the Assembly of the Council of Europe in presenting the Macmillan–Eccles plan. 'The continental tradition', he declared, 'likes to reason from the *a priori* from the top downwards, from the general principle to the practical application ... The Anglo-Saxons like to argue *a posteriori* from the bottom upwards, from practical experience.' But then he struck a different note – this time patronising the English. 'Of course, the Scottish people, who are the intellectuals of Britain, know there is nothing to be frightened of: one should accept everything *en principe*, get around the table, and start the talks.'[30] This, as was noted, contradicted the previous passage in his speech. At the end of it, nobody quite knew what he was saying.

At the end of the debate, the Assembly agreed to adopt the Macmillan–Eccles plan. But the decision was irrelevant, first, because France, Germany, Italy and the Benelux countries had already started their discussions to flesh out the Schuman Plan into a treaty to form the European Coal and Steel Community (ECSC), and, secondly, because the Korean news had underlined the urgency of resistance to communism – and, consequently, the creation of a European Army. Churchill himself, on 11 August, proposed it. 'We should now send a message of confidence and courage', he said, 'from the House of Europe to the whole world. Not only should we re-affirm, as we have been asked to do, our allegiance to the United Nations, but we should make a gesture of practical and constructive guidance by declaring ourselves in favour of the immediate creation of a European army under a unified command, and in which we should bear a worthy and honourable part.'[31] Macmillan himself was much more cautious. He noted that Churchill had no clear or well-defined plan. 'He was an old man trying to give a new lead to the world he had helped to save.'[32] Moreover, the Conservative Party, much as Churchill was held in affection and admiration, would not easily go along with the idea of a European Army.

But none of that mattered very much in the end. The Council of Europe was becoming little more than the 'talking shop' that Salisbury had predicted. The true debates had moved elsewhere – to Paris where René Pleven produced his proposal for a European Army in October 1950, to Brussels where the six candidate countries of what was to become the European Coal and Steel Community were thrashing out the details of their treaty and to London where the Korean War was weighing ever more heavily on the political debate.

The autumn of 1950 dragged on. It was cold and wet. Eddie Devonshire's death in late November was duly recorded. 'A very melancholy day. Dorothy, Maurice and I went to Chatsworth ... As the coffin was lowered into the grave, the sun was setting behind the hill. I fear the sun has gone down on Chatsworth for a long time – perhaps for ever.'[33] Christmas was spent at Gosses with his family in almost continuous snow and ice – Macmillan staying in bed a good deal of the time and reading, yet again, the first three volumes of Edward Gibbon's *Decline and Fall of the Roman Empire.* The only light note was the theft on Christmas Day of the Stone of Scone from Westminster Abbey. 'What a strange and delightful interlude', he wrote, 'in the great world tragedy – a sort of Scottish harlequinade.'[34]

By the spring of 1951 it had become clear that the Labour Government was in terminal difficulties. The original intention of the Conservatives not to try to force a second General Election had worn thin and there was a series of late-night sittings – and even all-night sittings – designed deliberately to harry the Government to destruction. Abroad, the Chinese spring offensive in Korea threatened to overrun South Korea again – there was talk of using the atom bomb against the North Koreans and their Chinese allies – and in Iran the new Prime Minister, Mohammed Mossadeq, was threatening to nationalise the Iranian assets of the Anglo-Iranian Oil Company. It is little wonder that in this succession of midnight votes and international crises Ministers' health suffered. Attlee was taken into hospital with duodenal ulcers, Bevin, who had been ill for some time, died in mid-April (to be succeeded as Foreign Secretary by Morrison – 'this dirty little cockney guttersnipe', Macmillan called him[35]) and Cripps had been forced to resign as Chancellor, to die the following year. On top of all that, on 23 April Bevan, along with his junior Ministers Harold Wilson and John Freeman, resigned over the imposition of charges on false teeth and spectacles. In short, the Government gave every appearance of breaking up.

All this, of course, was cheering to Macmillan. He was now convinced that it was only a matter of time before the Conservatives were returned to office. He was also cheered by the sale of shares in Macmillan's American company – some £1.2 million pounds arrived in the parent company's account. There was a trip to Sweden in March, which he enjoyed, and, for the first time, Dorothy – with Catherine – came to stay during the May meeting of the Council of Europe in Strasbourg (they had driven across France – breaking the handbrake and puncturing a tyre in the process). Moreover, he and Dorothy were planning a summer holiday and, best of all, the main house at Birch Grove was now empty and ready for the furniture which had been in store – and subjected to assaults from moths – since the beginning of the war.

By early September the Conservatives were leading in the Gallup poll, the Macmillans were on their holiday in Scotland, walking across the hills of Arran from Lochranza to the Cock of Arran to look at the remains of a farmhouse, then back to see the churchyard at Lochranza where Macmillan's forebears had been buried, then back to the mainland and driving to the northernmost tip of Scotland. All in all, it was a happy time, only marred by Dorothy dropping him off at Inverness to take a train back to London and 'continu[ing] visits in Scotland for another week ...'[36] (Bob Boothby, of course, lived not far away.)

It came as something of a surprise when, on 19 September, Attlee announced the dissolution of Parliament for 5 October, with polling day in the General Election set for 25 October. Other Ministers, and most Conservatives, expected him to soldier on. The timing was the more curious in that the Egyptian Government denounced the treaties with Britain which had allowed the stationing of British troops in the Canal Zone and dual control of the Sudan. At the same time, Korea was still in danger and on 4 October Mossadeq ordered all British employees of the Anglo-Iranian Oil Company to leave Iran. Finally, at the end of September, the Chancellor of the Exchequer, Hugh Gaitskell, had announced a startling fall in the United Kingdom foreign exchange reserves. It certainly was an odd moment to call a General Election. But there it was. Another race had begun.

The campaign which followed was destructively bad-tempered. Apart from the customary scare stories about how Labour would nationalise everything and complete the move to a totalitarian communist state, or how the Conservatives would cut social security and leave old people to die in penury, the main attack on the Conservatives, and on Churchill himself, was launched by the *Daily Mirror*. By the end of the campaign the newspaper had become little short of hysterical. On 23 and 24 October it screamed 'Whose Finger on the Trigger?' and asserted with confidence that Churchill was aching to take the country back into war.[37] Churchill was so angered by these attacks that he (unwisely) sued the *Mirror* for libel.

Macmillan, in his analysis of the result, thought that the *Mirror* campaign had heavily influenced the Election. That may be so, although politicians always think that the media have a determining influence on Election results (as, for that matter, do those who work in the media). Most analysis, other than Macmillan's, shows that the truth was rather different. In October 1951 the electorate was as polarised as it was in

February 1950. In the event, the Conservatives in 1951 scored 48.0 per cent (as against 43.5 per cent in 1950), and Labour scored 48.8 per cent (as against 46.1 per cent in 1950). The substantive change was that the Liberal Party, having fielded 475 candidates in 1950, had virtually run out of money and only fielded 109 candidates in 1951. The result was that the former Liberal vote was split between the two main parties. In the event, the split turned out (nationally) to be almost two to one in favour of the Conservatives, with a slight tendency to favour Conservatives in marginal constituencies – although there was no north/south variant, as Macmillan claimed.

The upshot was that although overall the Labour Party won a greater share of the popular vote, the Conservatives won a clear – if small – majority of seats in the House of Commons. The Liberal vote in vital constituencies had made the difference. In other words, it can reasonably be said, as did many Labour supporters at the time, that the Conservatives only won the 1951 Election because the Liberal Party had run out of money.

None of that was of particular concern to Macmillan (although he did spend a good deal of effort in his memoirs analysing the result). What mattered to him personally was that his majority in Bromley went from 10,688 to 12,125. Moreover, and much more important, it was clear that the 'hell' of Opposition had come to what he thought would be its predestined end – and, as it happened, it would be not quite for eternity but for a very long time. In other words, the Tories were back in the business which they believed belonged to them – and to them only.

13

'Shall I Ever Be Foreign Secretary?'

Throughout the day of Saturday 27 October 1951 Macmillan, like all aspiring ministers immediately after General Elections, sat by his telephone waiting for a summons to Churchill's house in Hyde Park Gate where Cabinet appointments were being settled. Attlee had driven to Buckingham Palace as soon as it had become clear that Labour had lost the Election, and Churchill had in turn kissed hands in the early evening of Friday as the new Prime Minister. But, as it turned out, Macmillan waited in vain. The first news he heard was on the radio at six o'clock on the Saturday evening. Apart from the Prime Minister himself, it was reported, nine Cabinet Ministers had been appointed – Eden as Foreign Secretary, Lord Woolton as Lord President, Salisbury as Leader of the House of Lords, Maxwell Fyfe as Home Secretary, Monckton as Minister of Labour, Lord Ismay as Dominions Secretary, Butler as Chancellor of the Exchequer, Lyttelton as Colonial Secretary and Lord Leathers as Minister for Co-ordination of Transport, Fuel and Power. The three Lords, Woolton, Salisbury and Leathers, were said to be 'Overlords' to supervise Government policy. That was all. Before anybody could react, Churchill had decided that a good day's work had been done and had gone off for the weekend to Chartwell.

Macmillan was both surprised and angry. He was on the telephone immediately to his closest friend and ally, Harry Crookshank, who made matters worse by saying that he thought that Churchill might have decided on a much smaller Cabinet and that the list was final. There was nothing more on the nine o'clock news, and a further conversation with Woolton shed no more light; so Macmillan sat down and finished the book he was reading at the time – Walter Scott's *Waverley* ('What a grand story, and what a noble story! ...'). If that was to be the end of his career, so be it.

The following morning the summons came. He was required to present himself at Chartwell on the Sunday afternoon. Dorothy drove him over from Birch Grove and, on arrival punctually at three o'clock, was immediately invited by Mrs Churchill to a long walk in the Chartwell garden. Macmillan was left to go in to see Churchill – as always smoking yet another of his long cigars. Much to his surprise – and consternation – Churchill asked him to take charge of a new Ministry of Housing and Local Government, with a seat in the Cabinet – albeit at a junior level. Macmillan replied that he had hoped to be Minister of Defence. But Churchill was firm; he was keeping that job for himself. (He had, in fact, asked Lord Portal, former Chief of the Air Staff, to take the job, but Portal had turned it down. Churchill had then decided on Field Marshal Alexander, but it would take four months before he could be disengaged from the Governor-Generalship of Canada.) Macmillan then asked what the new Ministry, apparently to be named the Ministry of Housing and Local Government, was meant to do. Churchill cheerily admitted that he had little idea, and then called in Sir Edward Bridges, the Head of the Civil Service and Sir Norman Brook, the Secretary to the Cabinet (and a supply of whisky). It soon appeared that nothing had been decided except that the new Ministry would take on about half the old Ministry of Health and a slice of Town and Country Planning. It was all, to Macmillan's ordered mind, very confusing.

Just before Macmillan went out to start talks in earnest with the civil servants, Churchill asked him whom he would like as a junior Minister. After a few names had been tossed around, they settled on their fellow MP, the forty-five-year-old Ernest Marples. Marples, in fact, was almost a character opposite to Macmillan. He was bumptious and talkative (the grandson, as it happened, of a head gardener at Chatsworth), had educated himself, sold newspapers for a living and had worked for a time as a bookie's 'dodger' before starting his own engineering company. At the outset of the Second World War he had volunteered, joined the Army as a private, had been promoted up to sergeant major but never to a commission as an officer. After the war he had been elected to Parliament, had started up the firm of builders Marples-Ridgeway, and had seen it grow in no more than two or three years into a major construction company. Finally, he had astonished his Parliamentary colleagues by his taste in clothes – notably his liking for electric blue suits and orange-coloured shoes. But he had energy, and he knew how to run a company. In short, he was the ideal ally for the bookish – and occasionally languid – Macmillan. (In fact, he was more than just an ideal ally. At least one civil servant of the day thought that Macmillan owed much of his success to Marples – who rolled up his colourful sleeves and actually got the work done.)

Apart from the daunting administrative problem of carving out a new department from two other departments and fitting it into the old Local Government Board building on the corner of Parliament Square, there was the problem of the housing target. At the Conservative Conference of 1950 – which Macmillan had not bothered to go to – a fit of enthusiasm had propelled into Conservative policy a target to build 300,000 houses a year. Nobody, of course, had any idea how it could be done. By the 1951 General Election, however, the target had turned into a pledge – and much was made of it in the campaign. Macmillan and Marples were thus landed with a promise which most believed impossible to meet, a new department and, to cap it all, a new Permanent Secretary, Sir Thomas Sheepshanks, whom neither of them thought up to the job.

Churchill had, in truth, been very cunning. Macmillan thought that his support of Churchill over the years and his ability to make witty conversation had won undying support – and that a senior position in any Churchill administration was more or less guaranteed. But it was not as easy as that. Churchill, in fact, had never much taken to Macmillan as a person. He thought him pompous, and there were times when he thought him untrustworthy. Furthermore, Mrs Churchill, whose opinion could never be disregarded, did not like him at all. She thought him too obsequious when it served his purpose and too fond of lecturing those he knew to be less intelligent than himself. Nevertheless, Churchill valued Macmillan's abilities. He therefore set him a test. If he succeeded, it would make his career. It was, as Churchill was quick to remind him, up to him.

Given this doubtful hand to play, Macmillan quickly set about his business. He was quite aware of the pitfalls. As a Minister in a department whose task was to spend money he would have to persuade the Treasury of his case and, in particular, the Chancellor, Rab Butler. He would also have to persuade his own colleagues that the only way to meet the promise given to the electorate was to engage in a sustained programme of local authority housing.

The first matter, he knew, would have to be dealt with directly between him and Butler in Cabinet, and even as early as the following Thursday there was an exchange between the two. Butler raised the whole matter of what he claimed was a disastrous economic inheritance. Public expenditure, including housing, must be cut. Macmillan, obviously concerned not to have an open row, nevertheless protested that the housing pledge could only be met with Treasury cooperation. The message was simple. Butler would be responsible if financial constraints meant that the commitment was not met – and, it went without saying, for the consequent inevitable electoral damage.

The second matter would have to be dealt with with greater subtlety. Macmillan and Marples had quickly decided that the only way to achieve the housing target was by subsidising local authorities to build for rent.

In other words, council housing was to have the top priority. That, of course, ran against the traditional Conservative ideas of a 'property-owning democracy'. At the time the chief proponent of the idea was Salisbury, Dorothy's brother-in-law, of course, and now leader of the House of Lords.

It was no doubt awkward. But Macmillan manoeuvred his way around the challenge. In a speech to the House of Commons on 4 December he announced that 'we wish to see the widest distribution of property. We think that, of all forms of property suitable for such distribution, house property is one of the best.'[2] As a long-term aim, that might have been desirable. In the short term he believed nothing of the sort. Council housing for rent was the only way to meet the political objective he had been set – and which he was determined to achieve. The thought that Salisbury was irritated (in fact, by now he regarded his brother-in-law by marriage irredeemably untrustworthy) was neither here nor there. The target had to be met, not only for the credibility of the Conservative Government but also, it need hardly be said, for the sake of Macmillan's own political career.

There is no doubting the enthusiasm with which Macmillan set about his new task. Sheepshanks remained nominally in charge of the Ministry, but he was rudely pushed aside in favour of a recruit whom Macmillan had known at the old wartime Ministry of Supply, Sir Percy Mills. Even the new Ministry was organised along Beaverbrook lines. A Ministerial Council was set up to speed the process of allocation of materials to local authorities. Mills set up ten Regional Housing Production Boards. The Minister for Materials, Lord Swinton, was cajoled into allocating what-ever he had at his disposal to local authorities for housing; and the Treasury was under continual bombardment not to stem the flow of funds to local authorities.

In the midst of the hectic programme for the new Ministry, Macmillan had also to respond in Cabinet to the clear refusal of his colleagues, particularly Butler and Salisbury, to find anything useful in the European ventures which he – and Churchill – had pursued when in Opposition. When Maxwell Fyfe in late November asked for a view on what he should say at the Council of Europe about the Schuman Plan, the Cabinet view seemed almost wholly negative. Butler said that '[the] Plan is unpopular with Unions in mines and steel. [We should] make propaganda at home to make it clear we aren't hand[in]g over our mines or works to the Schumaniacs.' Macmillan tried a rescue bid: 'Likely it won't be ratified. Might be a chance for a new attempt in wh[ich] we c[oul]d join.'[3] Yet Butler's views were echoed by others. In truth, there was no doubt that the tide in the new Cabinet was flowing against

Europe. But there was, equally, no doubt that Macmillan would make sure that the matter was very far from settled.

The last open joust of the year with Butler in Cabinet came on 20 December. Butler was presenting his civil investment programme for 1952. Macmillan had already objected that the programme would cut housing investment. When it came before Cabinet he said that 'on [the] basis of finishing in a year we sh[oul]d complete 230,000 in 1952 ... on P[rogra]mme 1953 w[oul]d be worse than 1952 ... We may fail ... At least let me try ... Reduced standards ... 2 bedroom house vs 3 etc ... May I start housing ... ?'⁴ Macmillan's plea – particularly in advocating a reduction in building standards to get to the politically required figure – was decisive. The official Minute recorded that 'there was general sympathy with the Housing Ministers that they should be free to try to build as many houses as they could within whatever allocation of labour and materials might be made to them'.⁵ In other words, the figure of 300,000 was by then politically sacrosanct – whatever it might cost in terms of reducing standards of housing or changing categories to suit the purpose.

But that was not the end of it. On 21 December, in a meeting at the Treasury, Macmillan made 'a grand assault on the Treasury planners ... In a talk, I made it clear to Butler that I wd resign if my plan for working up to 300,000 by 1954 was not accepted ... So far as Rab can be pinned down, he seemed to accept this ...'⁶ Butler's acceptance, in fact, marked the general recognition of what had become evident political reality. The housing pledge had given the one clear dynamic to the new Government. (Some even said that the longed-for wartime spirit had returned.) As a consequence, by the end of 1951 Macmillan was already seen as a Minister who could not possibly be ignored.

Moreover, as a bonus, the big house at Birch Grove had by then been restored and brought into domestic action. For the first time for twelve years he was able to sleep in what he regarded as his proper home. Furthermore, the return to Birch Grove House also signalled an improvement in the Macmillan marriage. Dorothy had put all her – occasionally explosive – energy into the restoration of the house and, although the two were still living apart, the relationship was both cordial and respectful. Besides, the shooting was good (fifty pheasants and a woodcock bagged on 12 January), Maurice was a shade more restrained in his drinking and Sarah had found an acceptable boyfriend by the name of Andrew Heath. All in all, it made for an altogether more settled home life – and at least Dorothy was aware of, and sympathetic about, the demands made on her husband by his political career. As though in celebration, he had put on weight, his hair had taken on a distinctive shade of grey, his three-piece pin-striped suits with watch chain and breast pocket handkerchief seemed better fitting – and the snarl in his smile seemed less pronounced. In short, he was looking every bit a confident Tory Minister.

Early in 1952 the politics, too, were going well. Macmillan managed to resist Salisbury's opposition to his Bill to create new towns on formerly agricultural land and made a good speech about housing to a large audience in the Albert Hall on 22 January. True, there were ominous signs from Egypt and the British balance of payments was apparently in somewhere near free fall – Butler 'seemed not to have a real grip of the situation . . . I do not believe the Treasury has ever been so badly served as now.'[7] At that point, however, all political activity came to a sudden halt on 6 February, when the Cabinet was summoned to be told solemnly that King George VI had died. It was then time for a good deal of ceremony – ten days for the dead King to lie in state and be buried (Dorothy and Macmillan watched the funeral procession from his flat at 90 Piccadilly before going by train to Windsor for the service) and for a few more days to greet the new Queen Elizabeth.

All that done, with suitable pomp and circumstance, the political game then resumed. Almost immediately, the country seemed to be in the middle of an economic crisis. Australia, which had emerged from the war with large sterling balances, had started a programme of industrial investment which required US dollars to buy essential capital equipment for the purpose. The resulting Australian purchases of US dollars had led to a corresponding drain on the United Kingdom gold and dollar reserves to buy the sterling back to support a fixed exchange rate.

Faced with this, the Treasury produced a plan. It was certainly radical, if perhaps rather ill-considered in its expected effect. The proposal, code-named ROBOT, was to block almost all foreign-owned sterling balances and to make the rest convertible at will – at a floating exchange rate. The plan was then looked at in secret by a group of Ministers headed by Churchill (Macmillan was kept out of it) and was first presented to Cabinet on 28 February. As Macmillan later pointed out (although he refused to give an opinion until he had had time to study the plan) it was 'a most revolutionary and vital decision' which they were called on to make.[8] Butler made the presentation, only to find Eden, who flew back from a visit to Portugal for the second meeting on the same day, vehemently opposed. The Treasury then produced an alternative which would have involved large cuts in imports (including timber for housing). That, in turn, was thought to be altogether too pessimistic and was never seriously considered.

In the end, after a long and desultory argument at a third meeting on the matter – Macmillan's only comment was about possible political fallout in the Commonwealth – Churchill became so alarmed by Eden's hostility and threats of resignation (although Eden had a known habit of threatening resignation at regular intervals) that he concluded the meeting by saying that he had 'sympathy with the Chancellor of the Exchequer [but the] large diff[erenc]e of view, wholly on merits, means that it w[oul]d be [a] v[ery] g[rea]t risk to adopt this bold course'.[9] That was that, but Macmillan, curiously enough, in a postscript thought that Butler's scheme had the makings of a good idea. He went on to note, however, that Butler was both tired and very uncertain of himself, and that 'he should have fought harder for it . . .'.[10]

The next problem was Europe. In the Cabinet's previous discussions, all the brave words of Strasbourg seem to have been forgotten. But Macmillan saw no reason to let the matter die. Although it meant straying beyond his brief, and consequently annoying Eden, he wrote a paper for discussion at Cabinet alongside a predominantly hostile Foreign Office paper submitted by Eden. Macmillan's paper, entitled 'The Future of the Council of Europe' argued – at considerable length and with many reminders of what his colleagues had said when they were in Opposition – against the negative attitude in the Foreign Office both on the Schuman Plan and on the European Army. His paper argued for a much more enthusiastic attitude to both, with Britain taking a lead on both matters in the Council of Europe. Preferably, he went on, the European Coal and Steel Community and the European Defence Community should be subordinate to the Council of Europe itself.

Macmillan presented his paper to the Cabinet meeting of 13 March. Anthony Nutting, standing in for Eden who was ill with flu, presented the Foreign Office paper. Macmillan then put his case, but, try as he might, his presentation fell flat. Apart from Maxwell Fyfe, all his colleagues followed the Nutting/Eden line. Churchill said, 'I never contemplated [an] amalgam Army.' Salisbury complained that Macmillan 'would like to see [the] U.K. [as a] leading and full member of [a] Continental bloc . . . I w[oul]d not like to see it pass Cab[inet] th[a]t we all favoured acting like [a] continental nation.' Churchill chimed in again: 'There is the Channel – can't smudge that out. Nor the once great Empire.' He then said that he did not accept the 'whole of [Macmillan's] thesis'. The Cabinet then approved Eden's paper. 'H.M.', the Cabinet Secretary noted laconically, 'registered dissent.'[11]

In fact, there was not much more he could do. He had trespassed on Eden's territory and had been roundly rebuffed. He thought about resignation but quickly decided that there was no point in it – it would not have helped his cause and would have brought his career to an immediate full stop. All he could do was to note wearily in his diary that

'I don't believe [Churchill] realises the sense of disappointment or even anger of those he led in 5 years work in the European Movement'.[12] He then sent a Minute to Churchill warning him of this and then, rather forlornly, wrote that 'I leave world politics and return to my "rabbit hutches" (as he will call "The People's House")'.[13]

That was not the last disappointment of March 1952. Towards the end of the month Macmillan heard that Andrew Heath had been taken ill with pleurisy and a tubercular abscess on his lung. He had been rushed to hospital and operated on. Sarah and he had been due to marry in late April – and that, of course, now had to be cancelled. But there was a further complication. What Macmillan might not have known (since in the climate of the time such things were frequently kept by daughters from their fathers) was that Sarah had become pregnant. Not unnaturally, she confided in her mother, Dorothy, who insisted that she get an abortion – on the grounds that if she went ahead and had the (illegitimate) baby it would ruin Macmillan's career. The abortion was duly done, quite when and where is not known (perhaps, as these things often were, it was done abroad). In fact, and tragically, the operation was bungled and Sarah was left permanently unable to have children of her own.

Macmillan may or may not have known about all this. Boothby, on the other hand, certainly did (presumably because Dorothy told him). It was, he later said, 'the one thing I could never quite forgive Dorothy, the one wicked thing she did ... I think it was all part of her guilty conscience, but it killed [Sarah] ...'[14] Be that as it may, there is no doubt that Dorothy herself was taking a very grave risk. In those days, procuring an abortion was a criminal offence. Even though Sarah may have had the operation abroad, if the whole murky business had come out in the press there is no doubt that Dorothy would have been, to say the least, seriously embarrassed – as would, in consequence, Macmillan.

That aside, during the spring and early summer of 1952 Macmillan was fully occupied with taking his legislation through Parliament. But he was becoming more and more aware of a sense of drift. 'The more I reflect on the situation,' he wrote on 21 June, 'the more dangerous the present drift of HMG seems to be ... So far, P.M. is obviously postponing decisions, and Butler is also (I think) playing for time ... Meanwhile, we drift – like our predecessors ...'[15] But the drift, such as it was, did not last very long. The Treasury still very clearly wanted a reduction in council house building to meet their overall economic objectives. Butler, for his part was anxious to cut the Minister for Housing down to reasonable size. 'In dealing with the Min. of Housing,' he minuted his officials, '"the hungry sheep look up and are not fed".'[16] Macmillan was fully aware of this. 'I cannot help feeling that there is a certain piquancy in the struggle,' he wrote in his diary, 'because Butler dislikes and fears me.' He himself professed to like Butler, who had 'great charm. But it has been cruelly said that in politics there are no friends at the top. I fear it is so . . .'[17]

For a time, the political battle was intense and closely fought. But by the time Parliament rose for the summer Recess it was clear that Macmillan had won. The figure of 300,000 was again deemed sacrosanct. In fact, Butler had made a tactical mistake. In the midst of the housing argument, he had tried to revive the idea of floating the sterling exchange rate. That had irritated Churchill, who had in the end come down firmly on Macmillan's side. 'Don't accept need to modify our hous[in]g p[rogra]mme to wh[ich] we are deeply comm[itte]d,' he told Cabinet on 17 July, 'and is our only success.'[18] That, at least for the moment, was the end of the matter. Macmillan, much thus relieved, was able to leave London at the end of the month, first to visit the areas of Devon which had been badly flooded and then to Scotland for a week's grouse shooting.

The break certainly did him much good. The long battle with the Treasury and had left him tired and depressed. Furthermore, he had been sleeping badly. Besides, the break allowed him more time for reading (in fact, at this time he was branching out in his reading – not just his constant and reliable favourites of English literature but now Flaubert and Hugo – in French, although he found Flaubert's French difficult – and Villari's lives of Machiavelli and Savonarola).

Suitably refreshed, by the end of the summer Macmillan felt that the Government was much steadier and that the Conservatives had recovered a good deal of political ground. Housing completions were satisfactory – he was confident of achieving 252,000 in 1952. Moreover, the first debate at the Party Conference in October was on housing. Macmillan was given a wildly enthusiastic reception when he rose to reply to the debate – and an even wilder one when he sat down. But his feet were firmly on the ground. 'It really is rather comic,' he noted, 'after all the years of conflict and unpopularity. But it will not last. It is all right to put up the houses. But the next job will be to put up the rents . . .'[19]

In fact, Macmillan had started work on a paper for Cabinet – called, perhaps overambitiously, 'The Grand Design' – which would ask for authority for an overall housing policy for the period after the 300,000 target had been met, probably in 1954. His objective was to produce a general statement of policy in which unpopular measures – greater freedom for councils to raise rents and increases in valuation for the purposes of domestic rates – would be presented alongside more popular measures – to repair derelict houses and to promote housing co-ownership, all of it to be published in a White Paper. Not content with that, he was urging his officials to hurry up with the reform of Town and Country Planning.

1952 thus ended busily but happily. Dorothy and Macmillan went to early communion on Christmas Day, and later to Matins with the Faber and Amery grandchildren, before they all settled down to their feast. 1953 started well, too. Eden, with his wife Clarissa, stayed for a night at Birch Grove and appeared much less nervous and tetchy than usual. Macmillan, in the course of a long and open talk, told Eden that everybody assumed he would take over as Prime Minister when Churchill retired. Eden accepted that but replied that nobody knew when Churchill would go. Sometimes he hinted that it would be soon – perhaps after the Queen's Coronation due in June – but at other times he hinted that he was fit and able to go on for a long time. It was all, at least for Eden, rather depressing. But Macmillan, needless to say, then took the opportunity of sounding Eden out on his own prospects. The Foreign Office, Eden replied, would have to go either to him or to Salisbury. (Macmillan thought that Eden would prefer Salisbury but was not sure that a Foreign Secretary could properly sit in the House of Lords.) The matter was then suitably left in the air, leaving Macmillan to wonder 'Shall I ever be Foreign Secretary?'[20]

February brought more floods, and another round of ministerial visits, this time in Norfolk. February also brought another dose of flu, leaving Macmillan with a bad cough even after his temperature had returned to normal. March, however, brought something much more serious. In great pain, he was admitted to St Thomas's Hospital in the afternoon of the 28th. The diagnosis was not entirely clear, but it seemed that he either had an infection of the gall bladder or a troublesome gallstone. After few days' treatment, the pain went away, but as a precautionary measure his doctors advised that he should have his gall bladder removed.

By coincidence, it so happened that Eden was having the same problem. After some hesitations, his doctors diagnosed gallstones in his bile duct and advised immediate operation. In fact, it was not until some days later that Eden finally went into hospital. In spite of all the preparation, the operation went badly wrong. A second operation at the end of April, to clear up the results of the first, went just about as badly. The only solution seemed to be to have further treatment in the United States. Yet all that took time and trouble, and it was not until June that Eden was able to travel.

There was worse to come. On 23 June, the very day Eden was having his operation in America, Churchill, at the end of a dinner for the Italian Prime Minister, Alcide de Gasperi, while leading his guests into the drawing room only managed a few steps before slumping down into a chair. He had had a massive stroke. The following day he went to Chartwell with his doctors in close attendance. Butler and Salisbury were summoned and a press release issued disguising, at Salisbury's request, the true nature of the illness and merely stating that the Prime Minister was in need of a complete rest. On 29 June Butler took the chair at Cabinet and revealed to his colleagues what had happened. 'It was a terrible shock to us all,' Macmillan recorded, 'although revealed so discreetly. Many of us were in tears, or found it difficult to restrain them . . .'[21]

Not more than two days later, however, Macmillan was answering a debate in the House of Commons on school buildings – making 'the best Parliamentary and debating speech I have ever made'.[22] That done, he found himself invited down to Chartwell for dinner the next day. As soon as he saw Macmillan Churchill 'cried out "I must congratulate you on a magnificent Parliamentary triumph. It was a masterpiece."'[23] Macmillan was quite obviously taken aback. He was expecting an invalid. Instead, Churchill appeared in high spirits. He had already done some three hours of talking on the telephone and dictating but, to Macmillan at least, he hardly seemed tired. His left arm was still very weak, but he made a joke of it. Pouring out some champagne – with a steady hand – he shouted 'you see, I don't spill precious liquor'.[24] In fact, his doctors were as astonished as Macmillan at Churchill's apparent recovery – while counselling caution about the future.

With both Churchill – however cheerful – and Eden – however depressed – out of political action for the foreseeable future, Macmillan was anxious to stay in the thick of it. But his doctors were adamant. His gall bladder must be removed. If it was not done soon – there was no question of waiting until the autumn – his life might be in danger. On 6 July, therefore, he was driven to St Thomas's for the operation, which was performed successfully two days later. His gall bladder was full of stones and his bile duct had been probed to make sure that no stones had entered it. As he said himself, 'I was almost knocked out for a week.'[25] There were, of course, many letters (including a charming one from Butler) and telegrams, but it was not until 20 July that he was up to having visitors, apart from Dorothy's daily visit of no more than a few minutes. Maxwell Fyfe, David Eccles, James Stuart all wanted to talk about the succession to Churchill. He was back again to reading Voltaire (in French – 'how much easier classical French is than modern French. There are no hard words!'[26]).

On 28 July Macmillan was back in Cabinet, defending 'The Grand Design' and announcing that completions for the first half of the year had totalled 145,000. Moreover, he was confident that the target of 300,000 would be reached, at least in 1954 and possibly even in 1953. The only difficulty was that the availability of materials, and the ability of the building industry to produce, might let them down. Eccles, as Minister of Works responsible for the industry, disputed that, saying that productivity was improving at a fast rate and that there would, on present estimates, be no shortage of materials. This would leave room for the expansion of private sector building – and a reduction in council house building – which Macmillan was advocating.

But at the end of his presentation Macmillan slipped in another rider. He hoped that the White Paper would be published before the end of the Session and debated during the Debate on the Address of the new Session in the autumn. Nevertheless, he went on, 'Once this *is* touched off, we must see it thro[ugh]. Means no dissolution for 18 months. Must get it thro[ugh] and working before Gen[era]l Election.'[27] He was supported by James Stuart, speaking as Scottish Secretary. Macmillan's last rider does not appear in the official Cabinet Minutes. But he and Stuart had made their position quite clear. Once 'The Grand Design' was launched, there could be no question of a General Election for a year and a half. Well before then, they had in mind that Eden would be back in action and that he (rather than Butler) would have taken office as Prime Minister.

On 30 July Sarah finally married Andrew Heath at Horsted Keynes parish church. She wrote to Macmillan – such was the relationship that they communicated by letter – to ask him, as was customary, to give her away. Dorothy had wanted her to wait another six months, but Macmillan wrote back to her that he was content for her wedding to be at some date between July and September. He did, however, add: 'You have had a long wait and a very difficult time, which I think you got through with great courage and good sense ...'[28] In the light of this exchange of letters, it may be that he did know about her abortion after all. (With his strongly held religious views Macmillan might well not have approved of abortion.) Nevertheless, and although still on a severe diet after his gall-bladder operation, he put up a good front on the day.

Throughout the early summer of 1953 the Churchill succession was by far and away the main topic for political gossip. By August Eden was back in London, very thin but looking healthy and relaxed. He had seen Churchill who, he told Macmillan, was still dragging his left leg, nursing a weak left arm and from time to time speaking thickly. Perhaps, Eden thought, he simply could not go on. But suddenly, on 10 August, Churchill appeared in Downing Street and started again to announce himself as a Prime Minister who had fully recovered his health. He was much looking forward to following up a speech he had made – on 11 May, before his illness – proposing a meeting with Georgi Malenkov, who had become the Soviet Premier appointed after Stalin's death, together with President Eisenhower.

Churchill's recovery amazed the whole political world. By the end of August, he was holding court at Chequers, the Prime Minister's official residence. In fact, he was only there for a weekend (he had been told by his son-in-law, Christopher Soames, that if he wanted to remain Prime Minister he really had to use Chequers from time to time, much as he might dislike it) before going on holiday to the South of France. During that weekend, Macmillan and Dorothy were invited there to dinner – and to stay the night. On the following morning Churchill (still in bed, as was his habit) explained to Macmillan his intention to remain Prime Minister as long as he could meet the physical challenges of the House of Commons and the Party Conference. Yet Macmillan, when he heard this, privately had his doubts. In telling Crookshank about what Churchill had said and his own doubts, he thought perhaps 'that history would accuse us all – Rab, Bobbety [Salisbury] and the politicians in the Cabinet – of weakness and cowardice. We know the Emperor has no clothes, and we dare not say so . . .'[29]

The crucial tests came in early October. On the 2nd, Churchill chaired Cabinet and 'excelled himself, in control of the situation and in showmanship'.[30] Eden was back, and Macmillan managed to get approval for his White Paper, thanks not least to Butler's support. Yet the big test was to be the Party Conference at Margate. 'We were all terrified about how the Old Man would get on,' said one of his secretaries.[31] Butler, Macmillan and Eden all had 'tremendous welcomes . . . But, of course, amid all the speeches and amusement of the Conference, the excitement was concentrated on the Saturday afternoon. How would Churchill come through his ordeal? The answer was magnificent. He spoke for 50 minutes, in the best Churchillian vein. The asides and the impromptus were as good as ever. His voice seemed sometimes a little weak, and once or twice flagged . . . At the end, of course, he was completely done . . .'[32] The Emperor had shown that, after all, he was not short of clothes.

Business, at least for the moment, was back to usual. Macmillan's White Paper, now entitled *Houses – the Next Step*, was published on 3 November. Press conferences and debates followed, and in the course of those Macmillan was told by his officials, on 15 November, that it only needed 45,000 more houses to be completed during November and December to reach the magic target of 300,000. He even felt confident enough to intervene at Cabinet on 26 November, in a discussion about what Churchill might say in his forthcoming meeting with Eisenhower at Bermuda on the European Defence Community. '[We] must recognise', he said, '[the] growing weakness of France ... [They] started the fe[deral] idea at a time when G[ermany] was weak & they th[ough]t *they* w[oul]d dominate it ... If they had b[ee]n content with a looser assoc[iatio]n we c[oul]d have b[ee]n in it.' He went on to say, with support from Eden, that we should 'p[ost]pone all the federal structure & and go on with the European Army' (of national forces under national commands).[33]

Christmas 1953 was another happy time. 'The house is like the old days – quite full ... All the children seem very well. Anne and Michael Faber came to tea – so we had all 7 grandchildren, for the first time for many months ... D and the girls sat up half the night, filling stockings, preparing presents and the like ... The tree in the Hall was very fine – reaching almost to the top of the house ... Dorothy, most of the children went to Communion at 8 a.m. ... The church was very full at Matins ... I read the lessons as usual ... We had two full pews ... After tea, the presents to all – including indoor servants ... Altogether the whole ritual in its full form!'[34] It was the sort of atmosphere in which Macmillan, in his mood of a would-be aristocrat, felt completely at home.

On 18 January 1954 Macmillan had his moment of triumph. He was able to announce to Cabinet that the figure for housing completions in 1953, to be announced in February, was 318,750. There was much congratulation. That was followed by further congratulation at the Cabinet meeting on 10 February, where it was noted that Macmillan on that day had reached the age of sixty. All that, however, was only a pleasant prelude to what turned out to be a spring of hard Parliamentary labour. Long hours were spent in the House of Commons on the Housing Repairs and Rents Bill, followed almost immediately in mid-March by the Second Reading and subsequent Committee stage of the Town and Country Planning Bill.

April then saw the first of a series of rows about the new hydrogen bomb. The United States had exploded the bomb in the Pacific, and the size and power of the explosion had set off something close to panic. The House of Commons wanted urgently to know what influence Britain had over its possible eventual use. In a debate on 6 April Churchill responded to the attacks made on him by Labour politicians on radio and television by revealing suddenly that it was the Labour Government which had relinquished the British right of veto over its use. The revelation, such as it was, went down very badly. It was tantamount to accusing Labour ministers of having abandoned the defence of the country. Attlee countered effectively – pointing to the NATO alliance, which gave the necessary safeguards, as a Labour creation. There was then a period of '20 minutes of storm and cries of "resign" "dirty" and so on ... Bob Boothby, with a characteristic gesture of disloyalty, walked out ... it was [Churchill's] greatest failure since [his] speech on the abdication.'[35]

The rows about the hydrogen bomb in the House of Commons, however, were nothing compared with the row which blew up in Cabinet over Churchill's proposal to meet Malenkov. He had been to see President Eisenhower in late June, and on the way back he had sent a telegram to Molotov, the Soviet Foreign Minister, suggesting such a meeting. Eden, who was on the ship with Churchill, had tried to dissuade him but to no avail. Butler had seen a draft of Churchill's telegram but restricted himself to a few textual comments. The rest of the Cabinet had been left in the dark. When they heard about it there was something close to uproar. After a series of difficult Cabinet meetings the row exploded on 23 July. Eden complained that his advice had been ignored. Salisbury, supported by Crookshank and Macmillan, pointed out that if collective Cabinet responsibility was to be maintained they must be fully informed about what they were to be responsible for. Churchill then lost his temper and said that he had a perfect right to send messages to other heads of government without consulting the Cabinet. Salisbury hinted at resignation.

In the end, the row petered out, not least because the Soviets wrote inviting the United States, France and Britain to a Four Power meeting. But the damage had been done. Eden had been shocked by Churchill's behaviour – he told Macmillan that 'the old man is really a crook! He hasn't told the truth!', to which Macmillan replied that 'this almost child-like determination to get his way at all costs ... must be, partly at any rate, a result of his mental illness'.[36] Gradually, over the late summer and early autumn, there was emerging something of a serious conspiracy to tell Churchill that his time was up.

But it was not to be quick. From time to time, Macmillan was given to moaning. 'The miracle', he wrote in August, 'is that we have been able to get along as well as we have ... these interminable Cabinets, full of reminiscences and monologues, are becoming an intolerable burden ... Eden and I and others who felt exhausted and fed up (e.g. Salisbury, Crookshank etc.) could retire quietly and unostentatiously into private life. But I told [Eden] that one really cannot resign because one is not made Prime Minister!'[37] Butler, too, was clear that Churchill had to go. But none of them could work out how it could be done. As James Stuart told Macmillan, 'it is impossible to *remove* Churchill. It would be too risky; he has all the cards. It would damage the Party in the country and in the HofC.'[38] Compounding the problem was the Government's relative popularity. It had survived the economic problems of the earlier years; the terms of trade had turned back in favour; rationing was gradually being relaxed; and the nation was starting to feel good about itself again. Besides, the Labour Party was in the middle of a truly spectacular row as the result of Bevan's provocations to Attlee and the Labour leadership.

It was thus no good making out that Churchill should retire for the good of the Party. As a result, by the end of September Eden and his supporters were reduced to muttering simply that something had to be done – but they did not know what. As it happened, Churchill then turned the tables on them. He started what he called a 'reconstruction' of his Government. In fact, it was little more than recognition of the wish of Alexander, who had served loyally but ineffectually for two years as Minister of Defence, and Lord Simonds, who had been an equally ineffectual Lord Chancellor, to retire. Churchill, however, used the opportunity to dangle all sorts of exciting prospects in front of his Ministers – but only seeing them one by one and never in groups. Macmillan was offered the Leadership of the House of Commons and the title of Lord Privy Seal – but only if Crookshank would agree to take over as Home Secretary. (Maxwell Fyfe was to be promoted to the House of Lords, as Lord Kilmuir, to be Lord Chancellor.) But Crookshank did not want to be Home Secretary, and that meant that Macmillan in turn refused to take Crookshank's job.

In the end, Churchill agreed that Macmillan should move to Defence. For the next six months he was to take on a job which he had originally wanted but which now, with a fading Churchill interfering the whole time, was little more than a bed of nails. So it proved. 'This new Ministry of mine is a queer kind of affair,' he wrote in late October. 'I have no power; yet I am responsible for everything – esp if it goes wrong. The P.M. is always busy about defence affairs – on Wednesday the Defence Committee sat under his Chairmanship for nearly 6 hours. (It's true that it cd all have been done in 20 minutes.)'[39]

For Macmillan, it was something of a nightmare. In Housing he had been left to get on with his job. In Defence, he was under what turned out to be random harassment from Churchill. Furthermore, Churchill, in the celebrations at the end of November for his eightieth birthday, had announced himself full of health and vigour. In fact, on 22 December 1954, at a meeting of his senior Ministers – Eden, Salisbury, Woolton, Butler, Crookshank, Stuart and Macmillan – he suggested that he was now thinking of retiring not before July 1955. Macmillan ended the year alone with Dorothy at Birch Grove, suffering from lumbago, with poor shooting – and a good ration of depression.

The lumbago, and a cold to match, went on throughout January.

Worse still, on the night of 24 January the house at Birch Grove had been burgled. All the Macmillan silver, all Nellie's jewellery, as well as all the forks and spoons, had been removed. On the morning of 26 January Churchill called in sympathy and asked him to go round to No. 10. 'I found him in bed,' Macmillan wrote in his diary, 'with a little green budgerigar ... sitting on his head! ... A whisky and soda was by his side – of this, the little bird took sips later on. Miss Portal sat by the bed – he was dictating ... The bird flew about the room; perched on my shoulder and pecked (or kissed) my neck; flew to Miss Portal's arm, back to the P.M.'s head, while all the time sonorous "Gibbonesque" sentences were rolling out of the maestro's mouth ... The bird says a few words, in a husky voice like an American actress (I did not know that budgerigars could be trained to speak) and occasionally sips a little whisky ...' Macmillan could not help being won over. Really,' he concluded, 'he is a unique, dear man with all his qualities and faults ...'[40]

That, in truth, was to be the problem for the would-be conspirators. Try as they might, they all were constrained by a residual devotion to Churchill – who had, after all, led them through some of the most difficult moments in British history and whose generosity, when he felt prepared to give it free rein, knew no bounds. But the political realities weighed heavily. On 8 March 1955, after the successful launch of the White Paper announcing Britain's intention to manufacture the hydro-gen bomb, Churchill lunched with Eden and told him that he intended to resign on 5 April. 'It seems settled', Macmillan noted the following day after his own lunch with Eden, 'that Churchill will resign on 5 April.'[41]

But that was far from the last word. On 11 March a telegram arrived from Makins, then British Ambassador in Washington. It relayed an American suggestion that Eisenhower might visit Paris on 8 May, the tenth anniversary of VE Day. The objective would be to encourage the French to ratify the agreements – successfully negotiated by Eden – which, after the stillbirth of the European Defence Community, were designed to be the basis of Western European Defence. There would at the same time be a celebration of the newly acquired sovereignty of the Federal Republic of Germany. Moreover, Makins went on the say that Eisenhower might be prepared to start planning a meeting with the Soviets to reduce tensions.

This was enough for Churchill. He could see the opportunity, long desired, for a Four Power meeting at which the Soviets would agree to a basis for world peace. 'Of course,' he said to Colville, 'this meant all bets were off: he would stay and, with Eisenhower, meet the Russians.'[42] The next morning he wrote to Eden to tell him. Eden wrote an angry reply, demanding that the matter be discussed at an early Cabinet. In the meantime, Eden consulted Butler and Salisbury, who both felt very strongly that Churchill should stick to his promise. At the Cabinet meeting of 14 March Eden openly challenged Churchill to say whether he was going back on 'the arrangements you have made with me'. Churchill replied that it was not a matter which should be discussed openly in Cabinet. Salisbury countered that 'it is clear that certain plans are known to some members of the Cabinet; would it not be better if they were known to all?' Butler then weighed in by asserting that it was not a question of loyalty but whether an Election may become necessary. 'You have always said that you would not lead the Party at another election.'[43] He was already concerned that the economy might deteriorate and make a May Election essential.

'The ensuing days were painful.'[44] On 27 March Churchill heard that the new Soviet Premier, Nikolai Bulganin, had spoken favourably about Four Power talks. The following morning he sent for Butler and told him to see Eden and say that the timetable had to be changed. On 29 March he asked the Queen whether she would mind, and, when she said she did not, he went to what was meant to be a farewell dinner with the Edens. In fact, such was the emotion of the moment and so amiable was Eden himself (and the prospects of a Four Power meeting seemed, after all, still so distant) that he changed his mind again. The next day he told Eden and Butler that the timetable still held. He would resign on 5 April.

On the eve of the event, there was a splendid dinner in Downing Street, attended by the Queen and the Duke of Edinburgh and all the great of the land. When all the guests had gone, Churchill and Colville went up to his bedroom. Churchill 'sat on his bed, still wearing his Garter, Order of Merit and knee-breeches ... Then suddenly he stared at me and said with vehemence: "I don't believe Anthony can do it."'[45] The verdict was clear. In fact, Churchill's verdict had not escaped Macmillan who, as it happened, was forming his own view. Earlier in the year he had lunch with Lord Moran 'whom I have known for many years as Churchill's medical adviser – [as] Sir Charles Wilson ... a man of great shrewdness and wit ... [he] thought that Eden wd have great difficulty in standing the strain. The state of his inside is not good, and he ought to be careful. If the artificial bile channel ... silts up again ... it will be very serious ... Moran has a very shrewd idea of the whole position.'[46] It was an opinion to which, as might be imagined, Macmillan listened with the greatest care.

14

Ambition

Harold Macmillan, the newly appointed Foreign Secretary, arrived by car on the morning of 12 April 1955 at the entrance of the undoubtedly grand – but to the outside observer somewhat overblown – building in King Charles Street which houses, if that is the suitably dignified word, what is now known as the Foreign and Commonwealth Office. In his memoirs, he modestly recorded that he was much bewildered by its size and complexity, that the lift at the ambassadors' entrance was out of order and that as a result he got lost in the basement passages. That may have been so, and modesty was perhaps in order on that day. Others had noted that when it came to the public eye modesty was not one of his characteristics. He had, after all, learnt all the tricks when he was Minister of Housing – and he had learnt to play them well. On 5 April, for instance, the day on which Churchill had said a tearful farewell to his Cabinet, Lord Woolton noted that 'very amusingly, Harold Macmillan again stopped and posed in the middle of the roadway before joining me in my car and then waved to the crowds as we passed them. I agree', Woolton went on, 'that a public man must be something of an actor; I wonder whether it is necessary to be a showman as well. Winston, of course, has always done it; Eden does it in a very gentlemanly way, bringing his hand up to the semi-salute. But there is nothing semi about Harold; he sort of says "give me a cheer", and waves to them although they are not waving to him.'[1]

Macmillan claimed in his memoirs that the Foreign Office, as it then was named, marked the 'summit of my ambitions'.[2] As with other such assertions in his memoirs, this needs to be treated with caution. He had been told very clearly by Lord Moran that Eden could easily break down under stress, and it was not difficult to imagine circumstances under which this might happen – although nothing was on the immediate horizon. But what was obvious was that, were it to happen, Macmillan's only serious competitor for the succession to the position of Prime Minister would be Rab Butler. As Foreign Secretary, he was in a prime position to tip the competitive odds in his favour. Furthermore, he had seen in Cabinet that both Eden and Butler could be pushed – that both of them had something of a soft centre. At the age of sixty-one, he could in addition easily reflect that Gladstone, after all, had formed his last administration in his eighties.

There were other, more domestic, advantages as well. 90 Piccadilly could be abandoned in favour of a flat in the official Foreign Secretary's residence of 1 Carlton Gardens. Dorneywood, the other official residence – an elegant but uncomfortable country house – he could do without, as he told Eden on his appointment. He preferred his own home at Birch Grove. Admittedly, he was assigned a detective to follow him wherever he went, which was a nuisance, but that was only a minor difficulty compared with the privileges of travel, accommodation, service and general cosseting which the Foreign Office accorded (and still accords) to its ministerial head. Official dinners were another nuisance, particularly since he had given up drinking alcohol at the beginning of the year (although he was still smoking cigarettes). Nevertheless, given all that, Macmillan showed every appearance of enjoying the privileges and the position as much as any of his predecessors.

As it happened, there was not much time to take root. Eden, with the agreement of his Cabinet, had decided on a May General Election. Butler had produced a Budget to cut sixpence off the standard rate of income tax, a threatened railway strike had been settled and the opinion polls looked healthy. Accordingly, on 6 May, Parliament was dissolved for an Election on the 26th. There was no doubt about Macmillan's continued membership of the House of Commons. Bromley was safe – and his adoption meeting passed off without difficulty. In fact, he was able to devote some time to supporting Maurice, who was fighting a Labour marginal at Halifax (his father's abstention from alcohol had been an obvious signal). All things considered, there was no reason why he should not win Bromley comfortably and continue in his duties as Foreign Secretary. So comfortable was it that even during the campaign there were trips to Paris and Vienna, the first to meet Eisenhower's Secretary of State, John Foster Dulles, and the second to sign the Treaty to release Austria from its post-war Four Power control.

In the event, Bromley was duly won (Macmillan's own majority went up by over 1000). Furthermore, the overall result of the Election was a Conservative working majority and a second Eden Government. Macmillan was duly reappointed to the Foreign Office. It was then time for him to return to King Charles Street – and to grapple with the problems which had been put aside during the campaign. First, however, there was the matter of getting to know in rather greater depth the people he would have to deal with.

The head of the Foreign Office at the time, as Permanent Under-Secretary, was Sir Ivone Kirkpatrick. His deputy, who would succeed him in 1957, was Macmillan's old friend from the wartime Mediterranean, Harold Caccia. Another old friend, and by now almost constant companion, was John Wyndham in Macmillan's Private Office. Caccia was easy enough to deal with – in spite of his almost visceral resistance to any British involvement with continental Europe. Kirkpatrick, on the other hand, was a more difficult fish. A small, good-looking, intensely energetic Irishman, outwardly he presented all the classical features of a successful British diplomat. He had been wounded in the First World War and, once recovered, had been sent to Holland to run a ring of spies. Thereafter, he had entered the diplomatic service and gradually moved up the ranks until, in 1933, he had been appointed first secretary at the British Embassy in Berlin. There he had acquired expertise in German and German affairs (he was Rudolph Hess's interrogator when Hess arrived in Scotland in May 1941) and an intense dislike of both – a dislike which was delivered in the most acid tones to anybody who would listen. But he was, in the words of one, 'so sharp that he cut'.[3] Finally, over the long years he had become devoted to Eden – and in consequence tended to regard Eden's successor as something of an unwelcome incomer.

If Kirkpatrick was not always easy to deal with inside the confines of the office, Macmillan's foreign counterparts presented quite a different series of problems. Apart from West Germany, Governments in continental Europe seemed to come and go, and with them their Foreign Ministers. On the other hand, the one relationship which Macmillan particularly prized, and which he was determined to make a success, was with the United States of America. In May 1955, there was no doubt that the key to that relationship was the US Secretary of State, the notoriously difficult Dulles.

'The only religious leader, lay or clerical', it was written of him, 'ever to become Secretary of State',[4] Dulles had spent his life as a lawyer and office holder in a strict Presbyterian Church. Physically, he was impressive: tall, bulky, with a craggy, gloomy face and down-turned mouth (Churchill, who, like Eden, could not abide him, called it a 'great slab of a face'[5]), he was given to shuffling along with his hands in his trouser pockets muttering disconcertingly to himself. Equally disconcerting was his habit of breakfast meetings, where he ate an almost endless succession of boiled eggs while delivering himself of long and rambling monologues. Macmillan found him to be 'sometimes . . . rather dreamy – as if he were thinking of something else. Then he does not look at you . . .'[6] Yet, at the same time, Macmillan confessed that he could not help liking him.

As for the problems on the Foreign Office agenda, the furthest away geographically, but most immediate in demanding attention, was the dispute with China over the Chinese claim to their offshore islands. The Nationalists, after the Communist victory in 1949, had retreated to the islands, the largest of which, the site of the capital of the Nationalist rump government, had been baptised by the Portuguese colonialists as Formosa – the 'Beautiful' (later, of course, to be named the less beautiful 'Taiwan'). There had been a conference of African and Asian countries at Bandung in April at which various compromise proposals had been put forward but none satisfied at the same time both China and the United States. There was in practice little that Britain could do in the matter while the United States was unclear what its policy should be. The most Macmillan could do was to avoid giving any guarantee of any sort to Formosa that it would not in the end be swallowed up by Communist China.

Moving closer to home, as it were, was the problem of Egypt and the Middle East. As far back as July 1952 a military coup in Egypt, led by General Mohammed Neguib and Colonel Gamal Abdel Nasser, had overthrown the monarchy. Of the two, Nasser was by far the more intelligent – and, equally, by far the more charismatic. Nasser, as a nationalist, had shown his colours early on. He wanted an end to the British military presence in Egypt – particularly the garrison in the Suez Canal Zone. By 1953 Eden had himself started to negotiate with Nasser over the withdrawal of the large force of British troops and supporting personnel in the Zone. In February 1955, Eden and Nasser had met in Cairo to celebrate an Anglo-Egyptian Agreement – apparently ushering in, according to the Egyptian Government a 'New Era of Co-operation and Mutual Understanding'[7] – signed the previous year. Moreover, American and British officials were at work on an ingenious plan, given the code name 'Alpha', to link Egypt with Jordan by a land corridor across the Israeli-held Negev. The package came with proposals for an international zone at Jerusalem. The final product was to be a lasting settlement between Israel and the surrounding Arab states. As a complement – and encouragement – to such an arrangement, Britain had agreed in April 1955 to join the pact signed between Turkey and Iraq – known as the Baghdad Pact – whose object was to frustrate incursions into the Middle East by the Soviet Union. At least for the moment, the Middle East seemed to have been a marked diplomatic success.

Even closer to home was the problem of Cyprus. The island had become a Crown Colony in the aftermath of the First World War, much to the irritation of the two-thirds of the population who were of Greek origin. A number of half-hearted proposals had been made to attempt to satisfy the objectors, but in July 1954 Henry Hopkinson, Minister of

State for Colonial Affairs, had told the House of Commons that Cyprus, in effect, could never expect to be fully independent. In fact, Hopkinson was only echoing what had previously been said. Moreover, it was clear that with the evacuation of the Suez Canal military base Cyprus would become the main base for British Armed Forces in the Mediterranean and, as such, could certainly 'never' be 'fully' independent. Hopkinson's assertion, however, commonplace as it might have seemed at the time, led to uproar. It was the word 'never' – always unwise in politics – which inflamed the Cypriot spirits. The Greek Government immediately declared support for independence from Britain under Archbishop Makarios III, the elected spiritual and political leader of the Greek Cypriots. To make matters worse, on 1 April 1955 a guerrilla organisation, known as EOKA, under the leadership of a Colonel Georgios Grivas (wartime leader of the ferociously right-wing 'X' Group and no friend of the British) announced their intention to secure union with Greece. Their method was violence and, to that effect, they launched a series of spectacular bomb attacks.

The last major problem was Europe. The European Coal and Steel Community had proved a surprising success – rather to the irritation of those in the Foreign Office who had been convinced that it would unceremoniously collapse. Worse still, from their point of view, the French Government elected in February 1955, under Edgar Faure, was showing dangerous signs of supporting Monnet, the President of the High Authority of the ECSC, in his proposal to the six member states that they should move further – to create a joint body for nuclear energy and – even more improbably – a customs union. Furthermore, now that West Germany was securely anchored in NATO, Adenauer was also showing signs of supporting Monnet's endeavours. Monnet's original idea of a customs union of the Six was, in fact, being carried forward with the greatest enthusiasm by the Benelux countries, with Spaak, now Belgian Foreign Minister, the Dutch Foreign Minister Jan Willem Beyen and the Luxembourg Foreign Minister Joseph Bech in the lead.

Yet looming over and above all these particular problems was the central issue of the post-war world: the relationship between the Communist bloc and the West. During the Election campaign in May 1955 the Conservatives had announced their intention of summoning a Four Power conference to discuss, and with any luck resolve, two major concerns: the status of Germany and the arms race. Eden put the organisation of the event at the top of Foreign Office priorities. Like Churchill before him, Eden had become convinced that all major problems could be solved, seemingly at a stroke, by meetings of heads of governments. 'It is wonderful', Churchill remarked with a sly smile when told by

Macmillan of Eden's enthusiasm, 'what a difference it makes to your views about a top-level meeting when you get to the top.'[8]

Macmillan duly set about his business – to address the wish of the Prime Minister for a Four Power 'summit'. The Cabinet agreed to set up a special ministerial committee to advise on the matter: Eden, Butler, Salisbury, Selwyn Lloyd (Minister of Defence) and Macmillan himself. 'The circulation of these deadly papers (all possible plans are canvassed and debated)', he recorded, 'is severely limited. The code name is CANUTE.'[9] He planned a visit to the United States in mid-June to prepare a conference agenda with Dulles and State Department officials. That would be followed by meetings with the French before the final run-in to the conference itself, to be held at Geneva in the second half of July.

What had almost passed him by in the excitement of an impending Four Power conference was that the Foreign Ministers of the ECSC member states had met on 4 June at the Sicilian city of Messina. They had decided that their goal should be no less than 'the development of common institutions and the progressive fusion of national economies and the progressive harmonisation of their social policies'.[10] In the midst of Macmillan's preparations for his United States visit Anthony Nutting, his Minister of State, 'begged Eden' to let him go to Messina,[11] but Eden ignored the request – nor was there any support from Macmillan himself.

On 21 June Spaak and Beyen arrived in London to explore British attitudes to the Messina proposals. They were met by Butler – Macmillan by then having left for the United States – and a group of Ministers of whom only Thorneycroft could be regarded as 'pro-Europe'. Butler spoke loftily of the importance of the Organisation for European Economic Co-operation (OEEC) whose budget he had, in fact, cut in 1952, and the difficulties the United Kingdom might have in joining the kind of organisation Spaak and Beyen had in mind. But somehow, in his customary Delphic language, he contrived to leave the impression that the British door was still at least half open.

Fortified by this, on 30 June a formal invitation arrived from Beyen inviting the British Government to participate in the work of the committee set up at Messina under Spaak's chairmanship, which was due to report on 2 October. Macmillan by then had only just returned from San Francisco (reading *Catherine the Great's Memoirs* – 'people used to disappear suddenly . . .'[12] and noting that 'Anthony [Nutting] has taken control of the F.O. and is no doubt enjoying himself'[13]). He was just in time to read a Foreign Office paper explaining in some detail that a European customs union, as proposed, would damage OEEC and might lead to a 'discriminatory bloc' in Europe against the rest of the world.[14]

This was not at all the way Macmillan wished to play it. In fact, at the discussion in Cabinet on 30 June he argued at some length that Britain should indeed be represented on the Spaak Committee. Moreover, on the nature of the representation, Macmillan afterwards managed to convince a reluctant Butler that 'representative' should be what it said, in other words, 'representative' rather than, as Butler wanted, 'observer'. Accordingly, Mr Russell Bretherton, an Under-Secretary at the Board of Trade, was appointed to lead a British delegation – with instructions 'to leave open the possibility of our joining or entering into a close association while avoiding any positive commitment'.[15] That was all very well. But Bretherton soon recognised his dilemma. 'If we take an active part in trying to guide the final propositions into a form which is acceptable to us,' he wrote, 'it will be difficult to avoid the presumption that we are in some sense committed to the result.'[16] It was a fair point, but the response from his superiors, across all departments in London, was that they were sure Bretherton would be able to steer the Six into the proper path of a loose association to which Britain could subscribe.

While Bretherton, dutifully following his brief, was spending a difficult summer in Brussels, the Four Power meeting was taking place in Geneva. There was, of course, much trumpeting – and an apparent expression of eternal goodwill between President Eisenhower and the new Soviet leaders, Nikolai Bulganin and the Party General Secretary Nikita Khrushchev – but in the end nothing much came out of it. The West put forward unrealistic proposals for the re-unification of Germany on the basis of free elections. The Soviets put forward equally unrealistic proposals on disarmament. Neither side expected their proposals to be accepted. There was further discussion on the Chinese offshore islands, but by then the matter had receded into the diplomatic background. By the end of July, and further meetings with Molotov in Paris, Macmillan was able to return to London – only to deal with the news that EOKA had launched a series of attacks in Cyprus on police stations in Nicosia and Kyrenia and that they had been enthusiastically supported by Athens radio.

During August Macmillan did not have much of a holiday. He prepared yet another paper on 'Alpha' ('I am beginning to feel more and more doubtful about the whole plan') – and, in the meantime, complained both in his diary and to those who would listen about Eden's persistent interference – 'telephoning direct to Sir Ivone Kirkpatrick ... which I must not allow'[17] and 'writing minutes on telegrams; it is a nuisance, especially when he is not even in London ...'.[18] Even reading Aldous Huxley's new book, *The Genius and the Goddess*, gave him little pleasure, and he badly missed the opening of the grouse season. It was thus in a rather grumpy mood that he prepared for the conference on Cyprus due to start in London on the 29th.

In spite of all that, he still had time to write a rather curious paper on the economy, requested, he noted carefully, by Eden (and whimsically entitled *Dizzy with Success*). In it he stated roundly that 'our trouble is that there is too much money bidding for the labour available'. He went on to advocate the classical measures – cut Government expenditure, reduce the monetary base by tightening credit, stimulate saving and encourage production. Surprisingly, however, at the end of his note Macmillan returned to Butler's (ROBOT) proposals of 1952 to free sterling from a fixed exchange rate. Noting that 'our currency (having freed commodity markets and decided to support transferable sterling) is virtually convertible – if you know how', he went on to say that 'having done all the things set out [earlier in the note] we might well take the plunge ... but do *not* devalue, to a fixed rate. Go onto a *floating rate*.'[19] The paper went to Eden – and to Butler. But Butler, who said in reply that he agreed with much of what it recommended, was certainly not going to go through 1952 all over again. (Nor, as it happened, was Macmillan himself when he became Chancellor.) *Dizzy with Success*, as is often the fortune of such documents, thus gently fell by the wayside.

The Cyprus conference at the end of August 1955 again achieved very little. The Turks maintained that Cyprus was Turkish territory and the Greeks maintained that the answer was self-determination (which in practice meant union with Greece). There was a vague understanding on all sides that some move towards self-government for Cyprus would be made, but it was left to the Cypriots themselves to start negotiations on the mechanics. But before that could happen there was an explosion of violence and a state of emergency – bringing an end to negotiation – was duly declared.

By that time there had also been further political turbulence in Egypt. Colonel Nasser, by then apparently firmly in control, had made a deal with the Soviets, through the medium of their satellite Czechoslovakia, for the supply to Egypt of 100 Mig aircraft, 100 tanks and other weapons, with a team of Russian technicians in support. On 23 September Macmillan went to see Eden with the draft of a telegram he proposed to send to Dulles. 'I am proposing to Dulles', he told Eden, 'a *very* stiff and almost threatening protest, in the name of the President and the P.M., to Nasser. We really cannot allow this man, who has neither the authority of a throne nor of a Parliament, to destroy our base and threaten our rear.'[20] Eden agreed with the text of the telegram. But just as Macmillan was leaving, Eden took him aside. 'How would I like to leave the F.O.,' Macmillan was asked, 'and go to the Treasury? I confess I was somewhat staggered. "When?" "At once." "What about Rab?" "He can be Lord Privy Seal and Leader of the House." "Have you spoken to him?" "Yes, last night. He seemed rather to like the idea." ... I said I must think about it.'[21]

There was certainly much to think about. But there was little time for thinking. Macmillan had to set off for New York to see Dulles, and, almost incidentally, to see Molotov to prepare the ground for another Geneva conference. At New York airport he was met by another old wartime friend, Pierson Dixon, by then British Ambassador to the United Nations. Dixon told him immediately that Eisenhower had suffered what appeared to be a major heart attack. Macmillan and Dixon then sat down to digest the news and to see whether an appropriate phrase could be inserted into the speech which Macmillan was due to make at a meeting of the United Nations Assembly on 30 September. All that done, and done with reasonable success, Macmillan flew to Washington to meet yet another of his old wartime friends and now British Ambassador to the United States, Roger Makins. There he was due to meet Dulles and the Vice-President – in fact, in Eisenhower's incapacity, temporary President – Richard Nixon.

The meetings, in Macmillan's account, went well. He was 'rather favourably impressed' with Nixon. 'He struck me as intelligent and not without force and dignity ...' Dulles, too, although in a gloomy mood, agreed with Macmillan about Nasser and the Soviet arms deal – and asked 'if we had enough troops to re-occupy Egypt and I said "not in Suez. They are moving out fast. But it could be done from Cyprus, no doubt." However, at this stage, that did not seem practical.'[22] The upshot of the meeting with Dulles was that a moderately fierce message would be sent to the Soviets – but to the Soviet Foreign Ministry only and without the signature of either Eden or Eisenhower.

Rather than having time to think about his future, on his return to London on 4 October Macmillan ran into another storm. Two Foreign Office officials, Guy Burgess and Donald Maclean, who had vanished in 1951, had reappeared in September in Moscow. A Soviet defector in 1954 had revealed that the defection of 'B and M' (as they were by then affectionately called) was the result of a tip-off from a 'Third Man' – called after the main character in the film of that name made about post-war Vienna – inside the British Government. It need hardly be said that there was a swarm of journalists around any spot where the Third Man might be – or, such is the nature of their trade, any spot where the Third Man might possibly have been, whoever he was. There were vociferous calls for an official inquiry. On 20 October Macmillan reported to the Cabinet on the matter. In his paper of the previous day he had written that such calls should be ignored. 'Nothing could be worse', he wrote, 'than a lot of muckraking and innuendo. It would be like one of the immense divorce cases which there used to be when I was young, going on for days and days, every detail reported in the Press.'²³ The Cabinet agreed. A White Paper would be issued – and little more was said. ('Divorce cases', of course, referred to the 1930s – just when Dorothy herself was beseeching him to give her one.)

Late in October, Macmillan set off again for Geneva and for the second round of the Four Power conference. On his way there, he stopped in Paris, partly to see Dulles to prepare the (unpromising) ground for the conference and partly to set out to Eden his conditions for accepting the Treasury. His letter, typed by Dorothy at Birch Grove and sent from Paris in the diplomatic bag, illustrates the strength of his negotiating position – and the toughness of the negotiator. His conditions were clear: Butler should not be Deputy Prime Minister; as Chancellor, he, Macmillan, must be undisputed head of the home front, under the Prime Minister; and he should be consulted about appointments to the Board of Trade. 'I thought it best to be quite frank,' his letter ended. 'If you don't agree, I shall quite understand. If you do, I am willing to try. Yours ever, Harold . . .'²⁴

Having sent his letter to Eden, Macmillan went on to Geneva – arriving on the day, 26 October, on which an embarrassed Butler was delivering to the House of Commons an 'Autumn Budget'. Macmillan knew perfectly well why he was being offered Butler's job. Eden had lost confidence in his Butler. 'Rab', it was said, 'is "no good any more". He must have had some sort of breakdown since his wife died . . .'²⁵ On his return to London on 5 November – the Geneva conference had been adjourned – Macmillan was able to scotch requests for a public inquiry into the Burgess and Maclean affair (he noted in his diary, yet again, that 'my speech is said to be the best I have ever made'²⁶) before setting off again to Geneva for the reconvened conference.

In fact, there was hardly any point in going back there. The conference came to a desultory end without any substantive conclusion. Nevertheless, rather than staying in London thinking about his future, as he had promised Eden, Macmillan on his return stayed no more than a couple of days before setting off for an extended tour of the Middle East which was to occupy the rest of the month. At this point, Foreign Office officials were wondering whether the Foreign Secretary was spending too much time away from the office. Ministerial responsibility for the Foreign Office was left, as usually happened when Macmillan was on his travels, in the hands of Anthony Nutting, the Minister of State. This was not at all to official liking, since business could not be properly done at long distance and, more important, Macmillan, in truth, neither liked nor trusted Nutting. In fact, on occasions he treated his own junior Minister with something near to contempt. While Macmillan was at Geneva, for instance, when Eden wrote to him for an answer to a question of little importance – which Nutting gave, on official advice – Macmillan wrote from his hotel in Geneva in his own hand to Kirkpatrick. 'I would much prefer Nutting' – he was 'Nutting' rather than 'Anthony' at that point – 'not to answer PM's minutes.'[27]

As it happened, Macmillan would have been better advised to stay in London during that particular November. On the 2nd, Beyen turned up to brief the British Government on the content of the Spaak Committee's report and the meeting of the Six which had taken place subsequently in Brussels. He met Butler, who reminded him of the need to avoid harming the OEEC and explained the difficulties which Britain might have with the Commonwealth if she were to consider joining the new common market. Nevertheless, Butler went on, the Six would always find Britain 'sympathetic' and 'European'. Thus encouraged, Beyen further said that the French were uncertain about the whole project and 'Western Germany's attitude was schizophrenic'.[28]

This gave Butler the opportunity he wanted – to scupper the whole project. If the Germans could be persuaded to pull out, that would be the end of it. At a meeting of the Cabinet Economic Policy Committee on 11 November – at which the Foreign Office was represented by the Marquess of Reading – Butler set out the plan. 'The impulse for a common market', he said, 'arose from the desire of certain sections of opinion in Europe for greater political integration ... the United Kingdom should avoid joining a common market, at any rate for some time to come ...' The Committee agreed with him, and decided that 'United Kingdom representatives at Brussels should continue to be non-committal on the question of the common market but that at the meeting in December it should be stated without ambiguity that we could not join in such a project ... Meanwhile, our views ... should be explained informally to the United States Government ... and also to the German Government, in the hope that this would lead them to adopt a more realistic policy towards such proposals.'[29] In other words, the Germans were to be put firmly in charge of the sabotage mission. Lord Reading was then given the task of giving the Germans their marching orders.

Macmillan was, of course, still in the Middle East – and maintaining radio silence on the matter. He knew perfectly well that Butler was now in a dilemma. On 18 November Butler was to see Spaak. He could not reveal the Cabinet Committee decision taken only a week before. On the other hand, he had to make the same friendly noises he had made to

Beyen. He therefore vacillated. But Spaak pressed the case. Then, as Robert Rothschild, Spaak's Chef de Cabinet, noted, 'the warmer Spaak became, the colder and colder Butler became'.[30]

By the time Macmillan arrived back in London at the end of November the damage had been done. The British decision – almost inevitably – had leaked. Adenauer was irritated and Spaak was furious. It was no good trying to make up ground. At a meeting of the Council of Europe Assembly in early December a junior Minister at the Foreign Office was told simply to hold the line. Macmillan himself appeared at the meeting of the Western European Union and defended the British view to an angry Beyen and an even angrier Spaak. He claimed that 'we would welcome and assist the plan, although we could not join, so long as a proper relation could be established between the inner and outer circles – the 6 and the 15 – Messina and OEEC'.[31] But at the same time he was telling the British Ambassador in Bonn to emphasise to the West German Government that 'the political cohesion of Europe would be damaged by the Six, and it would be deplorable if all OEEC stands for were to be jeopardised for the shadow of a Common Market which either never came to anything or if it did proved harmful to the worldwide movement towards freer trade'.[32] In other words, Macmillan, in spite of his expression of goodwill to Beyen and Spaak, had signed up to the plot to sabotage the nascent European Economic Community (EEC). It was not just that he had failed while in the Middle East to intervene in the Butler discussions. He was now committed to wrecking the whole project.

On 13 December Macmillan finally accepted the post of Chancellor of the Exchequer. It had been agreed that Salisbury, as Lord President, would have preference under the Prime Minister and that Butler, as Lord Privy Seal, would come next and chair the Cabinet in Eden's absence. Macmillan wrote his letters of farewell to Dulles, Makins and others, gave a party in King Charles Street for his officials (who complained, reasonably enough as it happened, that they were to 'be landed with that bloody Selwyn Lloyd'[33]) and, with genuine reluctance since he had enjoyed the job, moved down Whitehall to the (slightly) more austere offices of the Treasury. Later, in his memoirs, Macmillan said that he regretted the move. Dorothy 'was extremely unhappy at the final decision ... instinctively – for she had an inborn and inherited shrewdness about public affairs – she felt the change was a mistake. On looking back on it, I feel sure she was right.'[34]

Dorothy may or may not have had 'an inborn and inherited shrewdness about public affairs' (whatever that may mean) but she certainly disliked the prospect of moving from Carlton Gardens to No. 11 Downing Street. She was 'appalled at its unsuitability for a residence nowadays'[35] and objected to the garden, which faced north and was almost without sun at any time during the year. Nevertheless, whatever he might have said later, Macmillan knew he had made the right decision. He had made himself indispensable. Eden, having discarded one Chancellor, could not possibly discard another. It was a position of immense strength – and Macmillan knew it. After Christmas at Birch Grove, and during the New Year break at Wyndham's grand estate at Petworth, in the middle of the usual days spent shooting he wrote a paper – apparently well considered (according to Macmillan's memoirs, although no copy seems to have survived), but, again rather whimsically, entitled 'First Thoughts from a Treasury Window'.

Like Chancellors before and since, Macmillan claimed to have discovered a terrible mess (and, of course, blamed his predecessor). 'The position is *much worse* than I had expected. Butler has let things drift, and the reserves are steadily falling,' he noted in his diary.[36] 'First Thoughts' set out what he believed should be done. Throughout January 1956 he worked with Treasury officials on a paper to the Cabinet. 'If my colleagues accept it,' he noted, 'I believe we may save the economy from complete collapse ... but the plan is *very tough* and will be politically unpopular.'[37] In order not to reverse Butler's pre-Election reduction of sixpence on the standard rate of income tax, Macmillan's plan proposed severe cuts in Government expenditure – and the abolition of the subsidy on bread and a big increase in the price of milk. In the Treasury view, this was the only way to bring the public finances back into balance and, consequently, to restore confidence in sterling. At first Eden was horrified about the proposals for bread and milk but at a meeting of the Cabinet on 26 January acquiesced in Macmillan's general plan, while asking for the whole thing to be put off until the Budget in the spring.

It turned out to be Macmillan's first confrontation with Eden as Chancellor to Prime Minister. On his way to the United States, Eden wrote from the *Queen Elizabeth* to Macmillan to say that 'I have been giving much thought on our voyage to your problems and I hope it may be useful if I put some reflections down'. The reflections were simple: 'if it can possibly be avoided it would be a real advantage to hold over any further statement or action until the Budget ... As viewed from here, I am sure you would gain, and so would the Government, if the Budget were made a great occasion, and the only one.' Macmillan's reply to this friendly – in fact rather ingratiating – letter was not only abrupt but downright rude. 'I got your letter of 29th January from the ship last night. Of course it would be nice if we could do everything in a single operation. But we can't.' He then spelled out his programme and ended with a threat: '... I must ask you to accept this programme, without which I could not feel that I was doing my duty to you and the country.'[38] In the end, it was no contest. Macmillan was playing to his strength. Eden conceded the point.

On Friday 3 February, Macmillan and Dorothy left Carlton Gardens for good. A weekend at Birch Grove was spent working on a speech for a pending by-election and reading a biography of Baldwin written by Baldwin's son – as well as a life of Sir Francis Burdett which Macmillan's had published in 1931. The following Monday, Macmillan camped in No. 11 Downing Street (Dorothy joined him the next day) and prepared for more arguments in Cabinet about the bread subsidy. Eden reported at Cabinet on 9 February on his visit to Washington ('PM looked very fit on his return (he got back this morning) and has obviously enjoyed himself. Selwyn Lloyd (For Sec) looked rather exhausted[39]). He said that the Americans were still '"sold" on Messina – which they do not understand. It will be the EDC [European Defence Community] story all over again.'[40] In the subsequent discussion, nobody apparently noticed that the French elections of January had returned a government under the Socialist Guy Mollet which was determined to pursue the Messina project. Macmillan, on the other hand, was much more concerned with the argument about the bread subsidy – by 15 February he was waving his letter of resignation in front of the Cabinet Secretary, Sir Norman Brook – and the debate in the House of Commons on the death penalty (he was, as might be supposed, in favour of hanging).

Macmillan finally negotiated an acceptable compromise on the bread subsidy. But no sooner was that done than he crossed swords with Thorneycroft on his Monopolies Bill. In an obviously impatient mood, Macmillan complained about the meeting on 22 March. 'I had a meeting with Thorneycroft and his advisers this morning. But I find it rather painful so early in the morning. He shouts at me (with a cockney accent) as if we were a public meeting . . .'[41] He then went on to write a hectoring note to Eden on 5 April announcing that 'the present view of my advisers is that the crisis will come between August and September. I would say that on present form the betting is pretty heavy odds on compulsory devaluation. Most foreigners are sceptical even now of whether we can avoid it . . . I must not disguise from you that this is a real test for the Government and the Party. If we live up to it, you and your administration will earn first respect, and then renewed confidence. No personal considerations, or national hesitations, should stand in the way.'[42] In other words, Eden could take it or leave it.

Macmillan was nervous about his Budget. In an effort to get Butler's general support for what he was proposing, including – just possibly – a rise in income tax, he asked for a meeting. That did not go well either. Butler vacillated – and Macmillan was unforgiving. 'He [Butler] is in a mood of self-pity,' he wrote in his diary. 'It is the reaction after his wife's death. She was a woman of tremendous character and he depended on her vitality and strength. Now he is alone . . .'[43]

On Budget Day, 17 April, Macmillan stayed in bed most of the morning. He could eat very little. 'The nervous strain of these speeches', he wrote in his diary, 'seems to get worse as one gets older.'[44] In fact, he need not have worried. His speech was said to be the funniest Budget speech since the war. Commenting on the unreliability of economic forecasts, he stated that 'there is no true science which can give us certainty in this uncertain field. What passes for such is more like astrology than astronomy. Lyndoe or Old Moore may turn out to be just as reliable as Professor What's His Name or Dr So and So . . . some of our statistics are too late to be as useful as they ought to be. We are always, as it were, looking up a train in last year's Bradshaw [list of railway timetables].'[45] The Budget's economic content aroused little controversy. It was widely understood that corrective measures were necessary, and the complaints that the 1955 Election had been 'bought' by Butler's pre-Election Budget had been fully aired at the time of his subsequent autumn Budget.

Macmillan's novelty was the proposal to introduce a new type of National Savings Bond which carried no interest but which would be the subject of a monthly lottery draw. The Bonds would have the catchy title of 'Premium Bonds'. They were all part of the campaign to increase private saving. Public saving through taxation was no more than a product of war and its aftermath. Macmillan illustrated this with another sally. 'Does anybody read Dickens nowadays – except, of course, the Russians? If so, they will remember Mrs Pardiggle in *Bleak House.* "My family", boasted this philanthropic lady, "are not frivolous. They spend the whole amount of their allowance in subscriptions, under my direction . . . they enrol their contributions, according to their ages, and their little means." Just so – first pay out far more money to the people than is good for them to have. Then take it all off them again by taxation. It is as simple as shelling peas.'[46]

Much of the next few weeks was spent in tedious argument with colleagues about the cuts which Macmillan had promised in his Budget. But there was another matter which had suddenly risen to the top of his agenda. Thanks to the French Elections of January 1956, the prospects for Messina and the Spaak Committee had changed. Even the Foreign Office was now coming round to the view that the Common Market might well become a reality. Reacting quickly, on 6 February Macmillan had instructed Treasury officials to prepare an alternative to Messina. Noting their resistance, he had minuted that he did not like 'a European bloc excluding Britain, but he would not join the Six'. He was not opposed to their customs union but he 'wanted to join it with the Commonwealth – but to have no part in any supranational or federal tendencies'.[47]

The Treasury working party worked with speed. But before any decisions could be taken, they had to wait for a meeting of the Six, called in Venice on 17 May to discuss the Spaak Committee report (to which the British had not been invited, even as observers). As it happened, the Venice meeting was successful beyond expectations (at least the expectations of British Treasury officials). The Six agreed to proceed to the drafting of a treaty based on the Spaak Committee's report, and to reconvene in Brussels on 26 June to consider the draft.

In response to this, on 31 May a meeting of Ministers, chaired by Macmillan and held at the Treasury, agreed to put forward one of the alternatives suggested by the Treasury working party – a partial free trade area with Europe by which tariffs would be removed on imports to the United Kingdom (and vice versa) on industrial goods only (excluding those in which the countries of the Commonwealth expressed an interest). This quickly became known as 'Plan G'. On that basis, there was, as Ministers agreed, no question of the British wishing to attend the meeting of the Six in Brussels.

The following day Macmillan sent a minute to Eden. Entitled, again whimsically, 'Half Time' (in other words halfway between the Budget and the summer Recess), he reported on the difficulties of achieving the reduction in Government expenditure which he had promised in his Budget. The villain of the piece, he claimed, was defence. 'Some £700 million a year', he wrote, 'has been added to defence expenditure since the Korean War ... we should deliberately take some chances ... it may be better in our present economic plight to leave a ship or an aeroplane uncompleted ...'[48]

There was little reaction from Eden. As June moved into July, Macmillan was at his most gloomy. 'The Government's position', he wrote in his diary of 21 July, 'is very bad at present. Nothing has gone well. In the M[iddle] East, we are still teased by Nasser and Co; the Colonial Empire is breaking up ... At home, taxation is very high; the inflation has not been mastered ... The people are puzzled; the Party is distracted; Eden gives no real leadership in the House ...'[49] On top of all that, Maurice was only just returning from an extensive treatment for alcoholism in Switzerland, and on 27 July Nasser announced his intention to nationalise the Suez Canal Company. It was almost too much, and only Jane Austen could hold the cure. 'Read and finished *Emma*. There is nothing like Miss Austen's novels for a state of fatigue such as I seem now to reach by the end of every week ...'[50] Yet the fatigue, and the gloom about the state of the British economy, were as nothing to what, in the next few months, was about to come.

15

'We *Must* Make Use of Israel'

The town of Aswan in southern Egypt, perched on the eastern bank of the River Nile just below the rough water known as the First Cataract, is nowadays a widely advertised tourist attraction. The feluccas, visitors are told, catch the gentle breezes in their sails and glide lazily about the still waters, conveying their charges to the islands in the river and the historic sites. The faces and physique of the steersmen are indeed beautiful – of obvious Nubian origin, more Sudanese than Egyptian. The sun is high even in the northern winter months, and fragile visitors from northern Europe do well to take with them a good sun block. In the summer months the heat is of an intensity that northerners can hardly bear.

In fact, nowhere in southern Egypt was hotter, so it is claimed by those who stayed there, than the Old Cataract Hotel, a venerable British construction without any distinguishable form of air conditioning. Yet it was in this hotel that engineers and architects met in the early 1950s to plan the construction of a new dam on the Nile. It would, they planned, be higher than the existing small construction and would once and for all block the annual inundation of the river resulting from the melt of the winter snows in the Ethiopian mountains. The purpose was simple: to allow a rational development of agriculture and industry on the long banks of the river as it makes its steady way northwards towards Cairo and the Mediterranean. It all sounded very well. But, although the sweating planners were not to know it, Aswan was as a result about to become not just a tourist site but the origin of the greatest international conflagration since the Korean War.

The project of the Aswan High Dam was taken up by the International Bank for Reconstruction and Development (IBD – but usually known simply as the World Bank). The financing was discussed both within the Bank and with its major contributor, the United States, which, in addition to supporting the Bank, was to ask Congress for additional funds for the project. Britain, or, to be more specific, the Treasury, was also brought into the negotiation – although no extra funds were required from the British Government.

The negotiation proceeded slowly, as such things generally do, but by the autumn of 1955 an offer had been sent to the Egyptian Government. Rather to the surprise of the donor countries and the World Bank, instead of accepting the offer outright, the Egyptians showed a regrettable tendency to wish to examine the small print. As a result of their examination, they concluded that the contract would have given the World Bank, and its American president, more or less total control over the Egyptian economy. Furthermore, they knew that the Americans had no high opinion of Colonel Nasser. There was, they thought, the definite smell of a rat.

The rat became rather more obvious when the Americans reacted angrily to the decision of the Egyptian Government, on 16 May 1956, to give formal recognition to the People's Republic of China. There were many in Washington who now believed that Nasser was no longer a friend at all. The belief became a conviction when in June it became known that Dmitri Shepilov, the Soviet Foreign Minister, was in Egypt with an offer to finance the Aswan High Dam on favourable terms and to bid to buy the whole of the Egyptian cotton crop. The Secretary to the Treasury, George Humphrey, was particularly hostile. Accordingly, on 19 July, Dulles saw Eisenhower and told him that although 'the Egyptian Ambassador was returning to Washington with the publicly announced intention of accepting the US–UK–IBRD offer of financing, which was originally made on December 16, 1955 ...'¹ the offer should be withdrawn. Eisenhower could do no more than agree.

Later in the morning, Makins was summoned from the British Embassy to be given the news – and to express diplomatic surprise that the British Government had not been consulted. At four o'clock in the afternoon a startled Egyptian Ambassador, Ahmed Hussein, was told bluntly that there would be no World Bank or American money for the dam after all. Seven days later, Nasser, by then a properly elected President of Egypt, accepted the Soviet offer and immediately published a decree, to the universal approval of the Egyptian public, taking the Suez Canal Company into Egyptian ownership. Its revenues, Nasser explained in a series of radio broadcasts, were essential to service the financing of the dam – and hence to the future prosperity of Egypt.

Whatever the rights and wrongs of the dancing around the financing of the Aswan High Dam, the news of the nationalisation of the Canal came as a shock both to Britain and the United States. Eden, on 26 July, kept a select few of his dinner guests waiting after he had been told of the event by his Foreign Affairs Private Secretary, Guy Millard. The French Ambassador, Jean Chauvel, and the US Chargé d'Affaires, Andrew Foster, were summoned. Eden told them, in tones that were meant to be of the sternest, that Nasser could not be allowed to succeed – or, indeed, survive. In his mind, the two issues, Nasser's survival and the security of the Canal, had become inextricably linked.

At the meeting of the Cabinet on the following morning, on Eden's prompting, it was agreed that 'HMG should seek to secure, by the use of force if necessary, the reversal of the decision of the Egyptian Government to nationalise the Suez Canal Company'.[2] To manage the crisis, a Cabinet Committee was set up, consisting of Eden, Salisbury, Macmillan, Selwyn Lloyd, Lord Home and Monckton, to be known as the Egypt Committee. The Cabinet then went on to approve military action as a last resort and to authorise Eden to write to Eisenhower to tell him as much. Eden, in his letter to Eisenhower of the same day, duly followed the Cabinet decision. 'My colleagues and I', he wrote, 'are convinced that we must be ready, in the last resort, to bring Nasser to his senses ... I have this morning instructed our Chiefs of Staff to prepare a military plan accordingly.'[3]

Eisenhower was duly alarmed – not least because he was at the start of his campaign to secure re-election on 6 November. He immediately sent Robert Murphy, Under-Secretary at the State Department and – more relevant at the time – Macmillan's former colleague (and, up to a point, friend) in wartime Algiers, to London. His brief was simple: 'to see what it's all about' and then 'just go over and hold the fort'.[4] Murphy straight away was collared for a lunch in Downing Street on 30 July, where Eden and Macmillan 'gave him the impression that our military expedition to Egypt was about to sail. (It will take at least six weeks to prepare it, in fact.)'[5] Murphy was sufficiently alarmed to send a panic message to Washington. As a result, Dulles was told by Eisenhower to drop all his current engagements and make haste for London. Eisenhower then wrote a letter for Dulles to deliver in person to Eden, stating that he 'personally [felt] sure that the American reaction [to the use of force] would be severe' and asking Eden and Macmillan to think again.[6]

On the evening of 1 August Dulles and Murphy went to see Macmillan. 'We had an hour's talk,' Macmillan recorded. 'I told Foster, as plainly as I could, that we could not afford to lose this game. It was a question not of honour but of survival.' But Macmillan then went on to raise the stakes. 'We must either get Nasser out by diplomacy or by force,' he asserted, in an effort to 'keep the Americans really frightened ... We must have a) international control of the Canal and b) humiliation or collapse of Nasser.'[7] Dulles certainly was alarmed, if not, perhaps, frightened. For the first time it had become clear that senior members of the British Government, led by Eden, Macmillan and Salisbury, wanted not just the restoration of the Canal but no less than the total destruction of Nasser and his Government.

Whatever their views on Nasser, that was not at all what Dulles (and Eisenhower) had in mind at that moment. They were quite prepared to offer support over the Canal – and to see what might be done about Nasser in the longer term. But removing an elected Head of State and Government by force was quite another matter. On the other hand, they were worried that the Soviet arms deal with Egypt and the Soviet agreement to finance the Aswan High Dam, if successful, might bring with them Soviet political domination of the Arab Middle East. Their position at that point was, to say the least, delicate.

Undeterred by American pleas for caution, the Cabinet decided the following morning to move ahead with the plan to use force. Macmillan, however, was sceptical about the limited plan produced by the Chiefs of Staff. At the meeting of the Egypt Committee after Cabinet on 3 August, Macmillan first reported on an unpleasant meeting he had had with the Deputy Chairman and General Manager of the Westminster Bank who had claimed that the bank might have to freeze the funds of the Suez Canal Company if a court decided that Nasser had acted legally. More substantially, however, he provoked discussion in the Committee about a memorandum he had written and sent to Eden. 'I feel', he wrote, 'that we *must* make use of Israel against Egypt, if the military operation is actually undertaken.'[8]

There it was. For the first time, someone in authority, no less than the Chancellor of the Exchequer, had raised the matter of Israel and had argued the necessity for – not to put too fine a point on it – collusion. Eden and Lloyd were, in fact, rather shocked at the suggestion. But Macmillan went further than raising the matter in the Egypt Committee. On 5 August he and Dorothy were invited to dinner with Churchill at Chartwell. After dinner, he was alone with Churchill and Christopher Soames. Churchill had been shown the military plan by Eden and asked Macmillan what he thought of it. 'I said', Macmillan wrote, 'that unless we brought in Israel, I didn't think it could be done . . . Churchill seemed to agree with all this . . .'[9] Later that evening, Soames called Macmillan and told him that Churchill was going to see Eden the next morning and tell him so.

Macmillan then wrote a paper for the Egypt Committee, with the uncompromising title of 'Action against Egypt'. After criticising the existing plan, the paper ended by stating roundly, 'I hope further thought will be given to the Israeli question.'[10] Eden refused to have it circulated to the Chiefs of Staff – partly because he was still uncomfortable with its contents but partly because he thought that Macmillan was trying to upstage him by dragging in Churchill in support of his collusion idea. By then, of course, Macmillan had made sure that the Minister of Defence, Walter Monckton, would make enough copies. He also knew that the Chief of the Imperial General Staff, Sir Gerald Templer, was all for the idea – and had told Macmillan that he was grateful to him for suggesting it.

After a short midweek stay at Birch Grove ('we went to Pooks – where our tenant has a TV – to see a TV programme of Grannie (Evie Devonshire) at Hardwick House. She really did it splendidly, in spite of her 85 years'), reading a life of Dickens and complaining that 'I *am* very tired and feel rather old ...',[11] Macmillan returned to London to find a note from Eden inviting him to take a few days off. There was nothing sinister about the invitation – Macmillan, in those days, was one of Eden's most faithful supporters. Eden thought that Macmillan had been long in the firing line and, in the spirit of a fellow Etonian, thought he might need a rest. Besides, there was to be a conference, starting on 16 August, of maritime nations, including the signatories of the 1888 Suez Convention, summoned to London to discuss what was hoped would be a concerted plan to allow traffic on the Suez Canal to be guaranteed internationally. All Ministers would have to be at full attention for that. Eden's invitation was gladly accepted and Macmillan went off to Bolton Abbey for the grouse shoot (in dreadful weather, as it happened).

As holidays go, it was short and, at least to some extent, sweet. In spite of the weather, the shooting had not been too bad. But on his return he found a stern warning from Sir Edward Bridges, Permanent Secretary at the Treasury, conveying 'some of the rather uncomfortable thoughts which I have been having in the last few days; e.g., as to the immediate results in the whole Middle East of armed intervention in Egypt'. Apart from the consequences to sterling Bridges raised the wider matter of the political and economic problems (not least, the effect on the supply of oil) to which it would give rise. Refreshed, however, by his holiday, Macmillan was in no mood to listen. In his own handwriting he replied to Bridges: 'we *must* either obtain a diplomatic success, which will eventually mean that Nasser will go the way of Mossadeq; or impose our will by force. If we fail in *both*, I think our strength and life will begin to wither away. The general view in the Middle East and East is that the Europeans – and particularly the British – have "had it". This is what this row is really about.'[12]

For Macmillan, that was the truth of the matter. On 18 August, the London Conference then in seemingly interminable session, he and Dorothy had dinner at the American Embassy with Dulles. Dulles reported to Eisenhower the next day. Macmillan, he told Eisenhower, had said that 'there are only three choices: (1) Nasser voluntarily takes a proposal along the lines of the US paper [for an international body of Canal Users to guarantee passage of the Canal]; or (2) we compel Egypt to take it; (3) we accept Nasser's refusal. In the last event, Britain is finished and so far as I am concerned I will have no part in it and will resign.' Macmillan said this, Dulles noted, 'most soberly, yet strongly'. Dulles, however, went on to note that the Labour Party, and Gaitskell in particular, had broken ranks and were calling for United Nations intervention. 'I have no doubt that Nasser is fully aware of the situation and may calculate that if he stands firm the result will be not solid strength against him but perhaps a labor government which would be softer.'[13]

Macmillan was even more indiscreet with Dulles a few days later. Taking Dulles by the sleeve into a private room at a reception given by Eden for the participants at the London Conference, he said that he would like to speak to Dulles privately. He then asked Dulles whether he planned to stay on as Secretary of State after Eisenhower's hoped-for re-election. 'He said that', Dulles recorded, 'because he was thinking of perhaps going back to take over the Foreign Office in the reasonably near future and that his decision in this matter would be influenced by whether I would be his vis-à-vis in the United States. He spoke of the very happy relations ...' But Macmillan went even further. He 'urged me most strongly to take on the negotiation with Nasser. He said he did not have confidence that anybody else could pull it off.'[14]

Leaving aside the question of whether or not Eden was thinking of replacing Selwyn Lloyd (for which there is no detectable evidence, although Dulles noted, in a separate conversation, that 'Mr Lloyd showed obvious emotional strain'[15]), there is no doubt that Macmillan had a point when he thought that the delegation which had been appointed to persuade Nasser of the virtues of the London Conference was about as ill equipped as it was possible to be. The Conference had signed up to a proposal – backed by eighteen countries out of the twenty-two invited (the Soviet Union had been making mischief) – for a new Convention to internationalise the Canal. The head of the delegation, although Dulles was formally the Chairman, was the Prime Minister of Australia, Robert Menzies (known colloquially as 'Pig-iron Bob' after he had broken a strike of steel workers in Sydney). It was not, as Macmillan observed, a sensible choice. Menzies was a brash Australian, tough and undiplomatic, and he did not either like or trust Egyptians. Australian soldiers, he was apt to say, had seen too many of them in the war.

There was not much more that Macmillan could do. Treasury business was quiet; official discussions on Plan G continued (it was noted, almost as an aside, that the Six had resolved their remaining differences and were drafting a Treaty – to be signed in Rome the following year); a paper was written on 'The Economic Consequences of Colonel Nasser' to show the Cabinet how little Britain could afford the loss of oil; and, by way of relaxation, George Eliot's *Middlemarch* was duly read. The paper was then discussed at the Egypt Committee without enthusiasm, along with a new plan – to be known as 'Musketeer' – presented by the newly appointed general commanding the military operation, Sir Charles Keightley (another wartime acquaintance but a less happy one – from the days of the Cossack repatriation), and it was time for a break at Birch Grove. On 30 August Macmillan stayed in bed all morning, consoled by the two Amery daughters – 'they are very sweet and come to my bedroom in the morning "to pass the time of day" in the most friendly manner. They are naturally much excited about the twins [Catherine Amery had just given birth to twins] – whom they have not yet seen.' In fact, for the next three days he spent most of the time 'in bed or in my smoking room' to escape the bad weather and reading half of Villari's *Savonarola* – 'and have got tired of it'.[16]

The beginning of September brought no good news. The Menzies delegation were kicking their heels in Cairo. Eisenhower wrote further to Eden that 'now the London Conference is over our efforts must be concentrated on the successful outcome of the conversations with Nasser ... possibility of later appeal to the United Nations ... I must tell you frankly that American public opinion flatly rejects the thought of using force ... Moreover, I gravely doubt we could here secure Congressional authority even for the lesser support measures for which you might have to look to us.'[17] The warning could hardly have been clearer. Furthermore, the British press were getting restive – some papers demanding action, others accusing Eden of 'warmongering'.

There was some relief for Macmillan when Spaak came to lunch on 4 September to talk about the proposed Common Market and the possibilities of British association along the lines of Plan G. Spaak urged Macmillan to be quite firm and not to shrink from force over the Suez Canal, but on Plan G he was more reserved. It all depended, as Macmillan agreed, on whether British Ministers were prepared to make the first moves. The next day, the Economic Policy Committee of the Cabinet met and – rather to Macmillan's surprise – warmly endorsed Plan G.

But the relief was short-lived. Three days later it became clear that the talks between the Menzies delegation and Nasser had come to nothing. The Egypt Committee met to consider a new military plan put forward by General Keightley – to be known as 'Musketeer Revise' – for a direct assault on Port Said, at the head of the Canal. They also had to consider a new scheme put forward by Dulles for a Suez Canal Users Association (SCUA), based in Rome, which would organise its own pilots and collect dues, out of which partial payment to Egypt would be made. (Nobody, in fact not even Dulles, was confident that it would work.) The following weekend at Birch Grove allowed Macmillan a Saturday afternoon off – sitting in the garden reading and surrounded by six or seven grand-children – and a half of Sunday – to greet Ronnie Knox after church ('we had Daniel 3 – the fiery furnace – which the children greatly enjoyed'[18]) and talk with him over lunch and tea, before driving back to London in the early evening.

On Wednesday 12 September Parliament met for a two-day debate on Suez. In the Commons it was rowdy. Gaitskell, leading for the Opposition in moving a Motion of Censure, came out flatly against the use of force and demanded referral of the whole matter to the United Nations. Eden, in reply, spoke effectively – and confused the Labour benches by first appearing to agree to a referral to the United Nations – to roars of Labour approval – and then retracting. ('Boothby, characteristically, made a fighting speech yesterday and was in full retreat today.'[19]) In the Lords, Kilmuir, in a calmer atmosphere, expressed his view that Nasser's action had been a flagrant breach of the 1888 Suez Convention guaranteeing rights of passage and that the use of force would be perfectly legal. (His view, in fact, was wholly contrary to the considered opinions of the Attorney-General, the Solicitor-General, the Legal Adviser to the Foreign Office and every other legal opinion apart from that of one Oxford professor. The Cabinet, almost as a matter of course, accepted the Lord Chancellor's view.)

By the middle of the month of September everybody was clearly getting very tired. Eden was starting to show signs of breaking under the intense stress. Macmillan himself wrote that he was too tired to sleep. On the 14th an exhausted Cabinet met to spend the whole morning on Plan G; the Egypt Committee in turn met, yet again, in the afternoon to discuss Suez. On the 17th, Dulles arrived again in London to launch SCUA – and to be hectored by Macmillan and Salisbury at a dinner at the American Embassy. By the 20th, Macmillan was writing that he was reading *Vanity Fair* ('How good it is! I try to read an hour or two every day, however late. Otherwise, one w[oul]d go mad ...'). Eden then told him that there was trouble in the Tory Party but that he was quite determined. 'It was 1938 all over again, and he could not be party to it ...'[20] All in all, it was time to leave aside the second London Conference, called to set up the fledgling SCUA, and to get away. It so happened that there was a perfect excuse – the annual meetings of the International Monetary Fund

(IMF) and the World Bank. Thus, on the evening of 21 September, Macmillan flew to New York.

The journey was in part one of sentiment. It was the hundredth anniversary of Nellie's birth in Indianapolis. Accompanied by Roger Makins (ambassadors always have these strange duties), Macmillan flew on to Indianapolis to celebrate, if that is the right word, the event. The two were met at Indianapolis airport and immediately confronted by a barrage of excited journalists' questions about Suez. 'When asked how far he thought Nasser would go in the Suez dispute,' one exclaimed, 'Macmillan commented "Well, I've seen him. I saw Mussolini when he started . . . I think Nasser's going the same way."'[21] Quickly whisked away so as not to offend the Italian community of Indianapolis, they were then entertained to luncheon by some hundred or so 'notables' where he was given 'as my mother's son, a wonderful welcome by these very sincere folks. How I wished this c[oul]d have happened while she was alive . . .'[22] From there they flew to Bloomington and to Indiana University to receive a degree as doctor of laws 'in the presence of an audience of several thousand students and others . . . there were a number of prayers, speeches etc., as well as a Brahms something or other played by the University orchestra'.[23]

The highlight of Macmillan's journey into sentiment, however, came the next day. After a tour of the university, Macmillan and Makins were driven to Spencer. There was an enthusiastic reception committee, including some who said that they remembered Nellie and her parents. Macmillan read the lesson at Nellie's Methodist Church – the parable of the talents – and was then 'called forward from his seat in the eighth row by the Rev. Charles W. Ballard. He related the story of his mother and the background of his Hoosier ties. At one point he said, "I owe my mother everything."'[24]

Macmillan's own account was more emotional. For once, he was not acting a part. 'I found it rather difficult to get through, without breaking down, and I really felt that my mother was there watching us and enjoying the satisfaction of so many of her hopes and ambitions for me. When I remember all that I owe to her, it's difficult to express what she did for me.'[25] Even after all the years, his account strikes the reader immediately as a – surprisingly moving – moment of truth. For all the acting, the plotting, the aristocratic pretence and the endless immersion in books, Macmillan, at the age of sixty-two, nearly broke down when giving an address about his mother.

But the moment was brief. He and Makins drove back to Bloomington and flew, through a dreadful storm, to Washington. They were there in time to have a cheerful dinner with George Humphrey and his wife.

Humphrey was, Macmillan wrote, 'not very easy to persuade of our economic position' (in addition, Humphrey had been a consistent opponent of US involvement in the financing of the High Aswan Dam) but 'I had a [frank] talk with him after dinner and hope to see him again during the week'.[26] There was hardly time to notice that the United Kingdom on that day – much against Dulles's advice – had submitted its case to the Security Council of the United Nations.

If the journey to Indiana was one of sentiment, the stay in Washington was one of reality. Board meetings of the World Bank and the IMF are usually themselves formal – and mostly unentertaining – affairs but on the sidelines they are useful occasions for informal chats about the issues of the day. One of these took place on the morning of 25 September between Macmillan and the President – and by then, formally, the Republican Presidential candidate – Eisenhower.

The meeting was an event which has generated much controversy. On that morning a message came through to the British Embassy that Eisenhower would like to have a friendly chat with Macmillan – provided he and Makins were smuggled into the White House by the back door. They duly went in 'an ordinary car (not the Rolls) and we were taken to a little used and private entrance ... The President seemed to me in very good health ... His colour was good; he was clearly active and interested – and very keen to win this election ... His manner could not have been more cordial ... it was just like talking to him in the old days at St George's Hotel in Algiers.'[27] So far, as it were, so good. Moreover, the meeting lasted unexpectedly long and, at its end, Eisenhower showed Macmillan the narrow 'fairway' through the White House garden which led to a street lamp outside the railings. Eisenhower said that the distance was 270 yards – and that he could hit a golf ball in the general direction but that he had never managed to reach the lamp.

Cordiality aside, Macmillan came away from the meeting able to reassure Eden, in the firmest terms, that Eisenhower would not object to the use of force against Nasser. The question which has puzzled historians is why he felt so confident. Makins himself, for instance, although writing some thirty years after the event, had what appears to be a clear memory of the occasion. Referring to the meeting, he wrote, 'much to my surprise it was a purely social call, and the issue of the day was not discussed at all. It was a chat between three old friends. It was subsequently recorded that it was this interview which convinced him that Ike would not, in practice, oppose unilateral action by us against Egypt, but there was nothing in the conversation which could really have persuaded him that this was the case, except that Ike didn't raise the subject.'[28]

Macmillan, on the other hand, wrote in his diary that Eisenhower had spoken about the United Nations – that it could not be controlled – had asked why the US, UK, Germany and France could not form a group 'and try to settle all these things ahead of time' and, about Suez, had said that 'he was sure we must get Nasser down … The only thing was how to do it …'[29] Eisenhower's own account of the meeting only partially refutes Makins's later memory. When Dulles called him later in the morning to find out what Macmillan had had to say, Eisenhower replied that Macmillan had 'talked very much more moderately (about Suez) than he had anticipated … he cheerfully admitted that the issue was Nasser rather than the Canal … they had had "a nice chat" … Macmillan rather thought the Users Association is a good thing … reiterated that nothing was said which might cause Dulles concern.'[30]

Makins's own memory, however, normally so accurate, does not tally with his own official (and contemporary) report of the same meeting. ' The talk', his report went, 'soon turned to the Suez Canal question … The President said that this was the most "worrisome" problem with which he had to deal … He had one regret, namely the way in which the question of the High Aswan Dam had been handled … The President said that in the present climate of opinion we should have to go very carefully on the Suez affair … The President expressed interest in the threat to the Suez refinery … he added that if Nasser himself tried to secure control over other oil interests in the Middle East our case against him would be greatly strengthened. Mr Macmillan referred to the remarks which had been made by Mr Dulles in his TV interview of September 23 about the use of force which had been very helpful to us. The President was aware of them and also expressed approval.' It was only on item eleven of Makins's report that 'The remainder of the conversation covered personal or domestic political matters'.[31]

Macmillan, of course, picked up Eisenhower's comment. 'The President was aware of them and also expressed approval.' Dulles had indeed been interviewed on television two days earlier – and could not have been more helpful to Macmillan's cause. The interviewer had led with the question: 'London reports this morning that the British and French feel they would have your tacit consent to shoot their way through the Canal if the United Nations fail to secure a settlement. Is there any truth for those reports?' Dulles replied: 'No, there are no truths to those reports. We have not discussed at all what might happen if the United Nations' efforts should fail. I have pointed out … in the speech which I made last Wednesday night … that I do believe that peace and justice in international law are two sides of the coin, and you can't always count on nations not using force unless there is some alternative which conforms to international peace and justice, and I think there [Suez] unless we can work out some system here which is just, which recognises the real rights of users, then I don't think you can expect to go on forever asking people not to resort to force ...'[32]

Macmillan was thus, reasonably enough, quite clear from Dulles's comments, however strategically inelegant, and Eisenhower's endorsement of them, that Britain would have the support needed for the use of force. But there was to be a rider. On the afternoon of the 25th Macmillan went on to see Dulles himself. 'I had a private talk', Dulles recorded that evening, 'with Harold Macmillan ... I said that I hoped nothing drastic would happen through British action which might diminish our chances [of Eisenhower's re-election]. Macmillan said he recalled that we had been helpful in their election situation and he would bear that in mind. I said I felt that there was a basis for some reciprocity and he quite agreed. We discussed the plans for diminishing Nasser's prestige and I expressed the view that this could be done by economic and political means more effectively than by military means ... Mr Macmillan said ... that the present military situation was such that they could without undue expense hold action in abeyance ...'[33] In simple terms, Dulles was telling Macmillan that – whatever he had said on television – nothing should happen before 6 November, and Macmillan was responding not just that he fully understood the message but that military action could easily be postponed.

On the next morning, after a meeting of the International Monetary Fund, Macmillan had a further private talk with George Humphrey. For three-quarters of an hour Humphrey talked about British–American cooperation. 'He had such charm of manner and such a jaunty way of expressing himself', Macmillan later wrote, 'that I began to wonder what was the real purpose of the talk ... Finally, he said in the most emphatic way that America must see the United Kingdom through any of her troubles ...'[34]

That was enough. Macmillan returned from America convinced that Eisenhower would be re-elected and that he would, if the British and the French used force, 'lie doggo'.[35] Makins, too, left Washington on a high note. He had been persuaded by Macmillan to return to London as Permanent Secretary at the Treasury in place of Bridges, who was due to retire. He was flattered to find, on his return to his desk at the British Embassy, 'the splendid photograph of you [Eisenhower] so generously inscribed'.[36] At that point there seemed to be no clouds anywhere near the political horizon. The only problem was that Dulles had clearly told Macmillan that any military action must wait until after Eisenhower's re-election.

On his return to London on 1 October Macmillan spent most of a morning reporting to Eden on the results of his visit. Also on the table was a letter from Bulganin claiming that the British and French were acting wholly irresponsibly, as colonial powers, and were consequently a threat to world peace. That, they decided, could safely be ignored. But Eden could not refrain from writing to Eisenhower pointing out that Nasser was obviously in Soviet hands – the parallel, in his view with Mussolini's subservience to Hitler being self-evident. But all that was to no avail. Dulles again slipped. Under pressure from the American press, on 2 October he conceded that 'there were differences between the three governments ... in out of NATO areas the British and French were "encroaching in some form of manner on the problem of neo-colonialism" and the United States was to be found "playing a somewhat independent role"'. Anthony Nutting was with Eden when the report of the Dulles press conference was brought in. 'With a contemptuous gesture', Nutting later wrote, 'he flung the piece of paper across the table, hissing as he did so, "And now what have you to say for your American friends?."'[37] It was all becoming too much for Eden. Three days later he was admitted to hospital with a high temperature. As Lord Moran had warned, his health was starting to break down. Moreover, there were rumours about that his doctors were only keeping him going by extensive use of drugs.

Eden's stay in hospital was short. But when he came out he heard that Mollet and his Foreign Minister, Christian Pineau, had been flirting with the Israelis (and that 'the Jews have come up with an offer'[38]). At the same time, Selwyn Lloyd was opening the debate in the United Nations claiming the righteousness of the Franco-British case. Keightley, too, was saying that 'Musketeer Revise' could not be postponed. It is little wonder that Macmillan was writing, in his last entry before his diary fell silent (either it was not kept or, more likely, it was destroyed) 'our anxieties are not growing less. The Suez situation is beginning to slip out of our hands.'[39]

The October 1956 Conservative Party Conference in Llandudno, such as it was, came and went. Eden's speech on the 13th managed deftly to steer the difficult course between suitable belligerence and respect for the United Nations. But on the following day, Sunday 14 October, everything became very much more complicated. Carefully shepherded in by military escort, two visitors arrived at Chequers. Albert Gazier, the French Minister for Social Affairs, had come with General Maurice Challe to explain a plan – apparently dreamed up by Challe – for serious collusion with the Israelis. The Israelis, Challe's plan went, would attack Egypt. The British and French would then issue an ultimatum telling both sides

to stop, and, when one refused (obviously the Egyptians), send in forces
to enforce the ultimatum, separate the two sides – and occupy the Canal
and get rid of Nasser.

It was all very simple, and Eden was immediately much taken with
the idea. He promised a considered British response within days. On the
morning of Monday 16 October, Guy Millard rang round a group of
Ministers and asked them to turn up in Downing Street for a meeting
which would be private – and not minuted. Macmillan, Monckton,
Anthony Head (Secretary of State for War), Alan Lennox-Boyd (Colonial
Secretary) and the Chiefs of Staff (including, of course, the Chief of the
Imperial General Staff, Sir Gerald Templer) all duly arrived. Selwyn
Lloyd was summoned back from New York (and difficult, but not entirely
fruitless, negotiations on the 'Six Principles' with the Egyptian Foreign
Minister, Mohamed Fawzi, and the Secretary-General of the United
Nations, Dag Hammarskjöld). He arrived late – and jet-lagged. Nutting
stood in for him for the early part of the meeting.

'Eden opened the meeting', Nutting's account originally ran (it was
cut out of the published version of his book by the Cabinet Secretary of
the day at the time of publication), 'with a full account of Sunday's
meeting with Gazier and Challe. He did not mention Lloyd's negotiations
with Fawzi in New York, concentrating exclusively on the Challe plan
and making no attempt to disguise his enthusiasm for it. When he had
finished, Macmillan was the first to speak. Ponderously, he intoned his
belief that we should support the French and the Israelis. Recourse to
the UN, the Menzies mission and the Canal Users' Association had got
us nowhere, he said. We must break out of the stalemate which we had
reached, and the French plan, although fraught with difficulties and
dangers which he did not minimise, seemed to offer the best way out.'[40]

Nutting attempted to argue against the Challe plan. The Americans,
he said, should be consulted. Eden exploded: 'I will not bring the
Americans into this ... Dulles has done us enough damage as it is. This
has nothing to do with the Americans. We and the French must decide
what to do and we alone.'[41] Only Monckton supported Nutting (saying
that 'I did not like the idea of allying ourselves with the Jews and the
French ...'[42] and duly resigning as Secretary of State for Defence – only
to spoil his case by remaining in the Cabinet as Paymaster-General).
Macmillan, apparently, seemed to have remained silent. Eden and Lloyd
then left immediately for Paris to tell Mollet and Pineau that the British
Government agreed with the Challe plan.

Lloyd reported to the Cabinet on the morning of 18 October on the
result of the proceedings in the Security Council. There was general,
and dutifully solemn, approval of the result. The Council had voted

unanimously to the proposition that 'the operation of the Canal should be insulated from the politics of any one country'. It was noted, of course, that the Soviet Union had – undoubtedly only to make mischief – vetoed the second part of the British and French resolution which had, after all, been no more than the decision of eighteen user nations at the London Conference. It was also noted that there was apparently to be a further meeting, perhaps in Geneva, where the Egyptians were to be invited to put forward their proposals for a negotiated solution.

All that done, the Cabinet then went on to the real meat: Eden's report of his meeting in Paris. It was guarded, but the result was clear. 'The Cabinet should therefore be aware', the official minute runs, 'that, while we continued to seek an agreed settlement of the Suez dispute in pursuance of the resolution of the Security Council, it was possible that the issue might be brought more rapidly to a head as a result of military action by Israel against Egypt.'[43]

By that time Macmillan, and the rest of the Cabinet, knew that the matter was settled. There would be war – of some sort. The details of the war that was to be became clearer when Eden, almost dragging Lloyd along with him, went to a meeting on 22 October at a villa on the outskirts of Paris, hard by the porcelain factory of Sèvres. It was there that the Challe plan was put into words. The Israelis would attack Egypt; Egypt would defend herself; the British and French would tell both of them to stop; when they failed to do so, British and French forces would intervene. At a meeting of the Cabinet the next day, Ministers were told that 'from secret conversations which had been held in Paris with representatives of the Israeli Government, it now appeared that the Israelis would not alone launch a full-scale attack against Egypt . . .' and that 'grave decisions would have to be taken by the Cabinet in the course of the next few days'.[44] The final version of the deal was then sealed – and signed – with the French and Israelis at Sèvres at a further meeting on the 24th. It was, of course, as the 'Sèvres Protocol' stated, all to remain a deadly secret. (Needless to say, however, the Israelis, the French and one of the Foreign Office officials present at the signing each pocketed a copy of the document.)

On the 25th, Eden told the Chief Whip, Edward Heath, that only he, Lloyd, Macmillan and Butler were to know about the details of the Sèvres Protocol. But it was not as easy as that. Salisbury got wind of it, Lloyd told Nutting about it and Head, who had succeeded Monckton at Defence, certainly knew about it. But Eden was still not prepared to tell the full story. After a desultory meeting of Cabinet on the 24th (discussing, strangely enough at the time, Salisbury's proposals for reform of the House of Lords), Eden, at a further meeting on the 25th, suggested that 'if Israel launched a full-scale military operation against Egypt, the Governments of the United Kingdom and France should at once call on both parties to stop hostilities ...'[45] Kilmuir reiterated that the action would be defensible in international law. On hearing of the decision, Nutting finally decided to resign.

On 29 October, the Israelis, as had been agreed, attacked Egypt. The Cabinet met on the 30th and duly approved a draft of a statement to be made that evening to a House of Commons which had reassembled after the summer Recess. The deception continued. Not only was Parliament to be misled but the Cabinet continued to deceive itself in its approval of the draft of the Franco-British ultimatum. 'It was proposed', the minute goes, 'that if, at the expiration of twelve hours from the delivery of these notes [requiring both sides to stop hostilities and to withdraw their forces to a distance of ten miles from the Canal], one or both Governments had failed to comply with the requirements stated in them, British and French forces should intervene in order to enforce compliance.'[46] Macmillan reported that gold and dollar reserves were dwindling and that it was important to try to secure American support of sterling. (Oddly enough, the Cabinet then went on to discuss a memorandum from Macmillan asking for approval of arrangements to improve compensation to the occupiers and owners of land used for open-cast mining.)

Macmillan had by then made his point, and the Cabinet had approved Eden's proposal to write to Eisenhower asking for his support. The letter duly went. 'As you know,' Eden wrote, 'the Russians regarded the Security Council proceedings as a victory for themselves and Egypt ... When we received news of the Israeli mobilisation we instructed our Ambassador in Tel Aviv to urge restraint ... Egypt has to a large extent brought this attack on herself ...'[47] Eisenhower immediately wrote back. 'We have learned', his reply went, 'that the French had provided Israel with a considerable amount of equipment ... Late last week we became convinced that the Israeli mobilization was proceeding to the point where something more than mere defence was contemplated ... volume of communication traffic between Paris and Tel Aviv jumped enormously, alerting us to the probability that France and Israel were concerting detailed plans of some kind.'[48] In other words, the Americans knew that something was up. When their Ambassador to the UN, Henry Cabot Lodge, met Britain's Ambassador, Sir Pierson Dixon, to suggest referring the whole business to the Security Council, Dixon was 'completely unsympathetic'. (In fact, Dixon was near resignation on the matter.)[49]

At 12.30 p.m. on 31 October the Cabinet met again. There were only two items of business. Butler reported that the Labour Party had decided to table a Motion of Censure for debate on 1 November. It was agreed that this should be a two-day debate. The only other item was Suez. Eden told the Cabinet that the Israelis had accepted the terms of the Franco-British ultimatum but the Egyptians had refused. 'In these circumstances,' the official minute runs, 'the Commander-in-Chief of the Anglo-French forces had been authorised to put into operation the approved plan for enforcing compliance on the two Governments. At dusk that evening he would begin air operations designed to cripple the Egyptian Air Force.'[50]

The crooked die was thus cast. The Cabinet was unanimous both in the action – and the deception. Yet nobody seemed to have noticed that the Soviets were preparing their tanks to crush the uprising in Budapest or that Eisenhower's bid for re-election was only six days away. Among all those in the Cabinet on that day, Macmillan, after his sentimental journey to his mother's birthplace and with his affection for Eisenhower, might have been the one to point all that out. Dulles, after all, had warned him that nothing should be allowed to disturb Eisenhower's re-election. But, on the day, he kept his silence, rowing along with the rest of Eden's duplicitous crew.

'The Last Gasp of a Declining Power'

When he heard of the Franco-British bombing raids of 31 October, Eisenhower flew into one of the most spectacular of all his rages. In spite of all his friendly advice to Eden, in spite of Dulles's warnings to Macmillan, as he shouted to all who would listen, the British and French were not just blundering into an absurd misadventure but were going out of their way to derail his re-election to the Presidency. His language, it was said, was a wonder to hear. William Clark, Eden's Press Secretary, for instance, was the recipient, holding the telephone receiver well away from his ear, of a stream of what can only be described as military language from the President – who thought, as it turned out, that he was talking to Eden himself. But it was not just a question of Presidential obscenities. Winthrop Aldrich, the US Ambassador in London, recorded that the whole United States administration, from Eisenhower down, was deeply offended with the British and French '. . . not only not letting us know, but actually deceiving us as to what would happen . . . the President just went off the deep end . . . he wouldn't have anything to do with Eden at all. He wouldn't even communicate with him.'[1]

Eisenhower was just as angry with Macmillan. He felt that Macmillan, his old comrade in arms, ought never to have been a party to such outright deception. Dulles, too, was furious. George Humphrey, who had been so pleasant to Macmillan in September, was almost beside himself. In fact, so angry were they all that when the whole thing went to the UN Security Council on a Soviet Resolution of outright condemnation of the British and French it looked as though the United States would join with the Soviet Union in support. The US, in fact, had already, and ominously, joined forces with the Soviets on 30 October in support of a Resolution calling on all members to refrain from the use of force or from threatening force – which Britain and France had summarily vetoed, thus adding another drop of petrol to Dulles's already fiery mood.

Fortunately for the British and French, wise American heads calmed things down. Late in the New York morning of the 31st, an uncomfortable Dixon saw Cabot Lodge, the US Representative at the UN, and asked 'in this hot situation' for 'a cool review of the position as between friends'.[2] Although his relations with Dixon were hardly cordial after the British veto on the previous day, Lodge, after securing Dulles's reluctant agreement, gave at least a diplomatic inch, agreeing both to withdraw US support from the Soviet Resolution of condemnation and, more important, to persuade the Soviets not to take it to a vote. The price, however, Lodge pointed out, was US support for a Yugoslav proposal to summon a Special Session of the General Assembly to debate the matter under the 'Uniting for Peace' procedure, set up in November 1950 to enable the Assembly to act in cases where the Security Council was deadlocked.

At 5 p.m. the next day, Thursday 1 November, the General Assembly accordingly met in Special Session. Before it was a Resolution, moved by Dulles, for an immediate ceasefire by all parties involved in the Suez Canal dispute. The debate was – by UN standards – unusually rowdy. At about the same time, as it happened, the House of Commons in London was in the middle of yet another, and rowdier, shouting match. (In the meantime, as almost nobody seemed to notice, the Franco-British seaborne armada was lumbering towards Port Said at five knots, carefully shadowed, and occasionally harassed, by the US Sixth Fleet.) But in his speech to the Commons Eden – when he could be heard – made an important concession. He said clearly that if the UN were willing to take over the task of maintaining peace in the Suez Canal area no one would be better pleased than the British Government.

Taking up the theme, Dixon repeated it to the General Assembly as its debate dragged on, whereupon Lester Pearson, the Canadian Prime Minister, suggested to Dulles the formation of a United Nations Expeditionary Force (UNEF) to do the job Eden was proposing. Dulles refused to allow an amendment to the ceasefire Resolution but, after the Assembly, at 4 a.m. on the Friday morning, had voted in favour, he immediately stood up to say that if Canada introduced a Resolution along the lines Pearson had suggested the United States would support it.

On hearing this on the Friday in London the British Cabinet, too, endorsed Pearson's proposals at two meetings (Macmillan, as it happened, was not present at either), although Butler pointed, reasonably enough, 'to the difficulty of reconciling a statement along the lines proposed [acceptance of a ceasefire and UNEF] with the continuance of the Anglo-French operation against Egypt'. Lloyd, also, asserted that 'if no concessions were made to [US] feelings, it was possible that oil sanctions might be used against us. We might then be compelled to occupy Kuwait and Qatar ...'[3] Leaving aside the obvious beginnings of panic, Eden called Pearson with the result of the Cabinet meeting. The Canadian

Resolution was then duly tabled and set down for debate on Saturday 4 November.

Yet Eisenhower was still not placated. In fact, he was almost immediately dealt yet another blow. During the Friday night Dulles suffered acute abdominal pains. He was rushed to hospital and at 7.30 a.m. on Saturday 4 November he was operated on for cancer. Herbert Hoover, the Assistant Secretary of State, was therefore immediately thrown into the fray. That in itself was as it should be. Hoover was, after all, an expert on oil – which was a vital part of the whole dispute. But he had nothing like Dulles's authority, and Eisenhower came more and more to rely on George Humphrey. Indeed, such was Humphrey's mood that British Treasury officials were by then alarmed enough to start to warn Macmillan that 'whatever rights the British had under the International Monetary Fund statutes might not be exercisable if a UK application did not have the support of the US Administration'.[4] In other words, whatever the UK entitlement to automatic draw down from the IMF, the US might try to delay matters and, if it came to further stand-by arrangements, the US, if Humphrey so wished, could insist on conditions which the UK might find unacceptable.

The House of Commons met again on the Saturday morning to the now customary uproar. Lloyd was shouted down, Gaitskell was accused of being a 'traitor' and the Speaker suspended the Session. Later in the day the General Assembly met again and after further bad-tempered debate voted at 2 a.m. (New York time) on Sunday 4 November to authorise Hammarskjöld to negotiate a ceasefire and to set up a UN force. The Egypt Committee then duly met, yet again, at 12.30 p.m. (London time) on the Sunday to hear the news from the UN – together with the new request from Hammarskjöld for a ceasefire by 8 p.m. and his refusal to allow Franco-British forces to be part of UNEF.

There was even more on their agenda. There was a report from Head, who had flown to Keightley's headquarters in Cyprus the previous day and had returned with the message that British and French paratroopers were ready to go into action at first light on Monday the 5th. There was also a further report from Dixon, first, that Israel had announced its acceptance of a ceasefire provided Egypt did the same and, second, that there had been some discussion in New York about oil sanctions (according to Lloyd, when he heard this Macmillan 'threw his arms in the air and said "Oil sanctions! That finishes it"'). Finally, a Reuters bulletin from Vienna reported that Soviet tanks were on the streets of Budapest and the Hungarians were fighting them – in some cases with their bare hands.

It was in this febrile atmosphere that the Egypt Committee delib-

Dorothy canvassing in Bromley during the General Election of May 1955

The Cock of Arran

Macmillan speaking to Tory students, December 1948

At Conservative Party
headquarters as Shadow
Minister, January 1950

The Minister for Housing interviews a prospective customer, 1952

Macmillan (with Bill Deedes) gives the first-ever party political broadcast, May 1953

Macmillan and Dorothy at Birch Grove House in the summer of 1955

Macmillan placing a
wreath at his grandfather's
grave in Spencer, Indiana,
September 1956

The Minister for Housing interviews a prospective customer, 1952

Macmillan (with Bill Deedes) gives the first-ever party political broadcast, May 1953

Hugh Gaitskell with his daughters

Macmillan as Foreign Secretary with John Foster Dulles and Antoine Pinay, June 1955

Macmillan as Foreign Secretary and John Wyndham returning from a trip to Paris, July 1955

Macmillan and Dorothy at Birch Grove House in the summer of 1955

Macmillan placing a wreath at his grandfather's grave in Spencer, Indiana, September 1956

With Dwight Eisenhower
in Bermuda, March 1957

With Milton Eisenhower at Johns
Hopkins University, June 1958

Television report of Macmillan and
Eisenhower's conversation during Eisenhower's visit of August 1959

Protests in Trafalgar Square over Suez, 4 November 1956

Ships sunk to block the Suez Canal, late November 1956

erated – if panic can be described as deliberation. The idea of invading Kuwait and Qatar, in the event of oil sanctions, was, at least for the moment, put aside – it was better to try to placate the US to avoid sanctions in the first place. But there was still a major problem. In the light of the acceptance by Israel and, by then Egypt, of a ceasefire it was not easy to see any reason for Franco-British intervention. In other words, there was no *casus belli*. Nevertheless, the refusal of Dag Hammarskjöld to allow Franco-British forces to be part of UNEF was quite unacceptable. By then, it was clear that nobody quite knew what to do next. On that uncertain note, Eden decided that the whole matter would have to be referred to the full Cabinet.

So it was that at 6.30 p.m. on Sunday 4 November the already weary – and, in Salisbury's case, ill – Ministers assembled at No. 10 Downing Street. As they did so, chattering as usual in the anteroom, they could distinctly hear the noise of a demonstration taking place in Trafalgar Square. 'There was a steady hum of noise,' Lloyd recalled, 'and then every few minutes a crescendo and an outburst of howling or booing.'[6] Once in the Cabinet Room, Eden told them about the UN Resolutions. He also said that he had received a letter from Hammarskjöld which made it clear that 'it now lay wholly within the capacity of the United Kingdom and French Governments to bring the hostilities in Egypt to an end'.[7] A reply had to be sent not later than midnight London time. There were, he went on, three possible courses of action: to allow the initial phase of the occupation to go ahead as planned, to postpone landings for twenty-four hours or to defer military action indefinitely. Each course had its dangers. Postponing or cancelling would make it virtually impossible to resume the attack and 'we should fail to achieve our main purpose of establishing an impartial authority between Egypt and Israel' (the fiction was still maintained).[8] On the other hand, 'there were serious political disadvantages in refusing to suspend military action in defiance of majority opinion in the United Nations'.[9]

After a long discussion, and an adjournment during which he told Salisbury, Butler and Macmillan that he would resign if the decision went against carrying on with military action, Eden went round the table asking each Minister for his view. Macmillan, Lloyd, Home, Alan Lennox-Boyd, Head, Thorneycroft, Eccles, Sandys, Stuart, Gwilym Lloyd George and Hailsham were for carrying on. Butler (reluctantly), Kilmuir, Heathcoat Amory, Macleod, Salisbury and Buchan-Hepburn said they would do what the Prime Minister wished. Monckton and the Earl of Selkirk were for postponement. There it was. '[It was] Agreed that subject to the concurrence of the French Government the initial phase of the Anglo-French occupation of the Suez Canal area should be put into effect . . .'[10]

British and French paratroopers duly landed at Port Said at first light on 5 November. Just before that, the UK and French Governments had received a fierce letter from Bulganin threatening attacks on Western Europe. Bulganin also wrote to Eisenhower proposing a joint US/Soviet force – which American officials in Washington thought was no more than a camouflage for the Soviet action in Budapest. Eden, trying to recapture lost ground, wrote a cringing letter to Eisenhower ('Dear Friend, It is a great grief to me the events of the last few days have placed such a strain on the relations between our two countries . . .'[11]). Eisenhower drafted a taut reply – which, in the event was never sent – and, still not placated, at a meeting in Washington later in the morning said that 'with regard to the oil problem faced by the French and the British . . . the purposes of peace and stability would be served by not being too quick in attempting to render extraordinary assistance, and the Vice-President [Nixon] reinforced this view'.[12] In other words, even with the Canal by then hopelessly blocked, the US was certainly not going out of its way to help its two firmest allies – now branded as 'aggressors'.

Bulganin's threats, on the other hand, had in fact been of some help to the British and French 'aggressors'. They had concentrated the American mind. In rejecting the Soviet proposal for a joint US/Soviet force, the United States officially made it clear, as it was obliged to do, that any Soviet attack on Britain or France would be met with a full NATO – which meant, of course, United States – response. Furthermore, when the Soviets, on the evening of 5 November, attempted to initiate a debate in the Security Council about British and French non-compliance with the decision of the General Assembly to halt the 'aggression', the US voted against them.

Thus, by the evening of 5 November, it was all finely balanced. The Franco-British assault had been successful – half of the Canal area had been occupied without major casualties. The Soviets had damaged their cause by threatening, in effect, to start a Third World War. Oil supplies to the belligerents were dwindling, but there was enough in reserve, at least for the moment. But the difficulty was that both Presidential and Congressional Elections were to take place on the following day. Since it was impossible to predict the result, nobody could tell which way the United States, with a new President (or a re-elected President) and a new Congress, would jump. Yet it was clear to Eden that, with the speed of events, he could not wait. Accordingly, the Cabinet was summoned to meet again at a quarter to ten on the morning of 6 November – this time, since it was the day of the State Opening of Parliament, in the

Prime Minister's room in the House of Commons. It was a matter, they were told, of the greatest urgency.

The received version, as it were, of what happened on the night before, on the morning of the meeting and in the meeting itself has been told and retold, to the point where it has gained almost legendary status. Macmillan, in his capacity as the Chancellor of the Exchequer, is said to have told the Cabinet that there had been a dramatic attack on sterling, orchestrated by the American authorities; that some £100 million had been lost from the UK reserves as a result. Furthermore, in the middle of the meeting, the version goes, he received advice that the United States was going to block the UK application to draw down its quota (gold tranche) with the IMF unless the British and French agreed to an immediate ceasefire. Faced with this, and the impossibility of defending the sterling parity against the American attack and without IMF support, the Cabinet had no alternative but to back down under American financial might. The Americans, so it goes, had thus brought down a daring and possibly great venture, the importance of which, in their innocence, they had not understood, by financial blackmail of two of their closest allies.

This version is derived from Macmillan's own memoirs and, at least to some extent, is filled out in the official biography and the auto-biographies of other Ministers of the time (all written, of course, years after the event). In his memoirs, Macmillan wrote that 'losses [to the UK reserves] ... in November were to be $279 million, largely, if not wholly, in the first few days'. Moreover, 'selling of sterling by the Federal Reserve Bank ... seemed far above what was necessary to protect the value of its own holdings'. He then went on to write that 'I would not have been unduly concerned had we been able to obtain the money to which we were entitled from the International Monetary Fund [the UK 'gold tranche' amounting to $236 million] ... Accordingly I made the necessary soundings. I telephoned urgently to New York; the matter was referred to Washington. It was only while the Cabinet was in session [on the morning of 6 November] that I received the reply that the American Government would not agree to the technical procedure until we had agreed to a cease fire.'[13] The official biography then takes up the tale. 'He [Macmillan] told the Cabinet that there had been a serious run on the pound, viciously orchestrated in Washington. Britain's gold reserves had fallen by £100 million [$279 million] over the past week ...' It was Macmillan's interventions to explain this to the Cabinet on the morning of 6 November which 'decided the issue'.[14]

This account has been generally accepted, albeit with some doubts from time to time, by historians of the period. 'The reality was', one has written, 'that it was the economic and financial implications of the crisis resulting from American hostility which were paramount', at least in bringing about the premature halt of the adventure.[15]

There are, however, some very serious difficulties with the whole version. In fact, not to put too fine a point on it, it is not supported by any contemporary documentary evidence. First, the figure Macmillan claimed in his memoirs as the loss to the British reserves in the first part of November ('$279 million, if not wholly, in the first few days' in his memoirs and £100 million in the week prior to the meeting, in the official biography) is quite simply wrong. Macmillan himself, after all, had minuted Eden on the day before the meeting – 5 November – that there was 'speculation against sterling in Continental markets also . . . the reserves [had fallen] by $36 million over the first three days of November . . . but there was some relaxation of pressure in all markets on Friday'.[16] That is borne out by the official figures. The recorded loss to the UK reserves between 29 October and 5 November was no more than $45 million, a perfectly containable figure (given that at that point the UK gold and dollar reserves stood at $2206 million). It is confirmed by Macmillan's own statement to the Cabinet on 29 November. In Norman Brook's laconic notes: 'H.M.: In Nov. we lost 44/78/102/54 [$m]: Panic week 10–17.xi. Due to withdrawal fr[om] Europe into dollars & Swiss fr[ancs] via sterling.'[17] Put simply, the 'panic week' was the third week of November, well after the ceasefire had been decided.

Secondly, the allegation that the Federal Reserve Bank was leading a charge against sterling is unfounded. US Government sterling holdings, held at the Federal Reserve, at the end of September 1956 stood at approximately £30 million. By 31 December 1956 they had declined to £26 million. The selling, if that was what it ever was, can hardly be described as 'vicious' – and there was no evidence of the Federal Reserve selling sterling short. In fact, the Federal Reserve, operating on behalf of the US Treasury, seems to have been rather more than benign in its protection of the value of US Government (already minuscule) sterling balances. In other words, not only was there no run on sterling during the first week in November, but there was never any run at any time orchestrated by Washington. This, too, is confirmed by Macmillan's statement to Cabinet on the 29th that the move out of sterling, which caused the panic of the third week in November, came from Europe.

Thirdly, the telephone calls allegedly made by Macmillan on the night of the 5th were not recorded by the usually meticulous British officials – there are no transcripts of them in the National Archives. Nor were they recorded by the equally meticulous American officials. The best State Department historians could do subsequently was to state in an editorial note in their official publication that Macmillan 'recalled in his memoirs that ... he had requested the International Monetary Fund to repay the British quota ... No documentation concerning the British request or the American response has been found in Department of State files.'[18] As though that is not cautious enough, on enquiry it turns out that State Department historians, in compiling this note, sifted carefully through both US Treasury and IMF files. Equally, enquiry with the IMF itself shows that there is no record of an application at the time by the UK for any draw down of its gold tranche (but that, according to the official IMF historian, if such an application had been made it would immediately have been granted as a matter of right). In fact, there is no record of any attempt to convene the Executive Board of the IMF.

Finally, there is the matter of what Macmillan said (or did not say) to the Cabinet at the meeting on the morning of Tuesday 6 November. There is nothing, either in the official Minute or in the Cabinet Secretary's notes of the meeting, which supports the account of a 'decisive' Macmillan intervention. In fact, the official Minute shows that not only did Macmillan not make a 'decisive' intervention but that he made no intervention at all. The Cabinet Secretary's notes are truncated to half a page (Brook must have been told to keep his pen in his pocket) and are of little help on whether Macmillan said anything or not. Nor, as a matter of fact, is there any record of Macmillan leaving the meeting (an event always meticulously recorded by the Cabinet Secretary) to receive a message. As Guy Millard, Eden's Private Secretary at the time, writes: 'I certainly do not recall a dramatic event such as Macmillan leaving the Cabinet to take a message and then returning crest-fallen or despairing,'[19] although he adds that Macmillan might not have left, if indeed he did leave, via the Private Secretaries room.

In short, the received version simply does not stand up to any scrutiny based on official records. But, that left aside, it would be wrong to suppose that Macmillan's influence on the crucial decision was entirely negligible. In fact, what almost certainly did happen was that on the morning of the 6th Macmillan saw Selwyn Lloyd before the Cabinet meeting and told him that 'in view of the financial and economic pressures we must stop'.[20] Anthony Head further reported that 'Macmillan put the fear of God into the Cabinet on finances ...'.[21] Others were no doubt given the same treatment. Butler, for instance, was convinced that Macmillan had moved because of 'the loss of 279 million dollars in that November'.[22] There is no existing evidence that Macmillan spoke in a similar vein to Salisbury, but since Salisbury turned out to be the leader, along with Butler, in proposing a ceasefire when the Cabinet finally met, it takes little imagination to conclude that Macmillan had found the opportunity to have a discreet word with him too.

By the time Ministers did finally assemble in formal session it turned out that only three, Lloyd, Head and Stuart, supported Eden (buoyed as he was by his successful – and dignified – broadcast to the nation of 3 November) in his wish to carry on with military operations. Others were opposed or, at best, doubtful. The truth is, in Guy Millard's words, 'based on conversations at the time . . . that by this time the majority of the Cabinet had lost the will to continue.'[23] The decisive moment came when Salisbury told the Cabinet, 'we have played every card in our hand, and we have none left.'[24] The long debate was finally brought to a conclusion when Ministers were summoned to hear the Queen's Speech opening the new Session. Somewhat hurriedly, a ceasefire was duly agreed and, almost as an afterthought, the French were suitably informed (much to their fury).

Macmillan had perhaps not intervened at the meeting. But he had not needed to. His work had been done earlier. He knew perfectly well that Eden had lost the game – but there was no point in upsetting an already nearly hysterical Eden by letting his fingerprints, to use modern jargon, be all over what Eden would have thought of as a plot. He also knew that the game itself was lost. As he said later in the day to the Foreign Editor of *The Times*, Iverach McDonald, '"It was risky from the beginning – perhaps it was too risky."' McDonald went on to write that 'they all realised that there had to be a cease-fire. They did not take the Russian threats seriously but there was a risk of the war eventually spreading . . . the third world war . . . As Macmillan said, "America would win it, but *we* should all be killed."'[25] That was the truth of the matter. The time had come to recognise that the venture had failed. Macmillan knew that – perhaps as early as the morning of 4 November when he first heard of the threat of oil sanctions, and in his early morning conversations with his Cabinet colleagues he had quite certainly made his view abundantly clear.

The only question then was how the matter could be settled with at least some degree of dignity. It was of the utmost political importance for the Cabinet – and for Macmillan personally – to construct plausible reasons for what was in practice an embarrassing retreat. The first instinct for all of them was to adopt the age-old formula: declare victory and leave the battlefield. The point was made in the Cabinet discussion. 'If we agreed to break off hostilities at once,' the Cabinet Minute runs, 'we could maintain that we had achieved our primary objectives. The fighting in the Canal area had been brought to an end; and the United Nations had agreed in principle that an international force should be established in the area.'[26] Norman Brook's notes of the meeting confirm that it was

Eden himself who made the statement. It was, of course, quite untrue. The primary objectives had been to collude with Israel to occupy the Canal and get rid of Nasser. But that point could be suitably finessed.

The second instinct was to adopt another age-old formula: blame somebody else. For this, Macmillan provided the answer. It was quite simple. The Americans were to be blamed. Again, this was untrue – but it was plausible (and popular with those Conservatives, known as the 'Suez Group' who were both anti-American and all for pressing on). Of course, American diplomacy had been, to say the least, cack-handed – as Eisenhower himself later admitted with regret – but they had good reason to be offended. Be that as it may, the blame was duly, and with suitable fanfare from Macmillan, Eden, Butler and Lloyd in their memoirs, apportioned.

For Macmillan, apart from the realisation that the whole thing had been a dreadful mistake, there was a personal factor. Selwyn Lloyd thought that 'he was emotionally affected'[27] by the hostility of the American administration and, in particular, of his old friend Eisenhower. He had, after all, spent much of his life nurturing Anglo-American ties, and had only recently spoken with a distinct lump in his throat at his mother's childhood church in Spencer. But he had been rejected, and, like any other jilted lover, was hurt and angry – and lashed out with accusations of blame. Certainly, in later life Macmillan, in calmer moments, was open about his failure to read Eisenhower correctly and much regretted the damage done to Britain's relations with the United States. The love affair was, after all, to be renewed. Yet what he was much more reluctant to do – in fact, never did – was to admit that the whole Suez venture was shameful. As one British observer has written, 'It was not so much that the affair marked the end of Britain as a Great Power: it marked our end as a *good* power, one that could normally be expected to act honourably. It was for me what Munich had been for a slightly older generation and Iraq would be for a younger; but whereas Munich and Iraq were understandable if deplorable acts of *realpolitik*, the sheer irrationality of the Suez adventure still fills me with melancholy amazement.'[28] Macmillan, even in later years, never accepted the verdict. It had all been, he was to claim, for the best.

After 6 November, political life started a new chapter. Eisenhower turned out to have won his re-election by a wide margin. Nevertheless, his victory was not entirely sweet. Both Houses of Congress had been lost to the Democrats – who were even more fiercely opposed to the Franco-British action than their Republican opponents. This made for problems. When Eden called Eisenhower on the morning of 7 November it seemed as though the waters were becoming calmer. 'After all,'

Eisenhower said, 'it is like a family spat.'[29] Yet when Eden suggested a meeting, bringing Mollet along with him, Eisenhower quickly shut the door. He pointed out that he would have to consult the leaders of the new Congress and that all that would take time. Moreover, he went on, 'I am heartened by the news that there is a cease-fire in Egypt and sincerely hope that the UN force will promptly begin its work and that the Anglo-French Forces will be withdrawn from Egypt without delay. Once these things are done, the ground will be favourable for our meeting.'[30]

Macmillan met the same difficulty when he tried to relaunch the proposal to draw down on the IMF and to negotiate a further standby arrangement. He had assumed that the agreement to cease fire would unlock American approval. This turned out to be wrong. In fact, the American position was hardening. Not only did they want the ceasefire to hold but they wanted British and French troops out of Egypt altogether. The Economic Minister in Washington, Lord Harcourt, had a meeting with Humphrey on 8 November and was told firmly that 'for the United States to offer financial aid to the United Kingdom and France in the light of our actions in the last ten days would be totally unacceptable politically ... for some considerable time'.[31]

By 12 November panic was finally beginning to set in. 'We cannot continue to lose reserves at the present rate,' a Treasury Minute runs, 'and continue at the same time to hold sterling at its present value.'[32] It was clear that the continuing blockage of the Suez Canal – and the consequent difficulties in supplies of oil – was starting seriously to affect financial markets. In the meeting of the Cabinet on 20 November Macmillan 'said that the Cabinet might shortly face the grave choice of deciding whether to mobilise all our financial resources in order to maintain the sterling/dollar rate at its present level or to let it find its level ... during the first week in December he would have to announce the loss of gold and dollars during November. This figure might be as high as $300 millions ...'[33] Macmillan also wrote a morose letter to Humphrey ('it seems impossible at the moment for me to meet you personally, much as I would like to do so') explaining all his problems and hoping that Humphrey would 'come to the NATO meeting in Paris in December and that we could have private talks there'.[34]

During the previous evening – of 19 November – there had been more drama. At ten o'clock Macmillan, at his own request, went to see Aldrich at his home. 'Eden', Aldrich reported, 'has had a physical breakdown and will have to go on vacation immediately, first for one week and then for another, and this will lead to his retirement. Government will be run by a triumvirate of Butler, Macmillan and Salisbury. While Macmillan did not say so specifically, I gather that the eventual setup will be Butler Prime Minister, Macmillan Foreign Secretary, Lloyd Chancellor of the Exchequer, with Salisbury remaining Lord President of Council. Possibly Macmillan might be Prime Minister. First action after Eden's departure for reasons of health will be on withdrawal of British troops from Egypt. Macmillan said, "If you can give us a fig leaf to cover our nakedness I believe we can get a majority of the Cabinet to vote for such withdrawal" ... Macmillan is desperately anxious to see the President ... apparently consideration being given to appointment of Macmillan as Deputy Prime Minister ...'[35]

Eden's decision was duly announced by Butler to the Cabinet on the following day – the day on which Macmillan was telling the Cabinet that in the financial markets time was short. The announcement had two decisive effects. The first was to land Butler with the job of running the Government in Eden's absence – and, more particularly, of defending the Government's actions over Suez in a continuous and unpleasant rearguard action in the House of Commons. The second was to concentrate political minds on the prospect of the succession. On 22 November, as it happened, the two effects coincided. Butler had to mount the defence of actions which he had only reluctantly supported and of the subsequent climbdown, to the derision of the Labour Opposition and the mutinous silence of his own side. The announcement that one battalion would be withdrawn from Port Said did nothing to cool the spirits. (When telling Aldrich the news of the battalion's withdrawal earlier in the day Macmillan confided to him conspiratorially that 'Cabinet changes which he has previously forecast will take place within the next few days'.[36])

That same evening, however, the odds on the Cabinet changes forecast to Aldrich by Macmillan suddenly shifted. It so happened that Butler had been invited to address the '1922' Committee of Conservative backbenchers – not always the most agreeable audience and certainly not Butler's favourite one – to explain and justify the Government's position. As a matter of prudence, he thought he should invite Macmillan to accompany him. The plan, agreed by both of them beforehand, was that Butler should angle his speech to appease the right wing of the Party while Macmillan would speak to the left. This in itself was unwise, and the meeting turned out, from Butler's point of view, to be a disaster.

Butler spoke first. He did not take too long. He was factual and accurate – but flat. He was followed by Macmillan – who had decided that this was the time to put on one of his (carefully rehearsed) performances. As so often in important moments in his career, Macmillan produced another bravura show. It was thirty-five minutes of true theatre, including 'a *tremolo* on his own advancing years'.[37] 'One of the most horrible things that I remember in politics', one of Butler's supporters was later to write, 'was ... seeing the way in which Harold Macmillan, with all the skill of the old actor manager, succeeded in false-footing Rab. The sheer devilry of it verged on the disgusting.'[38] Macmillan's own verdict, however, was more restrained. 'I held the Tory Party together for the weekend,' he said, 'which was all I intended to do.'[39] But there was no doubt about which of them had put up the more impressive show.

Once Eden had left the London scene altogether – for a holiday in Jamaica at Goldeneye, the house of James Bond's creator, Ian Fleming – Butler and Macmillan decided that, whatever the rivalry, they had to work together to keep a very difficult show on the road. The news on sterling was bad and getting worse daily. In fact, it was Butler who set about digging Macmillan out of a very nasty hole. As Chancellor of the Exchequer he had come to know Humphrey well. When he heard that Butler had taken over the running of the Government, Humphrey called him from his Georgian home. He 'had shut himself with the telephone in the meat safe so as to avoid the intrusions of his family. "Rab," he said, "the President cannot help you unless you conform to the United Nations resolution about withdrawal. If you do that, we here will help you save the pound." Then I put him on to Harold Macmillan, my successor as Chancellor of the Exchequer, who stood shoulder to shoulder with me in those desperate and humiliating days.'[40] Humphrey's subsequent message to Macmillan finds no place in his memoirs but was presumably the same.

It was thus quite clear what the 'fig leaf' was to be. In fact, Humphrey had already made it clear at a meeting in Washington on 20 November. After commenting on the possible succession in Britain (he favoured Butler, to which Eisenhower responded that he had always thought most highly of Macmillan 'who is a straight, fine man and so far as he is concerned the outstanding one of the British he served with during the war') he had said that by drawing on the IMF together with a standby arrangement Britain could raise some $560 million. In addition, the US Export-Import Bank could establish a credit line to pay for imports from the US. 'We *are* in a position', he had gone on to say, 'to supply the "fig leaf" which the British say they need to cover their nakedness in withdrawing from the Suez [sic] ... providing they start to get out of the Suez at once.'[41]

There was nothing the Cabinet could do but accept the 'fig leaf' offered. At the meeting on 28 November Macmillan stressed that to secure the sterling position it would be necessary to reinforce the reserves by recourse to the IMF. 'For this purpose,' he went on, 'the good will of the US Government was necessary; and it was evident that this good will could not be obtained without an immediate and unconditional undertaking to withdraw the Anglo-French force from Port Said.' Although there was some muttering about the possible reaction of Conservative backbenchers in the House of Commons, Butler, in summing up, said that 'it appeared to be the preponderant view of the Cabinet that we should announce, in the next few days, that we were now prepared to withdraw the Anglo-French force from Port Said as rapidly as possible ...'. [42]

Thus did the British Government retire from the Suez Canal venture with its tail firmly between its legs. Yet the announcement of the withdrawal had the desired effect. Humphrey turned out to be as good as his word. Macmillan was able to make a statement on 4 December that the UK's gold tranche at the IMF was to be drawn down immediately and that a credit facility with the US Export-Import Bank was to be put in place. Moreover, Dulles – still no more than convalescing – and Humphrey were to visit London and Paris on 12 December. Churchill, too, weighed in with a long letter to Eisenhower regretting the misunderstandings and frustration which had occurred and fervently hoping that the Anglo-American relationship could be repaired. Eisenhower replied in his own hand (although he could not help reiterating to his staff that there were possibly 'some blessings in disguise coming to Britain out of this affair, in the form of compelling them to accept the Common Market'[43]).

Humphrey arrived in London and met Macmillan for a discussion of the further financial arrangements – an IMF standby and possibly a supplementary loan directly from the United States. But Humphrey would not have been human if he had not pointed out to Macmillan that the unpleasantness over the IMF position and the consequent run on sterling in the second half of November could largely have been avoided if Macmillan had followed the French example and had drawn the gold tranche – and arranged a standby from the IMF – well before there was talk of military action. (In fact, just after the Franco-British attack on Egypt, Humphrey had instructed his officials to try to unwind the French standby – only be told firmly that it was impossible unless France was formally put in the dock at the United Nations for threatening world peace.)

It would take a long time for relations between Britain and the United States to be restored to anything resembling equanimity. The Suez affair, and the deception involved, had been too damaging. But at least Macmillan lost no time in trying to mount a British Government – and personal – rescue operation. He was quick to see that it was much better to look to the future rather than raking over endlessly the ashes of the past. With this in mind, he asked to see Dulles on the fringes of the NATO meeting in Paris on 12 December. It was to be 'a long and confidential conversation'.

Macmillan started, Dulles reported, by recognising that 'there had been a certain loss of confidence on the part of the President, myself and others because of the Suez operation and the deception practised upon us in that connection. He indicated that he, personally, was very unhappy with the way in which the matter was handled and the timing, but that Eden had taken this entirely to himself and he, Macmillan, had had no real choice but to back Eden ... He said the British action was the last gasp of a declining power and that perhaps in two hundred years the United States "would know how we felt".'[44]

It was, of course, a somewhat novel interpretation by Macmillan of his role in the whole affair. Furthermore, it sits, to say the least, uneasily beside the record of Macmillan's wholehearted embrace of collusion with the Israelis and the consequent deception of the United States (and the House of Commons). Nor is Macmillan's plea that he had no option but to support Eden very convincing. After all, Nutting, Edward Boyle (Macmillan's junior Minister at the Treasury) and William Clark had all resigned. But he knew perfectly well that resignation would have meant the abrupt and permanent end to his political career. At his age there could have been no comeback.

Dulles received all this, as might be expected, somewhat quizzically. Although he liked Macmillan, he knew that there was a big game playing out in front of him. Moreover, he knew that Macmillan could not in all honesty escape his share of responsibility for the whole fiasco. Whatever Macmillan's professed love for his mother's country, he had connived at, and endorsed, the deception. In the bluster about Nasser as a modern Hitler he had made the mistake of imagining that 1956 was a rerun of 1938. Finally, he could have followed the French and put in place the same measures of support for sterling, which would have gone some way to avoid the subsequent humiliation. In short, Dulles knew that Macmillan's role in the Suez affair was – and, if the truth be told, still is – in those respects a sorry story.

Yet he also knew that it would be wrong to accuse Macmillan of failure of courage – of losing his nerve (Harold Wilson's famous jibe – 'first in, first out' is one such accusation). Macmillan was always courageous. In fact, in the Suez affair he was, if anything, overbold. Nor would it have been right to charge him with lack of realism. He was one of the first to see that the invasion had been a mistake – and, when such a mistake is made, to recognise the need to row back as quickly as possible. He was, as it happened, also politically skilled enough to avoid taking the blame.

In his talk with Dulles, Macmillan then went on to express 'his hope that some shift of government would make him or Rab Butler Prime Minister, but he said that it was not certain that this would happen. He said that after Eden returned, there would be a question as to whether he would resign at once on account of ill health. If not, he would probably hold on for six months ...' Having launched this missile, Macmillan then veered away and went on to encourage Dulles to dream up some 'big, imaginative plan for the Middle East ...'[45] Dulles took due note – but did no more than report what had been said to Eisenhower.

On 14 December Eden returned from Jamaica. Bronzed and fit, he was, the waiting press noted, a picture of health compared with the pale and careworn Butler who, out of duty, was at the airport to meet him. Smoothing his luxuriant hair which was ruffled in the breeze, he made a Prime Ministerial statement to the waiting press. 'I am more convinced than ever', he said, 'that we were right, my colleagues and I, in the judgements and decisions we took and that history will prove it so.'[46] Macmillan, however, when he heard this, was very much less sanguine. After all, petrol rationing was due to come into effect three days later. Moreover, the House of Commons was proving difficult to handle. Eden did, in fact, address the Commons with some of his old verve on 18 and 20 December. But when on a wind-up to an adjournment debate on the 20th Gaitskell pressed him for a straight reply on whether there had or had not been collusion he gave it. 'I want to say this on the question of foreknowledge and to say it quite bluntly to the House that there was not foreknowledge that Israel would attack Egypt – there was not.'[47] As it happened, it was the last Commons speech he ever made. It has, of course, gone down in history as his most disastrous.

On Friday 4 January 1957 Salisbury, having spent three days shooting over the New Year with the Royal Family at Sandringham, came back to his home at Hatfield. The next day a message came from Eden asking him to go to see him in Downing Street on the following Monday. Imagining that Eden wanted to discuss a difficult paper which was to come before Cabinet on the Tuesday, Salisbury duly turned up – only to find that Eden told him 'that he had had a bad report on his health and that he was afraid he would have to resign at once ... he had had a great deal of pain since he came back from Jamaica ... Horace Evans had advised that it was no use his trying to go on .... this view ... confirmed by three other doctors ... while the pain continued he could only sleep under dope ...'[48] There was no option other than immediate resignation.

That done, on Tuesday 8 December Eden went to Sandringham to submit his resignation to the Queen. The Tuesday Cabinet meeting was accordingly postponed. On the Wednesday afternoon, Salisbury was sought out by the Queen's Private Secretary, Michael Adeane, who told him that his advice would probably be asked about the succession. Adeane also asked 'whether I thought [the Queen] should seek advice from Sir Winston Churchill, who had let her know that he would be available for this purpose'. In reply, Salisbury said that Churchill should certainly also be consulted. In the evening of the Wednesday the Cabinet finally met. 'It was a short and very painful meeting. There was no agenda. Anthony, very bravely and without emotion, informed his colleagues of the doctors' report and of his decision to resign ... Then I [Salisbury] spoke and expressed our distress at this decision and our gratitude to him for his many kindnesses to us while we had been his colleagues, I was followed by Harold and Rab. All of us much moved. The Cabinet then ended.'[49]

Salisbury then retired along the corridor to the Privy Council Office next door, taking with him Kilmuir, the only other member of the Cabinet who, as a member of the House of Lords, was (politically) ineligible to be a candidate. Butler and Macmillan were told to stay away. The other Cabinet members 'trooped out into my ante room, where, I am told, they talked so loudly that they had to be restrained'.[50] The Ministers then came in one by one and apart from Buchan-Hepburn and Lloyd (who shocked Kilmuir by not expressing a preference) pronounced for Macmillan.

Salisbury then talked with Heath, the Government Chief Whip, and Oliver Poole, the Chairman of the Conservative Party. Heath said that Macmillan would be the right choice for the Parliamentary Party, and Poole, rather to Salisbury's surprise, took the same view. 'Conservative opinion in the country ...', Poole told him, 'had greatly admired Anthony's stand ... they were unwilling to apportion any blame for any failure on Anthony himself, who was their hero. They had therefore looked round for a scapegoat and had pitched on Rab, principally because he had very indiscreetly, during the previous autumn, expressed, in private conversation, doubts as to the wisdom of the Suez policy, and his remarks had been widely repeated ... He would therefore, at the moment, be a very unpopular choice with the rank and file of the Party in the Country.' By then, Salisbury thought that he had all the necessary information to enable him to give advice to the Queen, and 'I went home to dinner'.[51]

The one person whom Salisbury had failed to consult, however, was Anthony Eden. Macmillan himself was careful to record this. 'I gathered from Anthony', he wrote later in his diary – when it was resumed in the following month – 'that he had neither been asked for his advice nor had

[he] volunteered it.'[52] Why none of the Queen's courtiers had told her that it was at least customary to ask a retiring Prime Minister for his advice on a successor is for ever a mystery. For Adeane to suggest to the Queen that she should seek Churchill's advice but not Eden's verges on what is, in modern terms, constitutionally improper. (Seven years later, of course, the Queen herself went out of her way to take the advice of another ill and retiring Prime Minister – but that was for the future.)

At 11.15 a.m. on 10 January Salisbury went to Buckingham Palace to do his duty. He was followed by Churchill, who endorsed Salisbury's advice in favour of Macmillan. Just before 1 p.m. Adeane rang Salisbury to say that Macmillan had been summoned to the Palace. 'The next event,' Salisbury recorded, 'so far as I at 2.45 was concerned, was a message from Harold asking me to go and see him at no. 11. I walked along the passage and found him in very good spirits.'[53] Macmillan himself, however, seemed to have a different perspective. 'As I drove back to no. 11,' he wrote in his diary, 'I thought chiefly of my poor mother.'[54]

Part Four

CENTRE STAGE

17

The Tory Resurrection

When Macmillan kissed hands on his appointment as Prime Minister on 10 January 1957 he told Queen Elizabeth that his Government might not last more than six weeks. This has since been taken to be some sort of joke. But Macmillan was perfectly serious. He knew well that his Government was sitting underneath a particularly unpleasant Damoclean sword. If Eden's and Lloyd's lies to the House of Commons over Suez, if his own role in first suggesting and then supporting collusion with the Israelis and then endorsing the deceit practised on the United States, if all these were to come out into the Parliamentary limelight the sword would surely fall. His Government would then without a doubt be blown apart and he himself not just be out of office but thrown into the dustbin reserved for overambitious but failed politicians.

This being so, the immediate task was to ensure that the sword would remain in its place. It thus comes as no surprise to find that his first move after his appointment was to talk to his supporter – and partner in crime, as it were – Lord Salisbury. Salisbury, after all, had the political stature to bring down the sword by baring his – sometimes tender – soul about the whole Suez venture and Macmillan's own part in it. Second on the list of those to be muzzled was Selwyn Lloyd. He too could be a dangerously loose cannon. He had offered to resign on a number of occasions, and had been known to be a reluctant supporter of the use of force over Suez in the first place – and had been horrified at the Sèvres Protocol. Although he could be relied on not to speak out publicly – it was not just that he had lied to the House of Commons but also that he had a dubious private life – he could make a nuisance of himself, and of the Government, in the bars in the Palace of Westminster and in the surrounding clubs.

Third on the list was Rab Butler. Butler had every reason to be aggrieved. He had been led to believe by the press, and by his friends, that he would be the natural successor to Eden. Nevertheless, disappointed as he was, in the event he put on a dignified and generous face as a good loser. In return, however, he asked Macmillan for the job he coveted – that of Foreign Secretary. This, for obvious reasons, Macmillan was not prepared to concede. He had to keep Lloyd. The card that Macmillan played in his two meetings with Butler on 10 January was that it would be wrong 'for England's honour' to sacrifice Lloyd as well as Eden. 'One head on a charger', he said, 'should be enough.'[1] Butler, much to Macmillan's relief, accepted the strength of the card and agreed to take the Home Office in lieu. But he was not happy. Returning to his London home, Butler told the press, in his most sepulchral voice, that 'in public life one has to do one's duty. I would certainly not desert the ship at a time like this.'[2] That, more or less, was the sum of it.

Selwyn Lloyd duly agreed to remain as Foreign Secretary. In fact, it was Salisbury who turned out to be the most difficult of the three. He would be happy to remain as Lord President of the Council and Leader of the House of Lords. Yet Macmillan, when he saw him, proposed that a Minister of Fuel and Power should be given a much higher status than hitherto – and that the Atomic Energy Authority, up until then Salisbury's responsibility, should be transferred to the new Minister. Salisbury pondered this for a moment and then asked Macmillan where he stood on the matter of his pet project – House of Lords reform. Macmillan blithely brushed the question aside. After Salisbury had consulted Sir Edwin Plowden, the head of the Atomic Energy Authority, he wrote to Macmillan saying that Plowden found the proposal to change responsibility for the Authority quite unacceptable. But it was only after a few days that Salisbury heard that the proposal had been dropped. Worse still, he read in the newspapers that his protégé, Antony Head, had been sacked as Secretary of State for Defence and the job given to Duncan Sandys. 'I could not but feel', Salisbury wrote wryly, 'that all this was not a very happy augury of the relations which were likely to subsist between the Prime Minister and myself in the new Cabinet.'[3]

The main building blocks were by then in place. The remaining Cabinet posts more or less filled themselves and the junior ministerial posts, thanks to the guidance of the Chief Whip, Edward Heath, posed few problems – although Macmillan was quick to bring Marples back into government as Postmaster-General, along with Edward Boyle and his old friend Percy Mills. By Friday 18 January the list was complete and Macmillan could turn his attention to the arrangements in his office – and his new home.

In both of these, Macmillan was fortunate. In his Private Office he inherited from Eden as Principal Private Secretary, and duly kept, the very bright Frederick Bishop. 'Slim and remarkably boyish in appearance,' was one comment, '[Freddie] tended to be dry and precise on duty, though off duty ready to slip into lightheartedness.'[4] Philip de Zulueta was another – still in his thirties and relatively junior in the Foreign Office ('intellectual agility, charm, self-confidence to the point of arrogance and a readiness to be ruthless'[5]). Together with two others from the Treasury they formed an efficient, and, as it happened, devoted Private Office. The last recruit, to replace Eden's Public Relations Officer, William Clark, who had resigned the previous November over Suez, was a hitherto obscure official from the Colonial Office, then working at the United Nations in New York, Harold Evans.

Yet there is never any doubt that the secret to life in No. 10, if a Prime Minister makes it his principal home as well as his office, is his family. Again, Macmillan was fortunate here as well. Of course, there had been many family problems. He himself, for a start, had never been a particularly good father. He was accustomed to ignore his children from time to time when he felt like it and was certainly unsympathetic to weakness of any sort – drunkenness, sexual acrobatics, the occasional drug use – wherever any of it might occur. He was not an Anglo-Catholic for nothing, and one, moreover, brought up by his mother with a streak of Midwest American Puritanism. There had been, as well, the matter of not quite knowing (or perhaps knowing too well) the parentage of the youngest daughter. Furthermore, Dorothy herself had not been a sympathetic mother to her children once they had, as it were, flown the immediate nest. Finally, the whole Boothby affair had loomed for too many years – and menacingly – over both their lives.

But by the time Macmillan arrived in Downing Street as Prime Minister those traumas were largely in the past. As happens to all those who have reached the summit of their ambition, he felt himself able to relax. Dorothy, too, had settled down in her late middle age. The result was that both of them turned out to be affectionate to one another and also to be affectionate grandparents. Moreover, Dorothy's natural warmth of personality endeared her to all who worked in Downing Street, from the Private Office to the cleaners – all of whom enjoyed, as well, the sight of grandchildren on occasions, until it was forbidden, weaving their way on roller skates around the legs of anxious Cabinet Ministers.

The politics of the day were, of course, difficult. But Macmillan had made up his mind on one thing. At the very least, the Government needed to steady down after the ructions of the previous months. As an announcement of his intention, on the baize door between the Cabinet Room and the Private Office he pinned a notice written in his own hand. 'Quiet, calm deliberation', it read, 'disentangles every knot.'[6] Measured calm was also the rule in Cabinet meetings. '... There was an element of the dining club or the country house party about his conduct of

Cabinets and Cabinet Committees,' Lord Hailsham recalled later. 'There would be quotations from Homer, there would be vague historical analogies ... they would all be amusing and detached and very carefully thought out ...'[7] Yet it would be wrong to suppose that Macmillan was as 'unflappable' as his supporters claimed. When the mask slipped he could be irritable – and was known to drum the floor with his feet under the table at Cabinet meetings when things went wrong, while maintaining a studiously calm posture above.

On the broader front, there were several problems ahead, none of them by any manner of means easy. Morale in the Conservative Party was at a low ebb, relations with the United States and France were somewhere between bad and disastrous and the domestic agenda had been almost ignored in the long preoccupation with Nasser and the Suez Canal.

Of these, the easiest turned out to be Conservative morale. First of all, Macmillan decided to make a television and radio broadcast to explain as simply as he could the present situation and the difficulties the country faced. That was all very well, but, as it happened, the event brought its own little difficulties. 'About that time', he recalled later, 'there was invented a thing called a teleprompter, in which the written text went round and round. This had for me two disadvantages. First, being very short-sighted I could not see it; secondly, if I could just manage to read the words by screwing up my eyes, I presented the appearance of a corpse looking out of a window.'[8] Consequently, he learnt the text by heart and looked at his notes if he had forgotten the next words – and the broadcast was a reassuring success. Five days later, on 22 January, he was formally and enthusiastically installed as Leader of the Conservative Party, proposed by Salisbury and seconded by Butler (who, gratifyingly to everybody – including Butler himself – received loud applause). By that time, it seemed that the Party was just starting to crawl out from what had seemed to be a terminal slough of despond.

That done – and successfully done – Macmillan turned his attention to his other problems. He instructed Millard, by then handing over his job in Downing Street to Freddie Bishop, to report to him on the state of relations with the United States and France; he wrote to Salisbury, as Chairman of the Cabinet's Colonial Policy Committee, asking the Committee for something resembling a modern cost benefit analysis of the British Empire as it then stood; he invited Thorneycroft, the new Chancellor of the Exchequer, to present an assessment of the economic outlook; and, above all, he pressed Sandys into a thorough review of defence expenditure.

Millard duly reported that relations with the United States were as chilly as ever. Yet it turned out that this was mainly true at official level. Both Eisenhower and Dulles had sent Macmillan unusually cordial messages of congratulation. (Humphrey was much less pleased – he would have preferred Butler as Prime Minister and said so rather grumpily to Dulles.) Aldrich in London took up the baton, reviving the idea of a state visit to the United States by the Queen and suggesting a meeting between Eisenhower and Macmillan. The idea of a state visit was welcomed but, in view of the possible dangers immediately ahead, Macmillan suggested that this should be postponed until the autumn. He was, however, very keen to meet Eisenhower – but without Mollet, who, of course, was equally keen to mend fences with the Americans. At Eisenhower's suggestion, it was agreed that they should meet in Bermuda from 21 to 24 March and that Mollet should be invited to a separate visit to Washington, if possible in late February.

Aldrich was at the time on the point of retirement – much, given their friendship, to Macmillan's regret. When they met on 24 January Macmillan suggested, as a sort of farewell present, that Aldrich might wish to make the suggestion of a state visit to the Queen in his final audience. But at the same meeting Macmillan went very much further. He took Aldrich – almost recklessly – into his confidence. He said that he had only talked to Salisbury about the proposed meeting at Bermuda and that he was not proposing to take Lloyd with him there. Aldrich liked that, since Lloyd had made a speech two days earlier at the National Liberal Club which had been very critical of United States policy and was very much out of favour at the time.

'Somewhat to my surprise,' Aldrich's report to Dulles on the meeting goes on, 'Macmillan then said that he thought he ought to tell me, and he was willing to have me tell the President, that at the time of the reorganization of the Cabinet there had been serious consideration given to a change in the Foreign Secretaryship, but he had not wished to cause "two heads to roll" at that critical moment and for that reason Rab Butler had taken the Home Secretaryship with the idea that after about two months someone else would be made Foreign Secretary and Lloyd made Home Secretary. I got the impression from what Macmillan said at this point that the new Foreign Secretary might well be Salisbury.' If that was not possible because of Salisbury's membership of the House of Lords, Aldrich continued, 'I feel sure that the new Foreign Secretary will be Lennox-Boyd.'[9]

It was indeed a surprise. Macmillan had openly said that once the immediate Suez dust had settled he would move Lloyd out of the Foreign Office and into another job. The Home Office was the preferred choice.

Since Macmillan had taken Salisbury into his confidence on two of the most pressing matters of foreign policy, Aldrich's guess was probably right (membership of the House of Lords was no bar – Macmillan, after all, made the Earl of Home Foreign Secretary in 1962). There was no mention of Butler in Macmillan's conversation with Aldrich, but presumably he was to be marked down as the workhorse, even with the title of Deputy Prime Minister, to look after the domestic shop while the Prime Minister was on his travels – which was, in fact, what Butler turned out doing.

Aldrich went on to tell Dulles that the changes would probably not be in effect before the Bermuda meeting in the third week of March. In fact, of course, Macmillan's suggested Cabinet reconstruction never took place. Salisbury, Macmillan's confidant over the state visit and the meeting with Eisenhower at Bermuda, fell out of his favour over Cyprus and ultimately resigned from the Government in April. Lloyd and Butler thus kept their places. Nevertheless, the whole Aldrich conversation, even today, seems – to put it at its very least – constitutionally very odd. In fact, it may well be the first time in modern history that a British Prime Minister explained to a foreign ambassador, for relay to the head of a foreign state, the changes he was proposing to make in the government of the United Kingdom.

Be that as it may, it was, of course, all part of Macmillan's determined campaign to win back American friendship. That still remained an uncertain and sensitive nerve. But other things were going well. He and Dorothy had settled in No. 10. 'I have a good room as a study', he wrote, 'next to Dorothy's "boudoir" (she has arranged a working sitting room upstairs). The house is rather large, but has great character and charm. It is very "liveable".'[10] Shooting at Birch Grove had been particularly good – well over nine hundred pheasants had been killed – and his sixty-third birthday on Sunday 10 February had been celebrated appropriately in the presence of a clutch of grandchildren. Then, on the following weekend, he and Dorothy stayed for the first time at Chequers, which they found 'very comfortable ... but it has been rather spoilt ... there seems too much of everything ...'.[11] But, as he noted, the grandchildren much enjoyed playing about in the snow.

Politically, too, things were starting to fall into place. Thorneycroft, Macmillan's new Chancellor of the Exchequer, had lowered Bank Rate from 5.5 to 5 per cent and had produced encouraging estimates for public expenditure – but with suitable warnings about wage increases. Two by-elections – one in Eden's old constituency of Warwick and Leamington – had gone badly but not as badly as had been feared. Sandys's Defence White Paper, to be published in April, seemed to be on course. Salisbury had been, to say the least, unenthusiastic about Macmillan's proposed cost benefit analysis of the Empire and officials in both the Foreign Office and the Colonial Office were hostile to the whole thing; so the idea was quietly dropped.

There were still hurdles to jump over. Thorneycroft's proposals on the levels of wages which the economy could stand led to threatened strikes, above all by the shipbuilding and engineering unions; the Sandys defence review, recommending large reductions in expenditure and the abolition of conscription, was running up against obstacles in NATO; and Nasser was still firmly in control in Egypt. That, indeed, was still the main running sore, and Macmillan was showing his impatience. 'The American administration is weak and legalistic,' he wrote in his diary, 'and has no real foreign policy at all, except to try to please and cajole the Arab states in the area of the United Nations.'[12] After a few days he wrote again: '... it looks as if the American passion for being liked by everybody has got them into a position of being trusted by nobody.'[13] Even Salisbury was fired up about it. He wrote to Lew Douglas, the former US Ambassador to London, reminding him of the two world wars. 'We have been in both,' his letter went, 'from the first day to the last. In the first we lost most of our friends: in the second we lost our children ... Were we to adopt the same policy as the Chamberlain Government in the years before 1939? ... We didn't expect the United States to come in on our side ... But we *were* terribly hurt when she joined in the hunt against us, with all the enemies of freedom, the Russians and all the rest, at a time when we had risked everything ...'[14]

It was with all this in mind, after a bad-tempered meeting in Paris with Mollet and Pineau in which Mollet complained about Sandys's proposed British troop reductions in Germany and tried, unsuccessfully, to persuade Macmillan not to pay dues to the Egyptians when the Canal was finally opened again, that Macmillan and Lloyd (Macmillan had changed his mind about Lloyd's presence there), arrived in Bermuda, in beautiful weather, on the morning of 20 March. After a few sentences of thanks to the Governor, the welcoming band and the reception committee, they were driven to the Mid-Ocean Golf Club at Tucker's Town, which had been taken over in its entirety for the British and American delegations. Later in the day Eisenhower arrived by sea (he had been trying to get a few days in the sun to shake off a nasty cough) to be met also by the Governor and his family, the band and, finally, Macmillan – himself by then nursing a dreadful cold. On the way to the Mid-Ocean Club Eisenhower 'talked very freely to me – just exactly as in the old days. There were no reproaches – on either side; but (what was more important) no note of any change in our relationship or the confidence he had in me.'[15] On arrival at the club they found Dulles, who had flown in direct from Washington.

In the evening, the four – Eisenhower, Macmillan, Dulles and Lloyd – met for dinner in Macmillan's suite on the first floor of the club. Dinner talk was mostly about wartime reminiscences, but after dinner they moved next door to Macmillan's sitting room for a more serious discussion. The first subject, naturally enough, was Egypt. Macmillan immediately raised the question whether the United States was 'going to wage political and economic warfare against Nasser or seek some arrangement with him ...'. Lloyd made 'a strong personal attack about Nasser and his unreliability'. This was altogether too much for Eisenhower who 'said we could not at the same time seek his co-operation and combat him'. Dulles added that he 'did not assume that we were required to support him internally as against internal forces and indeed we would welcome certain types of change in Egypt. However, that was different from an international campaign against him.'[16] That, as Macmillan mournfully recognised, was the end of the matter. The two sides were still a long way apart. It certainly did not help that a wild storm, infrequent at the time of year in Bermuda but fearsome when it comes, was blowing at full force and rattling the windows of the Prime Minister's suite.

There followed a rambling discussion on 'colonialism', during which Macmillan made the surprising statement that 'they were considering abandoning Hong Kong. It was a costly business to hold it ... it might be profitable to some of the Chinese traders in Hong Kong but not profitable to the United Kingdom.' Dulles countered that Hong Kong was one of the positions which it was important for the free world to hold and that if the United Kingdom aligned itself with the United States in total opposition to Communist China 'we might be able to help to hold it'.[17] After a discussion about Cyprus, Eisenhower spent some time complaining about the attacks made on the US in the British press. Dulles then took Macmillan aside and told him that Eisenhower had felt badly hurt by the 'particularly vicious and coordinated attacks on President Eisenhower personally'.[18]

By then it was clear that the mood was far from friendly. The following morning, in the first plenary session, Macmillan, as he wrote in his diary, 'managed to take the offensive from the start'. It was, again, all about Egypt. The British people, he said, felt let down. Eisenhower took this up 'rather sharply' and said that there had been no question of letting anybody down since the United States had made its position clear at an early date.[19] Yet again, the two sides were in opposition – and there were some exchanges that verged on anger.

After that, however, the atmosphere in the meeting improved, although the weather outside remained dreadful and neither Eisenhower's cough nor Macmillan's cold was getting any better. But it seemed as though the bitter diplomatic boil had been lanced. Eisenhower told Macmillan that the US would in principle provide intermediate-range ballistic missiles (IRBMs) to Britain, would join the Baghdad Pact and would accept – with reservations about the impact on other NATO members – the British defence cuts. In the end, they all managed to cobble together a communiqué which was suitably cheerful. It was accompanied by a series of protocols on the important decisions – in Macmillan's view 'the only real result of the conference'.[20] Quite exhausted, Macmillan then spent a good deal of the 23rd in bed, and early on the 24th Eisenhower packed up and left.

All in all, it had not been a bad conference – although perhaps not as good as Macmillan and Eisenhower subsequently claimed. Eisenhower, when he met Congressional leaders after the event, began by saying 'that in all of the many conferences that he had attended in peace and war this one gave him about the finest feeling as to the competence of the participants and the trust that could be put in them'.[21] Macmillan reported the same to the Cabinet. Yet when he touched down at London airport on 27 March, to be met dutifully by Butler, he had to deal with another problem. There had been an article in the *New York Times* about the official communiqué of Bermuda. Drew Middleton, the author of the article in question, had written that Eisenhower had suggested that the US and the UK re-establish their intimate wartime cooperation, 'including joint intelligence and planning systems',[22] but that Dulles had knocked those words out. Macmillan had only just seen the article as he boarded his flight. But he had already been bombarded by Eisenhower, by both cable and subsequent letter. The offence of leaking, the Americans claimed, had been committed by Peter Hope, the Foreign Office Press Officer. Macmillan wrote back to Eisenhower plaintively that he did not accept the attribution – but he was careful to make sure that a suitable rebuttal was planted in the London newspapers. That, as it turned out, was just about enough to satisfy Eisenhower. Cooperation in intelligence was duly restored.

It was then time to turn to the next piece of news – the proposed resignation of Lord Salisbury. It was to be, as expected, over Cyprus. Archbishop Makarios had been exiled in March 1956 from Cyprus on the grounds that he was too vocal in support of Colonel Grivas and EOKA. He had been held, of all places, in the Seychelles island of Mahé – in the middle of the Indian Ocean. By March 1957 Macmillan noted, 'I am sure we had better let him go. We may never find a better opportunity and we can't keep him ... in the Seychelles.' But the very evening after his return from Bermuda, 'Salisbury came to see me after dinner. He was very charming, but seemed determined to resign over something. He is in one of his resigning moods.'[23]

There was then an attempt to put a finger in the dyke. On the evening of 28 March Butler called Harold Slater, Salisbury's Parliamentary Private Secretary, with a message from Macmillan to the effect that Lennox-Boyd had spoken to the Conservative Commonwealth Committee in the afternoon about Cyprus and that 'the meeting was pronounced a great success'. Moreover, Butler himself was to address the 1922 Committee later. 'The political situation there is therefore good,' Slater went on, 'and gives no cause for disquiet.'[24]

It was no good. Salisbury thought it a matter of principle. He wrote to Macmillan, one letter for publication and one more personal, explaining that Makarios's assurance that he would invite EOKA to abandon its campaign of violence but on the understanding that the state of emergency in Cyprus would be lifted was simply not enough. He therefore tendered his resignation. Macmillan wrote back – two letters, again one for publication and one, in his own handwriting, more personal (and unctuous). He said, 'I cannot tell you with what grief I got your two letters ... You will hardly realise what a sad loss you will be to all your colleagues ... But to me it means much more. I have taken on a very difficult job, in circumstances almost unparalleled in political history. I wish you could have been with me to see it through ... One thing comforts me – you refer to our old friendship. That we can surely keep. Yours ever, Harold.'[25]

In his diary, Macmillan was much less friendly. 'In pondering over Lord Salisbury's resignation at this particular moment,' he wrote, 'I came to this conclusion. All through history the Cecils, when any friend or colleague has been in real trouble, have stabbed him in the back – attributing the crime to questions of conscience.'[26] Then, a few days later he wrote, again in his diary, 'Lord Salisbury's resignation has left scarcely a ripple on the surface. The Cabinet, much as they all like him personally, feel like a man who has got rid of an inflamed tooth.'[27] So much, as it were, for Dorothy's brother-in-law.

Political life, as always, moved quickly on. The Defence Estimates were published, in the form of a White Paper, without much opposition. Even better, shipbuilding and engineering strikes had been called off. In early April, Macmillan and Dorothy went travelling together – to Ayr for the conference of Scottish Conservatives and on the way, with their grandsons, to Oxford. On 13 April, they were playing golf together at Ayr – 'for the first time for half a year ...

there was a lot of press and photographers (which rather impeded the game) ...'[28] He was also deep into *The Presbyterian Tradition*, a book which he had found in Ayr (and which diverted him from his reading of *Dr Jekyll and Mr Hyde* – which he then polished off in the next half-day).

On return to London, Macmillan found that Salisbury had written to *The Times* advocating a fresh approach to get some sort of agreement with Nasser and then go to the Security Council with it. Lennox-Boyd did his best to explain to Salisbury that his plan was unrealistic, and wrote to Macmillan saying so. But by then Macmillan was no longer interested. 'I fear you will not convince Ld S,' he wrote back in his own hand. 'He is not in a mood to be convinced. His letter ... is to be followed by a motion on the Order Paper by our right wing, who now regard him as their leader.'[29] Macmillan went on to note in his diary that 'he may have felt rather peeved that his resignation made so small a stir'.[30] It was, of course, both brutal and unfair.

It was perhaps not a fitting prelude for the Easter of 1957. Macmillan may have thought that he made up for it by going to church twice on Easter Day (which also happened to be his thirty-seventh wedding anniversary). He may even have liked one of the lessons of the day which he read – from the Book of Revelation: 'I am the Alpha and the Omega'. He may also have enjoyed the sight of some seven hundred cars parked at Birch Grove and more than two thousand visitors to the gardens. But what he surely would have enjoyed was the thought that his first six weeks had passed without the feared collapse of his administration, that there was now a prospect that the Suez Canal episode could be buried, that the British economy would no longer be threatened by a shortage of oil (petrol rationing was lifted on 15 May) and industrial unrest, that he had survived Salisbury's resignation – in short, that with a bit more luck his Government could hold on.

The next major test was the final debate in the House of Commons on Suez. Negotiations over how the Canal would be managed dragged on, but in the end the Egyptian Government refused to allow the Suez Canal Users Association any place in the future scheme of things. It was by then clear that France and Britain would have to concede. Accepting responsibility for the fiasco, Mollet resigned as French Prime Minister. Macmillan, on the other hand, set out to convince his colleagues – and the House of Commons – that humble pie was the only possible dish of the day. During a long Cabinet meeting on 10 May (just before the meeting Macmillan had heard about the death of his brother Daniel's wife) there was some muttering, but the conclusion, bizarre as it may seem, was that 'we had now extracted the maximum advantage from the present situation and that the Egyptian proposals represented the best arrangement for the administration of the Canal which we could possibly hope to achieve in the short term'.[31]

The debate in the Commons took place on 15 and 16 May. Macmillan was nervous about the result. He had heard that Salisbury was organising a campaign against him and was in touch with Eden about it. Nor did he think that he would get much help from the Americans. During his visit to Bonn the previous week, he had been told by Adenauer that 'Dulles had told him a) that Bermuda was a failure b) that the British had no foreign policy and were finished. I have always rather liked and stood up for Foster Dulles. But it may be that people are right in dubbing him "double-crosser".'[32] In fact, Macmillan was so gloomy about the Commons vote at the end of the debate that he genuinely thought that his Government might collapse.

In the event, it went much better than he had feared. His own opening speech, as he admitted himself, was poor. He was flustered by the constant barrage of catcalls from Labour. But Gaitskell was no better, and Macmillan's wind-up speech on the second day was certainly very much better. Thanks to some very effective whipping by Heath, the Government won the vote and 'the whole Tory Party stood up and cheered me. At the Speaker's chair, I turned and bowed. It was an extraordinary and spontaneous act of loyalty, which touched me very much.'[33] As if that was not good enough, as a bonus, at the end of the debate, the news came through that the British hydrogen bomb had been successfully tested, and the press account of the debate on the following morning – almost uniformly unfriendly to Macmillan over Suez – was swamped by the reporting of the (supposed) British triumph. Nevertheless, whatever the publicity and the rows in the Commons, the Government had survived. Furthermore, the whole Suez episode started to drift out of the news. Almost immediately, opinion polls also started to turn in the Conservatives' favour. It was time, Macmillan decided, to be optimistic again.

The first clear sign of optimism was Macmillan's approach to his old friend John Wyndham. Wyndham had retired from the Foreign Office (for the second time, as it happened) to do battle with the Treasury over death duties due on the large estate which he had inherited at Petworth. On 21 May Macmillan wrote asking whether Wyndham would be willing to join 'the old firm'. He said that he had hesitated until then since he had not believed that his administration would last more than a few weeks. 'But we seem now to have got over quite a number of jumps in this Grand National course, and having just managed to pull the old mare through the brook with the same jockey up, and the Cecil colours fallen, I am plucking up my courage.'[34]

The truth was that Macmillan had come to realise that life for a Prime Minister can be lonely. He had noted at Bermuda that Eisenhower seemed to be like a cross between king and prime minister – and that meant he was rather a lonely figure with few confidants, and glad to have somebody to talk to. The same was true of him, and when he recalled the days with Wyndham in North Africa, of the expeditions to the mountains and the days spent bathing naked in the sea at Tipasa, he came to the conclusion that he had found the ideal person. Wyndham, it need hardly be said, jumped at the chance.

Much less happy, however, was a visit to Downing Street on 12 June. Macmillan's old mentor, Ronnie Knox, came from Oxford with bad news. He had a cancer, which he thought had disappeared but had come back, this time on the liver. After his lecture on St Paul's Epistle to the Romans (the most theologically complex of all St Paul's Epistles, and on which Knox was an acknowledged authority), he arrived in Downing Street in time for lunch. 'We had luncheon and dinner together,' Macmillan wrote in his diary, 'and I was able to be with him for a short time after dinner ... Poor Ronnie is dying and he knows it and bears it with great fortitude ... The only comfort is that no friend I have is better prepared for the journey.' The next day 'I took Ronnie to Paddington Station and left him in the hands of a friend, to travel back to Mells. I fear we shall not meet again. He was calm; but I'm afraid when I left him I could not hold back my tears.'[35] It had been an emotional parting. But the following day, Macmillan took a large family party to the ceremony of Trooping the Colour. After that, he retired in solitude to read Scott's *Waverly* – a familiar text, and, in its familiarity, comforting for someone in obvious sorrow.

All governments welcome the end of the Parliamentary year, prefaced by the long summer Recess and concluding, all being well, with a short session in October. Ministers are tired and are glad to be relieved of Parliamentary inquisition. In July 1957 Macmillan gave the event a particular welcome. Moreover, a conference of Commonwealth Prime Ministers had come and gone in late June. It was with something of a light heart, therefore, that he went to give an address to the mainly Conservative Party faithful assembled in a football ground in Bedford on 20 July. His purpose was to echo the warning he had recently received from Thorneycroft about the possibility of renewed inflation. Whether intentionally or not – opinions have been divided ever since – he introduced his warning with the declamation: 'Let's be frank about it; most of our people have never had it so good.' He then went on to say that there was prosperity such as the country had never known (which is no more than stating the obvious at a time of post-war economic growth). But his message was simple: 'Is it too good to last?'[36]

Rare are the moments when politicians give to the electorate, in Enoch Powell's phrase, 'a tune they can whistle to'. Macmillan himself, at the time, did not seem to realise it. He wrote in his diary that 'the speech was well reported in the Sunday Press and I think helped to steady things a lot'.[37] But at the same time he was having to deal with an appeal for help from the Sultan of Muscat and Oman, at the southern end of the Persian Gulf, where there had been a popular revolt led by a religious leader. The Royal Air Force was told to intervene and duly did so with some effective rocket attacks. Apart from all else – more difficult Cabinet meetings on Cyprus and another visit from Dulles (apparently 'much more friendly and helpful than at Bermuda'[38]) – he was looking forward to a holiday.

It was a good, if short, holiday. In the early part of August at Birch Grove, there were in all nineteen grandchildren around and about; and Churchill and Clementine Churchill came to a happy family lunch. But it was too short. The Muscat business had to be dealt with – Dulles had to be persuaded not to support the Arab League in the Security Council over Muscat and Oman. At the same time there was a heavy speculative attack on the French franc which, along with rumours in London that Thorneycroft was about to let the pound float, was starting to transfer itself to sterling. It was certainly time for another break.

In the second half of August, there was much shooting to be done, at Bolton Abbey particularly, where, on 16 August, Macmillan recorded that he 'shot well and got just over 160 birds'.[39] By 22 August it was getting even better. 'We have had 5 splendid days on the moor and fresh air, exercise, and concentration in the attempt to execute difficult shots at these rapid ... targets has done me good.' Besides, 'John Wyndham has come.'[40] In fact, there is no doubt that Wyndham's return gave Macmillan the greater pleasure – greater even than the shooting.

On his return to London Macmillan found a personal message from Dulles. There were disturbing reports of the spread of communism in Syria, particularly among the younger officers in the Army. In the spring of 1957 the United States Congress had approved what came to be known as the 'Eisenhower Doctrine', which allowed the President power to use armed force to protect the independence of any nation against armed communist intervention. Since the Soviet Embassy in Damascus was actively orchestrating the Syrian left-wing Government, and since vital oil pipelines passed through Syria, the 'Americans are taking it very seriously and talking about the most drastic measures – Suez in reverse. If it were not serious ... it would be rather comic.'[41] In order to try to calm them down – another role reversal – Macmillan decided to send Freddie Bishop to Washington. As it happened, Bishop's mission was surprisingly successful in calming everything down.

On 29 August there was a Requiem in Westminster Cathedral for Ronnie Knox, who had died a few days earlier. There was a scare about Wyndham who had gone into hospital for what Macmillan feared was cancer, but which turned out to be a much less serious stomach complaint. Then it was a weekend for Macmillan and Dorothy with the Queen at the gloomy royal castle of Balmoral. They duly arrived there on the evening of Saturday 31 August.

The visit turned out to be more difficult than Macmillan expected. The Queen and Dorothy, coming as they did from the same social background, got on famously. Dorothy, too, was a great success with the princes and princesses. Macmillan, on the other hand, although he found the Queen 'as charming and intelligent as ever',[42] did not seem to strike a happy note with her. 'He lectured her ... and was not in the least interested in what she had to say ...' was one comment.[43] His first talk with Prince Philip went no better. 'He is *against* us being a nuclear power,' Macmillan wrote in his diary. 'I don't altogether like the tone of his talk. It is too like that of a clever undergraduate, who has just discovered Socialism.'[44]

The difficult situation was to some extent improved at a shooting party on the Monday, when six guns (including, strangely enough, Salisbury) bagged nearly four hundred birds. Prince Philip appeared to Macmillan to be more relaxed and helpful. The drive away from Balmoral, although through beautiful country was, however, marred by Dorothy's determination to stay in Scotland for almost the rest of the month (if previous experience is any guide, she presumably wanted to stay with Boothby at his Scottish home). Macmillan was thus left to make his way back to London and on to Birch Grove by himself.

During September telegrams went to and fro between London and Washington over Syria. More immediately pressing was the attack on sterling, which was reaching alarming proportions. Thorneycroft and his Treasury Ministers, Enoch Powell and Nigel Birch, were convinced that the root cause was domestic inflation and that this could only be held in check by control of the money supply. Macmillan's friend and private economic adviser, the Oxford academic Roy Harrod, disagreed. 'The idea that you can reduce prices by limiting the quantity of money is pre-Keynesian,' Harrod wrote. 'Hardly any economist under the age of 50 subscribes to it.'[45] Nevertheless, Thorneycroft persuaded Macmillan and his other colleagues. On 19 September Bank Rate was raised from 5 to 7 per cent, public investment was scaled back and credit limits imposed on banks. Needless to say, the measures were deeply unpopular – and, for the first time, raised doubts in Macmillan's mind about his Chancellor.

On 9 October Macmillan wrote to Eisenhower suggesting another meeting to follow up the progress made at Bermuda. His letter was well-timed. American confidence had been badly shaken by the Soviet success in launching the first satellite – known as 'Sputnik' – into space. 'In view of the extent of Russian power and technical capacity (the "satellite" launched this week has, of course, struck public imagination) couldn't we now pool all *our* resources to fight them ... This would involve getting rid of the Macmahon [sic] Act.'[46] This, for Macmillan, was the great prize – the repeal of the post-war Act of Congress preventing American administrations from passing on nuclear information to foreign countries.

A visit was quickly agreed. It was even welcomed by the American press (which had been enchanted by the Queen on her own visit). But there was very nearly a serious hiccup. A fire at the British nuclear installation at Windscale in the north-west of England threw large clouds of radioactive dust over north England and North Wales. If the news had got out, the whole nuclear programme, to which Macmillan was so attached, would have been thrown overboard. With the Americans it would have raised serious – and possibly conclusive – doubts about British technical abilities. There was only one thing to do. There was to be an inquiry, led by the most distinguished scientist, Sir William Penney. That, at least for the moment, was to be the end of it.

Macmillan, together with his retinue of private secretaries and officials, landed at Washington airport in the morning of 23 October. During the discussions, which took up most of the remaining day, he found Eisenhower 'much better than at Bermuda. He was brisk; confident; and seemed more sure of himself.'[47] Dulles was more forthcoming. NATO, he pointed out, was, in its original concept of maintaining large numbers of troops on the ground to defend against a Soviet tank assault, out of date. The future was nuclear – and there had to be some mechanism to ensure that the decision to use nuclear weapons, if it ever came, would have the general support of the non-communist world. Macmillan replied that 'he had sometimes thought of trying to create a new organization which would in many respects be a substitute for the United Nations, leaving the UN somewhat in the titular role of the House of

Lords', but that he had gone off the idea.[48] But nobody could think of anything that made more sense.

The plenary sessions on the following day went even better. Eisenhower referred to the McMahon Act as 'one of the most deplorable incidents in American history, of which he personally felt ashamed',[49] and Dulles, after lunch at the British Embassy, produced a draft of a 'declaration' to be entitled 'Declaration of Common Purpose'. There it was – in paragraph 3: the prize Macmillan had been hoping for – the end of the McMahon Act. After that, there was little more to do other than go through the formalities. Macmillan had got the two things he wanted: the restoration of the transatlantic friendship by which he set such store, and the repeal of the McMahon Act. It was no wonder that his press and television conferences on his return on Sunday 27 October found him in his best form, even after an overnight flight – confident, smiling and authoritative – and regretting that he had missed a good day's shooting.

When Parliament returned on the following Tuesday there was much to be done. There was a debate on the Thorneycroft measures of September – Harold Wilson from the Labour front bench accused Oliver Poole of a leak – a statement on the talks in Washington and a further statement on Windscale. In the excitement of the Wilson attack on Poole the Windscale statement passed without much comment. There was then a short break before the new Session, which was to be opened by the Queen almost immediately on 5 November (as it happened, it was Guy Fawkes Day). On the 2nd Macmillan had a good day's shooting (160 pheasants) and on the 3rd he stayed in bed almost all day. As he said himself, he was dog-tired.

But there was to be no let-up. After the State Opening there was the Windscale White Paper to be presented to Parliament (conveniently obscuring many of the major faults Penney had detected). By 12 November, after a series of meetings on the agenda for the December NATO conference in Paris, Macmillan came down with a bad cold. Always worried about the minor health problems of everyday life, he thought it might be pleurisy or even pneumonia. But by 17 November, after a long sleep, he had recovered enough to go to Paris to see the new French Prime Minister, Félix Gaillard, meet Adenauer in London in early December to try to persuade him (unsuccessfully) that the West German Government should pay more to support British troops in Germany, make a (heavily coached) television broadcast, and to have lunch with Churchill. ('He talked a lot about his father, to whom he is very loyal. From this point of view, he is not sorry to see the discomfiture of the Cecils.'[50])

On the morning of Saturday 14 December, Macmillan, with Lloyd, Sandys and a posse of officials, arrived in Paris for the NATO meeting after an uncomfortable night on the cross-Channel ferry. Dulles arrived in Paris soon after but in his first conversations with Macmillan seemed more worried about Eisenhower's health (he had had what seemed to be a minor stroke on 25 November) than anything else. Yet when Eisenhower himself arrived on the Sunday, he stood up in an open car in spite of the intense cold and waved his arms in the air at the crowd of Parisians – who all waved back with equal enthusiasm. Macmillan went to see him on the Monday morning to hear how he was. Eisenhower was sitting in a large room on the first floor of the American Embassy. He talked much about his health. He had been determined to go to Paris. (Those around him said that he would have resigned if his doctors had forbidden him to go.)

Eisenhower's state of health had so preoccupied the Americans that they had no clear plan for the conference. Macmillan managed to rescue what was turning out to be near chaos by proposing a clear agenda for both Foreign Ministers and Heads of Government. Ministers would meet in the morning and Heads of Government in the afternoon. In fact, so well did this arrangement work that an agreed position was achieved – siting of American intermediate-range ballistic missiles on European sites, together with a new approach to the Soviets to discuss disarmament questions generally. 'We have got the Americans', Macmillan noted rather smugly in his diary, 'to take a more realistic view of the psychological situation in Europe. We have got the Scandinavians off their moral high horse. We are beginning to get the Europeans out of the "Maginot Line" complex, and begin to look to their flanks.'[51] As it happened, there was a nasty jolt when the British press and the House of Commons received the outcome sourly – but Macmillan could afford to ignore them.

In fact, by the end of 1957 there was much which he could afford to ignore. After all, his administration had survived; the Labour Party in Parliament was ineffective; Suez had disappeared as a political issue; and there were encouraging signs of economic prosperity. Above all, he had mended relations with Eisenhower and Dulles. It was therefore with a reasonably light heart that he could leave London for Birch Grove for the Christmas holiday. On Christmas Day there was a family party of no fewer than twelve grandchildren and their respective parents – and brother Daniel. On both Christmas Eve and Boxing Day, Macmillan stayed in bed 'till luncheon and did little or no work all day. A walk with Daniel in the afternoon ... early to bed. I must start work seriously tomorrow. There is a lot to settle before we head for our [Commonwealth] tour.'[52] Indeed there was – not least, although he did not know it at the time, the resignation not just of his Chancellor of the Exchequer but of the whole Treasury ministerial team.

18

'You Almost Feel Yourself a Statesman'

On Monday 6 January 1958 the Macmillan Government suffered its first political heart attack. 'Dear Prime Minister,' Thorneycroft's letter of that date ran, 'I write to ask you to accept my resignation as Chancellor of the Exchequer. My reason can be shortly stated. I am not prepared to approve estimates for the Government's current expenditure next year at a total higher than the sum that will be spent this year.'[1] It could hardly have been worse. There were none of the customary courtesies – thanks for the opportunity to serve, pledges of continuing support for the Government, gratitude for past kindnesses and so on. Nor was there a personal covering letter. The whole thing was about as abrasive as it could possibly be. Similar letters, equally terse, arrived on the same day from Thorneycroft's two ministerial lieutenants, Enoch Powell and Nigel Birch.

The resignation of a senior Minister, let alone of a Chancellor of the Exchequer with his closest ministerial colleagues in tandem, is enough to threaten the life of any government; and the Macmillan Government was no exception. Its very heart, as Macmillan himself immediately realised, was in danger. Moreover, it quickly became known to the outside world that Thorneycroft's resignation had been delivered in the most brutal manner – quite extraordinary, it was noted, from one Old Etonian to another. The question was immediately asked whether the Government could possibly survive the damage. Pouring petrol on the fire, Thorneycroft and – particularly – Birch went out of their way in explaining that their resignation was on a matter of principle, that Treasury Ministers had been intent on winning the fight against inflation while others – unspecified, of course – were not.

Macmillan was both very worried and very angry. He wrote back to Thorneycroft in the iciest terms ('My dear Thorneycroft', and then, after reiterating the terms of the dispute, ' . . . I must add that your resignation at the present time cannot help to sustain and may damage the interests that we have all been trying to preserve.'[2]) Other Cabinet Ministers, when Macmillan read Thorneycroft's letter to them at the morning's Cabinet meeting on 6 January, were outraged. Heath, as Chief Whip, thought that it was treachery – a direct attack on Macmillan's leadership – and openly said as much.

In fact, the warnings of a crisis, like warnings of many physical heart attacks, had been evident over the previous months and weeks. The problem was the rate of inflation. The year on year rise in the Retail Price Index had moved from a comfortable 2 per cent in May 1957 to a very much less comfortable 4.5 per cent in July, where it stayed throughout the autumn. Thorneycroft had spelled out his own solution to the problem in the House of Commons on 28 October. 'There can be no remedy for inflation ...,' he said roundly, 'which does not include and indeed is not founded upon a control of money supply. So long as it is generally believed that the Government are prepared to see the necessary finance produced to match the upward spiral of costs, inflation will continue and prices will go up.'[3] In truth, Thorneycroft had never been much of an economic theorist but he had been convinced of an apparently magical cure for inflation – control of the money supply – by Powell's persuasiveness and the expert advice of a distinguished professor, Professor Lionel Robbins. Nevertheless, there was no doubting his new enthusiasm. As history has often shown, there is nothing like the zealotry of a recent convert.

The argument was thus between Thorneycroft's Robbins and Macmillan's Harrod, money supply theorists against 'Keynesians' – and, politically, Thorneycroft against Macmillan, Butler and most of the rest of the Cabinet. Specifically, it centred on the estimates of government current expenditure for the financial year 1958–9. Thorneycroft (overriding the views of senior Treasury officials – still robustly 'Keynesian') was insistent that the overall figure should not be higher than the projected outturn for 1957–8. This, he argued, would ensure that the money supply would be contained and the battle against inflation won. Since prices would inevitably rise during the year, this in practice meant a cut in real terms for those government departments which needed to fund already approved programmes. The argument had duly rumbled on in Whitehall, as these things do, over the winter, and by the end of the year, after seemingly endless meetings, officials had managed to narrow the difference between the Treasury and the spending Departments down from £150 million to just over £50 million, about 1 per cent of the total estimate for the coming financial year. The matter was then brought before the Cabinet on the morning of Friday 3 January to try to narrow the remaining gap.

The meeting lasted four hours and was, for the Cabinet of those days, exceptionally bad-tempered. Thorneycroft tried to hector his colleagues into accepting the conclusions of a paper he had circulated two days before – to raise prescription charges, to remove the entitlement of family allowances for a second child and thus save the £50 million. John Boyd-Carpenter, the Minister for Pensions and National Insurance, protested. In fact, he had his resignation letter in his pocket. Thorneycroft was then so offensive that Macmillan 'had difficulty in preventing some of the Cabinet bursting out in their indignation'. Nevertheless, after closing the meeting, he thought that it was worth another attempt at pacifying his unruly Chancellor. He saw Thorneycroft privately in London on the following Sunday morning – after a good and relaxing day's shooting at Birch Grove on the Saturday – to make his appeal, but 'I got the impression that he had made up his mind to resign . . . It struck me that he was in an excited mood, and he had obviously been pushed on by the Treasury Ministers, Birch and Enoch Powell. The first is a cynic; the second a fanatic.'[4] Nevertheless, even then he did not think that all was entirely lost and, after discussion with Butler and other colleagues, he called another Cabinet meeting for that very evening to try to engineer a compromise.

In the event, all efforts were fruitless. True, Thorneycroft was less offensive than before but he was still adamant. After a break for dinner the Cabinet reassembled at half past ten in the evening for a final shot. Macmillan was by then showing signs of panic. 'It was . . . clear by dinner', he wrote on the following day, 'that the greatest danger was the complete disintegration of the Cabinet – Treasury Ministers; Defence Ministers: Labour: and Social Ministers – all might resign (for different reasons) and there would be no alternative to the resignation of this govt.; a Labour administration; a dissolution; an election in which the Conservative Party would be in a hopeless and even ridiculous position, without policy or honour. This must at all costs be avoided.'[5]

The next morning the resignation letters duly arrived. But Macmillan had been, even in his near panic, supremely skilful. By going out of his way to find a compromise over the £50 million difference, he had, although he had failed in the attempt, secured the support of the rest of the Cabinet (apart from Reginald Maudling, who seemed to be prepared to sacrifice the second child's allowance) and thus avoid the terminal damage to his Government's heart which he, and others, had feared. His stage management after the resignations, too, was particularly artful. He moved quickly to fill the main vacancy, appointing a reluctant (but much more compliant) Derick Heathcoat Amory to the Exchequer in time for his meeting with the Queen at six o'clock that evening.

The public stage, as well, was carefully prepared. He and Dorothy were due to leave for their long-planned tour of the Commonwealth on the morning of 9 January. A Britannia aircraft, suitably equipped – a cabin with twin beds – was waiting for them at London airport. Macmillan let it be known that the trip would go ahead on schedule, as though nothing had happened. 'We started off from London airport as planned,' Macmillan's diary runs. 'Almost the whole Cabinet came to see me off.' Indeed they did, prompted by the Chief Whip. They raised their (mostly bowler) hats to him as, in striped trousers and short jacket, he prepared to mount the steps to the Britannia. ('I said a few words to the BBC, TV, etc., which I had prepared last night, about the Commonwealth trip and "our little local difficulties". This will annoy a lot of people, but I think it will give them a sense of proportion.'[6])

In the event, Macmillan just about pulled it off. There was, of course, a great media scene, made more frantic by the sight of the Prime Minister apparently abandoning his Government and taking off into the skies – leaving Butler to make the necessary junior Treasury ministerial appointments and generally to clear up the mess. Yet it was not so easily done. During the following week Macmillan, on his travels, was particularly nervous. 'I have had to deal with a great deal of business from home,' he wrote on 19 January. 'Butler, Chief Whip [Heath], and all the others seem to have kept things going very well. There is, of course, great confusion and perplexity in the Party ... Nevertheless, I have a feeling (from the reports) that the worst is over.'[7]

The first stop on the tour was Delhi. For Macmillan – and for Dorothy – it was a wholly new experience. Although Macmillan had met Commonwealth leaders, the meetings had always been on British or neutral territory. He had no first-hand knowledge of the teeming crowds of the Indian subcontinent, the strange devotions of South East Asia or the brashness of Australia. In fact, the further he was away from London the more difficult the whole enterprise seemed to become. It is little wonder that when he arrived in Delhi such was his nervousness that when he emerged from the Britannia at Delhi airport his instinctive gestures – in a sudden reversion to the ways of boys at Eton about to face their tutors – were to fasten the middle button of the jacket of his dark blue suit and to straighten his Old Etonian tie.

The Colonial Office had not been much help. The cost benefit analysis of the Empire, which he had demanded early in 1957, had occupied much official time but had only produced the lame conclusion that the Commonwealth was, in economic terms, neither an asset nor a burden. Sir Norman Brook, in fact, when he saw the result ruled firmly that it was not worthy of Cabinet discussion. In short, Macmillan had little briefing on how he was meant to behave. The result was that when a garland was hung around his neck he could do no more than produce a series of banal phrases which, in any other context, he would have avoided as quite ridiculous: 'my wife and I are indeed delighted ... this is the first time a British Prime Minister ... this is a unique occasion', and so on.[8]

Fortunately, his host, Pandit Nehru, lightened the whole thing up. Macmillan and Dorothy stayed at Nehru's home and both found their host 'able, full of charm, cultivated and ruthless – all great qualities in a leader'.[9] They were particularly impressed both by the lavish receptions and by the friendliness of the Indian crowds. The echoes of the British Raj were also much to their taste – Macmillan recalled the days in 1919 when he nearly became the then Viceroy's aide-de-camp. Dorothy was able to keep pace – her Cavendish and Lansdowne ancestors were duly brought into play. It all made for friendly and light conversation. Even so, Nehru could not resist a tease. 'I wonder', he asked Macmillan at one banquet – quizzically – 'whether the Romans ever went back to visit Britain?'[10] Macmillan, the classicist, was quick to see the joke – and the irony behind it.

Pakistan was less easy, although their hosts, President (and, as it happened, dictator) Iskander Mirza and his wife, were gracious enough and the food and wine were an improvement on Nehru's offerings – which Macmillan had pronounced to be uneatable and undrinkable. Yet the country was poor and politically unstable – and the people sullen. Macmillan noted, too, that Muslim religious leaders seemed to exercise great, if uncertainly directed, power. But by way of compensation there were more echoes of the Raj when he visited an officers' mess on the North West Frontier, decked with its trophies from the Afghan Wars, and swapped military reminiscences with the Pakistani (mostly Sandhurst-educated) officers.

After a brief stop in Karachi, where he made a speech about the vocation of Britain as a trading rather than an imperial nation (it was becoming one of his favourite themes), Macmillan and his party flew on to Colombo. There he found another Oxford product, the Prime Minister Solomon Bandaranaike. Bandaranaike, a Sinhalese Christian, had been Secretary and then Treasurer of the Oxford Union. 'He clearly models himself on Mr N[ehru],' Macmillan wrote, '... dresses like an Anglo Catholic priest at the altar, stole and all ... is a very rich man and the son of a very rich man ... is westernised ... makes friends with everyone ...' Macmillan, still far away from home, was only too happy to slip into the old and well-understood idiom of what he himself described as 'the capable, educated, liberal, North Oxford society to whom we have transferred power'.[11]

From Ceylon the party flew to Singapore for a stop of one night before flying on to New Zealand. But there was little time for rest, as there was a whole package of work waiting for him which had to be dealt with quickly (and which also contained the news that Thorneycroft had made a particularly good speech in his constituency). But if all that had to be done quickly, at least on the long flight to Auckland in New Zealand, in spite of a dreadful cold, he was able to catch up on his reading – Hardy's *Jude the Obscure*, Osbert Sitwell's *Great Morning* and Hugh Walpole's *Jeremy* – and noting regretfully that he had been so busy and so tired during the trip that he had not read anything since leaving London.

New Zealand, as might be imagined, was very much to his and Dorothy's taste. 'A really wonderful reception,' he wrote in what had become a rather sporadic diary, '... most attractive country and the people extraordinarily friendly and loyal.'[12] It was, without a doubt, one of the high points of the tour. But there was still business to be done. He heard that the government majority in the House of Commons had held up in the debate over Thorneycroft's resignation and that the tribunal set up to investigate the alleged leak of information on the change in Bank Rate had dismissed all the Labour accusations. He had also to deal with a proposal from Bulganin for a summit meeting – he even thought of going to Moscow to see Bulganin to discover what agenda he had in mind – and follow the negotiations with the Turkish and Greek governments over the proposals for Cypriot independence.

Frustratingly, all that had to be done at long range, so much so that by the end of January Macmillan was worrying about being away from London for so long. Not only was it 'very hard to keep track of all that is going on' but, in a politician's worst nightmare, Thorneycroft seemed to be taking advantage of his absence. 'I am beginning to suspect', Macmillan wrote, 'behind his rough and uncultured manner – rude and *cassant* [aggressive] to an extreme – a deep plot. He may be calculating on another sterling crisis this autumn and the break up of the govt in conditions which would allow him to seize the leadership of the party from me and Rab ...'[13]

Macmillan's nervousness – and Dorothy's too, for that matter – about the reception they might get in Australia came to the surface again when they landed at Sydney. An Australian diplomat had inadvertently been snubbed during the Singapore stopover and the Australian press had duly taken note. Before their arrival there had also been a good deal of ribaldry about Macmillan's 'pommie' accent. Yet, as it turned out, the Australian leg of the tour was in many ways the most successful. Both Macmillan and Dorothy became surprisingly adept at managing the informality of Australian crowds – Macmillan untypically making forays, rushing up to astonished bystanders, pumping their hands and saying 'How *are* you?' and 'Very nice of you to come!'. The Australians, equally untypically, loved the performance. There were fruitful talks with Menzies as well. In the end, in Melbourne, he was heard to remark that 'everybody's so much nicer to you in other countries than they are at home. At home you always have to be a politician; when you're abroad you almost feel yourself a statesman.'[14]

Macmillan was brought back to domestic political reality when the party landed at Heathrow at about midday on Friday 14 February. Butler was there with a detailed *aide-mémoire* describing in his customary lucid prose what had happened in the Prime Minister's absence while he had been minding the governmental shop or, as Butler himself preferred to put it, minding the baby. The problems, of course, had not changed: Thorneycroft, Cyprus, Bulganin, the Middle East. 'All important,' Macmillan wrote, 'and all insoluble!'[15] On top of that, the Conservatives had suffered a truly dreadful defeat at a by-election in the Lancashire constituency of Rochdale, not only losing to Labour but coming in third place behind the Liberals.

There was to be little relief. Still suffering from jet lag, Macmillan had found in addition that he could not shake off the cold he had caught in Singapore and the sore throat which had followed. On 19 February his doctor, John Richardson (who had looked after him all those years ago in Algiers), pronounced himself alarmed at the state of both larynx and chest. Macmillan himself thought that 'perhaps it was the start of cancer',[16] but the X-ray and the consultant's opinion calmed him down.

Yet there is no doubt that he was very tired, almost to the point of exhaustion, after the exertions of the Commonwealth tour. Equally, however, there is no doubt that the tour had been an outstanding success, both in enhancing his own standing as an international figure and in the confidence he gained, particularly in Australia, in engaging crowds directly and at first hand. One political magazine summed it up well. He appeared to be a new man. 'He spoke with the attractive diffidence of a schoolboy who had been abroad for the first time, desperately eager to communicate something of the vision he had seen.'[17] Nevertheless, he was still very tired. The weekends of 22 February and 8 March were spent mostly in bed, recovering physical strength – he was, after all, sixty-four years old – and catching up on his reading (starting Froude's twelve-volume *History of England* and finishing Robertson's two-volume *History of Scotland*, with *Pride and Prejudice* thrown, as it were, in between).

Of all the insoluble problems of late February, the most difficult was Cyprus. True, the new plan for an organisation of the British Armed Forces, not least the final abolition of Fighter Command, Britain's saviour in 1940, would cause 'a great row ... Neither Chiefs of Staff nor senior ministers will like it,' as Macmillan admitted. 'There will perhaps be some resignations. However, these seem to be endemic in my government.'[18] But that was wearily tolerable. Chiefs of Staff would forever complain and ministers could resign if they wished. Cyprus – the almost never-ending problem of how the island could possibly become independent of Britain without a ferocious confrontation between Turk and Greek – was worse. The plan produced by Lord Radcliffe at the end of 1956 for a part-elected, part-appointed assembly with a British Governor retaining control of defence and foreign affairs – and 'reserve powers' to veto legislation – had pleased neither side. But, equally, neither side was willing to stop the talking.

Yet it was Bulganin's request for a summit meeting that was currently top of Macmillan's agenda. Early in January he had written to Eisenhower a long letter on how to deal with the Soviets. He had suggested a series of meetings, writing of 'the next round of discussions with the intention of reaching agreement if the Russian approach [on nuclear testing] is genuine or of exposing their insincerity if it is not'.[19] Eisenhower, in response, had been much more cautious. In his note to Dulles he had written that 'it is easy to get entangled in such a proposition but not so easy to get out of it'.[20] Macmillan had then been warned off by Caccia in Washington, relaying Eisenhower's caution and pointing to the amendment to the McMahon Act on its way through the US Congress. Nothing should be allowed to upset its passage.

By the end of March, however, a cautious attempt to engage the Soviets in dialogue had been agreed with Dulles. The timing, as it happened, was fortunate. On 27 March Bulganin was unceremoniously bundled out as Prime Minister and Khrushchev took over. Quick to seize the moment, two days later Macmillan sent him the text of the statement agreed, although with some difficulty, by Dulles. 'It is clear', the statement read, 'that before a Summit meeting can meet ... preparatory work is required ... exchanges through diplomatic channels leading to a meeting between Foreign Ministers ... it is suggested that diplomatic exchanges should start in Moscow in the second half of April.'[21]

That kept the matter in play until the Easter of early April. Then, for Macmillan, at least, it was 'two whole days in bed ... finished Froude – 12 volumes – read also Churchill's *History of the English Speaking Peoples*. The chapters on the American Civil War are brilliant – the rest is dull ... Read Scott's *The Abbot* ... one or two good scenes ...' All the family, apart from Sarah, turned up for Easter – 'all the children [grandchildren] seemed well and happy. The Macmillan boys gave a house party in their new cottage – which is a sort of annexe to Pooks ... a capital party. They

cooked us a fine meal of scrambled eggs, sausages, kidneys, etc.'[22] There
was dinner with the Churchills as well. All in all, it was a happy, if
unseasonably cold, weekend, made happier by the thought that the
Thorneycroft challenge – if indeed there ever was one – was fading
fast.

Soon after Easter, Adenauer made an official visit to London. Both
British and Germans agreed that it was a success, not least because
agreement had been reached on the prickly question of the West German
contribution to the cost of the British Army of the Rhine. Adenauer said
that he was delighted with his visit (he apparently flirted shamelessly
with both the Queen and the Queen Mother at an official dinner at
Windsor). Macmillan, for his part, thought that the visit 'had helped to
counteract the poison which the French have been pouring into his
ears'.[23] Less successful, however, were the negotiations with the fiery
General Secretary of the Transport and General Workers Union, Frank
Cousins. In short, it was deadlock, and a potentially damaging London
bus strike was called by Cousins for early May.

In the middle of all this, there was a strange Parliamentary interlude.
A piece of legislation had been passed in both Houses of Parliament
and had received its Royal Assent on 30 April. Oddly, Macmillan does
not mention it in his diary and gives it only a glancing reference in
his memoirs. But although nobody at the time seemed to realise the
implications, the Life Peerages Act 1958 was the most striking –
and certainly most revolutionary – constitutional enactment of the
Macmillan Government. Over the course of time, as would become
evident, the Act, when fully implemented, would change the whole
complexion of the House of Lords. In short, it would turn the House
of Lords from a relic of the hereditary system into a professional
Upper House.

Speaking to the Second Reading of the Bill in the House of Lords,
however, at the beginning of the previous December, Lord Home, the
Leader of the House, had seemed wholly – and almost certainly was –
unaware of the Bill's potential long-term effect. The Government's
objective, as he put it, was to save the existing House of Lords from
impending collapse. He said that there had been 'agreement, if not
unanimity, on the introduction to this House of Life Peers. For this the
arguments are strictly and severely practical.' The small number of
Labour (hereditary) Peers, he went on, were maintaining 'a brave façade'
but they were bearing a strain 'which they cannot and should not be
asked to carry much longer, and this House is perilously near a breakdown
in its machinery'. In other words, Life Peers – and, astonishingly for the
time, women – were necessary to keep the Labour Opposition going. The

Prime Minister, of course, would consult the Leader of the Opposition in the Commons about nominations, but 'the emphasis would be on the appointment of persons who can help the working of Parliament'.[24] The Labour Opposition in the House of Lords claimed that the Bill was no more than 'tinkering', and in the House of Commons they wanted the abolition of the Lords and so could not be bothered with it. In that atmosphere of Parliamentary torpor, the Bill duly became an Act.

At the same time, as it happened, another European Parliamentary democracy was in very much deeper trouble with its own institutions. The insurrection in Algeria had led, by the end of April, to a rebellion by white settlers and their military allies against the French Government itself. During May, the Fourth Republic was in the greatest danger. There was much talk of civil war. By the end of the month it seemed clear to many that only the return of de Gaulle would be enough to calm everybody down. After a series of complicated negotiations de Gaulle, supported in the end by Mollet for the Socialists, agreed to take on the job of Prime Minister. He did, however, make it clear that the Fourth Republic, set up after the Second World War, had outlived its usefulness (if, indeed, for him it ever had any) and must be replaced.

At first, Macmillan was too much occupied with the London bus strike, a threatened railway strike, the proposal for a summit and the Cyprus problem – let alone a sudden flare-up in Lebanon (Nasser was apparently manoeuvring to try to get Lebanon to join the Egypt–Syria combination which he had proposed) – to pay much attention to events in Algiers and Paris. On 16 May, however, he suddenly took note of what was happening. The generals in Algiers had set up a 'Committee of Public Safety' in defiance of Paris. De Gaulle had failed to condemn it. 'De Gaulle', Macmillan wrote in his diary, 'has made an equivocal statement, but one which terrifies the French politicians. It is cast in his usual scornful but enigmatic language ... France is in turmoil – no one knows whether it will lead to the collapse of the Fourth Republic ... The only thing we have to rely on is the Anglo-American cooperation, which is closer and more complete than ever before.'[25]

It is this last comment which illustrates most clearly Macmillan's overriding priority in foreign policy. America was always to come first. In fact, almost to emphasise the point, it so happened that at the same time as the French Fourth Republic was collapsing he was due to receive a doctorate and make the address at 'Commencement' – the ceremony at which graduates receive their degrees – at DePauw University in Indiana. He was, of course, more than willing to revisit his mother's home state; but at the same time he wondered whether he could spend a day or two in Washington. Eisenhower welcomed the idea and dates were duly set down for early June.

That done, there was a moment for a short break – five days in Scotland with Dorothy at Glenalmond House (lent to them for the occasion) during which they played golf at Gleneagles on four out of the five days – and, on return to London, to have two teeth taken out in a difficult and subsequently painful operation. Two days in bed followed ('My face is better but rather swollen and my mouth very sore[26]). Then, after watching the Derby and dining at Eton, it was time to prepare for America.

The travelling party – composed of Macmillan, Dorothy, Norman Brook, Harold Evans, Freddie Bishop, Philip de Zulueta with secretaries and detectives – took off in their Britannia from London airport at midnight on 6 June. Selwyn Lloyd had wanted to come too, but had been told firmly by Dulles that if he were to come 'it would so alter the character of [the] visit as to elevate it to a conference from which it might be impossible to exclude the French and perhaps others'.[27] But Lloyd might have been glad to miss the trip. Two hours out into the Atlantic one of the aircraft's engines failed and it had to turn back. Macmillan had already gone to sleep and, although he was woken up to hear of possible impending disaster, decided that the best course of action was to stay in his bed. Fortunately, the Britannia was able to struggle back to London on three engines and take off again after suitable repair. Macmillan, the survivor of previous aircraft accidents, lay quietly in his bed throughout the whole dangerous adventure, reading Walter Scott's *The Fortunes of Nigel.*

The rather shaken party were welcomed at Washington airport the following morning by Dulles and a posse of State Department officials. There was immediate business to be done: arrangements for the exchange of nuclear information once Congress had passed the amendment to the McMahon Act and the British proposals for Cyprus for which Macmillan sought United States support. In the evening, there was dinner with Dulles, Christian Herter, the Under-Secretary of State, their wives – and Vice President Nixon. Although Macmillan's first encounter with Nixon had been friendly, this was quite the opposite. 'The Vice President', Macmillan recorded, 'poured out a monologue which extinguished any spark of conversation from whatever quarter it might arise ... This spate of banalities lasted for 3 to 4 hours ... I felt sorry for the Americans, who were clearly hurt and ashamed.'[28]

The next day, Sunday 8 June, was the day reserved for DePauw. The Britannia left Washington (without Dorothy, who was not in the least interested in Macmillan's Indiana roots, and, anyway, had intensely disliked his mother) and arrived at Indianapolis in time for Macmillan to be met by the President of DePauw, Russell Jay Humbert, and taken to lunch with the owners of the major Indiana newspapers at Humbert's home. It need hardly be said that he was given a true 'Hoosier' (the Indiana term for one of their own) welcome. On the journey from Indianapolis airport to Humbert's home in Greencastle, some thirty-five miles, there were flags, banners with 'Welcome Mac' or 'Welcome Home'. After lunch, again, on the way to the university there were more crowds – some six to seven thousand, Macmillan guessed.

The ceremony was long and – be it said – tedious. More than four hundred graduates were receiving their degrees, each one with its own citation. Macmillan's doctorate came next, after which he made his speech – lasting precisely twenty-four minutes, the timing required by the television companies which were carrying it coast to coast. As might be expected, there was nothing very original in the content. What was important, however, was that his message was unambiguous. This he certainly achieved. 'Macmillan Predicts Doom for "Imperial Communism"' was the headline of the *Indianapolis Star* the next morning. 'Calls Close Free World Ties Way to Speed Its End', it went on.[29] The owner of the paper, Eugene Pulliam, congratulated him at dinner later in the evening, and 'gave me a beautifully framed portrait of my mother (an old photograph, really) which had been found somewhere. It was a kind gesture.'[30]

There was then another doctorate to be collected at Johns Hopkins University in Baltimore, at their own Commencement. Eisenhower had himself, on behalf of his brother Milton, the President of the University, personally – and almost unctuously – invited Macmillan ('Dear Harold, This letter is a personal one ... complete freedom of decision without *any* slightest possibility of embarrassment ...'[31]) to accept the doctorate. Macmillan, of course, could not refuse, particularly since Eisenhower proposed to come with him in a helicopter taking off from, and landing back on, the White House lawn. But he did point out that no fireworks were to be expected, since his speech would be just about the same (slightly truncated due to time) as his speech at DePauw. All that duly done, on the next day it was a speech and questions at the National Press Club in Washington, and a further meeting with Eisenhower and Dulles.

During that meeting, as Macmillan wrote in his diary, 'Dulles put forward some very far-reaching ideas about the future, on which we must really do some work and have another meeting to discuss. What he wants to work towards is a unified system of government for the free world. Both he and the President feel that while this sense of unity and understanding exists between us we should try to create something definite to leave to our successors.'[32] In all this, of course, it was made clear that there was no room in Dulles's construction for the France of General de Gaulle.

In fact, de Gaulle's new Government had been the subject of a prolonged discussion. Dulles started it off but Macmillan quickly took over. '[De Gaulle] will want', he said, 'to resume the tripartite relationship but we will have to find some way of keeping him out of the things we don't want him in, such as Middle Eastern problems.' He went on to say that he 'expected de Gaulle to ask for an improved nuclear position for France'. Dulles immediately closed that door. 'It would be "extremely difficult"', he answered, 'to obtain Congressional approval of the type we are working out with the UK.' Eisenhower said that 'we cannot treat de Gaulle as if he were "like God" and the Secretary [Dulles] agreed'.[33]

After all that, and in a mood of some self-congratulation, Macmillan and Dorothy spent a nostalgic day in Ottawa and arrived back at Birch Grove on Saturday 14 June. Full of enthusiasm for the Anglo-American relationship, and with some confidence that the solution to the difficulties of Cypriot independence was not too far off, Macmillan set himself to prepare for a visit to de Gaulle at the end of the month.

It was to be far from easy. Macmillan certainly had a good idea of what he was up against. The British efforts to negotiate a free trade area (the old Plan G) between the Six and the rest of Europe, led, on the British side, by Maudling with a team of officials, would obviously make no progress until the internal political problems of France had been, in one way or another, resolved. 'With the *coup d'état* in Paris,' Macmillan wrote later, 'it seemed likely that all the previous discussions so carefully prepared and carried on with such detail and patience would fall to the ground. Both the European Community of the Six and the larger concept of the Free Trade Area would depend on the unpredictable decisions of the new ruler of France. I had to confess to myself that the prospects did not seem very favourable.'[34]

The British Foreign Office thought that under the circumstances the only thing to do was to exercise the maximum amount of charm. A memorandum from the Foreign Office put it succinctly: 'If we make the French feel cosy with us, that might have the effect of making them moderate their pretensions.'[35] Macmillan himself, on the other hand, thought about using a big stick. In trying to deflect the French from their nuclear ambition he thought to link French help with the free trade area, as a trade-off, with continued British defence involvement in Europe. 'I feel', he wrote to Lloyd on 24 June, 'that we ought to make it clear to our European friends that if Little Europe is formed without the parallel development of a Free Trade Area we shall have to reconsider the whole of our political and economic attitude towards Europe ... We would take our troops out of NATO ... We would withdraw from NATO ... isolationism ... surround ourselves with rockets and we would say to the Germans, the French and all the rest of them: "Look after yourselves with your own forces. Look after yourselves when the Russians overrun your countries."[36] Fortunately for Macmillan, his memorandum, private for Lloyd and Heathcoat Amory, never leaked out. Dulles certainly never got wind of it. Nor did Eisenhower. They would have been mightily surprised if they had.

But Macmillan and the Foreign Office had, not for the first nor indeed for the last time, read de Gaulle quite wrongly. De Gaulle – they should have known by now – was not susceptible either to wooing or to browbeating. In reply to Macmillan's friendly messages he had replied with equal cordiality, and the replies were genuinely meant. De Gaulle did indeed have friendly memories of the support which Macmillan had given to him in Algiers in 1943. But the interests of France, as always, came first. Furthermore, de Gaulle knew his bargaining strength. If the British wanted his support for their proposed free trade area there was one price, and one price only, which they would have to pay – to give help with France's programme for a nuclear strike force.

It was, of course, the help which Macmillan had sworn to Eisenhower, first in Bermuda in March 1957 and then more recently in Washington, never to give. Nor was he able to do so if he had wanted. Yet during his talks with de Gaulle Macmillan let slip that if the French wanted help with their nuclear programme they should apply to the Americans. Furthermore, although he understood the difficulty of conducting a nuclear test while the test ban talks were continuing in Geneva they ought to try to achieve some sort of nuclear experiment 'in order to qualify'.[37] That was enough for the General and his Ambassador in London, Jean Chauvel. They had heard what they wanted to hear.

None of that, however, helped Macmillan in discussions over the proposed free trade area. De Gaulle, while maintaining that he would always be prepared to listen to proposals, said firmly that French opinion was not favourable to the project. At that point Macmillan played his defence card. It had been a great effort, he said, for a traditionally isolationist Britain to keep four divisions on the European continent. If the Six threatened a trade war Britain would be driven back on itself with consequences for NATO and the defence of Europe. De Gaulle, ever the realist, was very much more impressed with this line of argument

and immediately undertook, on the free trade area, not 'to reply nega-
tively. That is not because of what you have said about NATO ... but
because of our desire to cooperate with you.'[38] The point was not conceded, but Macmillan's attack had struck home. Quite what that
meant in practice was, of course, as so often with the General, anybody's
guess.

Macmillan quickly realised that his visit had not been a success. De
Gaulle 'has, of course, aged a lot', he wrote in his diary. 'He has grown
rather fat; his eyes are bad and he wears thick spectacles; he no longer
smokes chains of cigarettes (indeed, he does not smoke at all); his manner
is calm, affable and rather paternal. But underneath this new exterior,
I should judge that he is just as obstinate as ever. I spoke very strongly
to him about the Free Trade Area, and the fatal political results that
would follow the present French attitude. But he clearly was neither
interested nor impressed ... like so many soldiers of his type [he] cares
nothing for "logistics" ... I am very apprehensive about European Free
Trade, for M. [Antoine] Pinay (whom de Gaulle has made Minister of
Finance) is a small man, with a small mind, and completely dominated
by the French "patronat".'[39]

On his return to London, however, there was some good news to
cheer him up. The London bus strike had finally faded out, the Gallup
poll (which had been showing a 13 per cent Labour lead in May) had
recorded a Labour lead of only just over 3 per cent in June, and Thorneycroft's dire warnings about inflation turned out to be unfounded (in
fact, the year on year rise in the Retail Price Index for July was to turn
out to be no more than 1.8 per cent). Yet that was only a brief respite.
On Monday 14 July, while taking a day off at Birch Grove, Macmillan
took an urgent call from Selwyn Lloyd. There had been a *coup d'état* in
Baghdad. The King, the Crown Prince and the Prime Minister had
apparently all been murdered. The British Embassy in Baghdad had been
torched. There was danger all round. In near panic, Lloyd almost shouted
down the telephone that if Iraq fell to Nasser or to the communists so
might Syria, Lebanon and Jordan.

Macmillan's immediate reaction was, as always, to turn to the Americans. Lloyd was sent off to Washington at short notice to sound out
Dulles. (De Gaulle, needless to say, was forgotten.) In a long telephone
conversation with Eisenhower on that evening, Macmillan learnt that
the United States was preparing to send troops to Lebanon in response
to President Chamoun's appeal. Macmillan wanted him to range much
wider – to be prepared to deploy troops wherever in the region danger
threatened. Eisenhower refused outright – an unusual display of bad
temper between the two men. But two days later a message arrived from

King Hussein of Jordan with an appeal for British troops. After much agonising ('I made each Minister express his view without any lead from me'⁴⁰) the Cabinet agreed unanimously to send two paratroop battalions to Jordan to protect Amman airfield.

In the panic, however, nobody had thought to ask Israel for rights to fly the British paratroopers over Israeli territory to Amman. The result was that the one flight from Cyprus which had overflown Israeli territory, had – very surprisingly – not been intercepted and had reached Amman. But the other flights from Cyprus were told in mid-air to turn back. Macmillan himself was badly shaken. 'This mistake . . .', he wrote in his diary, 'nearly led to a terrible disaster, which would (I think) have resulted in the collapse of all our policies and the fall of the govt . . . I waited throughout the morning in my study – trying to deal with other work and hiding my sickening anxiety . . . [Norman] Brook (who thought it was all his fault) was almost in tears.'⁴¹ It was only at about 1 p.m. on the day, while Macmillan was beginning to tell Gaitskell about what was happening in Amman, that Freddie Bishop sidled in with a note to say that the Israelis had agreed the overflight.

That crisis, at least for the moment, passed. But only three days later Khrushchev suddenly made an urgent request for an immediate summit meeting to discuss the whole matter of the Middle East. Macmillan was at church on the Sunday ('Litchfield, a fine church, good choir and a good sermon,' he noted⁴²) when an avalanche of telegrams poured in. He went immediately back to London. On arrival at Downing Street he found Dulles, who had arrived for a meeting with Ambassadors of Baghdad Pact countries in an effort to find a way for the United States to associate itself with the Pact without having to seek Congressional approval.

Over dinner with Macmillan, Dulles suggested a way to accommodate Khrushchev's request without losing too much Allied face: a special meeting of the UN Security Council which heads of government might attend. Other permanent members of the Security Council would, of course, have to be consulted. The first on the list was General de Gaulle. De Gaulle was then asked whether France would agree to the Dulles formula. The answer came back that she certainly would not. The reason, according to the British Ambassador in Paris, Sir Gladwyn Jebb, was that de Gaulle was, as he had been during the war, deeply suspicious of Anglo-American intentions in the Middle East. Furthermore, de Gaulle agreed with Khrushchev that there should be a meeting in Geneva. (He also apparently wanted to involve India in any discussion.)

In fact, de Gaulle's refusal of the Dulles solution had been unintentionally helpful. Since there could be no agreement on the venue – let alone the agenda – Dulles and Macmillan had no difficulty in replying to Khrushchev that it was a most interesting idea which certainly deserved further study. In other words, it could be quietly buried – until, of course, it was resurrected.

By late July, it was time for Parliament to go into Recess for the summer. Macmillan also thought it a suitable time to announce the first list of 'Life Peers', which duly appeared on 24 July. He had been meticulous in consulting Gaitskell, and the list which appeared, of ten men and four women, contained six Labour nominations. But heading the list, much to the general astonishment of those who cared about such things, was Boothby. It turned out, in fact, that Boothby had asked Macmillan for a Cabinet job but, failing that, had asked for a peerage. Macmillan was certainly not going to give him his Cabinet job, but was readily prepared to give him the peerage. The signal, of course, was easily read. Boothby's political career was over. He was politically finished – consigned to the political equivalent of the knacker's yard. It was a sweet, if in the end relatively gentle, revenge.

As July ended – with some unusual, almost autumnal rain and wind – Macmillan admitted to himself that he was still feeling very tired. But there was still no time for a holiday. The Cyprus negotiations around the Radcliffe Plan had at least been going reasonably well, if tortuously (although the attacks on British troops had not ceased), and Heathcoat Amory was steering the economy with cautious competence ('he is worth 20 Thorneycrofts!'[43]). Furthermore, the amendment to the McMahon Act had successfully passed Congress and a British–American bilateral pact was ready for signature. The main worry in early August was Jordan, where the Israelis – under heavy Russian pressure – had cancelled permission for overflights. The British troops there were, at least for the moment, stranded at Amman airfield. But at least the situation was, even if only temporarily, calm.

There was to be one more expedition before Macmillan could take a holiday. On 7 August he took off once again from London airport, this time in one of the new 'Comet' aircraft of RAF Transport Command – heading for Athens. He was going, he hoped, to finish once and for all the negotiations which would lead to a Cyprus settlement. It had become almost a personal matter – to achieve some sort of reconciliation of conflict in the region of the world which was closest to his classical heart. Selwyn Lloyd had told Dulles as much in a conversation they had had the previous May. 'He himself', Lloyd had told Dulles, 'was extremely sceptical as to whether the tripartite condominium [Macmillan's complex formula] would be accepted. Macmillan took a "starry-eyed" view of the matter and thought that this was a very idealistic, high-minded and imaginative proposal to which he attached much importance ... would insist on taking it on very much as a personal project and undertake the direct negotiations with Greece and Turkey on the spot.'[44]

It need hardly be said that Athens in early August is not the most convenient place for detailed negotiation on an arrangement between two governments, one of which, the Greek, regarded the other, the Turk, as barbarians, while the Turk regarded the Greek as useless and, be it said, effete. It was hot and unusually humid. At first, all the meetings went as badly as Lloyd had expected. The Turks, with some hesitations, had previously accepted the Radcliffe Plan. The Greeks, on the other hand, had found the plan wholly unacceptable – but were still prepared to discuss it.

The meetings with Greek Ministers took up much of the days of 8 and 9 August. On the second day, Macmillan made an emotional plea to Constantine Karamanlis, the Greek Prime Minister. 'I had seen something of Greek heroism in the War,' he said (in his diary version), 'and helped them ... in their struggle against communism ... the affection of the British people for the Greek people was as strong as ever ... we had made great sacrifices ... independence was over; interdependence must take its place. Modern Greece should set an example and not lag behind ...' Karamanlis was duly impressed. 'In reply ... Mr K became quite emotional ... They hated the Turks ... fought them for 500 years ... would fight them for Greek liberty whenever and wherever they could ... Having got all that off his chest, he felt better and we discussed [the Radcliffe Plan] very calmly until lunchtime.' On that note, Macmillan went off to look at the Acropolis ('which I may never see again') and the National Museum.[45] It was then time to fly to Ankara.

The Turkish Government put on a good reception for him, but in the detailed discussion the Turkish Ministers claimed that the Radcliffe Plan which their Government had accepted in London had been altered as a result of Greek pressure. A long wrangle ensued about what had been said or not said. 'The Turks were very rude, and accused us of bad faith. I was very rude back, and they withdrew, rather sullenly ...'[46] By the end of the meeting the Turks had agreed to support the Radcliffe Plan as it stood, and Macmillan was able to fly back to Cyprus with agreement (subject to the details) of both the Greek and Turkish Governments to the principles – if not the details – of the Radcliffe Plan.

There was then just about time for a small piece of nostalgia. On arrival in Cyprus, he went, unannounced, to have lunch with a battalion of the Grenadier Guards – commanded by the son of Charles Britten who had been in the 4th Division with Macmillan at Loos in 1915.

'I spoke a few words to them,' he wrote in his diary. 'I found all this very moving and I almost broke down in speaking, for it all recalled so many memories.'[47]

Safely back in London on 12 August, Macmillan spent much of the next day in bed. Hoping for a quiet few days, he started reading *War and Peace*. Apart from an exchange of telegrams with Eisenhower about nuclear testing, there was little more to be done and he and Dorothy were able, on 20 August, to catch a train to take them to Bolton Abbey – where a plentiful supply of grouse was waiting. (Apparently, not all of them had been shot by the Cavendish guests there the previous week.) Five days of shooting and reading, as well as some favourable poll results and press comment, were enough to restore the spirits – let alone the fresh air and rest to restore health. True, there were some troublesome riots in Nottingham on 23 August, primarily due to racial tension, which spread to Notting Hill in London by the end of the month. But Macmillan was quite content to leave that problem with Butler. There was also a problem with Dulles over the Chinese shelling of the offshore islands of Quemoy and Matsu. The British were in no doubt that China had a legal right to the islands. But it was better to keep quiet so as not to offend Dulles.

In fact, the affair of the Chinese offshore islands faded quickly. On 4 September the United States had threatened a nuclear strike on Chinese airfields if shelling of the islands was supported by bombing. That was enough. Khrushchev protested, but since he himself had never understood why the Chinese had started the thing in the first place (almost certainly, in fact, to 'derail Khrushchev's pursuit of détente with Washington'[48]) the protest could be, and was, disregarded. Nevertheless, the affair had a disturbing twist for Macmillan. Randolph Churchill had asked to see him 'to get a message from me to Winston (for the golden wedding) and to show me the wonderful *"Book of Roses"* which the Churchill family (and many leading artists) are giving to Winston and Clemmie. We got chatting about Far East and Cyprus ... He went off and wrote a "feature article" ... Unfortunately the editor [of the *Evening Standard*] asked whether he had seen me. Randolph said yes – and the article appeared as an interview.'[49] The embarrassing headline was 'Mac backs Ike'. The implication was that the British Government would support an American attack on China.

It was irritating, and it 'made a terrible hullabaloo'.[50] But it was not enough to prevent Macmillan from taking a ten-day holiday in Scotland during the second half of September. Dorothy had, yet again, gone north before him and met him at Wick airport on 13 September. There was golf, shooting, reading (Trollope took pride of place), the annual visit to

Balmoral – all in magnificent weather. It was with the greatest reluctance that he returned to London to get ready for the start of the next Parliamentary year. Above all, of course, his mind was turning to the biggest challenge of all – putting his Government and Party to the test before the country in a General Election.

19

The Prime Minister

'From time to time, in one of six of the more conservative London clubs (Pratt's, Buck's, the Carlton, the Beefsteak, the Turf or the Athenaeum), a tall, grey-haired man with a drooping moustache can be observed walking slowly – almost shuffling – up the stairs, alone. He walks in, orders perhaps a dry martini, and then may turn to talk to one of the members. He talks well, in a casual, relaxed way, with a sardonic wit. He has a habit of picking his teeth with concentration, and of brushing down the side of his moustache tiredly. Everything about him seems to droop – his moustache, his eyes, his mouth, his floppy cardigan. Even his black bow tie, which he wears in the evening, is tucked beneath his collar, in the Edwardian fashion. He is one of the few men in England who literally puts his tongue in his cheek when making a joke.

'His repertoire of languid gestures includes the pulling in of his mouth, tongue in cheek, as he prepares a quip; the pulling down of the corner of his eyes, while he pauses for a point; the fastidious wobbling of his hand, as he searches for a nuance; the opening of his mouth – squarely, like a trap – as he feigns amazement. He might be any aged clubman, imagining himself to be important. But in fact he is, of course, the Prime Minister ...'[1]

Thus one of the most acute observers of Britain at the end of the nineteen fifties. By then, let us say in the autumn of 1958, Macmillan had settled to the job of Prime Minister – never easy, in truth, whatever the new incumbent's previous ministerial experience and ambition – and to the domestic arrangements of No. 10 Downing Street. Yet none of them, nor even the home at Birch Grove, seemed to appeal to the donnish side of his character, the Balliol man and the devout Anglo-Catholic. He himself was fond of saying that he was part 'gownsman' and part 'swordsman', and it was in his meandering through his London clubs that the 'gownsman' found the most satisfaction. He was 'a supreme conversationalist. In an armchair, talking to two or three intelligent and sympathetic companions, he could fascinate and stimulate as few other men.'[2]

It need hardly be said that the companions were almost always men.

Furthermore, not only were they men but men of a certain class, and race. In that, Macmillan was a creature of his time and upbringing – snobbish, vaguely anti-Semitic, lofty and occasionally dismissive of 'servants' (among which were, apparently, the employees of the Macmillan publishing house). Women were, apart from his (errant) wife and a new friend, Ava, Countess of Waverley (the widow of one of Macmillan's former colleagues, Sir John Anderson), kept at a distance. Indeed, Ava Waverley was only acceptable because she '"had cultivated an unerring gift of flattering men who liked her", which explained "why women hate her" ... [Moreover] "she has a caressing, insinuating voice like the serpent of Old Nile."'³ (She was also rather fat and physically unprepossessing.) Other women, including, as it happened, Queen Elizabeth, found him the same boring Macmillan of the 1930s, never listening to what they said and insisting on treating them to long and stultifying lectures.

Macmillan's phonetics, too, were what today would be regarded as verging on the archaic. In fact, it was no more, and no less, than the Edwardian English – like his Edwardian tucked-in black bow tie – which he had been brought up to and which, depending on his audience, he continued to adopt like the actor he had learned to become. 'Off' was almost always pronounced 'orff'; 'lost' was, in the presence of Cavendishes, pronounced 'lorst'; and 'girl' became 'gel' or 'gal'. 'Political' generally was 'poelitical' and 'Parliament' was pronounced with all four vowels clearly enunciated. The phonetics, moreover, carried through into the language of his diaries. 'Luncheon' was never 'lunch', and when he drove anywhere in a car he always 'motored'. (The archaic language, in fact, went beyond his diaries and through to his memoirs – of the last volume Enoch Powell wrote that 'the reader has a recurrent sensation akin to that of chewing cardboard'.⁴)

In the age of television and radio all this could be irritating – and many thought it so. Macmillan himself never watched television. His outdoor recreation was shooting and his indoor recreation was reading books – an hour each day was set aside for the purpose, even in his days as Prime Minister – mostly of well-thumbed English classics. Television broadcasts were thus a particular challenge. It was not just a question of being unable to see the teleprompter. It was a question of being able to present himself as somebody who lived on the same planet as those whom he was addressing. The accent, the drooping eyes, the moustache, the snarl in his upper lip – none of that helped. Furthermore, although in the end he came across well, his ignorance of the television audience made him very nervous. On one occasion, on his way to deliver a speech to a dinner given by the British Broadcasting Corporation, he interrupted the briefing he was getting to ask – of a cartoon character almost everybody else had heard of – 'Who is Lenny the Lion?'[5]

Dorothy, too, was also a creature of her time and upbringing. But, apart from her sexual waywardness, she became a model wife for the occasionally fractious Prime Minister – jolly, charming, wholly without snobbery, always interested in other human beings of whatever class or race, adored by servants and full of the humour and life which made Downing Street such a joy for her grandchildren. To be sure, she still made sorties to see Boothby, but these now were more visits of old lovers rather than the flames of a new passion. Besides, she had put on weight and Boothby had started to look decadent. Almost in compensation for what had happened in the past, Dorothy had become the spirit of Birch Grove. On high days and holidays she would organise all sorts of parties for grandchildren, neighbours and neighbours' children – cricket matches, fireworks, tennis and so on – while Macmillan 'sat quietly reading in the summer house'.[6] Of course, there were expeditions to Chatsworth for big Devonshire occasions, but Birch Grove was, to say the least, a more companionable home – even though Macmillan was always comfortable when referring in conversation to the various Duchesses – and, indeed, Dukes – of Devonshire.

If the grandchildren were a source of delight both to Macmillan and to Dorothy, their children were certainly less so. All four of them, Maurice, Catherine, Carol and Sarah, had inherited what Macmillan called the Cavendish gene – propensity to alcoholism. Maurice had courageously struggled to rid himself of it, and by the end of the 1950s seemed to have done so – but his system had over the years suffered great damage. His wife, Katie, could not get on with her mother-in-law and thought her father-in-law was unfairly blocking Maurice's career in politics. Catherine, married to Julian Amery (Leo Amery's son and another product of Summer Fields, Eton and Balliol) in 1950, had been the most beautiful and lively of the Macmillan children, but had also succumbed to the Cavendish gene – and disappointment at her husband's snail-like political career. Carol, although herself for a time almost succumbing to the blight of alcohol, had in her marriage found a life away from politics. Insurance broking – her husband Julian later became Chairman of Willis, Faber – was a much safer occupation.

The whole atmosphere of family life, with its tensions, likes and dislikes, spilled over into No. 10 Downing Street. As it happened, in a rather different way, it also seemed to permeate Macmillan's Government. It was difficult to count, since Ministers were moved about (and in and out) from time to time, but one estimate is that his Government included thirty-five Ministers who were, one way and another, his own relatives. If so, that would have comprised more than a third of all his ministerial appointments. His Cabinet, too, was stuffed with Old Etonians. That, too, made for the feeling of an extended family. Everybody knew everybody else – perhaps, it might be said, only too well.

The problem for a Prime Minister, however, is that in a government of an extended family (or cronies, in today's language) he, or she, becomes more and more detached from the reality of life elsewhere. In Macmillan's case, the problem became evident from the end of the 1950s onwards. His constituency, Bromley, was safe, and needed little nursing. Holidays were spent in Scotland, shooting with like-minded and mostly aristocratic companions or at one or other of the Cavendish homes.

The routine of domestic life in No. 10 Downing Street was kept simple. Macmillan woke early, stayed in bed dealing with the box his private secretaries had put in his bedroom the previous night and only got up when it was time for breakfast – no more than tea and toast, with occasionally a boiled egg by way of variation. After shaving (he was particular about his moustache which was kept neatly clipped and was always careful about his hands) and dressing (he did not spend much effort on his clothes – Dorothy and Edith, the housemaid, had to look after them) he was ready for the day. Before lunch he had a glass of sherry or a gin and tonic but only water with the meal (the favourite, noted by Mrs Bell, the cook, was cold roast beef), the evenings being the time for whisky before dinner, wine with the meal and a glass of port afterwards – with a cigar or a cigarette – during a visit to one of his clubs. Lent, however, was usually a time for total abstinence.

The office routine was equally precise. Macmillan always kept his desk clear of clutter and all his books where he could easily find them. On the mantelpiece there were photographs of his father and the ruin of the (supposed) Macmillan croft in Arran. Private secretaries were summoned from time to time, as were shorthand typists from what was universally known as the Garden Room (not least because the window of the room in which they worked looked out over the garden). There were, of course, meetings, and people would come and go, but there was none of the frenetic and almost neurotic activity which Macmillan had inherited from Eden.

Nevertheless, although he cultivated the image, Macmillan was very far from 'unflappable'. As always with Prime Ministers, it was the preparation of speeches which was the most nerve-racking job – for all concerned. Once the date of the speech was known, preparation would start. Macmillan gave out a number of salient points which he wished included. The private secretaries then took over, consulted departmental officials where appropriate and produced a first draft. This was then worked on by Macmillan. At times he announced that he was ready to dictate. A secretary was summoned and a passage of the speech taken down, with passages from the draft complemented by his personal touch. When he was satisfied with the result, the word went out to turn it into 'psalm form' – a technique, and indeed a phrase, which he had learnt from Churchill. It was to be not more than one hundred words in large typeface on a small page, with spaces between lines. After more reworking, a final version emerged.

By the autumn of 1958 Macmillan had not only settled to the job. He was by then dominating the political landscape. The Gallup poll was showing good results. The economy was on reasonable track. The Labour Party was divided on so many issues that they were only able with difficulty to mount a coherent opposition. Those around him, whether they liked him or not – and opinions were sharply divided – recognised his supremacy. With his combinations of charm and arrogance, of snobbery and charity, of sudden subtleties and sly malice, of flashing intelligence and studied disdain, Macmillan, after just over eighteen perilous months in office, could now claim to have become a true Prime Minister.

20

'All the Political Domestic Mileage
He Can Get'

'You want to popularise abortion, legalise homosexuality and start a betting shop in every street. All I can say is that if you can't win the liberal nonconformist vote on these cries you never will!'[1] It was, as Macmillan said in later life, his favourite tease of Butler. In fact, it was very much more than a tease. The remark, however carelessly thrown off in a leisurely autumnal conversation, says much about Macmillan's true opinion of Butler. Their relationship, of course, had never been other than wary. Even if there was cordiality on the surface, there was no suggestion of personal friendship. Macmillan was by blood Scottish American, by education Summer Fields, Eton and Oxford, a Guardsman, a veteran of the First World War – who had married an English aristocrat. Butler was by blood wholly English, from an academic family which had provided governors for India, himself a son of the Raj, from a lesser public school and Cambridge, who had married money and, because of his disability, had never fought in a war. In other words, their two backgrounds, in terms of the Conservative Party of the time, could hardly have been more different. But it was not just a matter of background. By 1958 Macmillan's political mind, which was starting to give its serious attention to the next General Election, was wondering whether the Butler view of political life was, for the Party, an asset or a liability.

Of course, the wariness – almost suspicion – was not just a matter of votes at a General Election. It was also about the nature of the Conservative Party. There were differing political imperatives. Macmillan, an economic radical, was a social traditionalist. Social reform was of little interest and at times, for a Christian, even dangerous. Butler was the intellectual opposite, an economic agnostic but a social radical, particularly taken with loosening what he himself called 'legislation laced in Victorian corsetry', Britain's archaic and illiberal social laws.[2] Both, without a doubt, were exceptionally clever – and both, in their different ways, politically adept. Moreover, both were of acknowledged political stature. Yet there was, whatever the surface cordiality and the professed mutual admiration, an underlying – and quite marked – tension. In fact, it is no exaggeration to say that the tension between the two men, both personally and in their differing political imperatives, was the backdrop to the most important – and, from time to time, most uncomfortable – relationship of Macmillan's two administrations (and, as it happened, was, later on, to split the Conservative Party wide open).

By the end of the 1950s social opinion, at least the opinion of those who cared about such matters, was moving in Butler's direction. The sands were starting to shift under Macmillan's traditionalist feet. The social reformers had seized on the absurdity of literary obscenity trials, on the hounding of homosexuals, on the disgraceful state of the prisons and on the race riots of Nottingham and Notting Hill to argue the liberal case. True, it was not always plain sailing. Butler, for instance, had to spend much energy at successive Party Conferences explaining to the faithful why the Government was not proposing to 'bring back the birch'.

In fact, such was the mood of the Conservative rank and file that the reformers had to go to great trouble to keep their deliberations out of the public gaze. The forum for their discussion turned out to be a secretive group of Conservative ministers operating without – and away from – civil service support. The Steering Committee, as it was known, was formed of a small and select number of Cabinet ministers, with Michael Fraser from the Conservative Research Department as secretary and Macmillan himself as chairman. In Macmillan's absence the chairmanship fell to Butler. On the matters he cared about, Butler could rely for support on two other members of the Committee, Macleod and Heath. Together, the trio made a formidable group of advocates for social change – particularly effective, of course, during Macmillan's long absences abroad. Furthermore, it was the Steering Committee which mysteriously emerged as the body which was to draft the Conservative Manifesto for the next General Election.

Macmillan, as he said himself, was much more concerned with the management of the economy and the distribution of its dividend to the economically disadvantaged. He had gone out of his way to set out his stall, yet again, on 12 March 1958, in a speech to celebrate the twentieth anniversary of the publication of his 1930s pamphlet *The Middle Way*. In his – long and very carefully constructed – speech to the Conservative faithful on that evening he reiterated his conviction that the misery of the 1930s was a major injustice inflicted on people who could not, however hard they tried, do anything about it. In other words, the whole thing had been deeply unfair – and something which nobody with any sort of conscience should tolerate. For his part, he went on, he was determined to ensure that it could never happen again. Finally, just in case anybody had missed the point, he proclaimed that the Conservative

Party must always occupy the political middle ground. He omitted to mention, of course, although his audience fully understood, that the Conservatives were before long to face a General Election.

Later in the year Macmillan demonstrated in practice what he had announced in theory. On 22 October the Treasury produced a paper, over the signature of the Chancellor, Heathcoat Amory, arguing for stricter control over Government and public authorities' capital programmes to ensure that they were kept within the limits of available resources. If this was not done, the paper argued, the danger was inflation. Macmillan immediately saw in this an attempt to resuscitate the Thorneycroft agenda of the previous January. 'This is a *very bad paper*,' he wrote in its margin. 'Indeed a disgraceful paper. It might have been written by Mr Neville Chamberlain's ghost.'[3] Deflation rather than inflation was the danger. The Treasury should look, if anything, to reflation. In the face of such Prime Ministerial barracking the paper was hastily withdrawn. Reflation rather than deflation was the instruction. So be it. Not only did Heathcoat Amory cave in but Treasury officials started to recognise that the real Chancellor of the Exchequer resided not in No. 11 but in No. 10 Downing Street. Resistance to the Prime Minister's expansionist views would from then on have to be confined to Whitehall guerrilla warfare.

But it was not only the real Chancellor of the Exchequer who lived in No. 10. It had been evident for some time that the real Foreign Secretary lived there as well. Like many Prime Ministers before and since, Macmillan found foreign affairs much the most interesting part of his job. Obviously, he could not be his own Home Secretary, even if he had wanted to – Butler could be neither dominated nor dislodged. The Chancellor, Heathcoat Amory, had already been successfully decapitated. It was now a matter of ensuring that Selwyn Lloyd was little more than a bag carrier. Given that Lloyd was forever trying to resign and that his private life was the subject of much gossip, this was not too difficult. As Macmillan wrote in his diary, 'he really is an extraordinary capable and efficient man – as well as a wonderfully agreeable man to work with. He feels a great sense of gratitude and loyalty to me personally, for I have been able (by moral support, in private and in public) to help him through a bad time.'[4] In other words, it was settled that Lloyd would do whatever Macmillan told him to do. Moreover, Anglo-American relations were a strictly reserved Prime Ministerial fief. As attentive as ever (some would say obsequious), Macmillan wrote to Eisenhower to congratulate him on his sixty-eighth birthday ('My dear Friend ... It is now nearly sixteen years since you and I first met and I cannot tell you how much I value your friendship. We have done a lot together in war and peace

... Yours ever, Harold'.⁵) The relationship could hardly have been expressed more clearly.

Yet in the autumn of 1958 the going was far from easy. De Gaulle was proving as difficult as had been expected. He had already warned Macmillan that he was much displeased with NATO and that he would be making proposals for change. In fact, he went much further. On 17 September he sent a letter, with an accompanying memorandum, to Eisenhower and Macmillan setting out a plan for a world organisation under an American, British and French triumvirate. The letter and memorandum were marked 'secret', but, Macmillan noted, 'with incredible folly ... the General gave a copy to Spaak [the Secretary-General of NATO] and allowed the German and *Italian* ambassadors to see it.'⁶

Of course, it was not folly at all. It was done quite deliberately to achieve maximum effect. As de Gaulle himself wrote later, 'I called in question our membership of NATO which, I declared, was no longer adapted to the needs of our defence ... I therefore proposed that the alliance should henceforth be placed under a triple rather than a dual direction, failing which France would take no further part in NATO developments and would reserve the right under Article 12 of the Treaty ... either to demand its reform or to leave it.'⁷ His perfectly sensible point was that since the Middle East and the Far East were causing even more problems than central Europe, and given France's interests in those areas, it was only right that France should have a say in the military options available to meet crises. If that was not allowed, France would simply walk out.

Sensible, of course, his point may have been, but its presentation was badly handled. In fact, de Gaulle had decided to tell neither his Foreign Minister, Couve de Murville, nor Adenauer (who had been his guest at Colombey-les-deux-Églises only two days earlier) about his proposals. Couve promptly told Dulles that Spaak was responsible for their leaking out – and Adenauer was duly furious. The effect had been achieved – but perhaps not in the way de Gaulle wanted. (Dulles, in fact, later found out from Couve that 'none of de Gaulle's advisers share his rather extreme views about the triumvirate and NATO'.⁸)

It was time to talk to Adenauer. Macmillan had been due in any event for a visit to Bonn on 8 and 9 October. Once there, he found Adenauer 'very concerned. ... showed disgust and resentment. He had trusted de Gaulle ... Now he had struck a cruel blow at Germany ...'⁹ Macmillan, needless to say, was rather pleased at Adenauer's reaction. Anything which might wean Adenauer away from de Gaulle was welcome. He went on to suggest – unrealistically – that de Gaulle should be invited to write another memorandum, leaving out the offensive bits in the first, which could be openly discussed in NATO. Adenauer took that for what it was worth – but the two parted with expressions of cordiality and in a mist of (much appreciated) Rhine wine.

In his comments to Dulles, however, Macmillan took a different, and more realistic, line. He 'counselled against giving the impression that they were rejecting the memorandum out of hand'. He suggested that they should agree that 'there was a problem but that the proposals made were not necessarily the best ones to solve it and further exploration would be useful'.[10] Dulles replied that de Gaulle's proposal was quite unacceptable but agreed that they could not turn it down flat. State Department officials were accordingly instructed to prepare a response suggesting discussions at ambassadorial level along the lines Macmillan had suggested – but were told firmly that there was no need at all for them to hurry.

De Gaulle had also turned his attention to the British proposal for a free trade area. Macmillan in Bonn had tried to win Adenauer's support – in fact, he hoped that Adenauer's anger over de Gaulle's NATO initiative would work in his favour. He had also made the same threats as he had made to de Gaulle about British troop withdrawals from the European continent. Adenauer had been suitably impressed, but he was still hankering after a Franco-German rap-prochement and did no more than put on his customary impassive face. By 26 October, therefore, Macmillan was recording that 'the outlook for the European free trade area seems bad. The French are determined to exclude UK. De Gaulle is bidding high for the hegemony of Europe. If he could get peace in Africa and hold on to the Saharan oil, he might achieve it.'[11]

In the debate immediately after the State Opening of Parliament on 28 October (the ceremony was televised for the first time) Macmillan went on to tell the House of Commons that there were serious problems in the negotiations. Three days later, after a morning spent with the Canadian Prime Minister, John Diefenbaker ('... the problem with dealing with him is the same as with an adolescent boy – how to explain to him the facts of life without shocking him'[12]) he called a meeting with the Ministers most involved: Lloyd, Heathcoat Amory, Eccles (the President of the Board of Trade) and Maudling. They all agreed that if the French had made no move by the end of November negotiations should be called off.

The French duly obliged. On 6 November Couve de Murville called on Macmillan during a quick visit to London to tell him that there was little prospect of success. Macmillan snapped at him, saying that the French were just stalling. Macmillan then wrote again – angrily – to de Gaulle. 'I am deeply disturbed ... the Treaty of Rome ... can easily lead to a division in the European ranks rather than a bond of union ... Nobody has striven harder than I to put Europe in its rightful place in the world ... I beg you not to regard this as a technical issue. I hope you will give your close attention to it in its broadest political aspects ... we are already in a crisis which has the seeds of disaster for Europe in the long term ...'[13]

Macmillan was wasting his time. Not only did de Gaulle realise that he had Macmillan on the run but the Americans at the same time were tiring of the British complaints about the Treaty of Rome, and on 14 November Plan G, the original British response to the Treaty of Rome, was effectively killed. A press release from the French Ministry of Information announced curtly that 'it was not possible to create a Free Trade Area as wished by the British ...'.[14] De Gaulle's reply to Macmillan's letter was only slightly less offensive. All he could offer was the possibility of bilateral discussions – with the vaguest of agendas. British Ministers were suitably furious, the Foreign Office suitably aghast. Selwyn Lloyd called it 'perhaps the most critical development in Anglo-French relations since 1940'.[15]

On 26 November de Gaulle and Adenauer met in the small Black Forest resort of Bad Kreuznach – and decided to announce eternal Franco-German friendship. But help for Macmillan was at hand – from a surprising quarter. Another crisis had blown up. On 10 November, at one of the staged 'friendship meetings', to which thousands of Soviet workers were dragooned to welcome foreign dignitaries (in this case it was the Polish leader Wladyslaw Gomulka), Khrushchev announced that 'the time has obviously arrived ... to create a normal situation in the capital of the German Democratic Republic (GDR)'.[16] In other words, control of the Magdeburg corridor leading from West Germany, across East German territory and into Berlin, which the Soviets had exercised under the Potsdam Agreement at the end of the Second World War, was to be handed over to the East Germans. On 27 November, Khrushchev went even further. At a press conference in the Kremlin he announced that either the Western powers signed a German peace treaty, recognised East Germany and agreed to turn West Berlin into a demilitarised 'free city', all within six months, or the Soviets would meet their promise to hand over access control to the East Germans – and sign their own peace treaty.

Needless to say, there was consternation in Washington, London and, of course, Bonn. Adenauer quickly realised that it was no good relying on de Gaulle, however effusive the expressions of eternal friendship at Bad Kreuznach. France simply had not got the firepower – and was anyway too preoccupied with Algeria. Adenauer had no choice but to turn back to Britain. He therefore wrote to Macmillan asking him to intervene with Khrushchev – which Macmillan did, by letter, but to no effect. Adenauer then decided to invite himself to London, where he arrived on 7 December.

Adenauer was full of his own brand of righteous indignation, and made his point with some force. Macmillan had been enjoying a quiet weekend at Birch Grove ('a nice day, with about 220 pheasants – 5 guns') when, on his return to London, he was confronted by a very angry Adenauer. 'He, of course,' Macmillan wrote, 'wants to talk about Berlin. I want to talk to him about European Trade.'[17] The temperature of the conversation was high but by the end of it, whatever the language used – and the translation from German into English – Macmillan was left in no doubt that Adenauer regarded the whole Khrushchev initiative as a threat to the existence of West Germany itself.

Adenauer had made his point in Washington as well. But the question there was what, in practice, could be done. There were, officials pointed out, three difficulties. First, the Potsdam Agreement was not formally a treaty – and hence not binding on its signatories. Furthermore, it was an agreement between occupying powers, but, now that the United States, Britain and France, the former occupying powers, had recognised the sovereignty of West Germany they were no longer 'occupying powers'. The Potsdam Agreement had therefore become, as the Soviets pointed out, obsolete. The second difficulty was strictly practical, for instance whether it really mattered which – Soviet or East German – border guards would stamp the passports of travellers along the Magdeburg corridor. Finally, in a meeting in Washington on 11 December, Eisenhower was told, by an embarrassed Under-Secretary of State, that there were 'orders currently in effect directing personnel in the field to deal with GDR officials as agents of the Soviet Union ... the orders are the result of ambassadorial agreements ... [and] had been in effect since 1954'.[18] From beginning as a major Soviet threat, the whole thing, in the light of the facts, had become, to say the least, very muddy and uncertain.

Nevertheless, Eisenhower was insistent that 'we should make it clear to the Russians that we consider this no minor affair. In order to avoid beginning with the white chips and working up to the blue, we should place them on notice that our whole stack is in this play.'[19] Macmillan was very much more cautious. He was well aware, from the reports of the British Embassy in Moscow, that Khrushchev had no intention of starting another world war over access rights to Berlin. On the other hand, it was difficult to know what Khrushchev's real purpose was. The only thing to do, he concluded, was to seize the high ground – and go to Moscow to find out.

This was fraught with risk. He could not expect Dulles or Eisenhower to approve. Nor would de Gaulle be particularly supportive. As for Adenauer, the risk was that he might think Macmillan was simply doing what Neville Chamberlain had done in 1938 – selling out to force. The whole thing had to be carefully planned, and Macmillan spent the Christmas holiday of 1958 planning it. As it happened, the family Christmas at Birch Grove was a happy time – '4 children; 4 wives and husbands; 13 grandchildren; Daniel; and lots of nannies, active and retired ... It was a splendid party – the best I remember ... the home was wonderfully decorated ... dinner at 8.30 ... charades etc ... an exhausting day ...'[20] Macmillan's own mind, of course, was elsewhere.

The timing of his request to Moscow was very delicate. It was quite possible that the Soviets would turn him down. In fact, in early January 1959 they themselves made a new suggestion – sending a Note to the Western Allies proposing a peace conference at summit level. They even attached a draft of a German peace treaty. The suggestion obviously needed careful handling. At the time, Lloyd was recovering from a nasty operation to take out his tonsils, and Macmillan had to shuttle to and from the Middlesex Hospital to consult him – particularly important since Lloyd was due to join the Moscow party. It was better, Macmillan felt, to pause, to digest the Soviet proposal and to wait for a more favourable moment to suggest his own visit to Moscow.

There was therefore an interval – and time for a three-day visit with Dorothy to the north-east of England, starting at Darlington and ending at Newcastle. There were factory visits, lunches, dinners, speeches and so on. It was tiring for both of them – but exhilarating. Stockton was particularly welcoming, both to Macmillan and, even more so, to Dorothy. But the most striking impression was of the difficulties faced by manufacturing in the region. Order books were thin and managers nervous. It all served to reinforce Macmillan's view that the next Budget should be expansionist, a view reinforced, on his return to London, by the news that unemployment had risen.

By then Macmillan was losing his patience with Dulles and Eisenhower. If nobody else in the West was prepared to do anything, it was up to him to take the initiative. On 20 January, therefore, Caccia was told to write to Dulles about the proposed visit to Russia. This Caccia duly did. But Macmillan's instinct about the American reaction had been right. When Caccia's letter arrived on Dulles's desk, Dulles immediately called Eisenhower with the news. Dulles thought '[Macmillan] was campaigning'. Eisenhower said that he did 'not give much of a **** ... Let him go if he is that good ... they will come back with their tail between their legs ...'²¹ The message was then transmitted back to London – in rather more moderate language. Macmillan, when he received it, was almost fawning. He chose to interpret the American message in the most favourable possible way. 'The American reply', he wrote in his diary, 'has come and in the most friendly terms. They say, in effect, that they have complete confidence in me and I must do what I think best.'²²

Just in case there was any doubt, Dulles made the matter clear when he arrived in London on 5 February. 'I referred', the report of his talk with Macmillan runs, 'to stories indicating that the ... projected trip ... had been discussed in advance with me and approved by me. I said I thought it was undesirable that his statement to the House [of Commons] should contain such implications since, as he knew, I had considerable reservations about the wisdom of the trip at this time ...'²³ Having delivered this warning, Dulles went on to Paris before his return to America for a further operation and, as it happened, a final return to hospital.

With that not very friendly send-off, Macmillan, Lloyd and a party of officials set off for Moscow on Saturday 21 February 1959. Much to the delight of the British press, Macmillan wore Dorothy's father's fur coat and the white fur hat which he had acquired all those years before in Stockholm. At Moscow airport Khrushchev himself, flanked by Anastas Mikoyan, the Deputy Prime Minister, and Andrei Gromyko, the Foreign Minister, met the British party. The speeches were long but cordial. All in all, it was the best of starts. The Soviets were obviously trying to give the impression that an international thaw had set in.

Macmillan's Russian trip lasted in all ten days. The programme was crowded – almost absurdly so. There were two large dinners (poor food, Macmillan noted), two large receptions (bad wine but good vodka), three ballets (too long), visits to universities, collective farms, shipyards and factories as well as many hours of talks, both formal and informal. Not only Moscow but Kiev and Leningrad were on the programme. In discussions with the Soviets, Berlin and the Soviet proposals took up most of the time, but disarmament also figured, as did the nuclear test negotiations in Geneva and whether there should or should not be a summit meeting. All in all, it was exhausting, not least because there was almost no opportunity for the visitors to consult with one another

privately. Their residences, hotels and embassies were all heavily bugged –
except for a carefully constructed but uncomfortable room in the British
Embassy. At one delicate point, for instance, Macmillan and Lloyd had
to resort to standing in the snow in a wood, obviously keeping as far
away as possible from the nearby trees.

Macmillan, however, could not help respecting, and to some extent
liking, Khrushchev. He immediately understood that Khrushchev was
'the absolute ruler of Russia'. Even Mikoyan and Gromyko fell silent
when Khrushchev was on stage. 'Mr K', Macmillan wrote on his
return, 'is a curious study. Impulsive; sensitive of his own dignity and
insensitive of anyone else's feelings; quick in argument, never missing or
overlooking a point; with an extraordinary memory and encyclopaedic
information at his command; vulgar, and yet capable of a certain
dignity when he is simple and forgets to "show off"; ruthless, but
sentimental – K is a kind of mixture between Peter the Great and
Lord Beaverbrook.'[24]

The first two and a half days of the visit were all smiles. Admittedly,
there was no progress on the substantive matters, but Khrushchev went
out of his way, at a dinner at the British Embassy on the night of Monday
23 February, to praise Macmillan's 'frankness and understanding of the
interests not only of your country and of your side but also of our
country and our side ... such an approach makes it easier to find
reasonable solutions that could satisfy both countries, both sides'.[25] Of
course, Khrushchev had noted that Macmillan's views on the question
of access to Berlin were 'softer' (as Dulles also had spotted) than those
of his allies – particularly Adenauer – and he was going to exploit the
difference for all that it was worth. It was, after all, Soviet strategy to try
to drive wedges between the countries of the West. The tactics, of course,
could be adjusted as occasion required. His son Sergei wondered where
the Berlin crisis would lead, but '[there was] no clear answer. He intended
to act in accord with circumstances and depending on our partners'
reactions. He hoped to give them a good scare, and thereby extract their
agreement to negotiate ... What if negotiations didn't work? ... Then
we'll try something else ...'[26]

On the Tuesday 24 February, Khrushchev 'tried something else'.
While Macmillan and Lloyd were inspecting a nuclear power research
facility outside Moscow, and without warning them in advance, he
delivered a speech which, while underlining the welcome to the British
visitors and the wish for Russo-British friendship, was harshly critical
of Dulles and Eisenhower, brutally offensive about Adenauer and
contemptuous of the West's 'so-called people's capitalism'. Having
delivered this missile, Khrushchev and his colleagues turned up in

rollicking form on the same evening at a reception at the British Embassy, joking with Lloyd about the relative merits of Scotch whisky and Californian wine. Macmillan was 'overcome with faintness' and had to take a break of twenty minutes or so.[27] After recovering his composure, he quickly realised that he had to decide how to react to Khrushchev's speech, which, it was clear, would make all the headlines the following day and would be interpreted as a slap in the face for Macmillan personally (as indeed it was).

The Embassy reception finished, Macmillan and Lloyd retired to the dacha where they were, for the moment, housed. The next morning there was a clandestine consultation with Lloyd in the snow – away from equally clandestine ears. They decided that the most prudent course of action was to ignore the tone of Khrushchev's speech – and to carry on with their programme. Nevertheless Macmillan prepared, and learnt by heart, some firm sentences to deliver to Khrushchev when they next met.

On Thursday morning, 26 February, Macmillan duly delivered the prepared sentences. The Soviets, he said, would not succeed in dividing Britain from its allies. The allies were all quite firm and united about Berlin and the dangers of the Soviet ultimatum. Khrushchev, when he heard all this, was in return 'rude and provocative – talking about the Strang visit in 1939 and what Eden had said to him in 1956, and the result – our humiliation in Suez ... I replied that I did not accept such talk, and brought the meeting to an end. K then said that – owing to a toothache – he would not be able to go to Kiev with us – a special honour which he had [previously] announced ... Mr Mikoyan and Mr Gromyko would unfortunately not be able to come to Leningrad with us.'[28]

As soon as they heard this, all the Western Ambassadors, American, French and West German, immediately advised Macmillan to pack his bags and head for home. Macmillan ignored their advice – in spite of the Soviets leaking the absurd 'toothache' story to the press – and decided to carry on. His (correct) assumption was that this was no more than Khrushchev playing games. If he did cancel the rest of the visit, he realised (again correctly) that not only would the British press say that the whole thing had been a humiliating flop but the Soviets would say that, when faced with their powerful arguments, he refused to negotiate further.

So off they went to Kiev. Once there, they received a message from Khrushchev that his tooth had been successfully seen to – so he said, with help of a new British drill. When they arrived at Leningrad they found Mikoyan and Gromyko, after all, waiting for them full of smiles.

The trip then continued as though nothing had happened. Back in Moscow Khrushchev met them, and made a friendly enough speech. Macmillan was allowed to make a television broadcast 'without any censorship or interference'. There was 'no trouble about the communiqué; a ceremonial signature ... a drive to the airfield with Mr K in his car; a fine band and military parade'.[29] And that, in short, was that.

Back in London, Macmillan reported to the Cabinet. In Britain, his visit had been hailed as a great success. Nevertheless, it was in truth not at all clear what it had achieved. He could, and did, argue that the Soviets had offered a conference of Foreign Ministers if the West were not ready for a Summit, but they were probably prepared to do that anyway and, furthermore, Macmillan himself regarded that as a second best option. On the other hand, he had upset Adenauer by appearing lukewarm in defence of West German interests and, above all, he had reinforced American suspicions. From his bed in Walter Reed Hospital, where he had returned for what would prove to be the last stages of his cancer, Dulles immediately responded – telling Eisenhower that 'Macmillan is trying to get all the domestic political mileage he can get', that he 'didn't like the communiqué; that there were signs of weakness all through it' and, finally, that he was 'really worried that Macmillan is going to be prepared to compromise on recognition of the GDR etc'.[30] Christian Herter, Dulles's Deputy, who happened to be sitting beside him, nodded his agreement.

Macmillan's journeys to Paris and Bonn to explain himself to de Gaulle and Adenauer were not much more profitable. De Gaulle agreed with him that it was idiotic to start a nuclear war over the question of who stamped passports (which nobody had suggested) but did not think a summit meeting was yet the right answer to the German problem. Adenauer berated him for advocating what he called 'disengagement'. Macmillan tried to explain that all that he had suggested in Moscow was an agreed programme of 'thinning out' forces on either side of the border between West and East Germany, but Adenauer was not listening. In a private talk with Adenauer, Macmillan thought he had persuaded him to support the idea of a summit meeting – but he soon learnt that the French Government had finally turned the idea down. Adenauer, he assumed sadly but rightly, was certain to follow the French lead.

Seemingly undiscouraged, Macmillan persisted. The Soviets had sent a Note, which must be answered. There was, as yet, no answer agreed between the US, Britain, France and West Germany. For Britain, as he wrote himself, a summit meeting at the end of July or early August would (incidentally, of course) 'give me the maximum of manoeuvre regarding our own General Election'.[31] He therefore had to rely on convincing the United States. That, he knew well, could only be done face to face with Eisenhower in Washington.

'The Tories Must Wake Up!'

Nothing, in what proved to be a long run-up to the General Election, looked particularly easy. Even before he could leave for America to try to persuade Eisenhower of the dubious – but electorally advantageous – merits of a summit meeting with Khrushchev, Macmillan had three other problems to deal with. To be sure, the first, the Cyprus problem, was near resolution. In February 1959 the Greek and Turkish Foreign Ministers had agreed – much to the surprise of all involved – to the British plan for the allocation of ministerial responsibilities as a basis for independence. So far, so good; in fact, after all that time, so very good. Signature on an agreement was not far away. The other two problems, however, were much more troublesome. In Nyasaland, which had in 1953 been spatch-cocked into the Central African Federation with the two Rhodesias, the nationalist Nyasaland Congress Party had in the same February of 1959 started to riot against the federation in pursuit of full independence. The Nyasaland government declared a state of emergency, thus allowing the Federation authorities to aggravate matters by sending in Southern Rhodesian troops to put the insurgency down. On 3 March, they arrested Dr Hastings Banda, President of the Nyasaland Congress Party (known for his particularly distinctive fly-whisk), at his house, piled him – still in his pyjamas – into a lorry with seventy-two others and flew all of them off to prison in Salisbury. There was, of course, a fierce Parliamentary row. To the electorally sensitive Macmillan it was immediately clear the matter could not be hushed up. There had to be a suitably dignified investigation. While he was away in Moscow, therefore, the Lord Chancellor, Lord Kilmuir, dutifully appointed Sir Patrick Devlin, a senior judge, to lead it.

That put the Nyasaland problem at least into political suspense. But on the same day as Banda's arrest, there was another incident in Africa – this time in Kenya. Eleven Africans, detained in a 'rehabilitation' camp at Hola at the time of the Mau Mau emergency of a few years earlier (but never charged), had died as a result of savage beatings, apparently to force them to work on the local irrigation scheme. For the immediate moment, the matter was kept quiet. The Kenya government even issued a statement announcing that 'the deaths occurred after they had drunk water from a water cart ...'[1] The official line was all very well. But Macmillan – again electorally sensitive – knew that sooner or later the matter would burst into the political open.

It was against this background that Macmillan and Lloyd, on 17 March 1959, took off again from London airport for yet another transatlantic journey. They paid a quick visit to Ottawa, before arriving in Washington the following day. In fact, the prelude to their Washington visit, as they knew, had not been at all happy. There had even been some sharp exchanges about the programme. Macmillan, through Caccia, had suggested 'press conferences, appearance on the Hill ...' but Eisenhower 'was pretty hot about the Macmillan schedule. All the publicity he is seeking is outrageous ... told Herter to tell Caccia that if this is going to be a publicity operation [he] has no interest in it.'[2] Herter was equally vehement. 'It appears', he told Eisenhower, 'that they are trying to use this as a forum for their elections at home and to make Macmillan appear the leader in telling the American people where we are going.' In reply, Eisenhower said that 'if there is any reporting, [he] would do it and not Macmillan ... if Macmillan wants to make a report, let him do it in Britain'.[3]

In spite of all that, a programme was finally arranged. But the saddest part was a visit to Dulles in hospital. He was 'very thin and even emaciated' and quite clearly dying, so obviously so that Macmillan felt constrained not to argue with him. Dulles, in fact, was '*against* everything'. Sitting in a high-backed chair – with Eisenhower on a sofa and Macmillan and Lloyd on lower chairs – in the sitting room of his hospital suite ('furnished in a sort of Claridges style,' Macmillan noted), he pronounced himself against a summit meeting, against making any concessions to the Soviets and against any sort of arrangement with the GDR. Eisenhower, almost reverentially, remained silent throughout. At the end of an hour Dulles 'took my hand and clasped it in his two hands for quite a few moments when we said goodbye'.[4] Macmillan and Lloyd were so depressed by the meeting that they thought of going straight back to London.

Things went much better when the whole party transferred to Camp David, an elaborate – and self-consciously rural – Presidential retreat some thirty minutes by helicopter from the White House lawn. The discussion, which lasted for three hours or so during the afternoon (Eisenhower, rather to Macmillan's irritation, always had to rest before lunch) was wholly taken up with the question of a summit meeting and how to reply to the Soviets. But they could not agree, not least because Dulles kept calling from his hospital bed to find out what was going on.

Finally, tiring of the debate and of Dulles's calls, they all sat down to dinner and then watched a film – a western, which Macmillan, fastidious as he was, found, in his own words, 'inconceivably banal'.

The next day, they managed to arrive at a formula. On Eisenhower's suggestion, they decided that they would agree to a meeting of Foreign Ministers 'and that "as soon as developments in the Foreign Ministers' meeting warrant holding a Summit Conference" the Heads of Government would be glad to participate'.[5] The necessary telegrams to NATO allies were duly sent off. There was then some discussion of Macmillan's notion of 'thinning out' on the border between West and East Germany – the American Chiefs of Staff were having none of it – of nuclear tests and of the negotiations at Geneva, followed, the next day, by some desultory talks about the Middle East and British grievances over American protectionism.

Since it was a Sunday, church was marked in on the schedule. '[The] President and I left for church in a neighbouring village,' Macmillan recorded. 'It was called "Union of Evangelical and Reformed" – quite a nice service, with good singing and apparently much fervour.' Nothing could have been further from the Anglo-Catholicism of Oxford and Ronnie Knox. In fact, Macmillan at the time was equally sniffy about Eisenhower himself. 'With all his crudity, and lack of elegance of expression, he has some very reasonable ideas.'[6] By that time, Macmillan was tired and irritable. It was certainly time to go home. On the drive back to Washington, they called again on Dulles – it was the last time Macmillan saw him alive – and, on 24 March, the British party flew back to London. After he had reported to the Cabinet on his journey, Macmillan, by then thoroughly exhausted, was ordered by his doctor to take two days' absolute rest, with a heavy dose of Trollope. Macmillan dutifully obeyed – and in the two days and the Easter weekend which followed read six of Trollope's Barsetshire novels.

He thought that he had done well. But yet again his efforts had not made much impact, either diplomatically or electorally. Diplomatically, there had in fact been some serious fallout. He had upset Adenauer (Macmillan thought Adenauer was 'becoming an old and suspicious tyrant' and, when he made a speech highly critical of British foreign policy, thought he had 'gone a bit potty'[7]); he had failed to move de Gaulle; and Eisenhower was no more enthusiastic for a summit meeting than he had been before Macmillan's trip to Moscow. Electorally, there had been no impact at all. Gallup was still showing the two major parties level on voting intentions, and a detailed analysis by Conservative Central Office had concluded that, while the Government might just be returned to office in an early General Election, the risk of calling one was far too great. When a group of senior Ministers met over lunch in No. 10 on 3 April, they could only conclude that an early Election was out of the question and that, on present evidence, October would be the best option.

All of them, however, had much greater hopes for the Budget. They had reason. On 7 April Heathcoat Amory, almost fainting towards the end of his speech since he had had no lunch, announced generous cuts in income tax (from 8s. 6d in the pound to 7s. 9d in the pound at the top, with 6d off each of the lower rates), cuts in purchase tax, 2d off a pint of beer and incentives for businesses to invest. Not surprisingly, the Budget was very well received. In fact, the Gallup poll started immediately to move in the Conservatives' favour – a trend which was to continue throughout the summer. But it was still not enough. On 22 April, therefore, Macmillan told Conservative backbenchers that, whatever they might have thought, there would be no spring election. As he predicted, the news was satisfactorily leaked.

Nevertheless, the fever did not calm down. Gaitskell made an angry speech attacking Macmillan for trying to drag Eisenhower in to support the Conservatives at the next election. Macmillan took deep offence (not least because that was precisely what he was trying to do). 'He is a contemptible creature,' he wrote in his diary, 'a cold-blooded, Wykhamist intellectual and *embusqué* [the nearest equivalent in English is the American expression "draft dodger"].'[8] The comment was to set the tone for much of Macmillan's electioneering – proclaiming, with Etonian arrogance, that he was the right, indeed the only, person with the character to run the country, and accusing his opponent of little more than cowardice (Gaitskell had, in fact, tried to join the Army during the war but had been held back to work in a 'reserved occupation' as a Government economist). It was, to say the least, an unedifying start to what would be, in its later stages, an unedifying campaign.

On 11 May the Foreign Ministers Conference finally got under way in Geneva. Dulles had resigned on 15 April, his place taken by his Deputy, Christian Herter. Macmillan was not sure that the promotion had been wise. Certainly, Herter was a dedicated internationalist – he had, after all, been born and had spent the first nine years of his life in Paris. He had also, against all the odds, not only won the Massachusetts governorship for the Republicans but had been a successful, and much liked, Governor. On the other hand, he had not the force of personality of a Dulles and his relationship with Eisenhower was no more than distant. Since Eisenhower's touch in foreign policy was unsure – he had relied almost religiously on Dulles – and since he was in the last eighteen months of his Presidency (and forever worried about his health),

Macmillan suspected that the course of US policy, clear but sometimes obtuse under Dulles, would become foggy under Herter. Besides, Herter suffered from another disadvantage which Macmillan carefully noted – a curvature of the spine aggravated by arthritis – and could not walk without crutches (Macmillan, who had enough of his own, was always unsympathetic to, and sometimes even contemptuous of, physical disabilities in others). Nevertheless, as Eisenhower pointed out, there was little else he could do. It was true. In the last eighteen months of his Presidency he really had no other choice.

With Parliament in the mid-May Recess Macmillan took the opportunity for a week's holiday. Fortunately, there were to be few interruptions. Lloyd was still struggling with the seating plan for Foreign Ministers at the negotiating table, Devlin had not yet reported from Nyasaland and the Hola affair had not yet broken out into an open row. On 14 May, therefore, Macmillan and Dorothy left on the night train to Scotland. By a quarter past eleven on the following morning they were on the golf course at Gleneagles. Golf, indeed, set the tone for the whole of the next ten days: playing golf at Gleneagles, then driving north to Nairn on the Moray Firth for more golf. The weather was startlingly good, Dorothy's golf was on top form, and the two enjoyed themselves. All in all, it was at the end of a happy week that Macmillan took the night train back from Inverness to London. Dorothy – yet again – stayed in Scotland.

On 24 May 1959 Dulles died. But already, in Geneva, his absence had made itself felt. The conference was making no progress. Noting this, *The Times* of 1 June published a long article explaining all the problems and claiming that Macmillan would be replacing 'Selwyn Lloyd as Foreign Secretary "shortly"'.[9] It was, of course, quite untrue. But it was embarrassing, and Macmillan had to go out of his way to correct the impression in answer to a question in the House of Commons. That dealt with, early June brought the blow he had been expecting. The Hola 'massacre' had come out into the open and had been taken up by a vociferous Opposition. Not only that, but Macmillan himself, and at least some of his colleagues, knew that there really was no defence. 'Macleod later recalled his sense of outrage: "this was the decisive moment when it became clear to me that we could no longer continue with the old methods of government in Africa, and that meant inexorably a move towards African independence." Macleod believed that the same was true for Macmillan.'[10]

It was a difficult moment. Just as the arrangements for a successful signature to an agreement over Cyprus independence were being put in place, Macmillan was writing that 'we are in a real jam about the incident at Hola camp in Kenya'.[11] Lennox-Boyd seemed determined to resign, and Hailsham was excitedly recommending a public inquiry. On 4 June the Cabinet met to try to find a way out of the jam. After much agonising, they decided that the only solution was to present the whole incident as a certainly disgraceful event – but one for which Government policy could not be held responsible. On 10 June a White Paper was duly issued to that effect and put down for debate in the House of Commons on 15 June. The political temperature then rose a notch when it was announced by the Colonial Office, on 13 June, that an honour (by a stroke of supreme irony it was Membership of the Order of the British Empire) was to be awarded to one of those responsible for the camp. The debate, when it came, was noisy, hot – and personal, with Lennox-Boyd the Opposition's prime target. But like all such storms, it seemed gradually to pass. The House in the end accepted the Government view that the whole thing had, of course, been lamentable and a disgrace but that the fault lay in Kenya. In fact, it turned out that Lennox-Boyd's most effective critic was from the Conservative back bench, none other than Enoch Powell. The row rumbled on – but there was no longer much in it to threaten Macmillan or Lennox-Boyd. The press, Macmillan decided, was 'not too good about Hola, but not too bad'.[12]

Much more serious was the report of the Devlin Commission on Nyasaland. By an error in the Stationery Office the Colonial Office received an early proof on 12 July. It was fiercely critical of Government policy at all levels. 'Nyasaland has become,' it stated roundly on its first page, 'doubtless only temporarily, a police state where it is not safe for anyone to express approval of the policies of the Congress Party.'[13] Of course, the expression 'police state' was highly inflammatory – and Devlin knew it. Macmillan was furious. He knew that Devlin had been appointed by Kilmuir while he himself had been in Russia but did not know much about him. He soon made it his business to find out. 'He is a) Irish,' he wrote angrily in his diary, 'no doubt with that Fenian blood that makes Irishman anti-govt on principle. b) A *lapsed* R[oman] C[atholic]; his brother is a Jesuit priest; his sister a nun. He married a Jewess, who was converted, and was *received* a catholic. c) a hunchback. d) likely disappointed at not being made Lord Chief Justice. I am not at all surprised that this report is dynamite. It may well blow this govt out of office.'[14]

The final version of the Devlin Report was not in the hands of Cabinet Ministers until just before their meeting on Monday 20 July. They were also presented, when they arrived for the meeting, with a draft of the Government reply. This had been written over the weekend at Chequers by Kilmuir, Reginald Manningham-Buller, the Attorney-General, and

Julian Amery, but it was added to the report of the Governor of Nyasaland, Sir Robert Armitage. Cabinet ministers then read both documents
in the Cabinet Room before the formal meeting. The proposal before
them was that the Devlin Report and the Governor's reply, to be known
as 'Armitage's Despatch', should be published at the same time, on 23
July. Having quickly read (they were not left much time) the two documents, they were faced in the formal meeting with Lennox-Boyd's offer
of resignation.

Macmillan knew that he could not afford to lose Lennox-Boyd. The
General Election was not far off. Lennox-Boyd's resignation would take
with it his two junior Ministers, Lord Perth and Julian Amery, as well as
Armitage. The Government might be damaged beyond electoral repair.
When the matter came before the full Cabinet, Macmillan did not say
as much openly. But he put on his most solemn face in his presentation.
In fact, Macmillan played a very clever game. Without saying anything
specific, he had indicated his own view. Butler, in his Delphic manner,
did the same. Both knew that there are few instincts in a politician as
strong as self-preservation. The upshot was that each Minister in turn
said nobly that they all should stand by Lennox-Boyd and the Nyasaland
Governor. Macmillan then thanked them and said solemnly that if the
view had gone the other way he could not possibly have continued as
Prime Minister.

The two crucial debates, one on Hola and the other on Nyasaland,
took place in the House of Commons on 27 and 28 July. The first was
suitably hectic – attacks from the Labour MP Barbara Castle and from
Enoch Powell were particularly effective – but in the end fizzled out,
since the only time the Opposition could find for the debate was time
reserved for the Appropriation Bill, on which it was impossible to force
a vote. The debate on the Devlin Report – the Government Motion was
that only part of Devlin's report should be accepted – was even angrier,
many Labour members pointing out, quite correctly, that the Cabinet
had only refused to accept Lennox-Boyd's resignation to avoid electoral
embarrassment. But, greatly to Macmillan's relief, at the end of the debate
there was no Conservative rebellion and the Government's majority was
intact.

Parliament then adjourned for the summer Recess. Everybody
assumed that the General Election would be held in October, and the
political pace quickened. The Steering Committee was already busy
drafting the Conservative Manifesto – and incidentally bringing out the
underlying tension between Butler and Macmillan. 'We had reached
the passage', Butler wrote later, 'which stated ... my legislative aims for
the next Parliament. "We shall revise some of our social laws, for example

those relating to betting and gambling and to clubs and licensing, which are at present full of anomalies and lead to abuse and even corruption." The Prime Minister picked up the document, held it out two feet from his face, hooded his eyes and said very slowly, "I don't know about that. We already have the Toby Belch vote. We must not antagonise the Malvolio vote." Dutiful chuckles ... Ted Heath ... intervened by pointing out that we had already committed ourselves to such reforms. "Well," said Macmillan resignedly, "this is your province, Rab. I suppose you think it's all right."[15] Macmillan knew when he had to concede.

But he was by then working on another trick – how to get Eisenhower's support in the Election as far as possible out into the open. At first, things seemed to be going against him. The Geneva conference of Foreign Ministers was no more than sputtering on. Until that finished, there seemed to be no prospect of an electorally profitable summit meeting. Eisenhower, indeed, was fixed on the idea that 'the summit is a sort of post-graduate course, which the boys can only take if they first graduate with honours (at Geneva) ... So it is to drift along with the tide – with a half-crazed Adenauer, a cynical and remote de Gaulle, and an amiable but weak President.'[16] Then, much to Macmillan's dismay and almost without warning, Eisenhower invited Khrushchev to visit the United States in September. This, Macmillan immediately recognised, 'rules out any summit except the end of Sep[tember]. This, in turn, sabotages our General Election ... My own position will be greatly weakened. Everyone will assume that the 2 great powers – Russia and USA – are going to fix up a deal over our heads and behind our backs. My whole policy – planned for many years and esp during my premiership – of alliance and cooperation with America will be undermined.'[17] To make matters worse, Eisenhower then announced that in addition to a return visit to the Soviet Union he would be visiting Japan, India and Pakistan in October.

Macmillan saw his chance. He told Lloyd to tell Herter that 'if he does not come to the UK, this will be an insult to the Queen and to our whole nation which will never be forgiven ... I feel that, on reflection, he will see the necessity for treating us properly.'[18] The aim was simple: to get Eisenhower, one way or another, to visit Britain in the run-up to the General Election. He therefore wrote to Eisenhower proposing that the President call a summit meeting for the end of August or the first week of September. His letter, of course, fell on very stony ground. 'The President said he saw no reason why he should propose a summit meeting ... He said he has the feeling the British are trying to manipulate his activities with respect to an exchange of visits with Khrushchev, and a summit meeting ... He thought perhaps we should be more reserved in our discussions with the British ... He said it came with a very ill grace from Macmillan to express reservations about his seeing Khrushchev before a summit meeting when we recall the circumstances of Macmillan's trip to Moscow.'[19]

Macmillan had played his first card – and had lost. But he then played a second. On receiving a muted reply from Eisenhower, which did no more than say that the Geneva conference could not go on for ever, and perhaps there might be a summit meeting only of Western leaders, he wrote to Eisenhower that 'I am in broad agreement with the timetable which you now have in mind: ... A Western Summit before the end of August ... I hope that you will be able to press de Gaulle very strongly to fall in with your plan ...'[20]

This time Macmillan had boxed Eisenhower in. In fact, his mention of the Queen had been decisive. Eisenhower, ever courteous and respectful, could not ignore it. He would therefore have to call in to see the Queen on his way to Paris – if the 'Western Summit' was indeed to be held there. But de Gaulle had still not been convinced of the merit of a 'Western Summit'. The result was that on 3 August it was announced formally that Eisenhower had invited Khrushchev to visit the United States, that he would be making a return visit to the Soviet Union and that – Macmillan's prize – he would be making a visit to the United Kingdom at the end of the month of August. But there was more good news to come. It soon became known that the Queen might not be able to be in London to greet the President – as protocol demanded. On 4 August Herter sent a message to Eisenhower: 'Selwyn Lloyd told me this evening in the utmost confidence that Queen's difficulty in coming to London rpt London in connection with your visit is due to an indisposition which it is expected will prove to be due to a new pregnancy.'[21] Under those circumstances, Eisenhower simply could not refuse an invitation to Balmoral.

The Queen had been Macmillan's trump card – and her pregnancy had been the ace of trumps. Eisenhower's visit was thus becoming, as Macmillan wanted, a congratulatory (and self-congratulatory) cavalcade. The programme settled, Macmillan and Dorothy left for a ten-day holiday at Bolton Abbey. The weather was glorious, 'hot, sunny, and with little wind ... There were not a lot of grouse – tho' we got over 500 brace in the 5 days shooting'.[22] It was a welcome break and cheered Macmillan up enormously. He was even more cheered by a Gallup poll showing a Conservative lead on voting intentions of 6.5 per cent. He therefore wrote to the Queen warning her that he might soon be asking for a dissolution of Parliament.

At 5.30 p.m. on Thursday 27 August, Eisenhower and his party arrived at London airport. They were met by Macmillan and a suitable clutch of ministers and officials. After the customary speeches of welcome and an inspection of a guard of honour, Macmillan and Eisenhower then drove, in beautiful late evening sunshine and through lines of cheering crowds, to Winfield House, the American Ambassador's residence. In fact, the crowds were unexpectedly large (not that Macmillan minded) and much friendlier than some of the worried Americans had feared. 'There was the darnedest crowd you ever saw,' according to one of Eisenhower's staff.[23] The journey from the airport took two hours.

The next day Eisenhower flew to Balmoral to spend what turned out to be an agreeable, if slightly uncomfortable, two days with the Royal Family. On 29 August he flew south, accompanied by Prince Philip, landed at RAF Benson and drove with Macmillan, this time along minor roads where there were only 'occasional groups of people', to Chequers. Eisenhower went immediately for his pre-prandial rest. After lunch there was a short conference, after which Eisenhower, before going out to practise his golf shots, summoned his doctor, General Howard Snyder, complaining of slight dizziness and asking for his blood pressure to be checked ('BP: 132/84 HR: 72 with an occasional skip – I did not tell him about the occasional skip because he seemed to be a bit alarmed'). Seemingly none the worse, Eisenhower, along with Macmillan, Ambassador Whitney and Lloyd, went out to practise his golf. 'They used me as a target,' Snyder recorded ruefully. 'The President told me to get out there about 100 or 150 yards so they could use me for a target ... They came in in a very jovial mood ...'[24]

There was not a great deal of work done at Chequers. On Sunday the whole party went to church at Ellesborough (Macmillan read both lessons in his most elegant and aristocratic voice). After lunch, seeing that Eisenhower was getting a bit restless, Macmillan suggested a drive to Oxford for the afternoon. They visited Magdalen College, admired the hall and the chapel (including 'the cask of an old Norman, a man in Norman armor ...'[25]), went on to Christ Church and then New College. By the time they got back to Chequers Eisenhower was in obvious need of refreshment. Before dinner, his doctor related, 'he drank several gin and tonics, and one or two gins on the rocks ... They had three or four wines with the dinner ...' There was then a film 'to which the President did not stay'.[26] Given the President's consumption of alcohol, it was hardly surprising.

Seemingly unaffected by the previous evening, Eisenhower left Chequers in the morning. Macmillan had borrowed a white open Rolls-Royce from Douglas Fairbanks Jr, and the two rode in some style into London, through the City and up to the steps of St Paul's Cathedral. There they were met by the Bishop of London and shown the American

Chapel at the East End of the Cathedral. It had been reconstructed to include an area dedicated to American soldiers, sailors and airmen who had died on British soil during the Second World War. Both Eisenhower and Macmillan were mightily impressed – but less so by Canon Collins, 'fellow-traveller etc' who 'gave a ridiculous and offensive interview to the Press' and almost spoilt the party.[27]

In the evening there was the television broadcast, both President and Prime Minister having an apparently friendly chat in No. 10 Downing Street. It was blatant electioneering – but without an election. Such was the mood at the time that it was dubbed by its critics as 'the first of the election broadcasts'.[28] It was, of course, derided by Labour leaders as an electoral gimmick but, on the other hand, it was thought by the press to have been successful – and not too obviously partisan. Certainly, its audience ratings were high. In fact, both men were very nervous, and their performance was rather stilted – Macmillan's voice seemed to rise a tone or two and Eisenhower's eyes wandered about towards the camera – but the thing was done with reasonable dignity. The only complaint was from a radio commentator who thought that they should have held a press conference to answer specific questions rather than a general and woolly discussion. That, of course, was something Macmillan was anxious to avoid.

There were dinners on the evenings of 31 August and 1 September – the first at No. 10 Downing Street and the second, for Eisenhower's old wartime cronies, at Winfield House. Eisenhower in his speech reminded them that it was the twentieth anniversary of the German invasion of Poland. He concluded by inviting them to swap wartime stories with one of his favourite jokes: 'Now we will go to the room at the left and sit about with smokes and drinks, and I'll see whether any of you can be as big a liar as I may prove to be.'[29]

It was all very jolly. But when Eisenhower left on the morning of 2 September, Macmillan could reasonably reflect on a serious job well done. Moreover, Gallup was showing a Conservative lead of nearly 7 per cent. It was time to call a General Election, and on 7 September Macmillan left RAF Benson in a Heron aircraft of the Queen's flight to fly to Dyce airport – and from there to Balmoral. After a pause to discuss their electoral prospects in Scotland with his brother-in-law by marriage and Secretary of State for Scotland, James Stuart, Macmillan was driven to Balmoral for his audience with the Queen. Once there, he gave her a pedantic lecture on her right to refuse a request for a dissolution of Parliament (which she knew perfectly well already without the lecture – as, indeed, she knew perfectly well that it would be quite wrong, even ridiculous, for her to refuse the Prime Minister's request). The following morning he left again for London and a final Cabinet meeting before the announcement of dissolution at 4 p.m.

Macmillan spent the next two days working on speeches for the campaign with his speech writer from Central Office, George Christ, a genial and friendly man who had been Churchill's speech writer. (His name was pronounced with a short 'i', but Churchill was still fond of saying to his secretaries, 'Tell Christ to come down.'[30]) The omens were all favourable. The weather was set fair – it was due to be a particularly fine September – the poster campaign devised by the firm of Colman, Prentis and Varley featuring the slogan 'Life's Better under the Conservatives. Don't let Labour ruin it' had been much admired by professionals, and the Conservatives had adopted a cartoon by the *Evening Standard's* Vicky portraying Macmillan, in what was intended to be a derisory sketch, flying through the air like Batman – to the caption of 'Supermac'.

The early part of the campaign, however, did not go at all according to plan. For a start, Labour was helped by the timing. The Trade Union Congress was in session at Blackpool at the time, and the announcement of a General Election allowed trade union leaders to ensure defeat of a potentially damaging motion to cancel British plans for a hydrogen bomb. Then Gaitskell and Bevan, who had been on a visit to Moscow, were able to address the trade unionists as a united team, Gaitskell in particular adopting a new role as an international statesman, telling the delegates of his hard-nosed debates with Khrushchev. (The *Daily Express* managed to produce the headline 'Hugh and Nye defend the Empire'.[31]) Furthermore, the Conservative Manifesto, published on 11 September under the banal title *The Next Five Years*, was compared unfavourably with a slick Labour pamphlet, released at the same time, entitled *The Tory Swindle*. The launch of the Labour pamphlet, as it happened, went down well, not least because it was much helped by Randolph Churchill, who ensured maximum publicity by seeking an injunction to ban it.

Nor was the Conservative publicity any more impressive. The poster campaign was wound down when the Election was announced, its place to be taken by television broadcasts. These started off very badly. Heath later recalled his impressions when he eagerly watched the first one with other Ministers. 'It was meant to be a report on our term of office and there was Mr Macmillan sitting very comfortably in an armchair with his senior Cabinet colleagues around him. And Harold said "Well now, Rab, I think we've done very well, don't you?" And Rab said, "Oh yes, we've done awfully well, particularly the things I've been doing." And Iain Macleod then said, "Yes, well, I've done awfully well and we've all done very well indeed." After we'd had a quarter of an hour of this we were driven absolutely up the wall. And the next programme was just as bad.'[32] Nor was it just a question of television performance. The Labour Party, too, had taken the initiative in introducing daily press conferences, and the Conservatives were far too slow to follow suit.

Parliament was dissolved on Friday 18 September. The Labour Manifesto was published on the same day with the title *Britain Belongs to You.* Its most striking feature was a commitment to increase the old-age pension by 10s. a week. Both parties recognised that this was a telling move. Even Macmillan was starting to feel uncomfortable. When Heathcoat Amory came to see him to say that he would prefer not to remain in office after the Election, Macmillan was sharp: 'We cannot jug the hare until we have caught it ... All this talk seems to me to be taking victory for granted and I don't like it ...'[33] The weekend polls started to reflect the success of the Labour attack. The Conservative lead was dropping. By Friday 25 September things had got to such a point that the Conservative press was screaming. 'The Tories must wake up,' shouted the *Daily Sketch*, 'get off their dignified perches and make their voices heard.'[34]

It was on Monday 28 September that Gaitskell made his strategic mistake. In a speech in Newcastle he announced that under a Labour Government there would be no increase in the standard or other rates of income tax so long as normal peacetime conditions continue. This was followed by a press handout three days later which said that a Labour Government would remove purchase tax on essential goods. The two undertakings, taken together, played into Conservative hands. It had been one of their consistent themes that Labour could not be trusted with the economy, that they were a bunch of reckless spenders of taxpayers' money. It was, in fact, the Conservative strong point. Nearly a third of the electorate put economic management as the issue of most concern. On this issue, the Conservatives were easily in the lead. Instead of concentrating on the issues where Labour was strongest, such as pensions, Gaitskell had moved to the issue where Labour was weakest.

The Conservative counter-attack was led by the rumbustious explosions of Hailsham at press conferences in Central Office and by the clinically direct personal attacks on Gaitskell by Macmillan in the field. Apart from the constant insinuation, dropped to accompanying journalists, that Gaitskell was not fit to run the country because he had shirked fighting in the war, Macmillan, in a speech at Nottingham on 1 October, was open and direct. 'It was this addiction to figures,' he proclaimed, 'on which he built what seems now a false reputation, that led Mr Bevan to describe him as a desiccated calculating machine. That is now only a half-truth. I think he is still rather desiccated but his reputation as a calculator has gone with the wind.'[35]

The polls had already started to show a shift back to the Conservatives, and by then Macmillan was confident enough to change tack once more, to bring the prospect of a summit meeting back on the agenda – on the premise, of course, that it was he, rather than Gaitskell, who would be best fitted to stand for Britain. On 28 September, it had been announced from the White House – with the most convenient timing – that Khrushchev's visit to the United States had been such a success that the way was open for a full summit meeting. On 30 September Macmillan announced the event as yet another success for his Government. He only made one slip. He declared that the date for the summit would be announced within the next few days. There was hurried denial from the White House.

By the first weekend of October, the polls were showing that the Conservatives were widening their lead over Labour. There continued, of course, to be shows of optimism on both sides and to fierce campaigning in the marginal constituencies. Others, who should have known better, entered the fray. One such intervention, for instance, came from Field Marshal Montgomery, who declared roundly on 5 October that anyone who voted Labour 'must be completely barmy, absolutely off his rocker ... should be locked up in a lunatic asylum as a danger to the country'.[36] Labour's General Secretary, Morgan Philips, pointed out that if Labour voters had been locked up during the war Montgomery would have had to make do with half an army and that there was no limit to the idiocy of generals.

The last Conservative television broadcast was a strange affair. As a consequence of the previous poor showing, Wyndham had been asked to recruit a friend of his who apparently knew about these things, Norman Collins, a former BBC executive turned novelist. Collins, after hearing Macmillan speak once and noting his upright stance, advised that the final broadcast, on 6 October, should be by Macmillan standing alone, equipped with a globe of the world by his side, which he could twirl as occasion required. In their studio rehearsal Collins noticed that Macmillan was rather hoarse. A glass or two of port was called for. The final dress rehearsal was suitably done – and exactly within the time allotted. When Macmillan told Collins that he hoped he would do better on the night, Collins replied that it had already been recorded and was in the can. 'You are a remarkable fellow,' Macmillan replied. 'This is like going to the dentist to have a tooth out and to be told that it has already been drawn.'[37]

On 8 October, a dry autumn day, there was nothing more to do other than to calm the nerves. After the polling stations had closed at 9 p.m., Macmillan sat down with Dorothy in No. 10 Downing Street, watching the results on television as they came in. Exactly at ten o'clock the first result was announced – Billericay in Essex held by the Conservatives in spite of an influx of supposedly Labour voters from London spilling into the New Town. Two seats at Salford then showed a substantial swing to Labour, but at half past ten the inner London constituency of Holborn and St Pancras fell to the Conservatives. As the results came flooding in it became clear that the Conservatives would be returned with an increased majority on a poll of nearly 80 per cent. At 1 a.m. Gaitskell conceded the Election ('a curious modern Americanism,' Macmillan noted). At 2 a.m. Macmillan went to Central Office for a celebration where he 'had a fine welcome'. At 4 a.m. he went to bed 'happy but exhausted'. The following day, Macmillan and Dorothy went to the count at Bromley. His own majority was up by two thousand. All in all, it had been a wonderful electoral triumph. At his press conference in the evening and on television later, 'I tried to keep a humble note, stressing the need for national unity'.[38] If he failed to keep an entirely 'humble note', however, there was nobody who was going to blame him. Indeed, as he might have said himself, his mother would have been proud of him.

22

Le Double Jeu

In October 1959 the Conservatives were returned to power with a House of Commons majority over all other parties of one hundred seats. To the general astonishment, they had not just come back from the electoral dead after the Suez fiasco and the misery of Eden's resignation but, unlike even the biblical Lazarus, had come back clothed not in a shroud but in glory. Nor was there anybody who was in any doubt about who had been responsible. It was, as all agreed, the Leader of the Party himself, the Prime Minister and Member for Bromley, Mr Harold Macmillan. The gods, it seemed, had indeed smiled on him with their broadest smile.

Such was Macmillan's supremacy in his Party that he was able, in forming his new administration, easily to resume effective charge of the major departments of state (apart, that is, from Butler's preserve, the Home Office). Nobody complained. It was acknowledged that he had every right to do so, not just by virtue of his office or his Party's electoral success but – much more politically important – by virtue of his personal performance during the Election campaign. Nobody, for instance, who had watched the television programme with Eisenhower was left in any doubt that, in spite of his old-world appearance and language, Macmillan had exuded the sense of authority and aristocratic *bonheur* which his Party – and the electorate – had wished for. The touch of arrogance passed almost unnoticed. (After the event, as a matter of fact, in the privacy of his diary he noted that 'telegrams are pouring in, from Eisenhower, Debré, Adenauer etc down to the humblest folk'.[1] The 'humblest folk' were no doubt meant to know their station.) Equally, the murkier side of his campaigning was soon forgotten.

Under those circumstances, forming a Government was not too difficult, although Macmillan, of course, later claimed that it had been. Lennox-Boyd had decided to give up the political race. That meant that Macleod could go to the Colonial Office – an appointment much to Macmillan's satisfaction, since he was anxious to have an ally on Africa. The main problem was the chairmanship of the Party. Hailsham was apparently 'not safe . . . in a very over-excited condition and keeps giving ridiculous "press conferences" . . .'.[2] It needed some deft manoeuvring to persuade Hailsham to relinquish the job and to make way for Butler. Heath was rewarded by a ministerial job at Labour – replaced by (the much less effective) Martin Redmayne as Chief Whip. The question of who was to be Speaker of the House of Commons caused a minor difficulty, since Gaitskell claimed that the Labour Party was entitled to nominate whomsoever they wished. The suggestion was brushed aside and a Conservative duly elected. All in all, the few obstacles there were quickly disappeared and the new administration was constructed with reasonable despatch. Nevertheless, at the end of the process it was perfectly clear who was in charge.

On the other hand, in asserting his supremacy, Macmillan ran the risk that any future governmental failures could not easily be redressed by junior ministerial resignations. The finger of blame would point straight at the top. But it was a risk which Macmillan was perfectly ready to run. In fact, there is no doubt that the result of the General Election had raised his ambition, already high, up another step. He would now not just run things but, with his experience and what he considered to be his proven ability to persuade others to follow him, he would take initiatives to enhance Britain's prestige at home and in the world. Even more loftily, he would recapture the conceit of Algiers: the British Athens would again light the way forward for the American Rome. Last but far from least, when all that had been done, his legacy to history would rival that of Churchill.

Nevertheless, in spite of the dreams, Macmillan was, as always, prepared for political turbulence. In fact, even before the General Election, fought on a platform of 'Peace and Prosperity' when everything looked good, he had moments of doubt about the future. Seemingly unsure of where to go next, he had set up in secret a working party, under Sir Norman Brook and chaired by Sir Patrick Dean, to study Britain's place in Europe and the world. Moreover, on return to office, he quickly decided to set up, and himself chair, a Cabinet Committee to study in depth the future of British Africa, since, as he told Brook, Africa seemed to be the biggest problem 'looming up for us here at home'.[3]

At the time, this was probably the case. True, Archbishop Makarios was still raising last-minute obstacles to a Cyprus settlement, the Geneva negotiations on a nuclear test ban were moving, if at all, at snail's pace and the Soviets were not slackening the pressure over Berlin. But the Archbishop's bluff could, and would, be called, a further moratorium on nuclear testing had been agreed while talks continued and the Soviet problem could wait until the summit meeting of 1960. Indeed, as a bonus, Maudling's negotiations with the seven countries to form an industrial free trade area were coming to a successful conclusion, and a

Convention for a European Free Trade Area (EFTA) was ready for signature in late November.

It was therefore time to get down to the most difficult business – time, in short, to address the matter of Africa. Macmillan soon decided that the right course was a personal visit. The problems he had identified were, of course, interlinked: how to ensure a steady march towards black African majority rule in the remaining British African colonies, how to resolve the difficulties of the Central African Federation and how to edge the South Africans, with their Calvinist regime of apartheid, of fierce racial segregation, back to what the rest of the world considered morally acceptable.

As for the Central African Federation, a Royal Commission was in the process of formation, under the chairmanship of Sir Walter Monckton, to recommend a constitutional future for the Federation and its three elements. Nobody disputed the idea, but there were two difficulties: persuading the Labour Party to support it and, in parallel, securing acceptance for its remit from the bull-like Prime Minister of the Federation, Sir Roy Welensky, and the only slightly less aggressive Prime Minister of the white-dominated Southern Rhodesia, Sir Edgar White-head. As for South Africa and apartheid, there were no difficulties (other than holding his nerve), and Macmillan decided to take the thing head-on. He would say what he wanted to say in a speech with the highest profile; and the highest profile for the speech, and where it would be most telling, was the South African Parliament.

The three departments involved in Africa, the Foreign Office, the Commonwealth Relations Office and the Colonial Office, were mobil-ised in preparation for the Prime Minister's African visit. In practice, since Lloyd had little knowledge of, and even less interest in, Africa, in ministerial terms this meant Macleod and Home – who had sharply differing views on the right pace for black African advancement. It was obviously going to take time to marry them. Macmillan himself, however, was diverted from the task by yet another visit from Adenauer in mid-November. Adenauer wanted to complain again about British softness towards the Soviets. Macmillan became impatient. 'There was', as Lloyd reported to Herter, 'some plain speaking about this constant distrust, suspicion and unpleasant remarks and innuendos about the Prime Min-ister. Harold was pretty tough with him . . .'[4] In fact, Macmillan at one point was so rude to Adenauer that he thought Adenauer might walk out.

As it happened, Adenauer's visit was only one of a long string of diplomatic manoeuvres which Macmillan hoped would lead to a summit meeting with Khrushchev in the spring of 1960. De Gaulle had finally agreed to a 'Western Summit' in Paris in December. As though by way of preparation, Macmillan had started to read Proust (for the first time, at the age of sixty-four), not because he wanted to but 'I felt I *ought* to do this, because of the great influence which Proust has had on modern English literature'. He found the duty tiresome. 'I work away at Proust – partly in French, partly in English. But I can't make up my mind as to the real value of it all. I will finish the 12 volumes and then try to think about it.' A few days later he gave up: 'read Proust; I got tired of this.'[5]

Proust or not, the 'Western Summit' was due to start on 19 December. But Africa still intruded. On 3 December Gaitskell told Macmillan that the Labour Party would not after all nominate members of the Monckton Commission. Gaitskell, much to Macmillan's irritation, had tried to negotiate the Commission's terms of reference to include the possibility of dissolution of the Federation. When Macmillan refused, Gaitskell, after consulting his colleagues, simply declined to discuss things further.

More worrying, however, was the economic news. The Budget of April 1959 had stoked up the economy – as was intended. Then the Conservative Election victory had led to an upsurge – this time unintended – in both investment and consumption. There was a consequent increase in the trade deficit, up from £40 million to £50 million in November. By early December Sir Robert Hall, the Government's Chief Economic Adviser, was arguing for an immediate rise in Bank Rate. On 8 December, Heathcoat Amory made a widely publicised – but in truth rather lame – speech pleading for price restraint from manufacturers. Treasury officials, too, were put to work on a project for a deflationary 1960 Budget. But when he heard all this Macmillan would have none of it. There was to be no deflation. Even when Amory and Makins went on a formal visit to Macmillan they were told crisply that there was nothing to worry about. Nevertheless, when Makins left the Treasury on 1 January 1960 his successor, Sir Frank Lee, had become well aware that the economic weather forecast for the year was pointing firmly to dangerous storms ahead.

The economy might be what it might be, but Macmillan's mind was firmly focused on the 'Western Summit'. The time had now arrived. On the afternoon of Friday 18 December, therefore, Macmillan and Lloyd, together with officials, left for Paris, arriving at the grand and opulent British Embassy in time for dinner. The following day the four heads of government, Eisenhower, Macmillan, Adenauer and de Gaulle, met in a small room in the Élysée Palace with interpreters only. Everybody else was excluded. But the meeting was something of a revelation. For the first time since their wartime sessions in Algiers, Macmillan was open in his admiration of de Gaulle and the way he handled the thing. 'It was an extraordinary performance,' he noted in his diary, 'conducted by de Gaulle with great skill and grace . . .'[6] Business was concluded at admirable pace; and the upshot was that a summit meeting with Khrushchev would take place, and, given that, the best date was some time towards the end of April 1960. As to the place, Geneva was the obvious candidate – but de Gaulle was doubtful. '*Ce n'est pas très gai*,' he said. '*Le lac. L'esprit de M. Calvin. Non. Ce n'est pas très gai.*' ('It is not very cheerful,' he said. 'The lake. The spirit of Mr Calvin. No. It is not very cheerful.')[7]

Macmillan saw his chance – and took it. He suggested Paris, but qualified his suggestion with the condition that it would only be the first of a series of summit meetings, to be followed in due course by London, Washington and Moscow. Much to Macmillan's surprise – and pleasure – de Gaulle and Eisenhower agreed readily. There was to be a series of summits, one after the other. Finally, there was discussion of the agenda. It was, they agreed, to be left fairly general. Ambassadors should meet to fill out the key points. As for Berlin, Eisenhower thought that there might be some solution which Congress might accept. Adenauer, on the other hand, was grumpily intransigent – to the point where Eisenhower was very short with him. All that done, lunch – or 'luncheon' as Macmillan persisted in calling it – was served to, among others, a very contented British Prime Minister.

But if the first day had gone well for Macmillan, the second day went even better. After breakfast with Eisenhower ('I have never felt quite up to grilled chops and marmalade at that time,' Macmillan wrote later[8]) they left together for a meeting at the Château de Rambouillet, some fifty kilometres to the south-west of Paris. The château, set in a large park and gardens laid out in the formal French style, had been taken over and given to the state by Napoleon. Apart from its situation, its advantage was that de Gaulle was much more relaxed there than at the Élysée – which he disliked intensely, not just because of its absurdly rococo decoration but because the kitchens were so far from the private apartments that dinner always arrived cold. In fact, de Gaulle was so relaxed that he had played a trick. When Eisenhower and Macmillan arrived at Rambouillet, they found that Adenauer had not been invited until lunchtime. De Gaulle had been very clever. By this manoeuvre he had achieved precisely the kind of tripartite discussions he had asked for the year before. Furthermore, when he suggested that there should be regular tripartite discussions Eisenhower, much to Macmillan's surprise, readily agreed.

During the morning, the discussion ranged again over all the topics of current interest – the nuclear test ban talks at Geneva, Berlin, Africa and, rather more ominously, the future of NATO. By the time Adenauer arrived, the discussions had more or less come to a natural end. Adenauer then spent a good deal of the afternoon delivering a soporific lecture on the evils of communism. Macmillan, in a lapse from his usual good manners, could not avoid falling asleep. Waking later from his slumbers he found that the Foreign Ministers had not only discussed the problem of the economic division of Europe between the Six (EEC) and the Seven (EFTA) but had agreed that talks should be held under the aegis of the OEEC to narrow the differences.

The next day, back in Paris, Eisenhower's mood was less cordial – Macmillan thought he looked ill and was afraid that he might be having another heart attack. The truth, however, was that de Gaulle had made some caustic observations about NATO which had irritated him. Fortunately, there was little left to do. There was a plenary session in the morning to do little more than confirm the decisions on the summit meeting and send a letter of invitation to Khrushchev. Then came lunch, Eisenhower's departure for Madrid and Adenauer's for Bonn. Macmillan thought of going back to London but, before he could decide, an invitation came from de Gaulle for '*une tasse de thé* at 5.30, in the private apartments of the Élysée. Only Madame de Gaulle (whom I had not seen since Algiers days, but seemed rather younger) ... He spoke very freely and in a most friendly and even affectionate mood ... "*Cher Ami*" and all that ... this conversation at least gives me a chance of getting some European economic compromise (the Six and the Seven) with the only man who is capable of making it today.'[9]

Macmillan returned to London the following day and drove down to Birch Grove on the evening of 23 December in the highest of spirits. There were no more of the old snarls about de Gaulle – arrogance, vanity, pride, obstinacy, petulance and so on. The talk now was of a good atmosphere of confidence and friendship. As a Christmas present, Gromyko handed to Western Ambassadors Khrushchev's reply to the invitation to a summit meeting. It was 'yes': yes to Paris but the date of late April was inconvenient. After much telephoning to and fro, the date was fixed at 16 May 1960. In spite of the dreadful weather, Macmillan's Christmas turned out well. 'Altogether,' he noted, 'it has been a very happy time.'[10] The shooting at Arundel on the 30th was particularly good, the pheasants flying unusually high.

But Macmillan's mind was still very much on Africa, and, on 5 January 1960, after a visit to Sandringham to brief the Queen on what had happened and what was likely to happen (it took two hours, one before and one after tea), he was off on his journey. Dorothy came with him, as did an impressive array of official support: Sir Norman Brook, Tim Bligh (the successor to Freddie Bishop as his Principal Private Secretary),

John Wyndham (of course), officials from the Commonwealth and Colonial Offices, Macmillan's valet, Sydney Beecroft, and Dorothy's maid, Edith Baker.

But before he left there was one matter which the Queen had raised with him and which would need to be settled in his absence. The marriage of the Queen to Prince Philip had raised the question of what their descendants would be called. Both Prince Philip and his uncle Lord Mountbatten were insisting that the Queen's grandchildren should be called 'Mountbatten-Windsor'. 'The whole thing', Macmillan wrote, 'has been rather strange and painful ... Both the Prince and the Earl [Mountbatten] are very Almanac de Gotha ... The Earl wrote (and distributed) a book about his (obscure and unimportant) family. The Prince, it seems, thinks also all these things. I feel certain that the Queen only wishes (properly enough) to do something to please her husband – with whom she is desperately in love. What upsets me ... is the Prince's almost brutal attitude to the Queen over all this. I shall never forget what she said to me that Sunday night at Sandringham.'[11] It was a conundrum which was left to the Lord Chancellor to solve.

Neither Macmillan nor Dorothy had ever been to sub-Saharan Africa before. At their first stop, Accra in Ghana, they were greeted by large and enthusiastic crowds. It seemed like a repeat of their Commonwealth tour of two years earlier. Ghana, after all, had become independent and seemed, at least for the moment, to be pursuing a constitutional path. At their next stop, Lagos in Nigeria, however, Macmillan made a slip. In response to a journalist who asked about his plans for Northern Rhodesia and Nyasaland, he replied that 'the people of the two territories will be given an opportunity to decide whether the Federation is beneficial to them'.[12] Coming on top of remarks by Sir Hartley Shawcross, who had been recruited at the last moment on to the Monckton Commission, to the effect that he would not shrink from recommending that Federal territories should have the right to secede, this set Welensky's alarm bells ringing.

They were still ringing when Macmillan and Dorothy, after their short stay in Nigeria, arrived in Salisbury on 18 January. Macmillan tried to soothe the spirits by proclaiming his support for the Federation in a speech the next day and claiming that his Lagos remarks had been misreported. But he was not entirely successful. Although Welensky was mollified by the speech he was upset by the idea, which Macleod had been pushing, that Dr Hastings Banda would have to be released if there was to be any progress in Nyasaland. Welensky, in the end, accepted the idea in principle but stoutly resisted any suggestion that Banda should be released before the Monckton Commission made its long-awaited visit to Central Africa.

After a more relaxed stay in Northern Rhodesia and a less relaxed visit to a tense Nyasaland, Macmillan and Dorothy went briefly back to Salisbury before flying to Johannesburg. There was then a sightseeing tour of South Africa – Bechuanaland, the Northern Transvaal, the Rand, Swaziland, Durban, Bloemfontein and Basutoland, before their arrival in Cape Town on 2 February. Throughout the tour Macmillan seemed ill. Doctors thought that he was suffering from the common gastro-enteritis – but those who knew him better, and he himself, put his vomiting down to nerves before the major speech he was due to make to the South African Parliament. They knew, and he knew, that it was to be one of the most important speeches of his political career.

It needs hardly to be said that the speech had been many weeks in preparation, and almost everyone of consequence had been involved. The two prime movers were the High Commissioner for South Africa, Sir John Maud, and, of course, Tim Bligh, but there were signs of many other hands and nobody could be certain who was really responsible for the final version. Macmillan told Maud that we 'must philosophise not attack'. Maud agreed that 'the necessary courtesies must be observed, but they were after all dealing with ... a police state run by Transvaal thugs ... the main objective would be to get them to be less ostrich-like ...'.[13] The phrase 'wind of change', which was to capture the world's imagination so dramatically, had in fact been used by Baldwin in the 1930s. It had also been used by Macmillan in a speech on 9 January in Accra, but it had attracted little attention. Somebody, perhaps an official from the Commonwealth Office, just thought it worth using again.

At half past ten in the morning of 3 February 1960 (as it happened, the very day that Nelson Mandela was standing trial) Macmillan entered the Parliament building, the chamber of the old Cape Colony Parliament, to deliver his speech. As he entered and mounted the platform, there was no more than a polite ripple of applause (he had told the South African Prime Minister, Dr Hendrik Verwoerd, more or less what he was going to say and word had quickly got around). He then spoke for some fifty minutes to a largely silent audience. The speech, of course, had been most carefully constructed. The first third consisted of a history lesson – as usual, Macmillan brought in a mention of the Roman Empire. But then the tone changed. He spoke of growing African nationalism. 'The wind of change', he announced, 'is blowing through this continent, and, whether we like it or not, this growth of national consciousness is a political fact. We must all accept it as a fact, and our national policies must take account of it.' Then, later on, he went much further. 'As a fellow member of the Commonwealth it is our earnest desire to give South Africa our support and encouragement, but I hope you won't mind me saying frankly that there are some aspects of your policies which make it impossible for us to do this without being false to our own deep convictions about the political destinies of free men to which in our own territories we are trying to give effect.'[14] There was then a peroration, about how much Britain wanted to help South Africa but how difficult it all was. Macmillan then sat down – to audible muttering from his audience.

At the time, Macmillan's speech caused little sensation outside South Africa. Verwoerd, in a curmudgeonly reply, said that the white man had rights as well as the black man. He was widely reported in the South African press. There was then a difficult state banquet with Verwoerd and other South African Government Ministers and a few days sight-seeing before Macmillan and Dorothy were able to escape, taking ship on the *Capetown Castle* bound for Las Palmas in the Canary Islands – cheered on their way, as it happened, by crowds of South Africans of British descent. By that time, of course, the speech had been given international media saturation.

The speech quickly became known – and still is known – as the 'wind of change' speech. There were those who immediately grasped its significance – officials in the Colonial and Commonwealth Offices stopped writing policy papers, on the grounds that Macmillan had set out British policy once for all – and there were those, even to the present day, who came to recognise, and still do, that it marked one of the turning points of the twentieth century. A British Prime Minister had scented a breeze – of black African nationalism – and turned it into a wind. As a result, the British African Empire started finally on the long road to its dissolution.

The sea journey from Cape Town to Las Palmas was comfortable and restful. There was, of course, business to be done. Macmillan had to concede a rise of a full percentage point in Bank Rate and, in contrast, to refuse any further concessions to the awkward Archbishop Makarios over Cyprus. He heard, too, that the Cabinet had agreed Kilmuir's compromise arrangement with the Queen: that 'de-royalised' grand-children would carry the name of 'Mountbatten-Windsor' while those in line for the succession would retain the simple 'Windsor'.

Even more interesting, however, was a signal from his son Maurice. Quite fortuitously, Maurice had been having lunch with the Regius Professor of Modern History at Oxford, Hugh Trevor-Roper. It turned out that the Chancellorship of Oxford University was vacant, the previous holder of the office, Lord Halifax, having died in late 1959. The obvious candidate for the post, supported by a powerful group of heads of colleges led by Sir Maurice Bowra, was the undoubtedly distinguished former Ambassador to Washington, Sir Oliver Franks. But Franks was not universally popular. (In the true spirit of academic invective, for instance, one opponent referred to Franks as 'that bum-faced purveyor of last year's platitudes'.[15]) Trevor-Roper himself called Franks 'intellectually ordinary, and of dull, puritan, not to say sanctimonious virtue'. It went without saying that he was casting around for a competitor. He thought of Lord Salisbury but in the end decided that the man for the job was none other than the Prime Minister himself. He duly asked Maurice at lunch to ask his father whether he would stand, and a signal accordingly went out to the *Capetown Castle*.

Macmillan was tickled by the idea. Of course, he knew all about Trevor-Roper – he was one of Macmillan's authors – and did not underestimate the Professor's generally recognised maliciousness. He also knew that Trevor-Roper had an exaggerated view of the Prime Ministerial virtues – 'a gay, cavalier figure, ready for battle ... above all, a rebel ... in the great tradition of Disraeli and Winston as opposed to that other tradition of Bonar Law and Baldwin ...'.[16] Finally, he was clear that if there were a contest, and if he were to lose it, there would be some potentially serious political damage.

But it would, after all, be fun. When he arrived back in London on 15 February he duly consulted his closest Cabinet colleagues and the officials of the 1922 Committee. They all warned against the whole thing: he had nothing to gain and much to lose. He replied that the same was true of fox hunting, but people still did it – to which there was no obvious answer. His name duly went forward, and Trevor-Roper set about mobilising support. In fact, there was not much time, as the election was due to take place over three days at the beginning of March.

Before that could happen, however, the Africa story took another twist. Home had been in Salisbury trying to get agreement on the date of Banda's release. Macleod was insisting on release as soon as possible. Home, nervous of opposition from both Welensky and Whitehead, was much more cautious. In the end, Welensky insisted that Banda should not be released while the Monckton Commission was visiting Nyasaland – he threatened to call a General Election on the issue – but agreed that he could be released after the Commission had left. The proposal was approved in Cabinet on 23 February. But at the end of the meeting Macleod announced that although he accepted that the right decision had been reached his personal position was untenable and he would have to resign.

Everybody was puzzled. Macmillan even wondered whether it was a plot. In fact, there was an easy resolution. Macleod had unwisely told some of Banda's friends in Nyasaland that he would be freed almost immediately. That discovered, Macmillan devised the solution. He suggested to Macleod that Banda should be released three days before the 'Moncktonians' left Nyasaland, thus allowing those in favour of the Federation to give evidence while Banda was still in prison, and those against Federation to give evidence when Banda was a free man. The trick worked. Macmillan called Home in Salisbury and told him to sell the new compromise to Welensky and Whitehead. This Home duly did. 'Alec Home is splendid fellow,' Macmillan wrote in his diary.[17] The Cabinet duly endorsed the compromise at its meeting of 25 February.

Even apart from Macleod's near resignation, these were not easy days. Daniel, his brother, was in hospital after an operation for cancer of the colon. Dorothy had been ordered to take two weeks rest after her South African exertions. Heathcoat Amory – supported by Treasury and Bank of England officials – was spreading more gloom about the British economy. But the one matter which was to have a permanent impact on the future international status of the United Kingdom had, almost without notice, surfaced to the top of the political agenda. The matter was, quite simply, whether, in the nuclear age, the United Kingdom was able to defend itself alone against any future threat.

At Bermuda in May 1957 Eisenhower had agreed to site American intermediate-range Thor missiles in the UK. There was, to be sure, some confusion about who would control the firing of the missiles. But there was rather more confusion when Britain successfully tested its first hydrogen bomb in the same month. Since the only delivery system clearly independent and available to the British was an ageing bomber force, the Government decided to accelerate the programme, started in 1954, to bring into operation a liquid-fuelled ballistic missile known as Blue Streak. It turned out, however, that there were two insuperable problems: first, the missile launching sites were easily detectable and would be the first target for an enemy strike and, second, the sixty tonnes of liquid oxygen required for the launch could not be loaded in advance since it would freeze. The fuelling of the rocket took fifteen minutes – during which the whole site as well as the rocket would be obliterated. Added to those problems was the expense: £60 million up to the end of 1959 with an estimated final bill of £300 million.

On 20 February 1960 the Cabinet Defence Committee decided that there was only one course of action: Blue Streak should be cancelled and a relatively new airborne missile, known as Skybolt, should be purchased from the United States. This would have the advantage of prolonging the life of the British bomber force. Macmillan was duly authorised to see Eisenhower and make the request.

At the same time, however, he was enthusiastically following his revived friendship with General de Gaulle. On his return from Africa he had found waiting for him a memorandum on the matter written by Selwyn Lloyd. Lloyd pointed out that initially the emphasis of the Macmillan government's strategy had been to repair post-Suez relations with the United States. This had been successful, although 'the least satisfactory element in our relations has been the United States backing the Six and being so unenthusiastic about the wider European Free Trade Association of the Seven'. There was also mistrust over Berlin and the British attitude towards Communist China. 'In these circumstances,' Lloyd went on, 'we must preserve the best possible relations with the United States ... But should we not now try to make the same sort of effort with France as we did in 1957? Our assets are your personal relationship with General de Gaulle, the underlying French fear of Germany, and the fact that we do not object to tripartite consultation which they want.' In urging Macmillan to accept de Gaulle's invitation to visit him, Lloyd saw 'the programme for the new *entente*: (i) to further our present line vis-à-vis the Soviets; (ii) to keep Germany on the right lines ...; (iii) to reach a political settlement of the Sixes and Sevens somehow; (iv) to guard against the Americans indulging in any disastrous enterprises in the East'.[18] In other words, Britain was to play '*Le double jeu*' – the double game.

Macmillan needed no further encouragement. On Sunday 5 March he was told that he had been elected as Chancellor of Oxford University by a majority of 279 out of a total vote of 3500. 'Praise be to God,' wrote Trevor-Roper to his American correspondent, 'the party of the laity and the gaity has won. It is a glorious day ... Oh frabjous day! Calloo, callay! Of course ... it will not, in all probability make twopence worth of difference in the end ...'[19] Thus cheered, Macmillan made plans to go to see de Gaulle along the now familiar road to the Château de Rambouillet.

Dorothy and Macmillan, when they arrived on 12 March, were put to stay in the old tower of the castle where, it was said, François Ier had breathed his last. They found their whole apartment old and ugly – and the hot-water system did not work. In spite of all that, the discussions on the following day were notably friendly. De Gaulle thought that Khrushchev, his recent guest in France, was genuine in wanting some sort of agreement at the summit meeting but that the Germans were too worried about the proposal for 'thinning out' for it to be pursued. He went on to say that total and general nuclear disarmament was the ideal, but, failing that, 'France would continue to try to obtain a nuclear armament. The Americans had refused to give any help. He would be glad if it was possible for the United Kingdom to assist even with means of delivery.'[20]

Macmillan replied. 'I put the idea in his mind that we might be able to help him, either with American agreement or connivance. He seemed much interested. Did he want full control? Or would he consider a NATO, or WEU, or an Anglo-French control? He would reflect on this – the first was impossible. Germany would be the problem in the second. The third had its attractions.'[21] His offer is not reproduced in the official record in those terms, but there is no reason to disbelieve it. What is recorded, which has, understandably, a slightly different nuance, was that 'the Prime Minister explained the complications of the United Kingdom arrangement with the United States. General de Gaulle understood this. The Prime Minister said that the conclusion of the Geneva Tests agreement might provide an opportunity for some arrangement being made. General de Gaulle seemed attracted by this plan.'[22]

Whether Macmillan was wholly sincere in offering de Gaulle the measure of nuclear cooperation which he did is difficult to gauge. He certainly wanted de Gaulle's help in finding an accommodation between the Six and the Seven, but the extent of his offer is certainly surprising. Neither Lloyd (who was not at Rambouillet) nor the rest of the Cabinet had any inkling of it. But there is no reason to suppose that Macmillan's diary version is wrong. Sincere or not, this was the nearest Macmillan ever came to offering de Gaulle full Franco-British cooperation on the nuclear issue. Moreover, both the diary and the official record are clear that de Gaulle was very interested indeed in the prospect. True, de Gaulle went on to say that he thought the United Kingdom was always unwilling to choose between being part of Europe and having a special connection with the United States, but he was also very encouraged by Macmillan's clear support for tripartite discussions and his forthright statement that 'the United Kingdom would like to see a renaissant Europe led by France'.[23]

Whatever was said or not said, meant or not meant, all in all Macmillan was very pleased with Rambouillet. 'De Gaulle is certainly an extraordinary character,' he wrote in his diary. 'Now that he is old (69) and mellowed, his charm is great. He speaks beautiful, rather old-fashioned French. He seems quite impersonal and disinterested ... The visit was certainly successful in revitalising our old friendship ...'[24]

No sooner was that written than Macmillan was turning to America again. He decided to go to Washington to persuade Eisenhower to accept a new Soviet proposal at Geneva to ban nuclear tests in the atmosphere, space and underwater as well as most underground tests. It was a perfectly sensible move. After all, as he told the Cabinet on 22 March, 'we now had an opportunity to conclude an agreement which might be a turning point in the history of international negotiations on disarmament. The United States Government must be brought to appreciate the significance of this opportunity.'[25] Added to his transatlantic agenda, however, 'as well as the test problems, we want to get SKYBOLT and perhaps POLARIS out of the Americans. The dual operation', he went on, 'is rather a tricky one.'[26] Tricky or not, the decision was in line with the conclusions of Sir Patrick Dean's study, now known as 'Future Policy Review 1960–1970', which had just been presented to Cabinet. Leaving to others the Parliamentary battle over an incident at Sharpeville in South Africa, in which more than sixty black Africans had been brutally mown down by Afrikaner police, on Saturday 26 March, Macmillan set off again for Washington.

In their telephone call arranging the visit, Eisenhower and Macmillan had agreed that the whole thing should be as low key as possible. Eisenhower wanted 'to avoid any cabling on this and handle everything orally ... they discussed the cover for the visit and agreed ... to say that the President and Macmillan wanted to get together and to talk about the nuclear testing question; that anything else would get others' noses out of joint'.[27] Macmillan also told Eisenhower that Lloyd would not be coming with him.

All went to plan. On the Monday morning there was a meeting with Herter at the British Embassy. The first discussion was about the economic division of Europe between the Sixes and Sevens. Macmillan tried to play the card he had played with de Gaulle and Adenauer – that Britain would have to withdraw its forces from continental Europe unless a solution was reached. That met with little response. What encouraged him, however, was a State Department paper broadly accepting the Soviet proposal. That done, the meeting moved from the Embassy to the White House and immediately on to Camp David.

It could hardly have been better. By the afternoon of the Tuesday a joint declaration had been agreed on the Russian proposals – acceptance subject to negotiation on the details. But the second part of Macmillan's agenda had gone even better. 'We have got out of the Americans', he noted in his diary, 'a very valuable exchange of notes about SKYBOLT & POLARIS. They undertake to let us have the *vehicles* (by sale or gift), we making our own heads. This allows us to abandon BLUESTREAK (rocket) without damage to our prospects of maintaining – in the late 60s and early 70s – our *independent nuclear deterrent*.'[28]

Of course, it did nothing of the sort. Britain would for ever be dependent on the United States for technological developments – let alone spare parts and technical advice. Even more difficult, however, was the question of how to reconcile the purchase of future American delivery systems (Skybolt was not due to come into service before 1965) with the other part of the 'double game' – the wooing of de Gaulle to find a solution to the problem of the 'Sixes and Sevens'.

The question came up sooner than expected. On Tuesday 5 April, de Gaulle arrived in London for his long-planned state visit. It was to be, and indeed it was, a magnificent event. There were fireworks – the Cross of Lorraine exploded on the frontage of Buckingham Palace – fanfares, a ride with the Queen in an open carriage to address the two Houses of Parliament in Westminster Hall, a state dinner (Lloyd had written a particularly effusive speech for the Queen to read out), and crowds in the streets (and the pubs) singing the 'Marseillaise'. In short, London had been asked to put on her best party dress and had duly obliged.

De Gaulle was very taken with all this. In fact, he was so taken with the dignity of the thing that there was little opportunity for political discussion. He felt that to go to Chequers for political meetings would be a slight to the Queen. They were only to be fitted in with the programme of his visit as one Head of State to another. It was no more than good manners towards his hostess. As it happened, the first such convenient occasion occurred on the day of de Gaulle's arrival. At six o'clock that evening Macmillan, with only Philip de Zulueta for company, went to see de Gaulle, on his side only with his trusted aide, André Gérard. Bizarre as it seems, the place where the President of France received the British Prime Minister was Buckingham Palace.

Perhaps taken aback by the strange location, Macmillan started off by asking politely about the visit which Khrushchev had recently made to France. 'Very pleasant,' de Gaulle replied, and went on to say that he thought that Khrushchev was prepared to do a deal over Berlin at the summit meeting. As for Macmillan, he explained that the Americans had been very positive about the Soviet proposals at Geneva and that all looked set fair. Those courtesies completed, the two went on to the matter of the Sixes and Sevens. Macmillan said how damaging to the UK economy would be the raising of the EEC external tariff in July.

De Gaulle then riposted that 'he had to think about Germany'. But he went on to ask: 'Could the United Kingdom not contemplate coming into the Common Market?' (De Zulueta's English version translates the French *contempler* as 'contemplate'. It would, in the context, more accurately be rendered as 'think about'.) Macmillan replied that 'this was unfortunately impossible'. De Gaulle then probed rather more. '[He] enquired what the American position had been. [Macmillan] replied that different Americans had different views. [De Gaulle] said that he thought that the Americans were in favour of the Common Market. [Macmillan] agreed that this was broadly the case ...'[29])

There was an obvious dilemma. De Gaulle had remembered the hint at Rambouillet that there might be some arrangement for Anglo-French control of a nuclear force. If Macmillan was so insistent on the dangers to the United Kingdom of an economic division between the Six and the Seven, the simple answer was for Britain to solve the problem by joining the EEC and, in doing so, solve the French problem in creating a credible nuclear strike force under Anglo-French control. The fact that the Americans were 'broadly' in favour of the EEC would have accorded with Macmillan's suggestion at Rambouillet that the thing might indeed be done with their 'connivance'.

His problem, of course, was that he had just signed up with the Americans to buy Skybolt. That is why de Gaulle's suggestion that Britain should 'think about' joining the EEC (and, of course, join with the French in their nuclear ambition) was 'unfortunately impossible'. 'Unfortunately', as was to become evident, was precisely the right word. De Gaulle, impressed – and almost overcome – by the reception he had received, not just by the Queen and Parliament but by those on the London streets who remembered his stand for France in 1940, had held out to Macmillan the possibility of a friendly reception for Britain if she wished to join the EEC. There was, naturally enough, a price, and Macmillan, at the time, thought the price 'unfortunately' unacceptable. He had just committed himself to America.

Macmillan was again feeling tired. He had won a long battle with Heathcoat Amory about the Budget of 4 April and the tone of the Chancellor's speech which was to accompany it. 'Continued expansion' was now the main theme – much against the Treasury advice for 'retrenchment'. Washington and Camp David, followed by de Gaulle's state visit, had left him drained. Moreover, he was starting to feel despondent about the Government's performance. 'I feel', he wrote in his diary, 'the govt has lost a good deal of ground in the press and parlt *since* the general election.'[30] The break for Easter in mid-April did him good, as did his installation on 30 April, in glorious weather, as Chancellor of Oxford University. But he realised that all that was mere diversion. In the real political world, so much more depended on a successful summit meeting with Khrushchev in May.

The conference of Commonwealth Prime Ministers in early May passed off without a hitch – once it had been agreed that the racial policies of the South African government were a matter of internal policy. But while it was in session, there was a much more serious incident elsewhere. The United States – and Britain, for that matter – had been sending high-altitude aircraft, the Utility-2 (U-2), to overfly Soviet territory and photograph military-industrial sites and missile installations. The U-2 could fly at 70,000 feet, much too high for Soviet T-3 interceptors and right at the limit of the very inaccurate Soviet anti-aircraft missiles. All flights were personally authorised by Eisenhower or, in the British case, by Macmillan. After Khrushchev's visit to America and with the summit meeting agreed, both Eisenhower and Macmillan had stopped the flights. In early April, however, the Central Intelligence Agency persuaded Eisenhower that they needed photographs of the ballistic missile test site at Tyura-Tam in Kazakhstan, the industrial complex near Sverdlovsk and a possible launch site for intercontinental ballistic missiles at Plesetsk. The photographs apparently had to be taken during April, May or June, since the angle of the sun in subsequent months would mean a delay until the following year if those months were missed.

Eisenhower duly authorised U-2 flights for 9 April and 25 April. The first flight was, of course, picked up on Soviet radar but there was nothing they could do about it. The second flight was delayed by bad weather and did not take off until 1 May. Piloted by Gary Powers, the U-2 was also picked up on Soviet radar as it flew from its base in Pakistan across Kazakhstan and turned north towards Sverdlovsk. Anti-aircraft rockets were fired at it, one of which, by something of a fluke, detonated near Powers's U-2. The aircraft started to break up and lose height rapidly. The ejector seat had also jammed (Powers would anyway not have survived even if he had been able to eject). At about 18,000 feet Powers was able to get out, opened his parachute and landed almost on top of an astonished peasant who was working in a field on a collective farm.

Macmillan first heard of all this when he read a report of Khrushchev's speech to a meeting of 1300 Deputies in the White Hall of the Kremlin on 5 May. In fact, Khrushchev was quick to try to rescue a difficult situation. He shouted that he blamed 'imperialist and militarist circles, whose stronghold is the Pentagon'. They were trying, he went on, to 'torpedo the Paris summit or, at any rate, prevent an agreement for which the whole world is waiting'.[31] The State Department then made matters worse by announcing that a weather plane had gone missing over Turkey and may have strayed into Soviet air space. The US Space Agency, NASA, followed up by giving out details of the U-2 flight which were wholly fictitious. But Khrushchev, even then, was still trying to salvage the summit meeting. On 9 May he took the US Ambassador aside at a reception and told him that 'this U-2 thing has put me in a terrible spot. You have to get me off it.'[32] The next day the State Department issued a further statement, signed by Herter, that, contrary to previous hints, Eisenhower had personally authorised the U-2 flights. On 11 May Eisenhower told a press conference that 'the U-2 flights had been made with his knowledge and approval'.[33] Khrushchev was quick to see the consequence. The hawks in the Kremlin, led by the Defence Minister Marshal Rodion Malinovsky (de Gaulle called him the 'Rocket Marshal') and furious at Khrushchev's proposed defence cuts, would take centre stage. 'I was no longer in full control,' he said later in life.[34] From that moment, the summit meeting was doomed.

Macmillan, Lloyd and a group of officials arrived in Paris in time for lunch at the Embassy on 15 May. Khrushchev, shadowed everywhere by Malinovsky, had arrived the day before. At lunch there came a message that Khrushchev was asking to see Macmillan at the Embassy at 4.30 p.m. 'We are in trouble,' Macmillan wrote after the meeting. 'He made a speech, in violent terms, attacked the USA, President Eisenhower, the Pentagon ... He said that his *friend* (bitterly repeated again and again), his *friend* Eisenhower had betrayed him. He then proceeded with a formal declaration ... it would be impossible to carry on the summit conference unless President Eisenhower a) condemned what had been done by air espionage, b) expressed his regret, c) said he would never do it again, d) punished the criminals.'[35] It was, in fact, the same message as he had delivered to de Gaulle in the morning. De Gaulle, immediately realising that Khrushchev's demands were quite unacceptable, thought that the summit was no longer possible. But Macmillan, later that evening, did his best to persuade both de Gaulle and Eisenhower to have one more shot. Eisenhower refused to see Khrushchev by himself. All they could agree on was to wait and see what would happen the following day, 16 May.

It went as badly as Macmillan had feared. He had slept badly. When he went to have breakfast with Eisenhower (tucking into steak and jelly while Macmillan toyed with a boiled egg) the conversation was desultory. Macmillan was shown the opening statement which Eisenhower proposed to make in response to Khrushchev's statement, which by then had been circulated. It was, in his view, much too tough, but Eisenhower and Herter were not prepared to do more than tinker with it. At 11 a.m. the four Heads of Government took their places at a conference table set up specially in the Élysée. De Gaulle, who had been tipped off that Eisenhower wished to make a statement, invited him to do so. But before he could open his mouth Khrushchev claimed the right to speak. He pulled a large wad of typewritten script from his pocket and fired off. Shouting loudly and frequently repeating himself he not only reiterated his four demands but he made it clear that no summit was possible while

Eisenhower was President and that Eisenhower's return visit to the Soviet Union was no longer possible. After three-quarters of an hour of 'a mixture of abuse, vitriolic and offensive, and legal argument'[36] he sat down. Throughout his tirade, Malinovsky 'could be seen punctuating the speech with peremptory gestures and warlike grimaces'.[37] Eisenhower was seething with anger.

Eisenhower then read out his statement as calmly as he could. In the event it sounded reasonably emollient, but Khrushchev kept muttering throughout. It was then Macmillan's turn. According to de Gaulle, he 'exuded anxiety and distress'.[38] In an appeal for compromise, he claimed that 'the eyes of the world were on the heads of government and hopes of all the peoples of all countries rested on them'.[39] De Gaulle, who spoke next, was much tougher. He accused Khrushchev of deplorable diplomatic discourtesy. 'You have brought Mr Macmillan here from London,' he said, 'General Eisenhower from the United States and have put me to serious inconvenience to organise and attend a meeting which your intransigence will make impossible.'[40] As for the U-2, de Gaulle pointed out that a Soviet satellite had, the day before, overflown French air space without asking permission. He then suggested a twenty-four-hour adjournment. There followed a confused discussion about what might or might not be published until de Gaulle called a halt just after 2 p.m. On their way out, however, de Gaulle caught Eisenhower's elbow and told him 'whatever happens, *we are with you*'.[41] It was something that Eisenhower never forgot.

Macmillan made one last attempt to get the show back on the road. Eisenhower had gone back to the US Ambassador's residence in one of his most spectacular rages. His language was apparently in the finest tradition of the American military. That being so, General Snyder was immediately summoned to take the President's blood pressure. The result was not recorded but, Snyder noted laconically, Eisenhower 'had lunch and then rested ... Aside from private meetings with advisors, the President had no further activities.'[42] One of the 'advisors', of course was Macmillan, who arrived just after the US Embassy had issued a robust statement attacking both Khrushchev's assertions and his motives. Macmillan was not, at that point, particularly welcome. He had arrived without Lloyd – who was deeply upset – and found Eisenhower still resentful and, what is more, suspicious of Macmillan's intentions. He asked Macmillan 'what more could he do? I said I supposed he could "say he was sorry" or, preferably, a formal diplomatic apology.'[43] It was hardly the most tactful thing to say to the incandescent Eisenhower.

Macmillan had no more success with de Gaulle. The General saw no point in further discussion and suspected, like Eisenhower, that

Macmillan was weakening on substance in order to get something which could be presented as politically attractive. Nevertheless, he did not attempt to stop Macmillan from going off to see Khrushchev. At the Soviet Embassy Macmillan found Khrushchev 'polite but quite unmovable. The Marshal (silent, immovable, hardly even blinking) and Gromyko (also silent) as well as others were present . . . However, at the end of a very long talk I got the impression that he would not act without seeing me again.'[44] The point which Macmillan relied on was that, while apologies might be in order, to ask a Head of State to 'condemn his own people' was too much. 'He begged Mr Khrushchev to help find an honourable way . . . to prevent disappointing [the hopes of the world].'[45]

When Macmillan arrived back at the British Embassy late that evening, dog-tired, he knew that he had only one last chance. That quickly disappeared the next morning, 17 May, when Khrushchev, wandering around the Paris streets, reiterated his demands to accompanying journalists for a complete American climbdown. If this did not happen, he went on, the Soviets would up sticks and go home. When that word was spread – and arrived just as Eisenhower, Macmillan and de Gaulle were meeting at the Élysée to see what they should do – Eisenhower and de Gaulle agreed that there was no point in going on. The only matter to be settled for them was how to put the thing to bed – but, at the very least, putting the maximum of blame on the Soviets. The rest was to be a mere formality.

The three of them decided to invite Khrushchev to a meeting – to be presented as part of the summit conference – at 3 p.m. A letter was sent to Khrushchev to that effect. Khrushchev, who had been on a trip to the country, announced that he had only just got back, had had no lunch and was now going to have a bath. But if the meeting was not part of the summit he would turn up at five o'clock. If it was, he could not attend since Eisenhower had not apologised for the U-2. Eisenhower and de Gaulle wanted to make an announcement that there would be no summit – it was all over. Macmillan, 'with tears in his eyes',[46] pleaded again with them to make one final effort; Eisenhower whispered to Herter, 'You know, poor old Hal is very upset about this, and I think we might go as far as to meet him on this one point';[47] Herter demurred – and de Gaulle thought the whole idea too Byzantine. That was the end. At 4.15 p.m., a message came from Khrushchev restating his terms. De Gaulle, Eisenhower – and Macmillan – issued a communiqué saying that the summit would not now take place.

There was then a process of winding down. Khrushchev, carefully shepherded by Malinovsky, came to see Macmillan to say his goodbyes on the morning of 18 May. Eisenhower, too, stopped by. Later in the afternoon there was a long meeting at the Élysée to clear up the diplomatic aftermath. By then Khrushchev was giving a press conference. 'It was a terrible performance, reminiscent of Hitler at his worst,' Macmillan wrote. 'He threatens, rants, uses filthy words of abuse ...'[48] But there was not much anybody could do about it.

It had all ended in unpleasant farce. But the real loser in the whole fiasco was undoubtedly Macmillan. All the hopes of summitry, of Athens leading Rome, of the 'double game', all those hopes of October 1959 had vanished as winter snow in the fierce May sun. At dinner that evening in the British Embassy Macmillan was in despair. 'I rang the Chief Whip,' he told those around him, 'and asked him if I should resign now my policy is in ruins around me ... He told me to hang on ...'[49] Almost worse was the thought that Eisenhower, friendly as he had been, had snapped the bond of trust which Macmillan had forged between them after Suez. Eisenhower wrote to de Gaulle one of the most fulsome letters he had ever written: 'I leave Paris with the warmth and strength of your friendship, so amply demonstrated and renewed under the stress of the last few days, an even more valued possession than ever before. You and I have shared great experiences in war and in peace, and from these experiences has come, for my part at least, a respect and admiration I have for few men ... Certainly the word "ally" has for me now an even deeper meaning than ever before. I salute the staunch determination that you and your countrymen have shown.'[50]

On 19 May Macmillan wrote that 'I felt very tired today, with much pain in the region of my heart ... I can scarcely do anything this morning, either reading or writing ... We returned to London in the afternoon ... I went to bed, very exhausted. The pain is worse.'[51] Physically and psychologically, he seemed a broken man.

23

Enter JFK

Macmillan's chest pains after the Paris fiasco of May 1960 were not, as he imagined, a thrombosis, or even, as he claimed to his doctor, a heart attack. (Dr Richardson – by then Sir John – had already noted that his patient's complaints were becoming more frequent as he grew older – at times to the point of hypochondria.) It was simply that he was both tired and depressed. Richardson saw this, explained that the symptoms were similar to those of benign cardiac disturbance – and that the patient should not be too concerned – and then did no more than prescribe some sleeping pills. In other words, his advice was to have a good rest, stop worrying, calm down and everything would be all right. And so it turned out.

That was easily done. But what Richardson could not cure was the damage to the Macmillan Government. It had just suffered its second political heart attack. This time it was not just a matter of furious ministerial resignations, or even of suspected plots. This time it was the humiliating collapse of a major plank of the Government's foreign policy under the impact of what should have been, on any rational assessment, no more than a relatively minor security hiccup. But as if that was not bad enough – and it was certainly very bad – there was a second cardiac tremor at the same time. Yet another Chancellor of the Exchequer, this time Heathcoat Amory, was telling everybody who would listen that he now was determined to leave as soon as possible and retire to a peaceful private life.

The diplomatic fallout from the Paris fiasco was nearly as unpleasant as the domestic fallout. To be sure, Eisenhower did his best, as always, to help his old friend. Back in Washington, 'the President next mentioned the stories that have appeared to the effect that Macmillan had lost standing with the United States Government in connection with the Paris conference. He said that nothing could be further from the truth as far as he was concerned, and he assumed that this was true from the Secretary's standpoint as well.'[1] That may have been Eisenhower's personal view – and Herter may have nodded agreement – but it certainly was not the view of some State Department officials. Macmillan had, after all, spent two years trying to cajole them into a Summit Conference with Khrushchev, only to find everything blowing up in front of them.

Macmillan, like all Prime Ministers in political trouble, had to think quickly about what he should do. Resignation was no longer an option – he had briefly thought about that in the immediate aftermath of Paris but had been reminded it would be no more than a feeble gesture acknowledging defeat. The next option, of course, as often occurs to Prime Ministers in similar situations, was to move his ministerial pieces around the board to give at least an impression of authority. In fact, since this was the only option now available, Macmillan promptly set about the task.

First, there was the Treasury itself. If Heathcoat Amory was to go, he needed another Chancellor who would still do more or less what he asked. The answer was simple: Selwyn Lloyd. This in turn allowed him to move one of his favourites, Lord Home, to the Foreign Office. Accordingly, at the start of the ministerial merry-go-round – although Lloyd had not yet agreed to leave the Foreign Office – Home was invited on 3 June to lunch in Downing Street. Macmillan, after some introductory small talk, 'asked him whether, *if* I decided to ask Selwyn Lloyd to take the Exchequer (when D-H Amory goes) he would take Foreign Office'.[2] Home, understandably, was taken aback. He had no idea that he would be promoted so quickly. He replied that he would have to think about it; he was worried about his rather delicate health; he was concerned that the House of Commons might not take to a Foreign Secretary in the House of Lords. In short, he was flattered, but doubtful. He wanted time to reflect.

On the face of it, in terms of the politics of the day Home was not by any means the obvious choice. Macmillan himself had, after all, pointed out the difficulty of a Foreign Secretary in the Lords when Salisbury was spoken of as a possibility under Eden. Moreover, Home was a hereditary Earl at a time when life peerages had just been introduced. Furthermore, he had been a leading 'appeaser' at the time of Munich, as Chamberlain's Parliamentary Private Secretary, and had been found too delicate in health to fight in the war. If Macmillan was to hold that against Butler, he should – in all logic – have held it much more against Home. On the other hand, of course, Home was in many respects almost a Macmillan clone (but without the intellectual power) – Etonian, Christ Church, Anglo-Scot, in other words the sort of amateur, as Macmillan himself might have put it, who appealed to the would-be amateur aristocrat in himself. In sum, they spoke the same language and, unlike Butler, Home could be relied on to do what the Prime Minister asked.

Leaving him to make his decision, and by-passing a rather irritated

Butler, who wrote later that he would have liked the job of Foreign Secretary himself, Macmillan spent a pleasant four days on an official visit to Norway. It was a leisurely trip – an audience with the King, the odd speech and some rather desultory discussions about 'Sixes and Sevens'. But it was not without interest. In fact, Macmillan rather took to Norwegian politics. He even went so far as to approve of their 'applied socialism' which 'is of a fairly moderate kind'. He added – prophetically – 'I think both Sweden and Norway present the policies which Mr Gaitskell seeks really to impose on the British Labour Party. If he were to succeed, they too would win power and hold it for a long time.'[3]

Finally, after a week or so, Home made up his mind that he would take the job. After that, it was a question of following the merry-go-round and settling the consequential moves. Duncan Sandys went to Commonwealth Relations, and Hailsham, in spite of Macmillan's doubts about him, was felt just about safe enough to take over as Leader of the House of Lords. The two surprising appointments, as was quickly noted, were Thorneycroft as Minister of Aviation and Enoch Powell as Minister of Health. The former rebels had been welcomed back into the fold. The reason, although Macmillan would never admit it, was simple. After Paris, he scented danger. He was vulnerable. It was much better to have both of them inside rather than to leave them sitting, as Parliamentary snipers, outside. (Macmillan did, however, tell Norman Brook not to sit Powell opposite him at the Cabinet table since he could not stand forever to be looking at Powell's mad, staring eyes.)

The change which was the most politically significant was the move of Heath to become Lord Privy Seal and the Minister in the Commons responsible for foreign affairs. He was, to be sure, subordinate to Home, but he was to be given particular charge of relations with Europe. In fact, the move was both bold and clever. Not only did Macmillan promote one of his most fervent junior acolytes but, in doing so, he also opened another policy option. Maudling, who had hitherto looked after European affairs, had become disenchanted with the wrangling over EFTA and its relations with the EEC – the problem of 'Sixes and Sevens' – and had become openly anti-European. Heath, on the other hand, was almost embarrassingly pro-European. The new policy option, which had already formed in Macmillan's mind, was to solve the problem of 'Sixes and Sevens' by the simple expedient of ditching the Seven and joining the Six. He had, after all, already flirted with the idea of doing a nuclear deal with de Gaulle, and if that was the price for joining the Six, he was politically experienced enough to know that what might be 'unfortunately impossible' at one moment – for instance, in his Buckingham

Palace discussion with de Gaulle in April – could become perfectly possible the next.

Macmillan had been reminded of this, if indeed he had ever forgotten, from two directions. The first was in a long report from an interdepartmental committee chaired by Sir Frank Lee on the possible impact on the British economy of proposed tariff reductions within the EEC, which were to take effect in July 1960. The Lee Report, submitted in April, had come to the same conclusion as Macmillan – that the ideal solution for the problem of 'Sixes and Sevens' would be for the UK simply to join the EEC. (The 'Seven', it thought, could be conveniently bought off.) If that was not possible, the UK should try for 'near identification with the Common Market'.[4] The second came from his former Private Secretary and now deputy Cabinet Secretary, Freddie Bishop. Bishop had entitled it '"Joanna Southcott's Box" (named after a nineteenth century religious eccentric who claimed to be a prophetess). He said more or less what the Lee Report had said. Macmillan, as always impressed by literary and historical wit, minuted back to Bishop, 'I can see what they (the French) want, and I have always thought it worth doing. Support them in their general attitude towards NATO, give them the Bomb, perhaps some V-bombers, and generally support the idea of a confederation of Europe instead of a Federation.'[5]

There was still, however, the relationship with the United States. This, too, was going through some uncomfortable turbulence. For a start, Eisenhower was not well. He was tired, and anyway was coming to the end of his long term of office. There was also a nasty dispute about what had been agreed at Camp David in May about the precise siting arrangements of American Polaris submarines in Scottish ports, and who should control them. The British had proposed as a site Loch Linnhe, on the grounds that it was a reasonable distance from Glasgow. The Americans thought that Macmillan in May had agreed to a site on the Clyde perilously near Glasgow. As for control, the British proposed that if the submarines were required to launch their missiles within one hundred miles of the UK there should be joint control. The Americans replied that they were prepared to accept joint control if the missiles were launched within UK territorial waters but certainly no further than that. The matter was stated firmly by Eisenhower in a letter to Macmillan of 15 July. It was, as Macmillan had requested, 'a frank expression of my views'. 'The one hundred-mile proposal', the letter went on, 'could form a most difficult precedent with respect to the utilization of weapons in other waters, such as the Mediterranean or Caribbean ...'[6] In other words, it was quite unacceptable. Loch Linnhe was no good either.

Eisenhower ended by telling Macmillan to think again. The Cabinet duly met – and thought again. The Clyde it was.

By the end of July Parliament was winding down for the summer Recess. The new Cabinet was duly announced – to the predictable row over Home's appointment. In fact, the most apt comment came from the American Ambassador, Jock Whitney. 'Cabinet changes,' he wired Washington on 28 July 1960, 'apart from appoint of Lord Home not at all sensational and essentially shift of familiar faces to different desks. Dominance of Macmillan in all areas of major policy remains outstanding characteristic of this and previous Cabinet.'[7] That done, on 30 July the House of Commons went into recess and Macmillan retired, not to Birch Grove, where Dorothy was, but to Chequers. Again, he was worried about his health. Richardson arrived the following day to give him a thorough examination. Macmillan claimed that he felt 'mentally exhaust-ed'. Also, 'I think *people* are tiring, when it goes on in a continuous stream day and night.'[8] Richardson found, again, that there was nothing wrong with him which a few days' rest, and a fairly strict diet, would not cure. Macmillan, rather grumpily, decided to follow the advice and stay at Chequers – alone.

His stay there lasted for nine days, broken only by a short visit – his first since 1939 – to Chatsworth. It was perhaps just as well that he was out of London, since No. 10 Downing Street was closed down for major reconstruction. The foundations were far from secure – some of the original structure was literally built on straw – the vibrations from bombs in the war had caused the walls to bulge menacingly and the roof was leaking. In early August, while Macmillan was at Chequers and Dorothy at Birch Grove, the contents of No. 10, desks, files and furniture were moved to Admiralty House on the other side of Horse Guards Parade. For the former occupants of No. 10 it was, of course, very disruptive. Although the house itself was rather larger than Downing Street, and quite comfortable, the staff missed the comparatively cosy atmosphere of No. 10, and the move itself, needless to say, was as chaotic as might be expected. When Macmillan arrived there on 8 August he found that there were no bedrooms or sitting rooms – and duly beat a hasty retreat to Birch Grove.

Two days later, on 10 August, he was off on his travels again. This time it was to see Adenauer in Bonn. Adenauer was surprisingly welcoming – Macmillan suspected, probably rightly, that the welcome was due to the failure of the Paris Summit and the breakdown of Macmillan's attempts for an accommodation with the Soviets over Berlin. At first, Adenauer seemed reluctant to discuss 'Sixes and Sevens', but a pleasant evening overlooking the Rhine – as well as some carefully chosen bottles of

Riesling – persuaded him that the matter was too important, and the danger of a Brussels bureaucracy too serious (even though Walter Hallstein had been his own nominee as the President of the new European Commission), that a way had to be found to join the EEC and EFTA into one larger free trade area. Officials were put to work. Very pleased by the outcome, at half past ten Macmillan suggested to the old Adenauer that they might break up the party, leave officials there to talk further and, not to put too fine a point on it, retire to their respective beds. 'Dr A was very pleased by this idea. So, like truant schoolboys, we stole out of a side door, crept round the garden to the front door, got into our cars and drove home.'[9]

As it turned out, Adenauer's sudden enthusiasm came to nothing. On hearing of it, the French Ambassador to Bonn reported immediately to Paris. The answer came back swiftly. The French Government would not support any new proposals. In fact, the problem of 'Sixes and Sevens', it was inferred, was a matter for the United Kingdom itself to resolve and there was, for the moment, little more to be said. On the other hand, de Gaulle quickly sent another message to Macmillan asking, almost beseeching, him to press Eisenhower for a further 'tripartite' meeting in September. It is little wonder that Macmillan was bemused by two contradictory French signals. On his return to Birch Grove, on 14 August he simply 'stayed in bed until luncheon. Read and worked and dozed!'[10] and wrote a mournful letter to his friend Ava Waverley. It was the moment, as he told her, for more shooting, and he was hoping to get away for a few days.

In the event, he and Dorothy did get away to Scotland on the last day of August, escaping from a rash of strikes which seemed to have broken out one after another. Fortunately the weather was good, there were grouse aplenty and some good golf at Gleneagles. But it was not an altogether peaceful holiday. While they were there Macmillan heard that Khrushchev had decided to go to New York for a meeting of the United Nations at the end of September. The question, which he discussed with the Queen while on his annual visit to Balmoral in the middle of his holiday, was whether he should go as well.

The question also came up in Cabinet on his return after his fortnight in Scotland. Macmillan was not at all enthusiastic. He felt that he would achieve little by going. The major problems of the day were, of course, to be discussed – Berlin, the Congo (which had fallen into chaos after the Belgians had abruptly given it independence and, equally abruptly, had left the territory), nuclear tests – but none of these was easily solved. Furthermore, he was afraid Khrushchev would put on some sort of spectacular demonstration – and that he was better off not being there to witness it. In the end, however, he was persuaded by Home that it was important for him at least to show his face. Accordingly, on 25 September he took off, together with his customary entourage – but minus Dorothy – for New York.

Khrushchev had 'certainly not disappointed his advisors', in Macmillan's own words.[11] He had arrived on 19 September after a ten-day sea journey on a lumbering old ship, the *Baltika*, which had been built in Amsterdam for the Germans in 1940, had been expropriated by the Soviets at the end of the war, and twice renamed. He had occupied himself on the long voyage not just by reading papers and watching films but by playing practical jokes on his colleagues, particularly Gromyko, who suffered from seasickness. On arrival at New York, greeted by demonstrators carrying placards (one, admittedly not very poetic, read 'Roses are red, violets are blue, Stalin dropped dead, how about you?') he went into his own kind of overdrive. He immediately challenged Eisenhower to a face-to-face summit, went on to talk to journalists at every opportunity, sang the 'Internationale' from the balcony of the Soviet Mission on Park Avenue, and took off for Harlem to see Fidel Castro, Cuba's revolutionary leader, to embrace him fervently in the entrance of the Hotel Theresa. Then, on 23 September, he spoke for three hours to the General Assembly of the United Nations, demanding freedom for all colonial territories, abusing Eisenhower and Hammarskjöld, claiming that the office of Secretary-General should be abolished and that the UN itself should relocate to Switzerland or Austria. It was a bravura performance – which irritated almost everybody.

Macmillan spoke on 29 September. He was heard in dignified silence until he said that he regretted the failure of the Paris summit. At that point Khrushchev jumped to his feet and shouted, 'You sent your planes over our territory! You are guilty of aggression', waving his arms furiously and pounding the table in front of him with his fists.[12] He continued interrupting, to the point where Macmillan, over his shoulder, asked the President of the Assembly, in his most languid voice, whether he could possibly have a translation. The quip was, according to Macmillan's own version in his memoirs, 'thought very witty and effective'.[13] At least it seemed to silence Khrushchev.

The quip seemed to have passed Khrushchev by when Macmillan called on him later that evening at the Soviet Mission. They spent one and three-quarter hours in fruitless discussion, not least because Khrushchev was hoarse after all his shouting and, in fact, 'was subdued, speaking almost in a whisper'.[14] Macmillan himself found Khrushchev polite but distant. There was no mention in their meeting of a further meeting between Khrushchev and Eisenhower. That was confirmed when

Khrushchev returned Macmillan's call to say farewell – in a much quieter mood – on 2 October. (In fact, Khrushchev had one more explosion. After Macmillan had left New York, the debate dragged on and Khrushchev became more and more bored. Finally, when a Philippine delegate attacked the Soviet Union, he took off one of his sandals – he was always too impatient, or lazy, to tie up laces on to shoes – and used it to bang the table in front of him. The action, needless to say, made headlines throughout the world.)

By that time Macmillan had a further health problem. While in New York he had developed a noticeable limp, so obvious that there was comment about it in the New York press. It was, so he said, the result of the Somme wound of 1916, which always troubled him when he was tired. On his return to London on 6 October his leg was so painful that he had to have treatment for it in hospital. As it happened, his mood, already irritable because of the pain in his leg, was on the same day made immediately worse by the news that the report of the Monckton Commission on the constitutional future of the Central African Federation had leaked.

In fact, the leaker might well have been the Prime Minister of the Central African Federation, Roy Welensky, himself. He had written to his old friend Lord Salisbury on 21 September saying that he had just received his copy – and that it was 'a shocking document. Very briefly, the recommendations are that a secession clause should now be inserted in the [Federal] Constitution allowing any of the three parties to secede when they reach a certain degree of responsible government.' But, he went on, 'Macmillan gave me an assurance – I have it in black and white for what it's worth – that the Commission would not consider secession or any looser form of Federation.'[15] He also, in violation of all the norms of diplomatic behaviour, sent Salisbury some confidential attachments to the report. Salisbury read them 'as you may imagine, with the greatest interest, and have now, as you asked, burnt them'.[16]

It was not easy. Macmillan himself admitted that 'the Monckton Commission *has* gone beyond the strict terms of reference in one respect – the suggestion of a possible right to "secede" at some future date in some undefined circumstances'.[17] But he thought that Welensky ought in the end to approve the report since it recommended above all that the Federation should continue since it was in everybody's interest for it to do so. Both Salisbury and Welensky, however, felt that Macmillan was simply acting in bad faith – and that his true intention was to break up the Federation. They were neither of them in the least pacified by the official statement on the report's publication on 11 October admitting formally that Welensky indeed had a case. Macmillan tried to placate

Salisbury, who, he thought, 'is in a very sour and pessimistic mood',[18] by appointing Salisbury's (and Dorothy's) nephew Andrew, the current Duke of Devonshire, as Parliamentary Under-Secretary at Commonwealth Relations, but to no avail. From then on, and for the rest of their lives as it happened, Salisbury and Macmillan were hardly on speaking terms.

Macmillan's mood at the time was also rather 'sour and pessimistic'. He was suffering badly from the pain in his leg. He even told the Queen that he might have to resign because of it – but, when she heard this, rather disappointingly 'she did not react with the consternation he had expected'. (She was presumably relieved at the prospect of not hearing any more long lectures.) He also told Tim Bligh that 'we'd really better start thinking about the succession'.[19] Nevertheless, after cancelling an appearance at the Royal Opera House of a performance in honour of the King and Queen of Nepal, he was quite happy to take the overnight train to Scotland for some more shooting with the Homes.

There was at the time, of course, a good deal of frivolous comment about his overriding fondness for shooting and there were many cartoons poking fun at him. But, by the end of October, that changed. Political eyes were by then firmly focused on the US Presidential election. The two main candidates were studied, as might be imagined, with meticulous care. Macmillan already knew Nixon, who had won the Republican nomination, but he had not met John Fitzgerald Kennedy, the Democratic candidate. The omens, however, were not good. Kennedy's father, a self-made Irish American Catholic, had served an unhappy period from 1937 to late 1940 as US Ambassador in London. He and his wife had much enjoyed London social life, but had done little of note apart from advising Roosevelt in 1940 at all costs to stay out of the war since Hitler had already won and Britain was finished. But Macmillan saw at least a shaft of light. Such had been the Ambassador's enjoyment of London social life that his daughter had met and, in the course of time, married a Cavendish – Dorothy's nephew, William Hartington. His death at the end of the war in 1944, and her subsequent death in a plane crash, had cut what remained of the Cavendish connection, but Macmillan was clever enough to see a way to revive it. The appointment of another Cavendish, Andrew Devonshire, to a Government job was not just a sop to Lord Salisbury. It could prove most useful with the next President.

Kennedy duly won the election – albeit by the narrowest of margins. Macmillan then had to work out his best approach. He was not much helped by Jock Whitney, who, in a gossipy mood, described Kennedy as 'a strange character ... obstinate, sensitive, ruthless and highly-sexed'.[20] He also knew that Kennedy was not going to be another Eisenhower –

with shared wartime memories. Ruminating on this during a trip to Rome in late November to see the Pope, he came to the conclusion that the best approach was to set out in writing some broad ideas on international affairs and see how Kennedy reacted to them. It was a task which he decided to set himself for the 1960 Christmas holidays.

It was Kennedy, in fact, who took the initiative. On 16 December a message came from him through Caccia that he would welcome a meeting, possibly in March. Macmillan immediately sat down to draft a reply. It was to be by way of an aperitif to the main memorandum which he would write later, with one or two exciting ideas but not too pompous or lecturing or too radical. He duly spent the whole of one morning trying his hand at various drafts. The one thing which was ruled out, on the advice of Menzies (and the australian ambassador in Washington), was to try to pressure Kennedy into a summit conference before he was ready. He therefore ended up by suggesting, rather meekly, that the struggle with communism was essentially economic, and that capitalism should be directed towards winning it by concentrating on spreading economic growth and employment, particularly in developing countries. It was, of course, in a slightly different form, to be the theme of his memorandum – Western unity in the face of communism – but it was hardly a very exciting idea, and Kennedy's response, delivered through Caccia, was little more than polite.

The more considered memorandum – Macmillan's Christmas home-work – was apparently to be known as the 'Grand Design'. Although he stayed in bed all of 23 December thinking about it, he was up and about for Christmas Day – 'a very happy day' – and, at last, after days of fog and rain, 'a very jolly shoot – killing over 150 pheasants' on the 27th.[21] On 30 December, however, after hearing London gossip at lunch with Ava Waverley, he went – again by himself – to Chequers. There was to be more thought about the 'Grand Design'.

In the end, it turned out to be not too complicated. In fact, Macmillan's conclusions can be easily summarised. The communist regimes, he thought, particularly the Soviet Union and China, had been doing far too well for the past eight years. This was because the Western world was divided in the same way as Europe was divided in the nineteenth century. The West would not succeed against the East unless Europe was united and there was a general agreement between a united Europe and America. Since France was the key to Western European unity, and de Gaulle was the key to France, there had to be a joint and convincing effort to persuade him that the whole construct was in France's own best interest.

That, of course, was to be the trick. Macmillan's solution, as it had been all along, was to satisfy de Gaulle's nuclear ambitions in order to achieve the desired unity – starting with the resolution of the problem of 'Sixes and Sevens'. But to pay the price, conceding to de Gaulle his nuclear ambitions, he needed Kennedy's support. A programme was therefore set up with that in mind: the 'Grand Design' was to be agreed by departments and then by Cabinet; it was to be sold to de Gaulle at the end of January, to be squared with Adenauer in the middle of February; and, finally, after a meeting of Commonwealth Prime Ministers in early March, all would be followed by a visit to the West Indies at the end of March and, in the first week of April, by the conclusive visit to Kennedy in Washington.

The programme made a good start. Macmillan's ploy in appointing Dorothy's nephew Devonshire as a Minister paid off. The Duke and Duchess went to Washington for Kennedy's inauguration – and were given special treatment both by the new President and by his family. Devonshire was invited into the Presidential box for the parade and both were invited to the ball in the evening. When he returned to London Devonshire told Macmillan all about it – which gave the opportunity for another graceful letter of thanks. Moreover, Macmillan was able to add in his letter, flatteringly, 'what a great impression your inaugural speech has made in this country. Everyone here is struck by its content as well as by its form. We were particularly struck by your phrase about considering what the United States and other countries can together do for the freedom of man. In that search, however long and perilous it may be, we are your enthusiastic allies.'[22]

Nevertheless, it was obviously going to be a long struggle to get the 'Grand Design' agreed by all concerned. For a start, Macmillan's talks with de Gaulle at the end of January 1961 were hardly encouraging. Admittedly, Rambouillet was more comfortable. He and Dorothy were put in the same suite of rooms as before, but this time at least the rooms were heated, the bath water was hot and there were enough bedclothes. On the other hand, de Gaulle himself, although friendly, was in a rather prickly mood. He complained that 'tripartism' was not working well enough and 'he did not see how it was possible for the Commonwealth and the Six to make an economic community without destroying one or the other' and, on the suggestion that experts from both sides should meet to find a way forward, he replied that 'the experts in France had had such difficulties with the Common Market that it was true that they were daunted at the prospect of yet another negotiation'.[23] In the end, he grudgingly accepted that officials should hold talks on the matter during February – but he did not hold out much hope of success. The nuclear issue was left in the air. Not discouraged, however, Macmillan, for his part, came away thinking that they had made good progress.

The results of Rambouillet were quickly sent off both to Kennedy and Adenauer. Both, in turn, responded that it was all very interesting – and they looked forward (Kennedy with interest and Adenauer more doubtfully) to hearing what would happen next. What happened next, in fact, was that Macmillan became embroiled in a series of fierce but arcane domestic disputes – who should have been appointed Archbishop of Canterbury, whether the Queen had been right to get involved in a tiger shoot at the beginning of her visit to India, a spat over a publishing takeover – and an equally fierce but less arcane dispute about the future of Northern Rhodesia, with Macleod threatening again to resign if there was no progress towards African majority government and Welensky again threatening unilaterally to declare the Central African Federation independent of Britain.

That particular dispute quickly got very much worse. By the third week of March Macmillan was writing that he had had '3 weeks of continuous crisis – the worst I remember since the days before Suez . . . I have had very little sleep – sometimes not more than 2 or 3 hours a night . . . There have been 4 separate crises going on at once – 1. N Rhodesia (first stage) involving a possible break up of the Government and/or a revolutionary movement by Sir Roy Welensky. 2. Financial crisis, threatening collapse of sterling. 3. Commonwealth crisis . . . withdrawal of S Africa from Commonwealth. 4. S Rhodesia – second stage, with fresh threats from Sir Roy W and possible Cabinet crisis.'[24] Lord Salisbury had formed another 'watching group' of disaffected Conservatives ('rather a ragamuffin lot', Macmillan thought[25]).

On top of all that, another crisis was blowing up – this time in South East Asia. There had been a communist insurrection in Laos against the King and his Government. The communist insurgents, the Pathet Lao, had been liberally supplied with armaments in airlifts by the Soviets and had made some important military advances – largely because the Royal Laotian Army appeared to have no stomach for the fight. In what was his first international crisis, Kennedy was determined to stand up. He announced that a neutral and peaceful Laos, as had been agreed as long ago as 1954 in the settlement of the Indo-Chinese war against the French colonial power, should be supported by all countries with an interest in the area. Moreover, 'those who supported a neutral Laos would have to consider their responsibilities' and he 'had specifically referred to the obligations of the United States Government under the South-East Asia Treaty Organisation [SEATO] pact'.[26] That, of course, meant the use of force. His allies, including Britain, had the same obligations.

Macmillan was horrified. The idea of Britain committing troops in a South East Asian civil war – after the trauma of the Suez episode of not more than five years back – was almost more than he could take. Finally, at half past one in the morning of 23 March, his Cabinet agreed on a message to Kennedy pointing out all the difficulties of military inter- vention in Laos, the problem of Commonwealth reaction, the probable reaction in the United Nations, but, if he decided after all that to go in he would have (reluctant) British support. With that message, as it were, in his pocket, Macmillan, Dorothy, John Wyndham, Tim Bligh and (by now inevitably) his doctor Sir John Richardson, on the following morning, 24 March, boarded the RAF Comet for the West Indies.

The morning after their arrival in Trinidad a telegram came from Kennedy saying that he was very anxious to meet Macmillan to discuss the Laos question before a meeting of SEATO due to take place shortly in Bangkok. With his officials Kennedy had earlier complained about 'the weakness of allied support for our position ... he proposed that, if the British and French aren't going to do anything about the security of Southeast Asia, we tell them we aren't going to do it alone. They have as much or more to lose in the area than we have.'[27] He now wanted to guarantee British support for military intervention – under whatever banner it might ride.

Macmillan hastily consulted his senior colleagues. They all agreed that he should go to the meeting which Kennedy had suggested at the naval base of Key West in Florida but that they could not support sending even a token British force to South East Asia without further discussion. Macmillan accordingly took off from Trinidad early on 26 March and arrived at Key West in mid-morning in time for a meeting and discussion over lunch – before returning to Trinidad in the afternoon.

It was Macmillan's and Kennedy's first meeting. Macmillan was later said to be 'apprehensive ... as to whether the President would think he was a funny old man who belonged to the distant past and couldn't understand the problems of the day ...'.[28] Kennedy struck Macmillan as 'a curious mixture of qualities – courteous, quiet, quick, decisive – and tough'.[29] After Macmillan had explained his objections to a large military operation under a SEATO umbrella, Kennedy said that he had in mind a much more modest affair, designed to hold an enclave in Laos in order to demonstrate that he was not going to be pushed around by the Soviets. Macmillan had his doubts but agreed in the end that it might be politically necessary to take some sort of action. It was not a very happy compromise but at least it allowed Macmillan to see Kennedy face to face – and to leave for the return trip to Trinidad without an immediate rupture in their new relationship.

The next few days were spent pleasantly enough – and included Easter in Jamaica. Yet before he left Key West Macmillan had asked Kennedy, almost by way of polite enquiry, whether he had any particular preference for Caccia's replacement as British Ambassador in Washington. The answer came back like a bullet: David Ormsby Gore. He was, Kennedy explained, not just a distant relative and a pre-war acquaintance of his, but he was a particular friend of Kennedy's brother Bobby. Macmillan suddenly became aware both that there was a change in the Washington atmosphere – a President more or less dictating British representation there – but, almost more important, that there was a new '*éminence grise*' in the form of the Attorney-General, the President's younger brother.

On 4 April Macmillan and his party left for Washington and his second meeting with Kennedy. The next day was reserved for discussions at the White House, apart from a break just before lunch when Kennedy took Macmillan upstairs to meet his wife, Jacqueline. Kennedy and his Secretary of State, Dean Rusk, spent most of the time listening rather than talking, while Macmillan and his team went through the main elements of the 'Grand Design'. They laid stress on the need for unity of the free world in response to the communist advance, and the danger of a divided Europe – particularly the prospect of the Six being dominated after de Gaulle by a resurgent post-Adenauer Germany. 'It was really *most* satisfactory,' Macmillan recorded, 'far better than I could have hoped. He seemed to understand and sympathise with most of our plans. How far he will be able to go with de Gaulle to help me I do not know.'[30] What Macmillan meant by this was finding some way to bring France into the nuclear club. The theme was reiterated in a speech he made the next day to an audience of some four thousand at the Massachusetts Institute of Technology in Boston.

Kennedy was more forthright about Britain joining the Six. He and Rusk were certainly, as they said, worried about the prospect of a post-Adenauer Germany. Britain should join the EEC as a political counterweight to the de Gaulle France and to the future Germany. On hearing this message loud and clear, Macmillan said to George Ball, Kennedy's Under-Secretary of State, 'we're going to join Europe. We'll need your help, since we have trouble with de Gaulle, but we're going to do it.'[31]

Macmillan had been too quick. On his return to London, he sent, after careful preparation, a letter to Kennedy restating the 'Grand Design' and its premise – allowing de Gaulle into the nuclear club. On 8 May Kennedy sent an equally carefully prepared reply. 'There is one question,' he wrote, 'which I would like to clarify now. After a careful review of the problem, I have come to the conclusion that it would be undesirable to assist France's efforts to create a nuclear weapons capability. I am most anxious that no erroneous impressions get abroad regarding future US policy in this respect ...'[32] In other words, not only did Kennedy refuse to give Macmillan the entry card into the EEC which he had requested but he had told him on no account to hint to de Gaulle that there might be any change in US policy. The 'Grand Design', such as it was, had fallen on Washington's stony ground. If Macmillan wanted to pursue British entry into the EEC he would have to do it without his American entry ticket.

24

'I *Am* Ageing'

Kennedy had not been entirely frank. What he had not told Macmillan in Washington was that the Central Intelligence Agency had hatched a daring plan – bordering, in fact, on fantasy – code-named 'Bumpy Road'. The idea was to send a motley group of Cuban exiles on an expedition to Cuba to rouse what was expected to be an immediate popular revolt against the regime of Fidel Castro. As it happened, the plan, when put into action, turned out to be, as one historian put it, 'one of those rare events in history – a perfect failure'.[1] Landing at the Bay of Pigs in Cuba on the morning of 17 April 1961, without proper air support and having lost their principal supply ship, the fourteen hundred or so bedraggled exiles were met by some twenty thousand Cuban troops well armed with Russian weapons. The exiles duly surrendered with hardly a fight.

Gradually the news filtered through to the White House. When he heard the full extent of the fiasco, towards the end of a late-night meeting, Kennedy walked out – apparently almost in mid-sentence – and spent an hour by himself pacing up and down in the White House Rose Garden. It did not stop there. The next morning Pierre Salinger, Kennedy's Press Secretary, 'found him crying in his bedroom'.[2] The humiliation, for a young President who had come in with such high hopes, was crushing.

The plan for the Bay of Pigs invasion had been, of course, devised in secret, with surprisingly few leaks even in the Cuban community in Miami. The British Embassy in Washington had realised that something was afoot but were not quite sure what it was. When the true nature of the fiasco was revealed, the British, and the world, thought the whole thing a fine joke. But once the world's uproarious laughter had subsided, Macmillan was quick to see that Kennedy's humiliation had possible benefits.

First and foremost, Kennedy's initial enthusiasm for armed intervention in Laos had disappeared. It was no longer any good relying on overenthusiastic spies – or generals, for that matter – when the reputation of the United States was at stake and liable to ridicule. The result, as it happened, was a Presidential instruction to seek a negotiated ceasefire in

Laos and the reconvening of the International Commission in Geneva to decide the country's future as independent and neutral in its own right. So far, as it were, so helpful to Macmillan.

Secondly, Kennedy recognised that he would do well to pay rather more attention to what he might be told by those more experienced in foreign affairs. After all, as he said in an almost desperate appeal to Nixon for support, 'it really is true that foreign affairs is the only important issue for a President to handle, isn't it?' and then, 'I mean, who gives a shit if the minimum wage is $1.15 or $1.25, in comparison to something like this?' Even Eisenhower, whom Kennedy had previously thought to be merely ancient and grumpy, was wheeled in. 'There is only one thing to do when you get into this kind of thing,' the old General had told him. 'It must be a success.'[3] Eisenhower then went on to say that Kennedy would be wise if he paid attention to another ageing gentleman – the sixty-seven-year-old British Prime Minister. The point was duly taken. Kennedy, as always, was quick to learn. That, too, was helpful to Macmillan.

The result came soon enough. On 4 June the President and Mrs Kennedy arrived in London. It had been announced as a private visit, to attend the christening of Jackie's niece, the daughter of her sister, Princess Radziwill. The two came from a social triumph in Paris, where the glamorous young couple had taken the city by storm. Kennedy himself had emerged from a bruising encounter with Khrushchev in Vienna – and with an excruciatingly painful back. But although it was a private visit, Kennedy did not simply want to appear 'in the role of a cheerful uncle'.[4] There were, accordingly, to be official events (a dinner at Buckingham Palace, for instance) as well as a meeting and lunch at Admiralty House.

As he wrote after their visit (Macmillan had by then become 'Dear Harold'), 'London felt near home to us all.'[5] The remark was clearly meant. In fact, Kennedy's London visit in June 1961 marked the start of what was to become a surprisingly close personal relationship between the younger and the older man. But at first there was disappointment. Kennedy had to admit that his efforts to persuade de Gaulle of the merits of British entry into the EEC – and he had tried hard, as he had promised – had not been particularly successful. He reported that de Gaulle had been cordial but aloof ('very avuncular, very gracious, very oracular and very unyielding'[6]) – but that, perhaps by design, the social events, magnificent as they had been, had limited the time available for serious conversation.

De Gaulle's own position had been, ahead of Kennedy's visit, immeasurably strengthened by his success in April in neutralising an insurrection

Shooting party with the Duke and Duchess of Devonshire near
Bolton Abbey, 1960

Macmillan shooting left-
handed (due to weakness
from a war wound in his
right hand)

Macmillan, Dorothy
and six grandchildren
at Birch Grove House

Macmillan arrives in Moscow to be greeted by Khruschev, February 1959

Macmillan and Butler,
April 1959

The General Election
of October, 1959

Macmillan carried
through the breakers
during his visit to
Ghana, January 1960

The newly elected
Chancellor of
Oxford, April 1960

Macmillan at the United
Nations, September 1960

Macmillan's first meeting with Kennedy, Key West, March 1961

Dorothy playing golf at Gleneagles

In No. 10 Downing Street just before the move

Leaving No. 10 in August 1960, and returning in October 1963

General and Mme de Gaulle with the Macmillans in front of Birch Grove House, November 1961

" VOILA, THIS IS WHAT YOU CALL 'HIT FOR SIX', NON ..? "

'Vicky' in the *Evening Standard*, 15 January 1963

Macmillan walking with Lord Home in St James's Park, April 1963

The Queen leaving King Edward VII Hospital after seeing Macmillan, October 1963

Macmillan and John Wyndham, December 1968

Eileen O'Casey

Alexander Macmillan's marriage to Bridget Hamilton (Macmillan and Maurice supporting), September 1970

Old friends: Macmillan and Diana Cooper

in Algiers led by four senior French generals. At the height of the crisis he had appealed over their heads to the French Army and, dramatically, to the French people – and had won. At the time, the world had held its collective breath. Macmillan, at Birch Grove, had listened to de Gaulle's broadcast on the radio most carefully (there was still no television at Birch Grove apart from small sets in 'Nanny's' house at the lodge gates and in Pooks Cottage) and with the greatest admiration. This, at last, was the de Gaulle he had known in Algiers – unyielding in adversity and with limitless courage. He sat down and wrote an elegant and effusive personal message. In turn, the General replied with a suitably charming letter in his own hand. It was, once again, all smiles between the two.

Thus encouraged, and believing that de Gaulle might be mellowing towards the prospect of British entry to the EEC, on Sunday 18 June Macmillan summoned Ministers and a number of senior officials to Chequers to move his project forward. But, as he noted afterwards in disappointment, the discussions did not get very far. There was no unanimity among Cabinet Ministers about the merits of entry in the first place – Butler was particularly dubious. Furthermore, even during the weekend the whole issue was complicated by renewed rumblings from Welensky about the constitutional future of the Central African Federation, which had in turn stirred the right wing of the Conservative Party. Butler, and others, felt that disaffection over the Rhodesias would spill over into opposition to the EEC. In the event, the only agreement that was reached was to allow selected Ministers ('the St John the Baptists', Macmillan called them[7]) to set out on a tour of Commonwealth countries to test their governments' reaction to a possible British application.

While they were away on their journeys Macmillan tried to take a few days off at Birch Grove. He said he was not feeling well – he had a bad cold and had nearly lost his voice. Richardson said that he really needed a month's rest, but the rows over the constitutional proposals for the Rhodesias had become so bitter (Macleod and Home had fallen out – Home was even threatening to resign) that he was sent for in London to sort them out. 'I am beginning (at last)', he wrote, 'to feel old and depressed.'[8]

The problems were indeed piling up. Towards the end of June he reflected on them in his diary. There was Berlin (no solution in sight), Laos (civil war to erupt again at any moment), Europe (opinion on the Continent at best uncertain, at worst hostile to Britain), Central Africa and the Rhodesias (just a faint glimmer of light here – Home and Macleod made it up and Welensky at last seemed ready to accept the British constitutional proposals for Northern Rhodesia), the economic situation (getting worse) and, to cap it all, the Iraqis (threatening to overrun Kuwait). 'All this concentration of work', Macmillan reflected, '. . . has tired me greatly. It is quite an effort now to make an effort. But I cannot leave the ship now. I must try to get her into calmer waters before I do so.'⁹

It was a careful, and very deliberate, reflection, which marks a subtle – but significant – change. Until then, the idea of resignation or even of recognising a possible terminal point of his Premiership had never been given any more than a passing thought. Now, for the first time, the idea of resignation had risen to the surface of his mind – and had been recorded in his diary.

He was not alone in his reflection. Others had noticed the tiredness. One journalist was emphatic, telling Harold Evans, 'He's tired and worn out.'¹⁰ The London press was almost universally critical. They were even more so when Selwyn Lloyd announced, on 25 July, a series of measures designed to correct what had become a dangerous balance of payments deficit, including an expression which quickly joined other such expressions in political vocabulary – a 'pay pause'. 'Macmillan at Bay' was only one example – this from the *Daily Mail.*¹¹ It was said that he was slowing down, and when he made a poor speech, interrupted by Labour catcalls, when winding up the economic debate in the House of Commons, more than one commentator thought that his time was certainly up.

Macmillan seemed never to mind attacks from the press or even assaults from his opponents in the House of Commons. But on this occasion he did mind being roughed up in debate by Gaitskell, who had accused him of 'Edwardian nonchalance', and by Gaitskell's deputy, the rather less than sober George Brown. In a fury, he sat down and composed a paragraph which he intended to use in a future speech. 'Mr Gaitskell', his draft ran, 'accuses me of what he calls Edwardian nonchalance – what others have called unflappability. I think that if he had a little more experience of life, he would know that sometimes in dangerous moments it is advisable, even if one feels alarm, to cultivate an outward show of confidence. I learned that in early youth under fire on the battlefield. Unfortunately, for reasons which I wholly understand, this experience was not vouchsafed to Mr Gaitskell, Mr Wilson, Mr Brown, Mr Jay and the other leading members of the Labour front bench.'¹² It was Macmillan at his worst – arrogant, patronising and vindictive. But he was sensible enough to send his draft to George Christ at Conservative Central Office for his opinion. Christ tactfully replied that he liked the idea 'but I am not sure that it would come best from you'.¹³ That was enough. Macmillan retreated. The offending paragraph was never used.

Leaving behind his momentary tantrum, Macmillan soon realised that the deteriorating economic situation could in fact be used as evidence of the wisdom of applying to join the EEC. But, even so, the hurdles seemed to get higher by the day. The 'St John the Baptist' ministers returned to report to the Cabinet, on 18 and 21 July, that all members of the Commonwealth who had been consulted had serious worries. Some even thought that the Commonwealth would break up. But Macmillan pointed out at the meeting of 21 July that although that might be the case it was necessary to make a statement of some sort to Parliament before the summer Recess. Either they should say that they were now prepared to enter into negotiations 'which would show whether we could secure satisfactory safeguards for the Commonwealth, for our partners in EFTA and for UK agriculture' or they should say that they 'were considering the important issues raised by their consultations with other Commonwealth Governments and that a decision would not be announced until after the recess'.[14]

Faced with these alternatives, the Cabinet decided, in spite of outright opposition from Maudling and Hailsham and no more than lukewarm support from Butler, that 'the right course was to enter into negotiations with the EEC and to announce at once that we intended to do so'.[15] But Macmillan did not leave it there. With his mind on Kennedy and de Gaulle, it was, he asserted yet again, all part of the 'Grand Design'. 'The prospect of our membership might be held out as a step towards the larger concept of a union of the Free World. From inside the Community, indeed, we might hope to transform it into an outward-looking *group of nations* [italics in original], mindful of its responsibilities to the world as a whole.'[16]

On 27 July the Cabinet met again. Macmillan this time – unexpectedly – played truant. He was at the time in Admiralty House, apparently busy preparing his speech for the evening in the Commons. He may also have been feeling ill and nervously sick before what was to be a big Parliamentary occasion. Equally, all the Cabinet had to do was to confirm the decision of the 21st and to decide on the procedures. Yet it is hard not to believe that Macmillan's absence on the occasion – which, after all, was the point at which a British Cabinet finally decided on a truly momentous shift in British history – was deliberate and tactical. Butler, one of the most ambivalent supporters of Government policy on the matter, would have to chair the Cabinet and preside over the decision – something which Macmillan, ever the politician, could store up for future use if and when necessary.

The Cabinet duly decided that there should be a Statement in Parliament on 31 July announcing the Government's intention, followed by a two-day debate in the Commons on 2 and 3 August. In fact, and strangely, even at the outset, it was not entirely certain what the intention was. The Cabinet discussed two versions of the Statement, one of which proclaimed the intention to start negotiations with a view to success; the other, more muted, stated that the application was necessary under Article 237 of the Treaty of Rome to discover whether there was any possibility at all of success. In the course of the discussion it was noted that at least thirty Conservative MPs were supporting a Motion 'expressing opposition to any material derogation of British sovereignty ...'[17] The Cabinet, in the light of this, ended ambiguously. It was left to Macmillan to decide which of the two versions of the Statement should be used.

There was never any doubt about which version Macmillan would choose. He was clear that if the step was taken, as he had wanted it to be, it had to be taken with enthusiasm. The announcement was duly made on Monday 31 July. Macmillan noted that the Conservatives were 'anxious and rather jumpy'.[18] The US Under-Secretary of State, George Ball, thought that 'Macmillan attempted to slide sideways into the Common Market'.[19] The London press was hostile. Worse, however, was to come. Between the Statement and the Commons debate the press ran more rumours about Macmillan's health. He was, apparently, tired, failing and losing his grip. Two newspapers even picked up a report from Tokyo that he had suffered a heart attack. The alarm was immediately sounded in Admiralty House, and the Queen even asked him about it at the regular weekly Tuesday audience.

The press hostility then suddenly became markedly more offensive. But, as is frequently the case, it had been sparked by an episode which had nothing to do with the issues of the moment, Macmillan's health and the EEC. It so happened that the Lobby had been particularly riled by Macmillan's performance at a meeting on the Monday of the Statement. He had lunched at Buck's, had taken the pills which Richardson had given him – stimulants to help get him through the Statement – and arrived at the meeting 'with post-prandial glow ... swung the chairman's gavel perilously backwards and forwards, talked about the trenches and how they enabled you to appear calm when you felt terrified, said that he could still do the eighteenth in four and that he was now going to let off three or four hundred cartridges – on which cue he did, in fact, suddenly get up and go'.[20] The assembled journalists (themselves normally spectacularly bibulous) duly took the deepest offence. The Prime Minister's behaviour, all agreed, was outrageous. The personal attacks on him accordingly moved up in volume.

By the time of his opening speech on the Wednesday Macmillan was himself again. He put on a supremely professional performance and was listened to without interruption. Two days later he made a successful broadcast, most of which he had written himself. The Parliamentary

Session had thus come to a satisfactory, if slightly rocky, end. The press, of course, declared him to have 'bounced right back'.[21] But, whatever the mood in Westminster, there were still worries. Berlin was one – Khrushchev had started to squeeze again in his meeting with Kennedy in Vienna; a contingent of British troops had been sent to Kuwait; and the nuclear test talks at Geneva were at a standstill. With the arrival of the summer Recess, it was time to take a holiday, but, as Macmillan noted, there was never a good time for a Prime Minister to take a holiday.

Nevertheless, there was time to turn back to Trollope and to staying in bed in the mornings. 'Of course,' he admitted, 'it's a sign of old age and mental laziness to re-read books one knows so well. But I *am* ageing, and I do deserve a bit of mental relaxation.'[22] But, mental relaxation apart, the grouse were already waiting, and on 14 August he left for three days' shooting at Swinton (his party managed six hundred brace), followed by six days at Bolton Abbey (this time, for six guns, it was nearly one thousand brace). Then it was a train from York to Edinburgh where he was met by Dorothy and driven to Gleneagles.

The following morning, Saturday 25 August, Macmillan and Dorothy went out to play golf on the King's Course. Irritatingly, they were pestered by reporters and photographers. There was, in fact, some reason. The East Germans had blocked off access from east to west Berlin with barriers of barbed wire to prevent the daily exodus of three thousand or so refugees to the West. The journalists wanted to know whether Macmillan would be returning immediately to London to deal with what was obviously an international crisis. On the eighteenth fairway one particularly persistent journalist so annoyed Macmillan that he lost his temper. 'Nobody is going to fight about Berlin,' he snapped. Not content with that, he went on with 'I think it is all got up by the Press'.[23] Needless to say, the Sunday papers splashed his remarks on their front pages. It took all the skill of Harold Evans to calm things down. Moreover, the US Ambassador, David Bruce, cabled Dean Rusk that the 'Foreign Office spent [a] "ghastly" Saturday trying to explain away ... the Gleneagles remark ... PM ... sent message to President saying in effect he goofed'.[24] Macmillan did indeed send a shamefaced message to Kennedy. He also took the point: it was unwise to give impromptu press conferences on the eighteenth fairway at Gleneagles.

After that excitement, the annual visit to Balmoral passed off without incident. Macmillan seemed by then to be getting on better with the Duke of Edinburgh – who turned out to be a surprisingly good cook on a lunchtime picnic. Dorothy, as usual, afterwards stayed on in Scotland and Macmillan flew back to London. Immediately, there was business to be done: drafting a declaration after another Russian H-bomb test in the atmosphere, to be sent jointly with Kennedy and proposing to Khrushchev a halt to all tests in the atmosphere without exception, reading boxes, discussing with Martin Redmayne, the Chief Whip, about a possible ministerial and Party reshuffle, settling with Pierson Dixon, the British Ambassador in Paris, that he should lead the team of officials (Heath leading the ministerial team) in the negotiations over the EEC, and, finally, allowing a little time for a discussion with Maurice about the future of the Macmillan publishing house.

Soon, however, it was back again to Scotland. On 6 September Macmillan took the night train to Inverness, where he was met by Dorothy and driven to Nairn for a few more days of golf – as it happened, in beautiful weather. Much on his mind, however, was the reshuffle. The talk with Redmayne during his brief stay in London (Selwyn Lloyd had been brought in as well) had been in no great detail. In fact, what Macmillan had in mind was to replace Butler as Chairman with a younger Minister – he had Macleod as the favoured candidate. Yet Redmayne was already warning him that it would not be easy. The faithful, he pointed out, would not take kindly to what would appear as yet another Butler humiliation on the eve of the Party Conference in October.

Nor, indeed, was anything easy. By mid-September, back again in London, there were many diversions to take his mind off the reshuffle. The province of Katanga – mineral-rich and near neighbour of the Central African Federation – had decided to secede from the Congo, and the United Nations had decided to use force to claw it back. In the middle of it all Dag Hammarskjöld's plane had crashed and he had been killed, leaving the United Nations rudderless. Laos was still likely to erupt at any moment. Kennedy had suddenly decided that, far from resorting to force over Berlin, he was prepared to negotiate with the Soviets. On top of all that, Macmillan's old friend Harry Crookshank was dying of cancer, Macmillan himself was suffering from gout, the Conservatives were slumping in the Gallup poll and Dorothy was away in Ireland. In short, nothing was at all easy.

By early October, however, there had been a break in the gloomy clouds. Butler, in an anguished but selfless display of loyalty, had agreed to give up the chairmanship of the Party and the Leadership of the House of Commons. In a distressed comment, he wrote, 'I was told that I was too old and had anyway done the House for six years . . . But I now face singularly unpleasant resolutions at the Party conference [on hanging and birching] shorn of two plumes and retaining only the Home Office.'[25] Macleod, in turn, accepted the job of Chairman of the Party and Leader of the House of Commons, thus allowing Macmillan to put Maudling in as Colonial Secretary – and so avoid the constant rows between

Ministers at the Colonial Office and the Commonwealth Relations Office. Butler was to be given some (nebulous) responsibilities on Cabinet Committees, including the ministerial Committee overseeing the EEC negotiations, but could not, according to Macmillan, be given the title of Deputy Prime Minister. The fact that he had been doing the job anyway for some four and a half years seemed to be neither here nor there. All was settled in the end, however, and on 9 October the ministerial changes were duly announced.

Macmillan thought that he should explain the changes to Kennedy. To do this, he was able, rather than passing messages through the US Embassy, to talk directly to the President. A new American-designed secure 'scrambler' telephone had been installed, providing direct communication between Admiralty House and the White House. It was, of course, primitive by the standards of today. It broke down frequently and, in order to speak through it, it had to be activated on either side by a particularly inconvenient button. Nevertheless, it did provide a way for Macmillan to speak directly to Kennedy – without referring to his Foreign Secretary or his Ambassador. (The apparatus, of course, convenient as it was to Macmillan, could have caused chaos if either Home had been more assertive as Foreign Secretary or if the British Ambassador in Washington had been more prickly.)

In fact, Home seemed perfectly content to follow in his master's footsteps, and Harold Caccia, a Foreign Office career diplomat, was finally replaced by Kennedy's own nominee, David Ormsby Gore. Eminently suitable, Ormsby Gore, or simply 'Gore', as he was known in Washington, was a Conservative MP, a Foreign Office Minister, a relation by marriage of both Macmillan and Kennedy, the heir to a peerage and, on his appointment, the recipient of a knighthood. Indeed, so close was the family connection, and the friendship with both the President and his brother Bobby that one commentator claimed that 'apart from when the President was abroad, there were only three or four weekends during the ambassador's tenure and Kennedy's presidency when the Ormsby Gores were not with the Kennedys'.[26]

Nevertheless, when Ormsby Gore arrived formally in Washington he was faced with an immediate problem. Macmillan's proposal for a joint US–UK statement calling for a moratorium on atmospheric testing of nuclear warheads was still on the diplomatic table. At least, if the United States wished to test, Macmillan wanted to be fully consulted. But, as Kennedy's head of the National Security Council, McGeorge Bundy, pointed out, 'the Prime Minister is trying to get you hooked to an agreement not to test without his consent. This is dirty pool.' (By way of explanation, 'Pool' is sometimes known as 'Bar Billiards'.)[27] Kennedy ill

accepted the advice and said as much to Ormsby Gore – who duly assured the President that the Prime Minister would quite understand the position.

During the course of their conversation Ormsby Gore mentioned to Kennedy that Macmillan had invited de Gaulle to cross the Channel for a quiet talk about Berlin, to try to soften his hard line about negotiations with the Soviets and, of course, in addition to discuss the British application to join the EEC. In fact, the negotiations for the visit had not run altogether smoothly. Macmillan had invited de Gaulle to stay at Chequers. That was turned down, since it would appear to be some sort of official visit. Since de Gaulle had already made an official visit, and since the Queen would be absent, that would not do. The result was an invitation from Macmillan for de Gaulle and Madame de Gaulle to stay with him and Dorothy at Birch Grove.

Macmillan thought the whole arrangement inconvenient. Birch Grove House was not equipped for large official parties. In fact, without realising it, he had paid de Gaulle the greatest compliment – to be invited to stay in somebody else's home. In Britain such invitations were commonplace, but in France they were rare and much prized. De Gaulle replied with an emphatic and enthusiatic '*Oui!*' Indeed, only three years earlier he had himself paid the same compliment to Adenauer, inviting him to the modest house in Colombey-les-deux-Églises. In coming to Birch Grove, he hoped to revive his wartime friendship with Mamillan and, in doing so, achieve the same meeting of minds as with Adenauer at Colombey.

As with that visit to Colombey, there were in this visit to Birch Grove many logistical problems. Macmillan himself had to surrender his bedroom to make room for de Gaulle's large frame (fortunately, this time de Gaulle did not bring his own bed as he was apt to do) and sleep in the day nursery. De Gaulle brought with him not only a retinue of officials but also a store of blood plasma – he had a rare blood group – and suitable arrangements had to be made to accommodate the officials and the blood. (Macmillan found the matter of the blood a good joke – as it were, vaguely un-English. What his memoirs, in telling the story, do not reveal, however, was that fear of attempted assassination – amply justified in de Gaulle's case – had transferred itself to him. He himself, when he went to Swinton to shoot, 'came with two pints of blood which had to be kept in the fridge'.[28])

De Gaulle and Madame de Gaulle duly arrived on Friday 24 November. Dorothy was detailed to look after Madame, but the two quite clearly failed to get on. The contrast was obvious. Yvonne de Gaulle was a shy, retiring woman, small and stocky. She had a quiet charm but also a certain puritan severity in her character – an inheritance from her

Flemish ancestry. Deeply religious in the Catholic tradition of Normandy, she had been much involved in the campaign to close down the Paris brothels after the war. She was fiercely disapproving of adultery – and hence, it need hardly be said, far from a perfect companion for Dorothy. Dorothy, in turn, who was rumbustious, tall and, by then – not to put too fine a point on it – putting on weight, found Yvonne, apart from the fact that she spoke negligible English, 'a very difficult woman to entertain. She has a thing about people ... Won't go to the Hunt, nor the cripples' [sic] craft school, nor even ... the Pavilion at Brighton.'[29] In the end they settled for a drive to Beachy Head. What they talked about, if, indeed, there was any conversation, is sadly not recorded.

Macmillan did not do much better himself in his talks with de Gaulle. The first topic of discussion was Berlin. De Gaulle was firmly against negotiating with the Soviets. On the contrary, he seemed to be in favour of using military force to break through the barrier dividing the city, which had by then become a wall rather than barbed wire. The discussion went on a long time – with Home doing most of the talking on the British side. Macmillan at one point was seen to cover his face with his hands and seemed to go to sleep (de Zulueta and the French Ambassador both thought that he really did go to sleep) before exploding, 'Oh well, let's have a war then.'[30] De Gaulle took it quite calmly and later chided Macmillan gently for throwing a tantrum. But the most he would offer was to agree that the British and American Ambassadors in Moscow could meet the Soviets to explore 'the basis on which a negotiation might be possible'.[31]

If de Gaulle was not to be moved on Berlin, he was equally unmoved by Macmillan's arguments in favour of British entry into the EEC. True, he did accept that Britain had an important future role in some arrangement with other European states, but felt that 'there was no great hurry' and 'more time was needed'.[32] All in all, and in spite of the optimistic gloss which Macmillan put on the talks in public, in private he called them 'discouraging ... depressing'. 'Charming, affable, mellow as the General now is,' his diary goes on, 'his little pin head is still as small as ever ... inherited hatred of England ... sometimes when I am with him I feel I have overcome it but he goes back to his distrust and dislike, like a dog to his vomit.'[33] What had started as smiles had become some very ungenerous snarls.

De Gaulle's stubbornness on Berlin was duly reported to Kennedy. De Gaulle in his turn reported to Adenauer that Macmillan had made 'a great and sentimental drama' at Birch Grove.[34] Macmillan then went on to tell Kennedy that, in his view, the only way to get de Gaulle to bend was to keep up pressure on Adenauer who, on a recent visit to Washington, had apparently accepted the idea of negotiation with the Soviets over Berlin. Kennedy replied that he thought he still had Adenauer under control, but Macmillan in turn replied that he was afraid that de Gaulle would make him change his mind. At that point, Kennedy sent a message that it would be sensible to meet face to face to try to sort out a common position. It was agreed, on Macmillan's suggestion, that they would meet in Bermuda. The date was fixed for 21 and 22 December. Macmillan duly started his preparations.

There was in the meantime a pleasant diversion – in addition to some exceptionally good shooting. Earlier in the year he had received, along with Jean Monnet, a doctorate from Cambridge University. He was now to be granted the Freedom of the City of London. The ceremony was, as might be imagined, much to his taste – after all, the only two serving Prime Ministers who had been granted the honour before him were the elder Pitt and Churchill. The speeches were formal, needing no preparation, and the Grenadier Guards turned out to form a guard of honour. He hugely enjoyed the whole thing.

But there was also another crisis which blew up suddenly and almost without warning. On 7 December the Cabinet decided – nervously, it is true – to agree to a request from the United Nations to provide twenty-four heavy bombs for use in the Congo against the rebel forces of Katanga. The stipulation was that they should only be used against aircraft on the ground. But that was not enough to pacify the large section of the Conservative Parliamentary Party – some called it the Rhodesia faction – which supported the breakaway Katanga against the Congo as it supported Welensky and the Central African Federation against London. There was even talk in the press of one hundred Conservatives abstaining on a Commons vote on the issue. Harold Wilson, the Labour Foreign Affairs spokesman, told the American Ambassador that it was the most dramatic Parliamentary issue since Suez. Macmillan seemed seriously to believe that the Government might fall, and was badly worried. He even slept poorly for a few days. In the end, however, it turned out to be only a small, but admittedly violent, storm. In the vote on 15 December the Government had a very comfortable majority. By 19 December Macmillan could note that 'we have managed to get the two negro [sic] gentlemen [the respective leaders of Congo and Katanga, Cyrille Adoula and Moise Tshombe] to confer in some neutral spot'.[35] But Macmillan did record that there were between ten and twenty Conservative MPs who were very bitter against him personally and his 'progressive' colleagues in the Cabinet.

At midnight on 19 December Macmillan and his party – Home,

Brook, de Zulueta, three Foreign Office officials and his doctor, Sir John Richardson – left London airport for Bermuda. Kennedy's father had just had a stroke, prompting Macmillan to ask Kennedy whether he would prefer to change the meeting place to Washington or even Palm Beach, but Kennedy preferred to stick to the original plan. On 21 December he arrived in Bermuda. As in London, his back was horribly painful – he was unable to bend down to pick up a book or a piece of paper from the floor. Fortunately, a rocking chair was found which apparently helped a good deal.

The talks were friendly. It was agreed that they would negotiate with the Soviets over Berlin and that they would do all in their power to keep Adenauer in step and to try to bring de Gaulle into line. Both had recently received long letters from Khrushchev restating the Soviet wish for a peace treaty and indicating readiness to negotiate. On nuclear tests, the Soviets had recently tested a 100–megaton hydrogen bomb, which had led the Americans, in their turn, to decide to test in the atmosphere in the spring of 1962 unless there was a breakthrough in the Geneva discussions. The most convenient testing area for them would be the British Pacific island dependency of Christmas Island. Macmillan, almost dutifully, agreed to make the necessary preparations. Finally, Kennedy gave the strongest possible support for the British application to join the EEC. As McGeorge Bundy put it in his briefing to Kennedy, he should 'leave the Prime Minister in no doubt that the way to our hearts is through Europe . . . The British will lose their greatness, and Europe will not survive, *unless* a new, strong, increasingly unified Europe is formed.'[36]

All in all, Macmillan could afford to be pleased with the results of Bermuda, although 'these journeys tire me more and more each time and these discussions take a tremendous lot out of me. The London press continues critical of the Government. Happily, I think the Press, with its gossip and sneering and pomposity and pettiness – as well as its downright lies – is losing influence every day.'[37] He was glad to hear that Kennedy had the same problems with the American press. His tactic, which Macmillan was more and more to adopt himself, was to appeal directly to people by using television and radio.

Kennedy, too, could be pleased. He was beginning to get the measure of Macmillan. In the run-up to Bermuda, Dean Rusk had asked David Bruce for his assessment of the Prime Minister. The response is illuminating. 'I am neither an intimate nor a friend of the PM,' Bruce cabled back:

Few apparently are. His play, to use a gambling expression, is close; and his inmost thoughts are seldom open to penetration. He is a political animal, shrewd, subtle in maneuver, undisputed master in his Cabinet house. I have never heard of his being addressed with levity on serious governmental matters by subordinates or acquaintances, other than partisan opponents. If so, those heavily lidded eyelids would lift, and a contemptuous glance would stare them down.

His opponents think him a cold-blooded but formidable individual. Some liken him to Disraeli, though he lacks the flamboyance of a man who would change from a morning to an afternoon walking stick as the noon bell tolled in Gibraltar. Nor does he have Disraeli's fondness for exotic dress; rather his clothes are sometimes compared with those of English Dukes who have been accused of dressing in the cast-off garments of Irish beggars, though this does Macmillan sartorial injustice.

At times, he gives the impression of being shot through with Edwardian languor. It would be a mistake to infer from this that he is lacking in force or decisiveness, as it would be to deduce from what is called his 'Balliol shuffle' that he is not capable of swift action. In fact, he can featly [sic] spring onto his toes like a ballet dancer, and is a quick gun in the shooting field.

This is no mean man. He represents Edwardian and eighteenth century England in the grand tradition of the Establishment, and also has an extensive appreciation of contemporary public opinion. He has charm, politeness, dry humor, self-assurance, a vivid sense of history, dignity and character. To what extent he would bend conviction to comport with expediency one cannot say . . .[38]

25

'They Don't Really Smile'

'I began by wishing them a happy New Year, pointing out that it would be a *difficult* year, but one full of hope and opportunity.'[1] Thus Macmillan to the Cabinet at their first meeting of the year on 3 January 1962. As it happened, he was to be proved right only in part. 1962 was certainly to be a difficult year, indeed even more difficult than 1961. On the other count, however, he was to be proved badly wrong. There was to be not much opportunity and, at least for some of them, very much less hope. In fact, by the late spring of 1962, after a series of electoral disasters Ministers, and the Party in general, seemed to be losing heart. A visiting American journalist, C. D. Jackson, the publisher of *Life* magazine, spotted it. The Conservatives, he reported after his visit to Britain in June 1962, were 'politically ... not an army with an array of banners ... They don't really smile ... serious, sober, hard-working, concerned, thoughtful ... but ... not an army with banners.'[2]

Ministers were tired, as Macmillan himself noted in his diary early in the year. Most of them had, after all, been in office, one way or another, for just over ten years. Some of them, not to put too fine a point on it, were looking rather shop-worn. Macmillan kept on saying how tired he himself was – and at times he was indeed looking jaded. He worried, too, about his health – even a January cold became, in his mind, serious influenza and needed both Sir John Richardson's attentions and four days in bed. Moreover, he was under consistent and at times ferocious attack in the press. In Parliament, too, the Conservative right wing, led by Dorothy's brother-in-law, Lord Salisbury, seemed to be seeking every opportunity to embarrass him and, if possible, even to unseat him.

The major bone of contention between him and the Conservative right wing, as it had been for many months, was the Central African Federation. There was still no settlement on the future constitution of Northern Rhodesia and no decision on whether Nyasaland should be allowed to secede. Welensky, egged on by Lord Salisbury, was still muttering about betrayal. The 'Monday Club', named after a group of right-wing Tories who met on Mondays, and Salisbury's own 'Watching

Committee' were spreading what Macmillan regarded as poison. Maudling, who had taken over from Macleod as Colonial Secretary, had turned out to be even more radical in favour of African nationalism than his predecessor. Just as Macleod had rows with Home in his day, Maudling was having rows with Duncan Sandys. Resignations were again threatened, and Macmillan had, yet again, to step in to calm things down.

As if this was not enough, the 'pay pause' was going badly, both in its presentation and in its effect. A White Paper in January attempting to explain the Government's approach to future incomes policy was treated with something near to derision. Selwyn Lloyd, in presenting it, appeared 'stubborn', 'wooden', 'inarticulate' and 'unimaginative'.[3] On top of that, the deficit on external trade account for January turned out to be an alarming £67 million; nor was there much optimism about any possible improvement. In addition, there were threats of strikes on the railways, the London Underground and of a 'go slow' in the Post Office and the civil service ('How could the civil service go any slower?' Macmillan asked[4]). Moreover, Lord Radcliffe, in his review of security, had reported that 25 per cent of the paid officials of the civil service unions were communists. Not to be outdone, there were ministerial disputes – Butler and Heath were in the middle of a row about pessimistic remarks Butler had made to the press Lobby on the EEC negotiations.

Things were certainly going badly. Domestically, 1962 was indeed living up to Macmillan's prediction. But internationally things were not much better. Macmillan's visit to Bonn in mid-January was no more than moderately successful. He achieved some agreement from Adenauer on defraying the support cost of British troops in Germany but few – in fact, almost negligible – assurances on the EEC negotiations. Finally, Kennedy, although loudly proclaiming 'interdependence', was plainly not going to allow American defence manufacturers to lose out in bids for contracts. As Harold Watkinson, Macmillan's Secretary of State for Defence, minuted in February, 'it may well be that what the Americans mean by "interdependence" might be held by some parts of British industry to be "dependence".'[5]

All in all, it added up to serious political trouble, and Macmillan was quick to sense it. As he had done before when in trouble, he started to think about a reconstruction of his Cabinet. But when he thought about it he realised that there was an immediate problem: there could be no sensible reconstruction while responsibility for Central Africa was divided between two departments and two Cabinet Ministers. There was no point in appointing two new Ministers who would carry on the same rows as the old. In fact, he was tired of mediating between brawling

Ministers – and bored and frustrated by the problem itself. Following the advice of the Cabinet Secretary, Sir Norman Brook, he formed the idea of a new department, carved out of the Colonial Office and the Commonwealth Relations Office, to deal only with the affairs of Central Africa. To complete the offload, he wanted his most senior Cabinet colleague, Butler, to take charge of it. Butler was the best person to be involved in what had all the appearance of an intractable problem – and, as a bonus, it would allow Macmillan to get on with rearranging his Cabinet without interference.

The secret to the reconstruction was, of course, Selwyn Lloyd. Macmillan now thought him a flop as Chancellor – and, in fact, was by no means the only one to think so. The 'pay pause' had not just been badly presented. It had been badly planned at the outset. Many private firms had either automatic wage increases in line with inflation or compulsory arbitration built into employee contracts which could not be arbitrarily broken whatever the Government might say. The result was that the Government's own employees bore the brunt of the pause. Doctors, nurses, teachers, railwaymen, bus drivers, midwives – all were up in arms. Nor had Lloyd been more than lukewarm about one of Macmillan's pet projects, the National Economic Development Council (NEDC), which, together with the 'pay pause' (and its successor 'incomes policy') was designed in Macmillan's mind to recreate the 'Middle Way' of the 1930s – and, perhaps, to replicate the centralised planning of the economy which had worked so successfully in France.

Just in case Macmillan might have doubted his instinct that it was time for a Cabinet reconstruction, the electorate suddenly intervened – to volcanic effect. At a by-election on 14 March 1962 in the safely Conservative London suburban seat of Orpington (the neighbouring constituency to Macmillan's Bromley), normally faithful Government supporters let out a pained roar of protest. A Conservative majority in 1959 of 14,760 became a Liberal majority of 7885. Nor was Orpington an isolated case. At a by-election in Blackpool the Conservatives only just hung on against a Liberal challenge; in April, Liberals polled heavily in Stockton – in spite of Macmillan's own campaigning efforts – and in Derby North; and in June the Liberals only just failed to take West Derbyshire. Furthermore, an opinion poll at the end of March showed the Liberals ahead with 33.7 per cent, Labour second with 33.5 per cent and the Conservatives trailing with 32.8 per cent.

An analysis of the Orpington result by the Party Chairman, Iain Macleod, showed clearly that the main grievance of the middle-class voters who had deserted in such large numbers was over the 'pay pause'. The political answer was to produce a Budget in early April which might attract them back to the Conservative fold. Far from that, however, Lloyd insisted in Cabinet that inflation was the real threat and had to be kept under severe control. The result was a Budget which reduced purchase tax on cars, television sets and washing machines but, in a gesture of majestic folly, increased the tax on soft drinks, sweets and ice cream. Lloyd, needless to say, was immediately accused of taxing children's pocket money. It was a political disaster.

Macmillan had already reached the decision that Lloyd would have to go. The Budget only served to confirm it. But, worse than that, he also realised that he himself was now in danger. 'The Tories', he wrote, 'are very worried. Naturally, their disappointment must find an outlet. This must, in the long run, mean an attack on the leadership of the Party ... the enemies of the leadership, already numerous, have undoubtedly been strengthened. And Lord Salisbury is working hard, with growing power. He genuinely believes that the loss of our Conservative voters to the Liberal Party is due to our having followed too "liberal" policies! He thinks *reaction* is the cure, and he regards me as the arch-enemy of reaction.'[6]

The only bright spot in the otherwise gloomy electoral picture was that it was the Liberals rather than Labour who were creating the havoc. Macmillan saw this as a protest which could be reversed – rather than as deep movement for change. But the real danger he saw was that the Conservatives might panic. Immediately, in the days after Orpington, he made two speeches exhorting the faithful to hold firm. But his mood, even so, was bad and his spirit rather depressed – not at all helped by a painfully sore throat (needing another four days in bed) – while his mind was elsewhere, focusing on preparing for his next visit to North America.

The programme had already been fixed. At the end of April he was to go to New York, Washington, Toronto and Ottawa. In New York he was to address the American Newspaper Publishers Association on 26 April at their Annual Convention. The invitation had been discussed with Kennedy in Bermuda, who had approved. New York was to be followed by discussions with Kennedy in Washington. Once Macmillan's acceptance of the American invitation was announced, the Canadian press in turn asked him to speak at their Annual Dinner in Toronto on 1 May and Diefenbaker asked him to spend two days in Ottawa. As always with Macmillan's transatlantic journeys, it was building up to a very full programme.

The speech to the American Newspaper Publishers was particularly carefully prepared. In some rather lofty language, he set out to give his hosts 'some picture of my own country; how it stands today; what it is trying to do and how our people see their difficulties and their opportunities. A report to you, so to speak, on the health and outlook of your transatlantic cousin – something which, putting aside any question of sentiment, is perhaps of some significance to you.'[7] There was, as usual, an historical discursus. This was followed by an elegant description of the state of Britain (without mentioning Orpington) and, finally, an explanation of the British Government's aims in international affairs – with particular emphasis on the attempt to agree a nuclear test ban.

It was, and still reads as, one of Macmillan's best speeches – elegant, spirited at times and trenchant where needed. More than that, it achieved its effect. It was received with rapture by his audience. Not only was there a prolonged standing ovation but many inches of column space in the following days. In fact, during this visit Macmillan noted generally 'a greater friendliness to the UK than I remember before, pervading every aspect of our relations'.[8] In Washington, Kennedy met him at the airport, put on an impressive guard of honour, ferried Macmillan to the White House in his helicopter, went to dinner at the British Embassy (thus technically breaching protocol by setting foot on British territory) and going out of his way to be as agreeable as possible.

Macmillan found Kennedy much more relaxed than at Bermuda in the previous autumn. What he did not know was that it was due, at least in part, to Kennedy's improved health. Until October 1961 an array of doctors had relied on injections to assuage Kennedy's back pain and to treat his adrenal insufficiency (he suffered from Addison's disease) – procaine, amphetamine and various steroids – and, apparently, testosterone (he had caught the rather prudish Macmillan by surprise in Bermuda with his remark 'I wonder how it is with you, Harold? If I don't have a woman for three days I get a terrible headache'[9]). In the autumn of 1961 he had changed his medical team. The new doctor, Hans Kraus, was a rock climber who had trained the Austrian Olympic ski team. There was to be no nonsense. The patient's medication was brought under control (although Kennedy apparently still secretly took amphetamine from time to time) and a proper exercise plan set up. By April 1962 the improvement was noticeable.

Although the atmosphere was generally good, not very much came out of the formal Washington talks. In fact, on one issue there were some quite sharp exchanges. After Macmillan had made a 'classical' presentation of Britain's need to satisfy the legitimate interests of Commonwealth and EFTA countries, Kennedy made it clear that US support for British entry into the EEC was for political rather than economic reasons. He warned Macmillan that 'Britain could not take care of everyone in its wake as it joined the EEC. The political effect would be very serious. It would accentuate the US balance of payments problem, severely affect agriculture and could cause US withdrawal of forces from around the world.'[10] Kennedy's warning was in general terms, but George Ball, the US Under-Secretary of State, was even more trenchant on the possible damage to US trade. Indeed, Macmillan at times thought that Kennedy was weak in allowing 'Mr Ball (of the State Dept) ... to go on with his intrigues against us in Europe and the Common Market negotiations'.[11]

It was a shot across the bow. For the rest of the issues under discussion, however, Kennedy and Macmillan were in agreement. They would persevere with their attempts to negotiate with the Soviets (Macmillan found that Kennedy was becoming irritated with de Gaulle and Adenauer for their obstruction), they would produce more ideas to try to break the deadlock in negotiations for a nuclear test ban and, in the longer term, work towards a programme of disarmament. It was thus in a spirit of cordiality that Macmillan left Washington for his Canadian visit.

His speech in Toronto was as successful as his speech in New York (and more difficult, in that Canada was in the middle of a General Election). It was necessary, in spite of Kennedy's warning, to stress to the Canadians that the British Government was well aware of its obligations to the Commonwealth. But Macmillan still did not take to Diefenbaker. In fact, he said that 'he is a skilled operator – some would say a pure demagogue. Nobody likes him, but many fear him ...'[12] The official discussions, in the light of the current Election, could not add up to much, and Macmillan was anxious not to be used as an electoral asset for Diefenbaker – so there was no television chat. But he did accept the freedom of the city of Toronto, with a generous reception from a large crowd. As always, the approbation of a crowd was to him, as to almost all politicians, much to his taste.

On his return to Britain, Macmillan found that the atmosphere of political gloom had not lifted. The local elections had proved even worse for the Conservatives than expected. In his own constituency of Bromley, for instance, they lost all their council seats. The dockers had succeeded in breaching the Government's wages policy to the point where the whole thing was in danger of collapse. The press were more than ever critical, claiming that the Government was failing to enforce it (while – to Macmillan's fury – calmly awarding a 10 per cent rise to their own journalists). A renewed outbreak of the civil war in Laos had prompted Kennedy to send reinforcements to Thailand. Ministers were obliged – yet again – to consider the unpopular option of sending British forces to the Far East. At a meeting of the 1922 Committee Conservative backbenchers were openly critical of the Government. 'How long we can go on like this', Macmillan noted ruefully, 'I don't know.'[13]

Yet this was no time for moaning. Laos and the electoral disasters aside, the two problems of greatest concern, which had to be dealt with, were how to implement a successful and permanent incomes policy and how to join the EEC. On the former, Macmillan had already decided that Selwyn Lloyd was no longer up to the task of devising, let alone presenting, an incomes policy – and took the task on himself. On 20 May he summoned Ministers to Chequers for a full discussion of the economy, and on 28 May presented the Cabinet with a long – and to some of them sadly tedious – lecture. 'We are undoubtedly in a great difficulty,' he told them. But 'it is not a matter of wringing our hands upon a long period of failure. It is a matter of trying to see how we can take the next step forward.' There were homely references. 'We have ... the NEDC ... it is a tender plant and we must be careful with it. Still the NEDC has decided whether 4 per cent gross [sic] per annum is what we ought to try to go for ... It is not a thing you get by waiting, like a child that just grows as long as it eats enough ...'

But there was also real meat. 'Everybody knows it isn't just going to happen and they admit too that the growth in incomes must be parallel with the growth in production. And therefore anyone who is against an incomes policy should be denounced as either an anarchist, in favour of a sort of 19th century liberalism or free-for-all and devil take the hindmost; or willing to accept all the risks of continual devaluation ... ; or, and this is the class that we have got to address ourselves to, he may be ready to accept an incomes policy in principle but he may be sceptical about whether it will in fact be enforced fairly in practice. And since labour has the power to wreck any incomes policy the first task seems to me to persuade the Trades Unions and those who speak for labour that it is fair.'[14]

It was pure Macmillanism. The difficulty was that his Chancellor, Selwyn Lloyd, did not believe a word of it. Lloyd took the classic Treasury view that the main object of the governmental exercise was quite simply to keep the show on the road. It was no good the NEDC suggesting this or that. If inflation, or sterling, or, for that matter, any other of the economic imponderables seemed to be running out of control the prime objective was to take corrective action either in fiscal or in monetary policy.

The Macmillan view – that it was politically possible to engineer a better economic performance – was, of course, in line with French thinking, and should have helped with his second problem – how to join the EEC. In fact, as he kept on saying, on almost all substantive points, on how Europe should be organised and how government intervention should bring about national prosperity, he and de Gaulle were at one. Yet the final meeting of minds was proving ever more elusive.

On 22 May, Dixon reported on a conversation with de Gaulle, confirming his previous despatches that the General was, in one way or another, determined to keep Britain out of the EEC – but that if we played our cards well we could outwit him. Macmillan at the time was in his most anti-de Gaulle mood. 'He *loathes* England,' he wrote in his diary '– still more America – because of the War, because of France's shame, because of Churchill and Roosevelt, because of the nuclear weapon.'[15]

Macmillan, of course, had – yet again – misread de Gaulle. It was not a question of 'loathing England' (or Britain, for that matter). It was a realistic assessment of what France had to gain or lose in the transaction. If Britain were to play by all the rules and accept the Treaty of Rome as it stood – with minor transitional arrangements – de Gaulle accepted that it would be in France's interest for Britain to join, since Britain's entry would finally and irrevocably secure West Germany's anchor to the West and thus protect France from any future German revanchism. If, on the other hand, Britain were to bring along with it the whole baggage of the Commonwealth and the American 'special relationship', Europe would become an American dependency and, at some time in the future, Germany could fall into the Soviet embrace – with the consequent, and perhaps ultimate, danger for France. De Gaulle had lived through two German invasions and the memory of a third. A fourth, with Soviet support, was only a dim possibility – but a possibility none the less.

The truth is that in the spring of 1962 de Gaulle was playing for time. He was facing a referendum and, possibly, a General Election in October and, on the advice of his new Prime Minister, Georges Pompidou, and of officials in the Foreign Ministry, felt that he could not incur the opprobrium of keeping Britain out of the EEC until all that was safely over. All then depended on the result. If he and his Government were defeated or emerged seriously weakened, a veto would be politically impossible. The only tactic available in the interim was to sound sympathetic while raising doubts – and to play for time.

It was this tactic which de Gaulle adopted when he and Macmillan met at the Château de Champs on Saturday and Sunday, 2 and 3 June. The château itself, on the banks of the River Marne some twenty-one miles east of Paris, was an ideal spot for what Macmillan hoped would be a friendly chat. Built in the classic style of the late eighteenth century, early in its history it had reverted to the French crown owing to the conviction of its owner on a charge of embezzlement. For a couple of years it had been rented by the Marquise de Pompadour, who had spent far too much money redecorating the interior before tiring of it and handing the lease back. The gardens, one in French style and one English, designed by the nephew and pupil of the great Le Nôtre, were, and are, quite beautiful. It almost goes without saying that de Gaulle, in that setting, was a most courteous and attentive host. (He opened the discussions by saying that 'he was delighted to welcome Mr Macmillan. If he had his way they would meet every week.'[16]) Moreover, Dorothy found it more comfortable than Rambouillet – and probably the more comfortable in that Yvonne de Gaulle was otherwise engaged.

In the lead-up to the meeting, Macmillan had taken the trouble to see the outgoing French Ambassador to London, Jean Chauvel, and his replacement, Geoffroy de Courcel. In front of both of them he had dangled the idea of Franco-British cooperation on nuclear weapons. This, in truth, was not entirely honest. He knew perfectly well that the Kennedy administration would veto any passing of US nuclear technology to France. That had been confirmed to Ormsby Gore in Washington only a few days before Macmillan went to the Château de Champs. In fact, when it came to it in the discussions, Macmillan suggested that 'there might be a European organisation allied to the United States. There would be a plan for the defence of Europe. The nuclear power of European countries would be held as part of this European defence.' De Gaulle countered that under some circumstances 'the Americans might hesitate to engage the nuclear battle and that was why France must have a small deterrent of her own'.[17] In other words, de Gaulle knew perfectly well that Macmillan was hinting at something he could not possibly deliver.

The discussion then went on to the familiar topics: the Commonwealth, agriculture, Germany, and the change in the Community if Britain and the other EFTA countries joined. 'That was why', de Gaulle concluded, 'France had to look at this matter carefully.'[18] At the end of it all, nobody, perhaps not even de Gaulle, knew what the result would be, but Macmillan came away believing that the door was not permanently shut. On his return to London, he duly reported to Kennedy that de Gaulle 'was very frank and explained that Britain's entry into the Community would entirely change its character, not only economically but also politically. While he saw the advantages of a larger group he was afraid that the very increase in size might weaken the cohesion of the whole . . . But I do think that he accepted the seriousness of our purpose in entering into negotiations . . .' Disingenuously, Macmillan went on to write that 'we had no discussion about nuclear matters except that de Gaulle several times repeated his determination to secure a small deterrent force for France'.[19]

On his return to London, Macmillan was faced with another example of what he regarded as American diplomatic naïvety. He was already irritated by the efforts of George Ball, who, in vociferously proclaiming US support for British entry into the EEC, had only succeeded in bolstering de Gaulle's resistance. Now it was the turn of Robert McNamara, Kennedy's Secretary of Defense. In a speech in early June, Macmillan later wrote, '[McNamara] put forward with equal vigour and clumsiness a powerful condemnation of all national nuclear forces, except, of course, those of the United States. All others he attacked on the dual, if somewhat contradictory, grounds that they were "dangerous" and "lacking in credibility".'[20] Macmillan was furious. (De Gaulle, on the other hand, simply accepted McNamara's speech as confirming his own opinions.) In the current state of negotiations with the EEC the last thing Macmillan wanted to hear was the American Secretary of Defense saying that one of the major planks of British (and French) foreign policies lacked credibility. When Rusk arrived in London later in the month both Macmillan and Home complained angrily. The Labour Opposition, they told him, 'had them over a barrel'.[21] In short, if the 'special relationship' was to survive in health, they would welcome some greater sensitivity and diplomatic sophistication in Washington.

Fortunately for Macmillan, however, whatever its demoralising effect on the Government and its inflammatory impact in the House of Commons, McNamara's speech made few waves in an already turbulent British electoral sea. What was making waves, on the other hand, was the Government's apparent incompetence in the management of the economy. At lunch on 21 June Butler made the point. 'He feels', Macmillan wrote in his diary, 'that the present grave political situation is due entirely to the bad handling of the economic problem (or rather its bad presentation) by the Chancellor of the Exchequer and the Treasury. He felt that drastic action was necessary to save the situation.'[22] In other words, Lloyd had to go. The following day the Cabinet discussed Macmillan's paper on incomes policy. It 'makes me all the more angry with the Treasury and the Chancellor for their delay and lack of initiative. A whole year gone, and then the PM has to do it himself at the last minute.'[23] Redmayne, the Chief Whip, was singing the same tune. There had to be a change at the Exchequer before the start of the Parliamentary summer Recess. The relevant date, just in case Macmillan had not noticed it, was 3 August.

During the first week of July Macmillan brooded on the changes he had to make. Having brooded, he devised a plan. He then discussed it with those he trusted – Home, Norman Brook and Redmayne. All agreed with it. 'It will be personally terrible and I shrink from it,' he wrote in his diary. 'I am to talk with him [Lloyd] on Thursday [12 July] and try to give him forewarning in a nice way, with a view to the changes (which should be on a large scale) being announced at the end of the Session.'[24]

As it stood, it was a reasonable plan. But it ran into a snag. On 11 July, the day before Macmillan was due to break the news to Lloyd, Butler, who was privy to the plan, had lunch with Lord Rothermere and a group of his executives, including the Lobby correspondent of the *Daily Mail*. It was, apparently, a jolly affair and Butler, more than usually indiscreet, let slip that there was to be a major reshuffle – and that Lloyd was to be the main victim. The next morning the *Daily Mail* ran a banner headline: 'MAC'S MASTER PLAN'.[25] Underneath was the scoop: Lloyd, along with several other Ministers, was about to walk the plank.

It could hardly have been worse. It was the day of a by-election in Leicester North-East, and the Cabinet was due to meet to discuss incomes policy. In an uncomfortable atmosphere Macmillan was forced to deny that he was the source of the leak (and Butler said nothing). As the day wore on, the rumours swirled around Westminster. Just after four o'clock in the afternoon, Tim Bligh went to see Lloyd in his room in the Treasury and nervously told him that the Prime Minister wished to see him at six that evening – about the reshuffle. Lloyd asked whether Macmillan wanted him to resign. The answer came back: yes. Lloyd was stunned. Surprising as it may seem for an experienced politician, he had apparently not suspected anything.

The interview with Macmillan was a disaster from start to finish. For three-quarters of an hour Macmillan tried – and failed – to persuade Lloyd of the need for a radical reconstruction of the Government. Since Lloyd had occupied the two highest posts in the Cabinet – Foreign Secretary and Chancellor – and since he had said that he had no ambition to lead the Party, he pointed out that there was no other Cabinet post which would not seem like a demotion. Perhaps, Macmillan went on, he might like to make a third career in business. A peerage, of course, was a given. Lloyd replied that he did not want either a business career or a peerage. It was, as Macmillan wrote, 'a terribly difficult and emotional scene'.[26] Lloyd finally left to drown his unexpected sorrows with his friends in the House of Commons. Macmillan then sent for Henry Brooke, the Chief Secretary to the Treasury, and asked him to be Home Secretary, since Butler was to become 'first' Secretary of State (whatever that was meant to mean) and devote his time to Central Africa. Brooke agreed, rather reluctantly – he really wanted to be Chancellor. Macmillan then changed into evening dress and went off to an official dinner – the Queen and the Queen Mother were to be present – at the Savoy.

After the dinner Macmillan went back to Admiralty House and worked with Redmayne to put together a final list of ministerial changes. But the next morning he was rung by Home, who told him, in a state of great excitement, that Lloyd had seen John Hare, the Minister of Labour, during the previous evening and tried to persuade him to resign in protest at the rough treatment Lloyd had received – and that Hare had refused. Macmillan immediately suspected a plot. Immediate action was required. If he let the matter drift into the weekend there would be every opportunity for the plotters (perhaps Butler, perhaps Lloyd, perhaps Salisbury and others) to firm up their plans. He must purge the Cabinet without delay.

One after the other on that morning the victims were sent for. Percy Mills and John Maclay, the Scottish Secretary, went quietly. Watkinson found Macmillan 'tired and distressed. In emotional terms he told me that the Government was in crisis ... forebodings of Ministerial revolt ... he seemed much less than his normal calm and politically aware self.'[27] Kilmuir was next – another painful three-quarters of an hour with a long-standing friend and colleague. Kilmuir thought that Macmillan had lost 'both nerve and judgement'.[28] Finally, Eccles was offered his old job at the Board of Trade – but refused. He was then sacked, as he later put it, 'with less notice than a housemaid'.[29]

Macmillan was quite clearly in a panic. But having started the process he had to go through with it. In fact, he had to get the whole thing done in time to get the new list to the Queen at a Buckingham Palace Garden Party in the late afternoon. It would have to get to the Queen in time to allow her to sign it off and for it to be released for the seven o'clock news. It was close. At 6.10 p.m. the list was delivered to the Queen, who was just leaving the Garden Party. It was on the BBC at 7 p.m.

It was, as the wits kept on saying – and have been saying ever since – 'The Night of the Long Knives'. One-third of the Cabinet had been shown the door in what the press called a Stalinist purge. There was much talk of Macmillan's own future ('FOR MAC THE BELL TOLLS', as one newspaper put it[30]). Before 11 July, Gallup had shown an approval rating for Macmillan of 47 per cent. By 20 July that had sunk to 36 per cent. In the House of Commons, however, a censure motion from the Labour Opposition failed but Macmillan recognised that 'the storm is going to be quite hard to ride'.[31] The best quip came from a rising Liberal star, Jeremy Thorpe: 'Greater love hath no man than this, that he lay down his friends for his life.' The question then was whether he and his Government could survive. But, whatever the answer, there was no doubt that, as he went off to Birch Grove for the start of the summer Recess, Macmillan was not smiling at all.

26

'We've Got To Do Something for Harold'

August 1962 was a bad month all round. It was not just the weather, which was so appalling that it threatened to ruin the grouse shooting. Anglo-American relations were by then in near crisis. There was the simmering row with Washington over the Congo, and, as the month progressed, there were even worse disputes. At times, it seemed that the whole concept of 'Anglo-American interdependence' was in jeopardy. To be sure, McNamara's speech about the danger of national nuclear forces (other than American) had been offensive enough. But almost worse than that was what the British regarded as commercial treachery – for instance, a sudden American insistence in early August that their NATO allies buy from them a short-range surface-to-surface missile, known as Sergeant, 'on the favourable terms', as Macmillan later furiously wrote, 'more commonly arranged for vacuum cleaners or washing machines'.[1] The result was that an apparently technically superior missile developed by the British, Blue Water, had to be cancelled – at substantial expense to the British taxpayer. Macmillan made a feeble protest to Kennedy, but that was about all. The Secretary of State for War, Jack Profumo, who had only been in the job one month, was so upset that he offered to resign. ('The poor boy was nearly in tears,' Macmillan told Harold Evans.[2])

Even worse, it seemed, was to come. At the start of the grouse season in mid-August, Macmillan took a few days off to shoot at Bolton Abbey. It so happened that Ormsby Gore (who had by then become, both in Washington and in Macmillan's diary, 'David Gore') was there with him. A message came through to both of them from the US Embassy in London that the United States had apparently offered the US 'Hawk' missile to Israel. 'The Prime Minister came back rather tired from the moors one evening,' Ormsby Gore later said, 'to find a telegram to say that this is what had happened. He was very angry and sent off a rather intemperate telegram to the President . . .'[3]

'Very angry' and 'rather intemperate' are the mildest possible descriptions of Macmillan's mood and his telegram to Kennedy of 18 August. In fact, his telegram must rank among the most offensive ever sent by one head of government to another – let alone to a head of government who was also a Head of State. 'On returning from a very pleasant day's shooting at Bolton Abbey,' it started, 'I have just received the information that your Embassy in London has informed us that you have decided to supply Hawk missiles to the Israelis and that the decision will be conveyed to them tomorrow. This follows', it went on, 'two years of close co-operation during which we decided that it would be unwise to supply these weapons to the Israelis ... Dean Rusk gave a most categorical assurance to David Gore that your Government would consult us ... To be informed on Saturday afternoon that your Government are going to make an offer to supply on Sunday is really not consultation. I cannot believe', it ranted on, 'that you were privy to this disgraceful piece of trickery. For myself I must say frankly that I can hardly find words to express my sense of disgust and despair. Nor do I see how you and I are to conduct the great affairs of the world on this basis ... I have instructed our officials to let me have a list of all the understandings in different parts of the world which we have entered into together. It certainly makes it necessary to reconsider our whole position on this and allied matters.'[4]

As it happened, it appeared on further investigation that Macmillan had made a dreadful mistake. Untypically, he had shot immediately and from the hip. The explanation soon turned out to be simple: the US Embassy had got the message wrong. Macmillan then had to eat a large slice of humble pie. 'Dear Friend,' his message to Kennedy on the next day began. 'Since I sent my indignant message to you yesterday Lord Hood [Minister in the British Embassy in Washington] has telegraphed to say that he has had a talk with Mr Rusk which puts a different complexion on this affair, and that what you are going to say to the Israelis today is not mainly to do with missiles, but with refugees ... Meanwhile, this message is just to tell you how glad I am that my serious concern was all based upon a muddle between the various diplomatic messages. However, if you are dealing with Highlanders you must expect them to flare into a temper if they think they have a grievance.'[5] It was, of course, meant to be a joke, but Kennedy knew perfectly well that Macmillan was no Highlander, and, as a joke, it fell very flat. Kennedy did not think it at all funny.

As well as the dispute over the energetic US efforts to sell their missiles, there was disagreement over civil trade with Cuba. Kennedy wanted Britain to join in the US embargo. Macmillan saw no reason to stop profitable trade with Cuba simply to please the Americans. The Cubans, apparently, were interested in buying a fleet of London buses. But it was not simply a matter of buses. There were some ugly reports that the CIA were preparing a series of manoeuvres not just to dislodge Castro but to assassinate him. That was not only against all customary international procedure but, even worse, extremely stupid. Macmillan knew well that the more such clandestine activities were pursued the more the Soviets would have all the excuses to support Castro – and turn Cuba into a fully-fledged Soviet satellite. That was all the more reason for Britain to keep open its existing links with Cuba, if only to sell buses.

Another matter of contention with Washington in that difficult August was Britain's record on security. It was not just that Lord Radcliffe had openly declared that the British civil service trade unions had been infiltrated by communists. Every few years or so, as it seemed, there was the discovery of yet another Soviet spy in the midst of Whitehall. Often as not, he (or she) had managed to skip the country before detection or escaped from custody. The Americans, in particular the CIA, at the time thought the British security services to be little more than barely competent.

Certainly it came as no surprise to the CIA that, within a month, a sad and inadequate clerk in the British Foreign Office, by the name of John Vassall, was arrested. Vassall had been a cipher operator in the British Embassy in Moscow and had fallen into a KGB homosexual honey trap. He was photographed by the KGB 'naked, grinning into the camera; naked, holding up a pair of men's briefs which must have been mine'.[6] On his return to Britain and the Admiralty, Vassall, by then a minor Soviet agent, had proceeded to supply the Soviets with whatever information he could find. In fact, it did not amount to much. But there was worse to come. Vassall had been promoted to Assistant Private Secretary to the Conservative MP Thomas Galbraith, then Civil Lord of the Admiralty. Although subsequently moved to the Scottish Office, Galbraith's name came up high on a list of contacts when Vassall was arrested in September.

'We have arrested a spy who is a bugger and a minister is involved,' the Director of Public Prosecutions told anybody who would listen.[7] 'There will be another big row,' Macmillan noted wearily in his diary, 'worked up by the Press, over this.'[8] There was indeed a big row. It had all the hallmarks of an exceptionally good scandal – homosexuality, espionage, a hint of involvement in high places and a possible cover-up. In fact, so big was the row that Galbraith was peremptorily told by Redmayne, the Chief Whip, to resign and Macmillan was in the end obliged to drag out Lord Radcliffe again to conduct an inquiry into the matter.

All this happened while Macmillan was deeply engaged in another –

even more politically dangerous – row. The Commonwealth Prime Ministers had arrived in London to make their views known on Britain's application to join the EEC – and they were in no mood to mince their words. Although he had been fortified by Butler's now avowed support for Britain's application – delivered rather solemnly at a dinner with Macmillan in Buck's (in spite of Butler predicting 'the probable break up of the Conservative Party'[9]), Macmillan had the greatest difficulty in preventing a Commonwealth explosion. Even the Queen said that she was worried. As for Heath, who did his best to explain to the conference the progress of negotiations and the safeguards which Britain was demanding, and who was 'only accustomed to Europeans, who are courteous and well-informed even if hard bargainers, [he] was astounded at the ignorance, ill manners and conceit of the Commonwealth'.[10]

In response, Macmillan thought that it was time to explain to the nation (and the Commonwealth) what the EEC was all about and why Britain should enter it. Macmillan's new Minister without Portfolio (in practice, Minister for Propaganda), William Deedes, had told him that television was the medium to rescue the Government when it was in difficulty. 'The Government', Deedes had written, 'always has a mon-opoly of news value and to this extent a natural lead over other parties ... The leaders of television ... show an eagerness to get better relations with us ... we ourselves should not always be looking for "pinkies under the bed" ... there is scope for horse trading ... we may on occasions be able to secure appearances on particular subjects which suit us without a lot of fuss about balance.'[11]

Macmillan was impressed. If de Gaulle and Kennedy could go on television as national leaders rather than as party politicians, he saw no reason why he should not do the same. After a good deal of negotiation, intense drafting of a text and a number of rehearsals, the broadcast duly went out on the evening of 20 September. He watched it sitting quietly in Admiralty House with Dorothy, and was rather pleased with it. But he was subsequently very irritated when he heard from Evans that Gaitskell had demanded the right of reply. Not only that – and this was not just irritation but near panic – there were rumours that Gaitskell, either in his reply or at the Labour Party Conference in October, would commit his Party, if and when in government, to repudiate any agreement with the EEC. There was no doubt what this would mean. No govern-ment could negotiate in good faith with such a threat hanging over them. There would have to be an immediate General Election – with the latest Gallup poll giving Labour a clear eight and a half point lead and with Labour enjoying the support (such are the strange bedfellows of politics) of the Beaverbrook press.

It was obviously the crisis of the moment, and 'severe crisis, political or personal, make Scott a necessity. I have read *Woodstock, Kenilworth, The Abbott,* and am now started on *Waverley*.'[12] Even more Scott, however, was necessary when Home came to dinner on 3 October to tell him that Dixon had reported 'a bad interview with de Gaulle, who was glum, cynical and harsh – in his worst Algerian form (in the war)'. Moreover, 'the President [Kennedy] is angry with us for not being willing to join in a boycott or blockade [of Cuba] ... [and] for not being willing to join in boycotting Congolese copper ... (the Americans own most of the rest of the world copper supplies ...) ... we have found out that they have lied to us over the Israeli missiles [untrue, as it happened] and are still lying to us ... altogether we are in a very bad period with the US. This is sad and may do us both harm. Fortunately, personal relations with president and Rusk are good. David Gore is absolutely invaluable.'[13]

In the midst of these bad-tempered exchanges another and even more dangerous crisis was breaking. In September and early October 1962 the US Defense Intelligence Agency (DIA) had been observing what appeared to be a Soviet military build-up in Cuba. Spies reported the installation of SA-2 anti-aircraft missiles, a new weapon which was capable of bringing down a U-2 flying at its maximum height. It was also noted that the missiles could, if required, be used ground-to-ground and be nuclear tipped. Torpedo boats were also stationed there, carrying ship-to-ship guided missiles. Outwardly, Kennedy remained cautious. But it was well known that the US Chiefs of Staff had laid plans for an invasion of Cuba. All they needed was for the President to give the signal. When Kennedy revealed on 7 September that he was calling 150,000 reservists to the colours for twelve months that seemed to be the signal the Chiefs of Staff wanted.

But on 1 October there was a further and more sinister development. The DIA reported to McNamara and the Chiefs of Staff that there had been a 'first hand sighting ... of a truck convoy of 20 objects 65 to 70 feet long which resembled large missiles'.[14] It was, in fact, the first sighting of Soviet medium-range ballistic missiles (MRBMs) on Cuban territory. The sighting, of course, had to be confirmed and reinforced. On 9 October, therefore, Kennedy authorised a U-2 flight over Cuba as soon as there was suitable weather. On 14 October a U-2 duly overflew Cuba (safely) and took more than nine hundred photographs. The result was beyond doubt. There were three MRBM sites at San Cristobal and two intermediate-range ballistic missile (IRBM) sites at Guanajay.

From 16 October to 22 October Kennedy and his most trusted advisers, his brother Bobby, Rusk, McNamara, Bundy, Douglas Dillon, Roswell Gilpatric, Paul Nitze, Joint Chiefs Chairman Maxwell Taylor and Vice President Lyndon Johnson, the group which came to be named 'Ex Comm', spent the six days in the most intense – and hot-tempered – debate of the possible options in response: immediate invasion of Cuba, selective air strikes on the Soviet installations, and, on McNamara's suggestion, first a blockade around Cuba and then, if that failed, invasion. During the whole of that debate the Soviets (including Gromyko, on a visit to the United States at the time) continued to claim that they were not installing any offensive weaponry in Cuba. Equally, during those days none of America's allies were told about what the Americans by then knew beyond doubt.

By 22 October Kennedy and Ex Comm had decided on the least provocative of the alternatives – a blockade or, as it was to be called to avoid difficulties with the word in international law (or embarrassing references to the Berlin 'blockade' of 1948), a 'quarantine' on all ships, of whatever nationality, carrying arms to Cuba. The decision taken, Kennedy went on to say that he would address the American nation on television that very evening to explain his decision, the reasons for it and to ask for their support. Almost as an afterthought, Rusk then instructed the State Department to inform their allies around the world.

As it happened, the week in which Ex Comm was deep in agonised discussion passed by pleasantly enough in London. Even Ormsby Gore in Washington was only dimly aware that something was up. Kennedy had made a point of insisting that, by way of camouflage, he should keep all his outside appointments. The last thing he wanted was interference from outside or, even worse, leaks. He was wholly concentrated on the single imperative – the removal of what he perceived to be the greatest threat to the security of the United States since Pearl Harbor – and probably greater than that. Everything else was subordinate. As he said later to his brother Bobby, '"I don't think there was a choice." Bobby agreed: "Well, there wasn't any choice ... you would have been impeached," he said. "That's what I think," Kennedy declared. "I would have been impeached."'[15]

On 22 October, three weeks after the first sighting of MRBMs on Cuban territory, and the Ex Comm decision taken, Ambassador Bruce went round to see Macmillan. He brought with him 'a great dossier' and went on to speak of the 'excited, almost chaotic, atmosphere in Washington'.[16] Macmillan at first thought that invasion of Cuba was the best course, but soon realised that he would make no friends by suggesting it. When a copy of Kennedy's broadcast arrived in the late afternoon,

Macmillan, on Home's advice, was content to offer general support – which he reaffirmed in a later telephone call. He also sent for Maudling to assess the possible effects on financial markets when the news became public.

In truth, there was not much more that Macmillan could do. On 23 October the Cabinet was briefed. 'Ministers seemed rather shaken but satisfied.' Nevertheless, even in the middle of the crisis there was apparently still time for a jolly lunch. 'Hailsham, Keith Joseph, [Peter] Carrington, Michael Fraser and John Wyndham to luncheon. A merry party. John was very funny about the occasion when he was "privately vetted" by MI5. One of the dangers of a young man getting into enemy hands is being in debt. So the security people say "do you owe any money?" It's a routine question. "Yes" says John. "How much?" says MI5 officer. "Oh, about a million pounds" says John ... "Collapse of inspector" (as they used to say in the old *Punch*).'[17]

That done, the world crisis, as Macmillan himself called it, pursued its course. Given that there was not much he could do, Macmillan understood that his value to Kennedy was in keeping the Commonwealth and other NATO members informed and supportive. As the days went by and the tension mounted, Macmillan tried to make helpful suggestions – possible immobilisation of the Thor missiles in Britain or a proposal for a summit meeting – and Bundy kept in touch daily with de Zulueta, but Macmillan himself knew that 'not to do anything (except to talk to the President and keep Europe and the Commonwealth calm and firm) was probably the right answer'.[18]

At 10 a.m. on Wednesday 24 October the 'quarantine' went into operation. At the same time the US Strategic Air Command was ordered to move from 'Defense Condition 3' to 'DEFCON 2'. For the first time ever it was on full, wartime alert. Missiles were loaded and squadrons of B-52 bombers, with hydrogen bombs in their bomb bays, took off to circle around the clock in the skies above Greenland and northern Canada, refuelled by air tankers, waiting for the signal to head for their predetermined targets in the Soviet Union. US ground and sea units throughout the world were also put on 'red' alert. At the same time there were some elaborate and well-advertised rehearsals on the Florida coast for a full-scale invasion of Cuba.

In response to these alerts (which the Soviets picked up immediately but which were not revealed to NATO allies), Khrushchev at first sent an aggressive letter denouncing the 'folly of degenerate imperialism' and stating that 'we intend to protect our rights'.[19] On the following day, however, there were second thoughts. His tone softened – and a dozen Soviet ships turned away from the quarantine line. U Thant, the

Secretary-General of the United Nations, took the opportunity offered by a debate in the Security Council to suggest a cooling-off period. By the morning of 26 October, much to the relief of Ex Comm in Washington, it was clear that the quarantine was working. Nevertheless, even if the quarantine was working, the missile bases in Cuba were still under construction and the missiles were still there. 'We can't screw around for two weeks and wait for them to finish these,' Kennedy told Ex Comm. It was either negotiation or invasion – and Kennedy no longer believed that negotiation would work. Later in the evening he told Macmillan 'if at the end of 48 hours we are getting no place, and the missile sites continue to be constructed, then we are going to be faced with some hard decisions'.[20]

Overnight, however, there came a long letter from Khrushchev suggesting that if the United States promised not to invade Cuba the reason for the Soviet military installations would disappear. This seemed promising, but when it appeared in public the message was rather different. The Soviet Union, it said, would remove its missiles from Cuba if the United States removed its Jupiter missiles from Turkey. Kennedy himself was inclined to accept the condition, but the other members of Ex Comm pointed out that, if so, the European NATO allies would quickly draw the conclusion that the United States would not defend them in the event of a conventional Soviet attack. After four hours of wrangling they reached a conclusion: there would be no mention of the Turkey Jupiters in the formal response, but Bobby would go to see the Soviet Ambassador, Anatoly Dobrynin, and tell him that, while there could be no formal deal, the President would undertake to get the Jupiters out of Turkey – and would do so once the Cuban crisis was resolved. Dobrynin was also to be told that if this pledge was made public it would immediately be denied and become null and void. Bobby duly did as he was asked.

At 9 a.m. Eastern Standard Time on Sunday 28 October, Moscow radio broadcast the text of Kennedy's (official) reply and announced that it had been accepted by the Soviet Presidium. The crisis was over. Everybody could breathe more easily – including the British. Macmillan, of course, believed that they had been fully consulted throughout, and was at pains to say so. 'In fact,' he wrote in his diary, 'the President and Rusk (and, above all, the President's 'chief of cabinet' McGeorge Bundy) were in continuous touch with Alec Home, me; David Gore was all the time in and out of the White House. The whole episode was like a battle; and we in Admiralty House felt as if we were in the battle HQ.'[21]

Whatever those in 'battle HQ' may have believed, the truth is that

Macmillan was, throughout the whole crisis – and whatever he might have claimed – very much on the margin. It was a week before Kennedy even told him there was a crisis. He was not told that American B-52 bombers were in the air round the clock, waiting for the signal which would tell them to destroy the world within a few hours. He was not informed about the secret arrangement Kennedy made with the Soviets to remove the Turkey Jupiters – in fact, he was puzzled by the whole outcome. 'Why did [Khrushchev] suddenly abandon the Turkey–Cuba deal,' he asked his diary, 'and send the telegram on Sunday in effect throwing in his hand?'[22] As for Macmillan's influence on Kennedy's decisions, McGeorge Bundy said later, 'I don't think his advice on the Cuban Missile Crisis was very important' and, as for the telephone calls during the crisis, 'I don't think President Kennedy initiated many of those phone calls' and, if he did so, it was in the spirit of 'Let's see what Macmillan thinks, shall we call him up? ... more to touch base than because of a sense that he really wanted to know what Macmillan thought about a thing ...'[23]

Gaitskell made much, in the ensuing Commons debate, of Macmillan's lack of influence. He may well have been right; yet his attack lacked conviction. In the first place, he was still smarting from Macmillan's mockery of his ambivalence on the Common Market issue at the Conservative Party Conference in Llandudno in October ('She didn't say "yes"; she didn't say "no"; she didn't say "stay"; she didn't say "go"; she wanted to climb, but dreaded to fall; so she bided her time and clung to the wall' – delivered with impeccable timing[24]). Secondly, he could not plausibly claim that he would have done any better had he been in Macmillan's position. In fact, Macmillan could point out quite reasonably – and correctly – that it was his standing in NATO and the Commonwealth which had cemented the broad measure of support for the United States.

That may have been so, but it did not help him with the British press. It still seemed that anything he did – in fact anything at all – would do as a basis for attack. For instance, although Vassall had been found guilty and sentenced to eighteen years in prison, the press continued to hint darkly that there was more to come – that the whole affair was only the tip of a treacherous homosexual iceberg. Macmillan, for the first time, turned bitter and very angry. 'Fleet Street', he told the Commons during the Vassall debate, 'has generated an atmosphere around the Vassall case worthy of Titus Oates or Senator McCarthy ... a dark cloud of suspicion and innuendo.'[25] But his fulminations were to no avail. Not only were the press enjoying themselves, but the BBC itself joined in the fun. A new programme, *That Was the Week That Was*, based on a formula devised by a group of Cambridge undergraduates and designed to lampoon the pomposity (and, as they saw it, hypocrisy) of political life, rapidly won an audience of millions. Satirical magazines appeared, poking equal fun at authority. However much Macmillan might fret, there was nothing he or anybody else could do about it – as long as the law of libel was not infringed. The Prime Minister, in a flat cap, plus fours and smoking a pipe on the grouse moors, was an obvious – and, to the young, hilarious – target.

At the beginning of November 1962 Macmillan wrote that he was feeling very ill. At first he thought it was the result of the stress of the Cuban missile crisis, but he soon changed his mind. Dorothy had also been ill and Macmillan realised that he had caught her rather unpleasant bug. He had just about recovered in time for the Commons debate on the Vassall affair – the Labour front bench were now accusing not just Galbraith but Lord Carrington of treachery. It was, as Macmillan pointed out in his wind-up speech, bordering on lunacy.

Even though he was still convalescing, it was time to prepare for his next meeting with de Gaulle, to take place at Rambouillet in the middle of December. Before that, however, there was another diversion – and another spat with Washington. This time it was over the Yemen. In September the old Imam, who had ruled successfully (but with notable barbarity), had died. Three weeks after his death his son, Muhammed el Badr, was deposed by the Yemeni Army (all six tanks surrounding the royal palace) and replaced by Colonel Abdullah el Sallal, who declared himself president of a new Yemeni Republic. Sallal turned out to have the backing of President Nasser. The Saudis had disapproved of all this and had wished to restore the Imamate, but were unable to do so because half the Saudi Air Force had defected to Egypt (and Nasser) and the other half was grounded for lack of spare parts. Nasser had sent aircraft to support Sallal and had subsequently sent some 13,000 troops.

The reactions in London and Washington to these complicated events were in almost total opposition. The British were worried that the presence of Egyptian troops threatened the neighbouring colony Aden and the Aden Protectorate. The Colonial Office advised that there was no question of recognising the new Yemeni Republic and that the Egyptians must be told to leave immediately. The Americans, on the other hand, were pleased to see the crumbling of yet another piece of archaic empire and wanted to recognise the new Republic immediately. Macmillan himself (with the support of the Foreign Office) was not opposed to recognition but it required a number of calls – on a new and more efficient (and British) scrambler – to get Kennedy to stay the State Department's hand, at least for the moment.

Even more serious than a dispute about the future of the Yemen, however, was the question mark which suddenly appeared to be hanging over the Skybolt air-to-surface missile – the weapon on which the British were relying to bring their 'independent nuclear deterrent' up to date. By early November McNamara had come to the conclusion that Skybolt was simply costing too much. Furthermore, the test firings had gone badly. In all probability the programme would have to be cancelled. It certainly had to be reviewed. The question which then arose was how to break the news to the British. That, McNamara agreed, was his job. On 8 November, therefore, he saw Ormsby Gore and told him that Skybolt was being 'reconsidered'. 'Cancellation (he implied) was now a likely prospect ... Gore returned in shock ... a compatriot who saw him later in the day recalls that he "was like a man who'd learned the Bomb was going to drop, the end of civilization, and he doubted he could stop it".'[26] The next day McNamara spoke on the telephone to Thorneycroft, his counterpart in London, and delivered the same message, but said that he would like to see Thorneycroft – in London – to talk the whole thing through. It would be useful, he said, if he could go to London before the final Skybolt decision which he expected on 10 December (in fact, he was hoping for a decision from Kennedy on 23 November).

As McNamara had hoped, 23 November did indeed produce something resembling a decision: ' ... cancellation subject to consultation with the British on alternatives'. Nobody at the time (except for Thorneycroft – and then only in his own version of events – had uttered the word 'Polaris').[27] By that time Macmillan was in Scotland on a shooting party. 'Dorothy and I came up on Thursday night [22 November],' he wrote. 'Alec and Elizabeth Home are charming hosts and we have had a very agreeable party ... two very good days shooting, including two little grouse drives yesterday afternoon ...'[28] Macmillan, in fact, had felt the need to get away from the unavoidable publicity following the five current by-elections – all of which came in with predictably bad results. (The Conservatives lost two seats which they had previously held – Dorset South and Glasgow, Woodside – and in each case their vote had dropped by between fifteen and twenty percentage points.)

It was certainly a good time for him to be out of London. But the Skybolt problems did not stop just because he was in Scotland. Thorneycroft had told him on 11 November about the problem with Skybolt. Both knew perfectly well that without Skybolt the British V bomber force was soon to become useless, and, with it, the whole strategy of the 'independent nuclear deterrent'. In short, it was clear 'what Watkinson and the Prime Minister had swept under the rug two years before, and kept there: that Tory defense posture wobbled on a weapon which was marginal for those who had to make it and of dubious utility to them if ever made'.[29] The stakes could hardly have been higher. Thorneycroft knew that he would certainly have to resign if Skybolt collapsed without an alternative – unless he managed to put all the blame on the Americans. Macmillan, in his turn, knew that if Skybolt collapsed without an alternative it would be the end of 'interdependence' – and make entry into the EEC, and a deal with the French, not just important but necessary. It was a dilemma to be avoided almost at all cost. 'It might even force a choice between America and Europe' was a view at the time. 'McNamara's warning raised a horrid prospect: Pandora's box might open; those choices might emerge. The issue for Macmillan in November was how to sit on the lid.'[30] The way to do it was for both of them, Macmillan and Thorneycroft, to keep quiet – in the expectation that the Americans would in the end come up with a politically satisfactory alternative.

They both knew, however, that there was yet another complication. As Tim Bligh recalled later, 'for several months there had been growing an uncrystallized, uncanvassed, latent Cabinet sentiment against prolonging the effort to sustain the independent deterrent. Butler, our "Prince of Wales for 37 years" had never shared the PM's sense of its electoral importance ... Macleod had been impressed by McNamara's logic ... if a change had been put to the Cabinet in November, especially if it involved more money, all those latent feelings might have crystallized *against* going on ... the hell with it. The PM was not unaware of that ...'[31] On the other hand, they were all of them, the whole Cabinet, irritated by a lecture which Dean Acheson, Truman's Secretary of State (and, according to Macmillan, 'always a conceited ass'[32]), had given at West Point, in which he claimed that Britain had lost an empire but had not yet found a role.

It was against that background that McNamara arrived in London on 11 December. On his arrival he made a statement to the British press. Skybolt, it said, was very expensive, technically extremely complex – and it was no secret that all five flight tests attempted so far had failed. In other words, the programme was dead – before the 'consultation' had even started. There followed a long and bad-tempered exchange between Thorneycroft and McNamara during which McNamara persisted in refusing to make an offer of Polaris as a substitute for Skybolt. With that, they all went off, in separate planes, to a NATO meeting in Paris.

Macmillan himself arrived in Paris on the following Friday, ready for his meeting with de Gaulle at the uncomfortable Château de Rambouillet over the weekend. De Gaulle, as it turned out, was in his most confident mood. He had just succeeded in a referendum on a Bill to provide for direct elections to the Presidency instead of election by an electoral college – a Bill which the Council of State had declared to be illegal but which it consented to once the referendum had been won. The subsequent Assembly elections then produced a clear majority for the Gaullists. De Gaulle knew full well that he had finally come into his kingdom. Nothing was impossible.

The weekend started with a shoot on the Saturday morning. It was raining and Macmillan did not shoot well. His mood was made no better by de Gaulle appearing at the last stand and remarking with irritating interest on each bird that was missed. Yet when their talks started after lunch de Gaulle was courtesy itself, if rather condescending. There was a long discussion of international events and general agreement over Berlin and the attitude to the Soviets. It was when the discussion turned to the EEC negotiations that Macmillan sensed that things were going wrong. Accordingly, the following morning he asked Dixon to come from Paris with an interpreter (the previous day he had been speaking in French). De Gaulle was then joined by Pompidou and Couve de Murville.

At this point de Gaulle came out into the open. His plan for a looser kind of political union had been rejected by the other five member states. Revisions to the Rome Treaty were necessary. If Britain were to join, there would be more revisions. But 'it was not possible for Britain to enter tomorrow and the General felt that arrangements inside the Six might be too rigid for the United Kingdom. The Prime Minister had said that unless agreement was reached at once it would never be reached but President de Gaulle's view was that the United Kingdom and the Prime Minister had embarked upon a certain course which they would continue to follow.' The discussion dragged on. Macmillan made a long speech on the effect on Europe if the negotiations failed. There was then an unseemly wrangle about whether or not Britain was 'European'. Finally, de Gaulle said that 'he still foresaw difficulties at Brussels. In the Six as they existed . . . France could stop policies with which she disagreed . . . Once the United Kingdom and the Scandinavians . . . had entered the organisation things would be different . . . The result would be a sort of world free trade area which might be desirable in itself, but would not be European. After a pause, the Prime Minister said that this was a most serious statement. [It was], in fact, a fundamental objection of principle to the British application . . . should have been put forward at the very start . . . President de Gaulle said that this was not the case. France desired British entry into the Common Market. M. Pompidou observed that it was a question of dates.'[33] With that, the discussion ended. Macmillan, as he arrived back in London, was overheard saying 'I'm damned if I'll go there again'.[34]

There was no time for reflection. The next day Macmillan flew with his party to Nassau in the Bahamas to meet Kennedy. By then the decision to cancel Skybolt had been finally made. On his way to Nassau, Kennedy invited Ormsby Gore to join him in his plane for a talk. It turned out to be something of a revelation. With Gore's patient explanations, for the first time Kennedy started to understand the political dimensions of the Skybolt cancellation. The British V bomber force would be made useless. The British 'independent' deterrent would no longer exist. The Conservatives would be sunk. America would stand accused of bad faith. Britain would be ruled by anti-American Socialists. NATO might even collapse.

Kennedy was quick to grasp all those points. There is no doubt that he would, like McNamara, have liked to get rid of the British 'independent' deterrent. When Bundy was later asked what Kennedy felt about it, he replied crisply: 'A political necessity but a piece of military foolishness.'[35] But once Kennedy had understood the 'political necessity', in short, once the politics of Skybolt took centre stage, he and Ormsby Gore quickly devised a rescue formula. The United States, they agreed, would drop Skybolt as a weapon for themselves but development would continue for Britain. As an earnest of good faith the US would meet half the cost. This was to be the political rescue plan – to be called the 50–50 solution. Both Kennedy and Ormsby Gore were pleased with it.

Unfortunately, such was the speed of events, at that time they neither of them knew that McNamara had already looked at the solution and had rejected it. Nor did they know that Macmillan was now set on getting Polaris. He said as much to Kennedy when they went for an evening walk together. Nor was he very enthusiastic about another idea that was being studied in Washington – a multilateral, even mixed-manned, nuclear force (MLF), designed to ensure that allies could feel that they had some say in any decision to use nuclear weapons. Nor did he much like an idea that George Ball was promoting: a joint study to investigate alternatives to Skybolt – in other words, a device to buy time.

By then Thorneycroft had arrived in Nassau, tired after a bruising day in the House of Commons and then the long flight. He was also in a bad temper. It took all Ormsby Gore's diplomacy, and the crispness of Duncan Sandys, to stop him turning round and going home again. At the formal meeting the following morning he sat glumly while Macmillan made his long opening statement, reminding Kennedy of the history of

cooperation between the two countries and of the 'special relationship'.
Macmillan then followed with his pitch for Polaris, stating firmly –
among other things – that the effects of an agreement over Polaris on the
British EEC negotiations would be 'frankly, absolutely none'.[36] As for
proposed multilateral arrangements for nuclear fleets, or whatever they
might turn out to be, national forces would continue side by side with
any of those, at least for the foreseeable future.

Kennedy replied by recognising the history – and offering the 50–50
Skybolt solution. Macmillan turned it down. He was heartened to see
that McNamara was obviously disagreeing with his President. 'McNamara was a splendid chap,' Bligh recalled, 'he sat there saying "balls".'[37]
Kennedy then proposed the joint study idea put forward by George Ball.
Macmillan said, politely but firmly, that would only be postponing the
problem.

Macmillan then launched into another speech. There were plenty of
people in Britain, he said, who wanted to give up the whole thing. 'This
would be better', he went on, 'than putting a British sailor aboard ship
to have tea with the Portuguese. To give up would mean that Britain was
not the nation that had gone through its previous history ... Either
Britain must stay in the nuclear club or he would resign and we would
have a permanent series of Gaitskells.'[38] Almost as a last throw he added
that 'he would be prepared to put in [to NATO] all of his part of a
Polaris force provided the Queen had the ultimate power and right to
draw back in case of dire emergency similar to 1940'.[39]

Gilpatric, who was not present at the meeting, recorded the result.
'One of the reasons', he said, 'I think that – just as the British over-
reacted to the cancellation of Skybolt, we over-reacted to their over-
reaction – was that Macmillan had such an extraordinary power of
influencing an audience. I'm told that the speech he made on how, you
know, the destiny of England depended on a nuclear role, and his
government and everything else, apparently almost spellbound everybody from the President on down. I guess the reaction was "We've got
to do something for Harold." And so this thing was racked up. It was
not, you know, the kind of a well thought out, staffed, analyzed program
that we ... like to think that the Kennedy administration, once it got
under way, was capable of doing.'[40]

Macmillan had got his Polaris missile. The submarine and the nuclear
warhead were to be British built – but neither, of course, was worth
much without the delivery system. The price was that in future the
'independent' British nuclear deterrent would be assigned to NATO –
and hence under American command – unless there was some kind of
unspecified emergency. When the proposition was put to the Cabinet,

rather to Kennedy's annoyance since he thought that the deal was done, there was no more than grudging acquiescence. Butler and Maudling, for instance, wondered whether the game was still worth the candle. There was, however, a second price. Macmillan had been quite prepared to sign up to a multilateral nuclear force – whatever it was meant to be – but, in an effort to calm French nerves he also agreed that a similar offer on the Polaris missile should be made to de Gaulle. As it turned out, the manoeuvre was only too transparent and de Gaulle did no more than brush it aside.

1962 was drawing to a close. To finish it off, the weather descended into blizzards, alternating with periods of freezing temperatures – the worst winter since 1947 – all of which was near to bringing the whole of Britain to a halt. At the turn of the year, the Conservative poll ratings were dismal and there was the threat of a prolonged electricians strike. Unemployment was starting to rise, particularly in those areas where industry was vulnerable to the cold weather.

The economy was looking unhealthy. Even before the weather had hit, Macmillan had noted the regional disparities in employment, the imbalance between south and north – and the political consequences. In a note to the Cabinet in November, entitled 'Modernisation of Britain' he pointed out that 'while, politically, the country may be able to tolerate an average of 2 per cent, or even 3 per cent, of unemployment overall, it will not accept this if the figure is an average between 5 per cent in one place and 1 per cent in another'. He wanted a programme of action under the general theme of 'modernisation'. 'There is a great deal to be done and to be done quickly.'[41]

'1962 is over,' Macmillan wrote in his diary on New Year's Day 1963. 'It has been a *bad* year, both in home and foreign politics. The govt's position is weak and there is a general view that the socialists will win the general election.'[42] The enemy within, in the form of Gaitskell and his troops, were entrenched. It was time, and perhaps even past the time, to mobilise against them. It was the enemy without, however, who struck the harsher blow. On 14 January 1963, de Gaulle held his press conference. In the grand surroundings of the Élysée he announced that Britain was a maritime nation, insular and, in its nature and customs was profoundly different to the continental members of the EEC. Furthermore, if Britain were allowed to enter the EEC in the end there would be a colossal Atlantic community under American dependence. That was not acceptable. The negotiations for British entry should therefore be stopped – without delay. All this was announced with due theatricality.

Outwardly, Macmillan put on a brave face. Inwardly, he was almost inconsolable. He sent a letter to Ava Waverley that it was the worst time he had been through since Suez, wrote in his diary that 'de Gaulle is trying to *dominate* Europe', described Alain Peyrefitte, the French Minister of Information, as 'the new "Goebbels"' and Adenauer as 'the Pétain of Germany' and, after the French Government had succeeded in wrapping up the negotiations in Brussels, 'all our policies at home and abroad are in ruins ... We have lost everything except our courage and determination ... I was utterly exhausted and felt near collapse ...'[43]

While the shock waves of de Gaulle's press conference were reverberating around Europe there was another shocking domestic political event. On 18 January Hugh Gaitskell – quite suddenly – died. He had been in hospital for a little over two weeks with what appeared to be a simple viral infection. At the time there was scant cause for alarm, but it turned out that he had a rare immunological condition, systemic lupus erythematosus (in which the immune system turns on itself), for which there is still no known cure. He never recovered. At the age of only fifty-six, generally accepted at the time as a future Prime Minister, Gaitskell, in his death, left a tragic hole not only in the Labour Party but in the whole British body politic. Macmillan had never liked Gaitskell. 'I did not find him a sympathetic character,' his diary records. But he recognised that 'he was a distinguished man, with considerable political courage and ... skill'.[44] He was no more than moderately generous in his tributes, and was not above a quip about Gaitskell's memorial service in Westminster Abbey. 'The singing was exquisite,' he reported, '[but] I thought the lesson oddly chosen – it was the sheep and the goats – "goats to the left, sheep to the right" one might almost hear Saint Peter calling, in Parliament's last division.'[45]

At the time, Macmillan was in one of his most caustic moods. He took another swipe at the French – 'Couve de Murville (who is a pretty cold fish, anyway) behaved with a rudeness which was unbelievable ... French duplicity has defeated us all ... At home, there is a return of the old feeling of "the French always betray you in the end" ... neither the Government nor the diplomats have any idea what de Gaulle will do next. It is terribly reminiscent of the late 30s – waiting on Hitler.'[46] The only retort the Foreign Office (and Macmillan) could think of was to cancel the Paris visit of Princess Margaret. That done, Macmillan – and Heath, who had certainly made a name for himself in the negotiations with the EEC – went off to Rome to see the Italian Government, and to pay a courtesy call on the Pope – who he thought was sad and probably terminally ill.

In the event, on 14 February Harold Wilson was elected leader of the Parliamentary Labour Party by a majority of 144 to 103 over his nearest opponent, George Brown. 'Wilson got in fairly easily,' Mac-millan – still caustic – recorded. 'Poor Brown. I'm afraid Brown lost the Welsh and Scottish Labour MPs who (tho' his natural supporters) are mostly "teetotal" and would not vote for a drunkard. Wilson is an able man – far more able than Brown. He is good in the House and in the country – and, I am told, on TV. But he is a fundamentally dishonest – even "crooked" – man, almost of the "3 card trick" kind.'[47]

Macmillan's patronising – even disparaging – remarks about Wilson sit in contrast to the events of February and March 1963, which Wilson exploited with great skill. The collapse of the attempt to join the EEC, the petulance of the cancellation of Princess Margaret's French trip, the uneasy deal with Kennedy over the Polaris missile, further Egyptian infiltration in the Yemen and a pro-Nasser coup in Syria, the rise in unemployment – even the bad weather – told against the Government. Labour's lead in the Gallup poll of the end of March went to 15 per cent, and there was 'a wave of depression in the Party and the House of Commons. This has been fomented by my enemies . . . Salisbury, Nigel Birch, Selwyn Lloyd . . .'[48] The scandals, too, were coming thick and fast. In February, Charles Fletcher-Cooke, a junior Home Office Minister, was forced to resign when an eighteen-year-old was arrested for driving – without licence or insurance – Fletcher-Cooke's car at speed in east London. Then, on 15 March, 'I was forced to spend a great deal of today over a silly scrape (women this time, not boys, thank God) into which one of the ministers has got himself. It's Jack Profumo – S of S War. It wouldn't matter so much if it was just an affair of morality. But unfor-tunately, among the frequenters of this raffish and disreputable set, which centres round Lord Astor (Bill Astor), was the Russian Military Attaché . . .'[49]

In the middle of March 1963 Kennedy's special assistant (and, as it were, court historian), Arthur Schlesinger, spent three days in London. His report to Kennedy sums up the view of many outsiders – and many insiders for that matter. 'The Conservative Government', he wrote on his return to Washington, 'is in a sad state. It has held power longer than any government in modern British history (it is now in its 13th year), and it has run down dreadfully. Its solid achievements are largely for-gotten. People are bored with it and fed up with it . . . Today that government can do nothing right. It seems hopelessly accident-prone. It is detested by most of the press. It is derided on radio and television. Comedians make savage jokes about it. It sinks steadily in the public opinion polls under the weight of old age, unemployment, Soviet espionage, the Common Market failure, Skybolt and personal scandal. It reeks of decay; and the press and the opposition, sensing a rout, are moving in for the kill . . . it is hard to overstate the atmosphere of political squalor in London today . . . [and] the impression that the Government is frivolous and decadent, and that everything is unravelling at the seams.'[50]

27

'Butler Would Be Fatal'

At the end of a convivial luncheon of the 1922 Committee at the Savoy Hotel on 10 April 1963, the Leader of the Party and Prime Minister, Harold Macmillan, rose to speak. Through the clouds of cigar smoke and the fumes of brandy he explained that the immediate – and pleasant – matter was his response to a presentation by the Committee of a painting of the Chamber of the House of Commons, with himself portrayed as speaking from the Government Despatch Box, with his son Maurice sitting behind him and, in the usual obeisance to the great hero, with Churchill in his customary place. It was, as all present agreed when the painting was unveiled, a fine piece of work in a suitably traditional manner. Macmillan thanked them 'with sufficient warmth and grace combined (I was indeed much moved by this *unique* mark of affection)'.[1] But he then went on to announce that he had something perhaps more important to say to them. Although he recognised that, at the age of sixty-nine, he was hardly in the first flush of youth, he nevertheless felt able and willing to lead the Party (*Deo volente* – God willing – as he put it) into the next General Election.

His audience was encouraged – and at least some of them even elated – by the news. It was the first time that he had expressed his intention so clearly. It seemed that at least one uncertainty was resolved. Nevertheless, whatever he – and others – might have thought at the time, it was not to be his last word on the matter. In fact, in September and October of the year, whether in conversation with Dorothy and Maurice, or with one or other of his Cabinet colleagues (or in the privacy of his diary) he changed his mind with surprising regularity – either about whether he should stay or go and, if he should decide to go, on the timing of the event. In short, 1963 was to be in all respects a bumpy year.

Early April seemed as propitious a time as any for him to make his announcement. True, the satirists were having a high time ('You have never had it so often' or 'Life's better under a Conservative' were the enjoyable currency of the day) and the Gallup poll did not make happy reading – most recently recording a steady Labour lead of 15 per cent. None the less, Macmillan thought that after the rough weather of 1962 the Government was moving into at least some patches of sunshine. Butler seemed to be steering the doomed Central African Federation safely towards a quiet grave; the Yemen was, of course, still troublesome (and still the cause of some friction with Washington), but it was manageable; proposals for a federation of Malaysia were under way; British Guyana was demanding independence (and upsetting the Americans) but that could be contained; talks on banning nuclear tests were still stalled, but there was a glimmer of hope that Khrushchev might respond to another effort – and Kennedy himself was impressed by Macmillan's continued pressure; the detailed negotiations over the Polaris missiles were going according to plan (although the British Chiefs of Staff were far from enthusiastic about the idea of a Multilateral Nuclear Force); domestically, the Budget in early April had been reasonably well received; and Macmillan's long-term plan to reorganise the Ministry of Defence under one Secretary of State was still in Whitehall gestation. All in all, things were not too bad, and Macmillan thought that he could look forward with some confidence to a calmer year. He would, he thought, be able to lead the Party into those patches of sunshine – and win the next General Election.

There were, to be sure, some niggling worries. In January 1963 Kim Philby, formerly the head of the section of MI6 investigating communist activity, but since the late 1950s the *Observer* correspondent in the Middle East, had finally been identified as the 'Third Man' who had tipped off Burgess and Maclean in 1951 and allowed them to escape to Moscow. Philby had been interrogated in Beirut by an operative from MI6, had been told by the Soviets that his cover was blown, had admitted everything – and had skipped off. So far, so bad. But there was a further – and for Macmillan very much more irritating – complication. As it happened, in November 1955 Macmillan, then Foreign Secretary, had told the House of Commons that nothing could be proved against Philby and that he was not under any sort of suspicion (although even then quite a few in MI6 and the CIA knew better). It was all very embarrassing.

The Profumo case was another problem. Profumo had admitted in February that in 1961 he had become acquainted with Miss Christine Keeler, a girl, as the jargon of the time had it, of doubtful reputation (one of a string of such girls surrounding a fashionable osteopath – and portrait painter – by the name of Stephen Ward). It also appeared that, in addition to Profumo, another visitor to Ward's flat at the time was the Soviet Naval Attaché, Captain Yevgeny Ivanov. Ivanov was under surveillance by MI5 who suspected – correctly – that he was working for Soviet military intelligence. In fact, there seems to have been an attempt to turn him into a double agent. When all this reached the ears of Sir

Norman Brook in 1961 he had warned Profumo to stay away from Ward for reasons of security. Profumo immediately did so, finishing his month-long affair with Christine Keeler as well. But as the months went by she thought that there was a financial opportunity too good to miss and finally sold her part of the story (as well as an indiscreet letter which Profumo had written – starting 'Darling') to the London newspaper the *Sunday Pictorial*.

By March 1963 the whole Profumo/Keeler story was in general circulation among the London gossips. Nevertheless, no newspaper had dared to publish it in any detail for fear of litigation. This did not deter a Labour MP, Colonel George Wigg, a lugubrious and, if the truth be told, slightly sinister figure, from using the absolute privilege of the House of Commons for the purpose. On 21 March he had his moment. The main topic was, in fact, the fate of two journalists who had been sent to prison (much to Macmillan's satisfaction, as it happened) for contempt in refusing to reveal their sources in their reporting of the Vassall case. Wigg soon changed the debate's direction. 'There is not an Honourable Member in this House,' he proclaimed, 'nor a journalist in the Press Gallery, nor do I believe that there is a person in the Public Gallery who, in the last few days, has not heard rumour upon rumour involving a member of the Government Front Bench.'[2] He went on to invite Henry Brooke, the Home Secretary, to get up and say that the rumours – and here he referred by name to Christine Keeler – were false. Another Labour MP, Barbara Castle, followed up by referring to Keeler's failure to appear as witness at a criminal trial and hinting that her disappearance had been managed by people in high places. She, in turn, was backed up by Macmillan's old ally and adversary, Richard Crossman.

There was ministerial panic. It was obvious that Profumo would have to break silence. The House was sitting the following day and questions were unavoidable. After the evening debate ended, at nearly half past one in the morning, a junior Whip was duly despatched to haul Profumo out of bed in his home and bring him down to the House of Commons to the office of the Attorney-General, Sir John Hobson. This was not as easy as it might have seemed, since Profumo (and his wife) had taken powerful sleeping pills and the Whip had almost to break the door down to make himself heard. Just before three, however, Profumo arrived at the House with his solicitor, to be confronted not only by the Attorney-General but by Macleod, Deedes, Redmayne and the Solicitor-General, Sir Peter Rawlinson. Profumo was told that he either had to deny all the rumours immediately or resign. 'Look, Jack,' Macleod is said to have asked brutally, 'the basic question is "did you fuck her?"'[3] Profumo, half asleep, duly crumpled. He agreed a statement, to be made to the House later in the morning. Mostly, in fact, it spelled out the truth. But there was one sentence – and, as it happened, the only lie – which stood out: 'There was no impropriety whatsoever in my acquaintanceship with Miss Keeler.'[4]

Profumo's statement, still in draft, arrived in Admiralty House early in the morning of 22 March. Macmillan took one look at it, made two minor amendments – and thought that it would do. Just after 11 a.m., therefore, after no more than three hours' sleep, Profumo made his – by then heavily trailed – statement. It was, by any standards, robust. Not only did it include the lie but it went on 'I shall not hesitate to issue writs for libel and slander if scandalous allegations are made or repeated outside the House'.[5] He then sat down in his place between Macleod and Macmillan, 'who clapped [him] clubbably on the shoulder'.[6]

There, at least for the moment, the matter rested – but only for the moment. Most, indeed, accepted Profumo's statement at its face value. But there were doubters. Lord Aldington, for instance, the Deputy Chairman of the Party and Macmillan's old wartime colleague, told Redmayne that he was convinced that Profumo was lying (and was promptly told to shut up). Two Lobby correspondents relayed to Macleod's Parliamentary Private Secretary, Charles Longbottom, their suspicion that Profumo had misled the House and that the truth would, in the end, come out. Longbottom passed this on to Macleod (and, in his turn, was also told to shut up).

On 4 April there was a new twist. The Criminal Investigation Department of the Metropolitan Police (CID) opened an investigation into Stephen Ward on the grounds of living off immoral earnings. Christine Keeler was interviewed and, on 5 April, after a good deal of police pressure (and accompanying ribaldry), she signed a statement. She had indeed, her statement recorded, been Profumo's mistress in 1961 (her statement also went on to 'provide a plausibly detailed description of the interior of [Profumo's] house'[7]). The matter was quite clear. There could be no further argument.

The CID – presumably because they were so used to politicians 'having a bit of fluff on the side' that they did not think it of any consequence – failed to pass on Keeler's statement either to MI5 or to the Home Office. At the same time, however, Profumo sued *Paris Match* in France for suggesting that he had helped her avoid appearing as a witness in the trial of her West Indian attacker by fleeing to Spain. *Paris Match* duly retracted. He then sued the UK distributors of the Italian *Il Tempo Illustrato* for making a similar allegation, and received an apology in the High Court and token damages. As a result, without any knowledge of Keeler's statement and with the knowledge of Profumo's success in court, Macmillan thought that the thing was quietly settling down. Even the 'darling' letter was explained away. 'Profumo has behaved foolishly and indiscreetly,' Macmillan noted in his diary, 'but not wickedly. His wife (Valerie Hobson) is very nice and sensible. Of course, these people live in a raffish, theatrical, bohemian society where no one really knows anyone and everyone is "darling" ...'[8]

But it would not settle down. On 9 April Wilson wrote to Macmillan enclosing a letter from the Shadow Attorney-General, Sir Frank Soskice, and a memorandum from Wigg reporting on a conversation with Ward in which Ward claimed that he had knowledge of 'a great deal of extremely explosive material'.[9] The documents were referred to MI5, who reported on them to the effect that no further action was required 'from the security aspect. MI5 also said, at the time, that they had never been given any information about the relationship between Mr Profumo and Miss Keeler.'[10] On the question, which might be put in Cabinet, of whether the police had any knowledge of the truth of the Profumo/Keeler relationship, Bligh minuted that 'There is no information on this point'.[11]

Throughout the rest of April and most of May the Profumo affair rumbled on in the background. Macmillan noted a slight improvement in the Gallup poll but the May local elections went very badly. To try to shore up the Party's electoral position he created a joint Chairmanship of Macleod and Oliver Poole. It was not an easy formula, since it was always difficult to decide which of them was to do what. Their weekly meetings with Macmillan at first were awkward, too long and too indecisive. In the end, it took many weeks for the arrangement to settle down.

Nor was Macmillan at all content with the results of his international efforts. Khrushchev sent a discouraging reply to his letter, sent jointly with Kennedy, on nuclear tests, and Kennedy himself was pursuing too vigorously for Macmillan's liking the idea of a 'multi-manned' MLF. Moreover, the Southern Rhodesia Government was demanding full independence without more than a token concession to the African majority. If that was allowed, Macmillan was afraid that the other African states would walk out of the Commonwealth. All in all, May, in spite of beautiful weather and a garden at Birch Grove in full bloom, was proving a depressing month.

It all got very much worse when, on 24 May, Wilson wrote again. He enclosed a letter from Stephen Ward, in which he asserted most emphatically that Profumo had indeed lied to the House of Commons in his statement of 22 March. Ward had already seen Bligh on 7 May with the same message, but Bligh had then concluded that 'his remarks lay in a form of blackmail, namely that if the Government called off the

police enquiries about him he would not make a fuss about Mr Profumo'.[12] Finally, on 27 May, Wilson saw Macmillan in his room in
the House of Commons, and said plainly (if disingenuously) that 'the
Opposition were not concerned with the private life of a Minister but
felt that there were security issues at stake. Mr Ward was a "self confessed
intermediary of the Russians" ...'[13] He then followed up by asking for
an inquiry. Two days later Macmillan, having refused Wilson's initial
request, was worried enough to agree that the Lord Chancellor, Lord
Dilhorne, should look further into the matter. That done, Parliament
adjourned for the Whit Recess and, on Friday 31 May, 'Dorothy and
I then left for a short holiday in Scotland'.[14] For the purpose, he formally,
for the first time, handed the Government over to Butler. Profumo and
his wife, in turn (she apparently free from care), left on the same day for
a short holiday in Venice.

By then, three things were clear. First, nobody outside the CID (except
for the protagonists) had any inkling of the Keeler statement of 5 April on
what was, in fact, the truth. Secondly, and as a consequence, Macmillan,
Macleod, Redmayne and the others still believed that Profumo had been
honest to the House on 22 March. In fact, any other version was dismissed
angrily as 'Press tittle-tattle'.[15] Thirdly, however, Profumo himself realised
that the game was up. The enquiries into Ward's activities would certainly
lead the police to him. He would be questioned – and would have to
come out with it all. 'Having a Bellini cocktail that first night, he finally
told [his wife] the truth.'[16] It came to neither of them as a surprise when
Dilhorne telephoned the next morning and told Profumo to pack his
bags and come back to London. On the Sunday, avoiding the air routes
which would have attracted media attention, Mr and Mrs Profumo made
their miserable way home.

On the evening of Monday 3 June, Profumo rang Bligh and 'said there
had been a serious development and he wished to speak to the Chief
Whip as soon as possible. A meeting was arranged for Tuesday, June 4
and at this meeting Mr Profumo revealed the truth.'[17] Macmillan, by
then staying at Ardchattan Priory in Argyll, was immediately told by
Bligh, and suitable letters of resignation were drafted and exchanged the
same day. That done, Macmillan and Dorothy continued their holiday,
first to Iona off the West Coast and then across Scotland to Gleneagles.
There was more golf and another agreeable round of visits, to the point
where it was not until 10 June that they arrived back in London.

There they found mayhem. On 7 June Ward had been arrested and
charged with living off immoral earnings. On 9 June the *News of the
World* had begun the serialisation of the Keeler life story. Not only that,
but the hot June days in London were full of the most lurid stories of

Cabinet Ministers and senior judges engaging in the most imaginative of sexual antics. Macmillan and Dorothy could hardly take in – let alone understand – what was happening around them.

It was not only in London. The mood even spread to Washington. Bruce, from the Embassy in London, was sending excited telegrams – which Kennedy read with equal excitement and demanded that they be delivered directly to himself. (Kennedy's excitement, in fact, was not entirely innocent. When a Senator, he had slept with one Suzy Chang, a New York prostitute who by 1963 was living in London and was part of Ward's string. It was said that she wanted to tell her own story about her dinners with him at the 21 Club in New York – and about subsequent nights of passion.) Almost daily, Bruce sent his telegrams – relating, for instance, Keeler's description of Ivanov as a 'hairy chested Russian' and quoting her 'laments over her beloved Profumo, who was less fortunate than her lucky Jamaican lover'.[18]

'I do not remember ever having been under such a sense of personal strain,' Macmillan wrote in his diary. 'Even Suez was "clean" – about war and politics. This was all "dirt".'[19] For someone as uneasy about sex, let alone adultery, as Macmillan, it was all a dreadful business. But not only was it a dreadful business. There was little he could do about it. The House of Commons was due to debate the matter on 17 June, and Macmillan knew that he would have to defend not just the Government, the security services and the police – but himself. A bad slip could lead to a bruising vote against the Government and oblige him to resign. On 13 June Hailsham almost obliged – by a hysterical performance on the BBC. 'A great party', he shouted, 'is not to be brought down because of a scandal by a woman of easy virtue and a proven liar . . .'[20] It was a slip, but it was not such a bad one. It just made Hailsham look ridiculous.

There was, in fact, one bad slip. On 4 June Bligh had summoned Sir Joseph Simpson, the Commissioner of Metropolitan Police, to a 'general discussion about the [Ward] case – whether Mr P would be called as a witness and so on'. Bligh minuted that he told Simpson that 'it would be helpful, although the Prime Minister would not in any way wish to be thought to be involved in what the police were doing, to know what the timetable was likely to be in relation to Dr Ward and the police inquiries'. When he was leaving Simpson said that 'there were some newspaper people outside. I [Bligh] said that if anyone asked him what he had come for he should say that he had been discussing car parking arrangements for the Trooping.'[21] There is little doubt that the summons to Simpson, and Bligh's conduct of the meeting, if known outside, would have laid the Prime Minister's Office open to the charge of interfering with the course of justice – and would have been hard to defend.

Fortunately for Macmillan, none of this was known to Wilson when he opened the debate of 17 June. Wilson was at his most effective – forensic and caustic. Macmillan, in response, asked for the sympathy of the House. 'On me,' he said, 'as Head of the Administration, what has happened has inflicted a deep, bitter and lasting wound ... I find it difficult to tell the House what a blow this has been to me, for it seems to have undermined one of the very foundations on which political life must be conducted.'[22] Some thought his speech masterly, others thought that he looked tired and out of sorts. In fact, by far the most destructive intervention came from Nigel Birch on the Conservative back bench. It was a direct personal attack. He acquitted, he said (with something of a sneer) Macmillan of dishonour, but on the question of competence and good sense he did not think that the verdict could be favourable. In other words, Macmillan should go. Wigg, in turn, called Hailsham 'a sinister saint' and a 'lying humbug'. After much more in that style, the House duly went to a Division. Twenty-seven Conservatives abstained. The Government won. Macmillan, at least for the moment, had escaped Parliamentary disaster.

But he was still in a tight political corner. It was not just a question of avoiding defeat in the House of Commons. The media were on the rampage. The *Sunday Times* proclaimed that the Government had proved itself 'unalert to security dangers and indifferent to traditional moral standards'.[23] The Gallup poll for June recorded 52 per cent dissatisfied with the Prime Minister and a 20 per cent Labour lead on voting intentions. Macmillan told his Bromley constituents that all the calls for his resignation would, of course, be considered but that '"I would act neither in panic nor in obstinacy". This was interpreted to mean (as I intended) that I would hold on.'[24]

As it happened, help was to hand. First, on 21 June, Macmillan appointed Lord Denning to conduct a Judicial Enquiry into the security aspects of the Profumo affair, putting the whole affair *sub judice*. Secondly, Kennedy, who had '"ordered all ... cables from Bruce on that subject sent to him immediately"' had, because of his 'concern about Profumo fallout' (not to mention Suzy Chang) led him to wish to 'visit Macmillan in Sussex instead of London'.[25] Thirdly, on 2 July Khrushchev, speaking in East Berlin, suggested that the Soviets would be prepared to negotiate, and even accept, a partial nuclear test ban.

It was the last which was to pull the fat, as it were, out of the fire. Kennedy had accepted the idea, put forward rather tentatively by Macmillan, that two high-level negotiators should be sent to Moscow to see whether, and on what terms, a test ban treaty of some sort could be agreed. Kennedy had asked Averell Harriman, Under-Secretary in the

State Department and former Ambassador both to the Soviet Union and the United Kingdom, to do the job. Macmillan decided to appoint Hailsham as the UK negotiator. It was, perhaps, an odd choice. Hailsham, formidable lawyer as he was, had a tendency to shout when he was irritated – which was all too often. But it would, Macmillan thought, be a good test of Hailsham's possible leadership calibre – to see whether he could get on with Harriman and at the same time negotiate patiently with the Soviets. Everything – in all senses – was to play for.

On 29 June Kennedy arrived as planned for a short stay at Birch Grove – carefully avoiding London and possible Profumo unpleasantness. He had stopped in Ireland, 'where he had made a sentimental journey to "the home of the Kennedys" and [had made] a rather foolish speech about Liberty'.[26] On his way he had changed plan and stopped at Chatsworth to see his sister's grave. All that made him late and added to the general inconvenience. Kennedy himself had to be put in Nellie's old bedroom at Birch Grove – Macmillan had to move out. Rusk and McGeorge Bundy were put in spare bedrooms. Others were consigned to nurseries in the main house or to the outlying cottages. Neighbouring hotels and pubs were commandeered to house the security back-up. The whole area became a large security zone. But that hardly mattered. Crowds turned out in cheerful numbers to salute the young President. Macmillan, of course, did nothing to stop them – and certainly nothing to impede the television coverage.

In the event, Kennedy only stopped off for twenty-four hours. But from Macmillan's point of view two things were achieved. First, the President, after the Profumo revelations, had gone out of his way to demonstrate very publicly his belief in the Prime Minister's integrity. Second, in their talks Macmillan had persuaded Kennedy that some sort of nuclear test ban, however imperfect, should be their joint priority – and, furthermore, that any version of a multi-manned MLF would be difficult to sell to the British Parliament. More than that, however, Macmillan himself basked in the aura of the charismatic President (and looked forward to his next poll ratings). His memoirs tell (for the modern reader perhaps too sentimentally) the story of Kennedy's departure. 'It was time to go. He went, as he came, by helicopter . . . Hatless, with his brisk step, and combining that indescribable look of a boy on a holiday with the dignity of a President and Commander-in-Chief, he walked across the garden to the machine. We stood and waved. I can see the helicopter now, sailing down the valley above the heavily laden, lush foliage of oaks and beech at the end of June. He was gone. Alas, I was never to see my friend again.'[27]

Politically, Kennedy's quick visit had its intended effect. Although the polls continued to show a large Labour lead (20 per cent in Gallup in mid-July) Macmillan's own standing started to recover. From a satisfaction rating of minus 17 in June and July he was back to a much healthier minus 5 in August. But it was not just Kennedy's visit. Much of the improvement was due to the successful conclusion of the negotiations in Moscow over a nuclear test ban treaty. There had, of course, been much wrangling. There had been arguments about whether in addition there should also be a non-proliferation treaty. But on 25 July 1963, after ten days of tortuous negotiations, a treaty banning any nuclear explosion in the atmosphere, in outer space and underwater was initialled. When Kennedy telephoned Macmillan with the news, 'I had to go out of the room. I went to tell D[orothy] and burst into tears.'[28] Kennedy, in turn, wrote a generous letter to Macmillan thanking him for his perseverance. Even Kennedy's aides, in their later evidence, recognised Macmillan's role in bringing this particular ship safely to port. Nevertheless, Hailsham had much irritated Harriman in the course of the negotiations and the word was coming from Ormsby Gore that Kennedy had his doubts about Hailsham as a leader.

All that was (mostly) good news. But, closer to home, as it were, the ensuing euphoria had obscured another event which was to have its own particular significance. Just before Parliament rose for the summer Recess in early August a piece of legislation which was to have surprising – and far-reaching – effects received the Royal Assent. The Peerage Act 1963 allowed peers with hereditary titles to disclaim their peerages. Originally this was to be done only on succession or on the dissolution of Parliament, but an amendment passed in the House of Lords, and accepted by the Government, extended the window of opportunity to a period of twelve months from the passage of the Act. (Few at the time seemed to realise the effect it might have on the Conservative leadership. But it would be wrong to imagine that the Earl of Home and the Viscount Hailsham had failed to take note.)

While all this was happening, the police investigation into the ramifications of the Profumo affair was winding down. Ward, who had been on trial for eight days and had listened to, among others, Christine Keeler testifying against him and regaling the jury with stories of orgies, sado-masochism and wild licentiousness, committed suicide on 30 July. There was instant – and very widespread – shock. The media, particularly the press, stood accused. Their frenzy seemed, it was said, to have led directly to a personal tragedy. As a matter of fact, Ward's suicide effectively marked the end of media interest in the whole Profumo affair. Apart from the wait for the Denning Report, there was not much else. Moreover, as it happened, on 8 August there was a new sensation. A gang ambushed the Scotland to London mail train, in what became known as 'The Great Train Robbery', and made off with 'well over a million pounds'.[29] It quickly became the media story of the moment.

After a few days in early August at Chatsworth – in dreadful weather – Macmillan and Dorothy took off for a visit to Finland and Sweden. It was a rather desultory affair, of sporadic discussions with the leaders of both countries interspersed with some sightseeing. On their return to Birch Grove Macmillan saw Denning to give his evidence. Denning in turn 'took the opportunity to raise certain problems which he had in finishing his report. I suggested that he might like to discuss them with the Lord Chancellor (as head of the judiciary). I felt that I must be able to say (with absolute truth) that I had taken no part and had not discussed report (other than my own evidence) with Lord D.' None the less, Macmillan knew enough of Denning's conclusions to note after the meeting that 'I fear there will be trouble about *two* ministers, but how formidable this will be I know not'.[30]

By this time Macmillan was starting to have doubts about his April decision to lead the Party into the next Election. During the days at Birch Grove and then during a two-week holiday, first at Bolton Abbey and then at Swinton, he thought long and hard. But what he almost certainly did not know was that John Morrison, the Chairman of the 1922 Committee, had been to see Home to urge him to run for the leadership and that on 31 July Home had replied that he 'would see his doctor'[31] – the classic way of indicating assent. Others were taking an interest – Hailsham, Home and, of course, Butler.

'As I lie in bed in the king's room [at Bolton Abbey],' he wrote, 'reading and writing, there is no sound but of running water and a small sighing wind in the cedars and yews outside the windows. In this atmosphere I try to meditate about what I am to do ...'[32] The truth is that he could not make up his mind. Dorothy had stayed behind at Birch Grove, the weather was still dreadful, with rainstorms and high winds making shooting both difficult and tiring. The week, although restful, had turned out to be rather gloomy – not least because of a bad by-election result at Stratford. Swinton was more cheerful, but by the time he returned to Birch Grove at the end of August he was no further on in his meditation.

One week later, it seemed that he was becoming clearer. He would have to stay to deal with Lord Denning's report and the Commons debates which would follow. But 'I cannot go on to an election and lead in it. I am beginning to feel that I have not got the strength and that perhaps another leader could do what I did after Eden left. But it cannot be done by a pedestrian politician. It needs a man with vision and moral

strength – Hailsham, not Maudling.'³³ He now thought of a new plan –
resignation, to be announced at the Conference but not to take effect
before the Christmas Recess. In a letter to the Queen he wrote that he
had not yet made up his mind. Then, three days later, on 8 September,
he discussed the whole thing with Maurice (their relationship had latterly
markedly improved), who agreed that the new plan was right – but with
no resignation before the Christmas Recess. It seemed, yet again, that
his mind was made up.

Two days later, at Chequers, Macmillan had a long conversation with
Butler (without, of course, telling him about his new plan) and 'got a
good idea of his position. He would naturally (if I resign) accept the
premiership if there was a general consensus of opinion for him. But he
doesn't want another unsuccessful bid ... It is clear that in his heart he
does *not* expect any real demand for him. He would prefer to be Warwick
[the kingmaker] (which he could be) and not try to be king (which he
can't be). On the whole, he is for Hailsham.'³⁴ Then, on 18 September,
there was a conversation with Home – who thought Macmillan's reasons
for resigning were sound but who, when asked about a successor, said
'he favours Hailsham but fears that there will be complete disunity in
the Party and that great troubles will follow'.³⁵

The pieces at that point seemed to be falling into place. On 20
September Macmillan saw the Queen and told her of his latest plan –
although he was careful to stress that he had not finally decided. He
repeated both the plan and the *caveat* to Sir Michael Adeane, the Queen's
Private Secretary, who 'had chattered too much in the summer to too
many people'.³⁶ But by the next day he wrote in his diary that he had
finally made up his mind. 'I have now reached the definite decision to
announce that 1) there will not be a general election this year – 1963, 2)
that I will *not* lead the Party at the next general election but, following
Sir WSC's precedent in 1955, retire in time for a new PM to have a
proper time and some freedom of manoeuvre for the dissolution. But
I will *not* inform anyone of this except Lord Home, Lord Poole, Chief
Whip and Tim Bligh (of course, Dorothy and Maurice). I shall tell the
Cabinet on Tuesday morning before the Blackpool Conference and make
my speech on Saturday, October 12th.'³⁷

By then, Macmillan knew what Denning was going to say in his
report – and knew that it would not be too damaging. On 26 September
the report was published. It was, as might be imagined, an immediate
bestseller. In fact, Denning quickly concluded that there was no evidence
'for believing the national security has been or will be endangered'. But,
that being so, Denning had then launched out on his own (he was, it
need hardly be said, known for his austere Christian morality). He

proclaimed, 'I would normally regard homosexual behaviour or perverted practices with a prostitute as creating a security risk if it was of recent date.'[38] Denning went on to write paragraph after salacious paragraph on 'The Man in the Masonic Apron', 'The Headless Man' and headed his chapters 'Christine Tells Her Story', 'The Slashing and Shooting', 'He's a Liar' and 'Mr Profumo's Disarming Answer'. It is little wonder that the document sold 100,000 copies.

Macmillan, at least, was safe. Denning had offered some mild criticism of his inattention to the details and had identified one Minister – widely assumed to have been Marples – indulging in 'perverted practices'. But the upshot was that Macmillan could continue on his chosen path. In fact, that path was to lead him back, after the three years' exile in Admiralty House, to Downing Street. By the end of September, No. 10 Downing Street was operational again – and Macmillan and Dorothy were able to move back in on 2 October. 'The house is really nice –' Macmillan wrote on 3 October, 'not so fine a house or with such noble rooms as Admiralty House . . .'[39] but he was glad to be back at what had been for both of them a comfortable home.

On Sunday 6 October Home came to dinner with Macmillan – *à deux* – at Chequers, where the Macmillans had been spending the weekend. It was an occasion for frank speaking. Home made it clear that he was in favour of Macmillan's plan – to make an announcement at Party Conference and resign in January. Macmillan replied that he had discussed the whole thing with his son Maurice and felt that his family now all approved of his plan. The problem, of course, was how to get the right successor. ('Butler would be fatal. Maudling uninspiring – Hailsham, with Maudling and others in loyal support, might still win.'[40]) But as the conversation went on, both began to wonder whether Macmillan's plan would really work. It would mean that from the time of the Party Conference to January the Prime Minister would be under sentence of what amounted to political death. Furthermore, the scramble for the succession would start immediately and last for three months. Their conclusion was that Macmillan should think again – and hold another round of talks with his colleagues.

These duly took place in Downing Street on the following afternoon – of 7 October. First, Macmillan had a talk with the faithful Bligh, who told him that 'the Cabinet are rallying to me with great enthusiasm. Only one or two exceptions.'[41] Butler came next – and thought that Macmillan should stay. Dilhorne too thought the same, as did Redmayne and Duncan Sandys. At five o'clock Poole came – and thought that Macmillan should not risk a humiliating defeat in a General Election. At six o'clock, they were joined by others. The upshot was that all agreed that if Macmillan decided to go on he would have the full support of the Cabinet. By the time Macmillan went to bed he had changed his mind again. He was by then 'determined to inform the Cabinet that I had now decided to stay on and fight the General Election'.[42]

There was, however, to be a snag. Towards the end of the discussion Macmillan had felt the need to go to the lavatory to urinate. He went, and tried, but nothing emerged. He then went to bed, woke up in great pain and got up to try again. Again, nothing came out. By 2 a.m. the pain was so great that Macmillan called out to Dorothy to get a doctor. Since Richardson was on holiday Dorothy summoned his locum, Dr Stephen King-Lewis. King-Lewis duly arrived at Downing Street around 4 a.m. Alerted by Dorothy to the problem, he arrived with the right equipment – a catheter to be passed, under local anaesthetic and with an appropriate lubricant, down through the penis and into the bladder to drain it. The immediate problem was thus resolved.

But the resolution was only temporary. On the morning of 8 October it was evident that the problem persisted. At the Cabinet meeting Macmillan was still in pain, was indeed seen to be unwell, had been given a drink – probably of milk of magnesia to correct constipation – and abruptly left the meeting after an hour or so. That left his colleagues rather bemused – but they did have a rather desultory discussion about his future before most of them had to leave to catch a train to Blackpool. Dilhorne, however, had time to say that if Macmillan did stand down he was ready to organise soundings about a successor. Home followed, saying very clearly that since he himself would under no circumstances be a candidate he would be happy to help Dilhorne as umpire.

In fact, the reason Macmillan had left the meeting was that Richardson, alerted by King-Lewis, had not only set off immediately for London from his holiday in the Lake District but had told King-Lewis to summon Alec Badenoch, the leading urologist of the day. Badenoch arrived at about midday, was ushered in by Dorothy and proceeded to examine Macmillan – rectally – in a bedroom. Since Macmillan was still in pain, Badenoch – once his instruments had been taken from him 'by the butler and, under the supervision of [Badenoch], were "boiled up" [sterilised in boiling water] in another adjoining kitchen'[43] (the main kitchen was fully occupied with preparations for a party later in the evening) – introduced the catheter once again. He then told his patient not to drink anything if he wanted to go to an evening party for staff to celebrate the return to No. 10.

The question was what to do next. Richardson by then had returned hotfoot from the Lake District, and there was a consultation between him, King-Lewis and Badenoch before the evening party got under way.

Badenoch was clear in his diagnosis. Macmillan was suffering from a common condition in older men – benign enlargement of the prostate gland – which was obstructing the flow of urine. Since the condition had reached the acute level, it had to be dealt with by surgery. This was then agreed by all the doctors, and Macmillan himself. The conclusion was that he could go to the party but after that he should go into hospital that very evening. The surgery to the prostate would be a well-known procedure 'to relieve the obstruction causing his urinary retention'.[44] On the evening of 8 October, at 9 p.m., therefore, Macmillan was admitted to King Edward VII's Hospital for Officers. When he arrived, Badenoch immediately inserted a less temporary device, a catheter connected to a bag attached to the inner thigh to drain the bladder whenever necessary to make sure that, pending surgery, at least there would be little pain.

Badenoch was, as might be expected, to be proved right in his diagnosis. Macmillan's prostate enlargement was indeed benign. Macmillan, on the other hand, fearful as always about his health, wrote in his diary (once the pain was relieved he was perfectly capable of writing) that his doctors had told him that the enlarged prostate was 'by either a benign or malignant tumour'.[45] It is true that a rectal examination is not wholly reliable for diagnosis, but it does at least, according to urologists, provide the nearest thing to complete reassurance. For some reason, however, Macmillan, perhaps mindful of his friend Harry Crookshank's death from cancer, or perhaps because of something Richardson or King-Lewis might have said in an incautious moment, thought that there was at least a hint that he might be going down the same route – in short that he had cancer of the prostate.

On the following day, 9 October, Macmillan, by then comfortably in hospital, was able to reflect on what he should do. At first, he thought that nothing much had changed, that this was a temporary setback. But Badenoch had been clear. He had told him, and Richardson had confirmed, that the surgery would require time for healing, that a general anaesthetic for a man of his age would mean a prolonged period of recovery and that even after that he would have to take it easy for some considerable time. Macmillan's response to this advice was surprising. Far from being downcast, he was grateful – even happy. He told Badenoch that the whole thing had come 'as manna from heaven – an act of God'.[46] All indecision was now over. He could not possibly go on. That finally decided, he could now concentrate on his last remaining political task – securing a succession to his liking.

First of all, he had to make sure that his least favourite candidate did not win. He well knew that Butler would be the natural choice of the Cabinet – he had, after all, more or less done the job with great competence for a number of years when Macmillan was on his travels. But Butler was not particularly favoured by the Parliamentary Party and had little support in the more abrasive constituency Associations. If Macmillan left the announcement of his resignation until after the Conference – which would have been the logical course of action for a smooth succession – the Cabinet would be the decisive voice and Butler would stroll in. That was not at all what Macmillan wanted. He had to find a device to stop it.

The answer was to announce his resignation directly to the Conference. This would start – as Macmillan knew perfectly well – a very public campaign by the aspiring candidates. It would be a campaign that Butler, even if he wanted to, could not possibly win. It so happened that Macmillan's messenger to the Conference was immediately to hand. Home, as President for that year of the National Union, would be the right person to tell the Conference of the decision. Accordingly, Macmillan spent the morning of 9 October with his Parliamentary Private Secretary, Knox Cunningham, drafting an announcement – and getting it approved by the Queen. Apart from an interval for a sudden blockage in Macmillan's catheter which had to be relieved by the house doctor, they had a busy morning.

Home was summoned, and duly arrived at King Edward VII's. He collected his copy of the announcement and was told by Macmillan to read it out to the Conference as soon as possible after his arrival in Blackpool. Once in Macmillan's room in the hospital, however, he found, in conversation, that Macmillan had started to shift his ground. Hailsham, it seemed, was no longer the preferred candidate. Washington opinion had weighed heavily against him. Macmillan then suggested to Home that he might be prepared to allow his own name to go forward. Home put on a show of reluctance – and said that he would like to think about it. Nevertheless, knowing that he was armed with what amounted to political dynamite, he pocketed the announcement and prepared to set off for Blackpool the next morning – and to read it out, as promised, as soon as he arrived. Macmillan then settled down for the tests which his doctors required before surgery.

On Friday 10 October, the operation duly took place. Badenoch was, in the process, more than usually careful. He knew that he was dealing with a Prime Minister. He could not afford any mistakes. Eden's history was very much in his mind. He therefore recruited two other senior urologists, David Innes Williams and Joseph Smith, to be at his side. Macmillan, after a telephone call from Home, whose apparent reluctance seemed by then to have magically disappeared (after a conversation with his ambitious wife), was then prepared for the operation and taken to theatre at about 11.30 a.m. By one o'clock it was all over. The operation (known, technically, as an open retropubic enucleation of the prostate) had been a success. Macmillan recovered well, but the morphine treatment for the pain meant that 'I remember little about the rest of the day or the next day'.[47] The Queen telephoned three times and spoke on the third occasion to Badenoch, who reassured her that all was well. The Queen Mother rang as well. But it was not until 12 October that he felt able to understand what people were saying. His dreams, too, were disturbed. He dreamed that 'everyone was trying to destroy me and were all marching on the palace with that purpose. The Queens were protecting me . . .'[48]

As it happened, 12 October was also the last day of the Conference and the day on which Butler was to deliver the Leader's address, in place of Macmillan, at the end of proceedings. By then, out of all the mayhem both inside and outside the Blackpool Winter Gardens which followed Home's reading of Macmillan's message on the Friday, some things had become clear. Maudling's speech had been very flat; Hailsham had made the mistake of talking too much and, worse, of parading his baby, plus baby food, in the lobby of his hotel; and Home, who had made a good – if not outstanding – speech, was quietly canvassing support. Rumours then flew around about a possible Home candidature, but few of his Cabinet colleagues believed it. 'Don't be bloody ridiculous,' Macleod said to his Parliamentary Private Secretary. 'That's absolutely cuckoo. Alec told us in Cabinet he wasn't a runner.'[49]

But it was true. Home had, of course, deceived his Cabinet colleagues. When Butler paid Home the courtesy of inviting him and his wife to lunch on the Saturday before he gave the Leader's address, Home, in the course of the lunch, had stunned Butler with the news that he was indeed a candidate. Nothing could have been more calculated to derail Butler's final bid for the leadership on that very afternoon. Butler's address, in fact, was on a text inherited from Macmillan's speech writers. He could only do his best, altering bits here and there, but by the time he sat down it was clear that it had not been a success. As the Conference dispersed, the word was that Home was now the front runner.

By Monday 14 October, Macmillan was awake enough to take note of what had been going on. Redmayne came to see him in the morning and Dilhorne in the afternoon. Both had been Hailsham supporters but both had been put off by his behaviour in Blackpool and had switched to Home. 'But', Macmillan noted, 'the basic situation was the same – the Party in the country wants Hogg [Hailsham], the Parliamentary Party wants Maudling or Butler; the Cabinet wants Butler. The last ten days have not altered this fundamental fact.'[50]

The next morning Butler turned up at the hospital. Macmillan had by then drafted a 'minute of instruction' to the Cabinet on how to proceed from then on. As Prime Minister, he set out a process of consultation which should now take place – and, as Prime Minister, expected the Cabinet to agree to it. Dilhorne was to sound out the Cabinet; Redmayne was to sound out the other Tory MPs; Lord St Aldwyn (the Conservative Chief Whip in the Lords) was to sound out Tory peers; and Lord Poole was to take the temperature of the Party in the country. Butler duly accepted the instruction and went back to Downing Street to read it out to the Cabinet.

The Cabinet, in turn, could not reasonably refuse an instruction from the Prime Minister. But most were unaware that Dilhorne, Redmayne and St Aldwyn were by then firmly in the Home camp, or that Adeane had asked Home's wife the previous day (in confidence, of course, and 'without her husband's knowledge'[51]) whether her husband would take the job if it was offered. Furthermore, those charged with making the soundings were to report to Macmillan himself. In fact, having considered all the precedents of Prime Ministerial involvement (or non-involvement) in the choice of a successor, Macmillan had decided most definitely that he was going to be involved – that, in truth, he was going to keep the reins very firmly in his hands. He later claimed that it was because 'it was intimated to us quite clearly from the Palace that the Queen would ask for advice'.[52]

Moreover, he was enjoying himself. There was a stream of visitors, mostly Cabinet Ministers – much to the irritation of the hospital matron. He could even joke about it. When Badenoch asked him how his day had been, he replied: 'dreadful! I've just had a meeting with the ten biggest bores in the country!'[53] Nor did the Cabinet know that the choreography for a visit by the Queen to King Edward VII's had already been arranged. On the evening of 15 October, Adeane had spent an hour with Lord Swinton. 'He outlined the proposed drill', Swinton recorded at the time, 'that when Harold was ready to advise H.M. on his successor, the Queen would visit him in hospital and accept his resignation and receive his advice.'[54]

The soundings took place during the afternoon of Wednesday and all day Thursday 16 and 17 October. But there were suspicions at the time – and nowadays little doubt – that the questions were slanted. In fact, a number of MPs complained afterwards that the Whips were deliberately trying to get the answer which they knew Macmillan wanted. In fact, that turned out to be the case. The first to report was Redmayne: of the MPs canvassed, he reported Home having 87 first choices, Butler 86, Maudling 48, Macleod 12 and Heath 10. Home came out top on second preferences. Dilhorne reported next on the Cabinet. Astonishingly, he claimed that 11 supported Home, 4 supported Maudling, 3 Butler and 2 Hailsham. As one account put it, those figures were 'wildly inaccurate, perhaps even wilfully dishonest'.[55] St Aldwyn reported support for Home, and Poole, although he thought that Hailsham was the favourite, said that either Butler or Home would be acceptable. Macmillan had thus, by hook, as it were, or by crook, the result he wanted. On the evening of 17 October he telephoned Home to say that he would be recommending his name to the Queen.

No sooner had this happened than, almost as a matter of course in those days, the news leaked. Late in the evening protest groups formed. Macleod and Powell met at Powell's house in South Eaton Place (amid the debris of Powell's daughter's birthday party). Maudling joined them after dinner, as did Freddie Erroll (President of the Board of Trade) and Toby Aldington. Another group, Hailsham, Julian Amery and Thorneycroft, met at Hailsham's house in Putney. The two groups kept in close touch. All agreed that Home would be a disaster. They also agreed to surrender their own claims and serve under Butler. Redmayne, soon alerted to the revolt, sped round to Powell's house and did his best to convince the rebels to accept Home while they in turn tried to persuade him to accept Butler. After a protracted and angry argument in which neither side made headway, Redmayne agreed to report their views to Macmillan. Just to make sure that the Queen was aware of all this, Aldington telephoned Adeane and reported to him.

The problem that the rebels had was that Butler himself was not inclined to rebel. 'My only concern was for the Party,' he said in later life. 'Loyalty was of the essence.'[56] He realised only too clearly the chaos which would ensue if he joined the rebellion and openly challenged Macmillan – still the sitting Prime Minister. Gradually the 'Revolt of the Night' faded away. Its effect, however, was the opposite of what had been intended. When alerted the next morning by Bligh, Macmillan increased the tempo. But Home, too, had heard of the rebellion, and called Macmillan the same morning to say that, under the circumstances, he felt like withdrawing. Macmillan told him, in effect, not to be so silly. That done, the balletic arrangements got under way.

At 10 a.m. Bligh was despatched to Buckingham Palace with Macmillan's letter of resignation. Then, at 11.15 a.m., the Queen's car pulled up in front of King Edward VII's Hospital in Beaumont Street, the surrounding area having been sealed off for the event. Macmillan had been duly wheeled down to the board room of the hospital. He had put on a white silk shirt for the purpose but, since it was put over a battered old brown cardigan, the effect was comic rather than dignified. As he lay there, he had a bottle beside him – in case of a possible disaster of incontinence – and a bell to summon the sister who was posted outside the door. The Queen was met by the dignitaries of the hospital – and Badenoch – and was ushered in to see the patient, who at that point was still her Prime Minister (and remained so until she formally accepted his resignation).

The Queen was obviously upset. She spoke softly and unsteadily. But after some inconsequential talk – and her acceptance of his resignation – Macmillan asked her whether she wished to hear his advice. When she replied that she would, Macmillan read out the text he had prepared and advised her, in short, to move quickly. But, just in case there was trouble, she should, in sending for Home, use a formula in use in the nineteenth century – not to form a government but to see whether he was able to do so. She agreed. Back in the hospital, the Downing Street staff who had been in attendance were taking their leave of the man who was no longer Prime Minister. It was an emotional moment. Most of them, like Bligh himself, were in tears.

On the way back to the Palace, Adeane reminded the Queen that she need not accept Macmillan's advice, since when he had tendered it he was an ordinary Member of Parliament and no longer Prime Minister. Since Adeane had orchestrated the whole visit he presumably did not wish to be taken seriously. In fact, the visit, of course, had been unnecessary. If the Queen had wanted Macmillan's advice, she could have used the telephone. But once the visit was made, in the glare of publicity and in the knowledge that Home was Macmillan's preferred candidate, the fact that he was no longer Prime Minister (in which case his advice would have been binding), as he was when she arrived at the hospital, was neither here nor there. Having gone to the hospital and received advice – and then told Macmillan that she would not seek advice elsewhere – she could not just tear it up. Furthermore, as Adeane knew full well, the Queen personally much preferred Home to Butler. 'When she got the advice to call Alec she thought "Thank God". She loved Alec – he was an old friend. They talked about dogs and shooting together . . .'[57]

'We all understood', said a courtier, 'that Alec could not form a government unless Rab agreed to serve.'[58] But with the Queen's request in his hand, and not just as a result of Macmillan's – and Adeane's – dubious manoeuvres, Home held the aces. He was carrying the Sovereign's mandate. To refuse to serve under him, for Butler, would have meant at the very least the accusation of disloyalty – and almost of treachery. Butler duly agreed to serve and, one by one, the rebels of the night – apart from Macleod and Powell – followed suit.

The immediate result was that Home formed a Government. As for

Macmillan, no longer Prime Minister, he stayed in hospital rather longer than Badenoch believed necessary. It was not until 27 October that he finally emerged, with little publicity, to thank the hospital staff, the matron, the nurses, the house doctor and so on, and, walking carefully with a stick, made his way quietly to a waiting car and was driven away.

In all this, Macmillan (with the connivance of Adeane) had achieved his main objective – to prevent Butler succeeding him. Yet, in doing so, he had, like Samson at Gaza, brought down the temple with him. The Queen had been bounced into an unnecessary visit to his hospital which had locked her into accepting his choice of successor – thus committing, according to one commentator, 'the biggest political misjudgement of her reign'.[59] Moreover, thereafter, the 'royal prerogative', which Macmillan proclaimed as his determination to preserve intact, was at best very much diminished and in most cases simply removed, since the Conservative Party soon decided to follow the Labour and Liberal Parties and elect their leader, thus leaving the Queen normally no choice. Lastly, it soon became clear that Macmillan had chosen the wrong man. Home, with his half-moon spectacles and squeaky voice – never mind his proclaimed wish to use matchsticks to help with the problems of the British economy – looked in 1964 like a creature from another planet.

It all made for a sad end to Macmillan's Premiership. In his most successful years, 1957 and 1958, he had revived the Conservative Party after the Suez debacle, had established a Government of talent and one which could claim to be, by the standards of its predecessor and successor, reasonably successful, and had mended the fractured relationship with the United States. But as the years went by, like many Prime Ministers before and since, he seemed to become out of touch with the people he was governing. His language, the way he dressed, his shuffle, his affectations, all made him seem even more of an anachronism than was truly the case. His choice of Home as his successor, another anachronism, was, as he later admitted, a final, and fatal, mistake. According to many observers, not least Harold Wilson, Rab Butler would, as Prime Minister, have won the 1964 General Election. It is not the most cheerful epitaph for a Premiership – that the Prime Minister, at his departure, left behind him a Party which was to be out of power for six years.

Part Five

THE LAST ACT

The End of the Day

There was, as Macmillan had half expected, a political explosion. Iain Macleod and Enoch Powell, both of whom had refused all blandishments to serve under Home, stood at the front of an army of commentators to direct fire at the former Prime Minister. The attack followed three clear lines: Powell and his followers took the constitutional high road, stating that the offence lay in the way Macmillan had manoeuvred the Queen into accepting his nominee; Iain Macleod, on the other hand, complained, in an article in the *Spectator* published in the following January and supported by others in correspondence, that the whole thing had been stitched up by a toffs' 'magic circle', almost all of whom were Etonians; and a particularly vocal backbencher, Humphry Berkeley, insisted, in common with a good number of Conservative MPs, that Macmillan had had only one purpose – to deny Butler the succession by hook or, if necessary, by crook – and that by crook it had been.

All three lines of attack were fully justified. It was true that he had bounced the Queen. It was also true that he had favoured the Old Etonian Earl of Home. Finally, it was true that he had deliberately set out to deny Butler the succession. But such was the strength of the onslaught that Macmillan, even while still in hospital, felt that he had to mount a defence. This he did, both in a letter to Morrison, the Chairman of the 1922 Committee, for transmission to the Committee at large and, with greater venom, by writing passages in his diary which would be transmitted to posterity when he came to compose his memoirs. 'I have been very unfairly attacked about this,' he wrote. 'I feel that if I had not acted' (the constitutional point) 'there might have been complete disaster ... it is quite untrue that I was determined to "down" Rab' (the Butler point). 'It is true that I would have preferred Hailsham, as a better election figure. All this pretence about Rab's "progressive" views is rather shallow. His real trouble is his vacillation in any difficult situation. He has no strength of character or purpose and for this reason should *not* be PM ... The more I reflect on the events of the last week the more astonished I am at the failure of Rab, who was deputy PM and put in charge when I went to hospital, to *do* anything about the crisis. I had made it clear that I could not go on and he should have at least tried to get some method of testing opinion organised ... Lord Home was the only compromise candidate possible' (the toff and Old Etonian point). 'Incidentally, he was the best candidate of the four – but that is another argument.'[1]

On none of these three points does Macmillan's defence stand up to serious scrutiny. The episode of the Queen's visit to King Edward VII's Hospital had been there for all to see. There was no denying that almost all the main actors in the drama had been educated at Eton. Lastly, Butler had been a successful Home Secretary and Deputy Prime Minister, 'minding the shop' during Macmillan's travels and diligently managing the crises in the unravelling of the Central African Federation. (On the Butler point, as it happened, in the end – two years later – Macmillan recognised his mistake. He finally admitted that it would have been better if Butler had been his successor after all. 'Then we could have won the election in '64 ...'[2])

None the less, the fact that Macmillan felt it necessary to put down his defence in writing, even if only for posterity, shows the force of the attacks. They were deeply wounding, not just because they were evidence of his deviousness but because they questioned his honour. Moreover, his critics were still on the rampage. They went on to take him to task over his resignation honours list. A barony for Wyndham was far too much, and the revival of the title of baronet for Harold Evans, Knox Cunningham and Richardson seemed wholly eccentric. He himself was also criticised, in what seemed to many to be magisterial arrogance, for refusing the Queen's offer of an earldom, claiming, as he apparently did, that if he accepted and then died it would affect his son Maurice's position in the House of Commons (ignoring the possibility that Maurice would have every right to disclaim under the Peerage Act).

All in all, Macmillan, in the aftermath of his resignation, was not enjoying anything like a good press. Nor – to add to his dismay – was his health as good as he had hoped. Convalescence was taking time, and was not proving particularly easy. He was still in some pain, even after he left hospital, and had to be content with the minor entertainments of old age – being driven by Dorothy to Regent's Park, for instance, and sitting on a bench with a blanket over his knees. Depression took over from time to time and, as he wrote himself, he was 'on the point of bursting into tears for no reason'.[3] Of course, his mood was, in medical terms, perfectly understandable. He had just ceased to be Prime Minister after nearly seven years and he had had a serious operation. It is little wonder that he was taking time to adjust and recover.

But it was no good moping. He realised that he had to find something to do – and that meant returning, after all the years of absence, to his old career of publishing. With that in mind, on 31 October he paid his first visit to Macmillan and Co. The occasion was a meeting of the directors. Macmillan, when invited into their meeting, told them that he was proposing, with the agreement of his elder brother Daniel, to return to take an active role in the firm. Nevertheless, he went on, it would take him a month to regain his strength but after that, he would take over from his brother Daniel as Managing Director. What the other directors thought about this announcement is not known, but it can hardly have come as a surprise. Such was the nature of the firm in those days that the other directors took it as a matter of course that a member of the family could return whenever he wanted – and that a senior member of the family could return to a senior position.

Macmillan fitted easily enough back into the family firm. Even on his first visit he was asked to make a presentation to a Mr Harold Woods, who was retiring after forty-six years working for Macmillan's. 'On making the presentation,' the house newsletter reported, 'Mr Harold Macmillan commended Mr Woods on his long service and said that, as the firm had been in existence for 180 years, he could be proud of having served it for more than one third of its life.'[4] The arithmetic was dubious, but nobody noticed, and Mr Woods was then given the customary gold watch and a cheque for thirty pounds which had been collected from members of the staff (in other words, his fellow 'servants').

In fact, it was time, and more than time, for a change in the management. Daniel, intellectually brilliant though he was, had found much of the financial arrangements of the business tedious. Furthermore, in the firm's publications, books on classical history were favoured, as were educational books, but the general list – and the impressive backlist – had been neglected. Furthermore, after Daniel's wife had mysteriously drowned in her bath in 1957 and he himself had been diagnosed in 1960 as suffering from cancer, Daniel had become more and more short-tempered. It thus came as something of a relief when 'Mr Harold' in 1963 returned as Managing Director and Daniel moved up to Chairman. On 1 January 1964, the business was reorganised. A holding company was formed, Macmillan (Holdings) Ltd, of which 'Mr Daniel' became Chairman. Below that there were two operating companies, Macmillan & Co. Ltd, the book publisher, and Macmillan (Journals) Ltd, the publisher of *Nature* and, strangely, *The Nursing Times*. 'Mr Harold' became Chairman of both those operating companies.

By then, the original partnership had long been incorporated, and the shares in the successor company vested in the Macmillan Trust. Consequently, ownership of the new holding company passed as a matter of course into the hands of the Trust. Nevertheless, the management – and control – still rested firmly in the hands of the Macmillan family. Nobody was bold enough to question the direction of the business against the family's decisions. As for the staff, there were for them the familiar characteristics of many family firms. Any who could not accept the nature of the animal soon left. Those who remained were content to serve the family interest – either by being sycophantic and grateful for any act of kindness that filtered down from the top or by meekly referring all decisions of any importance to the family directors – and accepting them without argument.

Macmillan took a little time to settle in, but, once there, he started to deal with the problems which Daniel had left behind. 'I fear', he wrote later, 'that the last years of [Daniel's] long reign have left (and created) a lot of problems.'[5] He did not hesitate to wield the axe. Many of the senior staff were dismissed, some quite brutally, and the juniors were simply told that they were no longer required. The fiction list, which had suffered under Daniel's critical, and often cantankerous, attitude to authors, was gradually expanded. Much more significant, in terms of profitability, was the rise in paperback sales. Macmillans had a 51 per cent interest in the second largest paperback imprint, Pan Books, and also was able to make use of its backlist through the St Martin's Library imprint. Both, in the 1960s, caught the fashion of the day.

But it was not the same as life in No. 10 Downing Street. Macmillan lamented the lack of secretarial service. 'It seems strange', he noted, 'no longer to be able to ring the bell for a "young lady" at any time, day or night.'[6] He had also, since he had never learnt how to drive a car, to rely on Dorothy or a driver to get him about – and neither of these could be whistled up at will. Those were no more than minor problems – but irritating none the less. Yet his first month in a revived publishing career was completely overshadowed by a tragic and quite unexpected international event. On 22 November 1963, a day marked thereafter in every calendar of those living at the time, President Kennedy was assassinated.

There is no doubt that Kennedy's assassination was a terrible shock to Macmillan. He was staying with Wyndham (by then Lord Egremont) at Petworth when the news came through just before dinner on Friday 22 November. The house party was, of course, as stunned as the rest of the world, but for Macmillan the event was 'overpowering, incredible'.[7] It was almost like the loss of a son. He was pestered all weekend to go on television, but refused. He thought it wiser to speak in the House of Commons, which he did – movingly and much to the satisfaction of Ambassador Bruce – on the Monday. But the speech, and the emotion of the whole event, had so tired him out that he went straight back to Birch Grove and to bed.

There was another shock to come – this one minor, but closer to home. Ava Waverley, Macmillan's sad companion over recent years – her only close relation was her stepson, himself a busy doctor in Reading, and Macmillan had found himself almost in the position of a guardian – had been diagnosed with cancer of the liver. The diagnosis was not final, but a preliminary assessment was that she only had a few months to live. (In fact, the preliminary diagnosis turned out to be quite wrong. She lived for another ten years.)

As 1963 drew to its close Macmillan more and more felt the loss of Downing Street. Like other Prime Ministers before and since, he thought from time to time that he might be called back in times of national crisis, most probably to head a government of national unity, but, as with the others, the moment never seemed to come. Finally, at the end of the year, he stopped writing his diary – there was, in truth, nothing any more of great interest to write about. To be sure, the Denning Report was debated in the House of Commons before Christmas, but by that time there was little more to say about the whole affair.

When it came, 1964 was to prove both irritating and frustrating. There was one more speech in the House of Commons, on the presentation of a scroll to Churchill. There were the final nostalgic moments as he relinquished the Bromley constituency before the General Election of October 1964 – and the depressing experience of watching from the sidelines as Home led the Conservatives to defeat. Birch Grove House became more and more gloomy as the children moved away and the grandchildren grew up. Meals were often eaten in silence. He and Dorothy also often sat in different rooms for their solitary reading (they had long ago ceased to share a bedroom).

It was, however, again time to stop moping, and time for his memoirs. In August 1964, the fiftieth anniversary of the outbreak of the First World War, Macmillan started work. He was fully prepared. During the long years in office he had made a habit of telling his secretaries to copy documents to his personal files. Nothing was to be lost. Moreover, in his last days as Prime Minister, Bligh and others had copied a large number of official documents. It was, of course, quite wrong, as the Cabinet Secretary, Sir Burke Trend, sternly pointed out – but to no avail. By modern standards, indeed, such behaviour would have not only been inadmissible, indeed scandalous – but in those days only Burke Trend seemed to notice and, even then, he had no power to impose any restrictions.

The General Election of 1964 came and went. Labour returned to government with a slim majority. Maurice lost his seat and returned to a place in Macmillan's. At the same time Macmillan's own memoirs, originally planned to be three volumes, had already started to expand. It had been, and always was, a frequent (and self-confessed) fault. Once Macmillan put pen to paper prolixity took over. Moreover, his writing style had never developed like his speaking style. As a result, his memoirs read like his publications of the 1930s – turgid and hard to follow. Of course, as might be expected in any political memoir, they are full of self-justification and on a number of occasions, to borrow a phrase which recently gained currency, are economical with the truth. All that needs to be said, in fact, when confronted with the daunting work in its totality, is that the author was his own editor and publisher.

Just as Macmillan was embarking on the long journey of his memoirs the directors decided that the elegant but rather old-fashioned – almost Dickensian – offices in St Martin's Street (conveniently close to the Beefsteak) were no longer suitable for an expanding publishing firm. Besides, there had been an attractive offer for the building from a property developer. A search produced a much more modern building in Little Essex Street, on the slope going down from the eastern end of Aldwych to the Temple and the Thames (but, alas, much further away from the Beefsteak). It certainly had more natural light and was, in the provision of telephones and telex machines, up to date. Moreover, the directors at the same time decided to build an office for staff who had no need to be in central London, as well as a warehouse, at Basingstoke in Hampshire.

The move was completed in 1965 – but with much nostalgic regret for the past history of the firm in St Martin's Street. For Macmillan himself, as well, regret was a constant theme. Early in that year, in January, Churchill died (Macmillan, like everybody else, was much moved by the state funeral). Churchill's death was followed during the year by two deaths in the Macmillan family – the start, as it happened, of a melancholy succession. The first was of Joshua, Maurice's second son and an undergraduate at Oxford aged no more than twenty. Joshua, or 'Jishi' as he was called, was a young man of great charm – and full of youthful fun. But on a trip to Morocco he had been introduced to cannabis. From there he had moved on to heroin and cocaine. Treated for heroin addiction in Switzerland in the spring of 1965, he had returned to Oxford – where he took to mixing alcohol with the sedative Valium. One night he went out with friends, drank heavily and went back to his rooms. He then took about twenty tablets of Valium – and died in his own vomit.

The next death was of Daniel, just before the Christmas of 1965. In one way it was a release. The two brothers had not, in truth, had an easy relationship. Daniel had always liked to remind people that he was the elder brother (Arthur, the middle son, had chosen not to go into publishing and remained distant) and he was sometimes resentful of Macmillan's political success. Macmillan, on the other hand, was respectful of Daniel's intellect but critical of his business sense. After Daniel had been diagnosed with cancer, however, the relationship became more harmonious – but it could never be said that the two did more than live their lives at arm's length.

The next was Dorothy. In the spring of 1966, she and Macmillan made another expedition to Scotland. The return to Birch Grove was, apparently, serene. On 22 May, however, Dorothy was preparing to go to a point-to-point near Birch Grove. As she put on her boots in the hall she complained to her maid that she had a dreadful backache. A few minutes later she collapsed – and died instantly. (It was a massive heart attack. In medical terms, in fact, it was hardly unexpected. Although apparently in good health, she was carrying a great deal of weight, so much so that a door had to be removed to get her body upstairs.) Needless to say, the whole house was thrown into turmoil. Macmillan, who was asleep at the time, had to be woken up to be told the dreadful news.

Dorothy's death – there is no doubt of it – left Macmillan desolate. In fact, it changed the whole tenor of his old age. Of course, he was content with the tributes which were paid on her death – Hailsham (by then plain Hogg) said that 'she was one of the most gracious of ladies who ever occupied 10 Downing Street that I have ever known'.[8] Her grandchildren and their friends formed (and still do form, for that matter) a chorus of enthusiastic praise of the way she organised their entertainments at Birch Grove and her grandmotherly care and affection. Yet nobody who knew the history of her marriage and her waywardness could have believed that she was the soul of all virtue. As it happened, Bob Boothby, when he heard of it, also took her death badly. He drank heavily, and burnt all her letters in a moment of (probably alcoholic) grief. Coincidentally, at about the same time, Macmillan found a trove of Boothby's letters to her at Birch Grove. They were duly burnt, in their turn, by his daughter Carol.

After Dorothy's death Birch Grove House fell silent and empty. Macmillan decided to move into a bachelor flat, the former butler's rooms, which had not been used since the war and could only be reached through the kitchens and up a steep staircase. It was, more than anything, almost a replica of an Oxford undergraduate's rooms. There, surrounded by books, he could be by himself. When Mrs Bell, the Macmillans' cook for all those years, retired, and Edith Baker, their maid of long standing, died of cancer, his 'fortress', as he called it, became more and more untidy. Indeed, there were those who thought that he might be in danger of lapsing into the life of a recluse. The new cook only came in when required, and his chauffeur also lived out.

There were several things, however, that kept him going: publishing, Oxford, his memoirs and travel – and a (somewhat unlikely) renewed female acquaintance. But there were pluses. At the age of seventy, his mind was still active and, although he complained to Richardson from time to time, he was physically in good health. True, the shuffle was more pronounced (although, as always, the impression of old age was frequently exaggerated in the presence of others) and his voice was becoming more languid. But he was still agile when he wished to be and, for his age, able to travel without difficulty.

Richardson told him that he had to keep active – and this he did. There were frequent visits to Oxford. After Dorothy died, Macmillan treated his Chancellorship and the university as a Member of Parliament treated his constituency. He went at least three times every term – to dinners, to open new premises, to speak at formal occasions and to preside over the awarding of degrees. As always, his speeches, as on formal occasions in his constituency, were carefully prepared and delivered with what appeared to be spontaneity – full of wit and clever anecdotes. But in their substance they were firm. He believed that nothing in the university should change. The college system should be protected – like the regimental system in the Army – the tutorial method – one on one – should be preserved and, finally, the old centre of the university, by which he meant the colleges in the centre, should be carefully maintained as they would survive the construction of new colleges on the periphery. Above all, he thought that what Oxford offered was simply 'the best education in the world in the most beautiful city in the world'.[9]

Travel abroad was mostly on the firm's business – except when he was selling his own memoirs after they were finished in 1973. Over the years he visited Canada, Australia, India, Nigeria, Egypt, Japan, China, South Africa and, of course, the United States. As before on his travels, he showed a quite remarkable stamina. Wherever he went, he was, as a matter of course, received as an elder statesman – a part he played to perfection, acting as someone even older than he actually was and with eyesight which was worse than it really was (although it deteriorated markedly in the 1970s). His speeches were always much admired – one American newspaper described him as 'a living catalogue of the English-speaking political virtues at their best'.[10]

Yet he was lonely. Ava Waverley was no real substitute for Dorothy – she was preoccupied with running her salon for politicians in Smith Square (generally held, however, to be much less brilliant than the neighbouring salon of Pamela Berry). Anyway, those who knew her thought her, stocky and plain as she was, a 'bit of a battleaxe'. Fortunately, though, there was another, rather more lively, candidate. It is not known precisely when, but some time in the late 1960s Macmillan renewed acquaintance with the widow of one of the authors he had published in the early days of his publishing career. In the event, to the surprise of everybody who knew him (and her), it turned out to be a long-lasting, and strangely touching, relationship.

Eileen O'Casey had been born in Dublin in 1900 as Eileen Reynolds. Trained as a singer, she joined the D'Oyly Carte company as a chorus member in 1923. But her career there was not a happy one, the highlight being a six months' stint in the chorus of *Rose Marie* at Drury Lane in the summer of 1925. She therefore left to go to America looking for work. There were small parts in plays from time to time, but it was on one of her days (or weeks) without work that she picked up, and read a friend's copy of *Juno and the Paycock*. Immediately (and impulsively) she decided that she must – without question – meet the dramatist: Sean O'Casey. Back in Dublin she auditioned for O'Casey's *The Plough and the Stars* at the Abbey Theatre and then, under her stage name of Eileen Casey, she was given a role in the London production of the play in the summer of 1926. By that time she had met O'Casey, who turned out, dauntingly, to be twenty years her senior. None the less, it did not take long for O'Casey to propose marriage, which she accepted – and which lasted happily until O'Casey's death in 1964.

'A bloody terrible actress but a very beautiful girl' was O'Casey's verdict on Eileen. Whatever her acting ability, she was certainly beautiful. Brunette with red tints in her hair, with a clear Irish skin and grey-green eyes, she was reported by one of her friends to be a 'knock out'.[11] But even more than her beauty it was her character which men found so attractive – feisty and cheerful, adept in conversation and warm-hearted to anybody in trouble or sadness. Of course, by the time she and Macmillan renewed their former acquaintance she was nearing seventy, but she was still outstandingly good looking – and she had not lost her love of life. She had also not lost her love of languid, witty conversation, which Macmillan could provide in good measure.

Macmillan, in his old age, almost fell in love with Eileen O'Casey, and she, in her near old age, almost fell in love with him. There were weekends at Birch Grove, lunches at the Ritz and tea at Eileen's flat in Great Portland Street. The talk in the Macmillan family was of marriage. For instance, once, at Birch Grove, Macmillan asked Eileen to sit in Dorothy's chair at table – in front of the family. The message was clear. 'I know in my heart that he would have liked me to settle down with

him,' she said later, 'as we got on so well together ... [But he] found it
difficult to express affectionate feelings. I did not help matters, as I felt
so uncertain myself. I felt almost afraid of being committed to a life
which I did not think I could manage ... After a while I think Harold
and I both realised that it would not be possible for us to be anything
other than loving friends.'[12] Thus they remained as no more than loving
friends – although Eileen admitted in retrospect that she wished it had
been otherwise.

For Macmillan there were, too, the clubs. On his own in London, he
would spend the evening at one or other of them. The Beefsteak was his
particular favourite – and there are still members who recall his evenings
there, the old man keeping them up until two in the morning with his
reminiscences. As is usual with old age, they were anecdotal and repetitive – but their delivery was captivating. In fact, they tended to follow a
pattern. When all present were sitting comfortably, he would start with
the funeral of Queen Victoria, the procession led by Captain Ames, the
tallest man in the British Army. From there, it was usually a question of
the number of servants in the grand houses before the Great War, which
led on seamlessly to the battles of Flanders and the Somme and then to
the perils of the Second World War in North Africa. After the arrival of
Mrs Margaret Thatcher as Prime Minister in 1979 'the tone sharpened
and the speech trotted along, gathering pace as it reflected on the role of
the British as Greeks and the Americans as Romans and concluding in
fine scorn over the sale of the family silver'.[13]

On occasions, though, he still thought about a return to the political
stage. He even thought of standing again for the House of Commons in
the second General Election of 1974 and discussed with Eden (by then
the Earl of Avon) the possibility of forming a coalition government. But
he did not look the part. He had always, when required, acted old age
and, in genuine old age, could not reverse the act. 'Watching him shuffle
down the aisle at a memorial service, leaning on his stick with one hand
and resting on a grandson's arm with the other, Rab Butler exclaimed in
a stage whisper intended to be heard by half the church "It's all put on,
you know ... He can be very amusing, but he should really have been a
Cardinal Archbishop in the Middle Ages, where absolution from irregularity over the facts could always be obtained by a short visit to the
Vatican."'[14]

Shuffling or not, Macmillan liked in the summer to move at appropriate intervals, like a latter-day King Lear, to stay with his various
relations – mostly those on the Cavendish side, since the Macmillans,
obviously, had no grand estates. He was also much taken, and became
more taken in his late years, with the English nobility. His favourite

Duke, apparently, was Andrew, the eleventh Duke of Devonshire, and his favourite Duchess was Deborah, one of the Mitford sisters – and Chatsworth was thus a favourite stopping point. (Macmillan had got over the snubs from the Cavendish girls in the 1930s and towards the end of his life seemed to regard himself as one of their own. The Devonshires appear to have agreed – at least he was no longer accused of carrying the label 'trade'.)

The years, as they do, moved ineluctably on. Macmillan finally stepped down as Chairman of the Macmillan holding company, remaining as President. In March 1970 Sarah died – at the age of thirty-nine. Her marriage had failed, she had tried rehabilitation from alcoholism in Switzerland but that, too, had failed. In fact, she seems to have fallen over when drunk and hit her head, the resulting haemorrhage in her brain causing instant death. In 1972, John Wyndham died, aged fifty-two. He, too, had taken to alcohol. In 1980, Maurice suffered from a collapsed lung and was near death, only to recover, to live on as a near invalid and die four years later.

On 10 February 1984 Macmillan celebrated his ninetieth birthday. Apart from the general celebrations and the publication – by Macmillan's – of *A Life in Pictures*, there was an announcement from Buckingham Palace. The Queen, honouring her long-standing obligation to grant him an earldom whenever he chose to accept it, had been pleased to create him Earl of Stockton. In the event, there were those who cavilled at his choice of title – Stockton was, after all, a part of his history a long time ago. But nothing could spoil the birthday party – apart from the absence of Maurice, by then near his deathbed.

Macmillan's acceptance of an earldom coincided with – and may well have been prompted by – the final failure of his eyesight. Apart from his congenital short-sightedness, he had developed multiple cataracts and, worse, an inoperable degeneration of the retinas of both eyes. In short – the greatest deprivation – he could no longer read the books which had been his companions throughout his life. Books read and recorded on tape were no substitute for the written word. It was better to go and sit in the House of Lords. Apart from that, it was another club to be entertained – and the (then) younger members still speak in awe of the old man sitting in the (quaintly named) Bishops Bar well into the night, with his whisky, relating to other members the memories of a lifetime.

It took several months before he felt able to make his maiden speech. It had to be composed – and then learnt off by heart. There was no question of notes which could not be read. But when it came, on 13 November 1984, it was a supremely well-crafted and superbly theatrical performance. It was, of course, far too long by the convention of the

House of Lords, but nobody complained. Unsurprisingly, it turned out to be an attack – no more than thinly veiled – on the economic and social policies of the Thatcher Government. Undismayed, he followed it up in January with another speech in the House of Lords along the same lines. The next day – the first day on which the proceedings of the House were televised – he repeated his warning about the direction the Government was taking. There was to be one final blast. In November 1985, he made his last speech – to the Tory Reform Group. Again, it was an attack on the Thatcher Government's programme of privatisation. 'Selling the family silver' was again his theme – much to ministerial irritation.

It was not just ministers who were irritated. The press had started again to paint him as an out-of-date 'fuddy-duddy'. The world, it said (with some justification), had moved on, and Macmillan had not moved with it. It was also noted, more sympathetically, that he was becoming physically very frail. It was true. Before his November speech he had been seriously, and painfully, ill with pleurisy. He was troubled by gout and, by the end of 1985, almost totally blind (he could hardly see to eat his food). An attack of shingles was agonising and, as frequently happens, put a strain on his heart. As the months took their toll, he could only just manage, in the spring of 1986, to get to Oxford to award a degree to the Spanish King Juan Carlos, but a subsequent recurrence of pleurisy laid him low again. He revived enough to make his usual round of summer visits – to Chatsworth and to Scotland – and, finally, a last journey to Oxford. The Christmas of 1986 was spent with his children, grandchildren and great-grandchildren, but it was by then obvious that he was slipping away. On 29 December 1986, at the age of ninety-two, after saying quietly to his grandson 'I think I will go to sleep now'[15] he drifted off. So it was that his long and – all things considered – turbulent life came to a serene and peaceful end.

Epilogue

Harold Macmillan was the last British Prime Minister to have been born in the reign of Queen Victoria and the last to have fought in the First World War. (He was also, as it happens, the last British Prime Minister to sport a moustache.) He was in essence an old-style Tory – at least, to be more accurate, he made himself into one. These simple facts go a long way to explain why the end of his Premiership in 1963 has been seen as the end of a political era – some have said that it was the end of the Edwardians. Certainly, the prevailing mood of Britain, and the Conservative Party, changed after he left the stage. Of course, the change took time to become fully apparent. There was the unhappy interlude of the Home Premiership, when Macmillanism – if it can be called that – was given an uncertain extension of life, and there was the period when Wilson, Heath, and then Wilson and James Callaghan, struggled with the gradual disintegration of the post-war consensus. In fact, it was not until the 1980s that the full force of a new Conservative (or, perhaps more properly, Whig) doctrine, subsequently to be known as Thatcherism, made itself felt. Macmillan, it almost goes without saying, old-style Tory that he was, deeply disapproved of it.

Born into a puritanical Scottish-American household (with a domineering American mother), Macmillan was nevertheless educated in a quintessentially English manner. Summer Fields, Eton, Oxford and the Grenadier Guards were the training grounds for the English upper (and upper middle, since that was where he should be placed) class of his day, and all of them left their mark. Summer Fields and Eton taught him the virtues (and vices) of his class. Oxford sharpened his exceptional intellectual gifts and converted him – it is not too strong a word – to an intense Anglo-Catholicism. From there, his experiences in the First World War and in his subsequent constituency of Stockton, as he himself noted, served to instil in him the duty to mitigate, as far as possible, the injustices suffered by the less privileged – be they Guardsmen, Durham miners or Stockton steelworkers.

There are those who have said that this was all bogus, and that his proclaimed concern for the less fortunate was no more than show. The evidence is – on balance – against this view. For instance, he would never have chosen the title he did – Earl of Stockton – if that had been altogether true. On the other hand, there was no question of the less fortunate usurping the position of their social superiors. Macmillan was certainly no egalitarian, let alone Socialist. But he was a sincere Christian, and if his attitude towards the working class of the day was paternalistic, sentimental rather than revolutionary, it chimed well with his Christianity. Nevertheless, the general order of things – rendering to Caesar what was due to Caesar and, at the same time, rendering to God what was due to God – should not be disturbed. Politics was not, after all, about theology. If people wanted spiritual guidance, he often said, they should look to their bishops rather than to their politicians.

But politicians certainly could, and should, be looked to for guidance on how to manage a political career. In an illuminating moment, when asked which of all the peacetime British Prime Ministers he considered the greatest, Macmillan plumped not, as might have been expected, for Benjamin Disraeli but, surprisingly, for Sir Robert Walpole. He was, in Macmillan's view, the political master. To be sure, in his views about the economy, Macmillan was very much influenced by Keynes and his fervent disciple – and biographer – Roy Harrod. But politics were not just about economics. For lessons in how to be a politician he pointed to Walpole, and, in particular, to Walpole's two great maxims: to know 'what it concerned him most to know' and *quieta non movere* (more or less, 'let sleeping dogs lie').

Macmillan followed both of Walpole's maxims – almost to the letter. In explaining the first, Walpole had made it clear what it was that a successful politician needed to know about his fellow men – their strengths and weaknesses, their ambitions, their successes and their failures. He should be able flatter their strengths (to his advantage) and cut them down if they were weak. The secret, of course, was never to make a mistake. Macmillan took the lesson to heart. He spent a great deal of time reflecting on the characters of his colleagues and, in all his career, he made very few mistakes. Salisbury, Thorneycroft, Butler, Welensky – they were all, in their turn, brushed aside.

On Walpole's second maxim, the lesson was simple. Where there was no crisis, or where a crisis could be avoided, it was unwise to create one. Thus, not only should the prevailing social order not be disturbed but the existing rules should not even be revised unless revision was imperative for the maintenance of the prevailing order. Macmillan, again, learnt the lesson. In short, although he was on the Keynesian economic left of the Conservative Party he was at the same time on the social, markedly illiberal, right. (He was against the abolition of the death penalty, against making life easier for homosexuals, prostitutes and prisoners, against lowering the age of consent, and so on.)

Walpole also believed (as did another of Macmillan's mentors, Churchill) that politics was a profession which should be embraced at an early age. That was the way to success. Macmillan accordingly decided, from the early 1930s onwards, to educate himself to be a successful politician. Apart from studying political texts, he set himself to learn the practicalities of his chosen profession. He learnt how to act. He even taught himself (as did Harold Wilson) to be witty. He also studied the careers of other politicians in the greatest detail. (For instance, when he was a Minister under Herbert Morrison in 1940 he spent a great deal of his time, according to Morrison, advising his superior – although a political opponent – on how he should conduct his political career. Morrison even had to remind him from time to time that there was a war on. But it was, as Macmillan in his more relaxed moments would say, all part of the glorious game.)

If Walpole was in pole position in the glorious game, Disraeli was not far behind. Every page of his writing, Macmillan would tell anybody who would listen, was worth reading and re-reading. In particular, it was Disraeli who taught him that any politician who aspired to success had to master the House of Commons. The House, as Disraeli had pointed out, is a jealous mistress. Just as the highest compliment you can pay a woman, he had gone on, is to give her your time, you must be ready, if you wish to win the House of Commons, to do the same for her. Macmillan understood the lesson, and made himself always attentive to the House and its Members – and learnt to dominate the House when he spoke. Almost everybody from those days has his or her own anecdote of his speeches, and his visits to the Smoking Room, and it was no accident that in January 1957, after he had kissed hands as Prime Minister for the first time, he chose to celebrate not with his family but with the Government Chief Whip.

All those lessons were well learnt. But in one matter Macmillan was much less successful than Disraeli – in his relations with the monarch. He had duly followed Disraeli's example – flattery and an obsequious, almost oleaginous, approach, as evidenced in his letters – but Queen Elizabeth had been less impressed by Macmillan than Queen Victoria had been by Disraeli. There was also a certain – Balliol-type – inability to suppress a sense of intellectual superiority, which was no doubt justified but was none the less irritating for all that. The result, according to one courtier, was that when Macmillan visited Balmoral a junior secretary was detailed to take him for very long walks to get him out of the Queen's way. She was, in short, bored at being lectured and not being listened to.

If Disraeli was required reading and rereading, so was Trollope. He, too, gave Macmillan, the voracious reader, insights into the world of politics. But more than that Trollope, and the other great English classical writers of which he was so fond, helped him by encouraging long periods every day of relaxation – of reading and reflection. But they also taught him the benefits of pace – of pace in writing, of pace in reading and, above all, of pace in the conduct of meetings and conversation.

There was one area in which Macmillan developed his own version of pace – a technique for dealing with difficult people and difficult situations. In meetings, instead of concentrating on the difficulties, to the point of provoking resistance, he would, seemingly unpredictably, embark on a dissertation on a wholly irrelevant topic – about the relative merits of the American and British regimental systems, for instance, or the sad history of the ancient Greek city of Miletus. Just as suddenly, after ten minutes or so, he would then revert to the point at issue and his interlocutor (or his Cabinet), the mind lulled by the diversion, would, as often as not, agree to what he wanted.

If Macmillan's formidable personal political skills were the equal of those of Walpole or Disraeli, the question which needs to be asked, with him as with them, is what, in honest truth, was the point of it all. At one level, the answer is not too difficult. The ship of state, according to one Tory political philosopher, sails on the open seas. There is no port from which it came and there is no port of destination. The function of the captain and crew is to keep the ship sailing on, resisting the buffeting of the waves with touches of the rudder here and there, and making life for those on the lower deck as comfortable as circumstances allow. Beyond that, there is no objective – nor should there be. If the philosophy is rather bleak, it is certainly one which would have appealed to Macmillan. It is, after all, almost a paraphrase of Walpole's *quieta non movere*. It was the ultimate justification for remaining, under all circumstances, 'unflappable'. It was also the justification for seeking compromises, which, to his enemies and also to his allies, sometimes appeared as betraying a lack of nerve. The ship of state has to remain calm.

Yet, as with Walpole – and Disraeli, for that matter – the question put by Walpole's early biographer, Macaulay, remains open – whether the calmness which was sought was not for the peace of the country but for the peace of his own administration. As Macmillan himself said in his most languid voice, when asked for advice on the date of the General Election in 1978 by the then Prime Minister, James Callaghan: 'Dear boy' (his frequent, and to some irritating, mode of address), 'you have a nice town house, a house in the country, plenty of servants – I wouldn't give it up too early if I were you.' It was said only half in jest. It may just be, underlying it all, that in his – very private – view the only real purpose of the captain of the ship of state was to maintain his own position on the bridge.

Macmillan's personal life was much less successful than his political life. Physically, in spite of his constant complaints, he was healthy enough for a man of his time and background. Eyesight was always a problem, and the wounds from the First World War left him with a recurrent ache in his thigh – and a shuffle – as well as a limp handshake in his right hand. His handwriting, too, was always difficult to read and in his old age degenerated into an almost illegible scrawl. Apart from that, he stood well (when he wanted to), was agile enough (when he wished to be) and over the long years showed always remarkable stamina in travelling. Once his teeth had been straightened out he presented a reasonably handsome face to the world.

That was for the outside world, but in his own political and publishing world the face was not always so handsome, and he was far from universally liked. Bobbety Salisbury thought him a 'twister'. One Macmillan employee thought him a 'deeply unpleasant man'. On the other hand, a ministerial colleague 'loved the man', and Badenoch, his urological consultant, found him a 'brave, fascinating and delightful' patient. When he wished, he could be either witty and charming or, if occasion demanded, brutally and sarcastically rude. As for his family, he was on many occasions the latter. He was not one to tolerate weakness. Whether the alcoholism of every one of his children (and Sarah) was the result of what he liked to call the 'Cavendish gene' or whether it was the result of inadequate parental affection is a matter of medical debate. What is clear is that Macmillan either deliberately turned a blind eye or maintained that it could be overcome by a show of character strength. There was also, as frequently in his life, the possibility of prayer. (Rab Butler recalled being invited by Macmillan to kneel down with him and pray for Maurice's release from alcoholism.)

In fact, his relationship with Maurice markedly improved once the alcoholism had been mastered. Further than that, all that can, and should, be said is that he was a good and attentive grandfather. As for friends, they were, in truth, few and far between. Harry Crookshank was probably the closest (Macmillan sat for hours beside his bed, holding his hand, as he was dying of cancer). Women, at least until his later years, were for the most part something of an alien species. All in all, solitary reading was the preferred – and most rewarding – pastime.

Macmillan's wife Dorothy was also a child of her time and place. Brought up in the Cavendish household, she was never educated in a way to match Macmillan. In the custom of the day, she spent a good deal of her youth on outdoor pursuits – riding, shooting and so on. There was, of course, no question of her learning any domestic skills (one of the Mitford relations, who also lived in that rarefied world, said that 'nobody' could cook in those days – 'nobody', of course, referring to their own class and ignoring the millions of women who could not afford to hire other women to do it for them). She was snobbish, rumbustious and warm-hearted – and her language, apparently, could be from time to time truly dreadful.

Although she was a supportive wife when Macmillan reached the high offices of government, Dorothy will always be known for her outrageous affair with Bob Boothby. What is so startling about it is not that she became obsessed with someone whom many regarded as a bisexual rogue (or cad or bounder, depending on the strength of feeling and language) but that she was so flagrant and unapologetic about it. She made no effort whatsoever to conceal the affair from her husband or from her family and friends. In fact, she even seemed to go out of her way to throw it in their faces.

Macmillan had been, understandably, in despair. Day in, day out, over a period of years he suffered the humiliation of knowing that his wife was sleeping with another man, and that the other man was a Party colleague of his in the House of Commons. He had to put up with her telephone calls, letters – to and from – and visits to Boothby (his diaries frequently note with dry melancholy that after their Scottish holidays 'Dorothy stayed in Scotland', in other words with Boothby) but also face down the sniggers of those whom he saw daily and who knew that he was being cuckolded. It is not at all surprising that he broke down in 1931 and had to be shipped off by his mother to a sanatorium in Munich.

To survive such continued humiliation Macmillan needed all the willpower he could summon. At first, it was almost too much. There were thoughts, not of himself following her example and taking a mistress – he seemingly had a low sexual drive – but of suicide. Nevertheless, as 1931 moved forward and he recovered his mental balance he found ways of dealing with it all. In his convalescence he decided that he would not give Dorothy the divorce which she wanted (not that Boothby much wanted to marry her either). It was not just because divorce would have damaged his career – possibly irrevocably. The fact was that in his awkward – and emotionally strangulated – way he still loved her.

But he still had to cope with himself. The first step was to persuade himself that Dorothy was ill – and that she would recover from her illness in the course of time, provided she was treated, like a sick child, with tenderness and understanding. The second was to dedicate himself to his work. Publishing was not enough. Politics was the game he would play, and he would show those who laughed at him that he would come out on top. (The fact that Dorothy did not care for the political life presumably added a certain piquancy to his ambition.) The third was to assume a mask of impenetrable calm, to let the world know that there was really nothing to get upset about. It was known to others as 'unflappability'.

All that enabled Macmillan to survive. But it is not possible to hide emotions for long without side effects. The mask becomes second nature, and as the years went by, his mask became so much second nature that it became part of him. In other words, the mask became the face. Like all great actors, he seemed to become unable to slough off the act. Wilson said that he 'posed as a poseur', and there is much evidence from those who knew him, that, when caught unawares, he would scuttle back – automatically – into his act. The mask had indeed become the face.

Macmillan's legacy, as Prime Ministers and Presidents like to call it, can only be described as mixed. By the time he resigned, he had enjoyed a longer continuous period as Prime Minister than any of his predecessors since the Reform Act of 1832 with the exception of Lord Salisbury and Herbert Asquith. When he took office, the ship of state was in very rough waters. The Suez episode had generated great bitterness. Almost like the English Civil War, it had divided families and set brother against brother, sister against sister. Moreover, it had divided the British Commonwealth and frozen relations with the United States. On top of all that, it had brought the Conservative Party to the edge of electoral disaster. In his first two years he steadied the ship, restored relations with the United States and led the Conservative Party to electoral triumph in October 1959. These achievements should not be underrated. In fact, if he had retired, say, in the spring of 1962, some two and a bit years after his electoral triumph – and it was his triumph – he would now certainly be regarded as an exceptional Prime Minister (perhaps even 'great', whatever that means). After all, not only would he have served some five successful years in office but, on retirement, he would have left the ship sailing serenely on in calm waters.

In the light of the debacles of 1962 and 1963, of course, the legacy does not look quite so rosy. Even so, the achievements are genuine. In fact, it was in domestic policy rather than in foreign policy that the Macmillan administration could claim to be most successful. The reforms introduced by Butler at the Home Office (against Macmillan's inclinations) made Britain a more civilised place, and the economic policies followed by a series of Chancellors, closely supervised by Macmillan, made Britain a more prosperous place. In the later years there were, of course, accus-ations that it was also a more materialistic, more selfish and more decadent place, but those are complaints which tend to be heard from time to time whatever the colour or composition of the administration.

There was also one major foreign policy success for which Macmillan can take much of the credit: the gradual conversion of the British overseas possessions from Empire to Commonwealth. It was his realisation that Britain was no longer able to run an empire that was crucial. It was not that he thought highly of the imperial subjects. His opinions were no different from other Conservatives of the right (and he was particularly caustic about Macleod's idealistic view of black Africans). It was simply a matter of practicalities.

Against these successes must be weighed the failures. First was his overenthusiastic – and, frankly, sentimental – attachment to the British relationship with the United States. Like other British Prime Ministers before and since, he seemed to believe that there was some sort of mystical bonding between the two nations, and like other Prime Ministers he never truly understood that the United States, like all great powers, would in the end follow – without necessarily much regard for others – what it perceived from time to time to be its own interests. It was, and is, only at the (very narrow) margin that the United Kingdom could expect to be rewarded for following American ambitions. The conceit that Macmillan put forward, of the British as the Greeks (he meant, of course, the English as Athenians – nobody could think of the Scots or the Welsh as Greeks or of the English as Spartans) and Americans as Romans found no echo at all – other than merriment – in Washington. There was, to be sure, some residual American affection, particularly under Eisenhower, after the Second World War, but that disappeared over the Suez affair. Macmillan's personal relations with Kennedy were cordial on a personal level (Kennedy always enjoyed referring to Mac-millan as 'Uncle Harold') but Macmillan's influence during the Cuban missile crisis was negligible (the Americans thought that he was too accommodating to the Soviets) and the achievement of a test ban treaty owed as much to Kennedy's own skills as to Macmillan's constant pres-sure.

The margin of reward was, and is, narrow. In fact, the one moment a plea for reward worked was when Macmillan insisted on preserving a British nuclear force at Nassau in October 1962 – and Kennedy gave way, against his own better judgement and the overwhelming advice that a British nuclear force was at best irrelevant and at worst dangerous. But for Macmillan it provided a political answer to his Conservative critics who maintained that in 'presiding over the dissolution of the British

Empire' he was only intent on managing Britain's decline as an international power.

There was also the failure of his European policy. As he admitted himself, it turned out badly. In fact, the seeds of the failure itself were sown on Macmillan's watch. He was, after all, the Foreign Secretary who refused to take seriously the conference at Messina in 1956 which led to the formation of the EEC. From that strategic error all else flowed – and Macmillan, having ducked Messina in 1956, reaped the result in Paris in 1963. Many subsequently have put blame squarely on to General de Gaulle, accusing him at best of ingratitude, at worst of something near to treachery. This may be comforting for British historians, but the truth is that Macmillan simply failed to understand either de Gaulle or the apostle of European unification, Jean Monnet.

This was in large measure a matter of cultural infrastructure. Macmillan was a classicist. His mind was set towards antiquity. Although he spoke passable French, his diaries and memoirs show clearly that he had little sympathy for modern Frenchmen. Equally clearly, they show that he disliked Germans, and that he thought Italians, unlike the Romans, to be some sort of joke. He had no interest in music of any kind, no recorded appreciation of Italian Renaissance painting, little idea of the pleasures of French food and wine and little notion of the architectural glories of pre-1914 Germany. Holidays were taken not in continental Europe but in Scotland. Reading was mostly of the English classics, with occasional forays into Russian or French novels (there is no record of his reading Goethe or Dante, and Proust bored him). The result was an ignorance of a large swathe of European culture – and an underlying, wholly English, complex of superiority. (This is in contrast to Edward Heath, whose passion for classical music endeared him to the erudite officials in the European Commission – and, in the end, secured the successful negotiation which had eluded Macmillan.)

The political truth of all this was that Macmillan wanted – intellectually – to be involved in Europe but without being fully engaged in it. In Churchill's footsteps, he became wedded to the idea of a Britain with one foot tentatively planted in Europe (of loosely associated nation states) and with the other foot firmly planted across the Atlantic. The clearest possible vehicle for this was the Council for Europe, of which he was an enthusiastic supporter. It turned out, of course, that there were serious difficulties with this idea. First, it annoyed successive American administrations which, throughout Macmillan's tenure of office, persisted, sometimes irritatingly, in urging Britain to stop messing about and join the EEC. Secondly, it alienated continental European governments as their countries recovered from the ravages of war and grew in the confidence of never letting such war happen again. Thirdly, it exasperated Britain's continental European friends (and Jean Monnet).

It was to be neither one thing nor another. In fact, this is true of many of Macmillan's political endeavours. He was a monarchist who reduced the monarch's prerogative. He was a capitalist who persistently wished to intervene in the operations of the market. He was a British patriot who furthered the dissolution of Britain's empire. He was a European who was almost also an American. If he had been asked, he would probably have put himself forward as an example of the Aristotelian mean: nothing in excess; in other words, the middle of whatever road he was on. If that sounds ambiguous, Macmillan would not have denied it. After all, the world around him was ambiguous and its inhabitants devious. In the end, behind his mask – for better or for worse – so was he.

Notes

PART ONE

Chapter 1. 'The Old Rogue' (pp. 5–19)

1. BBC TV broadcast, 10.ii.1987.
2. Frank Johnson in *The Times*, 13.i.1987.
3. *Daily Mirror*, 11.i.1987.
4. *The Book of Arran*, vol. ii: *History and Folklore*, The Arran Society of Glasgow, Brodick, Kilbrannan Publishing Ltd, 1982, p. 197.
5. Rev. Gershom Stuart in *The Statistical Account of Scotland* (1794), p. 582.
6. Owen County, Indiana, Townships and Towns: www.owen.in.us/owenhist
7. R. L. Hamm in *Spencer Evening World*, 10.xii.1990.
8. Ibid.
9. Ibid.
10. H. Macmillan, *Winds of Change, 1914–1939*, p. 55.
11. Author conversation with Père Ploix, archivist at the Church of the Madeleine.
12. Marriage Certificate of Maurice Crawford Macmillan and Helen Artie Hill, 22.xi.1884.
13. Macmillan, *Winds of Change*, p. 41.
14. Ibid., p. 31.
15. N. Aldridge, *A Time to Spare: A History of Summer Fields*, Oxford, D. Talboys Publications, 1989, pp. 2, 3.
16. Ibid., p. 5.
17. E. Waugh, *Ronald Knox*, p. 54.
18. Macmillan, *Winds of Change*, p. 42.
19. Ibid.
20. S. Curtis, ed., *The Journals of Woodrow Wyatt*, vol. I, London, Macmillan, 1998, p. 146.
21. Eton College Book of Summer 1910.

Chapter 2. 'Balliol Made Me, Balliol Fed Me' (pp. 20–31)

1. Hilaire Belloc, 'To the Balliol men still in Africa'.
2. *Eton College Chronicle*, 9.ii.1987.
3. George Lyttelton (Eton housemaster), quoted in R. Davenport-Hines, *The Macmillans*, London, Heinemann, 1992, p. 147.

4. Quoted in A. Horne, *Macmillan: The Making of a Prime Minister*, vol. 1, *1894–1956*, London, Macmillan, 1988, p. 16.
5. Macmillan, *Winds of Change*, p. 37.
6. Valuation of Birch Grove in 1910: TNA IR58/40193.
7. P. Fitzgerald, *The Knox Brothers*, London, Macmillan, 1977, p. 119.
8. Waugh, *Ronald Knox*, p. 72.
9. R. A. Knox, *A Spiritual Aeneid*, p. 48.
10. Waugh, *Ronald Knox*, p. 96.
11. Quoted in Horne, *Macmillan, 1894–1956*, p. 18.
12. Ibid.
13. Ibid.
14. Knox to his sister, in Waugh, *Ronald Knox*, p. 106.
15. Quoted in Waugh, *Ronald Knox*, p. 107.
16. Quoted in C. Bailey: *Francis Fortescue Urquhart*, London, Macmillan, 1936, p. 32.
17. Waugh, *Ronald Knox*, p. 126.
18. Ibid., p. 124.
19. Knox, *A Spiritual Aeneid*, p. 117.
20. Quoted in Horne, *Macmillan, 1894–1956*, p. 25.
21. Ibid., p. 26.
22. Macmillan, *Winds of Change*, p. 45.
23. Quoted in Waugh, *Ronald Knox*, p. 128.
24. Ibid.
25. Macmillan, *Winds of Change*, pp. 45–6.
26. Quoted in Waugh, *Ronald Knox*, p. 171.

Chapter 3. 'I Was Very Frightened' (pp. 32–46)

1. Macmillan to Knox, 23.vii.1915; quoted in Horne, *Macmillan, 1894–1956*, p. 31.
2. King's Regulations 1912, para 242.
3. Macmillan, *Winds of Change*, p. 63.
4. Ibid., p. 67.
5. Ibid., p. 68.
6. War Diary of 4th Bn Grenadier Guards, 17.ix.1915; TNA WO 95/1223.
7. Ibid., 21.ix.1915.
8. Macmillan to Helen Macmillan, 23.viii.1915; War Diaries 1915; MS Macmillan dep.d.1/2.
9. Macmillan to Helen Macmillan, 26.viii.1915; ibid.
10. *Official History of the Great War; France and Belgium*, vol. 4 (1915, no. 2), p. 152.
11. War Diary of 4th Grenadiers, 25.ix.1915; TNA WO 95/1223.
12. Ibid., 26.ix.1915.
13. Ibid., 27.ix.1915.

14. Account of the capture of Hill 70 by 3rd Guards Brigade; TNA WO 95/1221.
15. Macmillan, *Winds of Change*, p. 76.
16. War Diary of 4th Grenadiers, 27.ix.1915; TNA WO 95/1223.
17. Macmillan, *Winds of Change*, p. 78.
18. Ibid., p. 79.
19. War Diary of 2nd Bn Grenadier Guards, 17.iv.1916; TNA WO 95/1215.
20. Macmillan to Helen Macmillan, 5.v.1916; War Diaries 1916; Ms Macmillan dep.d.2/2.
21. Macmillan to Helen Macmillan, 21.iv.1916; ibid.
22. War Diary of 2nd Bn Grenadier Guards, 19.vii.1916; TNA WO 95/1215.
23. Private Diary of Brigadier General Pereira, 9.viii.1916; TNA WO 95/1212.
24. War Diary of 2nd Bn Grenadier Guards, 26 to 30.vii.1916; TNA WO 95/1215.
25. Ibid., 10.viii.1916.
26. Crookshank War Diary, quoted in S. Ball, *The Guardsmen*, p. 56.
27. Operations carried out by 1st Guards Brigade during August and September 1916; TNA WO 95/1213; p. 2.
28. War Diary of 2nd Bn Grenadier Guards (narrative of events from 13 to 17 September 1916); TNA WO 95/1215.
29. Ibid.
30. Operations carried out by 1st Guards Brigade ..., p. 7; TNA WO 95/1213.
31. Macmillan, *Winds of Change*, p. 87.
32. Operations carried out by 1st Guards Brigade ..., p. 9; TNA WO 95/1213.
33. F. Ponsonby, *The Grenadier Guards in the Great War*, vol. ii, p. 59.
34. Macmillan, *Winds of Change*, p. 87.
35. War Diary of 2nd Bn Grenadier Guards (narrative of events ...); TNA WO 95/1215.
36. Private Diary of Brigadier General Pereira for 17.ix.1916; TNA WO 95/1212.
37. Macmillan, *Winds of Change*, p. 89.
38. Ibid., p. 90.
39. Ibid., p. 57.

Chapter 4. 'I Do Hope It Is Alright' (pp. 47–58)

1. Ninth Duke of Devonshire, diary entry for 6.i.1920; Devonshire MSS, Chatsworth.
2. Macmillan, *Winds of Change*, p. 108.
3. Macmillan to Cranborne, 2.vii.1919, quoted in Ball, *The Guardsmen*, p. 83.
4. Macmillan to Cranborne, 4.viii.1918, quoted in Ball, *The Guardsmen*, p. 76.
5. Macmillan, *Winds of Change*, p. 105.
6. Macmillan to Cranborne, 4.viii.1918, quoted in Ball, *The Guardsmen*, p. 76.
7. Macmillan, *Winds of Change*, p. 109.
8. Quoted in R. Davenport-Hines, *The Macmillans*, p. 169.
9. Ibid., p. 171.

10. Ibid., pp. 170–71.

11. The Colonial Office List 1920, p. 130.

12. Dowager Lady Jersey in *The Times*, 29.x.1937.

13. Macmillan, *Winds of Change*, p. 110.

14. Ibid.

15. Ibid.

16. Ninth Duke, diary entry for Good Friday 18 April 1919; Devonshire MSS, Chatsworth.

17. Memorandum as to strike conditions, 30.v.1919, p. 258; TNA CO 42/1011.

18. Devonshire to Milner, 2.vi.1919; TNA CO 42/1011.

19. Quoted in Horne, *Macmillan, 1894–1956*, p. 55.

20. Ninth Duke, diary entry, 7.xii.1919; Devonshire MSS, Chatsworth.

21. Ninth Duke, diary entry, 26.xii.1919; ibid.

22. Ninth Duke, diary entry, 27.xii.1919; ibid.

23. Ninth Duke, diary entry, 2.i.1920; ibid.

24. Lady Anne Tree, quoted in C. Booth and C. Haste, *The Goldfish Bowl: Married to the Prime Minister, 1955–1997*, p. 38.

25. *Daily Gazette*, Montreal, 9.i.1920.

26. *The Times*, 17.iii.1920.

27. *Morning Post*, 8.iv.1920.

28. *Bystander*, 28.iv.1920.

29. *Daily Sketch*, 22.iv.1920.

Chapter 5. 'I Had Never Been To Tees-side' (pp. 59–72)

1. *The Tatler*, 5.v.1920.

2. Quoted in Horne, *Macmillan, 1894–1956*, p. 61.

3. Macmillan, *Winds of Change*, p. 119.

4. Macmillan's son, Maurice, quoted in Horne, *Macmillan, 1894–1956*, p. 66.

5. Ninth Duke, diary entry, 6.xi.1922; Devonshire MSS, Chatsworth.

6. Macmillan, *Winds of Change*, p. 139.

7. Ibid., p. 140.

8. Ibid., p. 141.

9. *Stockton & Tees-side Herald*, 1.xii.1923.

10. Macmillan, *Winds of Change*, p. 145.

11. Ibid., p. 153.

12. Ibid., p. 155.

13. Ninth Duke, diary entry, 29.x.1924; Devonshire MSS, Chatsworth.

14. Author conversation with Lord Cledwyn of Penrhos.

15. HoC Debs, 30.iv.1925, cols 403–6.

16. Ibid., col. 406.

17. Ball, *The Guardsmen*, p. 107.

18. Booth and Haste, *The Goldfish Bowl*, p. 41.

19. Macmillan, *Winds of Change*, p. 218.

20. Ibid., p. 223.

21. Ibid., p. 226.
22. Churchill to P. J. Grigg, 21.xii.1927, in M. Gilbert, *Winston S. Churchill*, Companion Part 1, Documents; *The Exchequer Years 1922–1929*, London, Heinemann, 1979, p. 1149.
23. Macmillan to Churchill, 1.i.1928, in Gilbert, *Churchill*, p. 1159.
24. Churchill to Macmillan, 5.i.1928, in Gilbert, *Churchill*, p. 1172.
25. Macmillan, *Winds of Change*, p. 240.
26. Baldwin to King George V, 24.iv.1928.
27. Quoted in Davenport-Hines, *The Macmillans*, p. 191.
28. Macmillan, *Winds of Change*, p. 245.
29. *Stockton & Tees-side Herald*, 4 May 1929.
30. R. Rhodes James, *Bob Boothby: A Portrait*, p. 113.

Chapter 6. 'Why Did You Ever Wake Me?' (pp. 73–90)

1. Telephone interview with Sister Beate Klemm at the Neuwittelsbach Clinic, 25.x.2006.
2. Macmillan to Evelyn, Duchess of Devonshire, 20.ix.1931; Devonshire MSS, Chatsworth.
3. 'AWC' to Macmillan, 30.vii.1929; quoted in Davenport-Hines, *The Macmillans*, p. 180.
4. Lady Anne Tree, quoted in Booth and Haste, *The Goldfish Bowl*, p. 42.
5. Dorothy Macmillan to Cynthia Mosley, 14.ix.1932, quoted in Rhodes James, *Bob Boothby*, p. 116.
6. Macmillan to Urquhart, 10.ix.1930; quoted in Davenport-Hines, *The Macmillans*, p. 184.
7. Stuart Ball (ed.), *Parliament and Politics in the Age of Baldwin and MacDonald: The Headlam Diaries 1922–1935*; Headlam diary entry, 29.vii.1929.
8. Headlam diary entry, 18.vii.1929.
9. Macmillan to Sir Charles Heaton-Ellis, 2.xii.1929; Macmillan Constituency Correspondence, quoted in Ball, *The Guardsmen*, p. 116.
10. Headlam diary entry, 5.xii.1929.
11. Quoted in S. Dorril, *Blackshirt: Sir Oswald Mosley and British Fascism*, p. 49.
12. Quoted in Dorril, *Blackshirt*, p. 137.
13. HoC Debs, 29.x.1930, cols 80–81.
14. Bridgeman to Davidson, 2.xi.1930, quoted in R. Rhodes James, *Memoirs of a Conservative: J. C. C. Davidson's Memoirs and Papers, 1910–37*, p. 352.
15. N. Nicolson (ed.), *Harold Nicolson: Diaries and Letters 1930–1939*; Nicolson diary entry, 30.xi.1930. (Subsequent diary entries by Harold Nicolson refer to this volume.)
16. Macmillan letter in *The Week-end Review*, 27.xii.1930.
17. In D. Ritschel, *The Politics of Planning: The Debate on Economic Planning in Britain in the 1930s*, p. 83.
18. Nicolson diary entry, 30.v.1931.

19. Macmillan to Sir Charles Heaton-Ellis, 2.iv.1931; Macmillan Constituency Correspondence; quoted in Ball, *The Guardsmen*, p. 121.

20. Nicolson diary entry, 30.v.1931.

21. Memorandum of Sir Clive Wigram, 24.viii.1931, quoted in P. Williamson, *National Crisis and National Government: British Politics, the Economy and Empire, 1926–1932*, p. 342.

22. Macmillan to Evelyn, Duchess of Devonshire, 1.x.1931; Devonshire MSS, Chatsworth.

23. Headlam diary entry, 31.i.1932.

24. *State and Industry*, p. 10.

25. Boothby to Cynthia Mosley, 14.ix.1932, quoted in Rhodes James, *Bob Boothby*, p. 116.

26. Dorothy Macmillan to Cynthia Mosley (in 1932 but undated), quoted in Rhodes James, *Bob Boothby*, p. 115.

27. Macmillan to Evelyn, Duchess of Devonshire, 4.ix.1933; Devonshire MSS, Chatsworth.

28. Macmillan to Evelyn, Duchess of Devonshire, 10.iv.1934; ibid.

29. Headlam diary entry, 18.vii.1934.

30. Quoted in Ritschel, *The Politics of Planning*, p. 225.

31. *The Star*, 20.iii.1936.

32. Earl of Kilmuir, *Political Adventure: The Memoirs of the Earl of Kilmuir*, London, Weidenfeld & Nicolson, 1964, p. 45.

33. Death Certificate of Helen Macmillan.

34. Macmillan, *Winds of Change*, p. 482.

35. Dorothy Macmillan to Evelyn, Duchess of Devonshire, undated; Devonshire MSS, Chatsworth.

36. Harold Macmillan, *The Middle Way*, pp. 377–8.

37. Ball (ed.), *Parliament and Politics in the Age of Churchill and Attlee*; Headlam diary entry, 27.x.1938.

38. Macmillan, *The Middle Way*, p. 102.

39. Quoted in Horne, *Macmillan, 1894–1956*, p. 116.

40. Chamberlain radio broadcast, 3.x.1939; BBC Radio Archives.

PART TWO

Chapter 7. 'Very Much the Minister Nowadays' (pp. 93–108)

1. Lady Anne Hunloke (Dorothy's sister) to Evelyn, Duchess of Devonshire, undated; Devonshire MSS, Chatsworth.

2. Sir Henry Channon (ed. R. Rhodes James), *CHIPS: The Diaries of Sir Henry Channon*, diary entry, 16.xi.1939.

3. Nicolson diary entry, 6.i.1940.

4. Ibid., diary entry, 17.i.1940.

5. Ball, *The Guardsmen*, p. 214.

6. H. Macmillan, *The Blast of War*, p. 27.

7. Ibid., p. 28.

8. Nicolson diary entry, 19.iii.1940.

9. Channon, *CHIPS*, 19.iii.1940.

10. HoC Debs, 19.iii.1940, col. 851.

11. Ball, *The Guardsmen*, p. 207.

12. HoC Debs, 7.iv.1940, col. 1150.

13. Channon, *CHIPS*, diary entry, 8.v.1940.

14. Euan Wallace, diary entry 8.v.1940, quoted in Ball, *The Guardsmen*, p. 212.

15. Nicolson diary entry, 13.v.1940.

16. H. Evans, *Downing Street Diary: The Macmillan Years, 1957–1963*, p. 76.

17. Headlam diary entry, 24.vi.1940, in Ball, *The Guardsmen*.

18. Macmillan, *The Blast of War*, p. 108.

19. Headlam diary entry, 16.x.1940, in Ball, *The Guardsmen*.

20. Macmillan, *The Blast of War*, p. 110.

21. Quoted in Ball, *The Guardsmen*, p. 220.

22. Ibid., p. 224.

23. Headlam diary entry, 5.viii.1941, in Ball, *The Guardsmen*.

24. Lady Diana Cooper, quoted in P. Ziegler, *Diana Cooper*, London, Hamish Hamilton, 1981, p. 94.

25. Macmillan, *The Blast of War*, p. 140.

26. Ibid., p. 163.

27. Ibid., p. 166.

28. Ibid., p. 167.

29. Lord Hailey of Shahpur, 'Native Administration and Political Development in British Tropical Africa'; unpublished report of 1940–42, p. 49; quoted in R. D. Pearce, *The Turning Point in Africa: British Colonial Policy 1938–48*, London, Frank Cass, 1982, p. 26.

30. Macmillan to Cranborne, 1.x.1942; TNA CO 323/1848/7322.

31. Macmillan, *The Blast of War*, p. 185.

32. Ibid., p. 186.

33. Ball, *The Guardsmen*, p. 249.

Chapter 8. Greeks, Romans and Frenchmen (pp. 109–128)

1. USFOR LONDON to AFHQ 1.i.1943; Smith, Walter Bedell, Collection of WW2 Documents 1941–1945, #13, 1004; Dwight D. Eisenhower Presidential Library, Abilene, Kansas.

2. Macmillan to Dorothy Macmillan, 7.i.1943, Harold Macmillan, *War Diaries* [*HMWD*], p. 4.

3. A. Danchev and D. Todman, eds, *War Diaries 1939–1945, Field Marshal Lord Alanbrooke*, London, Phoenix, 2002, p. 351, entry for 28.xii.1942.

4. 'Une Déclaration de la France Combattante', Centre Historique des Archives Nationales, 20th Century Section [CHAN], 3AG1/251, 342.

5. Macmillan to Dorothy Macmillan, 7.i.1943, *HMWD*, p. 5.

6. Macmillan to Dorothy Macmillan, 26.ii.1943, *HMWD*, p. 7.

7. Ibid., p. 9.

8. Macmillan, *The Blast of War*, p. 244.

9. Macmillan to Dorothy Macmillan, 26.ii.1943, *HMWD*, p. 9.

10. Ibid.

11. Quoted in Horne, *Macmillan, 1894–1956*, p. 165.

12. In F. Kersaudy, *Churchill and de Gaulle*, London, Fontana, 1990, p. 241.

13. De Gaulle to Churchill, 17.i.1943, in Kersaudy, *Churchill and de Gaulle*, p. 245.

14. De Gaulle to Éboué, 12.i.1943; CHAN 3AG1/251, 371.

15. W. S. Churchill, *The Second World War*, vol. iv, London, Cassell, 1947, p. 611.

16. In Kersaudy, *Churchill and de Gaulle*, p. 252.

17. De Gaulle to Tochon, 23.i.1943; CHAN 3AG1/251.

18. Ibid.

19. C. de Gaulle, *Mémoires de Guerre*, vol. ii, Paris, Plon, 1956, p. 84.

20. *HMWD*, p. 10n.

21. Dorothy Macmillan to Macmillan, 23.ii.1943, in Horne, *Macmillan, 1894–1956*, p. 176.

22. Dorothy Macmillan to Macmillan, 5.ii.1943, in Horne, *Macmillan, 1894–1956*, p. 177.

23. Macmillan to Dorothy Macmillan, 26.i.1943, *HMWD*, p. 11.

24. Macmillan despatch, 13.ii.1943; NA PREM 3/442/6.

25. Macmillan to Dorothy Macmillan, 23.ii.1943, *HMWD*, p. 17.

26. Macmillan to Dorothy Macmillan, 3.iii.1943, *HMWD*, p. 32.

27. In Kersaudy, *Churchill and de Gaulle*, p. 242.

28. Macmillan to Dorothy Macmillan, 14.iii.1943, *HMWD*, p. 42.

29. 'The North African New Deal'; Memorandum by the Resident Minister in Algiers; NA FO371/36123.

30. Makins (Lord Sherfield) interview with F. Duchêne, *Jean Monnet, First Statesman of Interdependence*, New York, W. W. Norton, 1994, p. 110.

31. Macmillan, *The Blast of War*, p. 301.

32. Macmillan to Dorothy Macmillan, 28.iv.1943, *HMWD*, p. 73.

33. 'Note relative à la situation en Afrique du Nord'; CHAN 3AG/251, 1124.

34. A. Eden, *The Eden Memoirs: The Reckoning*, London, Cassell, 1965, p. 373.

35. Macmillan to Dorothy Macmillan, 20.iii.1943, *HMWD*, p. 46.

36. Macmillan to Dorothy Macmillan, 26.iii.1943, *HMWD*, p. 51.

37. Butcher diary entry, 8.iv.1943; Dwight D. Eisenhower Library, Pre-Presidential Papers, Box 166.

38. Macmillan to Dorothy Macmillan, 2.iv.1943, *HMWD*, p. 55.

39. H. Alphand, *L'étonnement d'être*, Paris, Fayard, 1977, p. 162.

40. Macmillan to Churchill, 29.iv.1943; NA FO371/36173.

41. Macmillan to Dorothy Macmillan, 5.v.1943, *HMWD*, p. 80.

42. Macmillan to Dorothy Macmillan, 9.v.1943, *HMWD*, p. 82.

43. Macmillan to Dorothy Macmillan, 18.v.1943, *HMWD*, p. 86.

44. Macmillan to Dorothy Macmillan, 20.v.1943, *HMWD*, pp. 87–8.

45. R. Crossman in *Sunday Telegraph*, 9.ii.1964.
46. Macmillan to Dorothy Macmillan, 21.v.1943, *HMWD*, p. 92.

Chapter 9. 'A Marriage Has Been Arranged' (pp. 129–152)

1. Title of Fourth Report from Macmillan to Churchill, 14.vi.1943; TNA PREM 3/442/6.
2. Original version of (expurgated) memo 'For President from Murphy', 30.v.1943; *Foreign Relations of the United States* (*FRUS*), vol. II, p. 127; quoted in Kersaudy, *Churchill and de Gaulle*, p. 284.
3. Fifth Report from Macmillan to Churchill, 'The Road to Recognition', 27.viii.1943; TNA PREM 3/442/6.
4. Record of conversation Macmillan/Monnet, 31.v.1943, *HMWD*, p. 97.
5. Record of conversation Macmillan/Murphy/de Gaulle, 1.vi.1943, *HMWD*, p. 100.
6. Ibid., p. 101.
7. Record of conversation Macmillan/de Gaulle, 2.vi.1943, *HMWD*, pp. 104–5.
8. Ibid., p. 105.
9. In 'A Marriage Has Been Arranged'; TNA PREM 3/442/6.
10. Ibid.
11. Ibid.
12. Ibid.
13. Text of FCNL Press release, *HMWD*, p. 108.
14. *HMWD*, p. 110.
15. Macmillan to Dorothy Macmillan, *HMWD*, p. 111.
16. Eisenhower to Combined Chiefs of Staff and British Chiefs of Staff, 10.vi.1943; *Eisenhower War Papers*, 2, no. 1050.
17. Butcher diary entry, 12.vi.1943.
18. *HMWD*, p. 121.
19. Ibid., p. 122.
20. Eisenhower to FDR, 18.vi.1943; *Eisenhower War Papers*, 2, no. 1057.
21. *HMWD*, p. 127.
22. Ibid., p. 131.
23. J. Harvey (ed.), *The War Diaries of Oliver Harvey*, diary entry, 14.vi.1943.
24. Record of conversation with General de Gaulle, 9.vii.1943; TNA FO 660/51.
25. Macmillan to Dorothy Macmillan, 9.vii.1943, *HMWD*, p. 145.
26. Macmillan to Dorothy Macmillan, 10.vii.1943, *HMWD*, p. 146.
27. *Sunday Telegraph*, 9.ii.1964, p. 4.
28. Macmillan to Eden, 3.viii.1943; TNA FO 660/106.
29. *HMWD*, p. 194.
30. *FRUS*, vol. II, p. 185.
31. *HMWD*, p. 194.
32. Macmillan to Dorothy Macmillan, 26.viii.1943, *HMWD*, p. 192.
33. Harvey (ed.), *The War Diaries of Oliver Harvey*, diary entry, 1.xi.1943.

34. *HMWD*, p. 224.
35. Harvey (ed.), *The War Diaries of Oliver Harvey*, diary entry for 8.x.1943.
36. Quoted in M. Gilbert, *Road to Victory: Winston S. Churchill 1941–1945*, London, Heinemann, 1986, p. 526.
37. Macmillan to Dorothy Macmillan, 16.x.1943, *HMWD*, p. 257.
38. *HMWD*, p. 269.
39. Poletti to McCloy, 27.ix.1943, quoted in M. Jones, *Britain, the United States and the Mediterranean War, 1942–44*, p. 94.
40. Churchill to Cadogan, 25.x.1943; Avon Papers; quoted in Jones, *Britain, the United States and the Mediterranean War*, p. 94.
41. *HMWD*, p. 280.
42. Commissaire aux Affaires Étrangères; note on 'Conversation avec M Eden', 10.xi.1943; CHAN 3AG1/425.
43. Ibid.
44. Catroux to de Gaulle, 23.xi.1943; quoted in Kersaudy, *Churchill and de Gaulle*, p. 304.
45. E. L. Spears, *Fulfilment of a Mission*, London, Leo Cooper, 1977, pp. 235–6.
46. *Ministère des Affaires Étrangères*, quoted in Kersaudy, *Churchill and de Gaulle*, p. 303.
47. *HMWD*, p. 295.
48. *HMWD*, p. 306.
49. Danchev and Todman, eds, *War Diaries 1939–1945, Field Marshal Lord Alanbrooke*, London, Weidenfeld & Nicolson, 2001, p. 467; diary entry for 8.xi.1943.
50. Ibid., diary entry, 18.xi.1943, p. 473.
51. Macmillan to Churchill, 8.xii.1943; TNA PREM 3/272/1.
52. Danchev and Todman, eds, *War Diaries 1939–1945, Field Marshal Lord Alanbrooke*, diary entry, 8.xii.1943, p. 493.
53. *HMWD*, p. 327.
54. *HMWD*, p. 335.
55. *HMWD*, p. 338.
56. *HMWD*, p. 339.
57. Makins to Alice Makins, 4.ii.1943; MS Sherfield.
58. Macmillan's last Report from Algiers, dated 3.i.1944; TNA PREM 3/182/6.
59. *Sunday Telegraph*, 9.ii.1964, p. 4.
60. Macmillan manuscript note to Makins, 11.x.1943; TNA FO 660/149.
61. Headlam diary entry, 6.xi.1940.

Chapter 10. 'People Get Very Peculiar After a Time' (pp. 153–175)

1. Dorothy Macmillan to Evelyn, Dowager Duchess of Devonshire, 17.v.1944; Devonshire MSS, Chatsworth.
2. Steel to Howard, 9.iii.1944; TNA FO 371/43654.
3. Dixon diary entry for 2.i.1944, quoted in Horne, *Macmillan, 1894–1956*, p. 217.

4. *HMWD*, p. 386.

5. *HMWD*, p. 351.

6. Macmillan to Mary (Moucher), Duchess of Devonshire, 18.iv.1944; Devonshire MSS, Chatsworth.

7. J. Colville, *The Fringes of Power: Downing Street Diaries 1939–1945*, diary entry, 4.iii.1944, pp. 476–7.

8. *HMWD*, pp. 408–9.

9. Makins to Sargent, 28.iii.1944; TNA FO 371/43654.

10. *HMWD*, p. 421.

11. *HMWD*, p. 422.

12. Dorothy Macmillan to Evelyn, Dowager Duchess of Devonshire, 17.v.1944, Devonshire MSS, Chatsworth.

13. Makins to Sargent, 14.vi.1944; TNA FO 800/277.

14. Eden diary entry, 23.vi.1944; Avon Papers AP/20/1/24.

15. Eden and Bracken to Macmillan, 16.vi.1944; TNA FO 371/43634.

16. *HMWD*, p. 455.

17. K. Young (ed.), *The Diaries of Sir Robert Bruce Lockhart*, vol. ii, *1939–1965*; diary entry, 22.vi.1944, *HMWD*, p. 324.

18. Ibid.; diary entry, 25.vi.1944, *HMWD*, p. 328.

19. *HMWD*, p. 476.

20. Dorothy Macmillan to Evelyn, Dowager Duchess of Devonshire, 28.vi.1944; Devonshire MSS, Chatsworth.

21. Dorothy Macmillan to Evelyn, Dowager Duchess of Devonshire, 14.viii.1944; Devonshire MSS, Chatsworth.

22. Macmillan, *The Blast of War*, p. 525.

23. *HMWD*, p. 502.

24. 'Organization [sic] of the Mediterranean Command for Rankin C Conditions'; TNA PREM 3/272/4.

25. *HMWD*, p. 505.

26. *HMWD*, pp. 506–7.

27. Dorothy Macmillan to Evelyn, Dowager Duchess of Devonshire, 14.viii.1944; Devonshire MSS, Chatsworth.

28. Macmillan to Mary (Moucher), Duchess of Devonshire, 9.ix.1944; Devonshire MSS, Chatsworth.

29. *HMWD*, p. 508.

30. Ibid., p. 537.

31. Ibid., p. 554.

32. Churchill to Eden, 7.xi.1944; Churchill Papers 20/153, quoted in Gilbert, *Road to Victory*, p. 1055.

33. *HMWD*, p. 581.

34. Ibid., p. 592.

35. Ibid., p. 597.

36. Harvey (ed.), *The War Diaries of Oliver Harvey*, diary entry, 21.xii.1944.

37. M. Soames, *Clementine Churchill*, London, Cassell, 1979, p. 364.

38. *HMWD*, p. 616.

39. Colville, *The Fringes of Power*, p. 539.
40. Ibid., p. 540.
41. Ibid., p. 541.
42. *HMWD*, p. 597.
43. Ibid., p. 707.
44. Ibid., pp. 715–16.
45. Churchill to Alexander, 7.v.1945; quoted in Gilbert, *Road to Victory*, p. 1336.
46. *HMWD*, p. 754.
47. Ibid., p. 756.
48. Ibid., p. 757.
49. 'The Robertson Order', quoted in *The Repatriations from Austria in 1945 [Cowgill Report]*, London, Sinclair-Stevenson, 1990, p. 30.
50. *HMWD*, p. 758.
51. Quoted in *Cowgill Report*, p. 156.
52. '*Macmillan at War*'; interview with Ludovic Kennedy on BBC TV 1982; quoted in I. Mitchell, *The Cost of a Reputation*, London, Topical Books, 1997, p. 42.
53. Colville, *The Fringes of Power*, diary entry, 19.v.1945, p. 600.
54. Dorothy Macmillan to Evelyn, Dowager Duchess of Devonshire, 28.vi.1944; Devonshire MSS, Chatsworth.

PART THREE

Chapter 11. A Stranger at Home (pp. 178–190)

1. R. Bruce Lockhart diary entry, 18.i.1946, in Young (ed.), *The Diaries of Sir Robert Bruce Lockhart (1939–1965)*.
2. Macmillan, *Tides of Fortune*, p. 29.
3. *Northern Echo*, 27.vii.1945.
4. R. Churchill to Macmillan, 17.viii.1945; MS Macmillan, dep.c.249b.
5. Churchill to Macmillan, 1.xi.1945; ibid.
6. Macmillan, *Tides of Fortune*, p. 35.
7. Cranborne to Salisbury, 7.v.1946; Hatfield House 4M 390/53–55.
8. R. Bruce Lockhart diary entry, 4.ix.1947, in Young (ed.), *The Diaries of Sir Robert Bruce Lockhart (1939–1965)*.
9. Headlam diary entry, 16.v.1947.
10. Headlam diary entry, 31.iii.1949.
11. Bruce Lockhart diary entry, 30/31.iii.1946, Young (ed.), *The Diaries of Sir Robert Bruce Lockhart*.
12. R. K. Law to Paul Emrys-Evans, 25.viii.1945; Papers of Paul Emrys-Evans, Department of Manuscripts, British Library, MS 53239, vol. 5.
13. Macmillan to Dorothy Macmillan (1947), quoted in Horne, *Macmillan, 1894–1956*, p. 310.
14. Ibid.
15. Ibid., p. 311.

16. Ibid., p. 312.
17. Headlam diary entry, 19.v.1947.
18. Ball, *The Guardsmen*, p. 293.
19. Macmillan, *Tides of Fortune*, p. 302.
20. R. A. Butler, *The Art of the Possible: The Memoirs of Lord Butler*, p. 145.
21. Quoted in A. Howard, *RAB: The Life of R. A. Butler*, p. 157.
22. Ibid., p. 156.
23. Butler, *The Art of the Possible*, pp. 148–9.
24. Headlam diary entry, 28.x.1947.
25. *Sunday Express*, 15.v.1947.
26. Quoted in M. Gilbert, *Churchill: A Life*, London, Heinemann, 1991, p. 872.
27. Macmillan, *Tides of Fortune*, p. 155.
28. Cranborne (Salisbury) to Emrys-Evans, 12.v.1948; Papers of Paul Emrys-Evans, MS 58264, vol. 1.

Chapter 12. 'This New Opportunity' (pp. 191–205)

1. Author conversation with Lord (Roy) Hattersley some time in 1987.
2. In B. Pimlott, *Hugh Dalton*, London, Jonathan Cape, 1985, p. 597.
3. Quentin Crewe, quoted in Davenport-Hines, *The Macmillans*, p. 243.
4. Macmillan to Dorothy Macmillan, 24.ii.1943; MS Macmillan dep.c.4/4.
5. In Davenport-Hines, *The Macmillans*, p. 244.
6. Ibid., p. 245.
7. Macmillan, *Tides of Fortune*, p. 161.
8. Council of Europe, *Congress of Europe, The Hague, 7–11 May*, p. 7.
9. Congress of Europe, The Hague, May 1948: *Resolutions*, London–Paris, International Committee of the Movements for European Unity, p. 5.
10. Macmillan, *Tides of Fortune*, p. 162.
11. Ibid., p. 163.
12. HoC Debs, 21.vii.1949, col. 1582.
13. Macmillan, *Tides of Fortune*, p. 166.
14. Ibid., p. 167.
15. Macmillan to Dorothy Macmillan, 22.viii.1949; MS Macmillan dep.c.11/2.
16. Macmillan, *Tides of Fortune*, p. 169.
17. Ibid., p. 176.
18. Ibid., p. 188.
19. Macmillan to Dorothy Macmillan, 6.ix.1949; MS Macmillan dep.c.11/2.
20. Macmillan, *Tides of Fortune*, p. 701.
21. Headlam diary entry, 28.i.1950.
22. Quoted in D. Kynaston, *Austerity Britain, 1945–51*, p. 391.
23. Macmillan, *Tides of Fortune*, p. 189.
24. J. Monnet (trans. R. Mayne), *Memoirs*, London, Collins, 1978, pp. 309–11.
25. Macmillan, *Tides of Fortune*, p. 192.
26. Ibid., pp. 194–5.
27. Ibid., p. 199.

28. HoC Debs, 27.vi.1950, col. 2159.
29. Quoted in N. Beloff, *The General says No*, p. 60.
30. Ibid.
31. Macmillan, *Tides of Fortune*, p. 217.
32. Ibid.
33. P. Catterall (ed.), *The Macmillan Diaries: The Cabinet Years, 1950–1957*, entry 30.xi.1950 (hereafter *HMD*).
34. Ibid., diary entry, Christmas Day 1950.
35. Ibid., diary entry, 21.vi.1951.
36. Ibid., diary entry, 8.ix.1951.
37. *Daily Mirror*, 23.x. and 24.x.1951.

Chapter 13. 'Shall I Ever Be Foreign Secretary?' (pp. 206–223)

1. *HMD*, 27.x.1951.
2. HoC Debs, 4.xii.1951, col. 2251.
3. Cabinet Secretary Notes [of Cabinet meeting] (Cab. Sec. Notes), 22.xi.1951; TNA CAB 195/10.
4. Cab. Sec. Notes, 20.xii.1951; ibid.
5. Official Minute of Cabinet meeting, 20.xii.1951; TNA CAB 128/23.
6. *HMD*, 21.xii.1951.
7. *HMD*, 24.xii.1951.
8. *HMD*, 29.ii.1952.
9. Cab. Sec. Notes, 29.ii.1952; TNA CAB 195/10.
10. *HMD*, 29.ii.1952.
11. Cab. Sec. Notes, 13.iii.1952; TNA CAB 195/10.
12. *HMD*, 15.iii.1952.
13. *HMD*, 17.iii.1952.
14. Quoted in Horne, *Macmillan, 1894–1956*, p. 341.
15. *HMD*, 21.vi.1952.
16. Butler MS note on (undated) Treasury paper; TNA T227/805.
17. *HMD*, 17.vii.1952.
18. Cab. Sec. Notes, 17.vii.1952; TNA CAB 195/10.
19. *HMD*, 10.x.1952.
20. *HMD*, 27.iv.1953.
21. *HMD*, 4.vii.1953.
22. Ibid.
23. Ibid.
24. Ibid.
25. *HMD*, 14.vii.1953.
26. *HMD*, 22.vii.1953.
27. Cab. Sec. Notes, 28.vii.1953; TNA CAB 195/11.
28. Quoted in Horne, *Macmillan, 1894–1956*, p. 342.
29. *HMD*, 1.ix.1953.
30. *HMD*, 5.x.1953.

31. Miss Portal in interview with author, 22.vii.2007.
32. *HMD*, 11.x.1953.
33. Cab. Sec. Notes, 26.xii.1953; TNA CAB 195/11.
34. *HMD*, Christmas Day 1953.
35. *HMD*, 6.iv.1954.
36. *HMD*, 23.vii.1954.
37. *HMD*, 25.viii.1954.
38. *HMD*, 28.viii.1954.
39. *HMD*, 29.x.1954.
40. *HMD*, 26.i.1955.
41. *HMD*, 9.iii.1955.
42. Colville, *The Fringes of Power*, p. 706.
43. *HMD*, 14.iii.1955.
44. Colville, *The Fringes of Power*, p. 706.
45. Ibid., p. 708.
46. *HMD*, 9.i.1955.

Chapter 14. Ambition (pp. 224–240)

1. Woolton diary entry, 5.iv.1955; MS Woolton 3 fol. 161.
2. Macmillan, *Tides of Fortune*, p. 582.
3. Sir Evelyn Shuckburgh, quoted in K. Kyle, *Suez*, p. 88.
4. Quoted ibid., p. 46.
5. Ibid.
6. *HMD*, 7.v.1955.
7. E. Shuckburgh, *Descent to Suez, Diaries 1951–56*, diary entry, 22.x.1954.
8. Ibid., diary entry, 31.viii.1955.
9. *HMD*, 13.vi.1955.
10. R. Lamb, *The Failure of the Eden Government*, p. 68.
11. Ibid.
12. *HMD*, 18.vi.1955.
13. *HMD*, 27.vi.1955.
14. Minute of 30.vi.1955; TNA CAB 128/29.
15. Lamb, *The Failure of the Eden Government*, p. 72.
16. Ibid.
17. *HMD*, 6.viii.1955.
18. Shuckburgh, *Descent to Suez*, diary entry, 31.viii.1955.
19. *Dizzy with Success*, note of 20.viii.1955; TNA FO 800/679.
20. *HMD*, 23.ix.1955.
21. Ibid.
22. *HMD*, 2.x.1955.
23. 'Disappearance of Two Foreign Office Officials, Burgess and Maclean', 19.x.1955; TNA CAB 129/78 (CP 9550 161).
24. *HMD*, 24.x.1955.
25. Shuckburgh, *Descent to Suez*, diary entry, 10.xi.1955.

26. *HMD*, 7.xi.1955.

27. Macmillan MS note on Nutting to Prime Minister, 9.xi.1955; TNA FO 800/686.

28. Quoted in Lamb, *The Failure of the Eden Government*, p. 75.

29. Minutes of Cabinet Economic Policy Committee, 11.xi.1955; TNA CAB 134/1226.

30. Quoted in Lamb, *The Failure of the Eden Government*, p. 76.

31. *HMD*, 14.xii.1955.

32. Quoted in Lamb, *The Failure of the Eden Government*, p. 84.

33. Shuckburgh, *Descent to Suez*, diary entry, 9.xii.1955.

34. Macmillan, *Tides of Fortune*, p. 697.

35. *HMD*, 22.xii.1955.

36. *HMD*, 30.xii.1955.

37. *HMD*, 19.i.1956.

38. Eden to Macmillan, 29.i.1956, and Macmillan to Eden, 2.ii.1956; TNA T273/312.

39. *HMD*, 9.ii.1956.

40. Ibid.

41. *HMD*, 22.iii.1956.

42. Macmillan to Eden, 5.iv.1956; TNA PREM 11/1326.

43. *HMD*, 28.iii.1956.

44. *HMD*, 17.iv.1956.

45. HoC Debs, 17.iv.1956, col. 758.

46. Ibid., col. 830.

47. Lamb, *The Failure of the Eden Government*, p. 89.

48. 'UK Economic Situation', 'Half Time'; Macmillan to Eden, 1.vi.1956; TNA PREM 11/1325.

49. *HMD*, 21.vii.1956.

50. Ibid.

Chapter 15. 'We *Must* Make Use of Israel' (pp. 241–257)

1. *FRUS*, vol. XV, doc. 473; 'Memorandum of a Conversation, White House, July 19, 9.40–9.52 a.m.'.

2. Minutes of Cabinet meeting, 27.vii.1956; TNA CAB 128/30.

3. Eden to Eisenhower, 27.vii.1956; Eisenhower Library, Ann Whitman File, International Series, Box #21.

4. Murphy in R. Murphy, *Diplomat Among Warriors*, pp. 461–2.

5. *HMD*, 30.vii.1956.

6. Eisenhower to Eden, 31.vii.1956; Eisenhower Library, Presidential Papers 1953–61, Ann Whitman File, Box #21.

7. *HMD*, 1.viii.1956.

8. HM diary entry, 3.viii.1956, MS Macmillan, dep.d.27. (The published version (*HMD*) reads 'he' rather than 'we'.)

9. *HMD*, 5.viii.1956.

10. 'Action against Egypt'; note by the Chancellor of the Exchequer; TNA CAB 134/1217.

11. HM diary entries, 5.vii.and 8.viii.1956, MS Macmillan, dep.d.27.

12. Sir Edward Bridges (untitled) note of 16.viii.1956; TNA T/273/380.

13. For President from Secretary, 19.viii.1956; Eisenhower Library, Ann Whitman File, Dulles–Herter Series, Box #7.

14. Memorandum of Conversation with Harold Macmillan, 21.viii.1956; Eisenhower Library, John Foster Dulles Papers 1951–59, General Correspondence, Memoranda Series, Box #1.

15. Ibid.

16. HM diary entries, 30.viii. and 2.x.1956, MS Macmillan, dep.d.27.

17. Eisenhower to Eden, 3.ix.1956; TNA T381/56.

18. HM diary entry, 9.ix.1956, MS Macmillan, dep.d.27.

19. *HMD*, 13.ix.1956.

20. *HMD*, 20.ix.1956.

21. Bloomington, Indiana, *Daily Herald – Telephone*, 22.ix.1956.

22. *HMD*, 22.ix.1956.

23. Ibid.

24. *Daily Herald – Telephone*, 26.ix.1956.

25. *HMD*, 23.ix.1956.

26. HM diary entry, 23.ix.1956, MS Macmillan, dep.d.27.

27. Ibid.

28. Makins, undated but some time after 1986; *Sidelights on Suez*, MS Sherfield 957.

29. *HMD*, 23.ix.1956.

30. Dulles/Eisenhower: Phone Calls, 25.ix.1956; 11.20 a.m.; Eisenhower Library, Ann Whitman File, DDE Diary Series, Box #18.

31. Record of Conversation, R. Makins, 25.ix.1956; TNA PREM 11/1102.

32. Transcript of NBC 'Meet the Press', Sunday 23.ix.1956.

33. Memorandum of Conversation with Mr Harold Macmillan, Chancellor of the Exchequer, 25.ix.1956; Eisenhower Library, John Foster Dulles Papers, General Correspondence, Memoranda Series, Box #1.

34. Macmillan, *Riding the Storm*, p. 137.

35. Quoted in Kyle, *Suez*, p. 258.

36. Makins to President, 25.ix.1956; Eisenhower Library, Ann Whitman File, DDE Diary Series, Box #17.

37. A. Nutting, *No End of a Lesson*, pp. 69–70.

38. Quoted in Horne, *Macmillan, 1894–1956*, p. 427.

39. Macmillan diary entry, 4.x.1956; MS Macmillan dep.d.27.

40. Nutting's original page proofs, in P. Murphy's 'Telling Tales out of School: Nutting, Eden and the Attempted Suppression of No End of a Lesson'; in Simon C. Smith, *Reassessing Suez 1956: New Perspectives on the Crisis and its Aftermath*, Aldershot, Ashgate, 2008, pp. 203–4.

41. Ibid.

42. Quoted in Kyle, *Suez*, p. 304.

43. Minute of meeting, 18.x.1956; TNA CAB 128/30.
44. Minute of meeting, 23.x.1956; TNA CAB 128/30.
45. Minute of meeting, 25.x.1956; TNA CAB 128/30.
46. Minute of meeting, 30.x.1956; TNA CAB 128/30.
47. Eden to Eisenhower, 30.x.1956; TNA PREM 11/1105.
48. Eisenhower to Eden, 30.x.1956; TNA PREM 11/1177.
49. Dixon, Double Diploma, p. 265.
50. Minute of meeting, 31.x.1956; TNA CAB 128/30.

Chapter 16. 'The Last Gasp of a Declining Power' (pp. 258–275)

1. Richard D. Challener with Winthrop W. Aldrich. Dark Harbor, Maine, 15 July 1964; John Foster Dulles Oral History; Public Policy Papers, Department of Rare Books and Special Collections, Princeton University Library.
2. Sir Pierson Dixon diary entry, 31.x.1956, in P. Dixon, *Double Diploma: The Life of Sir Pierson Dixon, Don and Diplomat*, London, Hutchinson, 1968, p. 265.
3. Minutes of meetings at 4.30 p.m. and 9.30 p.m., 2.xi.1956; TNA CAB 128/30.
4. E. Dell, *The Chancellors*, p. 218.
5. S. Lloyd, *Suez 1956: A Personal Account*, London, Jonathan Cape, 1978, p. 206.
6. Ibid., p. 207.
7. Minutes of meeting, 4.xi.1956; TNA CAB 128/30.
8. Ibid.
9. Ibid.
10. Ibid.
11. Eden to Eisenhower, 5.xi.1956; Eisenhower Library, J. F. Dulles Papers, Memoranda Series, Box #3.
12. *FRUS*, vol. XVI; *Suez Crisis July 26–December 31, 1956*; Memorandum of a conference with the President, 5.xi.1956; p. 986, doc. 500.
13. Macmillan, *Riding the Storm*, p. 164.
14. Horne, *Macmillan, 1894–1956*, p. 440.
15. R. Cooper: 'A Weak Sister? Macmillan, Suez and the British Economy, July to November, 1956', *Contemporary British History* (September 2008), vol. 22, no. 3.
16. Macmillan to Eden, 5.xi.1956; TNA T172/2135.
17. Cab. Sec. Notes, 29.xi.1956; TNA CAB 195/15.
18. *FRUS*, vol. XVI, pp. 1012–13, doc. 516.
19. Sir Guy Millard letter to author, 1.ii.2008.
20. Lloyd, *Suez 1956*, p. 209.
21. Quoted in Horne, *Macmillan, 1894–1956*, p. 442.
22. Butler, *The Art of the Possible*, p. 194.
23. Sir Guy Millard letter, as above.
24. Quoted in P. Hennessy, *Never Had It So Good: Britain in the Fifties*, p. 448.

25. Macmillan in interview with Iverach McDonald, quoted in Hennessy, *Never Had It So Good,* p. 448.
26. Minutes of meeting, 6.xi.1956; TNA CAB 128/30.
27. Lloyd, *Suez 1956,* p. 211.
28. Sir Michael Howard, *Captain Professor,* London, Continuum, p. 155.
29. Memorandum of a Telephone Conversation, Eisenhower/Eden 7.xi.1956; *FRUS,* vol. XVI, p. 1040, doc. 536.
30. Eisenhower to Eden, 7.xi.1956; *FRUS,* vol. XVI, p. 1056, doc. 545.
31. Embassy Washington to Foreign Office, 9.xi.1956; TNA T236/4189.
32. Note of a meeting in Sir Leslie Rowan's Room, 12.xi.1956; TNA T236/4189.
33. Minutes of meeting, 20.xi.1956; TNA CAB 128/30.
34. Macmillan to Humphrey, 20.xi.1956; TNA T236/4190.
35. Aldrich to State Department, 19.xi.1956; *FRUS,* vol. XVI, p. 1163, doc. 593.
36. Aldrich to State Department, 22.xi.1956; *FRUS,* vol. XVI, p. 1174, doc. 602.
37. Howard, *RAB,* p. 241.
38. Enoch Powell, quoted in Howard, *RAB,* p. 241.
39. Macmillan as reported by Nigel Birch and quoted in Howard, *RAB.*
40. Butler, *The Art of the Possible,* p. 195.
41. Memorandum of a Conference with the President, 20.xi.1956; *FRUS,* vol. XVI, p. 1166, doc. 596.
42. Minutes of meeting, 28.xi.1956; TNA CAB 128/30.
43. Memorandum of Conference with the President, 21.xi.1956; Eisenhower Library, J. F. Dulles Papers, White House Memoranda Series, Box #4.
44. Macmillan on the Suez affair in conversation with Dulles; Memorandum for the Record, 12.xii.1956; Eisenhower Library, J. F. Dulles Papers 1951–1959, General Correspondence and Memoranda Series, Box #1.
45. Ibid.
46. *The Times,* 15.xii.1956.
47. HoC Debs, 20.xii.1956, col. 1516.
48. '*1957*', a memorandum by the Marquess of Salisbury; undated but probably written soon after the events of January 1957; Hatfield House, 5M/diaries.
49. Ibid.
50. Ibid.
51. Ibid.
52. *HMD,* diary entry, 3.ii.1957.
53. Salisbury, '*1957*'.
54. *HMD,* diary entry, 3.ii.1957.

PART FOUR

Chapter 17. The Tory Resurrection (pp. 279–297)

1. HM diary entry, 3.ii.1957; MS Macmillan, dep.d.28.
2. *Daily Express,* 1.ii.1957, quoted in Howard, *RAB,* p. 250.
3. Salisbury, '*1957*'.

4. H. Evans, *Downing Street Diary: The Macmillan Years*, p. 29.

5. Ibid., p. 30.

6. Egremont (Wyndham), *Wyndham and Children First*, p. 170.

7. Quoted in Hennessy, *Never Had It So Good*, p. 542.

8. Macmillan, *Riding the Storm*, p. 196.

9. Aldrich to Dulles, 24.i.1957; Eisenhower Library, J. F. Dulles Papers, 1951–1959, White House Memoranda Series, Box #6, Meetings with the President – 1957 (7).

10. HM diary entry, 8.ii.1957; MS Macmillan, dep.d.28.

11. HM diary entry, 17.ii.1957; ibid.

12. HM diary entry, 22.ii.1957; ibid.

13. HM diary entry, 4.iii.1957; ibid.

14. Salisbury to Douglas, 11.iii.1957; Hatfield House, 5M/Personal: political.

15. HM diary entry, 20.iii.1957; MS Macmillan, dep.d.28.

16. Memorandum of Dinner Conversation at Mid-Ocean Club, 20.iii.1957; Eisenhower Library; White House Office, Office of the Staff Secretary; Records, 1952–61, International Trips & Meetings Series, Box #3, Bermuda – Substantive Questions (1).

17. Ibid.; Substantive Questions (2).

18. Ibid.: Substantive Questions (3).

19. HM diary entry for 21.iii.1957; MS Macmillan, dep.d.28.

20. HM diary entry, 23.iii.1957; ibid.

21. Minutes of the bipartisan Congressional meeting on 25.iii.1957; *FRUS, 1955–1957*, vol. XXVII, *Western Europe and Canada*, p. 768, doc. 294.

22. Editorial Note in *FRUS, 1955–1957*, p. 758, doc. 284.

23. HM diary entry, 27.iii.1957; MS Macmillan, dep.d.28.

24. H. Slater to Salisbury 28.iii.1957; Hatfield House, 5M/Box D.

25. Macmillan to Salisbury, 29.iii.1957; ibid.

26. HM diary entry, 31.iii.1957; MS Macmillan, dep.d.28.

27. HM diary entry, 5.iv.1957; ibid.

28. HM diary entry, 13.iv.1957; MS Macmillan, dep.d.29.

29. Macmillan MS note on TNA PREM 11/1791.

30. HM diary entry, 18.iv.1957; MS Macmillan, dep.d.29.

31. Minutes of meeting, 10.v.1957; TNA CAB 128/30.

32. HM diary entry, 12.v.1957; MS Macmillan, dep.d.29.

33. HM diary entry, 17.v.1957; ibid.

34. Egremont (Wyndham), *Wyndham and Children First*, p. 161.

35. HM diary entries, 15.vi and 16.vi.1957; MS Macmillan, dep.d.29.

36. Macmillan, *Riding the Storm*, p. 350.

37. HM diary entry, 26.vii.1957; MS Macmillan, dep.d.29.

38. HM diary entry, 31.vii.1957; ibid.

39. HM diary entry, 16.viii.1957; ibid.

40. HM diary entry, 22.viii.1957; ibid.

41. HM diary entry, 27.viii.1957; ibid.

42. HM diary entry, 1.ix.1957; ibid.

43. Confidential interview.
44. HM diary entry, 1.ix.1957; MS Macmillan, dep.d.29.
45. R. Harrod to Macmillan, 7.ix.1957; TNA PREM 11/2973.
46. HM diary entry, 9.x.1957: MS Macmillan, dep.d.30.
47. HM diary entry, 23.x.1957; ibid.
48. Dulles, 'Memorandum of a Conversation at the British Embassy, 23.x.1957';
Eisenhower Library, Papers as President of the United States, Ann Whitman
File, Dulles–Herter Series, Box #9.
49. HM diary entry, 24.x.1957; MS Macmillan, dep.d.30.
50. HM diary entry, 12.xii.1957; ibid.
51. HM diary entry, 19.xii.1957; ibid.
52. HM diary entry, 26.xii.1957; ibid.

Chapter 18. 'You Almost Feel Yourself a Statesman' (pp.298–317)

1. S. Crooks, *Peter Thorneycroft*, p. 94.
2. Ibid., pp. 95–6.
3. HoC Debs, 28.x.1957, col. 1124.
4. HM diary entry, 6.i.1958; MS Macmillan, dep.d.30.
5. Ibid.
6. HM diary entry, 7.i.1958; ibid.
7. HM diary entry, 19.i.1958; ibid.
8. Quoted in A. Sampson, *Macmillan: A Study in Ambiguity*, p. 137.
9. HM diary entry, 19.i.1958.
10. Quoted in Sampson, *Macmillan: A Study in Ambiguity*, p. 137.
11. HM diary entry, 19.i.1958.
12. HM diary entry, 24.i.1958; MS Macmillan, dep.d.30.
13. HM diary entry, 31.i.1958; ibid.
14. Quoted in Sampson, *Macmillan: A Study in Ambiguity*, p. 138.
15. HM diary entry, 14.ii.1958; MS Macmillan, dep.d.31.
16. HM diary entry, 20.ii.1958; ibid.
17. *Spectator*, 28.ii.1958.
18. HM diary entry, 14.ii.1958: MS Macmillan, dep.d.31.
19. Macmillan to Eisenhower, *FRUS*, vol. VII, Part 2, *Western Europe*, p. 794,
doc. 327.
20. Eisenhower to Dulles, *FRUS*, ibid., doc. 337.
21. In Cmnd 423 (1958): *Correspondence with the Soviet Union on Summit Talks*,
quoted in Macmillan, *Riding the Storm*, p. 480.
22. HM diary entry, 10.iv.1958: MS Macmillan, dep.d.31.
23. HM diary entry, 19.iv.1958; ibid.
24. HoL Debs, 3.xii.1957, col. 610.
25. HM diary entry, 16.v.1958; MS Macmillan, dep.d.31.
26. HM diary entry, 31.v.1958; ibid.
27. Memorandum of Conversation with the British Ambassador, 13.v.1958:

3. Macmillan's MS note on 'Public Investment and Reflation'; TNA PREM 11/2311.
4. HM diary entry, 31.xii.1958; MS Macmillan, dep.d.34.
5. Macmillan to President, 7.x.1958; Eisenhower Library, Papers as President of the US (Ann Whitman File), International Series, Box #24.
6. HM diary entry, 8.x.1958; MS Macmillan, dep.d.33.
7. C. de Gaulle, trans. T. Kilmartin, *Memoirs of Hope*, London, Weidenfeld & Nicolson, 1971, pp. 202–3.
8. Dulles to President, 17.xii.1958; Eisenhower Library, Papers as President of the US (Ann Whitman File), Dulles–Herter Series, Box #10.
9. HM diary entry, 8.x.1958; MS Macmillan, dep.d.33.
10. Editorial Note, *FRUS*, vol. VII, part 2, doc. 53.
11. HM diary entry, 26.x.1958; MS Macmillan, dep.d.33.
12. HM diary entry, 31.x.1958; ibid.
13. Macmillan, *Riding the Storm*, pp. 456–7.
14. Ibid.
15. Quoted in Mangold, *An Almost Impossible Ally*, p. 113.
16. Quoted in Taubman, *Khrushchev: The Man and his Era*, p. 396.
17. HM diary entries, 6 and 7.xii.1958; MS Macmillan, dep.d.33.
18. Memorandum of Conference with President Eisenhower, 11.xii.1958; *FRUS*, vol. VIII, *The Berlin Crisis 1958–1959*, doc. 97, p. 175.
19. Ibid.
20. HM diary entry, 25.xii.1958; MS Macmillan, dep.d.34.
21. Telephone Call Dulles–Eisenhower, 20.i.1959; Eisenhower Library, J. F. Dulles Papers, 1951–1959, Telephone Calls Series, Box #13.
22. HM diary entry, 22.i.1959: MS Macmillan, dep.d.34.
23. Conversation with the Prime Minister, 5.ii.1959; Eisenhower Library, J. F. Dulles Papers, Subject Series, Memos of Conversations, Box #12.
24. HM diary entry, 4.iii.1959; MS Macmillan, dep.d.35.
25. Macmillan, *Riding the Storm*, p. 603.
26. Sergei N. Khrushchev, *Nikita S., Khrushchev: krizisy i rakety*, Moscow, Novosti, 1991, vol. i, p. 416; quoted in Taubman, *Khrushchev: The Man and his Era*, p. 399.
27. Macmillan, *Riding the Storm*, p. 606.
28. HM diary entry, 4.iii.1959; MS Macmillan, dep.d.34.
29. Ibid.
30. Memorandum of Telephone Conversation, Dulles–Eisenhower, 4.iii.1959; Eisenhower Library, J. F. Dulles Papers, 1951–1959, Telephone Calls Series, Box #13.
31. HM diary entry, 8.iii.1959; MS Macmillan, dep.d.35.

Chapter 21. 'The Tories Must Wake Up!' (pp. 336–350)

1. Quoted in P. Murphy, *Alan Lennox-Boyd: A Biography*, p. 213.

2. Eisenhower Library; J. F. Dulles Papers, 1951–1959; Dulles to Greene, 9.iii.1959, Telephone Calls Series, Box #9.

3. Eisenhower Library; C. A. Herter Papers 1957–61, Telephone Conversation with the President, 9.iii.1959; Misc. Memoranda, Box #10, Presidential Phone Calls.

4. HM diary entry, 20.iii.1959; MS Macmillan, dep.d.35.

5. Macmillan, *Riding the Storm*, p. 646.

6. HM diary entry, 22.iii.1959; MS Macmillan, dep.d.35.

7. HM diary entries, 4.iv. and 9.iv.1959; ibid.

8. HM diary entry, 4.v.1959; ibid.

9. HM diary entry, 1.vi.1959; ibid.

10. R. Hyam, *Britain's Declining Empire: The Road to Decolonisation, 1918–1968*, p. 263.

11. HM diary entry, 9.vi.1959; MS Macmillan, dep.d.36.

12. HM diary entry, 17.vi.1959; ibid.

13. *Report of the Nyasaland Commission of Enquiry*, Cmnd 814, 1959.

14. HM diary entry, 13.vii.1959; MS Macmillan, dep.d.36.

15. Butler, *The Art of the Possible*, p. 198.

16. HM diary entry, 23.vii.1959; MS Macmillan, dep.d.36.

17. HM diary entry, 26.vii.1959; ibid.

18. HM diary entry, 27.vii.1959; ibid.

19. Memorandum of Conference with the President, 27.vii.1959; Eisenhower Library, White House Office, Office of the Staff Secretary, Records 1952–61, Subject Series, State Department Subseries, Box #3.

20. Macmillan to Eisenhower, 31.vii.1959; *FRUS*, vol. VIII, *1958–1960*, p. 1098, doc. 498.

21. Herter to Eisenhower, 4.viii.1959; Eisenhower Library, Papers as President of the US, 1953–61, Ann Whitman File, Dulles–Herter Series, Box #12.

22. HM diary entry, 21.viii.1959; MS Macmillan, dep.d.36.

23. Eisenhower Library, Admiral Evan P. Aurand Oral History (OH127) #1 on 1.v.1967 by John Mason.

24. Eisenhower Library, H. Snyder Papers 1910–1968, Box #9, Medical Diary re DDE, 29.viii.1959.

25. Ibid. 30.viii.1959.

26. Ibid.

27. HM diary entry, 31.viii.1959; MS Macmillan, dep.d.36.

28. D. E. Butler and R. Rose, *The British General Election of 1959*, London, Macmillan, 1960, p. 41.

29. Eisenhower Library, H. Snyder Papers, Box #9, 31.viii.1959 and 1.ix.1959.

30. Recollection of one of Churchill's secretaries.

31. *Daily Express*, 10.ix.1959.

32. Ted Heath, quoted in M. Cockerell, *Live from Number 10: The Inside Story of Prime Ministers and Television*.

33. HM diary entry, 16.ix.1959; MS Macmillan, dep.d.36.

34. *Daily Sketch*, 25.ix.1959.

35. Quote in Butler and Rose, *The British General Election of 1959*, p. 62.
36. Ibid., p. 66.
37. Wyndham, *Wyndham and Children First*, p. 186.
38. HM diary entry, 9.x.1959; MS Macmillan, dep.d.36.

Chapter 22. *Le Double Jeu* (pp. 351–371)

1. HM diary entry, 10.x.1959; MS Macmillan, dep.d.37.
2. HM diary entry, 18.x.1959; ibid.
3. Hyam, *Britain's Declining Empire*, p. 257.
4. *FRUS*, vol. IX, *1958–1960*, p. 113, doc. 43.
5. HM diary entries, 10.xi., 26.xi. and 30.xi.1959; MS Macmillan, dep.d.37.
6. HM diary entry, 19.xii.1959; ibid.
7. Ibid.
8. Macmillan, *Pointing the Way*, p. 105.
9. HM diary entry, 21.xii.1959; MS Macmillan, dep.d.37.
10. HM diary entry, 28.xii.1959; ibid.
11. HM diary entry, 7.ii.1960; MS Macmillan, dep.d.38.
12. R. Lamb, *The Macmillan Years*, p. 244.
13. Hyam, *Britain's Declining Empire*, p. 258.
14. Macmillan, *Pointing the Way*, pp. 475, 478.
15. R. Davenport-Hines (ed.), *Letters from Oxford*, p. 290.
16. Ibid., pp. 293, 297.
17. HM diary entry, 23.ii.1960; MS Macmillan, dep.d.38.
18. Foreign Secretary to Prime Minister, 15 ii.1960; TNA PREM 11/2998.
19. Davenport-Hines (ed.), *Letters from Oxford*, p. 307.
20. 'Points discussed with General de Gaulle at Rambouillet on March 12 and 13, 1960'; TNA PREM 11/2998.
21. HM diary entry, 13.iii.1960; MS Macmillan, dep.d.38.
22. 'Points discussed ...'
23. 'Points discussed ...'
24. HM diary entry, 13.iii. 1960; MS Macmillan, dep.d.38.
25. Minutes of Cabinet meeting, 22.iii.1960; TNA CAB 138/34.
26. HM diary entry, 25.iii.1960; MS Macmillan, dep.d.38.
27. Eisenhower Library, Herter Papers, CAH Telephone Calls, Box #12, Goodpaster to Herter, 23.iii.1960.
28. HM diary entry, 29.iii.1960; MS Macmillan, dep.d.38.
29. 'Record of a Conversation between President de Gaulle and the Prime Minister at Buckingham Palace at 6pm on Tuesday, April 5, 1960'; TNA PREM 11/2978.
30. HM diary entry, 17.iv.1960; MS Macmillan, dep.d.38.
31. Quoted in M. R. Beschloss, *Mayday: Eisenhower, Khrushchev and the U-2 Affair*, pp. 44, 45.
32. Ibid., p. 257.
33. Macmillan, *Pointing the Way*, p. 201.

34. Quoted in Taubman, *Khrushchev: The Man and his Era*, p. 447.

35. HM diary entry, 15.v.1960; MS Macmillan, dep.d.39.

36. HM diary entry, 16.v.1960; ibid.

37. C. de Gaulle (trans. T. Kilmartin), *Memoirs of Hope*, p. 250.

38. Ibid., p. 251.

39. 'Record of Meeting between the Four Leaders', 16.v.1960; TNA PREM 11/2992.

40. Quoted in Beschloss, *Mayday*, p. 287.

41. R. Aldous, *Macmillan, Eisenhower and the Cold War*, Dublin, p. 147.

42. Eisenhower Library, Snyder Papers; DDE Medical Record, 1 May 1960–31 August 1960, Box #8, 16.v.1960.

43. HM diary entry, 16.v.1960; MS Macmillan, dep.d.39.

44. Ibid.

45. 'Record of Conversation between the Prime Minister and Mr Khrushchev', 16.v.1960; TNA PREM 11/2992.

46. Beschloss, *Mayday*, p. 295.

47. Ibid., p. 296.

48. HM diary entry, 18.v.1960; MS Macmillan, dep.d.39.

49. Quoted in. Evans, *Downing Street Diary*, p. 114.

50. Eisenhower to de Gaulle, 18.v.1960, in Aldous, *Macmillan, Eisenhower and the Cold War*, p. 162.

51. HM diary entry, 19.v.1960; MS Macmillan, dep.d.39.

Chapter 23. Enter JFK (pp. 372–386)

1. Memorandum of Conference with the President, 24.v.1960; Eisenhower Library, White House Office, Office of the Staff Secretary, Records 1952–61, State Department Subseries, Box #4.

2. HM diary entry, 3.vi.1960; MS Macmillan, dep.d.39.

3. HM diary entry, 10.vi.1960; ibid.

4. 'Lee Report'; TNA PREM 11/3133.

5. Quoted in Mangold, *The Almost Impossible Ally*, p. 146; Macmillan to Bishop, 31.vii.1960; TNA PREM 11/2983.

6. Eisenhower to Macmillan, 15.vi.1960; TNA PREM 11/2940.

7. US London to State Department no. 494, 28.vii.1960; Eisenhower Library, White House Office, Office of the Staff Secretary, Records 1952–61, International Series, Box #14.

8. HM diary entry, 30.vi.1960; MS Macmillan, dep.d.39.

9. HM diary entry, 10.viii.1960; MS Macmillan, dep.d.40.

10. HM diary entry, 14.iii.1960; ibid.

11. HM diary entry, 24.ix.1960; ibid.

12. Quoted in Taubman, *Khrushchev: The Man and his Era*, p. 475.

13. Macmillan, *Pointing the Way*, p. 279.

14. Kohler to Herter, 30.ix.1960; Eisenhower Library, White House Office, Office of the Staff Secretary, Records 1952–61, International Series, Box #15.

15. Welensky to Salisbury, 21.ix.1960; Hatfield House 5M/U2.
16. Salisbury to Welensky, 21.xi.1960; ibid.
17. HM diary entry, 6.x.1960; MS Macmillan, dep.d.40.
18. HM diary entry, 2.xi.1960; ibid.
19. Evans, *Downing Street Diaries*, p. 123.
20. HM diary entry, 17.xi.1960; ibid.
21. HM diary entries, 25.xii. and 27.xii.1960; ibid.
22. Macmillan to Kennedy, 23.i.1961; JFK Presidential Library, President's Office Files, Box 127 'UK General 1/61–5/61'.
23. 'The Prime Minister's visit to Rambouillet 27–29 January 1961'; TNA PREM 11/3322.
24. HM diary entry, 24.iii.1961; MS Macmillan, dep.d.41.
25. Ibid.
26. Minutes of Cabinet meeting, 23.iii.1961; TNA CAB 128/35.
27. Nitze to McNamara, 23.i.1961; *FRUS*, vol. XXIV, *1961–1963, Laos Crisis*, doc. 10.
28. Lord Harlech to Richard Neustadt; Oral History Project, JFK Library; p. 28.
29. HM diary entry, 26.iii.1961; MS Macmillan, dep.d.41.
30. HM diary entry, 6.iv.1961; ibid.
31. George Ball, quoted in Mangold, *The Almost Impossible Ally*, p. 150.
32. Kennedy to Macmillan, 8.v.1961; JFK Library, President's Office Files, National Security Files, McGeorge Bundy Correspondence, 5/6/61–5/15/61, Box 398.

Chapter 24. 'I *Am* Ageing' (pp. 387–400)

1. Theodore Draper, quoted in R. Dallek, *John F. Kennedy: An Unfinished Life*, p. 363.
2. Dallek, *John F. Kennedy*, p. 366.
3. Ibid., p. 370.
4. McGeorge Bundy to Caccia, 14.iv.1961; JFK Library, Papers of JFK, Countries Box 127A, UK Security 3/27/61–4/30/61.
5. Kennedy to Macmillan, 10.vi.1961; JFK Library, National Security Files, Countries Box 170, UK – General 5/26/61–6/10/61.
6. HM diary entry, 11.vi.1961; MS Macmillan, dep.d.42.
7. HM diary entry, 18.vi.1961; ibid.
8. HM diary entry, 25.vi.1961; ibid.
9. Ibid.
10. Evans, *Downing Street Diary*, p. 153.
11. Ibid.
12. TNA PREM 11/3479.
13. Christ to Macmillan, 1.viii.1961; ibid.
14. Minutes of Cabinet meeting, 21.vii.1961; TNA CAB 128/35.
15. Ibid.

16. Ibid.

17. Minutes of Cabinet meeting, 27.viii.1961; TNA CAB 128/35.

18. HM diary entry, 5.viii.1961; MS Macmillan, dep.d.42.

19. G. Ball, 'Memorandum for the President', 7.x.61; JFK Library, National Security Files, Box 170, UK – General 8/1/61–8/20/61.

20. Evans, *Downing Street Diary*, p. 156.

21. Ibid.

22. HM diary entry, 10.viii.1961; MS Macmillan, dep.d.43.

23. Evans, *Downing Street Diary*, p. 159.

24. US London Embassy to Secretary of State, 28.viii.1961; JFK Library, National Security Files, Box 170, UK – General 8/21/61–9/15/61.

25. Quoted in Howard, *RAB*, p. 285.

26. J. Dickie, *Special No More: Anglo-American Relations, Rhetoric and Reality*, London, Hodder & Stoughton, 1994, p. 111.

27. McGeorge Bundy, 'Memorandum for the President – Talk with Macmillan', 27.x.1961; JFK Library, National Security Files, Box 170, UK – General 10/61.

28. Author conversation with Baroness Masham of Ilton, 7.iv.2008.

29. Evans, *Downing Street Diary*, p. 172.

30. Ibid., p. 174.

31. HM diary entry, 29.xi.1961; MS Macmillan, dep.d.44.

32. TNA PREM 11/3561.

33. HM diary entry, 29.xi.1961; MS Macmillan, dep.d.44.

34. Quoted in Mangold, *An Almost Impossible Ally*, p. 166.

35. HM diary entry, 19.xii.1961; MS Macmillan, dep.d.44.

36. McGeorge Bundy, 'Memorandum for the President', 19.xii.1961; JFK Library, National Security Files, Box 235A, Bermuda 1961 (file 1 of 3); Conference with Macmillan.

37. HM diary entry, 23.xii.1961; MS Macmillan, dep.d.44.

38. US London to Secretary of State, 13.xii.1961; JFK Library, National Security Files, Box 170, UK – General 12/11/61–12/31/61.

Chapter 25. 'They Don't Really Smile' (pp. 401–413)

1. HM diary entry, 3.i.1962; MS Macmillan, dep.d.44.

2. C. D. Jackson Papers 1931–67; Box #115, World Trip, Transcripts, UK, 1962 (1).

3. Evans, *Downing Street Diary*, p. 182.

4. HM diary entry, 15.i.1962; MS Macmillan, dep.d.44.

5. Watkinson to Macmillan, 13.ii.1962; TNA PREM 11/3779.

6. HM diary entry, 24.iii.1962; MS Macmillan, dep.d.45.

7. Macmillan's speech to the ANPA, 26.iv.1962; TNA PREM 11/3648.

8. HM diary entry, 6.v.1962; MS Macmillan, dep.d.45.

9. Quoted in D. Owen, *In Sickness and in Power*, p. 174.

10. State Department Circular to US Embassies, 1.v.1962; JFK Library, Papers of Arthur Schlesinger Jr, White House Files Box WH-36, Great Britain 5/61–1/64.

11. HM diary entry, 6.v.1962; MS Macmillan, dep.d.45.

12. Ibid.

13. HM diary entry, 17.v.1962; ibid.

14. 'Transcript of Prime Minister's remarks to the Cabinet on May 28th, 1962'; TNA PREM 11/3930.

15. HM diary entry, 19.v.1962; MS Macmillan, dep.d.46.

16. Record of a conversation at Château de Champs at 5.50 p.m. on Saturday 2 June 1962; TNA PREM 11/3775.

17. Record of a meeting at Château de Champs at 10.30 a.m. on Sunday 3 June 1962; ibid.

18. Ibid.

19. Macmillan personal telegram to Kennedy, 5.vi.1962; TNA PREM 11/3780.

20. Macmillan, *At the End of the Day*, p. 334.

21. US London to Acting Secretary of State, 26.vi.1962; JFK Library, Papers of Arthur Schlesinger Jr; White House Files Box WH-36, Great Britain 5/61–1/64.

22. HM diary entry, 21.vi.1962; MS Macmillan, dep.d.46.

23. HM diary entry, 22.vi.1962; ibid.

24. HM diary entry, 8.vii.1962; ibid.

25. *Daily* Mail, 12.vii.1962.

26. HM diary entry, 12.vii.1962; MS Macmillan, dep.d.46.

27. H. Watkinson, *Turning Points: A Record of Our Times*, Salisbury, Michael Russell, 1986, p. 161.

28. Earl of Kilmuir, *Political Adventure: The Memoirs of the Earl of Kilmuir*, p. 324.

29. Quoted in Horne, *Harold Macmillan, 1957–1986*, p. 346.

30. *Daily Telegraph*, 21.vii.1962.

31. HM diary entry, for 17.vii.1962; MS Macmillan, dep.d.46.

Chapter 26. 'We've Got To Do Something for Harold' (pp. 414–432)

1. Macmillan, *At the End of the Day*, p. 335.

2. Evans, *Downing Street Diary*, p. 211.

3. JFK Library Oral History; Lord Harlech interviewed by R. Neustadt, p. 20.

4. Macmillan to Kennedy, 18.viii.1962; T.406/62, TNA PREM 11/4052.

5. Macmillan to Kennedy, 19.viii.1962; T.407/62, TNA PREM 11/4052.

6. Vassall, quoted in D. Sandbrook, *Never Had It So Good*, p. 596.

7. Ibid.

8. HM diary entry, 25.ix.1962; MS Macmillan, dep.d.47.

9. HM diary entry, 21.viii.1962; MS Macmillan, dep.d.46.

10. HM diary entry, 12.ix.1962; MS Macmillan, dep.d.47.

11. Quoted in Cockerell, *Live from No. 10*, p. 82.

12. HM diary entry, 22.ix.1962; MS Macmillan, dep.d.47.

13. HM diary entry, 3.x.1962; ibid.

14. *FRUS, 1961–1963*, vol. X, *Cuba*; Editorial Note, doc. 436.

15. Quoted in Dallek, *John. F. Kennedy*, p. 560.

16. HM diary entry, 22.x.1962; MS Macmillan, dep.d.47.

17. HM diary entry, 23.x.1962; ibid.

18. HM diary entry, 4.xi.1962; ibid.

19. Quoted in Dallek, *John. F. Kennedy*, p. 563.

20. Ibid., p. 565.

21. HM diary entry, 4.xi.1962; MS Macmillan, dep.d.47.

22. Ibid.

23. JFK Library, Nunnerley Papers; McGeorge Bundy interviewed by D. Nunnerley 1970, pp. 2–3.

24. Cockerell, *Live from No. 10*, p. 85.

25. Quoted in Sandbrook, *Never Had It So Good*, p. 598.

26. R. Neustadt, *Report to JFK: The Skybolt Crisis in Perspective*, p. 37.

27. Ibid., p. 41.

28. HM diary entry, 25.xi.1962; MS Macmillan, dep.d.47.

29. Neustadt, *Report to JFK*, p. 49.

30. Ibid., p. 56.

31. Ibid., p. 57.

32. HM diary entry, 7.xii.1962; MS Macmillan, dep.d.48.

33. 'Record of Conversations at Rambouillet on Sunday 16 December 1962'; TNA PREM 11/4230.

34. Neustadt, *Report to JFK*, p. 86.

35. JFK Library, Nunnerley Papers; McGeorge Bundy interviewed by D. Nunnerley, 1970, p. 3.

36. Neustadt, *Report to JFK*, p. 90.

37. Ibid.

38. Ibid.

39. Ibid.

40. JFK Library, Oral History; R. Gilpatric interviewed by D. O'Brien, p. 88.

41. 'Modernisation of Britain', 30.xi.1962; TNA CAB 129/111 C. (62) 201.

42. HM diary entry, 1.i.1963; MS Macmillan, dep.d.48.

43. HM diary entry, 28.i.1963; ibid.

44. Ibid.

45. HM diary entry, 4.ii.63; ibid.

46. Ibid.

47. HM diary entry, 17.ii.1963; ibid.

48. Ibid.

49. HM diary entry, 15.ii.1963; ibid.

50. 'Memorandum for the President', Arthur Schlesinger Jr, 25.iii.1963; JFK Library, Papers of Arthur Schlesinger Jr; White House Files Box WH-36, Classified Subject Files, Great Britain 5/61–1/64.

Chapter 27. 'Butler Would Be Fatal' (pp. 433–453)

1. HM diary entry, 10.iv.1963; MS Macmillan, dep.d.49.

2. HoC Debs, 21.iii.1963, col. 820.

3. Quoted in R. Shepherd, *Iain Macleod*, London, Hutchinson, 1994, p. 295.
4. Ibid.
5. Ibid.
6. In D. Profumo, *Bringing the House Down: A Family Memoir*, p. 184.
7. Ibid., p. 186.
8. HM diary entry, 22.iii.1963; MS Macmillan, dep.d.49.
9. Profumo, *Bringing the House Down*, p. 187.
10. Note from T. Bligh to Prime Minister, 'Chronological Sequence of Events', 9.vi.1963; TNA PREM 11/4369.
11. Ibid.
12. Ibid.
13. Ibid.
14. Macmillan, *At the End of the Day*, p. 441.
15. Shepherd, *Iain Macleod*, p. 295.
16. Profumo, *Bringing the House Down*, p. 188.
17. 'Chronological Sequence ...'
18. London Embassy to Washington, 15.vi.1963; JFK Library, Papers of President Kennedy, National Security Files, Countries Box 175A, UK Subjects Profumo Matter 6/63–7/63.
19. HM diary entry for 7.vii.1963; MS Macmillan, dep.d.49.
20. Quoted in Sandbrook, *Never Had It So Good*, p. 619.
21. T. Bligh, 'Note for the Record', 4.vi.1963; TNA PREM 11/4369.
22. HoC Debs, 17.vi.1963, col. 945.
23. Quoted in Sandbrook, *Never Had It So Good*, p. 625.
24. HM diary entry, 7.vi.1963; MS Macmillan, dep.d.49.
25. Dallek, *An Unfinished Life*, p. 635.
26. HM diary entry, 7.vii.1963; MS Macmillan, dep.d.49.
27. Macmillan, *At the End of the Day*, p. 475.
28. HM diary entry, 27.vii.1963; MS Macmillan, dep.d.50.
29. *The Times*, 9.viii.1963.
30. HM diary entry, 16.vii.1963; MS Macmillan, dep.d.50.
31. D. R. Thorpe, *Alec Douglas-Home*, p. 293.
32. HM diary entry, 19.viii.1963; MS Macmillan, dep.d.50.
33. HM diary entry, 5.ix.1963; ibid.
34. HM diary entry, 11.ix.1963; ibid.
35. HM diary entry, 18.ix.1963; ibid.
36. HM diary entry, 20.ix.1963; ibid.
37. HM diary entry, 21.ix.1963; ibid.
38. Lamb, *The Macmillan Years*, pp. 480–81.
39. HM diary entry, 3.x.1963; MS Macmillan, dep.d.50.
40. HM diary entry, 4.x.1963; ibid.
41. HM diary entry, 7.x.1963; MS Macmillan, dep.d.51.
42. Ibid.
43. 'AWB and Harold Macmillan'; Memorandum compiled for author by David Badenoch (Badenoch's son) based on his father's account, 7.vii.2008.

44. Ibid.
45. HM diary entry, 8.x.1963; MS Macmillan, dep.d.51.
46. 'AWB and Harold Macmillan'.
47. HM diary entry, 12.x.1963; MS Macmillan, dep.d.51.
48. HM diary entry, 14.x.1963; ibid.
49. Sandbrook, *Never Had It So Good*, p. 653.
50. HM diary entry, 14.x.1963; MS Macmillan, dep.d.51.
51. Thorpe, *Alec Douglas-Home*, p. 293.
52. Macmillan, *At the End of the Day*, p. 508.
53. 'AWB and Harold Macmillan'.
54. Lord Swinton, quoted in B. Pimlott, *The Queen: Elizabeth II and the Monarchy*, p. 329.
55. Sandbrook, *Never Had It So Good*, p. 658.
56. Rab Butler in conversation with the author in the late 1970s.
57. Quoted in Pimlott, *The Queen*, p. 332.
58. Lord Charteris, quoted in Pimlott, *The Queen*, p. 333.
59. Ibid., p. 335.

PART FIVE

Chapter 28. The End of the Day (pp. 457–468)

1. HM diary entries, 19 and 20.x.1963; MS Macmillan, dep.d.51.
2. Quoted in Horne, *Macmillan, 1957–1986*, p. 582.
3. HM diary entry, 2.xi.1963; MS Macmillan, dep.d.51.
4. *Macmillan NEWS*, vol. i, no. 4; December 1963.
5. HM diary entry, 22.xii.1963; MS Macmillan, dep.d.51.
6. HM diary entry, 18.xi, 1963; ibid.
7. HM diary entry, 22.xi.1963; ibid.
8. Quoted in. Horne, *Macmillan, 1957–1986*, p. 585.
9. Quoted ibid., p. 598.
10. Quoted ibid., p. 596.
11. Author conversation with Eileen O'Casey's long-standing friend Robert Emmet Ginna.
12. Quoted in Horne, *Macmillan, 1957–1986*, p. 604.
13. Quoted in Davenport-Hines, *The Macmillans*, p. 337.
14. Quoted ibid., pp. 335–6.
15. Alexander Stockton, quoted in Horne, *Macmillan, 1957–1986*, p. 630.

Note on Sources

The Macmillan, Waverley and Sherfield Papers are in the Bodleian Library, Oxford. There is other Macmillan material in the Devonshire Collection at Chatsworth and much interesting tangential material in the Salisbury Papers at Hatfield House and in the Avon Papers in Birmingham. The National Archives at Kew (TNA) are the main UK public archive, and the Archives Nationales (AN) have a similar role in France. Primary source documents in the United States are more widely spread, but the main collections for my purpose have been the Library of Congress, the National Archives, the Eisenhower Library in Abilene, Kansas and the Kennedy Library at Columbia Point, Boston. All quotations from documents in all collections have been appropriately annotated in the chapter notes.

Select Bibliography

1. Macmillan's published writings

Memoirs:

Winds of Change, 1914–1939, London, Macmillan, 1966
The Blast of War, 1939–1945, London, Macmillan, 1967
Tides of Fortune, 1945–1955, London, Macmillan, 1969
Riding the Storm, 1956–1959, London, Macmillan, 1971
Pointing the Way, 1959–1961, London, Macmillan, 1972
At the End of the Day, 1961–1963, London, Macmillan, 1973

Other publications:

Industry and the State: A Conservative View, London, Macmillan, 1927
The State and Industry in 1932, private circulation, 1932
Reconstruction: A Plea for a National Policy, London, Macmillan, 1933
*The Middle Way: A Study of the Problem of Economic and Social Progress in a Free
    and Democratic Society*, London, Macmillan, 1938
The Price of Peace: Notes on the World Crisis, London, E. T. Heron, 1938
Economic Aspects of Defence, London, Macmillan, 1939
Ruin or Recovery?, London, Macmillan, 1949
The Middle Way: 20 Years After, London, Macmillan, 1958
The Past Masters: Politics and Politicians, 1906–1939, London, Macmillan, 1975
*A Reply to the Economist Article on Self-Government for Industry in the Issue of 2
    February 1935*; sine loco, 1935
The Colonial Effort; sine loco, sine nomine, 1942

2. Published correspondence and diaries

Macmillan, H., *War Diaries: Politics and War in the Mediterranean, January
    1943–May 1945*, London, Macmillan, 1984
Catterall, P. (ed.), *The Macmillan Diaries: The Cabinet Years, 1950–1957*, London,
    Macmillan, 2003
Geelhoed, E. B., and Edmonds, A. O. (eds), *The Macmillan–Eisenhower Cor-
    respondence, 1957–1969*, Basingstoke, Palgrave Macmillan, 2005

3. Biographies, part biographies and portraits

Ball, S. J., *The Guardsmen: Harold Macmillan, Three Friends and the World They Made*, London, HarperCollins, 2004

Beckett, F., *Macmillan*, London, Haus Publishing, 2006

Cockerell, M., *Live from No. 10: The Inside Story of Prime Ministers and Television*, London, Faber & Faber, 1988

Davenport-Hines, R., *The Macmillans*, London, Heinemann, 1992

Dell, E., *The Chancellors: A History of the Chancellors of the Exchequer, 1945–90*, London, HarperCollins, 1996

Edwards, R. D., *Harold Macmillan: A Life in Pictures*, London, Macmillan, 1983

Fisher, N., *Harold Macmillan: A Biography*, London, Weidenfeld & Nicolson, 1982

Hennessy, P., *The Prime Minister: The Office and its Holders since 1945*, London, Allen Lane, 2000

Horne, A., *Macmillan*, vol. 1, *1894–1956*, London, Macmillan, 1988

—— *Macmillan*, vol. 2, *1957–1986*, London, Macmillan, 1989

Hughes, E., *Macmillan: Portrait of a Politician*, London, George Allen & Unwin, 1962

Mangold, P., *The Almost Impossible Ally: Harold Macmillan and Charles de Gaulle*, London, I. B. Tauris, 2006

Sampson, A., *Macmillan: A Study in Ambiguity*, London, Allen Lane, 1967

Turner, J., *Macmillan*, London, Longman, 1994

4. General

Aldous, R., *The Last Summiteer: Harold Macmillan and the Politics of British Diplomacy, 1958–61*, Oxford, Headstart, 1997

—— *Macmillan, Eisenhower and the Cold War*, Dublin, Four Courts, 2005

—— and Lee, S. (eds), *Harold Macmillan and Britain's World Role*, London, Macmillan, 1996

—— and Lee, S. (eds), *Harold Macmillan: Aspects of a Political Life*, London, Macmillan, 1999

Ashton, N. J., *Eisenhower, Macmillan and the Problem of Nasser: Anglo-American Relations and Arab Nationalism, 1955–59*, Basingstoke, Macmillan, 1996

—— *Kennedy, Macmillan and the Cold War: The Irony of Interdependence*, Basingstoke, Macmillan, 2002

Baker, C., *Winds of Change: Harold Macmillan, Sir Robert Armitage and Colonial Policy in Nyasaland, 1959–60*, London, Institute of Commonwealth Studies, 1993

Ball, S. (ed.), *Parliament and Politics in the Age of Baldwin and MacDonald: The Headlam Diaries, 1923–1935*, London, The Historians' Press, 1992

—— (ed.), *Parliament and Politics in the Age of Churchill and Attlee: The Headlam Diaries, 1935–1951*, Cambridge, Cambridge University Press, 1999

Bange, O., *The EEC Crisis of 1963: Kennedy, Macmillan, de Gaulle and Adenauer in Conflict*, London, Macmillan, 1999

Beloff, N., *The General says No; Britain's Exclusion from Europe*, London, Penguin, 1963

Beschloss, M. R., *Mayday; Eisenhower, Khrushchev and the U-2 Affair*, New York, Harper & Row, 1986

—— *The Crisis Years: Kennedy and Khrushchev, 1960–1963*; London, Faber & Faber, 1991

Booker, C., *A Looking-Glass Tragedy: The Controversy over the Repatriations from Austria in 1945*, London, Duckworth, 1997

Booth, C., and Haste, C., *The Goldfish Bowl: Married to the Prime Minister, 1955–1997*, London, Chatto & Windus, 2004

Boothby, R., *Boothby: Recollections of a Rebel*, London, Hutchison, 1978

Brendon, P., *The Decline and Fall of the British Empire, 1781–1997*, London, Jonathan Cape, 2007

Butler, R. A., *The Art of the Possible: The Memoirs of Lord Butler*, London, Hamish Hamilton, 1971

Campbell, J., *Lloyd-George: The Goat in the Wilderness, 1922–1931*, London, Jonathan Cape, 1977

Card, T., *Eton Renewed*, London, John Murray, 1994

Chandler, A. D. (ed.), *The Papers of Dwight David Eisenhower: The War Years*, Baltimore, Johns Hopkins University Press, 1970

Clarke, P., and Trebilcock, C. (eds), *Understanding Decline: Perceptions and Realities of British Economic Performance*, Cambridge University Press, 1997

Colville, J., *The Fringes of Power: Downing Street Diaries, 1939–1955*, London, Hodder & Stoughton, 1985

Crooks, S., *Peter Thorneycroft*, Winchester, George Mann Publications, 2007

Dallek, R., *John F. Kennedy: An Unfinished Life, 1917–1963*, Boston, Little, Brown, 2003

Davenport-Hines, R. (ed.), *Letters from Oxford: Hugh Trevor-Roper to Bernard Berenson*, London, Weidenfeld & Nicolson, 2006

Dorril, S., *Blackshirt: Sir Oswald Mosley and British Fascism*, London, Viking, 2006

Egremont, Lord (John Wyndham), *Wyndham and Children First*, London, Macmillan, 1968

Eisenhower, D. D. (ed. A. D. Chandler Jr), *The Papers of Dwight David Eisenhower: The War Years*, vol. ii, Baltimore, Johns Hopkins University Press, 1970

Evans, H., *Downing Street Diary: The Macmillan Years, 1957–1963*, London, Hodder & Stoughton, 1981

Geelhoed, E. B., and Edmonds, A. O., *Eisenhower, Macmillan and Allied Unity, 1957–1961*, Basingstoke, Palgrave Macmillan, 2002

—— (eds), *The Macmillan–Eisenhower Correspondence, 1957–1969*, Basingstoke, Palgrave Macmillan, 2005

Harvey, O. (ed. Harvey, J.), *The War Diaries of Oliver Harvey*, London, Collins, 1978

Hennessy, P., *Never Again: Britain, 1945–51*, London, Jonathan Cape, 1992

—— *Having It So Good: Britain in the Fifties*, London, Allen Lane, 2006

Holmes, R., *Tommy: The British Soldier on the Western Front, 1914–1918*, London, HarperCollins, 2004

Howard, A.: *RAB: The Life of R. A. Butler*, London, Jonathan Cape, 1987

Hyam, R., *Britain's Declining Empire: The Road to Decolonisation, 1918–1968*, Cambridge University Press, 2006

Jarvis, M., *Conservative Governments, Morality and Social Change in Affluent Britain, 1957–64*, Manchester, Manchester University Press, 2005

Jones, M., *Britain, The United States and the Mediterranean War, 1942–44*, London, Macmillan, 1996

—— *Balliol College: A History, 1263–1939*, Oxford, Oxford University Press, 2005

Kaiser, W., and Staerck, G. (eds), *British Foreign Policy, 1955–64: Contracting Options*, Basingstoke, Palgrave Macmillan, 2000

King, A. (ed.), *British Political Opinion 1937–2000: The Gallup Polls*, London, Politico's, 2001

Knox, R. A., *A Spiritual Aeneid*, London, Longmans Green, 1918

Kyle, K., *Suez*, London, Weidenfeld & Nicolson, 1991

Kynaston, D., *Austerity Britain, 1945–51*, London, Bloomsbury, 2007

Lamb, R., *The Failure of the Eden Government*, London, Sidgwick & Jackson, 1987

—— *The Macmillan Years: The Emerging Truth*, London, John Murray, 1995

Lawrence, P. S. H., *An Eton Camera, 1850–1919*, London, Michael Russell, 1980

Murphy, P., *Alan Lennox-Boyd: A Biography*, London, I. B. Tauris, 1999

Murphy, R., *Diplomat among Warriors*, London, Collins, 1964

Neustadt, R., *Report to JFK: The Skybolt Crisis in Perspective*, Ithaca, Cornell University Press, 1999

Nicolson, H. (ed. Nicolson, N.), *Diaries and Letters, 1930–1939*, London, Collins, 1966

—— (ed. Nicolson, N.), *Diaries and Letters, 1939–1945*, London, Collins, 1967

Nutting, A., *No End of a Lesson*, London, Constable, 1967

Olson, L., *Troublesome Young Men: The Rebels Who Brought Churchill to Power in 1940 and Helped to Save Britain*, London, Bloomsbury, 2007

Owen, D., *In Sickness and in Power*, London, Methuen, 2008

Pimlott, B., *The Queen: Elizabeth II and the Monarchy*, London, HarperCollins, 1996

Ponsonby, F., *The Grenadier Guards in the Great War of 1914 to 1918*, 3 vols, London, Macmillan, 1920

Profumo, D., *Bringing the House Down*, London, John Murray, 2006

Ramsden, J., *The Winds of Change: Macmillan to Heath, 1957–1975*, London, Longman, 1996

Rhodes James, R. (ed.), *CHIPS: The Diaries of Sir Henry Channon*, London, Weidenfeld & Nicolson, 1967

—— *Memoirs of a Conservative: J. C. C. Davidson's Memoirs and Papers, 1910–37*, London, Weidenfeld & Nicolson, 1969

—— *Bob Boothby: A Portrait*, London, Hodder & Stoughton, 1991

Ritschel, D., *The Politics of Planning: The Debate on Economic Planning in Britain in the 1930s*, Oxford, Clarendon Press, 1997

Sampson, A., *The Anatomy of Britain*, London, Hodder & Stoughton, 1962

Sandbrook, D., *Never Had It So Good: A History of Britain from Suez to the Beatles*, London, Little, Brown, 2005

Shuckburgh, E. (ed. Charmley, J.), *Descent to Suez: Diaries 1951–56*, London, Weidenfeld & Nicolson, 1986

Smith, T., *The Politics of the Corporate Economy*, London, Martin Robertson, 1979

Thorpe, D. R., *Alec Douglas-Home*, London, Sinclair-Stevenson, 1996

—— *Eden: The Life and Times of Anthony Eden, First Earl of Avon, 1897–1977*, London, Chatto & Windus, 2003

Waugh, E., *Ronald Knox*, London, Chapman & Hall, 1959

Williamson, P., *National Crisis and National Government: British Politics, the Economy and Empire*, Cambridge, Cambridge University Press, 1992

—— *Stanley Baldwin: Conservative Leadership and National Values*, Cambridge, Cambridge University Press, 1999

Young, H., *This Blessed Plot: Britain and Europe from Churchill to Blair*, London, Macmillan, 1998

Young, K. (ed.), *The Diaries of Sir Robert Bruce Lockhart, 1939–1965*, vol. ii, London, Express Newspapers, 1980

5. Articles

Ashton, N. J., 'Harold Macmillan and the "Golden Days" of Anglo-American relations revisited, 1957–63', *Diplomatic History* (September 2005), vol. 29, no. 4, pp. 691–723

Ball, S. J., 'Selkirk in Singapore', *Twentieth-Century British History* (1999)

—— 'Banquo's Ghost: Lord Salisbury, Harold Macmillan, and the high politics of decolonization', in *Twentieth-Century British History* (March 2005), vol. 16, no. 1, pp. 74–102

Blackwell, S., 'Pursuing Nasser: The Macmillan government and the management of British policy towards the Middle East Cold War', *Cold War History* (April 2004), vol. 3, no. 3, pp. 85–104

Boughton, J. M., 'Northwest of Suez: The 1956 Crisis and the IMF', *IMF Staff Papers*, vol. 48, no. 3, International Monetary Fund, 2001

Catterall, P., 'Macmillan and Europe, 1950–1956: the Cold War, the American context and the British approach to European integration', Cercles (2002)

Catterall, P., 'The Prime Minister and his Trollope: Reading Harold Macmillan's Readings', Cercles (2004)

Cooper, R., 'A Weak Sister? Macmillan, Suez and the British Economy, July to November, 1956'; *Contemporary British History* (September 2008), vol. 22, no. 3

Deery, P., 'Menzies, Macmillan and the Woomera spy case of 1958', *Intelligence and National Security* (Summer 2001), vol. 16, no. 2, pp. 23–38

Fain, T. W., 'John F. Kennedy and Harold Macmillan: Managing the "Special Relationship" in the Persian Gulf region, 1961–63', *Middle Eastern Studies* (October 2002), vol. 38, no. 4, pp. 95–122

Francis, M., 'Tears, tantrums, and bared teeth: the emotional economy of three Conservative Prime Ministers, 1951–1963', *Journal of British Studies* (2002), vol. 41, no. 3, pp. 354–87

Goodlad, G. D., 'The premiership of Harold Macmillan: the Edwardian modernist', *Modern History Review* (1997)

Greenwood, S., 'Not the "General Will" but the Will of the General: The input of the Paris Embassy to the British "Great Debate" on Europe' (Summer 1960), *Contemporary British History* (2004)

Jarvis, M., 'The 1958 Treasury dispute', *Contemporary British History* (1998)

Jones, M., 'Macmillan, Eden, the war in the Mediterranean and Anglo-American relations', *Twentieth-Century British History* (1997)

Louis, W. R., 'Harold Macmillan and the Middle East crisis of 1958', *Proceedings of the British Academy* (1997)

Mark, C.-K., 'Defence or decolonisation? Britain, the United States, and the Hong Kong question in 1957', *Journal of Imperial and Commonwealth History* (January 2005), vol. 33, no. 1, pp. 51–72

Mauer, V., 'Harold Macmillan and the deadline crisis over Berlin 1958–9', *Twentieth-Century British History* (1998)

Rhodes James, R., *Eden and Macmillan*, London, Conservative Political Centre, 1997

Ruane, K., and Elison, J., 'Managing the Americans: Anthony Eden, Harold Macmillan and the pursuit of "Power-by-Proxy" in the 1950s', *Contemporary British History* (Autumn 2004), vol. 18, no. 3, pp. 147–67

Rubin, G., 'A spy at Woomera? How an airman nearly panicked Harold Macmillan and Robert Menzies', *RUSI Journal* (1 June 2004), vol. 149, no. 3, pp. 83–7

Tomlinson, J., 'Conservative modernisation 1960–64: too little, too late?', *Contemporary British History* (1997)

Waters, C., 'Macmillan, Menzies, history and empire', *Australian Historical Studies* (2002)

Williams, N. M., 'Harold Macmillan's private papers in the Bodleian Library, Oxford', *Contemporary British History* (1997)

Acknowledgements

Many people have been kind enough to help me in my task, and I cannot repay their efforts other than with my humble and very sincere gratitude. Ahead of the *péloton*, as it were, I must first thank Philip Bell, who has followed each chapter as it appeared in draft with what I can only describe as dogged and undeterred enthusiasm – and also his own immense wisdom. Philip has been my guide through most of the books I have written. I can only say that in all those cases, as in this, the final product has been very much improved by his friendly critiques. As if that bounty was not enough for me, Martin Gilbert and Nick Atkin generously volunteered to read through the final draft and make additional (as it turned out life-saving) corrections. Alex Stockton, too, has been good enough to follow my project about his grandfather with a kindly, helpful and friendly (although perhaps occasionally nervous!) interest.

Philip Murphy has – metaphorically – held my hand throughout the whole endeavour, pointing me always with alacrity to new sources where necessary. Edward Hampshire in the National Archives, Sophie Heywood in the Bodleian and other UK archives, Audrey Bonnery in the French archives, Agnes Ooms in the German archives, Debbie Drescher in Indianapolis, Sydney Soderberg in Abilene, Kansas, Lynn Farnell in Boston, Massachusetts, Joe Lindsley in Washington, DC, Fiona Hutchison in Edinburgh (and Arran) and Mia Stewart-Wilson and Julia Engelhardt, as picture detectives, have all researched diligently and imaginatively on my behalf. Together, they made an exceptional team. Christopher Arnander and Jane Nissen read the page proofs with their usual diligence and perceptive comments.

Libraries and archives, it goes without saying, are essential to the biographer's task. Pride of place, of course, goes to the House of Lords Library, courteous, helpful and efficient as always. Particular thanks to Elizabeth Hallam-Smith and Shorayne Fairweather – and also to the Library staff who work with them. But they were not alone. Veloise Armstrong in the Eisenhower Library in Abilene, Stephen Plotkin in the Kennedy Library in Boston, Jennifer Cole in the Mudd Library in Princeton, Connecticut, Monique Howell in the Indiana State Library, Indianapolis, James Boughton, the official historian of the International Monetary Fund in Washington, Helen Langley, Paul Cartwright, Colin Harris and Michael Hughes at the Bodleian in Oxford, Jonathan Smith at Trinity College in Cambridge, Robin Harcourt-Williams and Vicki Perry at Hatfield House, Andrew Peppitt and Diane Naylor at Chatsworth, Penny

Hatfield in the Eton College Library, Tessa Stirling and Sally Falk in the Cabinet Office, all have shown both kindness and patience – sometimes well beyond the call of duty.

Others have helped in a variety of ways, some great, some small: Magnus Linklater, Cita Stelzer, Sam Guskin, Simon Ball, Patrick Higgins, Robert Salisbury, Derry Irvine, Alistair Goodlad, Peter Carrington, Donald Logan, Michael Faber, Sue Masham, Piers Brendon, Mark Emberton, Trevor Smith, Charles Longbottom, Anthony Howard, David Badenoch, Guy Millard, Robert D. Graff, Robert Emmet Ginna. My thanks to them, and also, most particularly, to Andrew Wylie and his team at the Wylie Agency in London, Tracy Bohan, Laura Cullinane and Theo Collier of the Wylie Agency for their help and encouragement, and, of course, to my old friend and editor, Alan Samson, and his team, Lucinda McNeile, Elizabeth Allen and Helen Ewing, at Weidenfeld & Nicolson.

The author and publisher are grateful for the following permissions: Sally Sampson for extracts from Anthony Sampson's *Anatomy of Britain* and his biography of Macmillan; Virginia Makins for extracts from the Sherfield papers; David Badenoch for extracts from his memorandum to the author on his father's treatment of Macmillan's prostate problem; the Marquess of Salisbury for extracts from the Salisbury papers at Hatfield House; the Duke of Devonshire for extracts from the Devonshire MSS at Chatsworth; Sir Guy Millard for extracts from correspondence with the author; and to the Indiana State Library for extracts from documents in their library. Extracts are reproduced from the archive of the late Harold Macmillan by kind permission of the Trustees of the Harold Macmillan Book Trust. The author and publisher have made every effort to trace all copyright holders to obtain permission for various extracts quoted in the book. If any have been inadvertently missed, appropriate representations will be dealt with expeditiously.

Finally, my gratitude to my wife Jane for her constant and unflagging support. Not only has she read the drafts with the best critical attention but her insight into the processes of government in the period, as Rab Butler's niece and Winston Churchill's secretary, have been illuminating and, in many instances, decisive. I hope she feels that my dedication of the book to her, as well as my love, is at least in some small measure a reward.

Index

Soviet Union—*contd*
and Summit, 368–9, 370
British and Americans agree to negotiate with, 399
British spies, 416
Cuban Missile Crisis, 418–22
agree to test ban negotiations, 440
test ban treaty signed in Moscow, 442
brief references, 189, 337, 352, 353, 381, 394, 397
Spaak, Paul-Henri, 196, 228, 229, 234–5, 247, 326 *see also* Spaak Committee
Spaak Committee, 229, 230, 234, 238, 239
Spears, Louis, 85, 94, 146, 147
Spencer, Indiana, 11–12, 13, 14, 249, 267
Spencer, Captain Spier, 11
Stalin, Joseph, 113, 146, 164, 218
Stalingrad, 80, 106, 145
Stanley, Oliver, 67, 69, 78, 83, 106–7, 182, 183, 186
State Department, 139, 157, 172, 229, 265, 327, 364, 367–8, 372, 419
Steel, Christopher ('Kit'), 163
Stockton-on-Tees, 68, 80, 85, 181, 330, 403
HM as candidate for, 64, 65, 67, 71, 75, 79, 83, 169, 175, 180, 469
Stone of Scone, 203
Strachan-Davidson, J.L., 27
Strachey, John, 77, 84
Strasbourg, 196, 197, 203
Strategic Air Command, 420
Stratford by-election (1963), 443
Streatfeild, Sir Henry, 33, 38
Stuart, James, 65, 67, 100, 216, 217, 220, 221, 261, 266, 346
Suez Canal Company, 239, 242, 243, 244
Suez Canal, 289, 290 *see also* Suez crisis
Suez Canal Users Association (SCUA), 248, 251, 254, 289
Suez Canal Zone, 204, 227
Suez Convention (1888), 245, 248
Suez crisis, 242–73, 279, 282, 475, 476
'Suez Group', 267
Summer Fields preparatory school, 15–16, 20, 22, 469
Sumner, Humphrey, 29, 31
Swaziland, 358
Sweden, 195, 203, 374, 443
Swinton, 393, 396, 443
Swinton, Lord, 209, 450
Swithinbank, Bernard, 21
Syracuse, 140
Syria, 146, 147, 292–3, 307, 312, 431

Taranto, 142
Taylor, Maxwell, 419

Teheran, 185
conference, 146, 148, 159
Teitgen, Pierre-Henri, 194
Temple, William, 57
Templer, Sir Gerald, 245, 254
Thant, U, 420–1
Thatcher, Margaret, 5, 6, 466, 468
Thatcherism, 469
Thiepval plateau, 41
Thor missile, 361, 420
Thorneycroft, Peter
and *Industrial Charter*, 187, 188
and aircraft problem, 194
pro-Europe, 229
and Monopolies Bill, 237
and Suez crisis, 261
as Chancellor of the Exchequer, 282, 284, 285, 291, 292, 293, 294, 295, 299–300
resignation, 297, 298–9, 300
resignation debated in House of Commons, 303
HM has suspicions about, 303
appointed Minister of Aviation, 374
and Skybolt, 424, 425, 427
brief references, 304, 306, 312, 325, 451, 470
Thorpe, Jeremy, 413
Times, The, 69, 266, 289, 340
Tipasa, 124, 125, 133, 144, 150, 153
Tippecanoe, Battle of, 11
Tito, Marshal Josef Broz, 170–1, 173
Tochon, Commandant Loys: de Gaulle's letter to, 116–17
Tolbukhin, Marshal Fyodor, 170, 172
'Torch', 110, 111, 112
Toronto, 53, 404, 406
Tory Reform Group, 468
Town and Country Planning, 207, 215
Town and Country Planning Bill, 219
Trade Disputes Bill, 69
Trade Union Congress, 347
Transport and General Workers Union, 99, 306
Treasury, 70, 208, 209, 210, 211, 213, 231, 233, 235, 236, 238, 239, 241, 260, 297, 298, 299, 300, 325, 354, 373 *see also* names of Chancellors of the Exchequer
Treviso, 171, 172
Trevor-Roper, Hugh, 359, 360, 362
Trieste, 170, 171
Tschombe, Moise, 398
Tucker's Town, Bermuda, 285
Tunis, 126, 138, 149, 150, 159
Tunisia, 123, 124, 126
Turf Club, 93, 193, 318
Turkey, 62, 195, 227, 231, 303, 315, 421, 422
21 Club, New York, 439